Revised Edition

FIELDING'S
Worldwide Guide
To Cruises

FIELDING'S

Worldwide Guide
To Cruises

Antoinette DeLand

Revised Edition

William Morrow and Company, Inc. / New York

to

THOMAS KILLIP II, M.D.
(1903 to 1961)

always in grace with the sea . . .

FOREWORD

The true reward in the writing of anything comes from communication with the reader. So, I feel especially fortunate in the number of letters I received from cruise passengers who took the time to relate their own ship-board experiences, offer personal evaluations, and admonish me for minor gaffes. I now understand exactly what an "isthmus" is, and will never again put "per hour" after "knots"! The revision of any publication allows the luxury for some loving care and nurturing. There is time to replace lost commas, reflect upon the nuances of certain words, and even wonder why Plymouth, England, has been placed where Falmouth claims existence. An updating is also the opportunity for a little objective hindsight as well as that ever-tempting gaze into the future.

I would like to acknowledge my many colleagues whose fine reviews appeared in magazines, newspapers, and on radio throughout the country. Their kind mentions brought this book to the attention of many potential travelers, some of whom I have met aboard cruise vessels during the past year. Some of the reviews are excerpted on the cover, but the one that prompted perhaps the widest grin appeared in the *Buffalo Courier-Express*: "The great wonder of this book is its comprehensiveness . . . it is splendidly indexed for quick reference, yet written in a style which encourages front-to-back reading in trashy-novel style." (Well, it is often said, there is a trashy novel in all of us!)

The past year has been anything but calm for the cruise industry. Business, however, continues to boom as the 1980s roll along, and there are more exciting programs than ever before. This new edition boasts twenty-eight additional ship listings, eleven of which are new vessels and another eleven are "reborn"

7

vessels under new ownership. (The other six are ships now actively being marketed to North Americans.) The choice of vacations at sea continues to grow. While the Caribbean remains the mainstay—at least for North American departures—more ship lines are announcing West Coast sailings, and the diversity of Mexico is very IN this year. The Panama Canal appears to be as popular as ever, and the Pacific/Orient is enjoying a great resurgence in activity (where the thrill of coming alongside in those bustling ports is hard to beat).

This decade is also enlivening travelers' interest in our own wondrous country. Europe has its beautiful Rhine, the rivers Seine and Yonne, the cleaned-up Thames and the brown Danube, but North Americans are discovering their own historic waterways. The Mississippi will always be Number One, but there are now cruises along the Hudson River, the intercoastal waterway from Baltimore to Florida, as well as the Sacramento, San Joaquin, and Snake rivers which the early settlers first explored not so long ago. Alaska's Inside Passage deserves its popularity, but the Northeast/Canada and the St. Lawrence are equally breathtaking for both beauty and history.

With the additional number of berths available, competition couldn't be keener. Hence, there is a lot of talk these days of "free" this and that. Cash incentives, complimentary hotel stays, and "free" air fare are all being heavily promoted as ship line executives play the nervous numbers game. Now is the time to become an educated consumer, to look around carefully, and then to consult a knowledgeable travel counselor. Now is the time to remember what your mother always said, "Nothing in this world is free—it just gets built into the price you eventually pay." You should also beware of bargain basement offerings, because it is difficult to return a cruise that fell apart.

Alternatively, many cruise lines are now offering complete packages (Cunard, Norwegian American Cruises, Royal Caribbean, Royal Viking) that include the time at sea, plus air fare, port taxes, transfers between airport and pier, and hotel accommodations if necessary. It seems like a return to the Cooks Tour—and why not? Lindblad and R.K. Swan have been doing this for years, with great success. Cruises are sold on the fact that passengers can budget almost total expenditures in advance, but most ship lines have yet to offer the honest bottomline at a glance. (The biggest rip-off of all are the so-called port charges, which should either be absorbed by the ship lines or included in the published rate.) Shore excursions and tips should also be considered seriously in the future. Simplicity sells in this complex world, and contented cruise passengers soon follow.

Another overrated word in this industry lately is "luxury liner." There are some splendid luxury liners afloat, with accommodations and service and itineraries to match. I do not, however, consider paper plates on the breakfast tray to be the lap of luxury, and no self-respecting resort would dare such service. Be advised that your interpretation of luxury liner is not necessarily the same as that of an advertising copy writer.

Working diligently behind the scenes, to develop both consumer and trade awareness of the value and adventure of vacations at sea, is the twenty-eight-member Cruise Lines International Association (CLIA), with offices in New

York and San Francisco. Under the guidance of Bill Armstrong, Ron Lord, and Bob Kwortnik, the professional staff produces trade seminars throughout the U.S. and Canada, publishes a Cruise Manual for the trade, and juggles the diverse demands of over two dozen different personalities. (Only the heavens understand what humor is necessary, here.) CLIA suggests that all potential cruise passengers consult a qualified travel agent (who are responsible for some 95 percent of all bookings). Even seasoned travelers, high on repeaters' lists, are encouraged by their favorite ship lines to use their agent for all transactions. It doesn't add a penny to the cost of your vacation and, given the right person, you will make a new and sensitive friend.

I wish to thank all my CLIA friends for their continued support and consideration. There are also a few friends who work thoughtfully for the whole world of travel: Alice Marshall at Cunard; Ron Rubinow for NAC; Rich Steck at RCCL; Fran Sevcik at NCL; Joan Brower at AC&R; David Sutherland at Home Lines; Dick Barkle at Pan Am; Vincent Medugno at American Airlines, as well as Miami port director Carmen Lunetta and his staff. My friends Al Borcover, Travel Editor of the *Chicago Tribune*, and Norman Sklarewitz of Los Angeles both have offered helpful suggestions and frequent mentions. My editors at William Morrow & Company, Eunice Riedel and Naomi Black, have performed miracles in keeping this author happy (and no one ever accused me of being easy to please). My husband, Stephen Carter, continues his fine cartography, and has become a poetic chronicler of life at sea through photographs. Only our Peke, Mr. Ying, is annoyed at such conscientious ship research (so suitcases are now kept from sight and packing only allowed when the four-legged aristocrat is not around)!

Now about the star system. It continues to be an essential ingredient to the text, and is meant as a guide to the value of experience found aboard each vessel. Accommodations, food, service, itineraries, entertainment, shore excursions, and general on-board ambiance are all considered. (Hollow stars indicate newly launched ships.) I have also paid particular attention to readers' letters this year because, after all, they cared enough to write. The five-plus star category is again awarded to Norwegian American's *Sagafjord* and *Vistafjord* (which deserve it now more than ever) as well as to the entire Royal Viking Line fleet (*Sea, Sky, Star*). I think that Super Class aboard the *QE2* certainly deserves five-plus stars and might just be the most memorable experience afloat (although ordinary mortals don't fare too badly aboard this vessel, either). Finally, I must mention Lars-Eric Lindblad for sharing so many exciting areas of the world with cruise passengers and for making that "eighth continent"—the underwater world—available for all who wish to explore it.

The sailing schedules and rates listed in the back are as accurate as can be, but operational changes do occur. Therefore, consult your travel agent as well as the ship line before making definite plans. And after the cruise, why not send along your comments in care of William Morrow & Company? I would love to read them.

New York City   ANTOINETTE DELAND

CONTENTS

Foreword 7
1. Cruising—The Most Complete
   Vacation Possible 15
2. Choosing the Right Cruise 18
   Short Cruises 18
   Two-Week Cruises 19
   Long Cruises 19
   Air-Sea Packages 19
   Ship Personalities 20
   Freshwater Cruising 21
   Special-Interest Cruises 22
   Your Fellow Passengers 23
   How Much Will It Cost? 24
   Tipping 25
3. Before You Book 27
   What to Wear 27
   Ship-Board Facilities 29
   Ship Sanitation 29
   Shake-Down Cruises 33
   Booking Your Cabin 33
4. Before You Sail 36
   Luggage 37
   Immunization and Documents 37
   Money 38
   Electrical Appliances 38
   Embarking 39
   A Few Warnings 40
5. On Board 42
   Reserving a Table 42
   Eating Aboard 43

Drinking Aboard 46
Ship's Personnel and Services 48
Activities 50
6. Glossary of Nautical Terms 53
7. Ports of Call 71
   Bahamas and Bermuda 71
      The Bahama Islands 71
      Bermuda 72
   The Black Sea 74
      Bulgaria 74
      Romania 74
      USSR 75
   The Caribbean 76
      Barbados 76
      British Leeward Islands 76
      British Virgin Islands 77
      British Windward Islands 78
      Cayman Islands 79
      Dominican Republic 79
      Dutch Windward Islands 80
      French West Indies 80
      Haiti 81
      Jamaica 82
      Netherlands Antilles 83
      Puerto Rico 84
      Trinidad and Tobago 86
      U.S. Virgin Islands 86
   Central and North America 88
      Alaska and the
         Inside Passage 88

11

Mexico	90
The Mississippi River	92
The Northeast Passage	97
The Ohio River	100
The Panama Canal	102
The Far East	103
Bali	103
China	104
Hong Kong	110
Japan	111
Malaysia	115
Philippines	115
Singapore	116
South Korea	118
Sri Lanka	118
Thailand	119
The Mediterranean (see also	
Western Europe)	121
Egypt and the Nile River	121
France	123
Gibraltar	126
Greece	126
Israel	137
Italy	138
Malta	144
Morocco	145
The Suez Canal and the	
Red Sea	147
Tunisia	149
Turkey	150
Yugoslavia	154
The Pacific	155
Hawaii	155

Australia and New Zealand	157
The South Pacific	159
South America	162
Argentina	162
Brazil	163
Chile and Easter Island	164
Colombia	165
Ecuador	166
Galapagos Islands	167
Peru	169
Strait of Magellan	170
Venezuela	170
Western Europe (see also	
Mediterranean)	171
British Isles and Ireland	171
The North Cape	174
Northern Capitals	177
Portugal	181
Spain	183
8. **Going Ashore**	188
Information on Ports of Call	189
Buying Shore Excursions	190
On-Your-Own Shore Excursions	191
Changes in Itinerary	192
9. **Shopping**	193
Ship-Board Shopping	193
Shopping at Ports of Call	195
U.S. Customs	199
10. **Inland Waterways**	201
11. **The Cruise Lines**	214
12. **The Ships and their Ratings**	271
13. **Worldwide Ship Schedules**	357
Index	407

Revised Edition

FIELDING'S
Worldwide Guide
To Cruises

1. / CRUISING—THE MOST COMPLETE VACATION POSSIBLE

In *The European Discovery of America*, Samuel Eliot Morison described what he considered the first pleasure cruise in American history. It took place around 1536 when a London leather merchant named Richard Hoare chartered two vessels to sail to Newfoundland for the double purpose of catching some codfish and enjoying the cruise. Sixty persons are said to have signed on (including thirty "gentlemen"), but the excursion was hardly a success. The first ship was lost soon after setting sail, and although the second did reach Newfoundland the voyagers found nothing but misery there and had to eat each other to keep alive. When this ship eventually returned to England, there were few survivors—and one could say the tourist trade was set back several centuries!

In fact, it was well over three hundred years before people went down to the sea for the sheer joy of sailing, and several more decades passed before life aboard was at all comfortable. One inveterate traveler and recorder was our beloved Mark Twain, who left us with *Life on the Mississippi* and *The Innocents Abroad*. The latter described a year-long "great Pleasure Excursion to Europe and the Holy Land" in 1867, which he called "a picnic on a gigantic scale." The passage cost $1250, and five dollars per day in gold was recommended for shore excursions. Although his expectations that the excursionists would be "filling the ship with shouts and laughter" received some setbacks, he was grateful that at the end of the year he was still on speaking terms with many of his fellow passengers and had even made some friends. Above all, he recommended that people undertake such cruises "regularly," because his shore excursions had taught him that "travel is fatal to prejudice, bigotry, and narrow-mindedness."

This was also the time when Thomas Cook purported to organize the first "world cruise," which involved rail travel in addition to four ships. Begun with a transatlantic crossing from Liverpool to New York in 1872, this tour had been abandoned by many of its participants by the time it reached Cairo 220 days later. Fifty years later Cunard offered the first official world cruise—a four-month voyage on the *Laconia* from New York to New York. The 1922–23 itinerary included Honolulu, Shanghai, Hong Kong, Cairo, Naples, and other ports of call still popular today.

Cruises as we know them today began more or less in the 1920s, although on a grand scale and for a small segment of society. Transatlantic sailings and sea tours of the Mediterranean or South America were on three-class ships (four classes when there were immigrants). These cruises assumed the importance that a global voyage does today. Staterooms, as large as drawing rooms, sported heavy, hand-carved furniture. In first class, especially, you traveled with trunks of evening clothes and dinner jewels, servants who cared for them and you (and who slept somewhere below deck), and pets who stayed above. Except that ladies and gentlemen often separated after the evening meal for their own pleasures, life aboard was usually not much different from today. Some rules were never broken. If a young woman alone wished the pleasure of a charming steward for the night, she would most likely not acknowledge his presence the next morning because, good heavens, they had not yet been properly introduced!

Weekend party cruises were popular in the 1920s—from the East Coast to Havana, Bermuda, the Bahamas, and to Nowhere! Ships became floating speakeasies during Prohibition when liquor was legal (and very cheap) on the high seas. The low cost and steady flow of alcohol on cruises is still a lure, but most of us take to the sea for romance and adventure and for the temporary dream world that exists the minute we step aboard. The cruise vessel is a floating capsule of contentment as it transports us from one exotic port to another. And as we follow the progress of the ship on the navigation chart posted near the purser's office (and even place a dollar in the daily pool), the world looks so large and this voyage so small. Life at sea is such a fantasy of time and place that the glow lasts long after the cruise is over.

Sailing today is certainly safer and far more comfortable than it ever was before, despite the pint-sized staterooms and lack of ladies' maids and gentlemen's valets. Ships are better maintained, and passengers have far more consideration than a few decades ago. We have stabilizers to cut down the roll, air conditioning to keep out the heat, and plenty of ice in every bar. The first-class sections have all but been eliminated (except on the *Queen Elizabeth II* and

Stefan Batory). We cruise all over the world in the equivalent of the old cabin class, with food and service to match, entertainment that flies in and out so as not to bore us, and shore tours that activate our minds and senses as well as our pocketbooks.

When I told my travel agent about this book, she sat right down and wrote me a list of questions she proposes to clients to judge their seaworthiness. She likes first to compare the cost of a vacation at sea with one at a resort (or on an individual tour), where you usually pay separately for food, accommodations, entertainment, and all activities. If the advantage of just one rate for everything and no hidden extras (except what you intend to spend for shopping, drinks, and tipping) appeals to you, you may also enjoy the fact that all the many details of when, where, and what time things happen each day have already been solved by the ship lines. You not only leave the driving to them, but the food and entertainment decisions as well. They have even eliminated any language problem. You just sit on deck and relax.

Perhaps you are nervous that a cruise is too slow a pace for you, that it doesn't allow enough time in ports, or that there is too much group activity. Cruising is not an individual experience, and that is precisely why so many people enjoy it. If you are traveling alone, you can have instant companionship whenever you wish. Couples can be by themselves or seek others for conversation or cards. Children, no matter what age, make instant friends and become purveyors of all the news within this floating world. And if you're worried about being bored, there are so many different types of cruises available (see "Choosing the Right Cruise") that you can ship hop the rest of your life and never be satiated with the excitement of being at sea.

If you demand a place in the sun, then the Caribbean is your natural habitat, with its potpourri of colors and people and splendid tropical climate (and should you ever tire, Hawaii or the South Seas might entice your senses). If you're looking for adventure and wildlife, you'll love the Galapagos and Antarctica, the Amazon, or watching the whales off Baja. If majestic scenery fills your soul with wonder, then you should sail through the southern tip of South America, Alaska's Inside Passage, along the Saguenay River, or in and out of Norway's saw-toothed fjords. If you wish to stretch your mind as well as your legs in every port, the whole world is waiting for you, but you will especially enjoy cruises to Greece and Turkey, Israel and Egypt, the northern capitals, the British Isles, around South America, through the Indonesian archipelago, and the Far East. And if it's river life you like, try the small boats on the waterways of Europe, the paddle-wheelers on the Mississippi and Ohio rivers, cruises along the historic Hudson, and the barges along the Nile. You can be as enriched and fulfilled as you desire, or pursue each day at a snail's pace. This is the perfection of a cruise.

2. / CHOOSING THE RIGHT CRUISE

A while ago, I would not have considered myself among the true believers that the right cruise does indeed exist for just about everyone. After months of speaking with officials of some forty-five companies offering sailings on more than 125 passenger vessels all over this world, however, I am convinced there are many "right" cruises for anyone adventurous enough to come aboard. Once you cull through all the beautiful brochures; the singing of self-praises; the temptations of glorious food; and photographs of the most picturesque ports on earth, you will find several holidays-at-sea so well matched to your interests that you might even think they were custom made. The time to start shopping is now—that is if you plan to be on that passenger list this year.

SHORT CRUISES: Your first considerations will be time and money; how much can you spend on a cruise. If you're just discovering your sea legs, you certainly don't want to climb aboard a ship about to sail around the world. Most first-time passengers prefer to begin with three- or four-day cruise—to the Bahamas from Miami, to the Greek islands and Turkey from Piraeus, or a party weekend from the West Coast—just to ensure the sea air and salt spray agrees. If it does, you may wish to try a week at sea. A round trip from New York to Bermuda or the Bahamas (even to both) or a one-way cruise to Montreal can be made in seven days. From Miami you can visit three or four Caribbean ports or simply relax aboard the *Norway* with four full days at sea.

You can sail from Vancouver through Alaska's Inside Passage, or cruise among the Hawaiian Islands from Honolulu. Call at three ports in Turkey and four of the Greek islands in seven days, or concentrate on historic sites in Israel and Egypt on new "peace" cruises. Sail to Valparaiso at top speed from Buenos Aires through the Strait of Magellan, relax between Oxford and Windsor on the River Thames, or call at La Guaira and other ports in the lower Caribbean from San Juan. It takes less than a week to see the highlights of the Nile River monuments (but much more to really enjoy them), and seven days is terrific for the Mexican Riviera or the Galapagos Islands, or our very own Mississippi!

TWO-WEEK CRUISES: If you have two weeks set aside for life at sea, you can cruise from San Francisco to Alaska/Canada or from New York to the Northeast and Canada. You can cover more ports in the Caribbean, transit the Panama Canal, and sail up the Orinoco River. Two weeks is all it takes to cruise to the North Cape, circle the British Isles, or steam your way from New Orleans to St. Paul, stopping at all the river towns on the Mississippi. A four-teen-day cruise opens up the possibilities of more ports around South America, a tour of the northern European capitals from Hamburg, or the exotic islands of the South Seas from Sydney. Or sail down the Intracoastal Waterway from Connecticut to Florida, around the Indonesian archipelago from Singapore, or along the Nile.

LONG CRUISES: If you are among the lucky few who have more than two weeks to spend at sea, the world is yours. You can trace segments of the global voyages, join expeditions to Antarctica, sail from the Seychelles to the Red Sea, or cruise a goodly portion of the Amazon. Hop aboard repositioning sail-ings between San Juan and Vancouver, or take a slow boat from one coast to the other. You may even wish to stay a while in places you like best. Better yet, pick a cruise and build a longer trip around it. Several possibilities include the North Cape cruise, plus bus across Norway, Gota Canal to Stockholm, Silja Line overnight to Helsinki, Lindblad *Polaris* in the Baltic/USSR; Galapagos Islands plus Quito and Macchu Picchu; Greek islands and Turkey plus a week in Athens; Strait of Magellan plus overland travel in South America; canals of Burgunday plus Paris, or Chez des Amis throughout France; Mexican Riviera plus Chichen Itza and Tulum; Cunard Lines glamorous fourteen-day cruise and stay offer in the Caribbean; Alaska's Inside Passage plus Vancouver and Banff; and any stopover in the U.S. between port of embarkation and home.

AIR-SEA PACKAGES: Much variation is now possible with so many generous air-sea programs, stopover privileges, and open-ended plane tickets. The whole face of sailing away has changed drastically in the past decade due to the rise of air-sea packages (which about seventy-five percent of all cruise passengers now purchase). National Airlines (now Pan Am) pioneered this plane-to-ship idea in the 1970s and within a decade attracted almost a quarter-million passengers and fourteen different ship lines. Today's options include almost every line and almost every port, and much of the air transportation is even free!

When you sit down with your travel counselor to consider a cruise, measure carefully the advantages of all-inclusive air-sea packages. These feature cruise rate, reduced air fare, transfers from airport to ship, and often port taxes, all at less than the cost of each component individually. This is certainly a worry-free way to travel, for you are met at the airport and transferred to the cruise vessel without even having to claim your own baggage (it is transferred separately by the ship's personnel). You don't have to live in a major metropolis to qualify. Norwegian Caribbean's "Cloud 9" programs feature over eighty cities throughout the U.S., and other shiplines have even more. Royal Cruise Line has refined this air-sea concept so that passengers may fly to one port for embarkation and fly home from another. Air-sea also means cruise one way and fly the other, which the QE2 and British Airways have joined forces to promote. Pan Am flies passengers to Singapore, China, and South America for cruises. R. K. Swan charters a local aircraft for his Mediterranean and Nile River sailings. Air France will charm you into the mood for lovely barge trips in Burgundy and on other French waterways, and Lufthansa is proud to transport you to the Rhine. During the summer season Air Canada is solidly booked with Inside Passage passengers, and KLM promotes idyllic Dutch canal cruises. SAS will get you to vessels sailing the North Cape and the Baltic, while American Airlines shuttles passengers to San Juan. Sabena has discovered barging in Belgium.

SHIP PERSONALITIES: Whether you choose a fun-and-sun cruise, an adventure or cultural cruise, or a sailing with special scenery, you should pay particular attention to the type of vessel that suits you best. If you're not fussy as long as the vessel sails for your destination, you have a choice of ships of varying size, shape, and nationality. A ship really does have a personality, which is a mesh of many factors—crew, size, ports, and the people who sail aboard. For example, the French-flag and crew *Mermoz* is predictably temperamental and Gaulic with its French menu and complimentary wines at lunch and dinner. The QE2 can be rather stuffy and traditionally British, while the two small Cunard vessels (*Princess* and *Countess*) have more of a Barnaby Street reputation, with fish 'n' chips and all that. Princess Cruises flies the P & O Union Jack, but lacks traditional British stuffiness; and the seven-day *Sun Princess* is the swinger of the group. More elegant are the sister ships *Pacific* and *Island Princess* (also known as the "love boats"). If you hanker for some fun ships under the Caribbean sun, you'll find action around-the-clock on Carnival Cruise Line's four-vessel fleet (*Carnivale*, *Festivale*, *Tropicale*, and *Mardi Gras*) and on Commodore's *Boheme*, the "Happy Ship" that is cozy too.

The Greeks have a word for everything and it seems a cruise vessel for every occasion, from the sweet 180-passenger *Stella Maris* to the popular *Golden Odyssey* of Royal Cruise Line. In between fall many different types of ships belonging to Chandris, Epirotiki, Hellenic Mediterranean, K-Lines, and Sun Line. If you prefer the Italians, then you can find *buon gusto* aboard Sitmar, Home Lines, and Costa. Two Norwegian-flag lines, Royal Viking and Norwegian American Cruises, have northern European crew and ambience plus matchless service. Royal Caribbean and Norwegian Caribbean (Norwegian flag and officers, West Indian crew) boast a different type of atmosphere because of their total commitment to the Caribbean. Holland America, the oldest line in service after Cunard, is now registered in the Netherland Antilles and has retained its Dutch officers to complement a new all-Indonesian crew known for its charm and eagerness to please the passengers.

The once-proud American fleet is having its ups and downs. Gone are the *Mariposa* and *Monterey* of Pacific Far East Line. The famous Grace Line, which has been through several name changes in the past decade, is now owned by Delta Lines of New Orleans and still sends 100-passenger cargo liners around South America every *other* week; they offer four nice, steady vessels with an older clientele (no one really swings here), plus a friendly American crew and cooking to match. The new American Hawaii Cruises has brought the old *Independence* back to life as well as the *Constitution*, with a two-fold positioning on the Hawaiian circuit and occasional cruises from San Francisco. Both vessels, though old but well designed and sturdily built, have been converted into one-class, very casual "let's-see-Hawaii" vessels. If you don't expect the *Royal Viking Sea*, you will enjoy the experience. Other vessels flying the Stars and Stripes are much smaller and built mainly for freshwater or coastal cruising. American Canadian Line has the *New Shoreham II*, a 150-foot yacht that carries seventy passengers in the Bahamian Out Islands all winter and on the rivers and canals of the Northeast during the summer. American Cruise Line's newest *America*, the *Independence*, and *American Eagle*, also harbor hop in New England during the summer, run fall foliage cruises along the Hudson, and then sail down the Atlantic Intracoastal Waterway through the southern states in the winter. And a national treasure is the *Delta Queen* who keeps her younger sister, *Mississippi Queen*, company on the Mississippi and Ohio rivers all year-round with pilgrimages to ante-bellum plantations and tiny towns that are steeped in local lore and traditions of America's most romantic waterway.

FRESHWATER CRUISING: Freshwater cruising has a style of its own, and you might enjoy the Rhine river boats if you don't expect the same ambience as vessels that cater to Americans. Continental Waterways, Floating Through Europe, and Horizon Cruises have charming hotel barges that float slowly through England, France, and Holland and carry from six to twenty-four passengers. These are real gourmet cruises, with good conversation too.

The Russian-flag and crew vessels made a big splash a few years ago when Morposflot sent two of the newer, Scandinavian-built ships to our shores—the *Odessa* and *Kazakhstan*—which sailed from the East Coast and New Orleans to the Caribbean and were popular for their low, low rates. Americans were also frankly curious to see how their world neighbors behaved. The *Odessa* is no longer around, but did offer a pretty spartan cruise experience, for the crew was only jolly and amusing when on "show" at the once-weekly talent night. Frankly, I would rather spend a little more money and take a ship that enjoys sailing and passengers more. On the other hand, the flagship of Polish Ocean Lines, the *Stefan Batory* (ex-*Maasdam*) is more popular than ever, with excellent continental food and an interesting clientele who seem to be having a wonderful time taking the most economical sea route to Europe. The *Stefan Batory* also cruises the Saguenay River from Montreal and the Mediterranean from England.

SPECIAL-INTEREST CRUISES: If you prefer your cruise to be culturally enriching and intellectually stimulating, sign on with a company that devotes itself entirely to such mind-stretching experiences; but you pay plenty for the privilege. Most familiar is Lindblad, whose cruises have a loyal following and are often fully booked before the brochure is printed. Lars-Eric Lindblad, an intrepid traveler, never knows what he will brew next. The Nile and Antarctica have long been his habitat, and he added China as soon as his toe was in the door. Lindblad's greatest coup yet is the 36-passenger river boat *Kun Lun* he managed to wrest from the Chinese government for cruises on the Yangtze. The river voyage lasts only ten days, but it must be the most interesting expedition available. New as of 1982 is the M/V *Yao Hua*, or *Brilliance of China*, from Hong Kong or Nanjing. In addition to the *Lindblad Explorer*, which sails in the Far East and Antarctic, son Sven-Olof has chartered the *Pacific Northwest Explorer* for sailings around the tip of Baja California to watch wildlife in the Sea of Cortez, and the *Lindblad Polaris* has been launched.

Wildlife fans will also enjoy the Galapagos Island cruise, a unique experience for wandering among birds and sea lions in these relatively uninhabited Pacific islands. A newer company, Society Expeditions of Seattle, has also plunged full force into nature and culture oriented cruises; its *World Discoverer* sails the Amazon River and the waters of New Guinea and Melanesia, Antarctica, Iceland and Greenland, North and West Africa, and the Seychelles to the Red Sea. Exploration Cruise Lines, also of Seattle, now has a fleet of three small, unique vessels—the *Pacific Northwest Explorer, Majestic Explorer,* and *Great Rivers Explorer,* with exciting itineraries to match!

B.I. Discovery Cruises, a division of P & O Cruises, operates the *Uganda.* This sturdy but rather old vessel carries three hundred cabin passengers and six hundred students (in barracks below) on enrichment cruises throughout the Mediterranean. The cruises, strictly air-sea from Gatwick, are one hundred percent British; the price includes all shore excursions and guides. R. K. Swan, a second-generation travel expert, probably has the best enrichment cruises ever put together. Swan has chartered the *Jason* from Epirotiki for several years. She's hardly a luxury ship, but I doubt that the passengers have much time to notice. Swan gives reading lists, textbooks, and daily doses of archaeology, classics, botany, and the like. Although he claims that passengers come aboard to enjoy themselves, I think he would consider the program a failure if they didn't learn a little something. Swan's cruises cover the entire Mediterranean and the area around the British Isles. The sixty-passenger *Nile Star* offers the Middle East—two weeks of tombs and pyramids in the company of leading Egyptologists.

The Madison Avenue travel firm of Raymond & Whitcomb charters another Epirotiki vessel, the *Argonaut,* for cruises that encompass the entire Mediterranean, the waterways of northern France, the island world of Britain, and the Red Sea. These cruises, not quite so cerebral as Swan's, cater to college groups and museums and bring people together who share environmental interests. Others are run by Travel Dynamics aboard the very glamorous *Sea Cloud* or the spiffy Greek-flag vessel *Illiria.* Programs are superb and highly recommended.

YOUR FELLOW PASSENGERS: You are choosing your cruise companions when you decide which ship and which itinerary appeal to you. You will find more fun-loving, gambling, and drinking partners on a three- or four-day sailing aboard the *Sunward II* or *Emerald Seas* than on taking a two-month circumnavigation of South America. People who love beach parties and snorkeling will choose vessels in the Norwegian Caribbean fleet, because each sailing sets aside one day just for these activities. If you like to gamble, you will find plenty of fellow Lady Luck tempters on ships that feature full casinos on board as well as in every port. Cruise vessels that advertise double beds and convenient weekend departures are popular with honeymooners, who still prefer the one-week sailings in the Caribbean or to Bermuda, Nassau, and Mexico. Bridal parties may even board their cruise vessel early for nuptials and reception. Although many marriages are made at sea, the happy partners must wait until shore leave to be wed. The master of the vessel is no longer empowered to do the honors, but this doesn't prevent anyone from returning later for that honeymoon cruise!

Singles looking for action are almost certain to find it at sea on a wide variety of cruise vessels. High density passenger list ships are best for the singles scene, since these vessels carry more people in smaller than usual spaces and offer a better opportunity for being "thrown together in a storm." Try the *Sun Princess,* Cunard *Countess,* Cunard *Princess,* and the three Norwegian Caribbean seven-day ships for starters. Singles might also consider cruise ships with one thousand passengers or more, like the *Norway* and Carnival fleet, that have a reputation for continual social activities: deck games, parlor games, gambling, calisthenics, singles' parties, and so on.

The longer the cruise, the older the passengers. This is a general rule, but it works and makes sense. How many young couples can afford the time and money to sail around the world, or even a continent? Many retired couples take to the sea and discover a wonderful new realm that is both relaxing and stimulating; so they take longer and longer sailings, and some seem to stay aboard forever. Hence, you should not expect to find many swingers aboard the Delta liners, or any other 58-day cruise. If you wish to find a more youthful crowd at sea, take the shorter segments of longer cruises or limit your sailings to less than three weeks; then you will be satisfied with your fellow passengers' energy level.

Cruises can be perfect for families who wish to travel together. Children under sixteen years travel free on the *Delta Queen* or *Mississippi Queen* when sharing with two adults. Holland America, Sitmar, Home Lines, and Cunard (QE2), all have good facilities for young people as well as companions and counsellors during special vacation periods. Handicapped persons should not be deterred either. If you have a handicap, study deck plans to ensure maneuverability between public rooms, around open decks, and in and out of elevators (small vessels like the *Stella Maris* do not have an elevator). Find out whether the ship actually docks in port or whether passengers "tender in." The latter is inconvenient and can confine handicapped persons, especially in inclement weather and rough seas.

Geographic distribution might also determine your cruise companions. For example, Royal Cruise Line in San Francisco caters primarily to Californians. The New York-based ship lines draw most passengers from the Northeast Corridor (Washington, D.C., to Boston and Montreal). The Florida lines have the widest geographic distribution owing to the excellent and varied air-sea programs, but some vessels concentrate on the Middle-Atlantic and Midwest states. The San Juan-based ships also claim passengers from all over the country; everyone seems to fly down and back.

HOW MUCH WILL IT COST? Just what does a cruise cost? It's safe to say that prices are more than last year, but less than next! Prices vary with vessel, season, and itinerary. They are determined on quality of shipboard life, nationality of crew (Norwegians cost more than West Indians), and length and type of sailing (two weeks with Lindblad costs more than two weeks with Royal Cruise). The rock-bottom minimum per person, per day is $100, and that means an inside closet with upper/lower berths and a bathroom in which you can barely turn around. Better accommodations start with the bottom rate of $125 (per person, per day) and go up from there. Some vessels start higher, and you can't touch the deluxe cruise vessels for less than $200 per day minimum. Each vessel, however, has so many different sizes and placements of cabins that on one ship rates range from $100 to $450 (per person, per day) within twenty-three categories.

All ship-board rates are based per person, double occupancy. If you want a double cabin to yourself, you must pay the premium—which can be two hundred percent of the single rate. Because most rates are quoted per person for each cruise, comparing the per-person daily rate of several cruises can be confusing. My friends at Cruise Lines International Association, sensitive to this dilemma, suggest that you figure out the total vacation cost (not including presents and souvenirs). For example:

14-day Caribbean cruise	$2,800 per person, double occupancy
Port taxes	25 ” ”
Air fare add-on	125 ” ”
	$2,950 divided by 14 = $210.71

This cruise will cost approximately $210 per person, per day, double occupancy, which includes transportation, meals, all ports of call, and all entertainment during the fourteen-day sailing. If you are bringing the children along, or are travelling with friends, the rate per person will decrease because many ship lines offer discounts for third and fourth passengers in the same cabin. However, you must add incidentals to this price (drinks, tips, shopping, shore excursions, etc.) to find the real cost of your vacation. If you have a budget, you can figure your entire cost in the quiet of your home before you even depart.

While you should always choose your cruise on solid business sense, remember that the lower-priced vessels tend to be older and may cater to a crowd less well-heeled than you. Check prices, facilities, and benefits carefully and choose a good competitive rate. The best rates are often on excellent ships during the off-season. Keep in touch with what different lines offer in the spring and fall in areas where business may be slow at the moment. Some of the best current discounts are Holland America's Impulse Fare (for last-minute decisions) and Norwegian Caribbean's "Sail Saver," but other ship lines now follow suit as more vessels are launched. The "Sail Saver," similar to an airline stand-by fare, is aimed at people who just wish to take a nice one-week Caribbean cruise but are not fussy about which of NCL's vessels will accommodate them. The line assigns a room on whatever vessel has a vacancy at the last moment. You might also look in your local newspapers for all the cruise lines offering free air fare to and from the ship. Sitmar Cruises was among the first on trans-Panama Canal sailings, but a price war has certainly changed the face of the industry recently.

Your cruise should cost just what you can afford. With so many sailings and itineraries available throughout the year, never be shy about seeking the proper one for yourself. Whatever the status of your pocketbook and your own decisions, you can easily choose the right cruise and know exactly what it will cost beforehand. Port taxes range from $10 to about $60 (depending upon length of cruise), payable upon purchase of your ticket. You may also buy the complete shore excursion package at this time. The only other expenses you should have are personal—drinks, photographs, beauty shop, massage, and diversions such as skeet shooting. And tips.

TIPPING: Tipping is difficult and I commend Holland America Cruises for dispensing with it somewhat. Their policy is "No Tipping Required," but of course, passengers reward the crew for smiling service rendered. What most passengers are suggested to tip has risen a great deal (along with everything else). On many ships this suggestion is so subtle and the service so superb that you feel eager to give whatever you can. However, I have heard cruise directors tell passengers what to tip in such an authoritative manner that many people resented the entire situation. Tipping in the Caribbean at this year's prices is suggested to be two dollars per person, per day for the cabin steward and the same for the dining room steward—plus what you give to the bartender, deck steward, and maitre d'hotel for services rendered. A dollar a day per person is adequate for the busboy. On some Greek vessels in the Aegean you will be told to tip six dollars per person, per day. A union leader, stationed to receive your tip, will check off your cabin number. This means a couple will depart with eighty-four dollars less, even if they do not feel the service warrants that amount.

Tips are a personal matter, and you should use your own good judgment. Use what is written in your ship's manual as a guideline and take it from there. Above all, do not let this problem disturb your enjoyment of the cruise. And a final note: it is impolite to tip officers or cruise directors. They have done their job only if your cruise was the best vacation you ever had. Commend them by letter to the ship line.

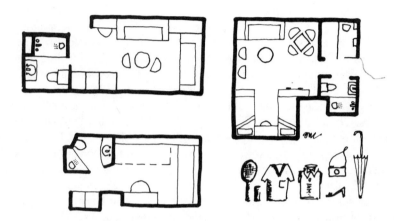

3. / BEFORE YOU BOOK

WHAT TO WEAR: With visions of seascapes and sunsets, and dreamy days spent at the rail watching flying fish—not to mention dancing on the moonlit deck—you may wonder if you will need a new wardrobe for your cruise. Unless your closet has nothing but designer jeans, you can probably pack right now and not purchase one new item for ship-board life. Cruise clothes are simply resort clothes, and you'll need the same basic outfits that you wear at home when casual by day and off to cocktails and dinner in the evening. Some cruise vessels require more clothes than others, due to more activities on board and on shore and a greater number of port calls and climate changes. A more formal atmosphere prevails on Norwegian American Cruises, Royal Viking Line, the QE2, and the *Rotterdam*, among others. On the other hand, life aboard the Lindblad vessels and other specialty cruises hardly dictate black tie or elegant jewels.

For most cruises, you will want very casual and colorful wear during the day. This means slacks and T-shirts for both men and women, with low-heel and comfortable shoes. One swimsuit and a cover-up (for walking through the public rooms and having buffet luncheon on deck), along with a pair of rubber flip-flops, are fine for a week's cruise. A pair of sneakers and espadrilles are perfect for walking on deck and sightseeing. (I never take expensive shoes for daytime wear, because many of the interesting sites are dusty and the old winding streets in port can be dirty and slippery.) Short shorts for everyone who looks good in them are perfect for lazy days at sea but are known to offend many inhabitants of host ports (especially in Haiti and the Dominican Republic). In general, you should dress moderately on shore and save the strutting, the open shirts, and the gold chains for the pleasure of your fellow passengers.

Many ship lines request that male passengers wear a coat and tie in public rooms after 6 p.m., so if this is not your style you should find another cruise vessel (or go to Club Med). For women, the evening is time for high heels, silk blouses, and romantic long skirts. Being on a cruise means getting dressed up almost every night. The first and last evenings spent on board are always casual—the first because you are probably tired from traveling, and the last because your suitcase is usually already packed and you dine in your onward-bound clothes. On a seven-day cruise, four nights will be called "formal," and on a fourteen-day sailing seven nights will require party clothes. Just how formal you wish to be depends upon your taste, the ambience on board your vessel, and the itinerary. Many cruise line spokespeople say that the night life in the Caribbean demands black tie at the Captain's parties, but only a dark suit in the Aegean. The reason: with many more days at sea in the Caribbean, passengers have plenty of time to primp; on Greek island and Turkey cruises everyone is just too exhausted from visiting a port (and sometimes two) every day.

Your ship-board clothing should be fun to wear and should more or less take care of itself. Few vessels offer dry cleaning services, but many now include launderettes and self-service pressing facilities on board. (Salt air can cause many lovely fabrics to become limp and lifeless on board.) Silk or synthetic blouses are best, with a variety of pants and skirts to mix and match. You may want a simple but colorful gown for the captain's party and the traditional photo of your meeting with the master of the vessel. For a seven-day cruise, I take four outfits for the evening (which is far too many, but I like the feeling of choice).

No matter what sunny part of the world your ship is sailing, always pack enough sweaters and wraps for the air conditioning on board, the breezy evenings on deck, and the early arrivals in port. You just never know, and it's terrible to be clothed in nothing but filmy see-throughs. Along with an extra pullover, bring some inexpensive and lightweight rain gear (jacket and folding umbrella). Spring and fall are unpredictable the world over, and my closet is full of umbrellas bought on vacations because I forgot to pack one. When you arrive in port, the purser will announce the weather forecast as well as the present temperature. However, a comfortable-sounding temperature can be either warm or cool, depending upon wind and clouds, and your tour bus may be air-conditioned, so always take an extra sweater.

The best way to decide what to wear is to study the cruise news, the daily activity sheet slipped under your door during the night. It will suggest proper dress for shore excursions as well as for the evening. If you're just beach-bound, you'll know what to wear; but you may need a windbreaker for an open boat ride across the bay.

SHIP-BOARD FACILITIES: Before booking, review the deck plan to reassure yourself that there is enough on board to be amusing for seven days or so. If you're the sporty type and like to keep in shape, look for the health center/gymnasium/sauna, and check that the sports deck is large enough. Since the average age of passengers has dropped considerably in the past decade and their interest in sports activities has risen, ship lines now take great pride in offering as many new and different programs as possible each day. Many vessels have golf driving ranges (a platform at the stern of the vessel at which you hit right into the sea), and Norwegian American even encouraged golfers to bring their clubs on four cruises this past season (and arranged play in ports). Jogging is, of course, the "in" activity at sea as well as on land, and your vessel will have a mile-route mapped, so there's no excuse for losing your style. As the thump-thump on the deck above can be a bother to sleepy passengers, the *Norway* requests joggers to please refrain from running before 8:30 a.m. (a good time when you're on vacation). If tennis is your fancy, check what is available. The baby Cunards have paddle tennis courts and some New York-based vessels, very strong on tennis instruction, will arrange play during the summer in Bermuda at Elbow Beach and in Nassau at Love Beach.

Diving has zoomed in popularity for passengers on Caribbean cruises. And no ship line caters more to the scuba crowd than Norwegian Caribbean, which offers "dive-in" programs aboard its five vessels (*Norway, Southward, Skyward, Sunward,* and *Starward*). Each ship calls at an uninhabited island in the Bahamas (Great Stirrup Cay or Little San Salvador) where passengers may snorkel on their own or join a group along an underwater trail. First-timers must attend classes in the ship's pool with a qualified instructor before they're allowed to take out the gear. The Caribbean is perfect throughout for snorkeling, but if you're a real addict and want to dive in every port, be sure your cruise ship calls at St. Thomas, St. Croix, the Cayman Islands, Barbados, Cozumel, Nassau and Freeport, or even in Atlantic-bound Bermuda. You can also rent Sunfish in most of these (and other) ports, have a quick turn around the bay on water skis, and do a little fishing.

Check the deck plan for the library or other quiet areas that may interest you. And if you have children, check the playroom. The swimming pools on board ship are really not for doing laps, but for lolling around and getting wet when you feel dehydrated from the sun. (But if the vessel shows two pools, plus a children's splash pool, you may be able to get some exercise in one.) The dining room arrangement, an important factor to check, often offers two sections—and you may note a preference immediately. When booking, ask about nonsmoking areas and whether the kitchen will serve special meals (low-sodium, kosher, etc.)

SHIP SANITATION: Everyone should be interested in the health record of the cruise vessel, which is available from any local office of the U.S. Public Health Service for vessels sailing from American ports. In 1975 the U.S. Pub-

Song of America

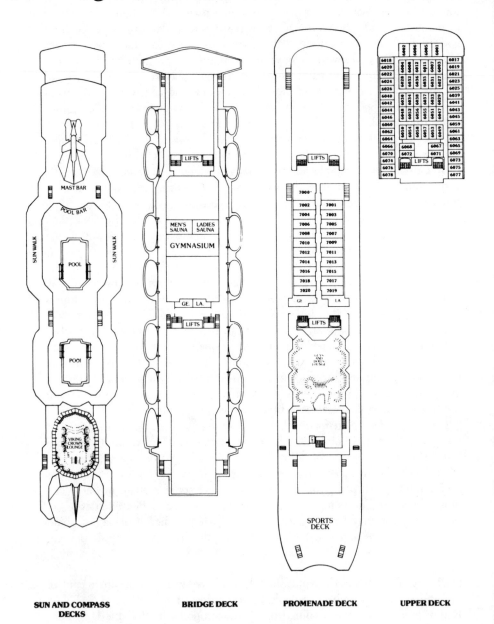

SUN AND COMPASS DECKS   **BRIDGE DECK**   **PROMENADE DECK**   **UPPER DECK**

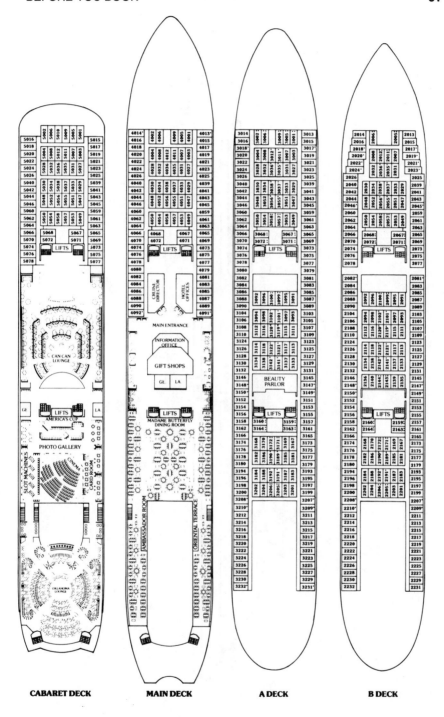

CABARET DECK **MAIN DECK** **A DECK** **B DECK**

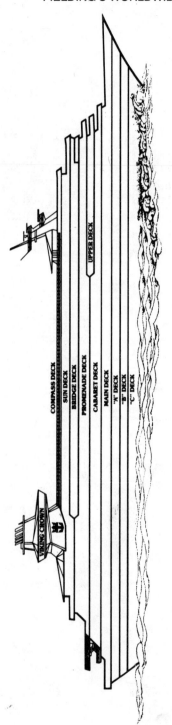

lic Health Service inaugurated a sanitation inspection program because occasional outbreaks of illnesses seemed caused by on-board sanitation. Inspections occur many times a year per cruise ship, and the crew is notified when the health officials are due aboard. Considerable publicity in the past drew attention to vessels that failed to pass the stringent tests (a score of eighty-five out of a hundred). Ship lines take great exception to the scoring and the rigorous standards. Strict or not, the tests benefit the passengers, who are captive audience for days and should expect the most sanitary conditions possible. Many ship lines have been very lazy in the past; I think a little adverse publicity is good for them. Contaminated food has caused illnesses to passengers aboard the *Skyward*, the *Song of Norway* and the *Festivale* (which was actually prevented from sailing by the U.S. Public Health Service and a shipload of passengers had to return home "cruiseless"), among others. However, these are isolated cases, and the health inspectors are determined to keep every ship line on its toes. Some lines have responded favorably, like Holland America and Cunard, who have placed a special officer on each flagship to monitor the kitchen and the sanitation.

SHAKE-DOWN CRUISES: Are you booking aboard a ship that is new to service, that has not been properly "shaken down"? Shake-down cruises work out the kinks (as in any new machine), but unless you're an invited guest or offered a huge discount for the privilege of being a guinea pig, avoid most newly launched or relaunched vessels for the first several sailings. Some shake-down cruises I have attended were memorable for many reasons, but I'm not sure I would do it again! Aboard one ship the second-sitting diners fell asleep in their plates awaiting service past 1 a.m. and the air conditioning went on and off. Aboard another inaugural cruise the ship went dead in the water for several hours and we were all disappointed to miss an exciting day's excursion. This was also the ship on which we drank coffee made from seawater because the supply of freshwater had long run out. On still another inaugural voyage the plumbing backed up, and a few hundred passengers were not allowed to embark in Southampton. One sold-out cruise to Bermuda was cancelled, and a month later the same ship's engines went dead for over twenty-four hours. On the first month of a new run, one line had problems with food, service, crew, shore excursions, and air conditioning. None of this is very amusing when it happens to you on your hard-earned vacation!

BOOKING YOUR CABIN: Be firm when you decide which cabin to book; it's your most important decision. First determine how much you can pay, because the variety in cabin categories is considerable. For example, a one-week cruise aboard the *Sun Princess* from Vancouver to Alaska's Inside Passage charges half the per-person rate in Category K (double room inside, with double bed and shower, on Capri Deck) of Category A (deluxe suites outside with queen-size bed, sitting area, refrigerator, tub/bath, on Promenade Deck). If you choose the lowest category and book an inside cabin, you and the deluxe stateroom occupants should be offered the same meals and choice of hours, entertainment, shore excursions, and so on. There may be some difference in cabin service—this is especially true on the *Queen Elizabeth II*—but most cruise vessels have crew that serve everyone equally with the same happy face.

If you plan to use your cabin only to sleep and change your clothes, or share it with another single traveler (the ship will assign a cabin mate), then by all means choose the lowest category and spend all your time out on the decks. However, if you and your spouse or companion plan to frequent the cabin or expect to entertain new-found friends, then spend a little more and book a larger, outside cabin that you will enjoy every minute. Request a cabin mid-ships where the ride is certainly smoother if you're prone to motion sickness. It's also better to be midway between the upper and lower deck, especially on transatlantic crossings that may be stormy. The deluxe outside cabins will have larger windows, while the rest of the outside categories feature the standard porthole. Whatever the aperture, never open it at sea, because it's very dangerous and because the ship is fully air-conditioned. With the advent of air conditioning, inside cabins became comparable to those with a sea view (except for knowing what the weather was like).

The category you choose to book will probably determine the layout of your cabin—upper and lower berths, two parallel lower berths (with uppers in the wall), two lower berths in "L" shape, or a double/queen/king bed. Deluxe suites with a separate sitting area (even another room) may also have a sofa-bed to accommodate additional passengers (if they are small). But whatever your category, unless you have booked the duplex suites on the QE2, expect to be shocked at the size. Lack of spaciousness in most cabins seems to have come full circle since the days of Charles Dickens. Dickens sailed to Boston in 1842 aboard the *Britannia* and was surprised to find his deluxe stateroom for three only a little larger than a closet. As the voyage progressed, however, Dickens and his cabin mates agreed that their accommodation was indeed quite spacious, especially if they all turned around in unison! You, too, will become accustomed to the small size. Unfortunately, as the price of new cruise ships rises, the amount allotted per cabin decreases. On the *Song of Norway*, two passengers cannot sit on the beds without locking knees, so try to travel with someone friendly. On the *Norway*, however, even the inside cabins with upper and lower berths are very spacious and comfortable. And the deluxe rooms (ex-*première* class of the *France*) offer a true feeling of grandeur—closet space even, and a bidet!

When choosing a cabin, no matter what category, consider your habits. If you are in bed by 9 p.m., stay away from the disco (which doesn't begin popping until 10:30 every night). If walking is a problem, select a cabin near one of the elevators. Do you need a bathtub? Will a shower do just as well? Some showers are so small that if you drop the soap you've had it. Do you need extra space to work; does the cabin have a telephone; do you wish to have a great deal of privacy? I have noted elsewhere that connecting cabins should be avoided unless you're purchasing both parts, because the so-called connecting panel is a conduit for conversations from both sides. Unless the connecting cabins have a proper, water-tight door between them, book a higher or lower category. Another common error, booking a deluxe cabin on Promenade Deck, allows everyone to watch you as they pass by. Passengers in these cabins on the *Song of Norway* complain mightily, and some even try to transfer to a lower deck. Discuss this and all the other nuances of cabin selection with your travel agent; then decide what category and its placement on the ship suits you.

In addition to beds (one to four), you can expect to find a dresser/vanity, a wardrobe, a chair or two, and a small table (for the champagne bucket and breakfast tray) in your cabin. On some of the newer vessels, the beds will convert to sofas by day (and may even fold into the wall). By popular demand, many ship lines are now offering a number of double-bed cabins, especially in the lower categories. And Carnival Cruise Lines claims that all its beds do convert into king size on the new *Tropicale*. If you prefer a larger bed to two twins, make your request when you book, and the ship line will try to accommodate you. In general, the line can no longer promise a specific cabin number when you book, but they will guarantee the rate and category you wish. When your tickets arrive, they will show the cabin number that you have been assigned.

4. / BEFORE YOU SAIL

When the cruise tickets arrive in the mail, you know you're on the way! It's a nice feeling just to grasp them and consider lazy days at sea, lunch on deck, adventuresome foods, personalized service, new ports, and new friends. Not to disturb the reverie, but while tickets are in hand, check the boxes and make sure the date and point of embarkation are correct. Since most ship lines no longer assign cabins when you book but instead guarantee a certain category (and rate), check to see that the cabin number on your ticket coincides with the category you paid for (occasionally, it will even be a grade higher). Also make sure the name of the ship is correct. Norwegian Caribbean Line officials claim that the majority of passengers who arrive for embarkation in Miami are not even aware which vessel they have booked, so don't laugh at this suggestion.

You might also read the passage contract carefully, for it details the ship owner's liability and cancellation charges. If you cannot use the ticket and do not give notice to the company within sixty days of departure, charges are levied (unless the space is immediately sold). If you decide not to sail in less than five days before embarkation, the total fare may be forfeit unless the ship line is sympathetic to the calamitous happenings that prevent your traveling. However, once you embark and begin your cruise (and then get sick or whatever), there is no recompense. (If the ship line must cancel a cruise, however, you will probably receive a full refund.) This contract also states the cruise fare (with all inclusions), procedures describing how to settle your account for any purchases on board, luggage restrictions (if any), policy regarding cabin changes, instructions to safeguard valuables, and a caution against carrying goods of a dangerous nature. These items are all detailed on, or along with, your ticket, in hope that no misunderstanding between passenger and ship operator will cause a future problem.

Baggage tags will accompany your tickets, and you should transfer the information on your ticket to that required on the tags. Some lines, like Royal Cruise, have color-coded tags so porters will immediately recognize on which section of the ship your bags should be placed. If you're traveling on an air-sea program and are met at the airport for transfer to the vessel, you will probably be requested to tag your bags with the ship's labels before you check them at the airport. This enables the ship line personnel to claim your bags upon your flight's arrival and transport them to the ship. If you neglect to follow these instructions, your cruise wardrobe may just sit in the baggage claim area until you begin to wonder why your cabin is so empty. Alternatively, if you fly into the city of embarkation on your own and did not follow the instructions sent to you (and tagged your bags too soon), your cruise wardrobe will be sent straight to the ship—while you run around the airport with visions of sailing away naked. Of course, bags do become authentically lost. If this happens to you, inform both the airline and the ship line at once; and don't leave the airport without filing a claim form and leaving your cruise itinerary (ports of call in order of appearance). I have known luggage to miraculously appear in the rightful cabin midway in a cruise, especially if the passenger is part of an air-sea program.

LUGGAGE: Luggage can easily become a problem, if you're not careful. Few of us can afford to rent the cabin next door just for our bags! One average-sized suitcase and one carry-on bag is quite sufficient for the normal seven-day cruise, especially if you plan to be casual by day. Pack your feathers and other fancies first, and put the casual clothes around them. If your spouse or companion prefers a fold-over bag, all the better; you can sneak in a few dresses or suits. Ships were once famous for the huge amounts of baggage they could accommodate. No longer. Space is at a premium on most of today's cruise vessels (especially those built in the past decade). So, just bring along what you can comfortably put in your cabin, either under the beds or in the wardrobe areas, because you don't want to fall over a suitcase every time you open the door. On ships offering longer cruises (more than a month or so), a proper baggage room for storage may exist. If you no longer have your wardrobe trunk from school or camp days, some companies will still come to your home, pack your clothing in a stand-up carton, and deliver it aboard your cruise vessel. At the end of the voyage, they will transport your wardrobe back to its proper home. All for a fine fee, of course (check with your travel agent or ship line for the most reputable and efficient firms).

IMMUNIZATION AND DOCUMENTS: If your cruise is confined to Caribbean or European waters, you probably will not need any immunizations. But if you are sailing for the Far East, be aware of requirements—for smallpox, cholera, typhoid, tetanus, hepatitis, and even yellow fever—imposed by some of the countries your ship will visit. If you cruise within the Galapagos Islands and certain other parts of South America, your doctor may advise that you take malaria-prevention medicine before and after your journey. Double-check each country's requirement *before* you sail so that your own doctor can administer the immunization and your arms will return to normal before embarkation.

You do not need a passport or visas for Caribbean cruises, but it often helps if you have some proof of citizenship (voter's registration or birth certificate will do). Elsewhere, you certainly must bring an up-to-date passport along.

The ship line should advise you of any visas necessary for the ports of call, and your travel agent will help you obtain them from the appropriate consulates. For China cruises, the ship line receives a blanket visa for all passengers aboard who plan to disembark and take tours handled by Luxingshe (China International Travel Service). If, however, your ship is calling at ports in the USSR and Poland, you may be requested to obtain your own visa, especially if you do not intend to take an organized shore excursion. (You also have to obtain your own visa for Japan, Australia, and other countries.) When you board your vessel bound for these wonderful and exotic places, the purser will require you to surrender your passport. This enables the local immigration and customs officials to clear the ship as soon as possible upon arrival in a port. You will not see or need your passport again (under normal circumstances) until your voyage ends. If you return to the same port of embarkation, you will receive your documents the evening before arrival. If the port of disembarkation is in a different country whence you departed, the ship line will keep your passport for clearance and return it to you directly after.

MONEY: All cruise vessels accept cash and travelers' cheques for payment of on-board extras (wine, drinks, boutique and gift shop purchases, and tips). Some ship lines now also accept credit cards for all these items, and a personal check is possible with advanced arrangements. The purser's office converts your dollars into local currency at certain hours if the supply on board is adequate. But this is not a bank, and the purser and his staff cannot reconvert your local currency into dollars (so don't ask, they often get mad). If the port officials are friendly and obliging, they will frequently allow a representative of a local bank to come aboard for several hours to handle passengers' monetary transactions. This helpful courtesy saves so much valuable time in port, be properly grateful when it occurs.

ELECTRICAL APPLIANCES: At this time you may also want to check if your hair dryer, electric shaver, and foot warmer will work properly in the cabin. Most ship lines have the correct electrical fixture in the bathroom for a shaver, but I have blown many a fuse trying to use my hair dryer on board. Hair dryers and travel irons are a source of consternation to most ship lines and should probably be left at home. If you must take your hair dryer, use it in the beauty salon where the outlets can handle it. (I would ask permission first and then offer a nice tip.) Never use an iron in your cabin; many vessels now have self laundry/ironing rooms by popular demand. Although all ships offer laundry and pressing services, it is nice to know one can press out a crease quickly, if necessary.

EMBARKING: When it's embarkation time and you know that your cruise ship will be returning to the same terminal, be observant. The departure is usually a blur and the returning a hassle, but if you have memorized the terminal's layout and know where you parked your car or where the nearest taxi service is you will feel better. For a 4:30 sailing, most ships begin embarkation around 1:30 p.m. If you embark on your own, do it early so you can relax and enjoy the getting underway. Local stevedores will carry your baggage onto the vessel and you will not see it again until it appears in the cabin. (In some of the smaller ports, you and your baggage will never part company, which can be more comforting.) If you carry expensive camera equipment or a great deal of jewelry, stop by the customs office in port and declare your valuables prior to leaving the country. This saves considerable time and embarrassment upon return.

Once up the gangplank, you will meet a steward who will show you the location of your cabin and introduce you to the cabin attendant. If you are expecting visitors and wish to have a small Bon Voyage party, the cabin attendant will bring ice and glasses, and deliver any flowers, champagne, or fruit that arrives in your name. Hors d'oeuvres or petits fours are a nice addition, and your room steward will try to oblige, but most ship lines require prior notification. Any special services at embarkation should be arranged for in advance, because the crew is so busy at this time. If your ship line encourages visitors, it will enclose some guest passes (usually two per passenger) along with your tickets. It may also enclose an order form for possible embarkation requests, as Holland America does, and the cost will be charged to your shipboard account for payment at the end of the cruise. (The hotel manager at Holland America tells me that sandwiches and hors d'oeuvres are just a few dollars a tray, but the bottled liquor will be more expensive than when at sea because of import taxes.) All of the ship's watering holes are closed by law in New York harbor and all along the West coast (but not in Miami), so the only alcoholic beverages available are by advance order (bottles only) or if you bring your own. The latter is perfectly acceptable, provided you imbibe in the privacy of your own cabin. You may also bring along your own party treats, but keep them to a minimum. Remind your well-meaning friends that you are embarking on a *cruise* and suggest they send the overloaded hampers off to someone who won't be served so many courses in the next several days. In any event, most Bon Voyage parties are less than two hours (visitors must disembark at least thirty minutes prior to sailing), so how much do you really need?

If you wish to have a large reception catered by the ship line, arrange the details through your travel agent. The line will handle refreshments and set aside enough space for you in one of the lounges. It is increasingly popular and convenient to have postnuptial parties on board your own personal "love boat." You may even plan an on-board ceremony, but you must bring along your own officiate since captains are no longer allowed to perform marriages, even at sea. For a full-blown wedding reception featuring a many-tiered cake, champagne, open bar, sandwiches, coffee, and live music for dancing, the ship's hotel manager will prepare one of the lounges for you, and your guests may board as early as noon.

Embark early enough to explore your new home, check out the pool area and deck chair situation, even plot which side of the ship is better for a tan. It's also a good idea to look in the boutiques (for future indulgences) and find the drugstore or gift shop, just in case the sun lotion or film supply runs low. And don't forget to locate your life jacket—usually under the bed or on the top shelf of the wardrobe—and study the deck plans on the back of your cabin door. Instructions for your life boat station and drill information also should be on the door. A drill will occur soon after sailing, or early the next morning if the first day of your cruise is spent at sea. When you hear the alarm, put on your life jacket and quickly walk up to your station on Boat Deck. Some ship lines take attendance, so don't fool around. The ship's photographer (whom you no doubt met upon embarkation) will record the event for posterity. You haven't been on a cruise until you have been immortalized in a life jacket!

A FEW WARNINGS: Basically, if you consider your cruise vessel a floating resort that transports you from one wonderful port to another as an added bonus, everything will be placed in proper perspective. For example, if you feel naked without your diamonds and emeralds (or wads of cash in your hip pocket) then bring them along, but place all valuables in a safe deposit box provided by the ship line (the very same boxes a hotel would provide) when not wearing or carrying them. I have rarely heard of a ship-board theft, but why offer the temptation?

If you plan to sun, take it easy; protect yourself with plenty of lotion. Many passengers forget that tropical sun is more intense than that found in most parts of North America. Too much sun for passengers on the *Norway* was such a problem that Norwegian Caribbean Line wisely transposed the port calls; the beach party at Little San Salvador now takes place after the shopping spree in St. Thomas. If your cruise takes you to new and exotic parts of the world, you might want to discuss the itinerary with your doctor or druggist, who might recommend an effective sun screen. Hats are mandatory if you are out touring along the equator all day, for a scalp burn is just as dangerous as any other.

Another danger may be to your camera, if you decide to bring it. The sea spray can damage lenses, and sand is "the end." The best advice is to visit your favorite camera shop with itinerary in hand and find out what lens, filters, film speed and type, and covers to use. Having the proper equipment is important if you're to enjoy taking your vacation photographs, especially at sea when so

many elements are working together (and some against you) at the same time—
and you're moving besides!

Speaking of moving, you may want to look into this funny thing called *mal de mer*. It's nothing but motion sickness, only you can't get off; accordingly, you have to cure the problem midstream, so to speak. There are now three methods to "cure" that feeling of being green: pills, shots, and patches. All three have pros and cons. The pills (by whatever brand name you wish to call them) tend to make you sleepy, and it is not wise to combine them with alcohol. The shot, available from any doctor or nurse aboard ship, works rather quickly, but my husband and another friend received a shot—for $3—aboard the *Atlantic* recently (during a freak summer storm on the Atlantic) and neither could sit down comfortably for two days! The "patch" is known as Transderm-Scop and is available by prescription, only. Aboard the *Norway* last summer, I met one of the distributors for this product and he said that NASA uses them on selected astronauts. However, it must be applied (behind the ear is best) *before* the cruise begins, and it only lasts 72 hours. The doctor aboard the *Atlantic* also informed me that it can cause dryness in the mouth, and occasionally slightly-blurred vision. You can eat and drink anything with the patch; with the shot, no coffee. (I have also heard recently that powdered ginger pills are also good—especially for health nuts.)

Since I dislike anything stronger than a Vitamin C pill, my own cure for queasiness is a nice hot cup of consomme (usually available on deck about 11 a.m.), some crackers (saltines are best), and deep breaths of sea air. One shipline executive also said: the best antidote for *mal de mer* is preoccupation. Joining in the many onboard activities is the best way to forget about the roll of the ship. In fact, that queasy feeling will most likely disappear, forever!

5. / ON BOARD

Getting underway never fails to make my skin tingle, my eyes mist slightly, and my knees a bit weak as I lift a glass of the bubbly in salute. Casting off and feeling the ship pull away from the pier is, indeed, one of the most exciting parts of being aboard. And the exhilaration exists whether you are sailing under the Golden Gate, past the Statue of Liberty, away from Dodge Island, or into the bustling harbor of Piraeus. As familiar landmarks disappear and the sun dips into the horizon, you know that adventure lies ahead. To fully enjoy the sailing away, I always like to have unpacked and treated myself to a quick tour of the public areas, so I can be out on deck, glass in hand, to toast the leave-taking. If you happen to be sailing from Piraeus, it's most likely cocktail time anyway, and the sunset is worth your dressing up. If you are aboard a Caribbean-bound cruise vessel, you may be in a more casual mood. In fact, the most familiar sight in Miami at 4:30 p.m. on any Saturday is a sea of orange life vests as the ships leave in formation with passengers preparing for boat drill.

RESERVING A TABLE: Before you really settle in, be sure to take care of your table assignment and meal hour preference, if you have not already done so. (Some ship lines handle this on shore and notify you by mail or by card in your cabin.) At sailing time, the maitre d' (or someone on his staff) will be receiving passenger requests outside the dining room or in one of the public lounges, so seek him out speedily if you want a good choice of tables. Unfortunately, most ship lines have two seatings for all meals in the dining room (exceptions include Royal Viking, Norwegian American, *QE2* first-class, plus the *Daphne* and *Danae* lovelies), which means that your stomach is fed either earlier than it is accustomed to or later than satisfactory. Meal hours vary somewhat among the lines, but the main seating is around 7:30 a.m. (breakfast), noon (luncheon), and 6:30 p.m. (dinner). Second or late seating hours are generally around 8:45 a.m., 1:30 p.m., and 8:30 p.m. Since you may avoid these schedules by having breakfast in bed or out on deck, and partaking of the luncheon buffet that is usually served around the pool, dinner hour is your only real decision. If you have young children, you will be encouraged to consider the earlier time period. The later seating is more fashionable, of course, and more suited to couples and swinging singles.

On most ships you may request, and be very firm about, a table for two. (I have always found this the most satisfactory, as my husband and I enjoy our quiet conversations at sea.) If this is not possible, however, ask for a table for six or eight, because at a table for four you may get stuck with a completely incompatible couple. Many ship lines claim that they are experts at putting people together in the dining room. I don't believe for one moment that any maitre d' or his staff can look at seven hundred different passengers in the space of an hour or two and match them perfectly. It's simply dumb luck, and if you luck doesn't hold and you find your table companions to be not your type, then take your case back to the maitre d'. In most instances he will be obliging, but his hands may be tied if the ship is fully booked. If you are traveling alone or in a group of singles, you will want the largest table possible. Explain this in a gentle way to the maitre d' and he will do his best. After all, he wants everyone happy (and many a romance has begun at the table).

EATING ABOARD: More has been written about food on board cruise vessels than about itinerary, ambiance, service, size of cabins, or anything else. Because at least five meals are served daily, you can have a "pig out" (as my husband calls it) from early morning to late at night. For starters, you can rise early (good heavens!) and have coffee on deck at 6:30 a.m. This may stimulate your appetite for the three choices of full breakfast available on most ships. You may return to your cabin for everything from the dainty Continental breakfast to kippers, assorted cheeses, and hot chocolate. If you want the proper sit-down service that you paid for, head for the dining room where your waiter will keep the java hot and you may have everything on the menu. Or, on many cruise vessels, you may have a pleasant buffet breakfast out on deck; although lighter than what is available in the dining room, this may include scrambled eggs, bacon and sausage, English muffins, toast, fresh Danish pastries, juice, fruit, and coffee/tea. Hours for this repast will be posted in your daily program. For the real sleepyheads, coffee and Danish may be served in one of the lounges until lunchtime. Just a few of the ships with outside service are the Cunard *Countess* and *Princess* (the cafe later turns out hamburgers), the *Oceanic Independence* (with a Parisian-style sidewalk cafe), the *Norway,* and the Royal Caribbean vessels (with a pool cafe on sun deck).

Not many ships continue the tradition of bouillon at 11 a.m., a hangover from the grand old days of translatlantic travel. Bouillon, always good for warming the insides as you sat under a steamer rug on a deck chair in the misty air, was also an excellent antidote for queasy stomachs. In the Caribbean you will probably not be served bouillon (instead you head for a cool, refreshing drink from the bar), but if you are cruising in the colder waters of Alaska, the Baltic, around the North Cape, or across the Atlantic, you can count on it (and it may be a lifesaver).

Before you have digested those waffles with whipped butter and rasher of bacon, lunch is being served. At sea (or in port) on pleasant days, a cold buffet is usually served near a swimming pool (and you may fill your plate while bikini-clad). Some ships also have hamburgers and hot dogs sizzling on a nearby grill. I always avoid the dining room at lunchtime, if possible, and love these outdoor buffets. Even if the weather is on the cool side, it's refreshing to sit on deck and inhale the sea breezes. Aboard the *Stella Solaris* one spring, we sat on deck with some fruit and cheese from the cold buffet, shared a bottle of local wine with new-found friends, and thought life was certainly splendid as the ship sailed away from Dikili and the ruins of Pergamum. Such a feeling would have been entirely lost in a packed dining room.

However, if you must have a hot lunch, the dining room readies a complete range of dishes for your palate. Soups, salads, and entrees change daily, and the chef prepares a special. I always ask the waiter what he advises before making a final decision. After all, he's been in the kitchen and knows what looks good. After a day or so, a wise waiter will know your preferences and begin to recommend dishes before you even pop the question. Every ship line features some sort of specialty that you will soon not be able to live without. The Sun *Princess* has the juiciest hamburgers afloat, while Sitmar serves fantastic pizza. Herring in every form can be found aplenty on Royal Viking, the *Lindblad Polaris* and Norwegian American vessels, and traditional southern "Steamboatin' Cuisine" is also a treat. The *QE2* has an excellent soup kitchen, and the other two Cunard vessels couldn't exist without their daily ration of fish and chips (with vinegar, of course). Greek vessels serve mounds of black olives, and a handful a day is wonderful for your skin as well as delicious with crusty bread and feta cheese.

Food becomes important at sea, and it's mind-boggling that so many meals are served to so many people so efficiently. Although Robert Dirks, Director of Marketing, Fontainebleau Hilton, refers to most ship-board cuisine as "banquet food," fine exceptions to this blanket judgment are Home Lines, Royal Viking, Norwegian American, and *Delta Queen*. I do not agree with many writers who tell you that every night aboard every ship you will have a gourmet meal and impeccable service. Nonsense! On most cruise vessels you will be very pleased with the taste and presentation of your meal. On others, well, it will be more difficult to choose a palatable and well-balanced dinner. However, if one meal does not pass the taste-bud test, there are certainly many more to anticipate. And, if you're curious about the amounts it takes to feed a shipload, the galley of the 1700-passenger, 800-crew *Canberra* caters an average of 7500 main meals a day; approximate quantities consumed are ⅓ ton fish, 1¼ tons meat/poultry, 1½ tons vegetables/potatoes, ⅓ ton flour, ⅓ ton butter and bacon, 4840 eggs, 3500 pieces of fruit, 6500 bread/rolls (baked on board, of course), 180 loaves of bread (each 2½ lbs. and baked on board); 2000 pastries made in the ship's confectioners shop. Not to mention 1374 menus printed daily for two seatings in two different restaurants. And you wonder why your cabin is so small—foodstuffs demand top priority for space!

Should you have the slightest feeling of hunger by late afternoon, full tea service in one of the lounges will feature sandwiches, pastries, and little cakes. Royal Caribbean serves ice cream sundaes at 4 p.m. in the pool cafe. Ice cream parlors (for the purchase of gooey concoctions), found on the *Norway* and the *Oceanic*, are popular gathering places throughout the day.

Finally, you hightail it to the dining room as the first note of chimes is struck for your dinner seating. (Most cruise ships request that you enter the dining room not more than fifteen minutes after the meal has been announced. This is a courtesy both to the kitchen and your table companions.) Most of these floating restaurants assume a new and enjoyable personality in the evening. The stewards are usually in a good mood because dinner is their favorite meal to serve, and their day is almost over. If the lights are low enough to hide your wrinkles but still find your plate, all the better!

Aside from the first and final evenings on board, which are casual and often awkward, your evenings in the dining room will be very special. You can expect a Captain's Welcome Dinner as well as a Captain's Farewell Dinner plus any number of other galas. Often featured are Spanish Night, Italian Night, French Night, Caribbean Night, Greek Night, American Night, Hawaiian Night, Norwegian Night, and two or three galas depending upon the nationality of your crew and the length of your cruise. If you are aboard a Greek-flag vessel, you might have a taste of what K-Lines Hellenic Cruises offers on its Soiree Grecque. For appetizers, the list reads: dolmadakia, taramosalata, tzatziki, amphissa olives, bourekakia, fried baby squashes, and ouzo special. This is followed by: shrimps Microlimano style, baby lamb Roumeli style or veal liver, roast potatoes and buttered artichokes, Greek salad (cucumbers, tomatoes, feta cheese, onions, black olives, oil and vinegar), assorted Greek cheeses, and for dessert a choice of baklava, kataifi, galaktoboureko, or kaimaki ice cream (or all four). And by the end of the meal, the sommelier has recommended a number of Greek wines. (The only item missing at this feast is the famous Avgolemono soup of chicken broth, egg, and lemon—delicious)!

And this is just one special evening! Royal Caribbean claims that you have a choice of some 1500 separate items on its weekly menus (but I suspect this includes all three meals). On some of the more elegant cruise vessels, you may order off the menu and have a steak every night if you wish. Settle any special diet needs before you book your cruise, because some lines will not cater to individuals but do carry enough different types of foodstuffs so that you may work around the problem. And if you're fussy (like me), you just may have to make do with soup and salad one night if everything else appears too heavy or greasy. Strictly speaking, I would say that the food on most cruise ships is good, and it's difficult not to overeat (especially when those luscious desserts come rolling in). Steaks, prime ribs, and fresh fish of all varieties are the best selections at sea. Sauces, like many wines, do not travel well, and I avoid any dish that arrives imbued. And stay away from anything that looks a bit old (sauces are sometimes used to cover up). A friend also suggests that the caviar now served aboard many vessels at the captain's gala dinners and a traditional treat at the Welcome Aboard dinner is barely passable. Since the good stuff is priced like gold and very rare these days, one can understand why ship lines must downgrade the class of their caviar.

On the other hand, many fine and memorable dishes will keep you from becoming bored at sea. How about reindeer meat with juniper berries, real Russian borscht and piroshki, rack of lamb à la QE2, freshly grilled Alaskan salmon, grilled baby calves' liver, duck a l'orange, and uncountable numbers of "omelette surprise" (baked Alaska) and special gateau! It's difficult not to indulge, so it's best to diet beforehand. Then, by the end of your cruise, you cannot complain that the sea air shrank your wardrobe.

In case you just can't make it to bed without another little snack, the midnight buffet begins about 11:30 p.m. and lasts until 1 a.m. or so. Here you will find deviled eggs, cold meats, cheeses, salads, lobster and shrimp, fresh fruit, and tempting little pastries. Some ships pay particular attention to this final meal of the day, especially in the Caribbean (Carnival Cruise Lines claims to have three different buffets on every vessel). If you happen to be sailing in Europe, you may not be honored with a buffet, or you may find only a simple table of cheeses, bread, and cold meats (such as Royal Viking arranges in its Sky Deck lounges, where I rarely saw anyone with nerve enough to partake, because the dinners on board were all so splendid).

DRINKING ABOARD: The captain of the *Dolphin*, a cozy vessel that cruises out of Miami twice weekly to the Bahamas, says the amount of alcohol consumed per day per passenger is directly related to the length of the cruise. He says that three- and four-day passengers drink more in each 24-hour period than do passengers on longer cruises. Well, for the getting underway, nothing beats those bubbles up your nose. It's traditional, and popping that cork is good for the soul! Norwegian American Cruises believes in this tradition so much that every one of its cabins includes a complimentary bottle of champagne for the sailing. It's a splendid gesture that other lines should imitate (the *Mermoz* should continue to provide champagne as it did for its tenth anniversary celebration, since this is the only French-flag vessel in the Caribbean). Now, where to enjoy your champagne . . . if you have a large cabin with terrace, you know where. Otherwise, out on deck to enhance every bittersweet moment of departure.

Most cruise vessels have several lounges with bars. Outstanding are the RCCL (Royal Caribbean Cruise Line) trademark Viking Crown Lounge, ten stories up and cantilevered from the smokestack, and the *Norway*'s Club International, the most elegant lounge afloat and a lovely hangover from French Line days. Once the vessel is underway and you have time to explore, you'll be surprised how many little nooks are tucked around where you have a preprandial cocktail, waker-upper, or putter-to-sleeper. With the exception of the Club International (which concentrates solely upon itself), I always venture toward the best view and find my spot for the duration of the cruise (a true creature of habit). Most vessels have some type of glass-enclosed lounge located on a high deck, so that you can be on top of (yet a part of) the sea below. On the *Stella Solaris*, the glassed-in Piano Bar has a panoramic view and the *Mississippi Queen*'s two-story, glass-enclosed Paddlewheel Lounge is among the most dramatic. On the Princess vessels, the view is best from the Starlight lounges. Royal Viking has its Discovery, Windjammer, or Stella Polaris room up on Sky Deck (by whichever name, the view is the same and always splendid). And so on. Every vessel has at least one spectacular public area, a quiet bar, and plenty of spots where the action congregates.

Drinks on board ship, no longer as inexpensive as they were, are still less than on dry land. If you are a teetotaler, you'll find plenty of juices (75¢), sodas (50¢), and colas in the can (75¢). Perrier is about $1.10, and beers range from American ($1.25) to imported ($1.50). Cocktails average $1.75 for the simple variety (martini, daiquiri, piña colada, margarita, Manhattan, side car, black Russian) and often only $1.25 on "special" (like bloody mary or screwdriver in the morning, Cuba libre at noon, and crème de menthe on the rocks after dinner). Cunard specializes in liquered coffees after dinner in the *Princess* and *Countess* main lounges, and you can always find ouzo on Greek ships, vodka on Russian vessels, and schnapps on Scandinavian-flag ships. Some vessels will serve wine by the glass from the bar, others will not—and this can be a problem to the many Americans who now prefer wines to hard liquor.

If you enjoy wine with your dinner, you'll love being at sea. The wine list is usually interesting, especially if you're aboard a Greek- or Italian-flag vessel and wish to try the many local brands at reasonable prices. Greek white wines might be retsina, Robola, Santa Elena, Hymettos, Santa Laura, Demestica; red wines of the same type are Chevalier de Rhodes, Naoussa, Monte Nero, Santa Laura, Demestica, and Lava. On Italian vessels, Soave Bolla seems to be the popular brand, along with Verdicchio, Frascati, and the straw-covered Chiantis. The more expensive French white and red burgundies, Beaujolais, California names, and even Blue Nun are on most wine lists, plus champagnes from sparkling German wines to vintage French at $25 a bottle. Greek and Italian wines are still in the $5.50 to $8 range, while the French *caves* are much, much more. Most lists have a number of bottles that are $10 and below, so why pay more for a vintage that was not made for rolling around on the sea all day?

If you wish to order wine, advise your dining room steward as soon as you are seated, for the sommelier can become very busy as the evening progresses and may not have time to chill or uncork the bottle properly. He knows the "cellar" and can offer worthy suggestions if you catch him before he is beckoned away and you have to wait forever for your choice. Some cruise vessels post the menus in advance and allow you to order your dinner wine early for more efficiency—a fine idea.

SHIP'S PERSONNEL AND SERVICES: The most important people in your personal ship-board life are your cabin attendants and the dining room staff assigned to your section. The names of your cabin attendants should be posted and visible as you enter your cabin for the first time, and in fact, he/she or they should be waiting to greet you and offer any assistance. These stewards or stewardesses are your link with the rest of the cruise vessel, for they know what time meals are and what to do about laundry, pressing, ice, or extra glasses for cocktail parties. They will clean your cabin when you depart in the morning and should have a sixth sense about what you might want upon your return from a long day in port or up at the pool. If you enjoy breakfast in bed, your cabin steward or stewardess will collect your order in the late evening and bring the tray at the appointed time the following morning. If there is a small service you wish to have performed each day (like tea at 4:00 or the ice bucket filled at 5:00), inform him or her as you get settled (and a small tip then may help). Your cabin attendants are chosen for their cheerful attitude and willingness to serve. If you find them the contrary and it threatens to ruin your cruise, discuss the situation with the chief purser. If there is space elsewhere on the ship, the chief purser may move you to another cabin. If there is not, you may have to settle for his reprimanding the proper person. My husband and I have had excellent cabin attendants and terrible ones. If you have strong feelings about your cabin service either way, reflect it in your tips (good service should be rewarded well).

The same goes for the dining room personnel. If the maitre d' has placed you at a table of stimulating people, the sommelier has suggested the most perfect wines each evening, and the stewards have been attentive and gracious at every meal, they should all be tipped appropriately. And don't forget how many times you have requested additional favors, like an extra dessert, a birthday cake for your husband, or farewell champagne for the table. You will have found your own favorite barman who, within a few hours of sailing, remembers your favorite brand and how much ice to add. If he also remembers your names, you belong to an exclusive club, indeed. And don't be surprised if your favorite steward or stewardess serves at other functions, like the luncheon buffet around the pool, afternoon tea in the lounge, or a private cocktail party. A good waiter is in demand throughout the vessel.

Other service personnel you may wish to know are the deck steward, the pool attendants (indoors or out), the gymnasium attendant, and any children's counselors. On deck, you may need assistance with setting up the chaises (some ships, like Home Lines' vessels, still charge for them), getting proper towels for swimming, and the accoutrements of deck games such as shuffleboard or table tennis. If you use the indoor pool, another set of attendants will service that area as well as the sauna and gymnasium equipment. Occasionally, an expert in physical fitness will be on board to instruct you in the use of the Nautilus or other machinery or to lead a class in calisthenics every morning and perhaps a little yoga at teatime (if you show up too early for tea on the QE2, you will run smack into the yoga session in the Queen's Room). Carras Cruises employed a most attractive woman on the *Danae*, who offered individual lessons in exercise that soon became the most enjoyable part of everyone's day! Eric Mason on the QE2 is certainly the dean and most seaworthy of all physical fitness experts. Eric, in his 60s, looks half his age, no doubt due to his daily jog about this vast vessel (and he's terrific at yoga, too.)

If you are sailing with the children, you will be delighted to know that they are entertained in their own part of the ship and you may not see them from breakfast to dinner time (after that, it's your responsibility). Many ships have separate children's playrooms and also add a set of young counselors to their service personnel during school vacation periods and the summer months. Young passengers have their own games, are tended while swimming, get their favorite junk food for lunch (hamburgers, hot dogs, french fries, and sodas), watch movies geared to their age, and even have their own tea parties. Children love ship-board life if there are others to play with. You may feed them an early dinner (in the cabin will do if you prefer to dine late yourself) and engage a steward or stewardess to baby-sit in the evenings. The chief purser will take care of this for you (it costs extra, of course), because baby-sitting is not part of your cabin attendants' normal duties.

If you wish to use the beauty/barber shop and spa facilities found on most cruise ships, make your appointments well in advance and make several of them to be sure (you can always cancel later). Beauticians and barbers on board have excellent reputations and will give you a new hairstyle for less than it costs at home (haircuts are especially reasonable for men). Most of these shops also offer pedicure/manicure treatments on availability. Make appointments especially early for evenings that feature a gala, because space in these shops is limited. The same goes for sauna or massage appointments. The price of such pampering is not included in the cruise fare, so you may wish to consider whether you really need a massage. Since the answer is usually "yes," book early for a mid- or late-cruise treatment. Directly after a strenuous port tour is the best time, and it will make you feel like a new person.

After you have learned the ropes of wining, dining, exercising, and pampering yourself with a manicure and massage, you may either collapse in a deck chair for the rest of the voyage or attend marathon activities. Foremost in your schedule should be the Captain's Welcome Aboard Cocktail and Dinner Gala on the evening of your first full day at sea. This is the most formal event of the cruise, and just how dressy you should be will depend upon your particular ship line. Most male passengers will appear in blacktie on Royal Viking and Norwegian American vessels, as well as first class on the QE2, while this event is very casual aboard the *Oceanic Independence*. Women are luckier in their dress because a simple long skirt and top will do nicely on any cruise for "formal" evenings.

At the captain's Welcome Aboard evening, the cruise director (or directrice) will ask your name and then introduce you to the chief purser and the captain. It's easy to tell which one is the *captain*, or master of the vessel, because he wears the most gold on either shoulder (usually four wide bars). The *chief purser*, who deals with the day-to-day running of the cruise and is general information officer, wears three gold (sometimes silver) bars on either shoulder and an insignia that looks like a clover. After you have been introduced to these two men and photographed by the ship's professional shutterbug (the photos will be on display and sale later), you are offered a drink (martini, Manhattan, juice, champagne) and an hors d'oeuvre or two. When all the passengers have been received, the captain introduces the rest of his staff. This will consist of the *chief engineer* (four stripes and a propeller) who makes everything work properly, the *chief radio operator* (three stripes and a radio signal), the *chief electrician* (three stripes and some electrical current), and the *doctor* (three stripes with red or three stripes and a caduceus). And then the *cruise director* will introduce his or her staff, and you are invited to the dining room for a splendid seven-course meal. On some ships, champagne, caviar, and baked Alaska are still part of the traditional welcome dinner.

The chief purser and the cruise director will be the most evident of the ship's personnel on your voyage. The chief purser and his staff handle all money transactions, stamps, and stationery; clear you through customs at ports of call; and provide general information. Whatever you need to know about the vessel and any scheduling you will find at the purser's office, which is open daily from about 9:00 a.m. and usually situated in the middle of the main public deck. Should you need the doctor, you will find his hours posted as well, and you will be advised what numbers to call in case of emergency. If you need to send a message or make a ship-to-shore phone call, the radio room is open to passengers at certain hours (but always closed by law in port). Communication with office or home is very expensive, so be prepared to pay plenty for the privilege. Most communication is excellent and swift, so there is nothing to fear about being way out at sea, and many cruise ships now advertise their use of satellites for telephone calls, placed in the privacy of your cabin. (It's called Progress when you can't even get away from it all on a cruise!)

ACTIVITIES: Your cruise director, responsible for the daily passenger activity list, will invite everyone to the main lounge on the morning of the first full day at sea to explain the myriad of happenings that is called a cruise. He will run down the basics—like the library, card room, and writing room (for books, bridge, and backgammon)—and offer the outdoor crowd such sports as shuffleboard, golf driving range, table or deck tennis, badminton, and volleyball (although not every ship offers every sport). He will also explain rules around the pool areas: what to do about towels, how to get and keep a deck chair, how to get beverage service. Then he will probably begin to check off the more sophisticated entertainment, like skeet shooting, wine tasting parties, ice carving lessons, dance lessons, trap shooting, lectures, and concerts. And we must not forget bingo, which is still everyone's favorite pastime—and the stakes can become very high!

Some vessels offer live musical entertainment (classical, jazz, and all that other stuff) at various hours during the day, while other vessels feature a concert of classical records every afternoon that is popular to read or rest by. And then there are lecturers invited on board free of charge in exchange for dispensing everything they know in an hour or two. I think this arrangement works best aboard the QE2, which is so large and invites so many lecturers on each transatlantic crossing or around-the-world sailing that a few are bound to be good. I, for one, would love to hear what Lillian Gish, George Plimpton, and Scott Carpenter have to say for themselves. I did not much care to hear George Gallup, Jr. (of the well-known poll family) dispense an air of gloom about America in the 1980s (alcoholism will be the country's number-one killer, he said) or a New York stockbroker tell how to buy short and sell long (or is it the other way around?). But, better luck next time. Actually, my favorite organized activity on board is language lessons, because if you're bound for a foreign destination it's very nice to know how to say, "How much is it, please?" and "Good morning." Language lessons are especially fun if you're on a long voyage and can build upon what you learn. The same goes for learning bridge or backgammon or how to do the cha-cha.

The tour guide or cruise director gives a travel talk before each port of call, explaining the schedule, what the shore excursions will cost (in the event you have not already purchased them), and what to expect in money exchange, shopping, and weather. If the cruise director is sophisticated enough, he will also explain what you can do on your own and not dissuade you from exploring without benefit of a paid guide. Usually these travel talks are accompanied by a film or slide show to familiarize you with the landmarks you will be touring. On the cruises that pay particular attention to in-depth sightseeing and archaeological sites (Swans Hellenic Cruises, Travel Dynamics, etc.), these lectures will be accompanied by reading lists, maps, and other accoutrements.

Unless you are aboard one of the very serious and intellectually stimulating cruises, your ship-board life will also feature elaborate evening entertainment and gambling. The latter ranges from a few slot machines to a full casino, complete with "bunny club" type croupiers. Here you can play roulette, 21, and blackjack to your heart's content, and some of these casinos are open from twelve to fourteen hours per day. (Just keep in mind that if they didn't make lots of money, the ships wouldn't continue to run the casinos.) Slot machines are the more casual form of tempting Lady Luck, and some vessels also go in for "horse racing" (using films in one of the lounges and accepting big bets on who will win). The jackpot does overflow from time to time, so if you're in the mood for a little gambling you will not be disappointed.

Aside from the races and travel shorts, you can also find full-length feature films that are first-rate. Actually, films are difficult to select for aboard ship, the energetic Irene of the Stella Solaris told me recently, because passengers complain if they're too violent, too sexy, or too dull. And whether the film is rated

PG, R, or X will provide plenty of comments. Although I have always found a goodly range provided—from *Bugs Bunny* to *Star Wars* to *10*—I have never found the time nor wanted to come inside long enough to see one! Most vessels do have splendid theaters though, which are also busy for religious services (some people even get married in them before the sailing), lectures, musical recitals, and full-length revues. The Saga Theater aboard the *Norway* is kept very busy with full-blown productions of musicals four times weekly, live concerts with great stars as Rita Moreno, and the Las Vegas-style spectacular revue called Sea Legs.

A little less spectacular, but equally enthusiastic, entertainment is offered in the largest lounge after the evening meal. This is one of the day's big events and a wonderful way to wind down. The shows are always energetic and some are topnotch (so enjoyable that you would even pay to see them). The best evening entertainment can be usually found aboard the ships cruising in the Caribbean, for passengers here are discerning and receptive to good acts. And you are soon aware if a ship line pays particular attention to its entertainment. For example, Royal Caribbean boasts that you never see the same act twice, as it shuttles groups between ports and its three vessels. Holland America, also known for putting emphasis on good shows, flies in a new group every week during the three-month world voyage. But however good a professional group can be, I always prefer the traditional cruise staff talent show to anything (probably because the faces are familiar.) This is where the Russians, Poles, Greeks, and other nationalities distinguish themselves in native dances, colorful costumes, a little clowning, and some singing. You may also have to endure a passenger talent show (less polish but always fun) and, without fail, the great masquerade party. If you enjoy dressing up and being someone else for a few hours, bring along a splendid costume and be the show stopper (I think you also win a bottle of something that goes by the name of champagne).

Late in the evening the main lounge continues to keep some passengers contented with soft music and dancing, while others scatter around the ship. This is the time I choose a quiet moonlit nightcap and my cabin. Elsewhere the action continues in a discotheque and doesn't even break while the midnight buffet is served. After all, the hours fly by, and A Club Called Dazzles aboard the *Norway* actually advertises a closing at 3 a.m. Oh well, that leaves just enough time for a short rest before early bird coffee at 6 and then the fun begins all over again!

6. / GLOSSARY OF NAUTICAL TERMS

No one wants to sound like an Old Salt, as they say, but learning some of the language of the sea will make you fee like an experienced sailor—especially if this is your first cruise. Study a few of the nautical terms listed below, and you'll be surprised at how quickly you will begin to say port and starboard without giving it another thought. Port, of course, is the left side of your ship (both words have four letters so that's easy to remember) and starboard is the right side.

ABEAM—anything perpendicular to the structure of the ship; off the side.

ACCOMMODATION LADDER—a lightweight ladder (also called Jacob's ladder), made of wooden slats or aluminum, that is slung from the ship to a dock or small boat. Pilots and other officials use this ladder to come aboard while at sea. Passengers use this ladder at some ports as well, when the vessel is anchored out and tenders are the only available transportation beween ship and shore.

AFT—toward the rear of the vessel, or to the stern.

ALLEYWAY—any passageway or narrow corridor of a ship. Sailors also use this term ashore to describe the narrow street behind port.

AMIDSHIPS—in the middle of the vessel; halfway between bow and stern.

AWNING—the same term as on land. Any canvas covering strung over an open deck area for protection from sun and rain.

ASTERN—behind the rear or stern of the ship; often refers to something in the wake.

ATHWART—across the width of the ship.

BALLAST—weight placed in the ship to keep her on an even keel when empty. The term also refers to any weight placed on board.

BAR—sandbar, caused by current or tide near the shore.

BEAM—width of ship at her widest point.

BEARING—compass direction, expessed in degrees.

BELOW—under the deck or on a subsequent deck farther down in the ship. Can also mean "at rest" or "off duty" for crew member.

BELLS—sounding of the ship's time, at half-hour intervals, from one to eight, beginning at 4:30, 8:30, and 12:30 anew.

BERTH—nautical term for bed, means where vessel docks in port as well as the beds in your cabin.

BON VOYAGE—French expression for Happy Voyage or Journey. When you tell your friends you are taking a cruise, they will say Bon Voyage!

BOW—the forward, or foremost, part of the ship.

BRIDGE—ship's command center, where all navigation and navigational decisions are made. It is located above and forward of the passenger areas, much like the cockpit of a 747 aircraft. This is the domain of the captain and his officers; passengers are admitted only by special invitation.

BULKHEAD—wall-like construction inside a vessel for subdividing space or strengthening the structure; partition wall.

BUNKERS—the space where fuel is stored.

CABIN—your bedroom or sleeping accommodation aboard ship. Also called a stateroom, depending upon size and situation.

CABLE—the heavy iron chain used for the ship's anchor.

CLASS—first, cabin, and tourist were the three classes passengers booked across the Atlantic for years. Under my definition, Cunard Line has the three-class system on the *Queen Elizabeth 2* transatlantic run (although they only admit to having two classes).

COLORS—refers to the national flag or emblem flown by the ship.

COMPANIONWAY—interior stairway leading from deck to deck.

COURSE—the ship's route during her voyage. The navigator used to plot the course every night according to charts and the sun, but computers do most of the work now.

CROW'S NEST—the lookout cage high up on the foremast.

DAVIT—the apparatus which secures the lifeboats at sea and from which they are launched. (Pronounced day-vit.)

DECK—each floor of a ship.

DISEMBARK—to go out from a ship. Opposite of embark.

DOCK—where the ship ties up. Also called pier, wharf, quay.

DRAFT OR DRAUGHT—the amount of water a ship draws or needs to keep out of trouble. The draft is calculated from the lowest point of the ship to the waterline.

DRILL—any exercise ordered by the master of the ship, like the lifeboat drill the first day out.

EMBARK—to board a ship. Opposite of disembark.

FATHOM—a measure of six feet; used in determining the depth of water by soundings. This term is familiar to all Americans, because Mark Twain, the pen name of Samuel Clemens (who spent his youth as a pilot on the Mississippi River), means "two fathoms sounded."

FLAGS—ships talk to each other with flags in an international code of signals that all nations understand. While the flag hoisted on a private yacht might say "Come over for a drink," the signals on a large ship leaving port will show if a pilot is aboard, whether a medical doctor is in attendance, and what type of cargo is carried. Signal flags are never flown at sea, except when a vessel is in distress. The ship's country of registry is flown from the stern, her country of destination appears from the yardarms of the foremast.

FREEBOARD—the outer part of a ship's hull between the waterline and main deck.

FREE PORT—a port not included in customs territory, or free from import taxes. For example, St. Thomas in the U.S. Virgin Islands is a free port and a favorite stop for Caribbean cruise shoppers.

FUNNEL—the smokestack, or chimney, of the ship.

GALLEY—the kitchen.

GANGWAY—the bridge between ship and shore. Also called a gangplank as it is generally nothing more than a plank of wood.

GROSS REGISTER TON—a measure of the size of a ship. One hundred cubic feet equals one gros register ton.

HATCHWAY—wide openings on deck allowing access to the holds.

HAWSER—a rope of sufficient size and strength to tow or secure a ship.

HEAD—toilet.

HELM—the entire steering apparatus of the ship. The expression "at helm" means whoever has charge of the ship's course at that time.

HOLD—the area below deck where cargo is stored.

HOUSE FLAG—the company flag or symbol flown from the mast, or a design on the funnel that designates who owns the ship.

HULL—also called hulk, the body of the ship.

ISTHMUS—a narrow strip of land bordered on both sides by water.

JACOB'S LADDER—a rope ladder usually with wooden rungs.

JONES ACT—the Jones Act of 1886, designed to protect American shipping interests, forbids foreign-registered ships from carrying passengers between U.S. ports. It is often strictly enforced by the U.S. Bureau of Customs. Puerto Rico and the U.S. Virgin Islands and some others are exempted.

KEEL—the backbone of the vessel. To be "on even keel" means to be in balance, or steady.

KNOT—a unit of speed for a ship. One knot is equal to one nautical mile (6080.2 feet), or approximately 1.15 statute (land) miles per hour. The speed of a ship is measured in knots.

LATITUDE—angular distance measured in degrees north and south of the Equator. One degree equals about 60 nautical miles.

LEAGUE—a unit of distance. In English-speaking countries, a league is approximately 3.45 nautical miles.

LEEWARD—the direction toward which the wind blows.

LIFEBOAT—a small launch designed to carry passengers in an emergency. Lifeboat stations are noted in every cabin. Lifeboat drills, mandatory on cruise vessels, require passengers to don their life vests and proceed to their boat stations (listed on back of cabin door).

LOG—the daily record in which details of navigation, weather, engine performance, and other aspects of ship's progress are kept.

LONGITUDE—angular distance measured east and west of Greenwich, England. One degree varies according to the earth's curvature.

MANIFEST—list of ship's passengers, crew, and cargo.

MASTER—the captain of the ship.

NAUTICAL MILE—6080.2 feet (land mile is 5280 feet).

PITCH—the rise and fall of the ship in rough seas, as opposed to the "roll" or rocking motion from side to side.

PORT—the left side of the ship looking forward, also indicated by red navigational light; harbor.

PORTHOLE—the round window in your cabin. Deluxe cabins have large, rectangular windows.

PROW—another word for bow or front of the ship.

QUAY—dock, berth, pier. (Pronounced "key.")

RAILING—something to keep you from falling off the ship; good to lean on in the moonlight or to watch flying fish.

REGISTRY—certificate of ownership. The country of registry is denoted by the national flag flown at the stern of the vessel.

ROLL—the sideways motion of the ship, as opposed to the "pitch" or up and down motion.

RUNNING LIGHTS—the colored lights required on all vessels at night to indicate her direction or course.

SAFETY AT SEA LAWS—according to the International Convention for the Safety of Life at Sea of 1960, all ships embarking passengers in U.S. ports must comply with the strict standards set forth at this convention.

SHE—yes, ships are always considered members of the female gender. It's an old tradition that even feminists have to accept. Longtime men at sea have their own reasons . . . but here are two. "It's not the initial expense that breaks you, it's the upkeep." "Because she shows her topsides, hides her bottom, and when coming into port, heads straight for the buoys."

SHIP TO SHORE—communications with land by radio telephone. Some ships now use a telephone link by satellite, which is faster.

SKIPPER—slang for captain. This term is not used on cruise ships, as the more formal "master" is generally employed.

STABILIZER—a retractable fin extending into the water on either side of the vessel to ensure smooth sailing in rough seas. Most vessels are now equipped with stabilizers of the Denny Brown type from England.

STACK—funnel or chimney of the vessel.

STAGE—a walkway protruding from the front of a "steamboat," that can be raised while cruising or lowered to embark passengers and/or supplies.

SOUNDING—see fathom.

STARBOARD—the right side of the ship looking forward, also indicated by a green navigational light.

STATEROOM—a sleeping accommodation aboard ship.

STERN—the aft, or extreme rear section of the ship.

SUPERSTRUCTURE—the structural part of the ship above the main deck.

TENDER—a smaller vessel, sometimes a lifeboat, used to carry passengers from ship to shore and vice versa.

TIME AT SEA—nautical time is like Navy time, based on the 24-hour clock. Hence, 8 a.m. is 0800 and 8 p.m. is 2000 hours.

UNDER WAY—indicates the ship is set to sail, the anchor has been brought up, and the lines let go.

WAKE—the trail a ship leaves behind in the water, the foam churned up by the propellers.

WATERLINE—the painted line dividing the ship between the portion that should remain above water and the section that is below.

WEIGH ANCHOR—to raise the anchor and prepare to get under way, a command given from the bridge.

WINCH—power-operated machine used to work the ship's cranes and/or davit.

WINDWARD—the direction from which the wind is blowing.

YARDARM—either outer arm of the yard (beam) of a square sail. The expression "when the sun is over the yardarm" means that cocktail time is approaching.

YAW—to deviate from the ship's course, usually caused by high seas.

ABBREVIATIONS

MS—Motor Ship
MTS—Motor Turbine Ship
MV—Motor Vessel
TSS—Turbine Steamship
SS—Steamship
USS—United States Ship

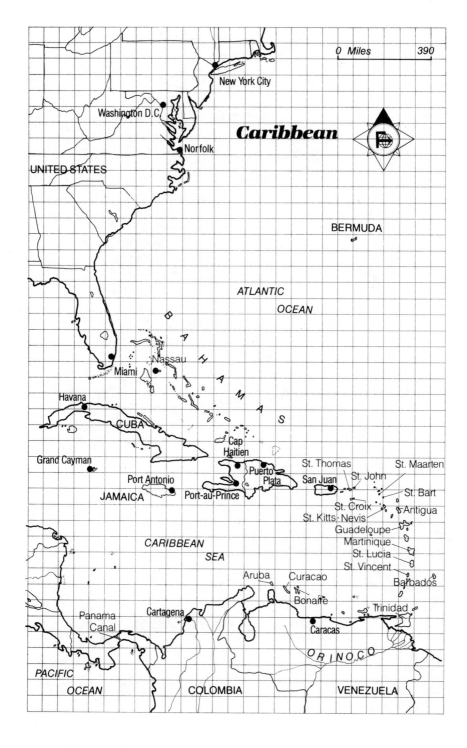

0 *Miles* 390

Caribbean

New York City

Washington D.C.

Norfolk

UNITED STATES

BERMUDA

ATLANTIC

OCEAN

B A H A M A S

Nassau

Miami

Havana

CUBA

Grand Cayman

Cap Haitien

St. Thomas St. Maarten

Puerto Plata St. John

San Juan St. Bart

Port Antonio St. Croix Antigua

JAMAICA Port-au-Prince St. Kitts·Nevis

Guadeloupe

Martinique

CARIBBEAN St. Lucia

SEA St. Vincent

Aruba Curacao Barbados

Bonaire

Panama Cartagena Trinidad

Canal Caracas

PACIFIC O R I N O C O

OCEAN COLOMBIA VENEZUELA

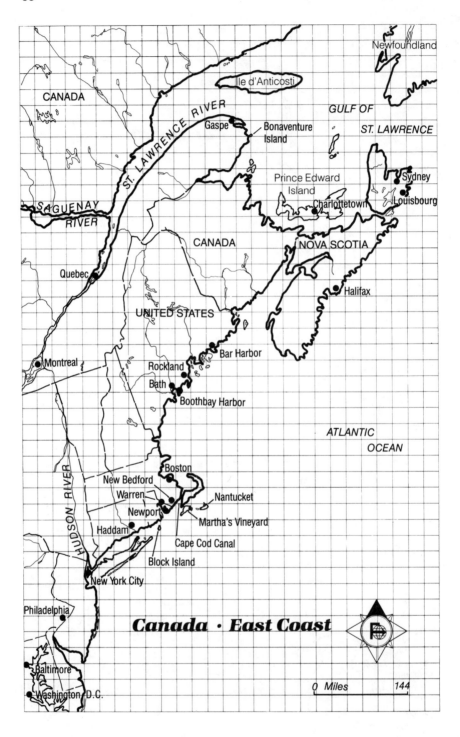

CANADA

ST. LAWRENCE RIVER

Newfoundland

Ile d'Anticosti

Gaspe · Bonaventure Island

GULF OF ST. LAWRENCE

Prince Edward Island

Sydney

Charlottetown

Louisbourg

SAGUENAY RIVER

CANADA

NOVA SCOTIA

Quebec

UNITED STATES

Halifax

Bar Harbor

Montreal

Rockland

Bath

Boothbay Harbor

ATLANTIC OCEAN

HUDSON RIVER

Boston

New Bedford

Warren

Newport

Haddam

Nantucket

Martha's Vineyard

Cape Cod Canal

Block Island

New York City

Philadelphia

Canada · East Coast

Baltimore

Washington D.C.

0 Miles 144

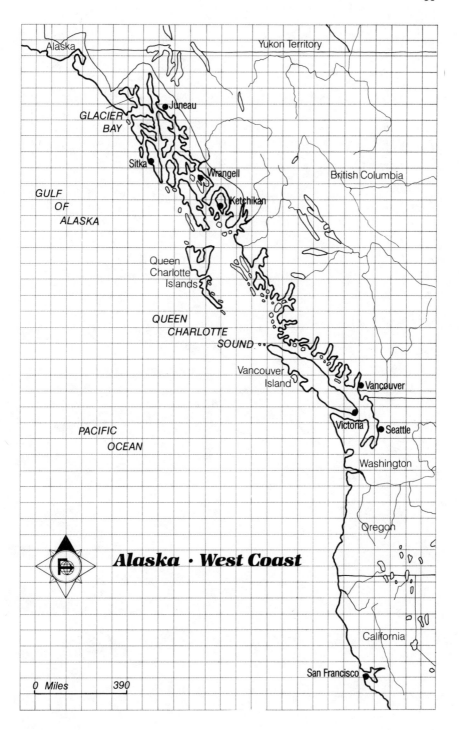

Alaska · West Coast

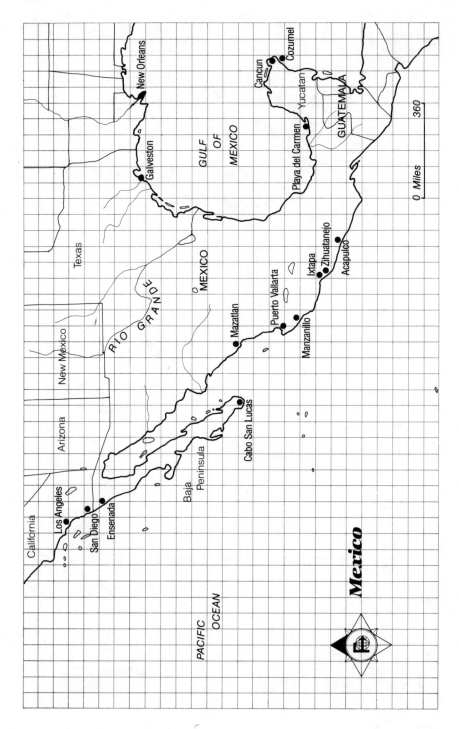

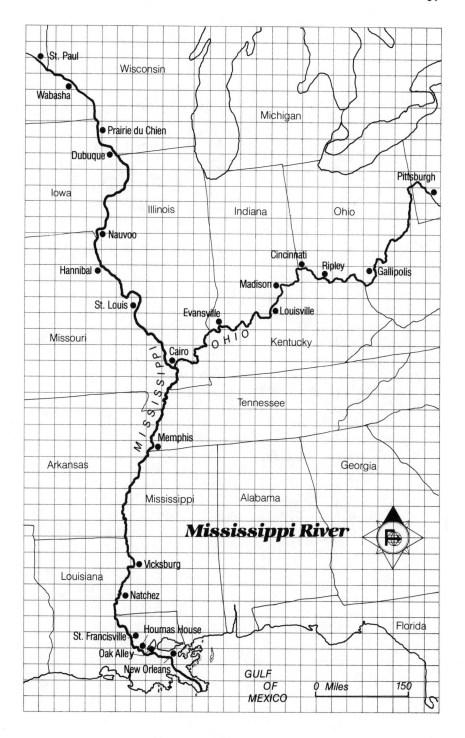

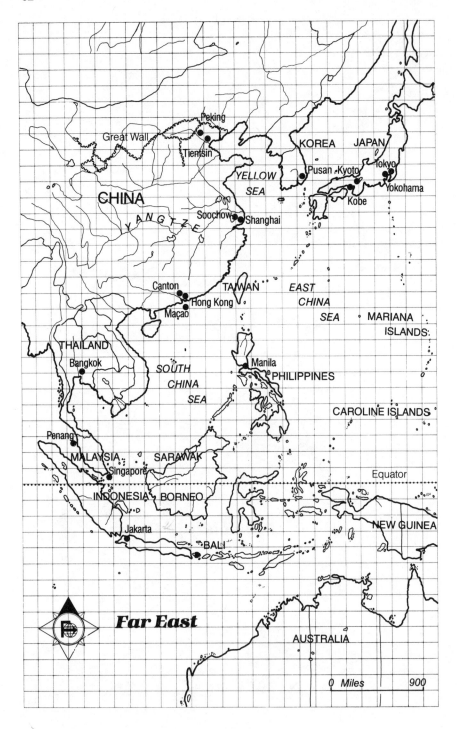

Peking
Great Wall
Tientsin
KOREA   JAPAN
Pusan Kyoto Tokyo
YELLOW
SEA   Yokohama
CHINA   Kobe
Soochow Shanghai
Y A N G T Z E
Canton   TAIWAN   EAST
Hong Kong   CHINA
Maçao   SEA   MARIANA
                        ISLANDS
THAILAND
Bangkok   SOUTH   Manila
           CHINA   PHILIPPINES
           SEA
                                CAROLINE ISLANDS
Penang
MALAYSIA   SARAWAK
Singapore   Equator
INDONESIA BORNEO
                              NEW GUINEA
Jakarta
          BALI

Far East

AUSTRALIA

0 Miles   900

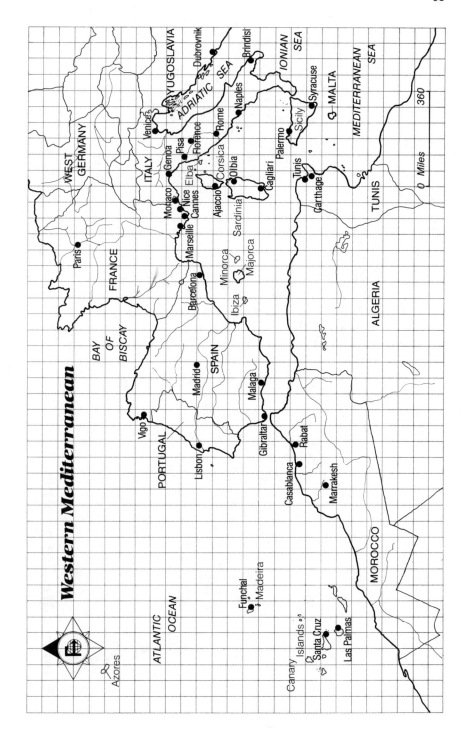

Western Mediterranean

ATLANTIC OCEAN

Azores

WEST GERMANY

FRANCE

Paris

BAY OF BISCAY

PORTUGAL

SPAIN

Madrid

Lisbon

Vigo

Malaga

Gibraltar

Barcelona

Minorca

Majorca

Ibiza

Monaco
Nice
Cannes
Marseille

Genoa
Pisa
Florence
Elba
Corsica
Ajaccio
Sardinia
Olbia
Cagliari

ITALY

Venice
Rome
Naples

YUGOSLAVIA

Dubrovnik
Brindisi

ADRIATIC SEA

IONIAN SEA

Palermo
Sicily
Syracuse

MALTA

Tunis
Carthage

TUNIS

MEDITERRANEAN SEA

ALGERIA

MOROCCO

Rabat
Casablanca
Marrakesh

Canary Islands
Santa Cruz
Las Palmas

Funchal
Madeira

0   Miles   360

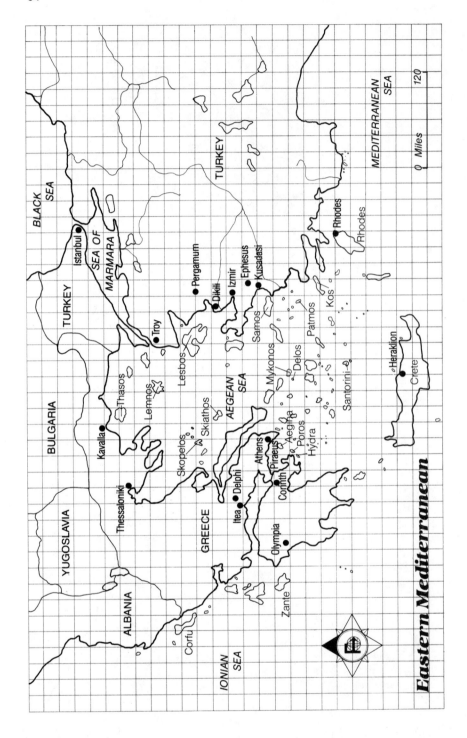

Eastern Mediterranean

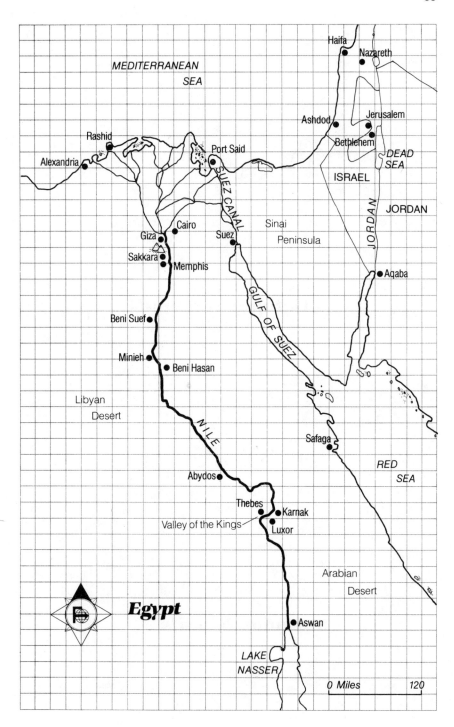

MEDITERRANEAN
SEA

Haifa
Nazareth

Rashid
Ashdod
Jerusalem
Alexandria
Bethlehem
Port Said
DEAD
SEA
ISRAEL

SUEZ CANAL

JORDAN
JORDAN

Cairo
Giza
Suez
Sinai
Sakkara
Peninsula
Memphis

Aqaba

GULF OF SUEZ

Beni Suef

Minieh
Beni Hasan

Libyan
Desert

NILE

Safaga

Abydos

RED
SEA

Thebes
Karnak
Valley of the Kings
Luxor

Arabian
Desert

Egypt

Aswan

LAKE
NASSER

0 Miles   120

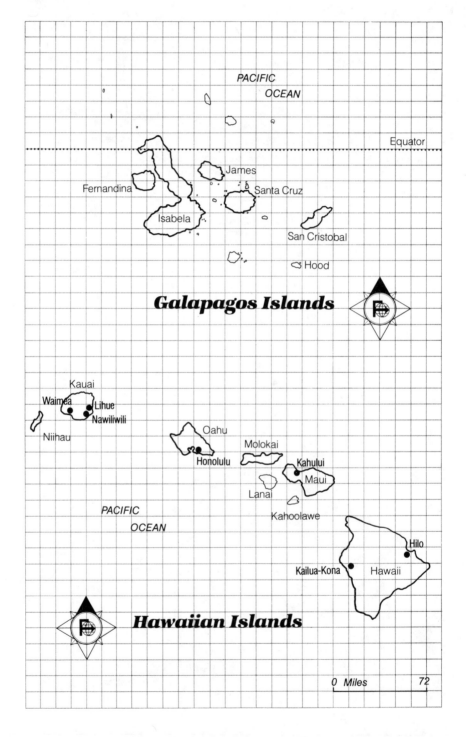

PACIFIC
OCEAN

Equator

James

Fernandina
Santa Cruz

Isabela
San Cristobal

Hood

Galapagos Islands

Kauai
Waimea Lihue
Nawiliwili
Niihau

Oahu

Molokai

Kahului

Honolulu
Maui

Lanai

Kahoolawe

PACIFIC
OCEAN

Hilo

Kailua-Kona Hawaii

Hawaiian Islands

0 Miles   72

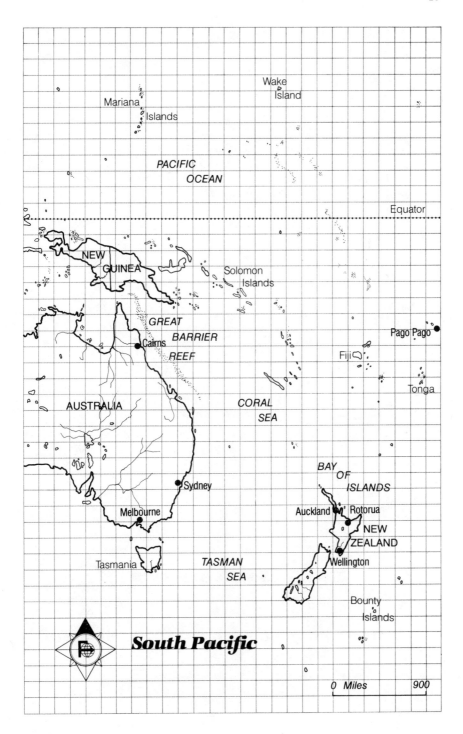

Wake
Island

Mariana
Islands

PACIFIC
OCEAN

Equator

NEW
GUINEA

Solomon
Islands

GREAT

BARRIER

Cairns

REEF

Pago Pago

Fiji

Tonga

AUSTRALIA

CORAL
SEA

BAY
OF
ISLANDS

Sydney

Auckland   Rotorua

NEW
ZEALAND

Melbourne

Tasmania

TASMAN
SEA

Wellington

Bounty
Islands

South Pacific

0   Miles   900

Antilles

CARIBBEAN
SEA

Cartagena

Caracas
Trinidad

VENEZUELA

ORINOCO

Bogota

COLOMBIA

Quito

Equator

ECUADOR

Guayaquil

AMAZON

Recife

PERU

BRAZIL

Salvador

Lima

Brasilia

PACIFIC
OCEAN

BOLIVIA

CHILE

PARAGUAY

Santos
Rio de Janeiro

Valparaiso

URUGUAY

ATLANTIC
OCEAN

Santiago

Buenos Aires

Montevideo

ARGENTINA

Puerto Montt

South America

Tierra del Fuego

STRAIT
OF
MAGELLAN

0 Miles   720

British Isles

Shetland Islands

Lewis

Orkney Islands

Hebrides Islands

Harris

ATLANTIC OCEAN

SCOTLAND

NORTH SEA

Edinburgh

Belfast

GALWAY BAY

IRELAND

IRISH SEA

Dublin

Holyhead

Liverpool

York

Conway

Hull

Waterford

BANTRY BAY

ENGLAND

WALES

Stratford-upon-Avon

ST. GEORGE'S CHANNEL

AVON

THAMES

Oxford

London

Southampton

Windsor

Plymouth

Dover

ENGLISH CHANNEL

Calais

Channel Islands

FRANCE

0 Miles 120

Paris

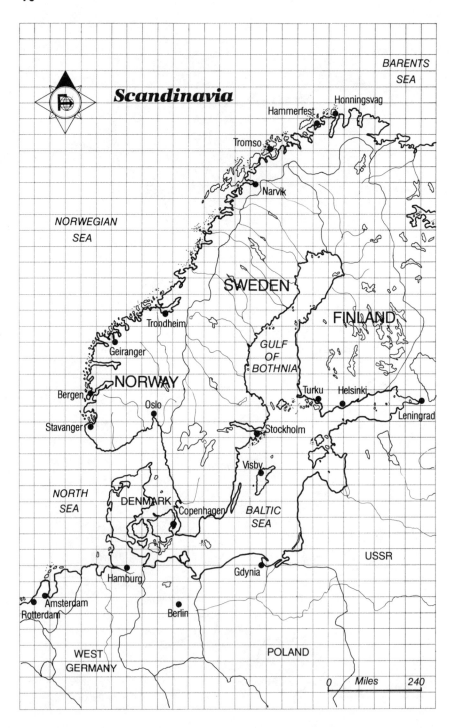

7. / PORTS OF CALL

BAHAMAS AND BERMUDA

THE BAHAMA ISLANDS

Christopher Columbus was the first tourist to this lovely archipelago that begins just fifty miles off the coast of Florida and stretches in a great southeasterly arc to within fifty miles of eastern Cuba and Haiti. Columbus arrived in 1492 on an island he named San Salvador. However, the Spanish never quite got around to settling these islands (seven hundred strong) that are scattered across some 100,000 square miles of the Atlantic Ocean. The British arrived in 1629 and ruled for about three hundred years, leaving behind a legacy in language, architecture, law, and some lovely manners. The Bahamas became self-governing in 1964 and independent in 1973, although they still belong to the Commonwealth and Queen Elizabeth II continues as head of state.

Ever since Columbus' visit, tourism has played an important role in the growth of these islands. Ponce de Leon came looking for his Fountain of Youth, and when George Washington stopped by in the eighteenth century he called them "Isles of Perpetual June." For cruise vessels, the center of tourism is **Nassau,** the main port and capital city on the island of New Providence. Nassau has retained some charming colonial overtones, although its Bay Street area has turned honky-tonk with the influx of fried chicken and hamburger chains, and the shopping is no longer exciting. But it's an easy town to explore from your vessel docked at Prince George Wharf. The government buildings are all around Rawson Square, which has a high-priced straw market in the middle. Try not to miss the statue of Queen Victoria and the 1797 octagonal structure that was once a prison but is now a public library. You might also want to have a look at Christopher Columbus, who stands in front of government house. If you like forts, three are within easy reach: 1790 Fort Charlotte, named after the wife of King George III; 1741 Fort Montagu, built to guard the eastern entrance of the harbor; and Fort Fincastle. Nearby is the so-called Queen's Staircase, a 102-foot-high set of limestone steps that number the sixty-five years of Victoria's reign. If you take a city tour you will also visit the Ardastra Gardens to see trained flamingos, and the Seafloor Aquarium to see dolphins perform. Or, you can take a three-hour catamaran cruise around the harbor, have a rum punch, and swim off one of the island's lovely beaches.

Just a hop, a skip, and a few dollars' taxi ride from Prince George Wharf is Paradise Island, an exquisite crescent-shaped beach famous for bathing beauties, nightclub entertainment, and gambling. Here are also some beautiful gardens and a fourteenth-century cloister, but no doubt you will want to take Lady Luck straight into the casino at the Britannia Beach Hotel and then enjoy the Las Vegas-style review in Le Cabaret.

Gambling is also the most interesting distraction in **Freeport**, on Grand Bahama Island, the second most popular cruise call in the archipelago. Here, El Casino is reputed to be the largest gambling den on this side of the Atlantic, and it certainly is the most frequented, especially by those on the four-day cruises from Miami. When you've had enough of the chips, browse around the International Bazaar for one of those famous T-shirts (my favorite is the one in French).

The Bahama Out Islands should not be overlooked either. More and more cruise vessels are calling among these little pieces of paradise. To accommodate the new *Norway*, Norwegian Caribbean Lines bought an island in the southeast called Little San Salvador. The line's other vessels also call at the Berry Islands for beach parties, snorkeling, and Sunfishing. Other islands that some of the smaller cruise vessels visit are Abacos in the north, long and skinny Eleuthera, and the Exumas.

No matter where you happen to go in the Bahamas you will be welcome. Many of the cruise vessels have excellent People to People programs in which Bahamian couples come on board to exchange experiences. Several islands have popular programs in which travelers can visit a Bahamian home. Often these visits make for enduring friendships.

BERMUDA

Britain's oldest colony sits out in the Atlantic Ocean some 600 miles due east of Savannah, Georgia, and approximately 775 miles (forty hours) southeast of New York, from where you will most likely sail. Since the late nineteenth century this tiny coral island with pastel-colored houses and quaint British customs has been a popular watering hole for cruise passengers. Warm winters used to attract the wealthy, who arrived with steamer trunks and servants for a long stay. Most cruises now last seven days—either Saturday to Saturday or Sunday to Sunday—from the first week in April until November.

Many cruise vessels dock at the pier on Front Street in downtown **Hamilton,** Bermuda's only city and its capital. Other ships dock in St. George and spend a day or two at the other end of the island. Hamilton, a nice, clean place, has interesting shops where, despite a few good buys, most British goods now unfortunately sell for exorbitant prices. If you're interested in pullovers and other woolens, check prices at home before you leave to see how they compare with Hamilton stores. My favorite shop is Bluck's, at the corner of Front Street and Bermudiana Road, where the beautiful and expensive china, crystal, silver, and antiques will knock your eyes out.

If you don't take the shore excursions and feel confident on the road, rent a motorbike the minute you disembark. It's the best way to get around as no rental cars are allowed and buses are poky. Remember to follow the rules of the road—drive on the left and always wear your helmet.

Exploring this 21-square-mile piece of land that geologists say lies on top of a submerged mountain is loads of fun, especially if you opt to do it with a friend instead of a crowd. Since your ship will stay three full nights in port if you're on the seven-day cruise, you'll have time to see everything. The Visitors Bureau (left as you leave the pier) has terrific maps and pamphlets and will answer any questions. When you go on your jaunts, be sure to take a swimsuit, because you will be tempted by many beautiful beaches. My favorites are the public beaches along the South Shore, especially Jobson Cove or Warwick Long Bay, where you can spend the whole day among cliffs, rocks, and sparkling sand. At the large supermarket along the way (if you're coming from Hamilton, it's just past St. Paul's Lane on the left) you can stock up on cold drinks and snacks. (Don't be shocked by the prices. Food is very expensive on this island.)

Try not to miss the Blue Grotto Dolphin Show in Harrington Sound (just before the causeway), the Crystal or Leamington caves, where stalagmites and stalactites form a forestlike maze, and Gibbs Hill Lighthouse. This is the oldest cast-iron lighthouse in the world, built in the 1850s, the view of the entire island from the top of its 185 steps is fantastic. Gibbs Hill Lighthouse is off the South Shore Road, just behind the fanciful highrise Southampton Princess Hotel. It's open from 9 a.m. to 4:30 p.m. daily, and admission is about twenty-four cents. What a bargain!

Save an entire day for **St. George,** the island's original capital and in 1609 the landing spot for the 150 passengers of the shipwrecked *Sea Venture*. St. George, my favorite place for browsing, has loads of charm and history. Even if you don't like churches, you'll enjoy St. Peter's, which dates from 1713. The head stones in the graveyard read like *Who's Who* (some Americans lie there). Across the street is the Confederate Museum and King's Square, where you can be photographed in the pillory and stocks. The Print Shop houses a working model of a seventeenth-century press, and the hostess at President Henry

Tucker house will entice you with some interesting history and gossip about the days of the American Revolution. Catty-corner to this house is the Carriage Museum, chock full of the custom-built carriages that were used until the advent of automobiles on the island in 1945. The St. George restoration project at Somers' Wharf is wonderful, and you can dine in old warehouses and shop in the less-crowded branches of the well-known Hamilton stores. If you want to take home a little artwork, stop at Rosecote (on Stowe Hill in Paget), where the island's artist laureate, Alfred Birdsey, lives. If you're lucky, you may see him wandering about—small man with a huge talent. But most likely you'll deal with son-in-law Tony Davis, the family businessman. Prints and originals cost less than a taxi ride and make lovely gifts.

THE BLACK SEA

Politics has its way even with cruises, and some ship lines are substituting Italian ports and more Greek islands for their previously popular calls at resorts on the Black Sea. However, I have decided to cover these resorts, despite the current political frictions, because I believe countries are not only governments, but also people—people like us who work, play, laugh, cry, and hope for a brighter future. Travel is often the first step toward a greater understanding of what these other people are all about.

BULGARIA

Varna is Bulgaria's largest seaport and the jumping-off point for visiting nearby resorts, such as Zlatni Pyassutsi (or Golden Sands) some eleven miles up the coast, renowned for the silky beaches that stretch some five hundred feet into the sea. Midway between the two towns is the coastal resort of Drouzhba, with its eighteenth-century monastery. South of Varna lies Bulgaria's largest and most popular resort, Slunchev Bryag, or Sunny Beach. A few miles inland the sixth-century Aladja Monastery is built right into the rocks. You can find traces of Bulgarian history all along the coast. Life here began in the seventh century when Finno-Tartar tribes mingled with Slavic settlers and held their own against the Greek and Byzantine empires in the south.

ROMANIA

The seaside resort of **Constanta** was built on the ruins of an old Greek colony called Tomis, where the poet Ovid is said to have spent his last years. The country actually was founded by the Roman emperor, Trajan, who conquered Dacia in A.D. 106 and called it Romania. Constanta (also spelled Constanza) today is a modern city with narrow streets and mosques left over from the days of the Ottoman Empire. Nearby resort towns along the coast are famous, year-round health spas for the treatment of nervous disorders and skin diseases. Pay special attention to the Romanians enjoying their beaches, for they are among the most independent and interesting of all the Eastern Bloc peoples. Some even say that their Latin heritage has never been stronger nor more apparent than now. The tourist shops offer romantic, richly embroidered scarfs and blouses, peasant skirts, rugs, ceramics, and charming handcrafts.

USSR

Yalta, the most famous of all Black Sea resorts, was a favorite with nineteenth-century Russian princes, who built many beautiful palaces along its shores. Originally a Greek colony, Yalta passed through the hands of Romans, Genoese, and Turks before becoming Russian at the end of the eighteenth century. Fifty years later Yalta was a major battleground in the Crimean War. Today this large seaport and spa backs up on Livadia, where the 1945 Yalta Conference took place. Livadia Palace, the White Palace, where the conference was held, was built in 1911 for Tsar Nicholas II in Italian Renaissance style. Every window looks out on a different view. Opposite the entrance is a marble column, which was a gift from the Shah of Persia to the tsar. This palace, like so many others in the area, is now a sanatorium. Yalta is the most interesting of all Black Sea resorts, especially for Americans. Franklin D. Roosevelt Street, one of Yalta's oldest avenues, leads straight into town, linking with Lenin Promenade. Monuments are everywhere—to Lenin, to Gorky, and to playwright Chekhov, who lived on Kirov Street from 1898 until his death in 1904 (his house is now a museum). The Alexander Nevsky Cathedral, built in the old Russian style in 1902, is open to visitors daily, but other churches are generally closed or have been turned into museums. In Alupka, the farthest town on the Yalta coastline, is a palace built by Count Vorontsov, a confirmed Anglophile and a favorite of both Alexandra and Nicholas. Vorontsov's palace (built between 1828 and 1846) was designed by an English architect who used Indian styles. An Arabic inscription repeated tenfold says, "There is no happiness but that which comes from Allah." This palace is now a museum of European and Russian paintings, with a bust of Vorontsov himself and a bust of British statesman William Pitt the Younger in the winter garden. The area has many other lovely palaces that can be viewed only from the outside, plus beautiful but crowded beaches.

Odessa, the third largest city in the Ukraine, is home port of the Black Sea Shipping Company, whose cruise ships sail from such faraway places as Vancouver and New Orleans. One would hardly call Odessa "The jewel of the Russian Riviera," as one ship brochure does, but it is certainly a city of note and history. A fascinating period was 1803 to 1814, when the Duke Richelieu was mayor and the city prospered from all the customs duties he collected. By the end of the nineteenth century Odessa was Russia's largest port and third most important city, after Moscow and St. Petersburg (Leningrad). Today Odessa is an industrial, educational, and tourist center that claims to have inspired poets and prides itself on its revolutionary past. Among many fine monuments cruise passengers can visit is another palace built by Prince Vorontsov in 1826, this time in the classical Russian style. The lighthouse in port also bears his name. A few of the famous old churches are open for services and tours, including the five-domed Uspensky Cathedral. An archae-ological museum has a large collection of artifacts from ancient Greek settle-ments along the Black Sea coasts. But the most striking monument of all is to the Russian poet Pushkin from the citizens of Odessa, a tribute to the four years (1820 to 1824) the writer was forced to live here in exile.

THE CARIBBEAN

BARBADOS

One of the most British of all the Caribbean islands, Barbados lived under the Union Jack from 1625 to 1966. The island took its name from the Por-tuguese who arrived in 1536 and thought the hanging roots of the banyan trees looked like beards, hence "barbados." Capital and main port of the island is **Bridgetown,** whose harbor police still wear the uniforms of Nelson's sailors. A statue of Lord Nelson stands in the town's Trafalgar Square, said to be some seventeen years older than its counterpart in London.

Exploring Bridgetown is easily done on foot at a leisurely pace. Begin with the activity-filled Careenage, or Inner Harbor, and the Pelican Village craft center, then head to Trafalgar Square for a look at old Nelson. St. Michael's Cathedral was first built in 1665, but the present structure dates from 1831. Too bad, because if George Washington really came to Barbados (along with his half-brother Lawrence) for a health cure, he worshiped on the site but not in this building. A house on Upper Bay Street is where he may have lived for a while, and one story says he even caught smallpox. Wander through other interesting lanes for local color before you take a taxi to the Barbados Museum at Garrison, about a mile out of town. If you have a chance, pay a visit to Sam Lord's Castle, a nineteenth-century mansion that is one of the more famous sites in the Caribbean. If you've opted for an organized tour, you will most likely stop at another Great House, Villa Nova, the former home of British diplomat Sir Anthony Eden. Beautifully renovated and furnished with Barba-dian antiques of local mahogany, it once dominated a large sugar cane plantation.

BRITISH LEEWARD ISLANDS

Lying north of Barbados, between Anegada and Guadeloupe passages, the Leewards consist of Antigua, Barbuda, Montserrat, St. Kitts, and Nevis. Of the group, Antigua is the most popular for cruise ship calls, although St. Kitts and Nevis are coming into their own.

ANTIGUA: This 108-square-mile island was discovered in 1493 by Columbus, who named it after Santa Maria la Antigua of Seville. The British colonized the island around 1623. Its capital and main port is St. John's, where you can see rum made and buy a barbecue pot, but the real attraction of the island is Lord Nelson's Dockyard in **English Harbour.** The romance and history of the harbor recall the days when the 25-year-old Horatio Nelson was senior captain of the Leeward Islands Squadron in 1784. He rose to commander-in-chief and was married on nearby Nevis in 1787, with the future King William IV as his best man. A residence built for the king when he was still the Duke of Clarence can be visited when the present governor is not using it. Nelson House, now a museum of Nelson and naval memorabilia, as well as the Master Shipwright's House, Sew Pit Shed, Mast House, Joiner's Loft, and Sail Loft are all part of this fascinating area. And don't forget the charming Admiral's Inn, where you can enjoy a rum punch before the drive back to the capital via Swetes Village and Fig Tree Hill. Or, you can skip all the sightseeing and take a tour of Buccaneer Cove for lunch and swimming. If you still want to be cruising, try the fantastic West Coast and a stop in Emerald Bay for swimming. Cunard will fly you to the island of Montserrat—fifteen minutes away by air— for a tour of the capital, Plymouth, and the smoking crater Soufrière, as well as a bit of the Irish who colonized this emerald isle in 1632.

ST. KITTS: Nearby St. Kitts was also discovered by Columbus in 1493. He named it after his patron saint, St. Christopher, who had carried him safely on a voyage to the New World. Often called the Mother Colony of the British West Indies, St. Kitts was first settled in 1623. From here people set out to colonize the other islands. The English fought over St. Kitts with the French for many years. In 1783 the Treaty of Versailles ceded it to the British at last. The island became an associated state of the British Commonwealth in 1967, but French influences are still intact in names like Basseterre, the capital and main harbor. Basseterre means "low land," and the harbor it describes has an Old World charm, with lovely colonial structures like Government House and the Old Court House. If you have four hours, you can drive around all of St. Kitts and stop at the 1694 Brimstone Hill Fortress at Sandy Point for a view of the nearby island of St. Eustatius.

NEVIS: Otherwise, you might as well carry on to the 35-square-mile **Nevis,** just two miles south. Surrounded by coral reefs, Nevis has at its center three high peaks that usually have halos of white clouds. Columbus thought this was similar to the snow-covered Pyrenees, so named the place Las Nievas. Shore excursions here stop at Fig Tree Church, where Admiral Nelson was married to the wealthy young widow, 22-year-old Fanny Nisbet. Other sites include the house in Charlestown where Alexander Hamilton was born in 1757, the 200-year-old thermal baths, and St. Thomas Church and its ancient tombstones.

BRITISH VIRGIN ISLANDS

TORTOLA: Although there are more than fifty British Virgin Islands, only a third are inhabited, and cruise vessels call only at Tortola. The English settled here in the 1520s, and the islands were granted a charter in 1773. They have been British ever since, although Tortolans use the U.S. dollar as well as their own Tortolan dollar that looks like a British fifty-pence piece. Half-day tours of the island are offered from Road Harbour, but the local cruises are best for seeing these lovely little islands. A launch cruise to "Treasure Island" crosses Sir Francis Drake Channel to Flanagan Island, Pelican Island, Norman Island (known as Robert Louis Stevenson's original Treasure Island), Privateer Bay, Peter Island, and Salt Island.

BRITISH WINDWARD ISLANDS

St. Lucia, St. Vincent, and Grenada are the most popular cruise stops in the British Windwards (which also include Dominica and the Grenadines).

ST. LUCIA: The second largest island in this chain, St. Lucia features Mt. Soufrière, the only "drive-in" active volcano in the world. You can drive up to the lip of the crater, cook an egg in the steam, and visit the sulfur baths. St. Lucia is believed to have been discovered by Columbus on St. Lucia's Day, June 15, 1502, although some scholars claim the Spanish arrived later. Early settlers had to contend with the Caribs, who were determined to keep the white man away. In the mid-seventeenth century the French arrived, and from then until the turn of the nineteenth century they fought with the British over possession of this island. Although the British finally won in 1802, everyone involved suffered a split personality. The French-sounding Castries is the island's capital and main harbor. Unfortunately, nothing colonial or interesting remains. A fire in 1948 completely destroyed the old town. Apart from the volcano excursion, you can take a tour across the causeway to Pigeon Island, now a national park, where British Admiral Rodney once kept pigeons.

ST. VINCENT: This island, eighteen miles by eleven miles, was named by Columbus when he arrived on St. Vincent's Day in 1498. Another piece of property that the Caribs hung onto for as long as possible, St. Vincent was declared neutral during the fighting between the French and the English in 1748, but it went to the British in the latter part of the eighteenth century. After the British Captain Bligh brought breadfruit here from Tahiti, it was nicknamed Breadfruit Island, and breadfruit is still a major product. This is another split-personality island with French names and British overtones. And it has *its* own volcano called Mt. Soufrière, but this one is semi-dormant. You can climb to its 4000-foot rim for a view of the crater lake below. Capital and main port of the island is Kingstown, which has some attractive nineteenth-century dwellings as well as a 200-year-old botanical garden. The Mesopotamia Valley has twenty-eight miles of rural beauty. If boat tours are offered to any of the Grenadines, hop aboard, especially if you like to snorkel in crystal-clear waters or swim at sparkling beaches.

GRENADA: Originally named Concepción by Columbus, who first saw it on August 15, 1498, this island is nicknamed the Spice Island. Again, the Caribs kept their 133 square miles of volcanic mountains, green valleys, and beautiful beaches as long as they were able. The British and the French fought over this small piece of real estate, but the British assumed possession in 1783. Grenada became a crown colony in 1877 and was granted its independence in 1974. Its capital and main port, St. George, is one of the most picturesque harbors in the Caribbean. On a protected harbor and blue inner lagoon, the town has pastel warehouses and gabled dwellings. A good walking tour takes about two hours, and you can enjoy such sights as Old Fort George, which has French origins, the Market Place, and Marryshow House. There are plenty of local arts-and-crafts exhibits, and you can fill your pockets with cinnamon, nutmeg, ginger, vanilla, bay leaf (laurel), and clove. Organized excursions feature a bus tour or a catamaran cruise to Grand Anse Beach for sunning and snorkeling. The bus goes through the Mt. Parnassus Valley by the famous nutmeg trees, stops for a panoramic view of the harbor from Richmond Hill, and drives on to Morne Jalous and the charming fishing village of Woburn. You meet your fellow passengers from the catamaran at Grand Anse Beach.

CAYMAN ISLANDS

These are known by locals as the Alligator Islands, because reptiles were once plentiful. Before that, our friend Columbus, who discovered them in 1503 on his fourth voyage, called them Las Tortugas for the many turtles. The islands are also famous for their ring of coral which has been the nemesis of more than three hundred ships whose hulls and buried treasures keep the intrigue level high. Life on Grand Cayman, twenty-two miles long and eight miles wide, is slow and casual, with the emphasis for cruise passengers on relaxation and beach parties. The small capital and main port of George Town is quiet, and its tax-haven status interests many visitors (Grand Cayman may yet become the Monaco of the Caribbean). There is free-port shopping, and you can purchase a gift package of frozen green-turtle steaks.

DOMINICAN REPUBLIC

After Columbus discovered this island, he installed his brother Bartolomé as governor. Bartolomé founded Santo Domingo, the oldest city in the New World, which drew the influential and adventurous in the first half of the sixteenth century. The independent Dominican Republic was established in 1844. Its capital and chief port is **Santo Domingo,** which boasts the oldest cathedral in the Americas, dating from 1514. Other sights are the Alcazar of Diego Columbus (built in 1510 and restored in 1957), the sixteenth-century Casa del Cordón, the National Museum, and the Palace of Fine Arts. Also here are a national theater, a national library, and the Museo del Hombre Dominicano on the Plaza de la Cultura.

A cruise call that I think is more a waste of time than anything else is **Puerto Plata** on the so-called Amber Coast. This is where Columbus landed—or ran aground—and founded the town of Isabella. From the harbor at Puerto Plata you can visit the restored fortress of San Felipe, which once guarded the settlement from British pirates and Carib Indians. If you wish to take the tour to one of the powdery beaches, I understand you might swim under the noses of some Dominican army machine guns.

DUTCH WINDWARD ISLANDS

Of these three small dots—Sint Maarten, Saba, and Sint Eustatiu (also known as Statia)—Sint Maarten is the most popular for cruise calls.

SINT MAARTEN: Columbus was here, too, on St. Martin's Day, apparently in 1493, but records say that he never went ashore. The island is divided, and only the Dutch side is called Sint Maarten. The larger French section is called St. Martin and is a member of the French West Indies. On the Dutch side, the capital and chief port, Philipsburg, has little to offer but a few narrow streets. Shore excursions descend onto the French side for a tour of small villages and local markets. Other than the seventeenth-century Fort Amsterdam, now very crumbly, the island has few historical sites. Beautiful scenery and interesting people are the main attractions. You can take a catamaran cruise aboard the *Maison Maru* to some spectacular beaches (bring your bathing suit) and caves that are not accessible from the road.

FRENCH WEST INDIES

Largest and northernmost of the French West Indies is Martinique, called the Pearl of the Antilles. Cruise ships also dock at Guadeloupe, and occasionally at Iles des Saintes and St. Barthélemy (or St. Barts, which used to be one of the best-kept secrets in the Caribbean).

MARTINIQUE: The capital and main seaport of Martinique is **Fort-de-France,** a city 100,000 strong that will remind you of New Orleans with its iron-grillwork-studded buildings. Although Columbus is said to have landed on the western coast of this twenty-by-fifty-mile island, he did not stay long enough to think of a name. So the naming was left to the French, who arrived in 1635 and used the Carib name, "Island of Flowers." In 1848 the islanders were granted full French citizenship, and in 1946 Martinique became a *département* of France, governed by a prefect appointed through the French Minister of the Interior.

Organized shore excursions take you north to **St.-Pierre,** once considered a little Paris but destroyed in 1902 by Mt. Pelée, the 4500-foot volcano. You can visit the museum that chronicles the terrible eruption. Then your drive goes almost to the base of the volcano and through forests of giant fern to Balata for a visit to the church that looks like a small replica of Sacré Coeur in Paris. Martinique was the birthplace of Napoleon's wife Josephine, and a museum in the village of Trois Ilets tells of the local beauty who became Empress of France. Other tours might include Absalon, a thermal resort, and Carbet, said to be where Columbus landed, or the restored eighteenth-century De Leyritz Plantation. A Kon Tiki tour, in a catamaran, features a Calypso steel band and complimentary rum punch. But you may just prefer to explore the bustling port of Fort-de-France on your own—graceful women in colorful native dress, side streets redolent of Creole cookery, a library, a cathedral, Fort St.-Louis overhanging the bay, and a statue of Josephine looking out toward her native village.

GUADELOUPE: This island is in two parts, like a butterfly with spread wings. Columbus discovered it in 1493 and named it in honor of Our Lady of Guadeloupe of Estremadura. The French settled here in 1635, but the English interfered for almost two centuries. The Treaty of Paris in 1815 finally made the island French, and in 1946 it was made a *département* with the same status as Martinique. Guadeloupe consists of Grande-Terre and Basse-Terre, divided by the Riviè Salée. Capital is **Pointe-à-Pitre,** a busy seaport that was a pirate haven in the eighteenth century (pirate spirits are said to still hover over the city) and that has quaint streets and European-style buildings.

Tours from Pointe-à-Pitre will take you across the bridge of the Rivière Salée to Guadeloupe's verdant rain forest and Parc Naturel, a botanist's paradise. A stop is made at Fort Fleur d'Épée, with interesting underground passages and dungeons. This was the keystone of French defense during the long battle against the British, and the view of the sea and other islands from here is spectacular. Other historic sites include Sainte-Marie, where Columbus is said to have landed, and Trois-Rivières, where relics and rocks bear inscriptions by the Carib Indians. Guadeloupe also has a La Soufrière volcano—which is only sleeping—with extraordinary views from the top (but watch out for the hot-lava bogs).

ILES DES SAINTES: This cluster of eight islands off the southern coast of Guadeloupe includes Terre-de-Haut, an occasional cruise call. Here you can explore the peaceful and charming harbor of Bourg and enjoy some of the best snorkeling that exists anywhere.

ST. BARTHELEMY: Dependent upon Guadeloupe but 140 miles north, St. Barts is considered by a loyal following to be the most chic island in the Caribbean. Its 2500 inhabitants are mostly of French-Norman and Swedish background. Its capital is Gustavia, known for fabulous French food and charming atmosphere, but don't let on where you heard this. Some of the smaller cruise vessels now stop in the harbor. *Zut alors!*

HAITI

This country of black magic and primitive paintings was discovered by Columbus in 1492. He named it Hispaniola, but the native Arawak Indians already called it Hayti, the mountainous country. Hispaniola still refers to the entire island, of which Haiti occupies one-third and the Spanish-speaking Dominican Republic the rest. The Spanish ceded the Haitian portion of Hispaniola to the French in 1697 and it was called Saint-Dominique until 1791 when the country reverted to the original Indian name. The history of Haiti has been turbulent. Often called the world's first black republic, it has been independent, more or less, since approximately 1806, although the U.S. assumed control between 1915 and 1924. The terror reign of "Papa Doc" Duvalier (1957–71) raised some dust which has now settled somewhat. Haiti is a fascinating and controversial country that you either love or you don't. (No gray area here.)

Capital of Haiti and main cruise port is **Port-au-Prince,** a city of incongruities and squalor. Its French, African, and West Indian cultural mix makes it exotic and colorful. With landmark buildings and the famous Iron Market, you can sightsee and barter over the bargains all day. Haitian art is well known now; primitive painting and sculpture is on every street corner, but you may wish to visit the Arts Center first, the Museum of Haitian Art, and a few local galleries before you purchase anything. Other tourist attractions in the capital are the voodoo relics in the Ethnographical Museum, the tomb of the late President Duvalier in Fort Dimanche, and Habitation Leclerc, a luxury resort hotel which was the renowned mansion of Pauline Bonaparte, Napoleon's sister. Tours out of town take you to Pétionville, the Land of Perpetual Spring, and the 3500-foot-high lookout called Boutillier, from which you can enjoy a panorama of the bay, city, and distant mountains. Your excursion may also include a local rum distillery that offers complimentary tastings and samplings.

About two hundred miles north of the capital is **Cap Hatien,** a more popular cruise port because of San Souci Palace and La Citadelle La Ferrière. Once the rich capital of Sainte-Dominique, "Le Cap" is Haiti's most historic town—and the least offensive to tourists. The two famous monuments built in the early part of the nineteenth century by the black emperor Henri Christophe—who controlled the northern part of Haiti—are about a twenty-mile drive from the port. San Souci Palace, which is similar to Versailles, was the most splendid structure in the New World and even the roofless ruins of the reception rooms, ballrooms, and royal compartments never fail to impress me. The Citadelle, which some call the Eighth Wonder of the World, was built by some 200,000 slaves and finished in 1817. Its walls, 140 feet high and twelve feet thick, house a garrison designed to hold 15,000 men and a suite of forty rooms for the emperor. The climb to the top is long and arduous, even by horse or mule, but it is well worth the effort for both the tour of this fortress and the view beyond.

JAMAICA

Another mountainous island, Jamaica has four peaks surpassing six thousand feet. Discovered by Columbus in 1494 and colonized by his son Diego, this lovely isle of streams and forests (Xamayca, the Arawaks called it) was under Spanish domain only until the mid-seventeenth century. The British seized it in 1655 and allowed it to become a pirate base. One of the greatest pirates of all, Henry Morgan, later became lieutenant governor of Jamaica. The island, independent for almost two decades, depends heavily upon tourism. Cruise vessels concentrate on the northern shore. **Port Antonio,** one of the cruise calls, is a beautiful little harbor with the majestic Blue Mountains (where that wonderful coffee comes from) as a backdrop. With little of interest to passengers, the port's biggest attraction is river rafting on the Rio Grande. The bamboo rafts are about thirty feet long and can accommodate three people—

two is more comfortable—plus a raftsman. It's a relaxing three-hour journey down the river, with time out for a rest in the shade or a dip in the cool, clear, fresh waters. Bathing suits are a must for this one.

The beach resort of **Ocho Rios** has been built around a pleasant, natural harbor. If your cruise vessel arrives in the late afternoon, don't miss the performance of local dances on the beach, complete with stars overhead and torchlights all around you. By day you can visit Dunn's River Falls, where the sparkling water rushes straight from the mountain to the beach below. It's fun to explore these beautiful falls, and you can even climb them if you are properly dressed—bathing suit and sneakers will do the trick. If you wish to get away from the water, an interesting plantation tour takes you to the 1200-acre Prospect Estate, where spices and cattle are big business.

Montego Bay, or Mo'Bay as everyone calls it, is the largest of these three Jamaican ports. Once the favorite of the international set, Mo'Bay's glitter is now long gone. Restored Rose Hall, once among the grandest of eighteenth-century plantation homes in the West Indies, attracts many visitors. The house, which has had two novels written about it, has enjoyed a notorious past. Its second mistress allegedly murdered three spouses and a lover and then was mysteriously done in herself. For a different kind of intrigue—a la James Bond (his creator had a house here)—catch a glimpse of the crocodiles and alligators in nearby swamplands. Some of these beasts, kept by a fearless young man, will do tricks for you as they did in the James Bond film *Live and Let Die.*

NETHERLAND ANTILLES

Aruba, Bonaire, and Curaçao (The "ABC islands") are popular pieces of Holland not only for their Dutch manner but also for their business acumen. These islands have long offered substantial tax credits to companies incorporated here, and one of the world's largest oil refineries is on Curaçao. So, while you explore the delights of Dutch treats in the sunshine, your cruise vessel may be refueling at an economical price. Lying off the Venezuelan coast, all three of these islands were settled by the Spanish.

CURAÇAO: Willemstad, the capital, might just be the most photographed port in the whole Caribbean; its narrow, eighteenth-century gabled houses are painted in every color. The island, discovered by the Spanish explorer Alonzo de Ojeda in 1499, greeted the first Spanish settlers three decades later. They didn't have long to get comfortable, however, because the Dutch arrived, established a colony, and named Peter Stuyvesant governor not long after, in 1643. It was here that Stuyvesant supposedly lost his right leg in an excursion against Sint Maarten. As you wander around this charming port, notice the many dutch-ingrained influences—in the little canals, the colorful floating market, and the old-style dwellings. Take a walk across the famous Queen Emma Pontoon Bridge, which swings open to let ships pass in and out of the harbor. Also interesting are Fort Amsterdam (now a seat of government), the 1769 Old Dutch Reformed Church, and the 1732 Mikve Israel—Emmanuel

Synagogue, which claims to be the oldest in the Western Hemisphere (but then, so do several others). If you fancy refineries, you'll love the one operated by Shell. Another local concern, Curaçao orange-flavored liqueur, offers a free sip at the Chobolobo Mansion (you can also buy some to take home in pretty Delft jugs).

ARUBA: Alonzo de Ojeda claimed Aruba for Spain in 1499, at the same time he discovered Curaçao, but the Dutch moved in here, also, in 1634. Aruba, much smaller and less prosperous than Curaçao (although it has a huge oil refinery), is only fifteen miles from the Venezuelan coastline and twelve degrees from the Equator. Its capital and main port, **Oranjestad,** is another delightfully Dutch harbor with old-style houses whose red-tiled roofs sparkle in the sunshine. Take a walk over to the schooner harbor and open market, then on to Wilhelmina Park and the nearby street lined with typical early Aruban buildings.

If you take an organized shore excursion, it may feature such tourist attractions as Frenchmen's Pass (where Indians allegedly fought the French), the natural bridge, and the rock formation garden of Casibari. In the tiny village of Noord an interesting church, St. Anna's, has an oak altar, handcarved in Holland in 1850 by well-known Dutch artist Van Geld. Some rather fascinating caves and grottos with hieroglyphics show evidence of Arawak Indian habitation. Aruba also has its own Palm Beach, complete with fancy resort hotels and gambling facilities, if you like that sort of thing.

BONAIRE: Noted for flamingos and excellent scuba diving, Bonaire was discovered by a band of men under Amerigo Vespucci in 1496. Second largest of this ABC group, it seems small and very quiet in contrast to its two sisters. The main port, **Kralendijk,** is storybook pretty, with its tiny harbor and pink fish market. Take a wonderful drive out to the Washington National Park, a game preserve and the first of its kind in this area. And if you aren't watching the lovely flamingos, you will want to be underwater watching the myriad colors of the world below. Visibility supposedly reaches to 65 feet below the surface, and all kinds of equipment can be rented.

PUERTO RICO

On any Saturday during the winter season as many as nine cruise ships may be making "turn arounds" in **San Juan,** the most popular port for seven-day cruises in the lower Caribbean. From early morning to late afternoon and early evening, these ships will be resting gently in their berths waiting to take on passengers for sailings to La Guaira, Barbados, St. Lucia, and the like. But San Juan holds her own as a port of call and is well worth an extra day or two to explore, either before or after your cruise.

It's not hard to see why Ponce de Leon exclaimed "puerto rico!" (rich port) when he arrived in the harbor in 1508 to establish a European settlement. Columbus discovered the island on November 19, 1493, during his second voyage to the New World, and the Indian inhabitants received him cordially.

When Ponce de Leon arrived fifteen years later to colonize the island for Spain, the chief of the Taino Indians greeted him and, following Indian custom for friendship, the two men exchanged names. Ponce de Leon became the first governor of Puerto Rico and moved the early settlement to the present site of Old San Juan in 1521. A 24-foot-square frame house was built for him here as a reward for his services, but he never lived to occupy it. However, the Ponce descendants inhabited the house, Casa Blanca, for 250 years. It is now a museum that illustrates Puerto Rican life of the sixteenth and seventeenth centuries. The former Spanish colony was ceded to the United States in 1898 as a result of the Spanish-American War, and Puerto Ricans have been U.S. citizens since the Jones Act of 1917. Spanish is still the primary language, although English is the tourist tongue. Old San Juan, which includes the seven-block-square quarter once enclosed by a city wall and the forts El Morro and San Cristobal, celebrated its 460th birthday in 1981—no small feat. This old section has tremendous charm, and the colonial architecture and ambience are being conserved. Lovely wrought-iron balconies and heavy, carved wooden doors and shutters decorate the whitewashed houses. Inside, the ceilings are supported by beams in such a way that each room is a work of art.

Walking is the most practical way to get around Old San Juan. You can easily design your own tour with a copy of *Que Pasa*, the tourism publication, in hand. (Get a copy at the Visitors Center in the square near Pier Number One.) El Morro, the sixteenth- to eighteenth-century fort built 140 feet above the sea, is the perfect place to begin. Stop next at the Plaza de San Jose, dominated by the statue of Juan Ponce de Leon that was made from a British cannon after an unsuccessful attempt on the city in 1797. This large square also houses San Jose Church, a former Dominican convent that is now the Institute of Puerto Rican Culture, and several renovated buildings that are now museums. On the right side of the square are a small Museum of Santos (small, wooden, religious statues which are a great part of the island's history and folklore) and the Pablo Casals Museum, which has the Maestro's cello. Calle Cristo, Old San Juan's most famous street, runs from the Plaza de San Jose to the harbor wall and is paved with bluish-tint bricks, *adoquines*, which were used for ballast in Spanish ships. Cristo Street runs down past the Cathedral of San Juan and El Convento Hotel (superb buffet is served in the courtyard of this seventeenth-century former convent) and dead ends at Cristo Chapel, built to honor a miracle that occurred on the spot in 1753. Adjacent is Pigeon Park, which overlooks the harbor and La Princesa Jail. Backtrack a bit and pay a visit to La Fortaleza, the governor's mansion, which is the longest continually occupied executive house in this hemisphere. (Museum times in San Juan are a trial, to say the least. If the guidebook says they're open at certain times—and they're not—try to convince the attendants. Mañana is the common word here.)

Shopping in Old San Juan is fun, especially if you're not in the mood for anything too grand. Some very expensive looking jewelry stores may tempt you (not me), but for straw items, hammocks, and inexpensive beach wear, the place is great. Take advantage of the factory shirt outlet that sells Hathaway,

Dior, and other name brands at terrific bargains, but I generally stay away from places such as Barrachina that send advertisements to the ships to entice you the day before your flight leaves. Compare prices before you buy anything—even a quart of rum. Remember, there's always an angle when you are offered something for nothing.

Save metropolitan San Juan and the excellent resort hotels on Condado and Isla Verde for a longer stay; life there is glamorous and exciting in the birthplace of the Pina Colada!

TRINIDAD and TOBAGO

Most southerly of the West Indian groups, Trinidad is the island on which government and commerce are located, while Tobago is the weekend resort, get-away spot. Columbus discovered Trinidad in 1498 on his third voyage to the New World and named it La Trinidad for the three hills around the bay where he anchored. The Spanish settled here a century later, but many battles with the British followed. The island was finally ceded to Britain by the Treaty of Amiens in 1802. Both islands ended their link with the monarchy in 1976 and became a republic.

TRINIDAD: From the capital and main port, **Port of Spain,** Calypso and steel bands originated and spread throughout the Caribbean. For people watching and a walk through the sights and sounds of this exciting place, begin at Queen's Wharf and walk north to Independence Square, Frederick Street, Queen Street, and the Red House (seat of government). You may also want to pay a visit to the Angostura Bitters factory and then continue to the 200-acre Queen's Park Savannah area, with its racecourse, cricket fields, and diverse architecture. The park's lovely Botanical Gardens, laid out in 1820 on a 63-acre plot, provide licensed guides who will show you around and be happy to explain the flora. Built on a peak over a thousand feet above Port of Spain is the 1803 Fort George, which offers the most wonderful all around, including the mountains of Venezuela.

TOBAGO: From Trinidad to Tobago, which some claim was Robinson Crusoe's island, the flight takes fifteen minutes. Tobago is completely unspoiled, and the weather is often better than on Trinidad. Here you'll find some exotic bird life, and the main town of Scarborough has a colorful market.

U.S. VIRGIN ISLANDS

Lying forty miles due east of Puerto Rico, the USVI were discovered by Columbus in 1493 during his second voyage to the New World. He christened them Las Virgenes, in honor of St. Ursula's legendary eleven thousand martyred virgins. On the island he called Santa Cruz (now St. Croix) he searched for fresh water but was chased off by the Carib Indians and sailed away. The Caribs kept the islands off limits for seafarers until 1555, when Spain claimed the territory. Throughout most of the century, however, the islands were contested by England, France, Holland, and Denmark. The Danish won and kept the islands until 1916 when they sold them to the United States for $25 million. This probably makes the U.S. the only governing power in the Caribbean that ever paid for anything! The package included St. Thomas, St. Croix, and St. John as well as several lesser land masses in the area.

ST. THOMAS: Charlotte Amalie, capital of St. Thomas, is the most important port in the USVI, not only for its charm and beauty—the town is named for a Danish queen—but also for all the duty-free shopping available to American cruise passengers. In this little town with cobblestone streets and quaint shops displaying gold watches and cases of liquor, Americans can purchase and bring back duty-free twice the amount allowed elsewhere. No wonder as many as nine cruise vessels dock in this harbor at one time.

If you don't wish (God forbid) to shop, you won't be bored. You can take a tour of this lovely 30-square-mile island, passing famous landmarks such as Bluebeard's Castle and lookout tower where the pirate could spot unsuspecting galleons. Continue your drive up Mafolie Hill and have a look at Louisenhoj Castle before catching the view from Drake's Seat of Magens Bay Beach, reportedly one of the ten most splendid beaches in the world. St. Thomas also has a magnificent underwater observatory, and a visit here is not soon forgotten. Called the Coral World Underwater Observation Tower, and located on a lush tropical peninsula on the northeastern shore of the island, the observatory/ tower's three stories rise from the sea some one hundred feet from shore. On the lowest level hundreds of tropical fish, coral formations, and beautiful deep-water flowers are visible. On the second level you will be surrounded by sharks, sting rays, barracudas, and huge sea turtles. The top level of the tower is an extraordinary geodesic dome with a spectacular view of St. John and the British Virgin Islands.

ST. JOHN'S: Another highlight is the excursion to St. John's, a ten-minute ride by motor launch across Pilgrim Bay (don't sit at the rail unless you are prepared to be drenched). At Cruz Bay you board a motorized surrey—complete with the fringe on the top—for the short but spectacular ride to Trunk Bay, which has been rated by the U.S. National Park Service as the world's sixth most beautiful beach. Trunk Bay has pristine white sands and coral green seas, and is wonderful for snorkeling. A short underwater trail leads to the best look at colorful tropical fish and coral. Don't touch the coral because it's sharp, and don't take souvenirs because that's against the law. You may also go to Coki Point under the auspices of the Virgin Islands Diving Schools, which will teach you how to approach this underwater world and then give you a diploma testifying to your accomplishments. For enjoying the coral reefs with much less effort, join the Kon Tiki raft party, which includes rum punches, a steel band, and swimming on the beaches of Honeymoon Bay.

CENTRAL AND NORTH AMERICA

ALASKA AND THE INSIDE PASSAGE

The 1000-mile-long sea corridor that skirts the west coast of British Columbia and Alaska, known as the Inside Passage, is a busy waterway from May to September. During this popular season as many as a dozen cruise vessels sail through what one might call the Last Frontier, our rugged forty-ninth state. The scenery compares favorably with the Norwegian fjords, both with sheer-rock cliffs, massive glaciers, and snowcapped mountains. Nature's more somber colors prevail in this spectacular setting. Be forewarned; the weather can be tricky—the locals say it's a *good* day when it's only drizzling! Hence, choose such cruises carefully—forget sunbathing and shopping and concentrate on shore excursions and equal time for absorbing the majestic scenery.

The longer cruises through the Inside Passage depart from San Francisco, while the shorter, seven- and eight–day sailings originate in **Vancouver.** This delightful seaport is considered Canada's gem of the Pacific for its fine weather, prosperity, rich cultural life, and interesting sights. Modern highrises of steel and glass sit beside Victorian structures in a beautiful setting between mountains and sea. The city, founded in the 1860s, has a wonderful historic section, Gastown, which is a renovated gaslight district. Two other areas of interest are Chinatown, second in size only to San Francisco's in North America, and Robsonstrasse, with chic European shops and restaurants.

You can head straight for 1000-acre Stanley Park on the northern edge of Vancouver, where you can swim in pools or from the beach, visit a zoo and aquarium, see century-old totem poles, or just stroll among the more than 100,000 trees. (By the way, hockey's Stanley Cup and this park were both named after the same man, Lord Stanley, Governor General of Canada in 1889.) If there is time, drive over the Lions Gate Bridge to see the lovely homes and the symbol of Vancouver, two mountain peaks known as the Lions. Your excursion may also include **Victoria,** a quaint English town that is the provincial capital of British Columbia. Reached only by ferry, Victoria seems dull compared to cosmopolitan Vancouver and rather too touristy for my taste. However, it has many totem poles and lovely gardens.

On board and underway, it's time to wrap yourself in a warm blanket, settle into a deck chair, and watch the view as the sunshine (you hope) warms the crisp air. Your first sight will undoubtedly be Lynn Canal, where fjords, fishing villages, and foothills will keep your camera busy. It's beautiful and rugged and somber, and it's easy to relax up here and slip into a slower pace. First port of call for many ships is **Ketchikan,** a city of some ten thousand or so that claims to be both the salmon capital of the world and totemland. Hence a tour of the city includes a salmon hatchery and Totem Park, where these handcarved poles portray legendary chiefs, mythical birds, and even Abraham Lincoln. Totem Bight State Park, a fifteen-minute drive north of Ketchikan, which has plenty more of these tall poles as well as a handcarved Ceremonial House, is the center of early Alaskan Indian culture.

Juneau, capital of Alaska, is a product of the 1880 gold rush. For the forty-ninth state, Juneau is considered sophisticated, and suburbanites live in modern, low-slung houses with beautiful views of mountains, glaciers, and the sea. One of the most impressive of several tours features Mendenhall Glacier, which is about one and one-half miles wide by one mile long. It has been retreating at the rate of approximately fifty feet per year (you stand where the glacier ended around 1940). If you prefer to save your glaciers for later, don't miss the good performances of Tlingit and Haida tribal dances and snacks of fresh, fire-baked Alaskan salmon. For a more adventurous (and costly—about eighty dollars per person—) salmon bake, catch one of the seaplanes parked along the waterfront for the half-hour ride to Taku Lodge. This forest-surrounded, log-cabin lodge offers a hearty lunch of salmon, homemade biscuits, beer chilled by glacial ice, baked beans, potato salad, coffee, and cookies—and there is time to walk it off before the flight back to Juneau.

Highlight of every Inside Passage cruise is **Glacier Bay National Monument,** about forty miles northwest of Juneau, accessible only by plane or boat. The scenery here is some of Alaska's most spectacular, and park rangers will board your vessel in the morning to comment on the history and habits of glaciers as you cruise along. The better part of a day is spent cruising slowly through Glacier Bay while you relax on board watching the ice floes pass by, occasionally hearing a glacier calve, or crack off, and learning about the rare wildlife that inhabit the area. Perhaps the sun will be brilliant this day, and your stewards will serve a wonderful buffet luncheon on deck.

The National Park Service, concerned about the survival of the endangered humpback whales that frequent Glacier Bay during the popular cruise months of June and July, wants to limit the number of cruise calls allowed in future years. So, when you book your cruise, be sure that it will visit Glacier Bay. My advice is not to trust the brochure but to have your travel agent confirm the exact itinerary of your vessel.

Final port of call on most Inside Passage routes is the former Russian settlement of **Sitka,** a town that lives in the past for the sake of its many tourists. On the site of an ancient Tlingit village, Sitka was founded by Aleksandr Baranof when he transferred the headquarters of the Russian-American Company here. On October 18, the 1867 ceremony in which the American flag replaced the Imperial Russian one is reenacted. Sites to visit in the area include the 54-acre Sitka Historical National Park, where Tlingit tribes made their last stand against the Russians and where Indian craftsmen now demonstrate their carving techniques. (The carvings for sale in town are rather pricey, I feel.) You can tour the onion-domed Russian church. It was rebuilt in 1966 after a disastrous fire, but the icons are original. The Alaska Pioneers' Home, the Russian cemetery, and a fine museum of local history and artifacts that span two centuries are also interesting. During the summer months a group of Sitka women perform tyical Russian folk dances.

MEXICO

Our neighbors south-of-the-border extend their arms in welcome to *norteamericano* cruise passengers who come for a taste of the continual feast of colors, sights, and beautiful beaches. Mexico's western coastline is one of the most popular of all cruise destinations, especially for ships originating from southern California. The so-called Mexican Riviera stretches from Mazatlán to Acapulco and includes Puerto Vallarta and Zihuatanejo. If you don't delude yourself into expecting Puerto Vallarta to have the crazy chic of St. Tropez, or Acapulco to be as sophisticated and glamorous as Monte Carlo, then you will enjoy what this Riviera has to offer.

Sailing directly south from San Pedro, California, the port for Los Angeles, many crise vessels call first at **Ensenada,** a peaceful little community just sixty-seven miles south of the California border, in Baja California (the lower peninsula that belongs to Mexico). Juan Rodríguez Cabrillo founded Ensenada in 1542. However, neither he nor Fray Junipero Sera (who founded San Diego) stayed, because they couldn't find fresh water in this beautiful, natural harbor. Today fresh water is found in underground wells, but this is still a frontier town with spectacular beaches and not much else—a pleasant but uninspiring cruise stop.

At the tip of Baja California are San José del Cabo and **Cabo San Lucas,** the latter more famous because the waters of the Sea of Cortes and the Pacific Ocean meet here. Sea lions frolic under nearby Los Arcos, natural rock arcades that are best viewed from small boats. Some cruise vessels simply sail by Cabo San Lucas and consider it seen, but others stop for a few hours for the small boat excursion to Los Arcos and a drink on the terrace of the Hyatt Hotel, which overlooks the Bay of Chileno. If you care to return someday, the fishing is considered some of he best in the world.

Mazatlán, one of the best harbors on Mexico's Pacific coastline, is noted for its shrimp industry, which feeds much of the U.S. market. Fishing here is also good, and marlin can be caught year-round. The fishing and the continual sunshine make Mazatlán a popular tourist town. Your shore tour will take you along the Olas Atlas section to the cathedral, Indian market, and outdoor cafes. You can watch high cliff-divers at Glorieta's Rocky Promontory, but it's more rewarding to shop for Indian handcrafts and Mexican silver. Or you can find your way to Las Gaviotas Beach and pay a visit to the new hotels that have grown up alongside this lovely stretch of the city. This is the perfect place for swimming and sunning.

Some people I know bought houses in a sleepy, slightly seedy little fishing village named **Puerto Vallarta** before it became fashionable; or shall I say "popular" since it's debatable whether or not this town has ever been "fashionable." Nonetheless, cruise brochures love to call it an "exquisite, picturesque seaside village." Don't expect too much, for aside from a few beaches and an area now known as "Gringo Gulch," Puerto Vallarta does not have a great deal to offer the quick visitor. There are some nice beaches in Puerto Vallarta, so plan to spend your time browsing, people-watching (both the swells and the indigents congregate in this town), and sunning. I thought the city tour was not worth my while or money, so don't feel guilty about passing it up. This is one of the many port calls you can do on your own and be the better for it.

While **Manzanillo** and its beautiful beaches are often the next port of call, **Zihuatanejo** is more interesting for its beaches and its similarity (although smaller) to Acapulco. As a town, it doesn't have much to offer except its five splendid beaches and a few nice restaurants. Shore excursions will take you to Ixtapa's sixteen-mile beach. The Mexican government is investing heavily in Ixtapa's future as a tourist attraction. The Palma Real Golf Club and some new hotels welcome you and help you relax in resort style. Other than that, what can one say but enjoy the scenery.

At last, **Acapulco.** A true resort. A port worthy of your time and a city with real bite to it. Acapulco is where even jetsetters take their honeymoons, not to mention brief get-away weekends. It has eternal sunshine, bikinis, no ties, siestas, nonlunches on the beach—whatever you like any time of the year. Although the official season runs from mid-December to the end of April, even Frank Sinatra has visited in the summer. And both the J. F. Kennedys and the Henry Kissingers spent their honeymoons here (albeit in private villas). If there is any real Riviera on the Mexican Pacific coast, this is it. One can play high or low here, either walking casually along "hotel row" or taking a tour to La Quebrada to watch divers plunge from a cliff 136 feet high into the sinister, swirling waters below. Acapulco is an exciting place with too many highrise hotels, too-crowded beaches, too-expensive shops, and never a moment to spare for anyone.

If you go on an organized shore excursion, you will see the city and, per-haps, the only historic monument around, Fort San Diego, which was origi-nally built in 1616 and rebuilt in the late eighteenth century after it was destroyed by an earthquake in 1776. Also here are a beautiful yacht club (where some 1968 Olympic events took place), a cathedral built in the 1930s, the west or older section of town that should become fashionable someday, a new convention/cultural center, and a public market. One sight not to miss is Las Brisas, overlooking Acapulco Bay, one of the world's most imaginative hotels. (You will most likely see the hotel jeeps, complete with fringed tops, buzzing all over town.) Some shore tours take you to way out of town to the Pierre Marqués Hotel and beach for lunch and swimming, which I found okay but not very exciting. Acapulco by night is exciting, as in most resort towns, but in my experience the taxi drivers here were well versed in the art of *bandido.*

If your cruise ship spends two full days at port in Acapulco, you may be offered the opportunity to visit **Taxco,** the city of silver. Taxco is 145 miles straight up from Acapulco, along a narrow highway that might make you ex-ceedingly nervous (it does everyone), but your attention will be diverted from time to time by the children along the side selling iguanas. It's all worth it, though, for Taxco is charming. Reportedly explored by Cortés (who noted the silver-mining potential), this cobblestoned, colonial town sits atop some rich silver mines, although more than two hundred shops furnish the town with approximately ninety percent of its income. Take a look at the Church of Santa Prisca and Casa Figueroa, the local art gallery and museum. There are also some interesting and vast caves in the area, Las Grutas de Cachuamilpa. Be certain to pack extra sweaters for the excursion to the caves; Taxco is 5700 feet above sea level, and the average temperature ranges only from sixty-six to seventy-six degrees.

The **Yucatán Peninsula** on the Atlantic coast of Mexico is a major tourist haven, for both its abundance of comfortable tourist facilities and its historical interest. This is the land of Mayan splendors. The best known and most remarkable ruin is **Chichén Itzá.** For cruise passengers it's a three-hour drive from the port of **Cancun.** Chichén Itzá is the chosen city of Kukulcán, the "Plumed Serpent," the incarnation of God who founded Mayapán as the civil center of the peninsula (while Chichén Itzá remained the religious center). Hundreds of structures here dot the more than six-square-mile complex that straddles the highway, the earliest buildings dating from the fifth century, and additional ruins (some not yet excavated) extend deep into the surrounding jungle. Most impressive is El Castillo, or the Pyramid of Kukulcán, which the Spanish used as a fortress. One of the many fascinations of this pyramid is the solar phenomenon that occurs during the vernal and autumnal equinoxes—the sun creates a shadowy serpent up its northeast side. Other points of interest in Chichén Itzá include the ball court, the Temple of the Warriors, and the Well of Sacrifices. A tour to this ancient site makes for a long day (about eleven hours), but it is worth the effort.

If you prefer to visit an ancient Mayan city closer to the seashore, you will want to see **Tulum,** a short drive from Cancun. This walled fortress by the sea was first viewed in 1518 and rediscovered only in the mid-nineteenth century. Tulum is one of the most ancient cities in Mexico, but all that remains now is the tower (or Castillo) of Tulum, a pyramidal structure sitting atop a forty-foot bluff. Down below lies the crystal-blue Caribbean. You may just wish to enjoy the beautiful sea from one of the empty, sweeping beaches of Cancun, a resort that some say is the best in Mexico. Both the flora and fauna are lovely here, and the water is so shallow that you can walk out "forever" before you reach any noticeable undertow. The Caribbean's newest spa, Cancun means "pot of gold" in one of the many Mayan dialects. So true.

Two other Mexican calls in the Caribbean are **Cozumel** and **Playa del Carmen,** both popular for their fine beaches, excellent underwater diving opportunities, and resort atmosphere, not to mention terrific beach parties.

THE MISSISSIPPI RIVER

As the principal waterway in the United States, the Mississippi River has touched the lives of all Americans at one time or another. "Ole Man River" is one of our nation's most moving folk tunes. Tom Sawyer and Huck Finn of

Hannibal are a part of every child's vocabulary early on. And many of us stumbled over the stinger "Mississippi" at some school spelling bee and then learned how to say it fast—backwards. The river flows south some 2470 miles from northern Minnesota to the Gulf of Mexico, offering a historic venue for cruises and an unparalleled view for passengers of a way of life that has endured along its banks—sleepy river towns that are slightly behind the times, plantations that show us what wealth there was in the land, and cities that have become industrial centers but still retain the charm of yesteryear.

Thanks to the Delta Queen Steamboat Company, cruises up and down the Mississippi River are available almost year-round on the only two overnight paddle-wheel steamboats left in America. You can choose the venerable old lady named *Delta Queen*, who is listed in the Register of Historic Places, or her baby sister, the *Mississippi River*, launched in 1975 but already a legend. Most of the cruises originate from **New Orleans,** that romantic, much-fought-over city founded by the French in 1718 on the first high ground above the Mississippi Passes, about ninety-five miles upriver from the Gulf. New Orleans was poverty stricken and sparsely populated in 1811 when the first steamboat, named the *City of New Orleans*, was built in Pittsburgh and launched on her first trip downriver.

By 1840, some 100,000 people lived in New Orleans, and it was the second largest port in America. Just before the Civil War the number of steamboats at her miles-long terminus numbered at least a hundred. Today the city is still a busy and colorful port, famous for Mardi Gras, Bourbon Street jazz, the French Quarter, Garden District, and the new Superdome. Time is well spent here either before or after your steamboat cruise. Other major ports of embarkation on the Mississippi are Memphis (as of 1983), St. Louis, and St. Paul.

Cruising upriver on the lower half of the Mississippi, your first steamboat landing is **Nottoway Plantation,** built in 1859 by John Hampton Randolph. Renowned as the largest plantation home in the South, Nottoway has sixty-four rooms and boasts twenty-two enormous columns enhancing its Greek Revival and Italianate architecture! Steamboat passengers may tour the grounds and mansion from the docking at water's edge, enjoying views of the river and century-old live oak trees from the largest of Nottoway's two hundred windows.

At the river's 153-mile mark is **Oak Alley Plantation,** first settled in the early 1700s by a Frenchman who had the foresight to plant two rows of oak trees from the house to the river. When the steamboat ties up at the water's edge, you walk to the Greek Revival mansion, built in 1837, beneath an alley of 250-year-old oaks with Spanish moss dripping from their solid bows. It's a truly wonderful experience, and if you close your eyes and breathe deeply, hoop-skirted Southern belles with velvet ribbon around their necks are stepping daintily down to greet you.

Another restored, antebellum-style plantation complex open to visitors is **Houmas House,** which is also approached from the river. (Perhaps you will recognize this house, for it has been in many television films and was the setting for *Hush, Hush, Sweet Charlotte.*) Named after an Indian tribe that once inhabited this spot, Houmas House commands a river view of several miles in both directions. The Greek Revival mansion dates from 1840, and from that year until the Civil War this 20,000-acre plantation was the foremost sugar producer in America. Houmas was spared the ravages of famine and fighting during the war because its Irish owner declared British immunity—a ploy that worked! Under new ownership and management in the 1880s, the plantation flourished again, reaching a record production of twenty million tons of sugar in one year. But success was short-lived. By the end of the century, the land was parceled off and the house stood in disrepair. It was purchased by a New Orleans doctor in 1940, who devoted the last twenty-five years of his life to planting formal gardens and to restoring the house and furnishing it with museum-quality early Louisiana craftsmanship. A tour of this house and grounds is a real treat.

Baton Rouge, capital of Louisiana, is situated at the 230-mile mark of the lower Mississippi and named for the red post that once divided two Indian nations here. Founded in 1719, the city was the site of a Revolutionary War battle that did not even involve a colonist—it was strictly between the British and the Spanish (who had possession of this territory). Today this gracious Southern metropolis has wide avenues lined with former plantation homes, like the 1791 Magnolia Mound, now a museum of Federal-period furniture. Baton Rouge is also known for Louisiana State University, whose Rural Life Museum is a reconstructed plantation settlement, and the Old State Capitol which overlooks the river from a bluff. The original 1849 Gothic structure that stood here was burned by Union troops during the Civil War (accidentally, they say) and reconstructed in 1882.

The next call for the Delta Queen Steamboat Company is the sleepy river town of **St. Francisville,** Louisiana, which boasted half the millionaires in America during the cotton boom of the 1850s. Today, the luxury and splendor this region knew is recalled only in the restoration of once-thriving plantations, foremost of which are Rosedown and The Myrtles. Rosedown Home and Gardens were built in 1835 by a wealthy cotton planter and his wife who spared neither money nor means to create a magnificent setting in the style of seventeenth-century France. The Myrtles was built in the early 1830s, and locals believe that the ghost of a former resident still roams the house. In the restoration, special care was given to the iron grillwork that surrounds a 100-foot veranda. Both these plantations are near Audubon state park and on the steamboat tour.

Natchez, Mississippi, lies at the 363-mile mark in the heart of the fertile Mississippi River delta. The antebellum homes here also reflect the wealth of early cotton planters who often used European architects and craftsmen. Many of the fine places here can still be visited because General Ulyses S. Grant spared Natchez Over The Hill (as it was called then) in his thrust south during the Civil War. Semiannual events in this gracious river town, founded in 1716, are the spring and fall Natchez Pilgrimage Cruises that bring passengers to view some of the more than two hundred antebellum properties in the best seasons. Some of the highlights of these tours are Stanton Hall, occupying an entire block and patterned after an Irish ancestral home; Connelly's Tavern where the first American flag in Mississippi was raised in 1797; a lovely Georgian home named Rosalie; Longwood, looking just as the workers left it when war broke out; and D'Evereux, where the most elaborate balls in Natchez were said to have taken place.

Just seventy-three miles upriver is **Vicksburg,** site of the siege of 1863. To this day the citizens of Vicksburg refuse to celebrate the fourth of July, for on that day their ancestors surrendered to the Union Army that had surrounded the city for three solid months. This peaceful town has many memories, war memorials, and cemeteries. The Old Court House Museum, former headquarters of the Confederates, has touching memorabilia from the period—receipts from the sale of slaves, Confederate money and clothing, and photographs of Mississippi River steamboats. A few of the local homes that survived are also worth visiting, especially Cedar Grove with a cannonball still lodged in the parlor wall. For a change of pace, your tour may take you to a scale model of the entire Mississippi River system at the Waterways Experiment Station (operated by the U.S. Army Corps of Engineers).

Memphis, Tennessee, at the 736-mile mark on the lower Mississippi, was planned in 1818 and named after the ancient city on the Nile. Hernando DeSoto supposedly came through here in 1541, stopping only long enough to build some barges to cross the river. Memphis became an important port and agricultural center in the 1800s, and the world's largest cotton market was established here in 1873. Located on Cotton Row, the Memphis Cotton Exchange is still active and handles more than four million bales each year. Tours in Memphis include a visit to the Exchange and, when weather permits, to a cotton field and working cotton gin. It's also fun to visit the old Beale Street haunts of famous blues musicians W. C. Handy, Elvis Presley's mansion "Graceland," Schwab's famous Five and Dime, and the Chucalissa Indian Village and Museum.

At the mouth of the upper Mississippi is the quiet town of **Cairo,** Illinois, whose prosperity was tied to the steamboat trade. Cairo's dreams of a future more exciting than Chicago's were dashed by the southern extension of the Illinois Central Railroad in 1855. However, memories of a glorious past linger, with landmarks like the restored Magnolia Manor and Holiday Park to give us an indication of once-abundant wealth.

St. Louis, Missouri, at the 180-mile mark on the upper Mississippi, was second only to New Orleans in the days of steamboat packets, and as the historic Gateway to the West, played host to thousands of famous and infamous settlers, traders, and trappers. Wagon trains bound for the West crowded the riverfront as pioneers formed some unusual alliances in their battle against the elements of the new frontier. Among enterprising Americans who made their home in St. Louis, at least for a while, were Abraham Lincoln and Charles Lindbergh, who christened his plane "The Spirit of St. Louis" in honor of the city whose business leaders believed in him. St. Louis has interesting buildings in all styles—from the much-photographed Gateway Arch on the riverfront to WPA projects and historic structures. The Old Courthouse was the scene of the notorious Dred Scott case, and the Anheuser-Busch Brewery is the largest in the world. The Jefferson Memorial has original documents relating to the Louisiana Purchase as well as some of Lindbergh's trophies commemorating his New York to Paris flight.

Everyone's favorite river town is still **Hannibal** (at the 308-mile mark on the upper Mississippi), where Tom Sawyer, Huck Finn, and Becky Sharpe played their pranks. The author of these escapades (Samuel Clemens) was born in nearby Florida, Missouri, but grew up in Hannibal where the arrival of the steamboat was about the only event to raise the dust (or a few waves) on a somnolent summer's day. While still in his teens Clemens boarded a paddlewheeler en route to New Orleans, and a combined career of river pilot/writer—and Mark Twain was born. Shortly after he left, the railroad came to save Hannibal from extinction when riverboat traffic diminished after the Civil War. Any visit to Hannibal is strictly a do-it-yourself tour about the town, wandering along the street with the whitewashed fence, the Pilaster House with law office and drugstore, and the birthplace of Margaret Tobin (known as the "Unsinkable" Molly Brown).

Nauvoo, Illinois, at the 375-mile mark on the upper Mississippi, was founded in 1839 by Joseph Smith and followers of the Church of the Latter-Day Saints (Mormons). But Smith and his disciples fled for their lives seven years later over a series of disputes with the non-Mormon community. However, they left behind some interesting Mormon-style buildings that have been restored by descendants of the original pilgrims. Nauvoo is also known for its fruit harvests, especially the vineyards that produce abundant native wine. And to enjoy with the wine, try some domestic bleu cheese.

As the Mississippi continues and your riverboat cruises upstream, **Dubuque,** Iowa, lies at the 579-mile mark, a commercial city in America's heartland. An air-conditioned motorcoach from the docking site takes passengers to visit the quiet backwater of **Galena,** known for a quaint atmosphere and its nineteenth-century architecture. The tour features a walk through the town's antique and specialty shops and former home of Ulysses S. Grant, our eighteenth president.

Prairie Du Chien, Wisconsin, is near the meeting of the Mississippi and Wisconsin rivers, where Indians are believed to have lived for some ten thousand years. The many tribes included the Woodland, Fox, Sauk, and Winnebago, and the Hopewell culture built huge burial mounds about two thousand years ago. The settlers built a fort on top of one of the mounds in 1812. It was burned and replaced by Fort Crawford in 1816, which still remains. Prairie du Chien was a thriving frontier settlement in 1826 when Hercules Dousman arrived as a confidential agent for John Jacob Astor, the American Fur Company millionaire. The Dousman family became rich from fur trading and built an enormous mansion named Villa Louis on one of the Indian burial mounds. This restored villa is a showplace of Victorian architecture and furnishings. You can also visit the original Astor Fur Warehouse and restored Fort Crawford, complete with hospital.

At one time, **LaCrosse,** Wisconsin, claimed the largest transportation organization on the Upper Mississippi—with two hundred steamboats landing a month. Three rivers meet here: the Mississippi, the Black, and the La Crosse. A stop at Grandad Bluff, 675 feet above the city, offers a view of three states: Wisconsin, Minnesota, and Iowa.

At **Wabasha,** Minnesota, in unspoiled wilderness, the two *Queens* dock at Read's Landing. Steamboats brought supplies up to this logging and fur-trading center in the early 1800s and took log rafts back down the Mississippi. The Wabasha Country Museum chronicles the regional history of steamboats and rafts, and if you're interested in a view of Sitting Bull's peace pipe, pay a visit to the Suilman Antique Museum. Visitors can enjoy a tour of the Anderson House Hotel as well, which opened in 1856 and to this day warms guests' beds with hot bricks. Wabasha is also the home of the Nelson Cheese Factory, where sampling is part of the tour.

Minneapolis/St. Paul, the twin cities on the upper Mississippi, mark the 839th mile and the final point of navigation on the river and the end of your steamboat cruise. In the old days, ox carts provided transit from this point northward, with as many as five hundred wagons per caravan shuttling between the steamboat landing and Fort Garry, which is now Winnipeg, Manitoba. The city of St. Paul grew up around the landing while Minneapolis blossomed next door. Twin City attractions include the Guthrie Theatre; a 36-foot-high-onyx Indian statue; Fort Snelling, established in 1825 by the U.S. cavalry; the home of the Betty Crocker testing kitchens; the Walker Art Center; and Minnehaha Falls.

THE NORTHEAST PASSAGE

From New York to Montreal, summer cruises are popular along the northeast coastline and through the passage of the St. Lawrence and Saguenay rivers. This is the so-called Northeast Passage, through which you will enjoy a wealth of historical sights. A special charm penetrates cruises in this section of North America—the beauty of the scenery and the flavor of these seafaring people. Along the way you will sail by centuries of our maritime heritage, from New York's South Street Seaport to Mystic, Connecticut, where America's last wooden whaleship, the *Charles W. Morgan,* lies in state. You may also see old sea captain's houses in Stonington, Connecticut, and the Bath Marine Museum, built along the broad waters of the Kennebec River of Maine.

One of the first islands to view after leaving New York is **Martha's Vineyard,** Massachusetts, which was settled in 1642 by Thomas Mayhew (who bought it for forty pounds). Edgartown, the Vineyard's first port and a major whaling center in the eighteenth and nineteenth centuries, still boasts many fine old mansions built by wealthy sea captains and ship owners. Whaling was also important to the development of nearby **Nantucket,** which means "faraway land;" it is also known as the "place of peace." Nantucketers caught their first whale in 1672, and the Whaling Museum on Broad Street declares this island was once the center of the world's whaling industry. Few cruise vessels stop here, so it is a treat if you can explore the town's cobblestone streets and old dwellings that remain much as they were 150 years ago. The island is a testimonial to historic preservation, and many of the finely restored buildings are open to the public. Herman Melville's whaling novel, *Moby Dick*, devotes an entire chapter to the island and its inhabitants.

Newport, Rhode Island, renowned as the playground of the ostentatious rich in the late nineteenth century, was once the most prosperous seaport on the eastern coastline. Now it is the yachting capital of the Atlantic, with three of the most prestigious races either starting or ending there—the Newport to Bermuda (even years), the Annapolis to Newport (odd years), and the America's Cup (every four years). Aside from the glittering mansions and the beautiful boats, Newport is noted for some fine eighteenth-century public buildings and its more than one hundred colonial homes that have been refurbished and made available for rent. The town houses the superb 1726 Trinity Church (called a matchless reminder of Colonial America) and the 1763 Touro Synagogue (the country's first) commissioned by Sephardic Jews from Portugal and designed in Georgian style by local architect Peter Harrison.

To call at **Boston** Harbor and Massachusetts Bay is to follow the route of the early European explorers to the New World. The first European settlement here was at Weymouth in 1623. In addition to the many interesting and historic places within the old city, Boston's waterfront has undergone an impressive revitalization and should be the starting point of your walking tour. And ferry boats will take you from Long Wharf to some of the more than thirty islands that dot the harbor. If you like sailing ships, don't forget "Old Ironsides," the *USS Constitution*, that was built in Boston between 1794 and 1797. The restored version graces the waterfront near the museum. There is something for everyone in Boston—excellent eateries, museums, universities, and historic sites. The one and a half-mile Freedom Trail links landmarks to capture the essence of early American history. This and other well-known walks make it impossible to be blasé about America, at least when in Boston.

Bar Harbor lies on the east coast of Mount Desert Island, off the rockbound coast of Maine. During the mid-nineteenth century Bar Harbor was a conclave of the very wealthy, and despite a devastating fire after World War II, some of the elegant summer cottages still exist. One prime example, the former wood and stone mansion of the late Nelson Rockefeller, was sold a few years ago for about one million dollars to a member of the Ford Motor Company family. However, Bar Harbor is no Newport; today the island is known more for Acadia National Park, with views from Cadillac Mountain. The island's succulent lobsters and clams often find their way into local bakes.

Halifax is Nova Scotia's capital and the largest city in the Maritime Provinces. Lord Cornwallis founded the city in 1749 and built the Citadel to guard against the French on Cape Breton Island at Louisburg. Once the mightiest fortress in British North America, the Citadel still dominates the capital but is now a park with military, marine, and provincial museums. The only shots fired from the Citadel these days are from the cannon at noontime, a well-preserved tradition. Halifax has a spectacular harbor, and water tours aboard the *Bluenose II* are available (but the best overall view is still from the fortress). A large redevelopment plan to save the city's lovely eighteenth- and nineteenth-century structures from destruction began in the early 1960s. Even the eighteen-acre Public Gardens on Spring Garden Road (originally laid out in 1753) have been preserved. Another interesting park is Point Pleasant, the only spot in North America where Scottish heather grows wild. Apparently the seeds were spread when British sailors shook their mattresses out long ago.

Off the coasts of Nova Scotia and New Brunswick, in the Gulf of the St. Lawrence, is **Prince Edward Island,** a garden province that explorer Jacques Cartier in 1534 called "the fairest land 'tis possible to see." Its capital, a popular cruise call, is **Charlottetown,** named after the consort of England's King George III. Charlottetown has great charm and an atmosphere reminiscent of Victoria, a city on Canada's western coast. In fact, Victoria Park overlooks Charlottetown's harbor and is the site of Fort Edward whose six-gun battery protects the harbor's entrance. Province House sheltered the Fathers of Confederation when they met in 1864 to plan the union of British North America and Canada. Visit the more contemporary home of Green Gables in Cavendish (on the island's north shore), which was the setting for the novel *Anne of Green Gables,* and stop at the post office nearby, the most popular on Prince Edward Island.

Gaspé Peninsula reaches out into the Gulf of the St. Lawrence at the southeast extremity of the Province of Quebec. When Champlain landed here, it was called Gachepe or Land's End by the local Indian tribe, the Micmacs. Gaspé is a rugged peninsula, with centuries-old, twelve-foot fir trees and streams filled with Atlantic salmon that have been spawning here for thousands of years. Take an excursion to nearby **Percé,** known for its incredible natural beauty and for Percé Rock where explorer Cartier anchored his three small ships in 1534. A small boat will take you out two miles to Bonaventure Island, a wildlife sanctuary where you can tour bird colonies with a naturalist and see thousands of gannets, gulls, puffins, and kittiwakes nestling in the cliffs.

The *pièce de résistance*—the **Saguenay River,** sinuous arm of the St. Lawrence, flows 450 miles from Lake Saint John and boasts sheer granite gorges that rise to 1500 feet. This is one of the most spectacular waterways in the world. You won't forget the sight of whales feeding here, where the Sanguenay and St. Lawrence rivers come together. From May through November, they surge upon this spot and often stay on the surface long enough for good photographs. A sail along the fjordlike Saguenay River will give you some feeling for what fur traders, explorers, and missionaries experienced centuries before.

Quebec City, perched high above the majestic St. Lawrence, is often called the Gibraltar of North America; its place in history was forged by its natural assets. The city, founded in 1608 by Samuel de Champlain, is situated along an eight-mile plateau atop solid rock. The highest point, some 360 feet above the river, is Cap Diamant, site of the famed Citadel. The only walled city in North America, Quebec has never lost its French heritage and lifestyle. It is a popular tourist center that is best explored on foot or by *calèches*, colorful horse-drawn carriages. Romance and drama come to life in this delightful old town whose seventeenth- and eighteenth-century buildings have been lovingly restored. Take a look at Place d'Armes, where settlers and Indian traders used to meet. And don't miss Le Chateau Frontenac facing the square—a beautiful old hotel where Roosevelt, Churchill, and MacKenzie King met to discuss strategy during World War II. Off Place d'Armes are streets lined with historic houses and the sites of the first girls' school in North America and the first Anglican cathedral constructed outside the British Isles. You can also see the Continent's oldest house of worship—Notre Dame des Victoires, built in 1688. Recapture even more history from Dufferin Terrace, two hundred feet above the waterway, where Champlain built his fort in 1620; the views are spectacular on a clear day.

Quebec is divided into an upper and lower town. Dufferin Terrace is part of the upper town, the historic center for administration and defense. The old town, along the waterfront, functioned primarily as a post for fur trading and other commercial enterprises. Quebec's heart is crowded with so many restored historic dwellings, museums, shops, and fine restaurants that even experienced travelers are surprised and delighted.

Montreal, Canada's chief port and richest cultural center, is located around an island at the junction of three bodies of water. This was such a natural point of interchange that when Cartier came upon it in 1535 he found a community of some 3500 Indians living there. These Indians were soon scattered by French settlers, explorers, and missionaries who were determined to make this site their Gateway to the West. Doubtless they would be very pleased to know that they founded the second largest French-speaking city in the world. Montreal's oldest landmark, Place Royale, is said to have been named by Champlain. The foundations of the city laid here in 1642, were given the name Ville Marie. The old section also boasts a Place d'Armes, rich with history and memories and with beautiful old streets leading away from it. In the eastern part of the old city are lovely homes, open squares, and an 1834 hotel where Charles Dickens once stayed. Many of these eighteenth-century dwellings have had French, English, and American occupants during the city's varied history.

Modern Montreal is just as much fun to explore. The heart of the city, Centre Town, has shopping streets, business districts, cafes and restaurants, and fine hotels. Montreal's underground system is also worthy of attention—a city in itself. Fascinating tours around the island take you to the former Olympic village and along the banks of the St. Lawrence. Of special note is a view of St. Lambert Lock of the St. Lawrence Seaway, a 9500-mile network of navigable waters extending into the body of this continent.

THE OHIO RIVER

The Ohio River flows almost one thousand miles from its source in Pittsburgh, Pennsylvania, to its confluence with the Mississippi River at Cairo,

Illinois. Like the Mississippi, the Ohio River was discovered and explored by the French, and many of its early settlers came from the not-so-distant East. The Ohio has played its role in the story of America: the last battle of the Revolutionary War was fought on its banks in Wheeling, West Virginia, and Ulysses S. Grant, general and president, was born near the shore in Point Pleasant, Ohio. The first steamboat, built in 1811 in Pittsburgh and named the *City of New Orleans*, paddled the entire length of the Ohio River.

Evansville and **New Harmony,** Indiana, are located near the 795-mile mark on the Ohio River. Evansville was established in 1812 when Hugh McCarey crossed the river so his wife could visit her family. The landing grew into a large shipping center for coal, oil, and lumber. In the late 1800s this area became known as Lincoln Land, and a Lincoln Heritage Trail winds through Kentucky, Indiana, and Illinois, tracing the life of our sixteenth president. Nearby New Harmony was settled in 1814 by a group of dissident Lutherans hoping to build a perfectly planned community. Your tour will take you to some restored communal Harmony houses as well as the Labyrinth, an elaborate shrubbery maze that leads to a small temple symbolizing harmony.

The home of beautiful women, bluegrass, the Kentucky Derby, and the best bourbon in the south—**Louisville,** Kentucky—is at the 603-mile mark on the Ohio River. The city is at its best during Derby Week, the first part of May when the southern belles come out and Churchill Downs is filled with spectators watching the famous "Run for the Roses." A special cruise is offered the first week in May, but if you miss it, some of the excitement and atmosphere can be found in the Churchill Downs Museum. Other sights include the Thomas Jefferson-style Manor House, built around 1810, which stands as the only example of his design west of the Alleghenies, and Bakery Square where an inner-city restoration now holds thirty shops.

Madison, Indiana, is considered the finest example of a typical American town. The town was laid out in 1810, and by the middle 1800s was the largest city in Indiana. Jenny Lind performed in the local pork house (which apparently surprised her). The town today is interesting; the many restored buildings reflect the Federal era, the Regency period, the classic Revival style, and the Americanized Italian villa. Many of the restored and furnished homes are open to the public for a do-it-yourself tour.

Located on the 470-mile mark of the Ohio River, **Cincinnati,** Ohio, is home to the Delta Queen Steamboat Company and a major industrial center of the Midwest. Located here are steel mills, machine-tool plants, and the bases of many leading consumer products as well as the Taft Museum, a well-known zoo, and the Cincinnati Reds. The first suspension bridge to span the Ohio River, completed in 1867, connects Cincinnati with Covington, Kentucky.

Ripley, Ohio, was a major station on the Underground Railroad for four decades prior to the Civil War, although it was considered primarily a quiet river town noted for the breeding of fine draft horses. Ripley citizens now breed Arabian horses for distinguished sportsmen. Visitors to Rankin House learn that the Reverend John Rankin sheltered more than two thousand escaped slaves and helped them find routes north. You will follow in the footsteps of Harriet Beecher Stowe who visited Rankin in 1851. Upon hearing the story of Eliza Hariss' midnight river crossing on ice floes, Stowe wrote the book that inflamed the nation, *Uncle Tom's Cabin*.

Gallipolis, Ohio, is located at the 270-mile mark on the Ohio River. The town was settled by a group of Frenchmen, almost five hundred strong, who crossed the Atlantic in 1789 for this very purpose. Much of the town's French heritage remains. The Gallipolis City Park houses the first log cabins built here. Ouc House Tavern, now restored, was the center of village social life and boasted a visit by the Marquis de Lafayette in 1825. Crafts passed down by the French settlers are still taught in the schools, and your city tour includes a visit to Bob Evans Farm, which covers over one thousand acres near Rio Grande and offers outdoor recreation activities.

Pittsburgh, Pennsylvania, is located at the junction of the Monongahela, Allegheny, and Ohio rivers and became important as early as 1758 as a strategic spot for exploration of the West. Fort Pitt was built by the British in 1764 and named for William Pitt, then Prime Minister. Pittsburgh flourished and steamboats were familiar sights here for transporting wheat, rye, barley, flour, and whiskey to other river ports as far south as New Orleans.

Today's Pittsburgh is no longer the smoky, polluted city it was, due to an ambitious urban renewal program during the last three decades. Visitors will enjoy touring the Fort Pitt Blockhouse, the Fort Pitt Museum, the Carnegie Museum, the Duquesne Incline, and many arts events. Left off of the itineraries of the Delta Queen Steamboat Company for a few years, Pittsburgh seems to have returned to favor.

THE PANAMA CANAL

The approximately eight-hour transit of the Panama Canal is a cruise highlight for passengers sailing between Pacific and Atlantic ports. In addition to lush tropical scenery and exciting historical commentary by a ship-board lecturer, the passage of this fifty-mile "big ditch" will take you through one of the largest man-made bodies of water in the world, the island-studded 166-square-mile Gatun Lake. The Panama Canal was opened to commercial ship traffic in 1914, just ten years after the United States began serious construction of the canal and almost four centuries after King Charles V of Spain ordered a survey (in 1524) to determine a possible canal route.

Building the canal was a great human achievement that involved more than just American engineering genius and administrative skill. The problems with sanitation brought about the solution to some monumental public health problems stemming from foul water and causing the rapid spread of malaria. If your vessel passes from the Atlantic or Caribbean side into the Pacific, you will enter the channel at **Limon Bay** at Cristobal breakwater, just before the Gatun locks and lake. One of the most interesting portions of the trip is **Gaillard Cut,** an eight-mile channel through solid rock that got its present name from the engineer in charge. It is often said that Gaillard Cut, more than any other section of the canal, gives the impression of an enormous man-made ditch. Which is just what it is. At the south end of Gaillard Cut are the Miguel and Miraflores locks, the Canal Zone city of **Balboa,** and the Pacific Ocean. Of course, if your ship is traveling from west to east, you will have to read this article backwards, but either way, passage of the Panama Canal is an exciting experience. Throw a Panama Canal party, as I did—wonderful! (And most cruise buffs insist that the canal should be transited twice—daylight and nighttime.)

THE FAR EAST

BALI

Bali is that paradise island off the eastern tip of Java that you've always wanted to visit—and once you have visited, you can't wait to return. It's been called the Morning of the World, but it's not even of this world—it's too peaceful, too perfect. To be on Bali is to be content. Local women walk barebreasted in the street, temple bells tinkle in the breezes, and everyday is a Hindu holiday. Life in Bali means a simple sarong, a motorbike, and some fruit. It hasn't always been so idyllic. Bali is a Hindu island in a Moslem archipelago, the 13,662 lesser islands and six large ones that make up Indonesia. Ruled by Dutch colonists for 300 years and occupied by the Japanese during World War II, Indonesia announced her independence in 1945. Twenty years of flirtation with Communism under Sukarno ended with one of the worst bloodbaths in modern history—some 300,000 Indonesian communists were killed, and whole villages (including some on Bali) were burned to the ground.

The capital of Bali's three million inhabitants is **Denpasar,** a scruffy, touristy town that has no relation to the rest of the island. It does have an art museum and a large market, and large resort hotels are centered on Sanur Beach, a few minutes from town. Despite the influx of Western comforts and customs, the Balinese are adamant about preserving their beautiful island—no building can be higher than a palm tree!

Ubud, about fifteen miles from Denpasar, has long been an artist's colony for both native and foreign craftsmen. Here you can visit the studios of painters who will be delighted that you came to call. The nearby village of **Mas** is famous for the finest woodcarvers in Indonesia. Their sophisticated and stylized figures of polished teak and dark ebony are quite different from the mass productions found in Denpasar. Balinese artisans also make wonderful hand puppets of buffalo parchment for a popular form of entertainment—shadow plays, where mythical princes and princesses come to life on a screen while the storyteller chants dialogue from familiar tales.

Entertainment in Bali comes from the temples, so intertwined are religion and theater. Dancing is everywhere and taught by imitation. Although the dances you see are staged for tourists, the impact is not lessened. Two of the most popular are the classical, feminine Legong, the dance of three divine nymphs, and the Ketjak, which features a male chorus of 150, who chant in place of the ever-present gamelon (an Indonesian musical instrument), and who become an army of chattering monkeys at the finale. You will not witness either of these two dances without feeling something of that special spirit that hovers tightly about this island.

Bali is also beautiful mountains and terraced rice fields, and Pura Besakih, the sacred temple on the slopes of **Mt. Agung.** The Balinese consider this mountain the navel of the world. It's an active volcano that frets and fumes and last erupted in 1963 (killing several thousand people who were told the gods would take care of them). But wherever you go on Bali, you must leave your cares behind. As a young Balinese once said to me, as he was planning the next day's adventure, "Now leave your sensitive American stomach behind, and we'll have a good time!"

CHINA

That the world's largest and most intriguing country is a favored destination for cruise vessels and their passengers is not difficult to understand. The first cruise passengers to visit China in recent times were aboard the *France* in 1974, but the ship docked in Hong Kong harbor, and passengers took the train from Kowloon to Canton for a three-day visit. Two years later groups from both the *Rotterdam* and *Queen Elizabeth II* followed the same route.

In February 1977 I was aboard the Greek vessel *Danae* as she made cruise-ship history by sailing up the Pearl River in the dead of night to dock in Whampoa, the port of **Quangzhou** (Canton). The *Danae* was the first Western passenger ship in twenty-seven years to dock at a People's Republic of China port. Today, in addition to frequent cruise calls, there is twice-daily hydrofoil service from Hong Kong to the port of Whampoa, about a forty-five-minute dusty but fascinating ride from Guangzhou.

At first glance Guangzhou with its three-million inhabitants looked like a drab, gray version of neighboring Hong Kong. As my initial reaction faded, a sense of the city's character began to appear. This old city, dating from about the third century B.C., has been a center for foreign commerce for more than 2000 years. The Portuguese, the first foreigners to appear in this area, arrived in 1514. By 1557 they had received permission to settle Macao—a province they still occupy (although the Chinese have managed the politics for some years). By the 1860s foreign traders controlled Guangzhou from the Shamian island on the Pearl River in the heart of the city, and remained there until 1949. You will pass by this rather forlorn-looking island many times in your travels about the city. Its once-bulging warehouses and churches have been converted to factories.

Tours of Guangzhou are rather standard and under the control of Luxingshe (China International Travel Service or C.I.T.S.). Visits will be made to the zoo, the largest in China, to see the giant pandas and the aviary, and to Yuexia

Park with its artificial lakes and Zhenhai Tower. The tower, constructed in 1380, has a fine view of the city and houses a pottery museum which is a good spot to observe the local residents. You will also visit a factory or two, sip tea with the approved spokesperson, and be expected to ask questions about production, birth control, and life in China. Lastly you will be allowed to peer through the iron gate at the Dr. Sun Yat-sen Memorial, dedicated to the "father of the Chinese revolution in 1911." He was born in Guangzhou and founded the Kuomintang or Nationalist party there in 1923.

If you are spending a few days in Guangzhou, you will most likely be accommodated at the Tung-fang (Dongfang) Hotel, which has huge, old-fashioned rooms, broad red-carpeted stairways, and lumpy beds that have mosquito-netting drawn about them each evening. The Tung Fang also has a cavernous dining room where Welcoming Banquets are often held. The Tung Fang is across from a theater, where Chinese opera and acrobatics are performed, and the Canton Trade Fair exhibition halls. If your visit coincides with one of the semiannual fairs (mid-April to mid-May and mid-October to mid-November), by all means request permission of your guides to visit. The fair is China's impressive display to the world of her more than 40,000 products—rooms and rooms of bicycles with the brand name Flying Cloud, sewing machines, sneakers lining four walls, machinery, natural resources, synthetics, and silks. Unfortunately, as a tourist, you cannot buy at the fair. Your shopping must be done either at the local Friendship Store or department store. Guangzhou also has a nice antique shop, but the guides again must be persuaded to let you stop here. While many of the items are what I would call antiquated rather than antique, the shop has some charming mementos.

The most famous restaurant for tourists in Guangzhou is the Ban Xi (also spelled Pan Hsi), a series of old tea houses connected by zigzagging bridges around and across an ornamental lake. Ban Xi is known for its dim sum, or little dumplings, and seems to serve an endless variety. One guide told me gleefully of a Japanese who dined there every day for a week and still did not exhaust the menu. If you think China is a classless society, your thoughts will fly away at the Ban Xi. The pavilions cater to different clientele—workers in one area, party members in another, while foreigners are served in a new, two-story pavilion overlooking a lake. As in all Chinese banquets, a sweet and a fiery wine for toasts, beer, and orange soda are the refreshments, followed by tea. But the desserts here are the best—especially the little cakes filled with chestnut puree and dusted with sesame seeds. A take-out service is just to the side of the entry hall.

Everything that has ever been written about **Shanghai** must be true, for this is one of the world's most fascinating cities. While today's Shanghai is a far cry from the notorious, bad old days of the 1930s and 1940s when sailors were "shanghaied," China's largest city and port has lost none of her excitement. Her eleven million or so inhabitants (who own and ride some two million bicycles) spread themselves out along the Huangpu, or Yellow River, while the mighty Yangtze is just twelve miles upstream. Shanghai is still the center of

China's trade and industry—a role that began with the Treaty of Nanking, which granted the British certain territorial trading rights in 1840. From then until the 1940s, the foreign communities lived in large mansions encircled and protected by their concessions (Shanghai International Settlement). So it is not surprising that the Chinese Communist party was founded in Shanghai in 1921 by, among others, a young student named Mao Tse-tung.

Because Shanghai has seen ships come from all over the world with goods and people, it has always been China's most cosmopolitan city. Shops are full of pretty things. Young girls wear colored ribbons in their hair and flowered blouses beneath their Mao jackets (which are really Sun Yat-sen suits). Couples hold hands in public and smile as you pass by. Your cruise vessel docks within sight of the Bund, that wide boulevard along the water's edge with handsome European-style buildings. From the deck of your ship you will recognize the former Palace Hotel (now called Peace) with its bronze-green roof and pointed tower. Once the most palatial hotel in the East (and owned by a prominent British family), it carries on as a survivor of the past, with old-fashioned rooms and atmosphere. Pay this place a visit if only to look at the sign that says "Ping Pong Room" (next to the Barber Shop). The coffee shop serves real coffee and cakes plus some fantastic-looking and intriguingly named cocktails that I did not try. The eighth-floor dining room has a great view of the harbor. Peek in next door at the banquet rooms, where high-level meetings are held.

Other buildings along the Bund once housed foreign banks and trading companies. The Bank of China now has the large building next to the Peace Hotel, and farther down is the Customs House whose one-hundred-foot clock tower chimes "East is Red" at least every hour. Behind the Bund is the real Shanghai, with narrow, winding alleys lined with low houses—tile roofs curving up at the corners—built around mysterious-looking courtyards. This is the Shanghai to explore, and you're perfectly safe to do so at all hours (although the city locks up early in the evening). Your ship is so convenient to the city that you can walk up to the Bund in a few minutes or call a taxi from the guard house (if you know where you are going and can speak a little Chinese). Walk along the Bund in the early morning when thousands gather to do their Tai-chi exercises. In the evening musical instruments and singing can be heard floating over the river. My favorite memories of Shanghai are of just standing along the Bund embankment, surrounded by curious but friendly Chinese, watching the parade of boats in the harbor.

Your organized tour of Shanghai will include a factory or two, a school or Children's Palace, and the Yu Yuan (Mandarin's Garden) which was built from 1559 to 1577 for Pan Yuntuan, an official of the Ming Dynasty. Although always very crowded, the garden is worth your time and is a preview to the wonderful imperial gardens you will probably visit in Suzhou (Soochow). At the restored Temple of the Jade Buddha, or Yu Fo Si, you will encounter large groups of devout Overseas Chinese (Chinese who do not live in mainland China). Shopping in Shanghai is, to me, the most fun of any city in China not only because of the variety of tempting and inexpensive gifts but also because the clerks are so friendly and helpful. The best place to shop is the Number One Department Store, the largest in the country, just around the corner from the Guoji or International Hotel. This store has floors and floors of jade, jewelry, bamboo flutes, sandalwood fans, and other Oriental treasures. On the ground floor, among household items of the cheapest quality, I found some wonderful, cream-filled vanilla cookies for a few cents a pound. At a store next to the Friendship Hotel a dozen hand-embroidered linen handkerchiefs cost but a few dollars. A friend bought some lovely chopsticks, but we had to draw pictures of rice bowls and the like to get our point across. And, down on the Bund where the British Embassy used to be is the state-managed Friendship Store, with glorious items from expensive rugs to T-shirts with the simple character that says "Shanghai."

Tianjin (Tientsin) is China's third largest city—after Peking and Shanghai—and like them is under direct control of the central government. The city possesses a fine harbor, built during the Japanese occupation of 1937 to 1945, which is often the getaway for cruise passengers to the North China Plain.

An important industrial center, the city is home of the famous Tientsin carpet, said to have originated in 200 B.C. Some eight major factories produce about 150,000 square yards of carpet each per year, and no foreign visitor departs this city without a tour of the Number One Carpet factory, employing more than 1400 people. This is the most interesting factory tour in China, for it allows you to follow the production of a carpet from beginning to end and justifies the price all the more. (If you plan to buy a carpet here, advise your guide. You may be able to purchase one at the factory, or you may be directed to a Friendship Store.) Tianjin also has a fine zoo, an antique shop (highly overpriced), and a comfortable and clean Friendship Hotel. The 74 mile trip to Peking takes about one and one-half hours on the train. The trip is a great adventure, especially if you are required to set your alarm for 4 a.m. and 5 a.m., as I was, to make the connection.

The center of **Beijing** (Peking) is Tien An Men Square, an area that covers almost one hundred acres and accommodates as many as a million people for the May Day festivities. Chances are your first view of Beijing will be from this square, which has the Monument to the People's Heroes in the center. Standing in this vast area, one senses the continuity of China through all her warring periods and revolution. Bounding the northern end of the square is Tien An Men, or the Gate of Heavenly Peace, whose five passages lead across five marble bridges to five gateways and the Imperial or Old Forbidden City. On the western side is the Great Hall of the People, where the National People's Congress meets and visiting dignitaries are honored in the 5000-seat banqueting hall. On the east end is a large building housing the Museum of the Revolution (in the left wing) and the Museum of Chinese Hichay (in the right wing). But the most impressive structure is the Chairman Mao Tse-tung Memorial Hall, completed in November 1977 after only ten months' construction time. Unfortunately, you will probably find the hall closed for "renovation."

All touring in Beijing is, of course, under the direction of the C.I.T.S., which has taken their interests into consideration when planning your activities. Fortunately, excursions are confined to exciting historical monuments and you are free from the obligations of visiting hospitals, schools, factories and the like. One half-day is set aside for touring the Temple of Heaven (Tien Tan) and the Forbidden City, where you can easily get lost for several hours. Another half-day will be spent driving to the Summer Palace, about forty-five minutes from the center of Beijing. Since the twelfth century the Imperial Court transported itself to this area during the summer to avoid the city heat, and the Summer Palace (Yiheyuan) grew into a sumptuous playground for the aristocracy. The 650-acre area has an enormous man-made lake for boating, pavilions with such names as Orderly Clouds, Joy and Longevity, Virtue and Harmony, and the famous Marble Boat that the Empress Dowager Tzu Hsi commissioned in 1890 with funds intended to expand the Chinese navy.

The highlight of any visit to China is a climb on the **Great Wall**, Wan Li Chang Chen, or the Long Wall of Ten Thousand Li (about 3000 miles). A comfortable tourist train whisks you from Beijing Station to Badaling, just over two hours away, with tea going and lunch returning. The scenery is spectacular as the train winds up into the Yian Mountain chain, and soon you see sections of the ancient wall undulating along the crests, between flowering trees in the foreground and snowcapped peaks in the distance. Just before Badaling the train stops (for quick leg stretchers and photographs) and then backs into the station. After a brisk twenty-minute walk from the station to the reconstructed section of the wall, the stiff climb begins, in the company of thousands of others from all over China and the world. The right-hand section (as you face the wall) is the less steep and therefore more popular with first-time visitors. And when you arrive at the top tower you'll know it, for a sign tells you (in Russian, Chinese, and English) not to go any farther. Indeed, the unreconstructed part of the wall is exceedingly dangerous. (The wall is slippery, so flat shoes with a tread are recommended. It can also be very windy, so hats, scarves, and windbreakers should be worn and taken off as you warm up. Layers of clothing are very important here.)

Some tours combine the **Ming Tombs** with the Great Wall. This makes for a long and arduous day, but it's better than to miss something. The Ming Tombs are in the foothills of Beijing, where the wind and water (Feng Shui) were considered favorable to enjoying the hereafter. This beautiful and peaceful area adjoins a huge reservoir which Chairman Mao is said to have helped build (as he also supervised the restoration of the Forbidden City, Summer Palace, and parts of the Great Wall). Entrance to the tombs is through the Avenue of the Animals, perhaps the most photographed stone carvings in China. The tomb generally visited is Ting Ling, or Tomb of Emperor Wan Li (1573–1620). The tomb itself is rather a disappointment, but the setting—especially the large square red tower and landscaping—is impressive. And do not miss the two small museums flanking the tower, which portrays a chronology of the excavations of the tomb as well as some of the treasures found—delicately beaten gold objects, silk brocades, and money.

No one leaves Beijing without a visit to the three-tiered Friendship Store and a sumptuous meal of the renowned Peking Duck. The Friendship Store on Chang An Jie caters to foreigners and thus has Mao suits, silk pajamas, dresses, and T-shirts in all sizes. It also sells such items as Happy Brain Pills, Flying Pigeon bicycles, hand-painted silk fans (for twenty-five cents apiece), rugs, furniture, food, and liquor. Not far from the Beijing Hotel, on Wangfujing, is a good handcrafts store, a fur shop, and a bookstore with revolutionary posters. Good antique shops line Liu Li Chang, or Glazed Tile Works Street, but again, be sure you differentiate between what is antique and what has been antiqued.

The most popular Peking Duck restaurant (and the one you will most likely visit) is known as the Big Duck by locals—as opposed to another called the "Sick Duck," because it is near a hospital. The feast here seems to go on forever, even before one comes to the platters of crisp, sliced duck served with green onions, brown sauce, sesame buns, or pancakes. For dessert come platters of sizzling apple fritters and bowls of cold water. To consume the delicacy, dip the hot fritter into the cold water and then immediately pop it into your mouth. It's perfectly wonderful!

It is easy to get around Beijing on your own, provided your guide is obliging and you have the time to explore or to visit friends. There are tourist buses at Beijing Station, a subway system, taxis for hire at the large hotels, and your own reliable feet—or you can do as the local inhabitants (both Chinese and foreign) do and hire a bicycle. But it's best to discuss any personal plans with your guide. The Chinese are easily offended by our abrupt Western ways and prefer to lead a harmonious group in which everyone does and sees the same thing.

The appropriate clothing for a China tour is just the opposite of what you would wear on board ship. You may need two wardrobes. As there are no formal evenings, long dresses and jewelry should be left on board. Casual, washable slacks, skirts and sweaters, or jackets and blouses are best for daytime wear, with something a bit nicer for evening. If you're staying in hotels in China, the laundry facilities are good for men but I wouldn't use them for most ladies' wear. As you will be walking a great deal, as well as climbing on and off of buses and trains, daytime shoes should be low-heeled and comfortable— again with something a tiny bit fancier for the evening. And then there's the climate. Beijing is bitter cold in the winter, rainy and cold in the spring, and hot as Hades in the summer. Autumn is pleasant. At any time dress in layers that can be increased or decreased as the temperatures change.

China is a photographer's paradise. If you intend to take many pictures, discuss your trip with a good camera shop. Because of frequent indoor shooting, and many fascinating subjects seen from moving buses and trains, you may have best results with high-speed film (400 ASA) for both prints and slides. If you want to draw a crowd quickly, take along a Polaroid-type camera. It's the best device yet for making fast friends anywhere in the world!

HONG KONG

I envy everyone who has the adventure ahead of sailing into **Hong Kong,** Jewel of the Orient, that 403-square-mile British Crown Colony sitting on the southern coast of China. Hong Kong is a dazzling collage of modern sky-scrapers lining the waterfront and winding their way up the Peak in Victoria; typhoon shelters where untold thousands live out their whole existence on small boats; and nonstop harbor traffic from all over the world. A bustling, dirty, city on the sea, it is home to some five million (no one knows the exact count) people. The majority are Chinese (including more than a million refu-gees), but just about every nationality is represented here.

Hong Kong has been the brightest jewel in the British crown since 1841, but relations with China, which completely surrounds it, have not always been good. During the years of the Bamboo Curtain, China used the colony as a money exchange (the Bank of China, with its two enormous lion statues, is a landmark). When times were tense China could cut off Hong Kong's supply of fresh water and pork. Relations now are friendly, almost loving, and the British governor of Hong Kong was invited to visit Peking a few years ago.

Passenger ships dock at the Ocean Terminal complex in the Tsimshatsui section of Kowloon. The clean, well-kept terminal houses a grand bazaar of shops, restaurants, banks, tourist facilities, the Harbour Village with traditional Chinese products, and whatever else one desires. One need never leave this three-story building that spills onto the Hong Kong Hotel, but there is much, much more outside. Hong Kong is a walking city, so put on your comfortable shoes the minute you arrive. Five minutes on foot from your cruise ship is Nathan Road, once a famous shopping street, flanked by the fabulous Penin-sula Hotel and the Sheraton, the New World Centre, and the elegant Regent Hotel. When your feet are tired, God forbid, have a cup of tea in the lobby of the Peninsula where, as the saying goes, you'll see the world pass by and proba-bly everyone you know if you sit long enough.

Two minutes from the terminal is the Star Ferry Building, easily found by its clock tower, where a cross-harbor ferry to Hong Kong Island leaves every few minutes. (Be sure to buy a first-class or upper-deck ticket so you can enjoy the scenery—it costs only pennies.) Victoria is the capital of Hong Kong Island, and Central District is its busiest section—deluxe hotels, office buildings, and elegant shops. Just behind the Hilton Hotel, another longtime landmark, is the Peak Tram station. The ride up this funny, wooden, cog railway is a must for the lovely residences along the way and the view from the top. Since the 1880s foreigners and wealthy Chinese have made this former mountain wilderness *the* place to live, even though it's often fogged in and thoroughly uncomfortable.

At the fishing port of Aberdeen you can eat fresh fish aboard a floating restaurant, or you can take a ferry to other islands like Lan Tao or Cheung Chau. Another popular tour is to the New Territories, Hong Kong's only rural countryside (held under a 99-year lease from China which expires in 1997). Most of the land out there is rocky, hilly, or swampy, but you can get a view of the mainland from a lookout point called Lok Ma Chau.

Although Hong Kong is often called the world's number one shopper's paradise, dining out is also continually exciting. Numerous continental restaurants exist, of course, but for Chinese cuisine Hong Kong is the closest thing to heaven. In my opinion, the dishes here are more interesting and tastier than in China because the ingredients are more suited to the Western palate. One of the best restaurants, right near Ocean Terminal, is the Jade Garden in Star House, which seats several hundred hungry customers in a series of rooms. It's especially popular on Sunday afternoons, when whole families eat merrily around tables set up for ten or more. In Hong Kong you can pick any Cantonese, Hunan, Szechuan, and other types of Chinese restaurants by just letting your nose lead the way. If your taste buds shout for Continental food, my choices always include Gaddi's at the Peninsula, Plume at the Hong Kong, Regent (nouvelle cuisine and best view in town), Pierrot at the Mandarin (complete with Picasso prints) and Lalique with champagne bar at the Royal Garden. If you're in the mood for a view of the whole colony, go to the top of one of the luxury hotels, all of which have nice cocktail lounges and restaurants (especially the Eagle's Nest at the Hong Kong Hilton).

JAPAN

Your cruise ship will come alongside Osambashi, or South Pier, in **Yokohama,** and if it's a clear day (and you're very lucky) you may be able to see Mt. Fuji in the distance—Japan's highest and most sacred mountain. Fuji-san, as the Japanese call it, is considered one of the two most beautiful conical volcanoes in the world (the other is Mt. Cotopaxi in Ecuador). But the volcano has not been active for more than 200 years, and Mt. Fuji has served as the favorite subject matter of poets and artists throughout Japan.

As a gateway for visitors to Tokyo and northern Honshu, Yokohama is a cosmopolitan port, although only opened to foreign trade since 1859. Twice devastated in this century (the 1923 earthquake and the 1945 air raids), it is now a city of three million inhabitants, including a large foreign community who add character from their homes up on The Bluff, their boutiques on Motomachi, and their bargain shops in Isezaki-cho. This is the shopping center of Yokohama, where the prices are less and the stores even more swinging than on Tokyo's Ginza.

A short cruise call, alas, cannot do justice to this Land of the Rising Sun. You will, though enjoy a small but delectable taste of what it means to say, "We Japanese." This nation flowered as early as the sixth century, when Prince Shotoku made his Constitution of Seventeen Articles and encouraged culture and education. Chronicles of the seventh and eighth centuries are still around, as well as the Manyoshu, a collection of some 4500 poems. Todaiji, a temple in Nara, has a repository holding some 9000 art treasures made by Japanese craftsmen or brought from around the world. Each subsequent century in this floating world that was Old Japan was more fruitful than the last. During the late sixteenth century, or Momoyama Period, Japanese arts flourished as never before, and these are the very arts you see and buy today. The tea ceremony, or *chanoyu*, was raised to the dignity of a national art. Kabuki, Noh, Bunraku, and other theater forms developed. Flower arranging became a national pastime, and paintings on scrolls and screens reached new grandeur. Today Japan is industrialized and computerized, but with all the changes, traditional arts are just as important to everyday life as they became during the Momoyama Period.

Tokyo has been the administrative capital of Japan since 1603, as Edo, but because of natural and man-made disasters the only thing remaining from this time is an iron post in the center of Nihonbashi that has always been used as the starting point for highways. This sprawling, bustling metropolis has a daytime population of about twenty million. (Avoid train and subway stations during the morning and evening rush hours. "Pushers" on the train platforms pack the cars with commuters, and it's not very comfortable, to say the least. And never try to walk against the flow of traffic in a train station or you'll be knocked flat.) Many visitors to Tokyo are a little afraid of the city and find it cold and impersonal. But, aside from the gray older buildings like the Imperial Diet and Library, Tokyo is just a series of small towns linked together. Many areas have not changed much in character since the turn of the century.

One of my favorite monuments in Japan is Meiji Shrine, a place of pilgrimage for the Japanese because it honors Emperor Meiji (and his empress), who opened Japan to the rest of the world in 1869 and encouraged Western ideas and social and land reforms. This Shinto shrine, destroyed in World War II but rebuilt in the 1950s, has beautiful gardens where you can enjoy every type of Japanese tree and flower. In the spring the *sakura* (cherry blossoms) are overwhelming; in summer a large iris garden boasts a hundred different varieties; and autumn brings pots and pots of *kiku* (chrysanthemums) along the paths. Even in winter the Meiji Shrine is not a bad place, for the days are sunny and bright and all the trees have been wrapped in burlap against the cold. You'll see many young couples spending the day at the shrine. You will also find couples and families enjoying Ueno Park, once the estate of a Daimyo and now a huge complex of museums, gardens, temples, a zoo, a pond, and even a pagoda. Nearby is the popular Asakusa Kannon Temple, founded in the seventh century by three fishermen, and now surrounded by one of Tokyo's many entertainment areas—the path to the temple is lined with souvenir shops.

Save some energy and money for the crowded Ginza, the famous silver street, lined with shops (where sweet-faced girls with white gloves bow and welcome you to each floor) and billboards. Stop in at the Sony Building and see what the latest invention is. If you're interested in Kabuki, the Kabukiza is just off the Ginza, and you may wander in for an hour or so and then leave. Everyone does, especially in the afternoon (the best actors play in the evening). Don't miss the Imperial Palace plaza, where swans float in the moats. You cannot visit the Imperial Palace, because the emperor and empress live there, but the grounds are open to the public on January 2 (New Year's) and April 29 (the emperor's birthday and a national holiday). You may enjoy day trips to

Nikkō, a national park in the mountains north of Tokyo that is famous for Toshogu Shrine, and to Hakone in the west, another national park with hot springs, where the views of Mt. Fuji are the best.

Gateway to the western part of Japan and situated on the edge of the beautiful Inland Sea, **Kōbe** has been an important port since Chinese and Korean cultural emissaries arrived in the fourth century. Kōbe is a delight, has a sister-city relationship with Marseilles and Seattle, and is famous for Kōbe beef and the choice Nada sake (Japanese rice wine). Kōbe is the starting point for luxury steamers that ply the Inland Sea, carrying sightseers to such interesting places as Beppu (a famous hot spring), Takamatsu, Shikoku, Shōdo, and Awaji islands. The area is dominated by Mt. Rokko, which you can ascend by cable car for a lovely view of the bay and sea.

But Kōbe is also known for its proximity to Kurashiki, the most delightful town in all of Japan and a treasure trove of folk crafts, plus the historic sites of Nara and Kyoto. **Nara,** capital of Japan from 710 to 784, is noted for beautiful temples and shrines. The most famous is Kofukuji, or Happiness-Producing Temple, which boasted 175 buildings at the height of its prosperity. All that remains is the reconstructed Kondo, or Main Hall, with a wooden image of Sakyamuni, now registered as an Important Cultural Property. The Five-Story Pagoda is another National Treasure (first built in 730 and rebuilt in 1426). My favorite spot is Kasuga Shrine, built in 768 by a member of the Fujiwara family, the most powerful in Japan (because, among other things, they supplied wives for the emperors), it consists of four small shrines—painted in vermilion and built in the Kasuga style of architecture—in a serene wooded setting. Don't leave Nara without feeding the deer that roam under the Japanese cedar, oak, and wisteria. And walk over to nearby Sarusawa Pond where the Five-Story Pagoda is often reflected in the still water. Japan's oldest existing temple is Horyuji, built in 607 just outside Nara. Horyuji, regarded as the fountainhead of Japanese art and culture, is headquarters for the Shotoku sect of Buddhism, named in honor of the progressive Prince Shotoku (574–622). Horyuji consists of several large buildings: Nandaimon (Great South Gate), Kondo (Main Hall), Shoryoin (Sacred Spirit Hall), Yumedono (Hall of Dreams), and a Five-Story Pagoda considered one of the oldest buildings in the world.

Temples and more will entice you to **Kyoto,** where the spirit of old Japan prevails. From Kyoto (cultural capital since 794), the country's arts flowed for more than ten centuries. Although it is Japan's fifth largest city and an important industrial center, Kyoto still exudes so much charm that visitors consider the city the culmination of their entire Japanese experience. Birthplace of most Japanese arts and crafts, it is also the center of the silk industry, and its Gion, or Pleasure Quarter, has worldwide fame. The Gion section, near the Kamo River, where dyed silks were once a common sight drying on the banks, is enchanting by day and night. The quarter is lined with wonderful restaurants offering traditional Japanese dishes as well as many different noodle shops. Gion is also the home of the Geisha, or Art Lady, who has trained since childhood in the subtle and refined ways of entertainment. The Geisha house is a very respectable place to be seen, although the cost of being so well taken care of for a few hours is almost prohibitive (and always was so, even in ancient Japan). If you are lucky enough to attend a Geisha party (Western women are welcome), it's a delightful experience. During the presentation of the meal, the Geisha and her Maiko (young assistant) will attend to your every wish, filling your tiny cup of sake over and over, even helping you manage the *o hashi* (chopsticks). All the while, you may admire her elegant kimono, powdered neck and face, sparkling white *tabi* (socks with one toe), and symbolic, ornamented wig. When the meal is finished, the Geisha and her assistant will sing, play the *koto*, and dance. The real fun begins as they entice guests to join in dances both nice and naughty. There is the Tanko-bushi (coal miner's dance), the Bon dance, the very naughty Ykuyuken (wading dance), and the Japanese baseball dance. It's all orchestrated to break the ice, so to speak, rather like charades or word games at a formal dinner. When the party is over, the Geisha will bow you gracefully from the room and return to her private quarters to await the next assignment or perhaps have a private visit with her patron.

Kyoto was laid out in checkerboard fashion—a plan taken from the Chinese—and originally called Heian-kyo (peaceful, tranquil capital), but the name was appropriately changed to Kyoto (capital city) because there was constant infighting in ancient Japan between church (the many Buddhist sects) and state (the imperial court). None of the temples was destroyed during World War II, because the Allied forces agreed to save the irreplaceable culture from the ravages of war. Kiyomizudora, or waterfall temple, is everyone's favorite and most closely spans the history of the city itself. It was never aligned with any one sect and survived by managing to remain on friendly terms with all. Approached by a long series of shop-lined steps, the temple has a superb view of the city from the top. For centuries the Japanese have made pilgrimages here and even bathe in the falling waters *(brrrh)*. If you are a gardener, Kyoto will enchant you with wonderful gardens, each evoking its own particular mood, within which are endless variations according to the weather, the season, and the number of visitors treading its path. If you linger long enough, a garden will change its mood as a bird flies in to perch, a pine needle falls, or a few rain drops alter the pattern raked in sand and bounce on the lily-strewn pond.

The gardens in Kyoto are often more memorable than the temples they adjoin. The garden at Ryoanji is famous for its rock symbolizing mountains, islands, and fierce animals. The garden of Ginkakuji (silver pavilion temple) epitomizes the spirit of Zen. The garden at Himeji Castle was designed without trees, so the shōgun would not be saddened by the sight of passing seasons. Himeji, in the center of Kyoto, on part of the site of the original Imperial Palace, was built in the sixteenth century (so is not even old by Japanese standards), for the Tokugawa shōguns, and its wooden pavilions have exceptionally beautiful carvings and paintings of the period. What I like best are the squeaky floors, intended to warn the shōgun of anyone approaching.

Kyoto is memorable any time of the year—spring cherry blossoms at the Heian Shrine; willow trees in summer at Uji Bridge; fall chrysanthemums; and snowflakes dusting the swans on Shinsen-en pond.

MALAYSIA

Penang is a relaxing, charming resort city with beautiful beaches and the blend of four cultures—Malay, Indian, Chinese, and Thai—with British overtones in its white, colonial architecture and civic monuments. It's an island-city where life hasn't moved along that fast since the turn of the century. Once you disembark, there is no need to rush about, because the tourist attractions are few. Hire a trishaw (a rickshaw that is peddled) and drive along Campbell and Carnarvon streets, where you can find goods from all over Asia. This is a so-called Free Port, which means the prices should be low, but compare before you buy. Above all, enjoy the local color of street hawkers, beautiful women in saris with their children, and old men falling asleep on the curbside. Indeed, one wonders how anything ever gets done in Penang since half the population seems to be having a snooze.

Fort Cornwallis is a pleasant spot in town and great for photographs, along with another colonial landmark, the Eastern and Oriental Hotel, where you can have a cool drink in the palm-fringed lobby or out on the lawn overlooking the harbor. For a view of the colonial side of Penang, take a drive through the old residential area where lovely, large homes were built long ago for British military and civil servants.

Penang has many Chinese temples (including a Snake Temple), Buddhist statues, and other religious monuments. My favorite outing is the funicular up Penang Hill for the lush view and a cool drink on the lawn of the restaurant/hotel. Penang Hill is one of the mountain retreats founded by the British in Malaysia and frequented during the oppressive summer heat. If you prefer beautiful beaches, tell the taxi driver to take you to "Batu Ferringhi" (Foreigner Mile), about twenty minutes out of town. Here you'll find lovely white sand, swaying palms, and casual, family-style hotels where Americans seek solace from the oil fields of Indonesia.

PHILIPPINES

The Philippines stretch some 1100 miles on a staggering 7107 islands, although ninety-four percent of the land area and population occupy only eleven islands. This nation of great natural resources and as yet unrealized industrial potential has too much disparity between rich and poor, understandable social unrest, and a potboiler political situation. Nonetheless, **Manila** is a romantic and historic capital edging a beautiful bay, an exotic mix of Malay, Spanish, and American Influences. The Philippines were discovered, more or less, by Magellan in 1521, and after colonization by the Spanish in 1571 were named for Philip II. For over three hundred years Spanish rule influenced culture, architecture, and religion. Then, following the Spanish-American War, the islands were ceded to the United States in 1898. After Japanese occupation during World War II, the Republic of the Philippines was proclaimed on July 4, 1946. Americans added a legacy of English to Spanish and Tagalog (the local dialect) and the idea of democracy as a way of life—although Filipinos have their own interpretation of democracy.

The Filipinos have given us two lifetime joys—terrific dance bands and the barong Tagalog, a loose-fitting, long-sleeved shirt that Filipinos wear from morning to night to keep cool in this hot climate. The more elegant variety is perfectly acceptable in place of coat and tie at the best restaurants and night-clubs. Leave your heavies behind on the ship when you dock in Manila, and head for the nearest shop—the styles have been modified to include pants suits and shirtwaist dresses for women, too.

Your first view of Manila will probably be from the Rizal Monument in the Luneta, a large park along the water. Rizal, a national hero and pride of the Malay people, was executed here in 1896, becoming the first Asian martyr to have opposed Western colonization. The Luneta faces Roxas Boulevard, the city's most famous street, and to the south you will see the pride of Madame Marcos—a new complex built on reclaimed land featuring cultural, design, theater, and convention centers. To the north is the renovated Manila Hotel, built at the turn of the century and once home to General MacArthur. (It's possible to book the suite of rooms he occupied, but the price is about $650 a night!)

Unfortunately, most of the fine old Spanish structures in Manila, including the seventeenth-century Manila Cathedral, were destroyed during World War II. However, St. Augustine Church, second oldest in the country, survived and is the most important landmark. Founder of the city, Miguel López de Legazpe, is buried here; the British left some fine woodcarvings during an invasion from 1762–64; the Spanish surrender of the Philippines to the Americans occurred here in 1898. St. Augustine's is located inside the former Walled City, or Intramuros Section, whose broad and impregnable walls were built by the Spanish in the sixteenth century to discourage potential invaders as well as to control a large Chinese community that lived outside.

Excursions from Manila include a hydrofoil ride to Corregidor, the island at the entrance of Manila Bay where Americans and Filipinos fought so hard in 1942, and a trip to Bataan Peninsula. Far more refreshing to the spirit is the drive south one hour to Tagaytay Ridge, where the air is cool at two thousand feet, and you can see a volcano within a volcano at Taal Lake. Farther south by one more hour is the most exciting excursion of all—shooting the rapids in a *banca* (canoe) at Pagsanjan Falls. The scenery is spectacular and the thrill is something to talk about for years!

SINGAPORE

About the only thing exotic about Singapore these days is the name, Singapura, which means "Lion City" in Malay. Billed as "Instant Asia," this city-island-state at the tip of Malaysia is renowned as a multiracial melting pot.

Living and working together in more or less perfect harmony are more than two million citizens who enjoy the highest standard of living in Southeast Asia. The majority are Chinese, of course, but they are joined by Malays, Indians, Pakistanis, Ceylonese, Indonesians, Europeans, and Eurasians.

Two men whose names are synonymous with Singapore are Stamford Raffles, an Englishman who founded a trading post of the East India Company here in 1819 because he predicted the island would become a crossroads of the East, and Prime Minister Lee Kuan Yew, a Cambridge-educated Chinese, who decided in the 1950s that his people should not be the "pawn and plaything of foreign powers" and set about putting the British back in their place. Some call his sixteen-year rule ruthless (he threatened to close down all British clubs that did not accept Chinese members), but his vision and vigor have made modern Singapore successful. What you see is what it is: clean streets (there is a stiff fine for discarding cigarettes); an uncorrupted police force; plenty of parks and housing projects; nonstop automobiles driven by affluent, hard-working people; and high rises everywhere. You also see the old (buildings) coming down with a fury, and the new going up. Singapore is in a constant leap forward, but some of us yearn for a little familiarity—for a little dirt and intrigue to remain as well!

Sailing into Singapore harbor is impressive. The busiest port in Southeast Asia and the third largest in the world, it harbors some three hundred vessels unloading raw materials or loading up with rubber, tin, and "Made in Singapore" products. The city itself is small and easy to explore on your own from your landing at Clifford Pier on Colliers Quay. While the downtown business district is becoming a monument to modern architecture like the multi-million dollar projects designed by I. M. Pei and John Portman for Raffles City and Marina Centre, there are still some pure Asian sights.

My first and most important stop is always Raffles Hotel. I sit under one of the whirling overhead fans in this charming bastion of colonialism, sip a cool drink, and dream of the romantic Far East of long ago. Somerset Maugham, Noel Coward, and Rudyard Kipling all wrote about Raffles, which began life as a tiffin house (an Anglo-Indian expression for lunch place) in the 1800s and was the birthplace of the Singapore (Gin) Sling in the 1920s. The hotel's colorful history parallels that of Singapore itself, and there is an encouraging sense of continuity under these fans—it's a world apart from the wrecker's balls outside.

I also love the Botanical Gardens, one of the best and most beautiful in the world, with exotic plants as well as a well-planned oasis of lily ponds, happy swans, orchard pavilions, and herbarium on eighty lush acres. If you like garish art, stop at the Tiger Balm Gardens, a place I have fortunately resisted on every visit. Save some time for shopping. The prices are on a par with Hong Kong, with, alas, not the variety in merchandise. At night Singapore is a different city. The Satay Club on Elizabeth Walk offers a meal for a song; Chinatown is alive with wonderful smells, and opera groups give street performances. If you like the wee hours, the Bugis Street show comes and goes as the very best in amateur transvestite entertainment, but it's not for everyone.

SOUTH KOREA

The Republic of South Korea's principal port and historical gateway from Japan and the Western world is **Pusan.** This city of two-million-plus inhabitants, once sequestered another million or so refugees as the only major area never to fall into Communist hands during the Korean Conflict. Situated on the southern tip of the peninsula and becoming a popular port of call for cruise vessels on the China circuit between Hong Kong and Kobe, its name *Pusan* derives from the Koryo Dynasty period (936 to 1392). Pusan refers to the mountain peaks that rise 2,500 feet behind the port and make the city around the harbor resemble something of a cauldron, or steaming pot.

The occupying-Japanese opened the port of Pusan to outside trade in 1876 and began construction of a railway northward in 1904. Although always considered a commercial and industrial center, the city is also now enjoyed as the main tourist center in the South. It boasts a splendid beach, a milder climate than most other places in both summer and winter, and some not-so-bad attractions. Optional shore excursions of the city offered by Pearl Cruises feature the Fish Market, the famous United Nations' Cemetery, and a panoramic view from the 387-foot Pusan Observation Tower. In proper weather, Haeundae Beach and neighboring resort hotel are both perfect for a few hours' relaxation.

Less than one hour along the excellent Pusan-Seoul Expressway is one of the country's largest and most interesting temples. This is the 35-structure-plus Tongdo-sa, built in 647 (during the reign of Queen Sondok) by the Priest Chajang. This priest, who studied in China and was considered a *taeguksa* or Great National Priest, founded many temples around the land; but this one is considered to be his most prestigious legacy. The Zen-sect *Tongdo-sa* means "To Save the World by Mastering the Truth," and its uniquely-different main hall *(Taeung-jon)* has been designated as National Treasure No. 144. Up in the hills around the temple are a dozen or so small hermitages where the resident priests retreat for enlightenment.

Another hour along the super-highway is Korea's *pièce de résistance*—the museum without walls that dates from the great Silla Dynasty (57 B.C. to 935 A.D.). This is *Kyongju*, which still boasts royal tombs, temple sites, Buddhist reliefs, and fortress ruins in impressive states of preservation. It is a full day (7½ hours) tour to this cradle of Korea's ancient culture and worth every moment. Here you will see many recent findings in the National Museum, visit several recently excavated Silla tombs, marvel at the beaten gold crowns and girdles, see the oldest observatory in the world, and wonder at other ancient sites. Kyongju offers inspiration to all of us, and the Korean government is paying considerable attention to the area as one of the country's most impressive tourist attractions. A special Korean luncheon at one of the new resort hotels on Bodrum Lake is also included in the tour.

SRI LANKA

Sri Lanka means Resplendent Land. It also means curry and rice, swimming in the Indian Ocean, graceful women in saris, men in dhotis, and serene monks. A favorite memory is of a monk walking down a road, barefoot and alone, oblivious to a sudden summer rain. Sri Lanka is both the ancient and contemporary name of this beautiful island that has been called Ceylon and that lies just thirty-one miles from the southern tip of India, and fifty-five miles (ten degrees) north of the equator.

Sri Lanka's first inhabitants came from northern India in the sixth century B.C. and their descendents were converted to Buddhism in the third century B.C. Indeed, we are told the religion was brought to Sri Lanka by a missionary son of India's famous Emperor Ashoka. The island seems to have been on an important trading route, for the Arabs appeared in the twelfth century. When the Portuguese occupied the coastal areas in the sixteenth century they called the island Celaio (Ceylon), a name that stuck for 450 years. The Dutch took over from 1658 to 1795, when they deferred to the British. In 1802, Ceylon became a British Crown Colony (except for the kingdom of Kandy which did not submit until 1815). She gained her independence from Britain in 1948 and reassumed the name Sri Lanka in 1972.

The best way to approach **Colombo** is by sea, the way the early visitors came, because the capital has a superb harbor (made even better by the British). The city is a hodgepodge of British colonial architecture, Oriental bazaars, and industrial suburbs. Your ship will dock in front of the Fort, the scene of many a battle but today a commercial hub with large banks, shipping offices, jewelry shops, and kiosks. The western fringes of the Fort dissolve into *pettah* (outer fort), which gives the appearance of an oriental bazaar—a rabbit warren of streets and nonstop haggling for just about anything in the world. Among other items, Sri Lanka is renowned for gems—rubies, amethysts, emeralds, aquamarines, garnets, topazes, and moonstones. South of the Fort is another complex, in the Galle Face section of the 72-mile Galle Road.

You'll want to see Victoria Park, now called Vihara Maha Devi, the Colombo Museum with its throne of the last king of Kandy, the performing elephants at Dehiwela Zoo, the President's Palace and Clocktower, and the sun setting over the Indian Ocean from the Mount Lavinia Hotel. Or you can cross the Victoria Bridge for a visit to Kelaniya and the 2000-year-old sacred shrine, where Buddha is said to have bathed in the river. The temple is called Raja Maha Vihare, and is one of the three most sacred places in Sri Lanka.

THAILAND

Bangkok is the most exhilarating and exasperating city in all of Southeast Asia. To say it is a city of contrasts is putting it mildly. It's hot and humid all the time, noisy, dirty from traffic fumes, and dotted with tawdry bars and shops (left over from the Vietnam War, when this was a favorite R & R)—yet the city has the most charming people on earth, beautiful traditions, and exquisite temples and houses. A curious melange of the old and new, with four million inhabitants, Bangkok has been the capital of Thailand only since 1780 when a General Chao P'ya Chakri became King Rama I and moved his court from Thon Buri, across the Chao Phya River. Today's Thailand (the former Kingdom of Siam) is still a monarchy, albeit modified, and the present King Bhumibol Adulyadej (Rama IX) and his lovely Queen Sirikit (he calls her his "smile") live in the Royal Palace in the center of town. They are much loved by their people, although it is no secret that some stern generals behind the throne really control things.

This is the city of klongs (canals) and wat (temples), and between the two you'll be well-occupied. Some say there are more than three hundred wat in Bangkok—which isn't too difficult to believe. These religious structures are a mixture of Indian, Chinese, and Khmer (Cambodian) influences, with the addition of Thai fancy in their colorful, multi-tiered roofs and curved gables. Adding even more local color is the endless stream of barefoot monks who wander about, their rice bowls extended for contribution while their saffron robes sway gently in the warm breezes.

The best place to begin a tour of Bangkok is the Royal Palace complex, a fascinating mixture of European and Thai architectural styles. In the compound is the most famous wat in the country, the Chapel of the Emerald Buddha (Wat Phrakaeo), a 31-inch statue sitting on a high altar. (Men are requested to wear coat and tie and ladies a skirt and appropriate shoes on the Royal Palace tour. And Thais remove their shoes when entering temples.) The Temple of the Reclining Buddha (Wat Po), close to the Royal Palace, houses a 160-foot statue of the Reclining Buddha, symbolizing the passing of Lord Buddha into Nirvana. In the courtyard of this temple is a bodhi tree, said to have sprung from a branch of the very tree under which the Buddha once rested. Another impressive temple is Wat Trimitr, the Temple of the Golden Buddha, with its five-and-one-half-ton seated Buddha of gold. My favorite landmark in Bangkok is Wat Arun, or Temple of the Dawn, on the banks of the Chao Phya River. Near it is the collection of the king's barges, ornately carved and gilded for ceremonial occasions. When you have had enough of wat, it's time for the klongs, where you will see another side of life. On these canals that wind through Bangkok are long, narrow boats loaded with fruits, flowers, vegetables, and handmade wooden products. See them early in the morning (6:30 a.m.) when the floating markets are in full force, and you will also observe the many families living along the banks as they rise for the day. (A guided tour is best for this excursion, but you can also bargain for your own boat.)

Thailand's National Museum is one of the most interesting in Southeast Asia. For a view of more personal treasures, visit Jim Thompson's House (open weekday mornings) or the charming Suan Pakkard Palace, former home of the Queen Mother. Both are good examples of typical Thai houses, which are actually exquisitely carved teak pavilions pieced together. Don't forget to look for the "spirit house" on the grounds. This interesting birdhouse-like object on a pole is kept filled with fresh flowers, food, and incense to appease spirits who first inhabited the land.

If you can make it through the smog and traffic, and the noise of the three-wheeled cycles that act as cheap taxis, see the beautiful Thai dances on the lawn of the Oriental Hotel. Here, in the somewhat cooler breezes of the Chao

Phya River, you will be treated to tales of the Ramayana, the Monkey King, and such, danced by local beauties wearing rich Thai silk costumes. It's worth the effort to get across town, and if you take taxis on your own, be sure you know how much to pay. The Thais haggle over everything, taxis included. You must set a price with the driver, and then disregard what the meter says as it ticks merrily on all the time. And remember, traffic jams are endemic in Bangkok, so leave for appointments early and be patient.

THE MEDITERRANEAN

EGYPT AND THE NILE RIVER

While many cruise vessels call at Port Said, then pack their passengers onto a bus for the three-hour ride through the desert to Cairo, the real gateway to Egypt and the Valley of the Kings is **Alexandria,** the country's second largest city. Founded by Alexander the Great almost by chance—he was enroute elsewhere but liked the fine harbor—Alexandria was an important trading and commercial center for the ancient world. Its lighthouse on the Isle of Pharos shone for centuries and was considered one of the Seven Wonders of the ancient world. Culturally, the city was also prominent, and its library had only one close rival—Ephesus. Politically, Alexandria was the base for Egypt's rulers—Ptolemy I and his son Ptolemy II, as well as Cleopatra, who lived here with her lovers Julius Caesar and later Mark Antony.

Poets have always loved Alexandria for its romance and color; Lawrence Durrell even dedicated his *Alexandria Quartet* to the place. However, in the present metropolis you will have to look around corners and through shabby exteriors to imagine the glories of yesteryear. Pay a visit to the Greco-Roman Museum with its busts of Alexander and various Roman emperors to realize that this was, indeed, a classical town; the Roman amphitheater; the catacombs used when Christianity tried to take hold; and the many mosques established after the Muslims conquered the land in the seventh century. A pillar once attributed to Pompey is now thought to be a victory column dedicated to the Roman Emperor Diocletian by his troops.

Outside of Alexandria—only ten miles—is a former residence of the royal family known as Montaza Palace. Here King Faruk abdicated on July 26, 1952 (a calendar with the date still hangs on the wall). The palace is as gaudy and overdecorated as Faruk and his family left it, but the lovely grounds have landscaped gardens and a small beach where you can swim. About an hour from Alexandria is the town of Rashid, where the Rosetta stone was discovered in 1799, which is worth a visit for those with time to spare.

But all roads lead to **Cairo,** the capital of Egypt and a city of mansions and squalor, peace initiatives (Americans are now treated well) and hostile looks (Muslims are sometimes insulted by the way we dress, so leave your skin back on the ship, please), and baksheesh (tips) everytime you turn around! If your time is limited, and it is for most cruise passengers, the best deal in town is the

Egyptian Museum, one of those rare museums that even those who usually don't like museums seem to agree is beyond description. But there are other museums of interest: the Islamic; the Coptic; the Center for Art and Life; the Papyrus Institute; and the Cotton Museum. Within Cairo you can also tour the early Christian churches in the Old City, an abundance of mosques, and a shop for every kind of souvenir possible—even have a caftan made while you wait. If you are adventurous, try an outrageously priced camel ride or an economical and thoroughly enjoyable sail on the Nile in the age-old, much-photographed, high-masted boat called a felucca.

But, no doubt, the Sphinx and pyramids are what you came to see, and your tour will take you to nearby Giza, actually considered a suburb of Cairo. Of the nine pyramids in the Giza complex, the Great Pyramid of Cheops is the most impressive and well known, and you may wish to visit only this one. Long ranked among the wonders of the ancient world, it was constructed about 2500 B.C. to ensure the Pharaoh Cheops of a trouble-free afterlife. (The Egyptians prepared themselves richly for what happened with death, while the Greeks were in love with being alive.) The pyramid took twenty years to build, and several thousand slaves moved more than two million blocks of stone. (Herodotus, the Greek historian, claimed that it took 100,000 men per year to do the job, but later historians say this is a slight exaggeration!) If this is the only pyramid that you desire to tour, you will find it the best example of what these luxurious resting places were all about. You may go inside all three of the Great Pyramids, but if you are tempted to climb them be forewarned that the stones have weathered over thousands of years and are very crumbly (and I certainly wouldn't want to lose you at this point). Alas, more than one tourist has fallen to his demise. Six smaller pyramids and many lesser tombs are in this area, as well as the Solar Boat (which may not be open to the public) used to ferry the body of the pharaoh from his palace in Memphis to this final resting place. Below the valley of the pyramids sits the majestic Sphinx, with the head of the Pharaoh Chephren (owner of the second pyramid) and the body of a lion. It measures some 240 feet long by 66 feet high but seems much smaller than you had imagined. Between its paws is an inscription that tells of a young prince who rested in its shadow and was promised the double crown of Egypt if he would remove the sand from its paws. Of course, he did, and that prince became the Pharaoh Tuthmose IV (whose reign lasted from about 1425 to 1417 B.C.), who had the inscription carved.

One-day tours will not include **Memphis** and Saqqara. If you have the time, though, go to this ancient city and its necropolis on the west bank of the Nile not more than a dozen miles south of Cairo. Memphis, capital of ancient Egypt during the Old Kingdom and part of the Middle Kingdom periods (from approximately 2700 to 1800 B.C.), was reputed to have matched the splendor of Babylon. Not much is left to see of all this past glory but a few statues and a lovely site covered by palm trees! Out in the desert lies the necropolis of **Saqqara,** the city of the dead. Here you will see a large complex of pyramids and tombs of the important personages of Memphis (try to visit in the early morning, afternoon heat can be intense). The most famous is the step pyramid of Zoser, the first pharaoh in whose name a pyramid was constructed. As he lived a very long time, what began as an elaborate tomb became a continually expanded stepped pyramid.

Sailing slowly on the **Nile River** in a small, air-conditioned ship is one of the highlights of worldwide cruising—for here are all the names of ancient monuments you have read about and always wanted to see. You pass by six thousand years of civilization, magnificent scenery, and ancient, unspoiled villages. A view of life on any river, and especially the Nile, is an unparalleled experience. In the company of your fellow passengers and guides you will understand why Herodotus wrote some 2500 years ago, "Egypt is the gift of the Nile."

The cruise ships vary from small, almost private yachts that carry not more than twenty passengers to larger, more luxurious vessels that hold about eighty passengers and come with swimming pools and on-board boutiques. You have a choice of from three days with stops of just the most popular sites to two full weeks on some six hundred miles of the river. Most of the vessels feature their own hand-picked Egyptologists who ensure that your mind is busy and not too muddled by all the dynasties, kingdoms, and gods and goddesses of ancient Egypt. (If you are especially keen on Egypt, choose one of the longer, upscale Nile cruises operated by Swans Hellenic of London or Lindblad. They are more expensive but worth every penny for the excellent lecturers and tours.)

A few of the more famous monuments that you will visit on your Nile cruise are the temples and tombs at Abydos, among the most ancient in all Egypt; the temple of Hathor (the cow-headed goddess) at Dendera; the temples of Karnak and Luxor commemorating the victories that made Egypt a great power in the ancient world; Thebes and the Valley of the Kings (as well as the Valley of the Queens); Aswan with Elephantine Island; and the great temple of Rameses II at Abu Simbel. In addition, you will see something of rural Egypt and the forty million people who live along the banks of the Nile in the very footsteps of their ancestors. All this adds to the appreciation of how vital this river was to the ancient world, and why the Egyptians believed that even their gods traveled upon these waters. Who knows—perhaps they did.

FRANCE

From Marseille to Menton, the **French Riviera** unfolds a spectacular coastline onto a blue-green sea. The Cote d'Azur, as an obscure nineteenth-century poet named it, has almost eternal sunshine, sparkling waters, and flowered hills. It's not surprising that painters, poets, and other artists continue to find their muse here.

Queen of the Cote d'Azur is **Nice,** a year-round vacation spot and the cultural center of the Riviera. The city was founded in 350 B.C. by Greeks from Marseille, who called it Nike (victory), and has always been a popular watering hole for royalty, especially when they were out of favor at home. Napoleon visited in 1794 (when he lived at 6 Rue Bonaparte, three blocks behind the port) and in 1796 (when, anguished by parting with Josephine, he wrote her a famous letter from here). The British discovered Nice in the eighteenth century as an alternative to their own dreadful winter weather. In 1820 the British colony paid for the magnificent boardwalk spanning the length of the Baie des Anges and appropriately named Promenade des Anglais. For over 160 years this promenade has been the meeting place for summer and winter visitors, with its one side facing the sea and the other lined with impressive facades of elegant hotels and mansions, public buildings, and casinos. Although the beach in this area is not sand but rather large pebbles, this deters no one—it's body to bronze body from May to September! East of the Quai des Etats Unis is the Castle, and behind the port is the Old Town, where narrow, winding streets are lined with medieval houses, wonderful food shops, a few interesting museums, and the famous casinos. Less swinging and more sophisticated is the Cimiez district, up in the hills, which boasts Roman ruins, the former residence of Queen Victoria and her retinue, and the Matisse and Chagall museums. (Both Henri Matisse and Raoul Dufy are buried there.)

If your time in Nice can be extended (I am not suggesting you jump ship, but some cruises do embark and disembark here), you can take exciting excursions in all directions. From Nice to Menton, you have a choice of three different routes, or *corniches*, as the French say. The Corniche Inférieure (lower road) takes you through Villefranche (which also gets its share of cruise calls), Cap Ferrat, Beaulieu, Monaco, and Cape Martin. The Moyenne Corniche (middle road) offers good coastal views and access to the medieval mountain town of Eze. But the high road will thrill you most. The Grand Corniche, built by Napoleon along the remains of the ancient Aurelian Way, is definitely not for the tender-hearted! It's a continual grade that's straight up and then down, but a chance encounter halfway through is worth wearing the lining of the car's brakes. This is the small village of La Turbie (population: 1800), which overlooks Monte Carlo 1400 feet below and offers splendid panoramas of the coastline. In the center of La Turbie sits the famed Alpine Trophy, commissioned by the Roman Senate in 6 B.C. to commemorate Augustus's victory over forty-four previously unconquered tribes (uniting Italy with Gaul and Germania); erected with the aid of slaves and elephants on the spot where the principal roads crossing the Alps met, it's an astounding sight to come upon way up here. Even the poet Dante was so impressed he dedicated some verse to La Turbie. You can read it on the plaque of a nearby house.

All three routes terminate in **Menton,** the easternmost town of the Cote d'Azur. Smack at the Italian border, this resort has the warmest climate of all, influences from both countries, and was another favorite of the British. Artist Jean Cocteau decorated the Salles des Mariages in the Town Hall and left enough memorabilia behind for a museum in his honor, in a seventeenth-century fort near the harbor.

Modern French artists so loved the Riviera that they left memorials. Marc Chagall and his wife donated some 450 works of art to the country he embraced when he left his native Russia, and the French government built a

museum in Nice, not far from the Matisse Museum. Between Nice and Antibes, in the little town of Cagnes-sur-Mer, is Les Collettes, where Pierre Au-
guste Renoir lived from 1908 to 1919, now a museum. Four miles from
Antibes is Diot, where Fernand Léger lived. After he died in 1955, his widow
dedicated a museum with the largest collection of his art works ever assembled.
In Antibes itself is the Picasso Museum, another great collection personally
donated by the artist (actually, it's on a permanent loan). I personally treasure
the Matisse Chapel in Vence. In 1947 the seventy-seven-year old artist created
this small chapel for Dominican nuns and then called it his "masterpiece . . .
the culmination of a whole life dedicated to the search for truth."

Just outside the medieval town of St. Paul de Vence is the Maeght Foundation, a gallery occupying a magnificent site overlooking the Mediterranean to
the south and the snowcapped Alps to the north. In a series of open and
enclosed courts, surrounded by pine trees, rosemary, and lavender, are works
by Braque, Chagall, Miro, Giacometti, Calder, Chillida, Ubac, and many,
many more. Within the town is La Colombe d'Or (the Golden Dove), one of
the region's most celebrated restaurants. Being lucky is sitting on the terrace
and watching the doves turn golden in the sun!

If your cruise ship calls at **Cannes,** you may wish to remain on the western
edge of the Cote d'Azur where the bikinis are said to be the briefest. Cannes
has been fashionable since the mid-nineteenth century, and since then the
Promenade de la Croisette has been sauntered along by everyone who's anyone. The harbor is packed with yachts during the season, and in the elegant
shops and casino are tanned beauties of all sexes. Things are even livelier at
bad-girl **St. Tropez,** the carnival town that Brigitte Bardot made famous a few
decades ago. You will notice varying types of chic-ness along the Riviera, and
St. Tropez is one extreme.

Traveling westward toward the Spanish border, your cruise ship may depart
from **Toulon,** which has a beautiful, natural harbor and is the home of the
French naval forces. During Roman times the port was famous for the purple
dye it produced. It was also the site of Napoleon's first important victory—
against the British—in 1793. During World War II this harbor was under
German occupation. The National Memorial to the Provencal Landing is up
in the peaceful hills, on the Corniche road to Mount Faron. The summit of
this mountain has superb views. Stop also at the square featuring the craft
workshops and studios—potter, weaver, ceramist, wrought-iron smith.

Marseille is the most famous name in this part of France, for it is the country's largest port and oldest city (founded in 600 B.C. by Greeks from Asia
Minor). This city is credited with France's national anthem, although the song
was actually written in Strasbourg as the war song of the Army of the Rhine.
During the French Revolution, however, Marseille's five hundred volunteers
heard the song and sang it along the way to Paris. By the time they arrived in
Paris the tune was well known and identified with them, and so it was renamed
the *Marseillaise* and adopted as the nation's anthem. In Marseille museums
might easily be bypassed, but people-watching is a must—find a sidewalk cafe,

have a coffee or a glass of local wine, and enjoy the variety of people that parade in this busy harbor.

Known as the Island of Beauty, **Corsica** has a rich and varied landscape that features beaches of honey-colored sand, secret coves, rocky crags, and rolling hills of pine, chestnut, oak, olive, and cork trees. Between the sea and the forests are scented herbs and bushes that perfume the air. "I'd know it if only from its fragrance," said Napoleon of the island on which he was born.

The main port of call for cruise ships to Corsica is **Ajaccio,** with a splendid harbor and a French-Italianate atmosphere. This is where old women walk slowly, slightly bent over and always dressed in black, cats dart about the narrow streets, and children play among donkey carts. You can visit the birthplace of Napoleon in town as well as the Napoleon room in the Hotel de Ville, or city hall, where you will find that nothing much has changed since the eighteenth century. Visit the Fesch Museum of Italian Primitives, and you'll understand a little more of this island France has owned for just over two hundred years.

GIBRALTAR

This 2.28-square-mile British Crown Colony, sitting strategically on a peninsula at the mouth of the Mediterranean, was ceded to Great Britain by Spain in the Treaty of Utrecht of 1713. Spain has been attempting to recover it ever since. Relations between the two countries were so tense in the 1960s and 1970s that Spain closed its border with Gibraltar. Today the border has reopened as talks on control continue. There are no natural resources here, other than a 1400-foot-high rock, a natural fortress that holds some of Britain's most sophisticated defense equipment. The commander of the fortress is also the Governor of Gibraltar and appointed by the Crown. About thirty thousand people live in Gib or The Rock, mainly of Genoese, Portuguese, and Maltese descent. The two official languages are Spanish and English. With little to see or do, it's a perfect cruise stop for just a few hours. You can visit St. Michael's Cave, with its huge stalagmite and stalactite formations and a natural amphitheater that was the setting for a beauty pageant the day I visited. You can also go up the Rock by cable car for a spectacular view of the Spanish mainland and the African coastline. Don't forget a brief stop to see the wild Barbary apes—but hang on to the handbag. These apes are famous for being impolite!

GREECE

The Piraeus is the proper name for Greece's first port, and one of the largest in the entire Mediterranean. Gateway to Homer's "wine-dark sea"—the Aegean—as well as to all of Greece and the monuments of the Golden Age of Western Civilization, it dates from the third milennium B.C. and reached its peak in the fifth century B.C. In 493 B.C., Themistocles started the Long Walls which joined the port with Athens, seven miles away. Only sections remain, the rest having been destroyed by the Spartans at the end of the Peloponnesian War in 404 B.C.

Athens—thirty minutes away by taxi, tour bus, or electric train—is home to more than one-third of Greece's nine million people, and it's difficult to do it justice in just one day. If you have extra time to spend abroad, spend it here. Syntagma, or Constitution Square, with the Parliament Building and Tomb of the Unknown Solider, open-air cafes that seat three thousand people for hours on end, banks and travels offices, is the center of city life. The Plaka area teems in daylight with shoppers, and at night revelers at the tavernas enjoy tantalizing food, a fine variety of reasonably priced wines, and entertainment. (Some tavernas have rooftop gardens where you can dine under the spell of the Acropolis.) The Acropolis dominates Athens from "rosy-fingered dawn" to sunset, and if your visit coincides with a full moon you are lucky indeed. Air pollution, however, is speeding the city's disintegration more than all the centuries of war, and you are no longer allowed to wander through the Parthenon or to view the caryatids in their rightful place on the portico of the Erechtheum. (They, poor dears, are now captive in the Acropolis Museum.) Just below the Acropolis is the Agora, or ancient marketplace, where excavations for the past half-century have been under the direction of the University of Cincinnati and the American School of Classical Studies in Athens. This is a wonderful place to roam, and the Theseum, a temple dedicated to Theseus, perches on a grassy knoll overlooking it all.

When you have visited Hadrian's Arch and the Temple of Jupiter, the National Archaeological Museum, and the smaller Benaki and Byzantine museums, taken the tram up Mt. Lycabettus, and wandered the many back streets, it's time to see the rest of Greece. The local CHAT tours (4 Stadiou Street) have comfortable day trips to Sounion (where the Temple of Poseidon overlooks the sea and the cape), to Delphi on Mt. Parnassus, and to the classical sites of Corinth, Mycenae and Argos, Nauplia and Epidaurus. Local buses are plentiful and a more adventurous way to get about. A trip to the Plains of Marathon, for example, is about one hour from Athens each way (unless, of course, you plan to run back). Rental cars are available, but gasoline is *very* expensive and you must know the rules of the road. If you park in an illegal zone, for example, the police teach a lesson by removing your license plates, making driving back impossible (and costly).

If the lure of the sea remains strong, excellent day trips from Palaio Phalero (between Athens and the airport) go to three nearby islands on a choice of cruise ships. (The cost for the day is about $40 including a lunch tray at sea, and the companies will pick you up and deliver you back to your hotel.) First call is usually at the island of Aegina, where a donkey ride through vineyards and pistachio fields will take you up to the Doric-style Temple of Aphaea or, if you prefer, you can have a swim in the bay of Aghia Marina. The next call is Hydra, an artists' colony with quaint, brightly colored houses along the waterfront. It's a wonderful place to stroll, shop, or sip ouzo. In the afternoon your ship visits the charming, unspoiled island of Poros, an important religious center in antiquity and home of the marble that was used, among other things, to build the Temple of Solomon. Poros—a weekend retreat of many Athenians who catch the hydrofoil on Friday evenings from Piraeus—has a beautiful harbor, windmills, fruit orchards, and olive groves. And then it's a two-hour sail back to Palaion Phaleron in the late afternoon, while you have a cool drink in the lounge and learn Greek dancing from the crew.

If you dock at **Itea** on the Gulf of Corinth and take the half-hour bus ride through Parnassus Country to **Delphi,** your route is through a sea of olives— probably the finest groves in all of Greece. First stop on your tour should be the Delphi Museum, with over ten thousand items found in the excavations begun by French archaeologists in 1892. Most impressive of the art works is the bronze charioteer, dating from 478 B.C., a barefoot, lifesize figure. Other works include stone friezes, toga-clad statesmen, a sixth-century B.C. sphinx presented by the island of Naxos to the oracle, and pottery fragments dating from the Mycenean period (1600 to 1100 B.C.).

Renowned throughout the ancient world, the Oracle at Delphi was often consulted for political reasons and thus thought to have changed the course of history many times. The woman who spoke was called a Pythia, and she had to fast three days and then bathe in the nearby Castalian Spring before she spoke. The upper precinct at Delphi includes the remains of the sanctuary, the Sacred Way leading to the Temple of Apollo, a fourth century B.C. theater, and a stadium where seven thousand spectators would watch the Pythian games every four years (it's a tough climb up to this one, but worth it). The lower ruins feature a large gymnasium, the Temple of Athena, and a lovely tholos, or round temple, whose purpose is unknown. The mystery makes it the most interesting structure of the lot.

During the Panhellenic games held in **Olympia** every four years a "truce of God" was proclaimed. Rivalries were abolished so all of Greece could come to Olympia in safety for the spirit of the competitions and social functions that followed. The greatest honor and achievement was to be an Olympic victor and to wear a crown of wild olives. The winner would be feted, paraded, and even immortalized in poetry and sculpture. The status of winners was great; even important generals would defer to a winner. The first Olympic games were probably held in 776 B.C. and were continued every fourth year until 394 A.D., when they were abolished by the Roman Emperor Theodosius II on the grounds they were a pagan ritual. The games were held in mid-summer under a full moon, and male athletes competed in the nude. Women were barred from the premises (and the events), but male spectators were encouraged to come from all over Greece and, indeed, the ancient world. The games were held on a site adjoining the Sanctuary of Zeus in Olympia, in the northwest area of the Peloponnese. This is where the Olympic torch is still lit today (with a magnifying glass and the rays of the sun) and then carried by runners to the location of the games, a tradition that began in 1936. As you walk among the ruins today, you pass through the fifty-century Temple of Zeus, the gymnasium, what is thought to be the oldest hotel in the world (to house specta-tors), the workshop of the sculptor Phidias (whose gold and ivory statue of Zeus here was one of the Seven Wonders of the ancient world), the house of Roman Emperor Nero (who introduced contests like singing into the games), and the fabulous stadium. (Perhaps one day the Olympic games will again be held here, where they belong.) The Olympia Museum displays artifacts found on the site (first excavated by French archaeologists in 1829 and continued by Hitler during World War II) and a scale model of the entire area. The Olympic Games Museum has a collection of memorabilia dating from 1896 when the games were revived in Athens.

Six of the islands in the Ionian chain—Corfu, Paxos, Lefkas, Ithaki, Kefallinia, and Zakinthos—lie off the western coast of Greece. The seventh is near the southeastern Peloponnese—this is Kithira where, according to Greek mythology, Aphrodite made her first appearance.

Of the Ionian group **Corfu** is an international tourist spot and popular cruise stop. It has an interesting history and provides a much-needed respite on sailings between Venice and Piraeus. All other Greek islands envy Corfu for its yearround greenness due to cypress groves and millions of olive trees. Of all the islands, Corfu is also the most un-Greek. Italian was spoken here for more than five hundred years, and the island was under the protection of the Venetian Empire from the fourteenth until the eighteenth century. Venetian occupation was followed by Russian, French, and British, the latter leaving a definite mark. The entire chain was ceded to Greece in 1864, and Corfu soon became a summer residence of the Greek royal family. Sailing into the port of Corfu you see the charming town nestled between two Venetian forts. The newer fortress (mid-sixteenth century) overlooks the port, while the older fort has a view of the Esplanade, or main square. The old Venetian-style town is fun to explore and good for shopping. Once in a while you'll happen upon a British legacy like the Royal Palace, the cricket field, and many of the statues in the Esplanade. Be sure to pay a visit to Saint Spiridon, the church dedicated to the patron saint, who is believed to have saved the island from plague in the seventeenth century and an invasion by the Turks in the eighteenth century. After you have wandered about the town, you may want to head for one of the beautiful beaches to sun on Corfu's famous golden sands. If your ship stays long enough, don't miss the Sound and Light performance (in English) in the Venetian Palace four nights a week.

Two out-of-town shore excursions of Corfu are known for fine views (and not much else). The first stop is Kanoni, a landscaped area named after the French canon that was once placed here. From this precipice you can photograph the so-called islet monasteries—the white convent of Vlachernae and the chapel on Mouse Island. When your eyes have absorbed the beauty of this setting, your tour will go on to the Achilleion, the former palace of Empress Elizabeth of Austria, which is now a casino/hotel near the village of Gastouri. The 200-year-old structure is rather hideous, due to the questionable taste of the empress as well as of Kaiser Wilhelm II (who owned it subsequently), but the proprietors and their guests certainly had lovely views from the terrace.

Focus of the Cycladic Islands is the deserted island of **Delos,** whose only inhabitants these days are some caretakers of its ruins and a few archaeologists. According to Greek legend, Delos arose from the sea just in time for Leto, Zeus's paramour, to give birth to Artemis and her twin brother, the sun god Apollo. This has always been a sacred island, and when the cult of Apollo was prominently practiced it became wealthy as offerings to the Temple of Apollo filled its coffers. It was the banking center for the Eastern Mediterranean, with money loaned out to other islands at an outrageous rate, and its inhabitants also did a brisk business in the slave trade. Then, in 88 B.C., Delos was caught in a dispute between Athens and Rome. To make his point for the Athenian side Mithridates, King of Pontus, completely devastated the island, carrying off all the valuables. Delos never recovered, and its commercial role was usurped by Rhodes.

Walking tours of ancient monuments in Delos take about two hours and give you ample evidence of the island's glorious past. The most impressive memorial is the Terrace of the Lions, where five archaic beasts (seventh century B.C.) still hold vigil, crouching on their hind legs. You will also see the remains of the Temple of Apollo, the Sacred Lake (now dry), and ruins of elegant villas in the Roman quarter with their delicate mosaic floors. Especially beautiful houses are the Dolphin, the Trident, and the Masks. If you have time, climb the steps up Mount Kynthos for a splendid view of the other Cyclades—Syros, Naxos, Paros, Tenos, and Mykonos.

If I had a genie I would wish to be transported from time to time to the relaxing nearby island of **Mykonos**. Mykonos has some much-photographed windmills, a church (they say) for every day of the year, and a whitewashed maze of narrow and charming back streets that were designed to confuse raiding pirates. Refresh your soul by sitting in a sidewalk cafe by the seawalls and letting the sparkling sun take over. Because of the pleasant atmosphere and cordial natives, Mykonos has drawn artisans from all over the world who paint, make sandals, weave, sculpt, design jewelry, knit, crochet, and who can even make you a dress in two hours. One wonders why the sign on the pier—"Help Keep Our Island Clean"—is necessary. I like best the sign in front of the statue in the town square, "Please do not park backpacks here." While days may be spent on the beach, evenings are always spent in town, watching people parade and then finding a superb little taverna for a leisurely meal (my favorite is Antonini's on the square).

Santorini, sometimes called **Thíra**, is the southernmost island in the Cyclades, and its eerie place in history is due to theories it may be the lost island of Atlantis. Recent excavations at Akrotiri reveal that a cosmic event in 1520 B.C. destroyed a flourishing civilization. As your cruise ship sails into the Bay of Santorini, note that this island, known as Strongyle or "the round one" in ancient times, is in five sections, of which Thíra is the largest. Soaring 900 feet above the sea and plunging 1200 feet into the submerged core of its volcanic crater—which seems fathomless—the island has a feeling of bareness, with rugged black lava cliffs topped by whitewashed houses and chapels that have a frenzied, surreal look about them.

From your cruise ship to shore is undoubtedly by tender, and from the shore up to the tiny, terraced town of Thíra you can either walk the winding and slippery eight hundred steps or pay a ripoff fee to ride a donkey. (While the ride is not one of my favorite travel memories, it is an experience you might want to try once! You may even buy a photograph of yourself to prove that you did it.) Once upstairs in the little town, you can shop around, have a coffee, or explore part of the island. If you have at least two hours before the tender leaves again, hire a taxi to visit the excavated site of Akrotiri, which is believed to have been contemporary with the Minoan civilization and then destroyed by the same holocaust of volcanic eruptions and tidal waves in 1300 B.C. If the site is closed, as it tends to be now on Sundays, you can take a twenty-minute taxi ride to the little town of Oca at the other end of the island, where it's fun to walk among the whitewashed houses built into the cliffs and look out at the sea below. (Your cruise ship will look very, very far away from up here.) Our taxi driver on this excursion stopped along the way to show us a charming little chapel dedicated to St. George. If you happen to miss Akrotiri, findings from the excavations are in a special series of exhibit rooms on the second floor of the National Archaeological Museum in Athens and include wall paintings, pottery, and a small person's bed.

The most important city in Macedonia was named after the stepsister of Alexander the Great, Thessaloniki. Founded in 315 B.C. by one of Alexander's generals, **Thessaloniki** (also called **Salonika**) has had a stormy history, primarily due to its situation at the crossroads of the main routes between East and West, Asia and Europe. As a proud and cultured city, it is layered with the legacy of the Romans, Saracens, Normans, Venetians, Turks, Germans, Balkans, and more Turks, peoples who passed through and often conquered. Despite the frequent destructive fires and wars the city endured, you'll find early Greek, or Macedonian, treasures, Roman monuments, Venetian ramparts, Byzantine churches, and occasional vestiges of the Moslem culture imposed by the Ottoman Empire (although when the Greeks recaptured the city in 1912, they destroyed all the mosques and minarets within reach). Ironically, Thessaloniki, which boasts the tomb of Philip II of Macedon, father of Alexander the Great, is also the birthplace of Kemal Ataturk, who became the father of modern Turkey. A landmark of the city is the fifteenth-century White Tower, constructed by the Venetians at the boundary of the no-longer-standing city walls. Nearby is the Archaeological Museum, with findings from Hellenistic tombs and a rich collection of gold from Macedonia and neighboring Thrace. A road from the White Tower leads to the university named after the philosopher Aristotle, who came from Macedonia.

Either before or after your cruise from Thessaloniki, take a tour around the old town to see the prominent Rotunda, an ancient Roman structure intended as a mausoleum but turned into a Christian church in the fifth century (and dedicated to St. George by Theodosius the Great, who commissioned some fine mosaics). In the sixteenth century the Turks made it into a mosque and added a minaret (which is still there). A few minutes walk from the Rotunda is the house where Kemal Ataturk was born in 1881, preserved by the Turkish government and open to the public.

The Arch of Galerius is another Roman monument, built by the Emperor Galerius in 303 A.D. to commemorate his victory over the Persians. It's surrounded by wonderful old houses and tiny Byzantine churches, and straight up behind are the ancient city walls, with a fourth-century atmosphere and a fine view of the harbor. Cruise passengers are also offered an excursion to Pella— the capital of Macedonia from the fifth century B.C. to 168 B.C. and the birthplace of Alexander in 356 B.C.—with fascinating ruins here as well as beautifully preserved pebble mosaics, streets, and sewer systems.

A one-week cruise itinerary from Thessaloniki, in cooperation with the Greek government (which likes to see the tourist dollar spread around), calls at the islands of Skopelos, Skiathos, Lesbos, Lemnos, and Thasos as well as the port of Kavalla. No longer on most cruise schedules is the all-male enclave of Mount Athos, where women have not been allowed for over nine hundred years (cruise ships with women aboard may not even sail within 500 yards of the main port). Mount Athos, a holy mountain harboring ancient monasteries of the Eastern church, once welcomed male visitors for a meal and overnight. Today, however, men must apply at the Ministry of Foreign Affairs and prove they have serious religious or scientific interests which warrant a visit to the community.

Kavalla, at the Thracian border in eastern Macedonia, is the port for shore excursions to Philippi, another ancient city at the crossroads of history. On the plains of Philippi important battles took place and legendary figures met their fates. St. Paul preached here and sowed the seeds of Christianity before he was detained in prison and finally forced to flee. Brutus is said to have seen Caesar's ghost on the Philippian plains, just before he and Cassius were defeated by Octavian and Mark Antony in the famous 42 B.C. battle. Ruins here include a large agora, or marketplace, a Roman forum, some baths, the prison in which St. Paul languished for a spell, and some early churches.

Skiathos and Skopelos are members of the Sporades, or scattered islands. Beautiful **Skiathos** is known for wild strawberry bushes and olive trees as well as for lovely bays and beaches that invite lounging in the sun. Shore excursions here are relaxing—a short tour of the village and then a quick transfer to one of the beaches. Less than two hours by sea is **Skopelos** ("rock"), green as well as rocky, where charming, whitewashed houses have colorful shutters and doors. The island is noted for its plentiful fruit, especially the plums that you can taste fresh or in various stages of being cured for export.

Lesbos, the third largest island in the Aegean (after Crete and Rhodes), is close to Asia Minor and convenient for excursions by small boat to Dikili, the Turkish port near the archaeological site of Pergamum. Lesbos has played an important role in Greek literature since the eighth-century-B.C. school of poetry was founded here. Native sons and daughters have included Aesop, the great storyteller, and Sappho, who wrote erotic lyrics to other women and was said to have practiced what she preached. Her poems were allegedly burned by the church in the eleventh century. Nonetheless, she left a legacy to the world in the word "lesbian." Legendary figures associated with this island include the lovers Daphnis and Chloe.

Lesbos has a large population (about 150,000), many olive trees (approximately eleven million), and multitudes of sheep and goats. From the capital city of Mytilini you have wonderful views of Asia Minor plus relics of the long Turkish occupation. The countryside is especially beautiful, and shore tours visit the fishing village of Petra up the coast, the pottery town of Agiasos, and the quaint harbor of Molivos (swimming is available nearby). Because Lesbos is so close to Turkey, you will see many Greek soldiers on guard around the island, but don't be put off—it's a way of life that is unfortunately thousands of years old.

The last two islands visited on this special itinerary from Thessaloniki are Lemnos (or Limnos) and Thasos in the Thracian Sea. **Lemnos** is the larger and has the better beaches (your shore excursion will probably take you to Santa Barbara). Rich in legend, this island was home of Hephaestos, blacksmith to the gods. Greek mythology says the Argonauts stayed two years on Lemnos (fathering a generation of children) during their search for the Golden Fleece. A Greek warrior, Philoctetes, was marooned here during the Trojan War. The capital of Lemnos is Mirina (Kastron), a small town dominated by its Genoese castle built in the Middle Ages. The town has a cool, dry climate as well as an inspiring view of Mount Athos—especially at sunset. **Thasos,** in contrast, is hot and humid. Once a prosperous island-state, it was known in the ancient world for gold, marble, and wine exports. The main town of Limin (also called Thasos) is built around the ruins of an agora, a theater, and city walls. The local museum is interesting, but the best finds, alas, were reportedly carted off to the Louvre.

As a member of the baker's dozen Dodecanese islands in the Eastern Aegean, **Koš** lies close to Asia Minor and is best known as the birthplace of Hippocrates, the father of medicine. The main port, founded in the fourth century B.C., has relics of former glories of the Hellenistic, Roman, and Byzantine periods. A twelfth-century Venetian castle lies in ruins to one side of the harbor, its walls lined with the shields of the Knights of St. John, who stopped here in the fourteenth century on their way home from the Crusades. (Of all the sites on Koš, the castle is the least interesting—especially if your cruise is calling at Rhodes). Just a few minutes' walk from the harbor you will find the ancient Greek agora as well as the temples of Apollo and Venus. For a splendid view from the top, climb up the tier of seats in the well-preserved theater. The museum on Liberty Square is also worth a visit. It has a 400 B.C. statue of Hippocrates, which was found under the theater, as well as a splendid Roman mosaic floor.

Two miles out of town on a beautiful hillside with pine forests, natural springs, and a view of the sea and Asia Minor, the Greeks built the Aesclepion of Hippocrates. One's imagination can run wild up here. Even historians admit they do not know what went on here in ancient times. You will find the

Temple of Asclepios, the god of medicine and healing, several curative rooms, plus a swimming pool and a stadium for physical therapy. Some believe that the Greeks performed surgery here, but the Romans built their baths on top of the "operating" rooms. In town natives will show you a plane tree that Hippocrates is said to have planted and lectured under, but botanists today doubt this.

Northernmost island of the Dodecanese, **Patmos** is considered to be the loveliest of all, with beautiful bays and capes and spectacular views at every turn. Although barren like most of Greece (especially in summer), Patmos has on its southern side that sparkling-white architecture found also in the Cyclades islands. Patmos is a place of pilgrimage, for here St. John the Divine received the revelations and wrote the book of Apocalypse (which he actually dictated to a disciple), in a cave that is now enshrined by the Church of the Apocalypse. Nearby, the pretty village of Hora has an eleventh-century monastery founded by St. Christodoulos, a former hermit, as a School of Virtue and Holy Purpose. (For those whose purpose was considered unholy, burning oil was ready for pouring atop the gate. A tour of this monastry is a must, although the lovely pebble beaches on the island also beckon. In the monastery compound is a treasury of costly icons and liturgical costumes and a library lined with glass cases containing over nine hundred handwritten books as well as some ninth-century illuminated manuscripts. You can also tour where the two dozen monks live, eat, and study. On the return to the port of Skala, stop in at the seventeenth-century house (if you can find it), a rich trove of folk art, furniture, and greenery.

Just over a mile from the shores of Turkey, **Samos** is another "Greece in Asia" island, known for its wine, its Temple of Hera (one of the wonders of the ancient world), and engineering marvels that still exist. Samos is characterized by mountainous terrain on which olives, dates, palms, poplars, and vineyards flourish. In the sixth century B.C. Samos was Queen of the Seas, due to its tyrant leader Polycrates, who used slaves from Lesbos to build the Temple of Hera, a harbor mole, and the mile-long tunnel that brought fresh water through the hills. Parts of the harbor mole and the tunnel are still around, but all that remains of the temple is a single, standing column a few miles west of Pythagorion (birthplace of the man who discovered that proportion forms the structural principle of the universe). Other sights on this lovely isle are two monasteries, the seaside village of Kokari, and many little mountain towns in sweet-smelling pine forests. If you are in the mood to taste a little of the local industry, visit the winery in Samos for a sampling of the new, young nectar of the gods. Some visitors also use Samos as the jumping-off point for a tour of the classical site of Ephesus (near Kusadasi in Turkey), while others head for the magnificent, uncrowded beaches.

When I asked Captain Michael Benas, the master of Sun Line's flagship, the *Stella Solaris*, which island in the Aegean was his favorite, he beamed and gave me a predictable answer, "Why, Rhodes, of course!" As we were sailing towards Rhodes at that very moment, I couldn't have been more delighted, for this island has long captured my fancy as one of the most enjoyable places in the entire world. **Rhodes** is the largest of the Dodecanese. Greek mythology tells us that the island rose from the sea and that Apollo took it as his domain, although he had to uproot some lesser gods who had already established squatters' rights. The island flourished as early as the eleventh century B.C. and reached its commercial and cultural prime in the fifth century B.C. Two centuries later the Colossus of Rhodes was known as one of the Seven Wonders of the Ancient World.

This 100-foot bronze statue representing the sun god straddled the harbor of the ancient port of Rhodes. It was erected in 290 B.C. by a local sculptor to commemorate the steadfastness of the Rhodians and as a warning against invasion. It seems that after an Alexandrian military man withdrew his troops in frustration when his one-year siege failed to intimidate the Rhodians, they simply melted down his machinery and made their colossus. Unfortunately the Colossus toppled over in an earthquake about fifty years later, and its site is now marked by two pillars topped with bronze deer—the symbol of present-day Rhodes.

Rhodes, about six hundred square miles in area, has three separate layers of history to explore—the ancient, the medieval, and the modern. The most splendid of the three ancient cities of Rhodes is Lindos, about a 45-minute drive from port to the western end of the island. Lindians worshiped the goddess Athena, who is said to have rained gold down upon their city. Her fourth-century-B.C. temple on the acropolis of Lindos is one of the oldest sites in all of Greece. The acropolis, a steep climb up from the small town below, has wonderful views of the Bay of St. John and the harbor where St. Paul is reported to have landed in 51 A.D.

Your cruise ship will dock within sight of the old town of Rhodes, which lies within the reconstructed medieval walls built by the Knights of St. John in the thirteenth century. (Some of the larger passenger vessels must anchor out and tender passengers in, however.) In the northern section of the old town are the Palace of the Grand Master and the former inns of the crusaders that still line the Street of Knights. A fifteenth-century Hospital of the Knights houses the Rhodes Archaeological Museum, which has fine exhibits, including the lovely Aphrodite Thalassia, found in the waters nearby and dating from the first century B.C. The medieval ramparts and buildings were all reconstructed during the Italian occupation, which lasted from 1912 to 1943 (all the good roads were built then too), and Rhodian guides will tell you that Mussolini had his eye on the 300-room palace as a summer residence (it's an impressive place, but I wouldn't want to live there). But Il Duce never got to fulfill this dream. An excellent Sound and Light show is aimed at the palace during the summer, and many ships stay in port for it. The English version begins about 9 p.m. And, if you prefer more sightseeing to shopping (the main area is Sokrates Street, the former Turkish bazaar), take a taxi to the mile-long Valley of the Butterflies—about twelve miles from the port of Rhodes along the western coastal road—to commune with millions of red and black butterflies that flutter through the trees.

Rhodes has thousands of foreign visitors (it's dubbed Scandinavian Haven) who fly in, come by overnight car ferries from Piraeus, or sail into the harbor on private yachts and sailboats from as far away as Australia. I love to walk along the breakwater, look at the boats, listen to the many languages spoken, and then sit in a waterfront cafe to watch the spectacle. This beats even the butterflies!

Crete is Greece's most southern island in the Aegean Sea and its largest (second in size only to Cyprus in the entire Mediterranean area). It is the legendary birthplace of Zeus, whose mother (Rhea) hid him in a cave lest his father (Cronos) swallow the baby whole, as he had all preceding brothers and sisters. (Cronos did not want any competition.) Crete is also the birthplace of Domenico Theotokopoulos (El Greco) in 1545 and Nikos Kazantzakis in 1883 (Whose *Zorba the Greek* is set here).

Heraklion (or Iraklion) is the most popular cruise port on the island, because it's closest to the Palace of Knossos and the fine Archaeological Museum. Although Heraklion has about seventy thousand inhabitants, only a few Venetian relics (a castle, a lion, a fountain, and a loggia) are of interest here. But it is the gateway to a view of the magnificent Minoan civilization, which flourished here from 2000 to 1450 B.C., and the wonderful tales of King Minos, the bull, Daedalus, the Minotaur, Theseus, and Ariadne. No visit to the island is complete without a tour of Knossos. Excavations were undertaken by Sir Arthur Evans in 1900 to uncover and reconstruct the palace, which was the center of a large town that Evans felt had a population of around 100,000 at its peak. The palace, which had 1200 to 1400 rooms, is built on a plan so complex that archaeologists believe it is the origin of stories about the Minoan labyrinth. The complex was not even fortified, which meant that the king, both a divinity and a monarch, was as confident as he was powerful. Evans's restoration features large red wooden columns made broader at the top than at the base, wall reproductions, the throne room, the queen's bathroom (she supposedly took milk baths), and the sophisticated sanitary system. You can see charred remains from the fatal fire of 1450 B.C. that makes it seem people lived here only yesterday. You can also walk down the oldest street in the world, once lined with homes of aristocrats, and peek into the huge garbage receptacle where broken pottery was thrown.

At the Archaeological Museum in Heraklion guides shout at the top of their lungs in every language possible. By all means avoid the frustrating tour here. Get away from your fellow passengers as quickly as possible, head upstairs for the frescoes, and then visit the 1:50 scale model of the Palace of Knossos and the cases downstairs. This museum is unique, in that it contains *all* the findings at Knossos and other sites in Crete. Not one object was carried off to European museums as happened so often at these classical sites.

If there is sufficient time before your ship sails, wander about the town a bit. The fruit market is spectacular, and you'll find interesting shops for souvenirs as well as tempting handwoven rugs in colorful Cretan designs.

ISRAEL

Whether your tour of the Holy Land begins in the well-equipped harbor of **Ashdod,** one of Israel's planned cities and perched on sand dunes, or in the three-tiered port of **Haifa,** populated since biblical times, you will find yourself on a journey like none other you have experienced before. Your cruise vessel may not be in port long enough for you to visit everything you would like, and you may have to choose between Jerusalem and Bethlehem, or the Nazareth/Tiberias/Sea of Galilee route.

If you are lucky enough to sail into Haifa, from the deep-blue sea to the top of "God's vineyards," Mount Carmel, you will enjoy panoramic views at every level: from the harbor with its broad bay, the Hadar or midsection business area; and the Carmel residential level of homes and parks and fine hotels. From Haifa, the heart of the Holy Land—Nazareth, Tiberias, and the Sea of Galilee—is easily accessible. Before you depart on your full-day tour give courtesy to Haifa itself, especially Elijah's Cave, where the prophet is said to have hidden from the wrath of King Ahab and his wife Jezebel, and where the Holy Family was sheltered on the return from Egypt.

The drive to Nazareth takes about an hour through Israel's largest and most fertile valley, an impressive array of fruit trees, vineyards, and green fields that were carefully nurtured from swampland. From the valley your bus will maneuver hairpin turns through the King George V Forest, and into Nazareth. Here is the Basilica of the Annunciation (built over the site of earlier structures), where the angel Gabriel is said to have announced to Mary that she would bear the Son of God. Nearby is a church where Joseph's workshop is thought to have been, and the synagogue Jesus attended. Two other historic sites are Mary's Well, where you will see women carrying jugs of water on their heads, just as they did in Jesus's time, and a Franciscan church where Jesus is believed to have dined with his disciples after the Resurrection.

From Nazareth the road leads directly to the Sea of Galilee, a tranquil freshwater lake thirteen miles long and some seven hundred feet below sea level. En route, you will pass by Cana, where Jesus is said to have turned water into wine, and you will glimpse of Mount Tabor, site of Jesus's transfiguration. The ancient town of Tiberias, built by Herod in honor of the Roman Emperor Tiberias, was a major center of Jewish life in the Holy Land (the learned men of Tiberias introduced grammar and punctuation into the Hebrew language). This resort is still noted for curative hot springs famed for more than 3000 years. From Tiberias you go on to the Church of the Multiplication of Loaves and Fishes and to the town of Capernaum, the center of Jesus's activities in the Galilee. On the return to Tiberias you will see the Mount of the Beatitudes, where the Sermon on the Mount was delivered and where Jesus is said to have chosen his twelve apostles.

Jerusalem, continually inhabited for more than four thousand years, is not only a great historical center but the cornerstone of the world's three great religions. Jews, Christians, and Moslems pay homage to their respective shrines. Jerusalem's inhabitants are thought to be members of the greatest melting pot mankind has ever known. The Old City, or walled section, of East Jerusalem is a living testament to that. Here you can visit the Wailing Wall (remnant of a wall that once supported the Temple Mount). Nearby is the gleaming Dome of the Rock, or Mosque of Omar, a Moslem sanctuary built over the spot where Abraham was prepared to sacrifice the life of his son and where Moslems believe that Mohammed ascended to heaven. On the Via Dolorosa, the route to Calvary passes fourteen Stations of the Cross marked for prayer. Pay a visit to the Church of the Holy Sepulchre, believed to be the site of the crucifixion. Also in the Old City are the Church of St. Anne, the Pool of Bethesda, and the Arch of Ecce Homo. From the Mount of Olives, you will catch your breath at the spectacular view of old and new Jerusalem before visiting the Church of all Nations, the Tomb of the Prophets, and the Garden of Gethsemane. From Mount Scopus the panorama includes the Judean desert and the distant Dead Sea. As your drive takes you through West Jerusalem, you will see the memorial to the six million Jews of the holocaust, Hadassah Hospital (largest medical center in the Middle East), and the Kennedy Memorial and Peace Forest where you can plant a tree for a small fee.

Bethlehem is seven miles south of Jerusalem from the Damascus Gate (it is traditional for pilgrims to walk it on Christmas). En route you will pass the Tomb of Rachel, wife of Jacob and mother of Joseph, and revered by Moslems, Jews, and Christians. At Bethlehem the Church of the Nativity on Manger Square is the principal shrine. The church is the oldest in the country, and the manger is believed to be in the crypt underneath the altar. Another historic site is the Milk Grotto, where Mary's milk is said to have turned the stones chalky white. And by all means, pay a visit to the bazaar where local merchants make a good living selling artifacts to the pilgrims.

ITALY

Italy's largest seaport, **Genoa,** is a spacious and attractive city that has some fifteen miles of quays receiving ships from all the seas of the world. A popular embarkation point for cruise ships sailing under the Italian flag, Genoa is an exciting port for the start of any adventure. The city is built up the side of a mountain and boasts many, many fine Renaissance palaces of the sixteenth and seventeenth centuries that overlook the bay (drive along Via Garibaldi and Via Balbi in the Porto Vecchio section). Genoa is midway on the Italian Riviera, which encircles the Ligurian Sea. The western end, or Riviera di Ponente, runs 101 miles to Ventimiglia and features such resorts as San Remo, capital of the flower section of this area and known also for its race course and casino. The eastern end, or Riviera di Levante, runs only seventy miles to La Spezia, a trading port and excursion center.

The rugged, rocky Portofino Peninsula is becoming a popular cruise call. **Portofino** is a small fishing village loved by artists. Except for the summer crowds and traffic, it's a rather sleepy, picturesque scene. My favorite walk is out to the lighthouse at sunset, to gaze out on the Gulf of Rapallo and along the coast to La Spezia harbor.

South of La Spezia is **Livorno** (Leghorn), an ancient trading port that one of the Medici princes linked by canal to Pisa in the sixteenth century. Pisa was a large commercial port in the eleventh century, rivaling Genoa and Venice, but her power declined after the fourteenth century, about the time the Leaning Tower was completed (it was built between 1174 and 1350). Since it began to lean, the tower has become Pisa's most renowned monument, and even native-son Galileo used it in the seventeenth century to work out his theory of gravity. The tower leans almost fourteen feet now, due to a fault in the design of the foundation as well as to the poor subsoil on which it was built. It serves as the campanile, or bell tower, to the adjacent twelfth-century Romanesque cathedral and fourteenth-century baptistry.

Some cruise lines use Livorno for the port of entry to Pisa at the mouth of the Arno River, as well as for excursions to **Florence,** where the purest Italian is spoken (Dante was a native son) and some of mankind's most magnificent masterpieces were made. The artistic capital of Italy from the fourteenth to seventeenth centuries, Florence has always been pleasing to the eye to great patrons—the Pitti, Strozzi, Pazzi, and Medicis, whose names still linger on palaces, public buildings, and in dedications. Florence remains an art center and its modern craftsmen do beautiful work in leather, silver, wood, gold, and fashions. The term "Florentine" reflects a special style, just as it was during the Renaissance when talents included Boticelli, Leonardo da Vinci, Raphael, Michelangelo, Buonarroti, Brunelleschi, Donatello, and Cellini. A visit to Florence is a delightful mini-course in the history of art—no musty class-rooms, just beautiful buildings still in use, and paintings and statues every-where. It's difficult to know where to begin, but the most practical place would be the Ponte Vecchio, that old bridge where the city began and which is now lined with shops.

If you have just one day to spend in Florence on a shore excursion, you will only get a taste of the beauty here. You won't want to miss the bronze doors of the Baptistry, or the Piazza della Signoria, the former center of political life and now the perfect spot to watch the action from a cafe or on the steps of the Loggia del Lanzi. The Pitti and Uffizi are two of the world's finest museums, but my favorite in Florence is the Bargello because it's small, is in a charming former palace, and has a lovely courtyard. It also has some interesting pieces by Michelangelo, Donatello, and Della Robbia. Save some time to walk around, have a *gelati* (ice cream) from a sidewalk vendor, and read the plaques on old buildings. The last time I was in Florence, I discovered Casa Guidi, at 8 Piazza San Felice, the former home of Elizabeth Barrett and Robert Browning.

On television I saw an old movie with the Bay of Naples in the background and an ocean liner anchored in the harbor; the hero had to choose between his wife on board the ship and a woman whose villa overlooked the bay. Well, the hero chose the woman with the villa, because of the magical quality of the bay.

Naples is the prime port for passenger traffic in Italy. It is also the birthplace of spaghetti and pizza (the real thing, not what we find in America) and the capital of bel canto. A fascinating, frustrating, and continually surprising city, it is a world apart from the rest of the country. Neopolitans are known for being independent, crafty, tenacious, and wary of strangers. Families here are the brotherhood of man—once a member . . . never out of mind.

Naples began as the Greek colony Neapolis, and although conquered in the fourth century B.C. by the Romans, never gave up Greek language or customs until the end of the Roman Empire. Since then, seven "royal" families have reigned over but never really ruled Naples. From ancient times the city has been a popular winter retreat, and the bay has a deserved reputation for providing interesting environs, including mountains, lovely capes, and islands. Today Naples is the jetty for cruises to Capri, Ischia, and Sorrento.

Naples is also the principal port for excursions to Pompeii, that ancient town smothered in molten ash in the year 79 A.D. from the eruptions of Mt. Vesuvius. The population of Pompeii—about 25,000 at the time, many of them wealthy aristocrats from Rome—had little warning. The entire area was quickly covered in hot lava and cinders, and was rediscovered in the seventeenth century. Excavations have been going since 1748, and today two-thirds of the city can be toured. It's an unforgettable feeling to wander among the uncovered ruins, to walk the stone streets still marked from chariot wheels, enter what were once luxurious villas full of exquisite frescoes and mosaics, and visit the Stabian Baths where both men and women exercised. It's as though the people of Pompeii have never left—their spirits still linger.

On the return to your ship you may want to visit Naples's old quarter (Quartiere Vecchio), the new castle (Castel Nuovo) built in 1282, and the National Museum located in a sixteenth-century palace full of treasures uncovered at Pompeii as well as at Herculaneum. Herculaneum was a nearby town buried in the same eruptions of Mt. Vesuvius but not excavated until the beginning of the nineteenth century. Historians have discovered that this town was for workers and the poorer folk, since instead of luxury villas they have uncovered what appear to be blocks of tenements.

If time allows, an excursion to the isle of **Capri,** a long-time haven for the international set, might be on your agenda. This island of dreams is four miles long and two miles wide, yet has some lovely wild and lonely spots, Blue Grotto sea cave, and 951-foot Monte Solaro (a chair hoist takes you up for a spectacular view). Or take a funny old convertible taxi up the Corniche Road to Anacapri, past the lovely villas owned by movie stars to the Piazza della Vittoria where you can sit in the sun, try the local wine, and drink in the atmosphere.

Since the reign of Emperor Trajan (53–117), Civitavecchia ("old city") has been the port for **Rome,** capital of Italy and cradle of Christianity. Called the Eternal City, Rome is thought by historians, poets, and artists to have no equal in all the world. A brief, one-day cruise call can never do justice to Rome, but it can give you a feeling for the many great monuments that have existed here for centuries. Unlike many other historic cities, Rome is alive, vibrant, and full of action, which makes its many ruins more appealing, its piazzas more exciting, and its many churches more interesting. Legend says the city was founded by twins Romulus and Remus, the offspring of Mars and Venus, who were abandoned in the Tiber River and brought up by a she-wolf. Ancient Rome was first a republic, then capital of an empire whose influence reached to England and Asia, and later divided into the Western Empire (Rome) and the Eastern Empire (Constantinople). Under the reign of Constantine (324–337), Christianity became the state religion and the era of the pagans versus the Christians began. And when there were no more emperors in the political forum, the popes wielded power and often assumed absolute authority.

Any tour of this metropolis actually encompasses three separate cities—ancient Rome, Christian Rome, and the Rome of the people. This last is the Rome you can't miss even on a quick visit—tourists sitting on the steps of Piazza di Spagna, policemen in white gloves, cars and buses going in circles, and the new next to the old and the ancient.

Ancient Rome consists of the Forum, the Palatine Hill, the Coliseum (where gladiator contests took place and early Christians were confronted with lions), the Arch of Constantine, the Imperial Forums, and the Baths. Also visit the Pantheon, the most perfectly preserved ancient building in the world, and the beginning of the Appian Way (Via Appia Antica), which was built in 312 B.C. and runs all the way down to the port of Brindisi.

Christian Rome centers on Vatican City, which (with 109 acres) is the smallest independent state in the world. By tradition, its Swiss guards wear uniforms designed by Michelangelo and all come from the same town of Valais, in Switzerland. Walking through Piazza San Pietro is an overwhelming experience. This square is an extension of the basilica itself, site of papal funerals and the enthronement of new popes. The Emperor Constantine built the first St. Peter's on this site in the fourth century; the present basilica dates from the sixteenth century and is the combined work of Bramante, Sangallo, Raphael, and Michelangelo—who designed the dome. After St. Peter's, you may wonder if it's worth visiting other churches in Rome. Yes, but only at a very, very, leisurely pace.

Dominating the Tiber River, and a personal joy, is Castel Sant'Angelo, built by the Emperor Hadrian in 135 A.D. as a mausoleum and turned into a fortress in the Middle Ages. It's connected to the Vatican by a tunnel—handy for several popes during difficult times. The interior is a museum of ancient weapons and some works of art. You can also see the prison cells and apartments of the popes (some combination!). From the top, the view of Rome is wonderful. I also like the seven hills of Rome, the white-marble Victor Emmanuel monument, Mussolini's balcony, and the Via Condotti where Gucci, Ginori, Valentino, and Bulgari display their wares. But the fountains of Rome will beckon, and if you do not stop to throw two coins over your shoulder into the Trevi Fountain (one to ensure your return to Rome; the other to fulfill a wish), then you have not really been to the Eternal City.

Ever-changing **Venice,** one of the most romantic cities in the world, was used by Shakespeare as the setting for *Othello* and *The Merchant of Venice*; Thomas Mann wrote *Death in Venice*; and in Ernest Hemingway's *Across the River and Through the Trees* the last line is, "Take me to the Gritti [hotel]!" Of Venice's many painters, my favorite is the eighteenth-century Venetian who so frequently recorded the play of light on canals that he was called Canaletto. In this romantic city you'll fall under the spell of gondolas, narrow canals, bridges, the sun setting on St. Mark's Square, funny houses in back alleys with their balconies and flower pots, palaces of the rich and noble, and the sound of water lapping as you walk along the quiet streets. Once under this spell, you're under forever.

The best way to approach Venice is by water, for the city is wed to the Adriatic Sea. Alas, the waters rise more each year and the city sinks. Although pessimists predicted the city would not be standing by the end of this century, the Italian government finally began a preservation project to give Venice a long and happy life.

Founded in the ninth century, Venice was made a republic with a Doge (leader), and soon enjoyed such great prosperity via the Crusades (which were much more an economic than a religious endeavor) that an empire evolved. The Venetian Empire, whose influence reached as far as Asia Minor, was at its height in the first half of the fifteenth century and began to decline after mid-century, just as the arts began to flourish. The sixteenth century gave us the painter Titian as well as a special style of architecture that became synonymous with grand palaces and civic buildings.

The best way to see Venice is on foot, following no specific route (but with a good map in hand). I like to begin and finish each day in St. Mark's Square, home of thousands of pigeons, unending aperitifs, old-worn charm, and elegant shops. The square changes personality by the hour. On the square is St. Mark's Basilica, a jumble of styles put together through the centuries, which has played host to innumerable historic events and figures. The interior decoration is dazzling, but pay special attention to the bronze horses over the doorway, brought back from Constantinople in 1204 by one of the Doges. Unfortunately, what you see today are copies of the original works because the priceless bronzes were deteriorating from air pollution. Take a ride up the bell tower (this is a real campanile) for an overview of all Venice, and then tour the Doge's Palace, for a taste of how the city's famous leaders lived and treated their enemies to the famous Bridge of Sighs.

Venice consists of 117 islands, 150 canals, and some 400 bridges! A ride on the Grand Canal is mandatory—either by gondola in the moonlight or water taxi during the day—for the two-mile stretch of the largest concentration of twelfth- to eighteenth-century palaces in the world. Stop, if you can, at the Rialto Bridge (with the famous hump) and visit the shops and galleries overlooking the canal. This is the business section of Venice and a good place to browse.

Across the canal from St. Mark's Square is the Island of San Giorgio, a few minutes away by water taxi. Here, in a peaceful and serene atmosphere, the church of San Giorgio Maggiore is in stark contrast to the Basilica across the way. Sit for a spell on the quay, waiting for the vaporetto to return, to view the hustle and bustle going on across the water! For a lighter diversion the Lido is a fashionable resort about a half-hour's ride by water from St. Mark's Square. It's known for its lovely beach, beautiful people, and casino. Another popular excursion is the island of Murano, a glass works since 1292. You can visit the main canal-street, lined with Renaissance houses, and the glass works and museum, but shop prices are high here.

Italy's islands—Elba, the Lipari, Sardinia, and Siciliy—are especially popular as cruise calls, for they offer a varied landscape and history. **Elba,** the largest in the Tuscan archipelago, is often called the Island of Sea Horses, but it is best known as the home of exiled Napoleon Bonaparte from 1814 to 1815. Here Napoleon reigned for less than a year following his abdication in Paris, and brooded over the view of his native Corsica. Cruise ships dock at Portoferraio, the sleepy capital of the island, guarded by two ancient forts. A walk along the waterfront and up the steps into the old section of town will take you to the Villa dei Mullini, where Napoleon often stayed and where he left mementos. A short ride from town is the Villa Napoleone at San Martino. Set in the beautiful hills, with terraced gardens overlooking the bay, this was the former emperor's summer residence, a mini-version of Versailles (but hardly so well kept—in fact, it's a *very* poor relative). Though the setting is lovely, I get a feeling of sadness.

The Lipari are an archipelago of seven small volcanic islands known for stark beauty and brilliant sunshine. Also known as the Aeolian Islands, because the ancients believed that Aeolus, the God of the Wind, lived here, the islands are Lipari, Vulcano, Alicudi, Salina, Filicudi, Panarea, and Stromboli. **Stromboli,** featured on the cruise circuit, has a smoking crater, vineyard-covered hills, and Moorish-style houses. The crater has minor eruptions of lava, and the spectacle of fiery stones falling into the sea is especially dramatic when seen from your ship at night.

Sardinia is a large island in the Tyrrhenian Sea, second in size only to Sicily, its southeastern neighbor. The island is said to have been colonized by the Cretans, which puts its first civilization around 2000 B.C., but a number of different peoples occupied it in rapid succession before the Spanish took over in the early eighteenth century. As a result, Sardinians have a keen sense of hospitality (they have no choice, one might say), honor, and are tough men and women of agriculture. **Cagliari,** Sardinia's capital, once a flourishing Carthaginian city, is now a busy seaport. It boasts a fine Roman amphitheater and a national museum of antiquities. St. Saturninus' Basilica dates from the fifth century and is thought to be one of the oldest Christian churches in the Mediterranean area. Cagliari's bustle is quite a contrast to the peaceful and rugged countryside, where native women wear long, pleated skirts and lace mantillas (left over from the Spanish days, no doubt) and shy away from the approach of strangers. Menfolk wear funny horned hats and are never far away from their dwarf-like donkeys.

Sardinia was put on the map of the international set a few years ago when the Aga Khan organized the development of the Costa Smeralda area on the northeast coastline. Here, where the scenery is spectacular and the sea an emerald green, he poured millions of dollars into luxury hotels, seasonal apartments, and yacht basins for his friends, and their friends. He used good taste—the buildings blend beautifully with the terrain and local Sardinian architecture. Those who do not come off yachts can fly into nearby Olbia for a visit to the eighty sun-filled beaches, or they can disembark for the day from cruise ships that dock during the season in the port of Olbia.

Sicily, the largest and most mysterious of the Mediterranean islands, home to some five million people noted for dark complexions—despite a few vestiges of the old Norman days in the occasional blond, blue-eyed baby. Sicilians are also reputed to have sinister characters, a sweeping and unfair appraisal drawn from movies about organized crime in the United States. The truth is, most Sicilians simply cultivate their vines, almond trees, fruits, and vegetables and have little to do with the outside world. Sicily is called the archaeological museum of Europe for its Greek temples and theaters, Roman bridges and aqueducts, Saracen mosques, Norman churches and castles. It houses so many interesting relics of European power struggles during the past two thousand years that it has many ports in which cruise ships call: Agrigento, with its Greco-Roman quarter and Valley of the Temples; Catania, which has been destroyed several times by eruptions from Mt. Etna; Messina; Palermo, the capital and chief seaport and the crossroads of civilizations for centuries; Syracuse, once the rival of Athens, with its beautiful bay and fine ruins of a former Greek city; and Taormina, a beautiful resort overlooking the sea and facing Mt. Etna.

Mt. Etna dominates Sicily in one way or another. It is the largest active volcano in Europe. In ancient times 135 eruptions were recorded, but the worst was in 1669, when the lava almost totally destroyed Catania. Already in this century Etna has erupted eleven times; another could occur at any moment. Nonetheless, visitors adore the ascent of the volcano to the huge black cone with fruit trees flourishing on its slopes. From Catania to the summit is about twenty miles, plus twenty minutes by cable car, and just under one hour on foot (high heels should not be worn on this climb). If you like to see the earth smoke and sputter, you will enjoy this excursion, provided you are dressed warmly enough. Otherwise, you may prefer a peaceful terrace in town and a glass of local wine. Later, stroll in the Bellini Gardens for a fine panorama of the city—and Mt. Etna.

MALTA

Your cruise ship will sail into **Valletta,** the capital that dominates the grand harbor of the Maltese Islands, Malta Gozo, and Comino. These islands have had their share of shipwrecks—Ulysses supposedly spent some time in the arms of Calypso on the island of Gozo, and Apostle Paul is said to have drifted to shore in about A.D. 60 and lived three months in a cave between Rabat and Mdina while converting the island to Christianity. These islands, strategically located in the middle of the Mediterranean, have been the center of a struggle between maritime powers for centuries.

The Maltese Islands are thought to have been affiliated with Sicily as well as North Africa. The first known inhabitants were Sicilian Neolithic farmers of about 4000 B.C. The Phoenicians arrived later (700 B.C.) and used the fine harbors for their trading activities. They left the basis of a language that is still in use today. But Malta's most interesting period dates from 1530 to 1798 when the Knights of St. John made their home here and built fortifications, palaces, inns, and churches. Shortly after the knights arrived, in 1565, an attack by the Turks was repulsed and brought great fame to Malta. (This military prowess was repeated from 1940 to 1943 when Malta resisted the Axis powers.)

Valletta, founded in the mid-sixteenth century, reflects the islands' rich heritage. For a tour of beautiful places in the capital, begin at St. John's Co-Cathedral and move on to the Palace of the Grand Masters and Armory. A fine national museum of archaeology is housed in the Auberge de Provence, one of the inns of the Knights of St. John of Jerusalem (who founded Malta). Later than these mid-sixteenth century structures but considered one of the oldest theaters in Europe, is the Manoel Theatre built in 1731 by one of the Grand Masters, Manoel de Vilhena. Outside of Valletta you can tour some unique sites, including the megalithic monuments of 2500 B.C., the Ghar Dalam Cave with fossils of animals that roamed some 170,000 years ago, a Blue Grotto that rivals the one in Capri, and the cave in which St. Paul is believed to have lived during his three-month stay in A.D. 60. (An account of his shipwreck can be found in Acts XXVII and XXVIII.)

The Maltese Islands also mean beautiful bays, beaches, and brightly colored boats called *dghajjes*, which you can take for touring the grottos and caves as well as for visiting the islands of Gozo and Comino. And when you're in the mood for shopping, the local crafts feature handmade tiles, plates, and glassware.

MOROCCO

The Kingdom of Morocco, at the westernmost point of North Africa, is the land of the Casbah, couscous, caftans, and Casablanca. Once part of the Carthaginian empire and later a part of the province of Mauritania under the Romans, Morocco was conquered by the Arabs, the Portuguese, the Spanish, and finally the French. It first became an independent Arab kingdom in 788 but broke up by the tenth century. Independence from France was finally gained in 1956. Couscous (made of semolina, meat, and vegetables) is the national dish and caftans are the native dress. The famous Casbah, though, is in Tangier, which is not a frequent cruise call, but Casablanca is. You can prepare yourself by catching the movie classic *Casablanca*, with Humphrey Bogart and Ingrid Bergman. Actually, the bustling city you sail into has no relation to the Casablanca of the 1940s; it is a thoroughly modern, twentieth-century city—the gateway to North Africa.

Casablanca has one of the largest harbors in Africa, and three gateways connect the old medina with the port. It's called "Casa" by those who live here and the "Great White City" by visitors. More new than old, Casablanca is also more Moroccan than French. It has both an old and new medina (the latter built by the French in 1921), a royal palace where the king stays when in town, United Nations Square, and Arab League Park. The most beautiful part of the city is the seaside residential area with lovely homes and romantic views. You may have heard of one quarter, Anfa, because Churchill, Roosevelt, and De Gaulle met here during World War II for the Casablanca Conference.

Just fifty-seven miles northeast along the Atlantic coastline is **Rabat,** capital of Morocco and home of King Hassan II. The drive is worthwhile. Only Moslems are allowed to enter religious monuments in Morocco, but you can visit the Quadias Casbah and Museum of Oudaia for a stroll through the gardens and the overwhelming displays of native arts and crafts. You may also climb the Tower of Hassan for a view of the city of Salé across the Bou Regreg. Take a walk through the medina, whose walls date from the twelfth and seventeenth centuries. Here you can peek at souk after souk, visit the old wool market, and pass by the mellah or Jewish quarter. And if an item grabs your fancy, bargain. The experts become serious only after your third offer.

The *pièce de résistance* in Morocco is the all-day tour to **Marrakesh.** This imperial, red-ochre city founded by the Almoravids in the eleventh century is the jewel of the Islamic world. Marrakesh, 150 hot miles from Casablanca, is an oasis at the edge of the scorching Sahara Desert. The temperatures during the summer months average over 100 degrees (F), which is why the city was once a winter playground for the rich and famous. (Winston Churchill used to stay at the famed La Mamounia Hotel, whose gardens came straight from the Arabian Nights.) The landscape of Marrakesh is dominated by the pink sandstone Koutoubia, or Mosque of the Scribes, which has a minaret 222 feet high. This great monument of Moorish architecture and decoration was built in the twelfth century. Below the mosque is the Djemma El Fna, the country's largest souk and greatest free entertainment center, where you can buy anything in the world from just about everyone. This is the most famous square in all North Africa; and if you survive it, you're on your way to becoming a native. Some say that the profusion of water-sellers, story-tellers, acrobats, soothsayers, dancers, and snake-charmers create an incredible biblical atmosphere (in the epitome of a Moorish town). Other sights to tantalize the senses include the medina and mellah, the sixteenth-century monument of Medersa Ibn Yussef, the royal tombs, Bahia palace and gardens (provided no guests-of-state are in residence), Dar Si Said (arts and handcrafts museum), and the many imperial gardens. Marrakesh is famous for its beautifully planned gardens replete with olive groves, especially the Aguedal and Menara as well as the Mamounia (attached to the deluxe hotel of the same name). These gardens are all the more impressive and inviting when you remember that the mysterious desert is but a step away.

THE SUEZ CANAL AND THE RED SEA

The opening of the Suez Canal in 1869 was honored by the presence of royalty, including such personages as the Empress Eugénie of Austria, for whom a palace was built at the foot of the Great Pyramids (now the Mena House Oberoi Hotel where you may have lunch). Italian composer Giuseppe Verdi wrote his spectacular opera *Aida* (with live elephants on stage) just for this occasion, and the royal guests reportedly received it with a tumultuous welcome at the newly constructed Cairo Opera House. What an inaugural for the 100.76-mile canal that joins the Mediterranean with the Red Sea!

It took a full decade to build the Suez Canal, and years of study and indecision passed before a shovel even touched the earth. The Suez is probably not the first canal on this site—scholars believe that a passageway of some sort existed between the two seas as early as the sixth century B.C. but was closed through neglect. From 1869 to 1980 the Suez closed only twice—the last time from the 1967 war to June 5, 1975, when it was reopened by Egyptian president Anwar Sadat. The western gateway to the canal is **Port Said,** a town that boomed during the late nineteenth century and is now known as a free port. You'll find little to do or see here, and most cruise ships call only as a courtesy and to offer full-day tours to Cairo, which comes into view at the end of a three-hour bus ride through the desert. (You can amuse yourself during the ride by counting the numerous checkpoints—rusted tanks left over from the recent battles—and the villages full of tents topped by television antennae.) From Port Said the transit through the canal to Suez takes about eighteen hours and passes by many little canal towns of which the prettiest is Ismailia. The city of **Suez,** the southernmost port of the canal, is a wonderful spot to view what you have just passed through (or if you are sailing in the opposite direction, what you are about to experience). Suez also sparks little interest for me, but it is another good embarkation point for visits to Cairo, since it's a reasonable two-hour drive from here.

Having transited the Suez Canal, your cruise vessel continues down the Gulf of Suez, between the Sinai Peninsula and Egypt's eastern desert. The first noticeable settlement of any size on this rocky, undeveloped Red Sea coastline is Hurghada, approximately 250 land miles south of Suez. From Hurghada you can see Mt. Sinai (Gebel Moussa) on a clear day. Just below the city lies the port of **Safaga,** from where all-day tours to Thebes, Karnak, and Luxor on the Nile River are arranged. The tours, although lengthy (twelve to fourteen hours), are wonderful, for you will visit the Valley of the Kings (tombs of Tutankhamen and Ramses VI) as well as the Temple of Queen Hatshepsut, eat an enjoyable lunch, and then ride by horsedrawn carriage to the Temple of Karnak. Following a visit to the Temple of Luxor, you may have time for a sunset sail on the Nile in a felucca before returning to your ship in Safaga for a late supper on board (according to the fine itinerary planned by Raymond & Whitcomb of New York). If your ship schedules another day in Safaga, try to fly down to the temple complex of Abu Simbel, about 160 miles south of

Aswan (at a cost of about $150 per person). Here you can explore the Great Temple of Ramses II and the smaller temple dedicated to his consort and queen, Nefertari. These two monuments were rescued from the floodwaters of the Aswan Dam in 1969, in a scheme that involved moving the temples, piece by piece, to a new site that was seven hundred feet away but two hundred feet higher. The project took four and one-half years and cost millions of dollars, and one engineer reportedly said that Abu Simbel qualifies as a wonder of both and ancient and modern world.

From Safaga your cruise vessel sails northeast to **Aqaba** in Jordan, a port town at the tip of the gulf that separates the Sinai and Arabian peninsulas. Aqaba is a biblical town, said to date from as early as the tenth century B.C. Known for its trading because of its location on the gulf, at one time it was a part of Egypt. Little of this past history remains, and the area now emphasizes splendid scuba diving on its beautiful coral reefs—equal to any throughout the world. As a result, Aqaba is becoming a fashionable, Middle East resort. Even King Hussein finds the thirty-minute flight from Amman (capital of Jordan) short enough to make him a frequent visitor to his villa on the beach.

Two unforgettable shore excursions, to Wadi Rumm and Petra, leave from Aqaba. **Wadi Rumm** is a great desert valley, about an hour's drive from the port, through which the famous T. E. Lawrence passed in his pursuit of the Turks during World War I. The route that Lawrence and his Desert Legion followed is fascinating, and your journey, either by car or camel train, will eventually end at the fort of the Wadi Rumm Desert Patrol which is also the home of several Bedouin tribes. Huge, red, stone cliff scenery; an almost perfect cloudless sky; and colorful Bedouin costumes combine to create an impression that boggles the mind. You may even be invited to a traditional Bedouin feast, although I understand that sheep's eyes are no longer served to foreign guests!

The rose-colored city of **Petra,** also known by the biblical name of Sela, lies in the desert near the Dead Sea and can be entered only through a narrow passageway that is just comfortable for humans and horses. Petra means *rock*, as does sela, and this narrow passage (or siq) is lined with towering cliffs of rosy-hued stone. Petra, one of the world's most unusual ancient sites, could date from as early as 2000 B.C. Through the centuries it was home to several different nomadic tribes, but the city reached its height under the Romans, who carved magnificent monuments out of the distinctive rock (the Treasury is the most perfectly preserved example). Later it became part of the Byzantine Empire, fell to the Arabs, and then was forgotten for centuries until it was rediscovered by a Swiss explorer in the early nineteenth century. What he found and what you see is a dazzling array of classical monuments, historic sites such as the Tomb of Aaron (the brother of Moses), and splendid views of the surrounding ancient lands. Petra's beautiful tombs and temples, and cliffs that change character with the rays of the sun, almost require you to set out with plenty of film and good hiking shoes.

TUNISIA

Tunisia's leading seaport is **La Goulette** (Halq al-Wadi), famous for its six-teenth-century fort (built by Charles V of Spain to safeguard his many con-uests in the Mediterranean) and its fish restaurants, which draw people from the nearby capital city of Tunis to the sidewalk tables. La Goulette is but a short distance from the capital the Romans once called Africa Vetus, and from the ruins of the ancient Mediterranean power of Carthage.

Approximately one million people live in greater **Tunis,** a typical North African metropolis that blends the old with the new, and the Oriental with the Occidental in a dizzying fashion. For here was a culture in which the con-quering sword of Islam smote the early Christianity of Byzantium and brought about a vigorous flowering of new art forms. In the eleventh century, Tunisia entered another aesthetic era as influences shifted from the eastern Mediterra-nean to the Moslem West of Andalusia (southern Spain). The art of this period, delicate and refined, appears in illuminated manuscripts, copperwork, carved wood, and stucco lacework. In the sixteenth century Tunisia became part of the Ottoman Empire, and Turkish art introduced a new dimension that became increasingly baroque. In 1881 the country became a French protecto-rate. It received its independence in 1956 and today is a nation poised (as they say) on the brink of change.

Nonetheless, as you drive through Tunis you will see a city whose layers of history are evident on every street corner. The medina, or inner city of shops and old houses, is considered one of the most beautiful in the Islamic world. There is the great mosque Djamaa Ez-Zitouna whose 184 columns were pil-fered from the Roman temples of Carthage. The National Library of Tunis, that the Turks used as a barracks, has a remarkable collection of illuminated Koran manuscripts, and the beautiful Palace of Dar Ben Abdullah is one of the Tunisian great houses. Outside the medina, boulevards and buildings with whitewashed fronts and light-blue shutters to filter the bright Mediterranean sun give the air of a French provincial town. (French is still the second lan-guage here, after Arabic.)

Just a short drive from this richness are the Carthaginian ruins of Punic and Roman Tunisia. The Phoenicians founded **Carthage** in 814 B.C., and the city became a Mediterranean power by the sixth century B.C., influencing civiliza-tions as far as southern Spain and the Balearic Islands. As the ancient Romans grew stronger and conquered lower Italy, they disliked the Carthaginians more and more and referred to them as Punics, which applied not only to the lan-guage they spoke (a dialect of Phoenician) but also to the fact that they were considered treacherous and perfidious. A series of wars broke out, known as the Punic Wars, and during the second Punic War (218 to 201 B.C.) a Carthagin-ian general named Hannibal crossed the Alps with the aid of elephants and invaded Italy, much to the disgrace of the Roman armies. Carthage was then totally destroyed, condemned to death by the Roman Senate in 146 B.C. The city, resurrected by Emperor Augustus, became a Roman province. The baths built in the second century A.D. under Antoninus Pius were among the largest in the empire. Built on the seashore near the site where the first Phoenician ships anchored, this magnificent structure measured seven hundred feet in length. Its sumptuous decorations were second to none. Other relics of these two Carthages that were nine centuries apart are the Necropolis, the city gate, a theater, the Tophet (where Carthaginians first offered human sacrifices, then substituted animals), and some interesting, beautifully decorated private houses.

Some shore tours also stop at Sidi bou Zid, a Moorish village along the coast from Carthage, and a photographer's paradise with its whitewashed houses untouched by the modern world. Here you can wander the steeply winding streets, past tiny shops, cafes, and benches crowded with village elders having a smoke. Where else, you may wonder, is the sky so blue, the cypress so green, and the bougainvillea so scarlet? Look across the Bay of Tunis to Bou Cornine, the twin-peaked mountain, and you will understand why this charming oasis is so popular with artists and lovers alike.

TURKEY

The little fishing village of **Dikili** on the edge of Asia Minor is a relatively new call for ships cruising the Aegean. A thrilling stop, Dikili is just a 35-minute bus ride away from the classical ruins of **Pergamum,** the ancient city that flourished for some four centuries (from the second century B.C. to the second century A.D.). During the height of its power Pergamum, a city of some 160,000 inhabitants, governed most of western and central Asia Minor. Bergama (its modern name) lies on a plain with the ancient Acropolis to the north and the Asklepeion to the southwest.

The Acropolis was the site of various kings' palaces, temples, a theater, and the second largest library in the ancient world (after Alexandria). The library is said to have contained approximately 200,000 papyrus scrolls, and when the Egyptians stopped exporting papyrus (they were becoming slightly jealous of the competition), the people of Pergamum simply invented parchment and continued writing books. The Egyptians, however, had the last word, for Mark Anthony carried away most of the library's contents in 41 B.C. as a present for his beloved Cleopatra. The beautifully restored theater, on the side of the Acropolis, features a white marble stage that hosts the annual Pergamum festival. Next to the theater sits a small temple dedicated to Dionysus, the god of wine. Archaeologists believe that this temple was placed on the first dead-end street in the world, for a covered walk led from here all the way down the hill to the Asklepeion, about a mile distant. The Asklepeion, a complex dedicated to the god of medicine and reputed to be the second largest hospital in the ancient world (after Epidaurus), specialized in psychotherapy. It was so popular that the coffers of Pergamum swelled from the many patients who came for treatments. The "cure" featured lolling in mud baths, getting lots of sleep, watching comedies (never tragedies) in the 3500-seat open theater, and running naked through the halls. Perhaps because of this last exercise, the treatment center had a central heating system.

A short 25-minute drive from the small port town of **Kusadasi** brings you to the archaeological site of one of the most extraordinary cities of the ancient world, **Ephesus.** In just a few hours' tour it is impossible to absorb this great and vast metropolis whose life spanned two thousand years, especially when one realizes that less than twenty percent of the city has been uncovered—and excavations have been going on for more than a century! Late Mycenean pottery from 1300 B.C. has been found in the area, but historians say the city was first settled around 2000 B.C. on a sheltered harbor around a sanctuary dedicated to the goddess Cybele (later held equal to Artemis). As the harbor silted in, the city was twice relocated—in 1000 B.C. (Ephesus II) and in 334 B.C. (Ephesus III). Today the sea has receded all the way back to kuşadasi and left a valley fertile for the growing of tobacco, fruit, and olives.

The Temple of Artemis at Ephesus was one of the Seven Wonders of the Ancient World, and at least one historian, Pausanias, considered it "the most beautiful work created by humankind." Artemis symbolized nature, virginity, and fertility and protected naval voyagers and wild creatures. The temple was destroyed several times but always rebuilt. Now, however, practically nothing remains so we can only speculate on its former beauty. The classical tour of Ephesus covers the remains of the third city, or Hellenistic period, as well as some monuments left from the following Roman era. I had been told by the cruise director of the *Stella Solaris* that Ephesus would be the highlight of my Aegean cruise, and this was true. The marble-paved streets lined with statues of important personages of two thousand years ago inspired me. Curetes Street, with its many shops and porticos, leads to the Library of Celsus and the junction with what is now known as Marble Road. On the right-hand side of this corner is every tour guide's favorite structure—the brothel! Scholars say it was constructed between 98 and 117 A.D. and featured baths, a public lavatory, and a series of small rooms on the second story. Mosaics depicting the four seasons and the usual pastimes of life inside a brothel have been found. Across the street from this building is an advertisement in the sidewalk—the head of a woman, a heart, and a foot pointing toward the brothel.

Arcadian Avenue leads from the huge amphitheater of Ephesus to what must have been the edge of the harbor in ancient times. The theater was renowned for its seating capacity of 24,000 and for its perfect acoustics. Now restored, it probably looks much like it did when St. Paul came to Ephesus in 54 A.D. to preach. If you have time and energy left after your tour of Ephesus, you can hire a taxi outside the gate at the end of Harbor Street and continue on to the Archaeological Museum, or drive up to the House of the Virgin Mary on Mount Solmisos (where it is believed she spent her final days) before you return to Kuşadasi for some light shopping and the comfort of your cruise vessel. (By the way, tax-free liquor is sold on the pier here during the late afternoon.)

The approach to **Istanbul,** the city that spans two continents, begins about thirteen hours prior to reaching the port. Your ship must enter the Dardanelles, the narrow strait that separates Europe from Asia and the Aegean from the Sea of Marmara. This is the gateway to a strategic area that has been both the bridge and battleground between the exotic East and the Western world for more than two thousand years. Istanbul has been known by many names in its many-layered history. Founded about the fifth century B.C., it was first called Byzantium after the mythical figure, Byzas. As a crossroad between the East and the West, the city fell to the Persians and then to the Greeks. In the first century A.D., the Romans added Byzantium to their empire, and it remained in their interest for the next several centuries.

In 330 A.D., the Emperor Constantine I renamed the city after himself and pronounced it the capital of the East Roman Empire. Although these later Romans built some fine monuments in Constantinople, few of the structures remain, because the city was on the Crusade route and thus went through several severe sackings. In the thirteenth century, Constantinople again fell to the Greeks and then finally landed with the Turks in 1453. The Turks built mosques for the devout, palaces and other places of intrigue for the sultans, and beautiful fountains for everyone. They also changed the name to Istanbul, meaning city of Islams, and made it capital of the Ottoman Empire. When the empire fell, Kemal Mustafa (also known as Atatürk) formed the modern Turkish Republic and moved the capital to the more central location of Ankara in 1922.

Istanbul today is home to about two million people and more than four hundred mosques whose domes and minarets make striking silhouettes on the busy skyline. It is truly a city of two continents, separated only by the eighteen-and-a-half-mile long Bosporus, the narrow strait that joins the Sea of Marmara with the Black Sea. Your cruise ship will dock in front of the old Customs House, or Yolgu Salonu, and you can see the newer section of the European side rising up before you. Across the Golden Horn, that inlet to the north, are the older quarters—Galata and Beyoglu. If you do an about face you'll be looking at the Asian side of Istanbul, which can be reached by numerous ferries as well as the only suspension bridge linking Europe with Asia. It's thrilling to sail into Istanbul (the only way I would ever want to approach this city), because you and your ship are immediately in the center of all the activity, the vibrancy, and the color that makes this area so fascinating. Churning, dirty, and busy Istanbul catches you in this crazy collage of colors, sounds, and smells as soon as you disembark from your cruise vessel.

One of your first stops should be the Blue Mosque, built by the Sultan Ahmed between 1609 and 1616, and covered on the inside with over 21,000 blue porcelain tiles that give it its popular name. One Turkish author writes that the exterior of the mosque, with its six slender minarets, "caresses the eyes like a beautiful flower." The interior is equally impressive because of the brilliant blue tiles overhead and the multipatterned Turkish rugs covering the stone floor. (You must remove your shoes when you visit a mosque, so carry a pair of heavy socks to counteract the dampness and chilliness of the stone floors.) Nearby sits another magnificent monument, Haghia Sophia, built by the Emperor Justinian between 532 and 537 with the aid of at least ten thousand slaves. The cost is said to have been some $7.5 million at the time, an amount that exhausted Justinian's treasury and forced him to impose new taxes. The ornamentation throughout was renowned, but little remains from the Fourth Crusader's final looting in 1204. In 1453, Sultan Ahmed converted this ancient sanctuary into a mosque and covered many of the beautiful mosaics with Arabic script and sayings from the Koran. Then Atatürk made Santa Sophia a museum in 1935, so that all could enjoy the beauty of the building. He encouraged the restoration of the mosaics. On a visit last year, I was told that plans have been made to uncover the mosaics in the central dome, which are believed to be especially fine, but the procedure will be complicated because the Arabic script covering cannot be destroyed in the process.

Any tour of Istanbul must also include the Mosque of Suleiman the Magnificent, possibly the most beautiful Islamic structure in the city. It was constructed between 1550 and 1557, by the order of the Sultan whose 46-year reign of the Ottoman Empire was considered the Golden Age of literature, science, arts, technology, geography, and military tactics. The interior of this mosque is light and airy, despite the tremendous size of the structure. The echo heard in certain parts is one of its most distinctive features. If you have time to go about on your own, take a taxi to a small, jewellike mosque (now museum) known as the Khora (Kariye in Turkish). Built around the seventh century, it houses priceless treasures in Giotto-style mosaics of the twelfth to thirteenth centuries.

Topkapi Palace, former home to the sultans and their six thousand or so retainers, is one of the most famous museums in the world. You may have even seen it in the movies. The palace contains the largest Chinese porcelain collection in the world, gathered by the sultans who believed that poisoned food served on this porcelain would change color and warn them. The palace has four rooms of ornaments made by the palace jewelers, some of which hold precious stones the size of your fist. Upstairs in another wing are the harem rooms, but they are only open at certain times, and not to large groups, so it's best to consult your guide if you wish to stay later to visit them. A separate room, open more often, gives an indication of the private lives of the sultans; and just outside, you can catch a glimpse of your ship in the distance. Before you leave Topkapi, follow the sign to the restaurant, stop at the first level, and take in a lovely view of Istanbul.

No visit to this city is complete without a tour to the largest oriental bazaar, or souk, in the world. Thousands of little shops comprise this covered bazaar, and untold numbers of peddlers try to entice you to patronize their stores (suede is a good buy). Most of the hawkers are downright annoying, but a few can be amusing, such as the man who promised he could find me a very nice flying carpet! Frankly, I prefer the smaller Spice (or Egyptian) Bazaar, which is quieter and redolent of the wonderful smells of local teas, pastries, and oriental spices. (If you're overcome by the aromas, you can take refuge in a very good restaurant here called Pandelis.) Another favored excursion in Istanbul requires you to hire a taxi and drive through the newer section of the European side—past the deluxe hotels and over the Bosporus Bridge to the Asian side. Two continents in one day is no small feat.

YUGOSLAVIA

Called the Pearl of the Adriatic, **Dubrovnik** is an almost perfectly preserved medieval town, a treasury of cultural and historic monuments documenting a thousand-year history. This is historic Ragusa, which grew up in the seventh century and became a city-republic in the fourteenth century, second only to Venice in strength. With a fleet of ships some three hundred strong, it was the most important trading center in the Balkans, linking the Danube River to the Mediterranean. The republic, governed by dukes, produced many important men of science and literature and lasted until 1806 when Napoleon entered the picture. Today the old walls and towers of Dubrovnik still rise dramatically from the Dalmation coastline. The city is the unofficial capital and tourist center of Yugoslavia, a country comprising the people and customs of Bosnia and Herzegovina, Montenegro, Croatia, Macedonia, Slovenia, and Serbia, as well as the autonomous provinces of Kosovo-Metohija and Vojvodina.

Cruise ships dock in the nearby suburb of Gruz, and your tour of the medieval city (where all traffic is banned) will undoubtedly begin at the western end through Pile Gate. From here the main street, or placa, runs to Ploce Gate at the eastern end and is lined with the most marvelous old buildings and archways. A rewarding walk runs from the circular fountain to St. Blaise's Church, which is dedicated to the patron saint and protector of the Republic who gave warning against and thwarted a Venetian invasion. In front of the church stands a fifteenth-century pillar, formerly the site for official announcements and now a gathering place for visitors from all over the world. Opposite Orlando's Pillar is the lovely, sixteenth-century Sponza Palace that was both the customshouse and mint for the Republic. Behind St. Blaise's Church, Gundulic Square memorializes a sixteenth-century poet. It is filled with Slavs in their colorful, native costumes selling produce in the morning and handcrafts later in the day. Dubrovnik's renowned Summer Festival takes place here in front of the cathedral and fifteenth-century Rector's Palace which displays fine furniture, paintings, sculpture, and silver.

To be a true visitor you must walk around the city walls (wear sensible shoes) and get a realistic view of what life was and still is like in this medieval town. You will pass such beautiful fourteenth- to sixteenth-century structures as the Dominican and Franciscan monasteries and cloisters (the former is at Ploce Gate, the latter is at Pile). You will also come upon the ruins of an old castle, built thirteen centuries ago; the simple houses of the townfolk; the Fortress of St. John; and wonderful views of the harbor. The walls end on the harbor, a perfect place to rest, sip a cool drink, and blend into the scenery.

South of Dubrovnik on the Adriatic coast, the Bay of **Boka Kotorska** (Gulf of Kotor) welcomes cruise vessels that call in the only classic fjord in southern

Europe. The town of Kotor lies at the foot of Mt. Lovcen in the province of Montenegro. The walled city has stood since medieval times. In its bay are tiny islands such as the one on which an orthodox church stands—the stalwart row to services.

THE PACIFIC

HAWAII

The glorious islands that make up our fiftieth state were formed from volcanic eruptions on the sea floor thousands of years ago. Inhabiting this landscape of red-hot volcanos, verdant mountains, paradisical valleys with daily rain showers, plus some of the most spectacular, unspoiled beaches in the world, is a potpourri of the earth's people: Polynesians, Orientals, Americans, Europeans, Africans, and the most exquisite combinations of all the above. What a pleasure to visit these islands—this land of "aloha" where everyone is gracious and friendly, the weather so sublime, and the sights so refreshing.

Most visitors to Hawaii arrive, alas, by air and thus miss the fun. Nothing is quite so thrilling as sailing toward Aloha Tower in Honolulu, past Waikiki Beach and Diamond Head (an extinct volcano that was the legendary home of Pele, the fire goddess), to be greeted by the Royal Hawaiian band, complete with floral leis (if you throw your lei into the sea and it returns to shore, islanders say, you will return to this land).

OAHU: Your first view of Hawaii is likely to be **Honolulu,** the state's capital and a thriving metropolis on the island of Oahu. This attractive city, where all types of people seem to live quite happily together, has a two and one-half mile coastline called Waikiki. The sobering tour of nearby Pearl Harbor, with its sunken battleships and memorial to lives lost on a fateful Sunday morning is the area's most popular attraction. If you're planning to spend a few days here, rent a car and enjoy the bustling Chinatown, the East-West Center at the University of Hawaii, Iolani Palace where Hawaii's two final monarchs lived, and Waimea Falls Park and Bay. Here, on the north coast of the island, is where waves up to thirty feet hit the shore to tempt only the most daring surfers.

HAWAII: American Hawaii Cruises, a U.S.-flag cruise line, offers weekly sailings from Pier 10 beneath Honolulu's Aloha Tower to four ports on three other islands. First call is at the Big Island of Hawaii, two hundred miles from Oahu at the southeastern end of the archipelago. This island claims some 22,000 different varieties of orchids as well as five volcanos (Mauna Loa and Kilauea are still active). The island's major seaport and only city is **Hilo,** where attractions curve around the graceful crescent-shaped bay. From Hilo it's a thirty-mile drive to Hawaii Volcano National Park and the gigantic Kilauea Crater. Kilauea is the legendary home of the Hawaiian goddess of fire, Pele. If you're lucky, you can watch her at play as lava fountains spring up from the floor of

Halemaumau Firepit. You can even walk through a long lava tube created by a molten stream centuries ago.

On the leeward side of the Big Island, the Kona coastline of nineteenth-century Hawaiian and missionary history, has the plantations that produce the world-renowned Kona coffee beans. The port of **Kailua-Kona,** a resort area at the edge of 8271-foot Mount Hualalai, has interesting remnants of the Hawaiian monarchy, for King Kamehameha I united the islands from here and ruled until his death in 1819. Have a look at the old stone walls, petroglyphs, the paved "highway" across the lava, and the crumbling platforms of Hawaiian temples upon which the monarch and his five great Kona chiefs walked. If you feel like an expensive taxi ride, two fabulous resort complexes are worth visiting—the thatched-roof huts at Kona Village, and the Mauna Kea, where former presidents play golf and movie stars play tennis.

MAUI: Many visitors agree with Mauians, who say "Maui No Kai Oi" or "Maui is the best ever!" Maui is the second largest island in the group, and **Kahului** is its principal seaport—although Lahaina (twenty-three miles away) is its historic heart and the first capital of the islands. This was the center of the whaling industry (1840–1865) and humpback whales from the Arctic still come to these Hawaiian breeding grounds during the winter months. But Maui is best loved for its magnificent scenery, especially the stunning white-sand beaches on the western shore, the lush Iao Valley that cuts through the island, and Halaekala National Park. It is said that Haleakala's enormous crater, with a circumference of twenty-one miles, could swallow all of Manhattan. It is called the House of the Sun, because Polynesian legend says that the demigod Maui captured the sun and held it captive to give his people more daylight hours.

KAUAI: Just ninety-five miles northwest of Honolulu, Kauai is known as the Garden Island because an abundant rainfall makes for a wide variety of native flora as well as for large taro, pineapple, and sugar plantations. Kauai claims to have the wettest spot on earth—the 5170-foot Mount Waialeale, with 486 inches of rainfall annually. It also has the only navigable rivers in Hawaii. The Wailua River, where the first Polynesians landed in the archipelago some one thousand years ago, has a motor-launch cruise impressive for lush vegetation and unique tropical varietals. Nearby is the beautiful cave called Fern Grotto, its entrance framed by huge fishtail ferns. And a short distance by road is Wailua Falls where, if you survive the steep trail, you can swim in the natural pool surrounded by hala trees.

Lihue is Kauai's commercial center, but large vessels must dock south of it in the deepwater port of **Nawiliwili,** beside freighters loading sugar. More historic is **Waimea** where Captain Cook landed in 1778. No doubt, Cook explored the island's biggest tourist attraction, Waimea Canyon, a miniature version of the Grand Canyon—best seen from Puu Ka Pele mountain and the lookout at Kaana Ridge.

AUSTRALIA AND NEW ZEALAND

AUSTRALIA: If I had to pick a good point to begin a South Pacific quest, it would have to be **Sydney**, capital of New South Wales and the oldest, largest (three million people), and liveliest city in Australia. This bustling metropolis is home to more than twenty percent of the country's population, and its beautiful harbor is both a welcome and familiar sight to every sailor. Imagine yourself coming into this port aboard a luxury cruise vessel, past the sparkling new highrises and the famous Opera House complex whose design is so evocative of billowing sails.

Sydney is often called the Cradle of the Country; it is the oldest civilized settlement in the southwestern Pacific (although one might question the criteria for being civilized). Nonetheless, history says that Captain Cook visited this harbor in 1770 and called it Port Jackson after a secretary of the British Admiralty. Actually Cook was only at the head of the harbor; and Captain Philip founded Sydney Cove on January 26, 1788, the anniversary of which is now celebrated as Australia Day. The best way to see Sydney is to emulate these founders; take a launch around the harbor to appreciate Harbor Bridge, the Opera House, and the skyline of the business district. Sydney has a small town mentality and a rather happy-go-lucky atmosphere—people seem to work only when they must, and the magnificent beaches north and south of the city are the most popular places to relax (the sun shines approximately 342 days of the year).

For a view of the city from fifty stories up, try the revolving restaurant at the top of the Australia Tower (actually on the forty-ninth floor), which takes two hours for a full 360-degree, effortless turn. Wander by Sydney's oldest building (the 1815 Cadman's Cottage near the passenger terminal) and the Argyle Arts Center where local craftsmen sell their wares. The latter is a large convict-built brick building that dates from the 1820s where convicts were once housed in the cellars. A stroll around Circular Quay brings you to the Opera House. Tours are conducted daily (except Saturday), and you can sit on the open-air terrace and watch ships sail by in the harbor. Other sites of interest include the Australian Museum (for a fine collection of aboriginal and South Sea art and the zoo). You are now in the land of kangaroos and koalas, and Taronga Zoo is one of the best in the world. For an even closer look, take a bus to Koala Park in Pennant Hills where you can cavort with koalas, kangaroos, and emus.

Sailing northward along the eastern coastline of Australia, your ship will enter the region of the **Great Barrier Reef**, a stretch of coral some 1242 miles long extending from Gladstone to Cape York. The reefs teem with marine and bird life; they are among the world's most beautiful natural attractions. In this area totaling more than eighty thousand square miles with over six hundred islands live several hundred kinds of coral, at least nine hundred different species of fish, and birds that migrate from as far away as Japan and Siberia. Other birds that are nearing extinction elsewhere survive well here. Cruising the Great Barrier Reef is intriguing, and some of the larger islands have resort facilities, many of which are great for water sports. Your cruise vessel may also call at **Cairns,** the most northerly city in Queensland, a tropical resort that serves as the base for excursions into the outer reef areas.

NEW ZEALAND: A certain amount of rivalry exists between Australia and her neighbor, New Zealand, and not all of it is simply on the surface. For example, New Zealanders are quick to point out that their country was not settled by convicts. Australians counter that they are not fifty years behind the times. Striking differences do exist between these two lands and cultures, which makes it a must to visit both. New Zealand is small compared to the vast continent next door. It consists of North, South, and Stewart islands which, together, about equal the size of the state of Colorado. Called the land of the Long White Cloud by Polynesians some six centuries ago, New Zealand lies halfway between the Equator and the South Pole and has some of the most spectacular scenery in the world. Sheep outnumber people by eighty to one at last count, and there are about five and one-quarter million acres of national parks. The largest and most famous is South Island's Fiordland National Park that comprises some three million acres of bays and fjords, of which Milford Sound is the most popular for local cruises.

New Zealanders refer to themselves as Kiwis (turkeylike birds) and say that they live upon God's Own Country, which was discovered by a Dutchman in 1642 (who named it Nieuw Zeeland). The islands were pretty much ignored until Captain Cook arrived aboard the *Endeavour* in 1769. The first English settled in 1840 near Wellington. These new Westerners had to contend with a large, native population who clung to their own considerable culture. These aborigines, the Maori, still number eight percent of the population and contribute a great deal to life in this land.

Windy **Wellington,** a port city that will remind you of San Francisco, is the capital of New Zealand and named in honor of the Duke of Wellington's victory over the French in the Battle of Waterloo. The city is built upon a series of steep hills at the southwest tip of North Island. To best understand the layout, climb to the summit of Mount Victoria (558 feet) where you can see the entire harbor and, sometimes, the tip of South Island just twenty miles across Cook Strait. A bust of Wellington rests on this summit, as well as a memorial to the American explorer, Rear Admiral Richard Byrd, who used New Zealand as a base for his Antarctic expeditions. Wellington is a pleasant, clean, and very British capital of about 350,000 with some pleasant but not overly exciting sights to see. It is a government town, and one of the largest wooden buildings left in the world houses the government headquarters.

Auckland, often thought of as the largest Polynesian city in the world, is a much more exciting metropolis of about 800,000 people. Situated at the separation of two seas, the Pacific and Tasman, and two harbors, the Waitemata and Manukau, the city has been built on top of seven extinct volcanos—in addition, the volcano called Rangitoto Island sits in Waitemata Harbor. A former Maori fortified village, Mount Eden is a 643-foot cone of an extinct volcano from which you can see the Pacific on one side and the Tasman Sea on the other. One Tree Hill, another former Maori site has one tree and a memorial to the Father of Auckland. The city offers a 300-acre park (where sheep graze close to the streets), a zoo where you can see the indigenous kiwi, a museum of transport and technology, and some lovely harbor cruises. Or you can take an excursion some 126 miles from the city to the Waitomo Caves to visit the Glowworm Grotto, eerie underground caverns illuminated by their many glowworms.

Far more interesting from a cultural point of view is **Rororua,** one of the country's prime attractions. Known as Sulphur City, this area about 150 miles south of Auckland is one of the traditional homes of the Maori people. From here, take an excursion to the thermal baths of Whaka, the Maori Arts and Crafts Institute, and the Ohinemutu Maori Village with its church and meeting house rich in local carvings. You can also attend a Maori concert and a typical Maori feast, which is cooked in the ground.

Sailing northward from Auckland, some cruise vessels call in the **Bay of Islands** for a brief visit to Russell and Waitangi. The latter is known as the birthplace of New Zealand history, for it was here that the Treaty of Waitangi was signed whereby, in 1840, the Maoris accepted the sovereignty of the British Crown in return for ownership of their traditional lands. Russell, across the bay from Waitangi, was the short-lived capital of this new colony; it still retains its Old World charm.

THE SOUTH PACIFIC

Following in the wake of Magellan were adventurers of the western world who discovered the paradisical islands in the South Seas that today are the last bit of exotica extant—Captain Cook, Captain Bligh and the crew of the *Bounty*, Robert Louis Stevenson, Henri Gauguin, and Somerset Maugham. Many who came to the far-flung Polynesian kingdom stayed. For where else is the sky so blessed with sun and blue, are the beaches so shining and sensuous, the waters so clear, and the flowers so brilliant? Among all this perfection live people who are friendly and relatively untouched by the world outside.

FIJI: Fiji is an archipelago of more than three hundred islands, which are the most populous and economically advanced of the South Sea group. A tropical paradise 1100 miles south of the equator, Fiji is the center of communication for the area. An independent sovereign state, it holds a population of over half a million. Its capital is **Suva,** and its prime minister is an Oxford-educated hereditary tribal chief. Suva is a thriving commercial port with duty-free shops, Government House, a museum containing local artifacts dating from two thousand years ago, and the University of the South Pacific. Everything goes here, and the mode of dress ranges from the sulu of the local population to the sari of the large Indian community to the many varieties of European dress. One short excursion from Suva takes you to Orchid Island, where the flowers grow wild beside vanilla, coffee, and tea. You can also see mongooses, iguanas, and monkeys.

Fiji is also known for its kava and fire-walking. The former is a beverage made from the root of a pepper plant; the latter is practiced by both the native-born Fijians and the Indians who were imported by the British for labor and who now make up more than half the population. The fire-walkers are followers of Maha Devi. Visitors may be invited to the ritual now and then, for a small fee, of course!

THE SAMOAS: The Samoas (American and Western) are considered the Heartland of Polynesia, and the same language and customs prevail on both sets of islands. Western Samoa is an independent Polynesian nation whose capital is **Apia**. American Samoa is an unincorporated territory whose native inhabitants are U.S. nationals but not citizens. Its capital is **Pago Pago** (pronounced Pango), made famous by author Somerset Maugham in a short story called "Rain." Anthropologist Margaret Mead also spent some time in American Samoa, which resulted in her book *Coming of Age in Samoa*; and Robert Louis Stevenson lived the last four years of his life in a large villa overlooking the port of Apia. While American Samoa is well subsidized by the U.S. and therefore rather rich, Western Samoa is poor. But the people on both groups of islands are simple and friendly, still ruled by the chieftain system and witchcraft. In fact, traditionalism caused both governments to issue a behavior code for tourists, which discourages revealing dress, requests no disturbances at prayer time, and advises how to eat and sit Samoan style (cruise passengers will probably not be bothered with the latter). Other than a few admonitions, Samoans just want you to enjoy the surrounding grace and beauty (and stay away from fiery kava and the local transvestites).

TONGA: Last of the Polynesian kingdoms and the only set of islands in the South Seas that has never been colonized, Tonga was a British protectorate and is now an independent nation within the Commonwealth. This group of 150 coral and volcanic islands, with a population of under 100,000, is one of the world's smallest nations. The name of its capital, **Nukualofa** (Land of Love), was chosen because Captain Cook supposedly referred to this archipelago as the Friendly Islands. Unfortunately, Tonga is very poor and rather feudal, and its present monarch (King Taufa Ahau Tupou IV) has had to rely on outside sources for funds (the USSR, Libya, and Japan); but he and his nobles hope that tourism will fill the coffers. Interesting sights around Nukualofa include the Royal Palace (which can be viewed over low walls but not visited), the Royal Tombs, and Ha'amonga Trilithon. The Trilithon is a stone calendar, erected about 1200 A.D. that predicts the summer and winter solstices. Not far from the capital in a village called Kolovai, flying foxes hang upside-down all day. They look like fruit and are considered sacred—only members of the royal family may touch them. For more natural phenomena, go see the blowholes where water shoots up sixty feet at high tide and visit the caves dripping with stalactites and stalagmites near the village of Haveluliku.

FRENCH POLYNESIA: French Polynesia consists of some 130 islands, of which **Tahiti** is the most familiar. The island was first sighted by Westerners in

1767 by the captain and crew of the English vessel *Dolphin*. A year later, French explorer de Bougainville claimed it for his country and left his name on the brilliant wild-flowers found everywhere here—the bougainvillea. Captain Cook arrived the next year aboard the *Endeavour* to set up a scientific observation post at Point Venus. Cook is also credited with giving Tahiti its name (from what he understood the natives call it), before he sailed away to discover the Society Islands, Australia, and New Zealand. He returned to Tahiti three more times; a monument to his memory stands at Point Venus. Another well-known captain to visit Tahiti, the infamous Bligh, was master of the HMS *Bounty*. In October, 1788, the captain and his crew began a five-month stay on the island. Just after the vessel sailed again, the mutiny occurred, and Bligh was left in a boat along with eighteen of his men and some provisions. The group survived and landed in Indonesia. (The true story is even better than the movie!)

Papeete, Tahiti, a bustling and noisy capital and port town must rebuff complaints that it has lost its paradisical charm as highrises replace interesting old buildings and powerboats replace outrigger canoes in the lagoon. But do not despair, just get out of town! Pay a visit to Point Venus, tracing the steps of the explorers and their men. Stop by the Museum of Discovery, with wax figures of captains Wallis and Cook and Frenchman de Bougainville as well as Tahitian chieftains and dancers. Some artifacts and engravings at the museum tell of the white man's arrival. **Papeari,** thirty miles southwest of Papeete, offers another museum of interest, the Gauguin Museum, which contains three original paintings as well as some drawings and doodlings made by the artist during his years on the island (it is said that he left some of his talent in one or two of the local population). And one thing is certain—you will eat very well (but not cheaply) on Tahiti.

Just twelve miles across the lagoon is **Moorea,** where nothing tempts you but sun, sand and the beautiful, clear swimming waters protected by an offshore coral reef. Drive around its thirty-seven miles for a look at famous Bali H'ai, the needle-shaped mountain actually called Mou'aroa. Another tourist attraction is La Belvedere, which offers the most magnificent view of Moorea and surrounding bays.

SOCIETY ISLANDS: Bora Bora and **Raiatea** are the best known of the Society Islands, so named by Cook because they look as if they are talking to each other. Bora Bora has one of the most colorful lagoons anywhere, and a pleasant excursion in a glass-bottom boat through the coral gardens can be a highlight to any day. Many small islets, or *motus*, make for pleasant swimming and sunning. This is a truly lovely island and a wonderful place to relax and enjoy nature's bounty. However, many visitors prefer Raiatea because it is less spoiled, and they find the people much more welcoming and friendly. It is believed that the original Maoris who went to New Zealand came from this island and from a river called Faaroa. Raiatea is not as beautiful as the better known Bora Bora, but it is certainly less touristy.

SOUTH AMERICA

South America! That magnificent land mass that bulges east to west below the Equator, and then slims down to a graceful point at Tierra del Fuego, is often misunderstood and rarely visited by its friendly northern neighbors who also call themselves Americans. Hardly a continent to ignore, it covers some twelve percent of the earth's surface, has a population of well over the two hundred million mark, and is growing rapidly. Its 6,866,000 square miles of land are bordered by the Caribbean as well as the Atlantic and Pacific oceans. South America claims the world's largest river, the Amazon (3915 miles); the world's three highest volcanos, Guallatiri (19,882 feet) and Lascar (19,652 feet) in Chile, and Cotopaxi (19,347 feet) in Ecuador; and the world's driest spot in Chile's Atacama Desert where the rainfall is barely discernible.

Culturally, this continent was influenced from the twelfth to sixteenth centuries by the fabulous Inca Empire that embraced some 25 million people and covered a territory that now includes Bolivia, Peru, Ecuador, northern Chile, and part of Argentina. Christianity was imposed upon the native population in the sixteenth century when the Spanish conquistadors and the Portuguese navigators began to colonize their discoveries, building churches and palaces lined with the newly found gold. The largest Spanish- and Portuguese-speaking population resides within the borders of South America; and races blend here unlike on any other continent. Called the ultimate in contrasts, South America boasts too much activity in all directions for any superlative to take hold. Here you can visit Machu Picchu (the mysterious legacy left by the Incas) and Brasilia (the ultramodern capital that symbolizes today's South America) in the same breath—and believe in both!

Traditionally, only one ship line offers regular sailings around South America, the American-flag Delta Lines, which operates 100-passenger cargo liners from the U.S. every two weeks. The ships sail clockwise around the continent. Other lines flirt with the area from time to time because it evokes the "new frontier," an untapped source of excitement for passengers, but none (at this time) boast frequent service. Some of the Costa Line fleet sail during the winter/spring from such ports as Santos, Rio de Janeiro, Buenos Aires, and Montevideo. It's a pity that more lines do not schedule at least one annual sailing around South America (as Royal Viking does so well each fall), because it is definitely the most relaxed and most comfortable way to see these ports. You can always spend a few extra days ashore, if you wish, and fly to meet your ship anon.

ARGENTINA

Buenos Aires, capital and port of Argentina, is considered the Paris of Latin America for its broad boulevards, sophisticated shops, art galleries, theaters, nightclubs, opera, and fine public buildings. It is also the city of Evita, where inflation can run extraordinarily high and where foreign business executives often hire 24-hour bodyguards as a deterrent to local terrorist groups. Despite the political and economic undercurrents, Buenos Aires still prides itself on its more than 150 beautiful parks and the best beef in the world. So, enjoy the romance and excitement of this city from the convenience of your cruise ship. Your city tour should include a visit to the Grecian-style Colon Opera House; Palermo Park on Avenida Libertador General San Martin (named after the national hero); the Plaza de Mayo and the pink Government House (known as Casa Rosada); the cathedral, which is one of the country's oldest buildings and where General José de San Martin is buried; and the Museum of Fine Arts. For a more charming and colorful view of life in Buenos Aires, you can visit La Boca, where local artist Benito Quinquela Martin helped change the scenery from slums to a picturesque fishing port. Don't miss the area museum stocked with his waterfront paintings. Some delightful restaurants are here too, where gourmet food is served with pride.

For a different look at this land of the *gauchos*, you can travel out of the city to a nearby *estancia* (ranch) for some congenial Argentinian hospitality which may include a sumptuous barbecue that would put even Texas to shame! Or you can take a two-hour cruise aboard a 160-passenger catamaran that allows a view of the Paraná delta area and a peek at the Luján, Sariento, Capitán, San Antonio, and Urion rivers.

Argentina stretches south some 2150 miles to Cape Horn at the lower tip of the continent. The bottom portion, called Patagonia (or Land of the People with Long Feet), boasts such fascinating place names as Tierra del Fuego and Ushuaia (the most southern town in the world). North of Cape Horn is the Strait of Magellan (see below).

BRAZIL

If I had to choose just one South American city to see, it would have to be **Rio de Janeiro.** Some say that this city has the most beautiful natural setting in the world. Truly, it competes with Hong Kong and San Francisco, and Rio is definitely a "fun capital," a city where the action rarely ceases from dawn to the following dawn. Brazilians love excitement, music, and the sun—and Rio has plenty of all three. Approximately sixteen beaches are within this beautiful fifteen-mile long bay—the most popular (and chic) is Copacabana, followed closely by Ipanema. If you want to "beach it" like a pro, go early in the day (8 a.m. to about noon) and wear as skimpy a suit as possible (remember, the "string" was invented here!). Leave everything you do not want to lose on the ship. Thievery is a real problem here, and some young natives are adept at stealing everything, whether one is wearing it or carrying it.

First among the city's attractions is the cable car ride to the top of Sugar Loaf, and then in the late afternoon, take a taxi or the cogwheel train up to the Corcovado Christ for a sunset view. The famed statue that symbolizes Rio in many photographs was designed by a French artist. Standing 120 feet high and weighing about seven hundred tons, the statue was inaugurated in 1931 and paid for by contributions from the citizenry of Rio. Impressive from any angle, the statue gives way to an especially thrilling panorama of this seaside city as the sun sets and dusk signals the illumination of lights below.

Rio is a city of great wealth and great poverty (if you look at the *favela* hillside shacks). You may notice considerable French overtones. Its largest park was laid out by a French architect, and the Municipal Theater is an exact copy of the Paris Opera House. The many elegant and expensive shops feature the latest fashion ideas from Paris, either originals or quickly turned-out copies. Many women of Rio spend a lot of time shopping and dressing and adorning themselves. Rio is also the hometown of Hans Stern, the world-renowned jeweler who combines much gold with Brazil's fabulous array of semiprecious stones. On your walking tours, you may come upon some magnificent baroque churches with gold-covered interiors, the worthwhile Museum of Fine Arts, and many exciting restaurants featuring freshly caught seafood and the local specialty *feijoada* (traditionally served at Saturday lunch so you can rest after eating such a large meal). If your time allows for sightseeing outside of Rio, drive to Tijuca Forest, once a private estate, and to Petrópolis where, in 1845, the Emperor Dom Pedro II built a summer palace that is now the Imperial Museum. Displaying items used by the Imperial family during this period, the museum is open daily (except Monday). The Emperor and his wife, Dona Teresa Christina, are buried in the cathedral nearby.

Just as I think Rio is an exciting tourist city, **São Paulo** is not. This metropolis of ten million is the industrial center of Brazil—sprawling, congested, and stacked with new skyscrapers. The "Paulistas" love it, but a friend who lives there laments: "When visitors come, there's no place to take them, little of interest to see!" Well, there *are* lots of new buildings, including the largest snake farm in Latin America as well as Edificio Italia, the highest structure in South America. São Paulo also boasts one of the world's largest parks, Ibirapuera Park, and three art museums. The city's port, Santos, claims the biggest dock area on the continent in addition to its lovely tropical climate and beautiful beaches. Given the choice, I would venture no farther than the beaches.

CHILE AND EASTER ISLAND

Chile has to be the longest, narrowest country on earth, for it measures 2625 miles from north to south and only 312 miles at its widest point. Ships sailing through the Strait of Magellan often stop at its southernmost city, Punta Arenas. More interesting, though, is the seaport of **Puerto Montt,** gateway to Chile's lake district. Beautiful Lake Llanquihue is surrounded by magnificent volcanos, including the eternally snowcapped Osorno. Puerto Montt has a zone of glacial channels that offer fantastic views wherever you look, and is noted for fine seafood.

Valparíso, Chile's main port, is colorful and enchanting. Founded in 1536, the old town and commercial section is built on reclaimed land along a low terrace, while the residential area clings to the slopes of the many hills surrounding the port. In between the two are narrow, twisting streets that delight tourists and photographers. Culturally, "Valpo" (as the locals say) has produced poets and writers, and its historical spots are many. For the best view in town, try the Miradero O'Higgins (named after the first ruler of the republic) located in the Alto del Puerto. Have a look also at the naval school, the Beaux Arts Museum, and the universities located here.

Just ten minutes along the coast from Valpo is the resort town of Viña del Mar, with beautiful beaches, lovely gardens and flowers, friendly atmosphere, and a large casino—one of the main attractions. But **Santiago,** on a 1706-foot plateau with the snowcapped Andes as an impressive backdrop, is the capital and center of Chilean life. Nature has endowed this setting with much favor; the city is built around beautiful hills. The most familiar is Santa Lucia which has two fortresses, a lovely park, and superb view. Santiago also abounds with man-made beauty, exemplified by its many churches (the cathedral dates from 1558) and more than a dozen museums. If you disembark in Valparaiso, look into the many excursions possible in Santiago Province.

One excursion, albeit far out and remote, takes visitors to the mysterious **Easter Island,** the most eastern member of Polynesia, 2300 miles west of the Chilean coastline. Easter Island is considered an open-air museum, not to mention an archaeological question mark overflowing with evidence that a sophisticated and complex culture once flourished on this remote piece of land in the Pacific Ocean. Easter Island draws many eager cruise passengers to its isolated seven by fourteen-mile shores to see the intriguing masonry-lined caves, the gigantic statues, the engineering and astronomical accomplishments, and the petroglyphs, as well as the attractive beaches and the hospitable Polynesian people (who call their island Rapa Nui). If you can't make the journey out this time, console yourself with the excellent introduction to these artifacts in Santiago's National Museum.

COLOMBIA

Cartagena is a popular call on cruises to the lower Caribbean, for it offers a taste of South America—a mere whiff of what lies below the equator. Colombia's 1200-mile coastline borders the Caribbean, and Cartagena de Indias (the proper name) is the most important gateway. Founded in 1533, the city never allows visitors to forget its early history, and ancient fortifications still protect the harbor—reminders of seventeenth- and eighteenth-century attacks by the French and British. The old city is appealing, with Iberian architecture, narrow streets made crooked to deceive pirates, and baroque monuments to Christianity. Don't miss the spectacular view from La Popa, a restored seventeenth-century monastery, and the colorful local market surrounded on three sides by the bay. If you prefer a more relaxed day, taxi to the splendid Hilton Hotel for a fresh tuna, a swim, and some lovely local shops.

ECUADOR

If your cruise vessel happens to call at **Guayaquil** (and only Delta Lines does at this writing), Ecuador's main port and largest city, my advice is to get out as quickly as possible. This metropolis of a million-plus people is a hot, dirty, sprawling flat area sprung from the Guayas River, about thirty-five miles from the Gulf of Guayaquil. That this city grew too big too fast is evident—don't try to mail anything from its *one* post office. It also has only one cemetery, which may be its most interesting feature. As one of my Quito friends said—typifying the rivalry between Ecuador's two major cities—"People are so brave to live in Guayaquil; but they are given nice burials."

The best way to leave Guayaquil and see something of the countryside is by the autoferro to Quito, a twelve-hour journey of just under three hundred miles. The autoferro is a single bus on rails, with a driver *(motorista)*, a conductor *(ayudante)*, reserved seats, a toilet in the back, and no food. It means planning ahead, spending the night in Guayaquil (where hotel rates are exorbitant), packing a lunch, and getting to Durán railroad station by 6 a.m. The train leaves approximately on time (at least by South American custom), and all seats not reserved by tourists are quickly occupied by locals traveling from one small village to another. In many of these villages, the autoferro is the only reliable source of communication, so the *motorista* and his *ayudante* deliver packages, messages, produce, and livestock along the route and pick up letters for the post office in Quito. Often, they will grab pieces of paper and envelopes from outstretched hands without even stopping. It's a unique performance, so try to get seats up front and watch.

If you're still sleepy the first few hours out of Guayaquil, don't worry, for the scenery is flat, tropical, and rather uninteresting. The spectacular views begin around 10 a.m. when the autoferro climbs one thousand feet up the Nariz del Diablo (Devil's Nose), a series of switchbacks and zigzags along a sheer gorge. From here it's a climb of ten thousand feet into the Andean highlands with breathtaking views of the snowcapped Mt. Chimborazo in the distance. If you're exceptionally brave, you are welcome to ride atop the autoferro, along with the chickens and the onions! The first and only rest stop comes around noon at Riobamba, capital of Chimborazo Province, a town known for its healthful, rarefied air at nine thousand feet.

From Riobamba the line climbs to Urbina Pass, the highest point at 11,841 feet, and then skirts the base of Mt. Chimborazo to Ambato, an important Indian market town. From Ambato to Latacunga the line skirts Mt. Cotopaxi, which is not only the highest volcano in the world (19,200 feet) but also one of the most perfect cones. Then you coast into Quito, arriving between 5 and 6 p.m. It's a long but fascinating day, and there's no better way to see the country in between.

Quito, capital of Ecuador, is a charming city spread out on an Andean plain some 9375 feet above sea level. Because of this height, sightseeing should be taken slowly, otherwise you may feel tired and weak. Quito lies on the Equator (the marker is about a twenty-minute ride from town), yet has a splendid climate of sunny days in the seventies and brisk, cool nights. The colonial section of Quito, founded in 1534 by Sebastián de Benalcázar, was declared a site of world cultural heritage by UNESCO in 1979 and is now being carefully restored. Among the many fine projects in progress is the courtyard and cloister of the Monastery of St. Augustine, dating from 1573. The inner city is marked by churches and palaces whose interiors shine with gold culled by the Spaniards from their newly conquered land.

In addition to some fine museums, including the Archaeological Museum in the Banco Central building, Quito boasts some excellent contemporary artists who add greatly to the local cultural attractions. You can visit the villa/workshop/museum of Oswaldo Guayasamin, the doyen of the artistic set, who dabbles in every medium from folkloric crafts to abstract sculpture to jewelry of 18-karat gold and semiprecious stones. Or you can visit the home/studio/shop of Olga Fisch, a delightful Hungarian octogenarian who has spent half her life in Ecuador and who won a Presidential award (of Ecuador) for her contributions to folklore. Olga designs lovely rugs and wall hangings from motifs found in Indian folkcraft and pottery. You can also see Olga's works in the arcade of the Colon Internacional on the edge of El Ejido Park. One of Quito's two deluxe hotels, the Colon is considered the "in" place in town, especially in the evening when the El Conquistador bar and restaurant, casino, and disco are all in full swing. The other deluxe hotel, Quito International, located in a residential area, offers a splendid view of the city and is quieter in the evenings.

GALAPAGOS ISLANDS

If you have never swum with a sea lion nor scratched the neck of a giant tortoise, one might say that you have not yet lived. Certainly, you have not yet visited the Galapagos Islands where these antics are commonplace and part of a thrilling cruise experience. The Galapagos form an archipelago of six minor and thirteen major islands covering some three thousand square miles across the equator in the Pacific Ocean. Discovered by Spaniard Fray Tomas de Berlaya in 1535, they were claimed three hundred years later by Ecuador, whose coastline is approximately six hundred miles due east. Shortly thereafter, Charles Darwin, the 26-year-old British naturalist, visited while board the HMS *Beagle*; the rest is history. Here Darwin observed the relationships of land- sea- and air-life; these observations guided him as he wrote his controversial theories concerning the origin of species. Scientists and naturalists still use the Galapagos archipelago to study behavioral patterns of animals and plants. The Darwin Research Station on Santa Cruz (or Indefatigable) Island is especially well known.

Some visitors refer to these islands as the world's zaniest zoo, for here a multitude of animals coexist in their natural habitat: sea lions, fur seals, land iguanas, sea iguanas, lava lizards, Galapagos tortoises, penguins, cormorants, frigate birds, blue-footed boobies, lightfoot crabs, and at least thirteen different varieties of Darwin's finches as well as many other birds. The wildlife is safe, since the Galapagos were declared a national park in 1959 and tourism is tightly controlled. Cruises of three-, four-, and seven-day spans are available on government-approved Ecuadorian vessels only, and passengers are accompanied on each island by guides trained at the Darwin Research Station. Ecuador's National Park Service, which manages the islands, requests that visitors leave nothing more than footprints and take nothing but photographs. Other more stringent rules advise visitors what cautions should be employed when observing the flora and fauna on the islands, and that introducing certain foreign objects can destroy the delicate ecological balance.

Within this archipelago approximately fifty different inlets and areas are accessible but the guides generally stick to the carefully marked paths on the less treacherous volcanic rock. Most landing parties use small boats, or *pangas*, that resemble lifeboats. Disembarking onto the islands for your twice daily (morning and afternoon) hike is often tricky and not recommended for the timid. Often to get ashore you must either jump feet first into the water (with pant legs rolled up and shoes in hand overhead) or jump onto slippery rocks. When a dock (or semblance thereof) is available, it seems an unaccustomed luxury. As your cruise within the Galapagos progresses, you will pick up a new language in addition to all the names of plant and animal life—"wet landings" and "dry landings." The islands generally visited are Santa Cruz (for the Research Station and giant tortoises), Santiago or James (for flamingos and fur seals), South Plaza (for land iguanas, sea lions, and swallow-tailed gulls), Hood or Española (for blue-footed and masked boobies, albatross from April to December, marine iguanas, and lava lizards), Floreana or Santa Maria (for flamingo), Tower or Genovesa (for frigate birds, red-footed and masked boobies, fur seals, petrels, and lava gulls), Isabela or Albermarle (for flamingos, Galapagos tortoises, flightless cormorants), or Fernandina or Narborough (for flightless cormorants, penguins, and marine iguanas), and Seymour (for frigate birds and blue-footed boobies).

Hood of Española (most of the islands have both an English and Spanish name) seems to be just about everyone's favorite. Here the hike lasts from three to four hours. You may become very fond of the blue-footed boobies, beautiful birds with blue feet and a rather dumb gaze that makes them appear like a dumbbell, or booby. They are charming when caring for their young or squawking that you mustn't get too close to the nest. In the proper seasons, you can also watch an albatross mating dance, rather like a fencing match with beaks, or even observe the new mothers feeding their young with an oil secreted from their body. And Hood has the Blowhole, where the surf pounds upon the lava-lined shore and then blows straight up through a huge natural hole in the porous rock—a big hit with children, who adore the Galapagos. As one brother/sister pair said to me last summer, "This is much better than Disneyland!" The Galapagos Islands are definitely for the young in mind and body. In addition to the strenuous shore excursions with wet landings and extensive hiking in the hot equatorial sun, entertainment is limited to evolution, ecology, and the forces of nature. The islands did not strike me as being particularly beautiful. One might even say that they are ugly—volcanic, spare, and arid. Although it's possible to swim almost every day, I only saw one beautiful beach—Espumilla—where I had a lovely sunbath and an exquisite swim. When friends snorkeling off the end of the beach sighted some baby sharks, I swam closer to the shore; but there was no danger. As the equatorial sun is direct and strong, burning is a hazard, so beachtime should be used sparingly if you are susceptible. I also recommend that you wear a large-brimmed hat at all times to prevent sunstroke.

The best cruise ship afloat in the Galapagos is the *Santa Cruz*, a ninety-passenger vessel built in Spain in 1979 just for these islands. The *Santa Cruz* has a charming captain named Carlos, an excellent crew, and good facilities. Her guides conduct tours in four languages (English, French, German, Spanish), give fine briefings before each shore excursion, and are ready to answer questions. For most tours the passengers are divided into four groups (Albatross, Booby, Cormorant, Dolphin) to alternate embarkation of pangas for shore. The cruises are highly structured, so passengers see the most in the shortest time. Wake-up call is 6:15 a.m., breakfast at 6:45, and departures to the islands begin at 7:30. Return to the ship about 11:30 a.m.; lunch starts at 12:30 while the ship sails to another location; afternoon excursions are scheduled between 3 and 6; and dinner follows at 7, succeeded by a briefing of the next day's activities. Bed down early!

To get the most out of your Galapagos experience, spend a full week cruising the islands and fly to and from your vessel from either Guayaquil or Quito. These charter flights aboard Ecuadorean Navy planes are very safe. The best time of year to travel here is probably June through September, when the weather is coolest, although the seas can be a bit rocky. Since the *Santa Cruz* sails between 2 a.m. and 8 a.m. most mornings, the tossings can be a detriment to sleep. Metropolitan Touring's twelve-passenger *Isabella* is also popular, although rather less elegant. Its size, however, does allow calls at some smaller islands.

PERU

Peru's main port, **Callao,** lies a convenient eight miles from **Lima,** capital of this nation that was once home to the spectacular Inca civilization and the subsequent center of Spanish power in the New World. Lima was laid out along the left bank of the Rimac River in 1535 by Francisco Pizarro, who named it Ciudad de los Reyes (City of Kings). Pizarro, slain six years later by his own men, is famed as the conqueror of the Inca Empire as well as the founder of the Spanish Empire in South America. The city is centered around the Plaza de Armas, just as Pizarro planned, but many of the fine colonial structures were destroyed by an earthquake in 1746 and have been replaced by modern buildings. Still, some survivors of the quake remain, and the churches lined with gold and intricate artwork are relics of a sumptuous seventeenth century. Lima claims the oldest university in the Americas, San Marcos, founded in 1551. Five thousand years of Peruvian culture lies within the Museum of Art, located in the 1868 Exposition Palace. The Museum of Anthropology and Archaeology displays more than eighty thousand objects discovered throughout the country, in addition to a constantly changing exhibition of exciting new finds. Historical monuments mingle comfortably with modern life, for Lima lives very much in the present and its commercial activity is indicative of a prosperous future. Limeños relish a beautiful city in which to enjoy life. If you are offered a sip of Pisco Sour, a local cocktail, expect a kick.

For those interested in pre-Inca ruins, the nearest site is twenty miles south of Lima in the Lurin Valley. Known as **Pachacamac,** the four-square-mile area is believed to have been a sacred city from 600 to about 900 A.D. The Temple to the Creator God here has 400-foot terraces, frescoed walls, and doors inlaid with semiprecious stones. Irrigation and reservoir remains are also evident. Peru's leading tourist attraction and *pièce de résistance*, however, are **Cuzco,** ancient capital of the Incas, and the mysterious fortress of **Machu Picchu** just seventy-seven miles away. Both take some doing to explore (Cuzco is 11,400 feet up in the Andes and Machu Picchu is another thousand feet higher), so plan ahead for full enjoyment of one of the most exciting excursions of your travels.

STRAIT OF MAGELLAN

This passage between the Atlantic and Pacific oceans that many have called the greatest natural wonder on earth is just north of Cape Horn. The spectacular 340-mile Strait slices off a small portion of Argentina and Chile, and its navigation is the highlight of any South American cruise itinerary.

The Strait was discovered in 1520 by the global circumnavigator Ferdinand Magellan as he explored the Rio de la Plata and Patagonia regions of Argentina. Passage through the Strait takes most ships about thirty-six hours, but this depends upon the seas which can be rough. Although much of the sailing takes place at night under the Southern Cross, you will want to be out on deck as much as possible; the majestic views equal or surpass Norway's fjordland and Alaska's Inside Passage. Often during the passage, Chile's Institute of Patagonia enlists passengers to spot whales and record data for a whale population study. A major portion of the world's whale population has been migrating to the peaceful environment of Patagonia and Tierra del Fuego. Passengers participating in the whale-spotting program are given full-color whale charts with illustrations and descriptions of the different species of whales, plus special forms providing space for information on type of whale spotted, time of day, latitude and longitude. When you've navigated from the Atlantic Ocean to the Pacific (or vice versa, as some ships sail), it's time to celebrate. After all, one does not do this sort of thing every day.

VENEZUELA

La Guaira is the bustling gateway to Venezuela's capital **Caracas,** which spreads along a valley some twelve miles from the sea via a winding mountain road. The city, founded in 1567 and christened Santiago de Leon de Caracas (after its patron saint), has lost most of its colonial character and is a major financial and commercial center with a nouveau riche atmosphere. An acquaintance who resides in Caracas said, "The already aggressive population has become even more so, because of all this new oil wealth." Nonetheless, the city is a major attraction in South America, especially noted as the birthplace of the continent's liberator and hero, Simon Bolivar. His family home, now called Casa Natal, is a national monument. Next door is the Bolivarian Museum which details the Conquest, Colonial, and Independence eras of South America. Also on the heroic tour is Cuadra Bolivar, another restored home of the Bolivar family (Simon was born of noble and wealthy parents in 1783) that has a tamarind tree in the garden that is said to have been taken from the Santa Maria hacienda near Cartagena, where Bolivar died an impoverished and forgotten man in 1830.

Visit the Colonial Art Museum, a beautifully restored mansion filled with art and objects from the Spanish-influenced colonial era; the Plaza Bolivar and cathedral (the latter dates from 1595); Quinta Caracas, where local artists can be found at their easels on the colonial-style patio; and the 400-acre University City, a former sugar plantation. Designed by local architect Villanueva in free-flowing concrete, University City gives me a jolting, futuristic feeling. Adjacent to the university, where fifty thousand students fill the campus each day, is the 175-acre Botanical Gardens—where you can refresh your spirit among elegant and abundant orchids and other tropical plants.

WESTERN EUROPE

BRITISH ISLES AND IRELAND

Every harbor in this varied island world called Britain and Ireland is loaded with history, pride, and tradition. Each has an individuality molded by adaptation to landscapes ranging from the isolation of the Shetland Islands to the subtropical Channel Islands to the highlands of Scotland, and the gentle lands of Ireland. Language has often kept these peoples together, while religion, politics, and plain stubbornness have set them apart. All share a fierce love for a rich past, however, and will proudly point out relics of the Stone Age, left-overs from Julius Caesar and four centuries of Roman rule, Saxon influences, and evidence that Saint Patrick really was here. Don't forget to appreciate the Norman towers, the country gardens, heather on the hillsides, and a misty climate that is thought to be good for your skin (since it is obviously not good for anything else). A cruise from the Atlantic Ocean to the Irish and North seas is one of the most worthwhile itineraries available.

The traditional gateway to England for seafarers, at least in modern times, is **Southampton.** Now the country's number one passenger port. Southampton dates from Saxon times. Both a local dwelling and a nearby abbey/monastery date from the twelfth century. One site not to overlook is the memorial tower to the Pilgrim fathers who set out for the New World on August 15, 1620, in a vessel called the *Mayflower*. Southampton is in Hampshire, whose most interesting city is Winchester—a historic center linked to the legends of King Arthur, with a cathedral dating from 1079.

The controversial **Channel Islands** are closer in culture and climate to France than to England. The two largest are Guernsey and Jersey, of which Guernsey is the more popular as a holiday (and tax) haven. The main harbor is St. Peter Port, a small town with not much more than its gentle hills and Victor Hugo's house. The French writer, exiled here from 1855 until 1870, lived in a small house overlooking the harbor, and his mistress lived nearby. He is said to have written some of his masterpieces here, including *Les Miserables*. If you cannot find the house (the way is tricky), you can at least communicate with a fine statue of him in Candie Gardens, which also have a lovely view of the harbor.

The white cliffs of **Dover** have been famous ever since Caesar is said to have sailed past them. Some interesting Roman remains here, discovered in the 1970s, include a fort, bath building, and painted house. The port also has one of England's oldest and best-known castles, built by Henry II in the twelfth century and used again during World War II. In Queen Victoria's time Dover was a seaside resort, but today it is better known as the closest car-ferry port to France.

Hull is the port for one of England's most delightful towns, historic **York,** which is still encircled by thirteenth- and fourteenth-century walls. York was also known as a Roman town and, in fact, became a bishopric during the reign of Emperor Constantine (around A.D. 315). Today York is most famous for its minster, a cathedral surpassed only by rival Canterbury. Called the Church of St. Peter, the cathedral was built on the site of a Roman fortress and is the largest medieval cathedral in England. Also of interest are the York Castle Museum, a collection of everyday objects displayed in a former prison; the Treasurer's House, dating from the eleventh century and built over some Roman ruins; and the Shambles, the best-preserved medieval street in the country.

The port of Leith is the gateway to **Edinburgh,** the cultural capital of Scotland. Edinburgh Castle dominates the city; its origins as a fortress are thought to have begun as early as the Bronze Age. The castle building dates from somewhere in the twelfth century. Edinburgh comprises the medieval "old" section and the Georgian "new" disticts. After paying a visit to the castle, walk along the Royal Mile to the Palace of Holyrood at the opposite end. Along the way you will see St. Giles Cathedral, John Knox's House (the fifteenth-century dwelling of the founder of the Scottish Presbyterian Church), and plenty of seventeenth-century timbered buildings with attractive overhangs. At the end is Holyrood Palace and Abbey, begun in the twelfth century, where Mary Queen of Scots is said to have lived between 1561 and 1567. (You can visit if the present Queen is not in residence.) Most interesting in the "new" towns is 7 Charlotte Square, a restored structure known simply as the Georgian House and headquarters of the National Trust of Scotland. This dwelling, an excellent example of eighteenth-century architecture, contains period furniture and decorative items. Also of great beauty is Hopetown House, the residence of the Marquess of Linlithgow. This huge country home (a mini-palace) is on the Firth of Forth, a pleasant drive away from Edinburgh. Don't leave the city without paying your respects to the monument of Sir Walter Scott, the favorite native son, which is in the East Princes Street gardens. (Some of Scott's characters are part of the statue's design.) You may also find a theatrical performance or an evening of colorful and energetic Scottish dancers while your ship is in port.

Just off the tip of Scotland lie the **Orkney Islands,** sixty-seven small islands that the Romans described in writings from the first century A.D., although megalith monuments date from about 4000 B.C. The islands were settled by Norsemen, who built some exciting monuments that have been restored—St. Magnus Cathedral, Earls Palace, and Bishop's Palace in Kirkwall (which means Church Bay). Kirkwall, capital of the Orkneys, is the focal point of their culture. The cathedral has enjoyed more than eight hundred years of worship, and an annual music festival is held every June here (alas, too early for most cruise calls). You may also visit the Neolithic chambered tomb called Maeshowe (built sometime before 2700 B.C.) and the Neolithic settlement of Skara Brae on the western coast. This complex of seven stone houses connected by covered alleys was inhabited probably between 3100 and 2450 B.C.

Some cruises sail up to the Shetland Islands, but these are a bit distant for most casual tourists. Closer to the mainland of Scotland and a bit warmer are the **Hebrides,** which consist of Inner and Outer groupings. Largest of the Outer Hebirdes is the island of Lewis and Harris, whose only town and port is called Stornoway. Apart from its Neolithic and Norse history, the island's biggest claim to fame is Harris Tweed, which has become Stornoway's best industry. It's not real Harris Tweed unless it's woven on this island. The lovely Island of Skye is a popular port of call in the Inner Hebrides. The scenery is magnificent and so is Dunvegan Castle, seat of the MacLeod clan since 1200. Open to the public, Dunvegan is said to be the oldest inhabited castle in all the British Isles.

Sailing southward between Britain and Ireland, some cruise vessels disembark passengers just below Conway Castle in the Welsh town of **Conway,** then reboard them in **Holyhead** on the island of Holyhead. This all-day tour of northwest Wales features a castle built by Edward I in 1284 and the surrounding town he laid out. The town is considered one of the most perfectly walled examples in Europe. Four miles south of Conway are Bodnant Gardens, seventy acres of plants and trees most suited to the wet climate of Wales. They overlook the lovely mountains of Snowdonia, through which you will drive on your way to Carnarvon Castle. Built by Edward I and finished in 1322, this well-preserved castle dominates the town's skyline. From the castle your tour will proceed across the Menai Strait and the island of Anglesey, to the port of Holyhead.

Eire, or the Republic of Ireland, is a delightful country to call upon, especially by the sea. Many charming port towns offer easy access to the heart of the land. **Waterford** originally settled by the Danes but granted its first charter by King John in 1205—is famous for beautiful hand-blown crystal. At nearby Cashel, the Rock of Cashel is said to have been visited by Saint Patrick in A.D. 450. The thirteenth-century Cathedral of Saint Patrick shares the rock with the Round Tower and Cormac's Chapel. In the southwest section of the country, **Bantry Bay** lies at the head of Glengarriff and the gateway to the great lake district of Killarney. If you do not visit Killarney, you have not seen Ireland! The three lakes, surrounded by lovely scenery and some interesting historical sites, are worth the drive from Bantry Bay. Also within the lake district is an 11,000-acre national park presented to the Irish people in 1932 by its American owners, who also restored the property's famous mansion. Known as Muckross House, it was built in the mid-nineteenth century and received many important figures of the day. The house is now a fascinating museum that details local Irish life of the last century. For another view of Ireland some cruise vessels call in **Galway Bay,** gateway to the strongest of Gaelic traditions. People here are among the most individualistic, and the living can be rugged. The sea breaks against the rocks with such force that the spray is constant. In the bay are the Aran Islands, populated first in prehistoric times and much later by Christian hermits. County Galway boasts a fine monastery, the Ross Errily Franciscan Friary, founded in the mid-fourteenth century, although most of its buildings date from the late-fifteenth century. Your tour may also take in Connemara, known for its beautiful scenery and fine ponies of the same name.

THE NORTH CAPE

From Stavanger to Spitsbergen, along Norway's western boundary, the cruise passenger is treated to an unending spectacle of some of the world's most exciting scenery. This is the land of fjords, and nothing equals it. Mighty fingers of snow and ice reach out as you sail by, while white-capped mountaintops glisten in the brilliant sun. The views are the same whether you choose to cruise along in a luxury vessel or in a cozy mail boat laden with locals. Chances are you won't be tempted much by sleep, for this is also the Land of the Midnight Sun. From mid-May to the end of July, as you sail farther and farther north, the sun stays longer and longer within sight, until you can't get away from it at all. When you reach the island of Mageroy, the most northerly point of Europe, the entire disc of the sun is visible twenty-four hours a day.

If your journey northward to the Cape begins in **Stavanger,** you will find a romantic seaport full of historic wooden buildings and a modern boomtown full of North Sea oil-riggers. The cathedral here was dedicated in 1125, and the marketplace has been the center of life since the ninth century. The oldest wooden house, built in 1704 and known as the Consul Fred Hansen House, is now a shop (so you can visit it). Stavanger is a good starting point for explorations to the southern arms of the fjords, Lyse and Ryfylke, as well as the peaceful and unspoiled fishing port of Haugesund.

A few hours north by sea is **Bergen,** the country's second largest city after Oslo, founded in 1070 by the Viking, King Olav Kyrre. During the Middle Ages, Bergen became Scandinavia's primary port for trading. Many buildings from this period still exist, despite the ravages of nature and man. Don't miss the medieval fortress of Bergenhus, built in 1262, the coronation site of King Haakon. Bergen, a cosmopolitan city proud of its university and music, was the early capital of Norway. Just outside the city is the former summer home of composer Edvard Grieg where he composed many of his famous works. Amid all this culture and history you can find easy excursions to some of the most beautiful natural attractions in all of Norway—Sörfjord, Samnangerfjord, Tokagjel Gorge, and Steindalsfjoss Waterfall. Hardangerfjord and surrounding countryside is a visitor's haven from spring to fall, for the area is rich in flowers, especially orchids. You may also see Granvinfjord, with its crystal-clear lake; the Hamlagrö mountain plateau; and the fertile Bergsdalen Valley. This is the classic "discovery route" and a splendid introduction to the natural resources that makes this country so special.

Eidfjord is the eastern extremity of the larger Hardangerfjord, and the village at the head of this fjord arm has served as a junction of eastern and western Norway for centuries. A shore excursion from the village takes cruise passengers along the banks of the river Eie (known for its abundance of trout and salmon) and into the majestic Mabodal Canyon. The bus ascends through the massive rocks and crags decorated with pines and wild flowers to the observation platform at the top, where you overlook the mighty Voringfoss Waterfall, one of the highest and most impressive in northern Europe—plunging six hundred feet to the floor of the canyon below.

The village of **Flam** lies by the end of Aurlandsfjord, which is at the tip of Sognefjord. Flam is famous for its twelve-mile electric railway that climbs 2845 feet to Myrdal through some dramatic panoramas. The train follows a serpentine path in and out of tunnels, but halts now and again so you can photograph some of the more spectacular waterfalls. From Myrdal station your journey will take you on to **Voss,** on the shores of Lake Vangsvatn. This village, known for its wealth of folklore, has a thirteenth-century Gothic church with a timbered tower, and a wonderful folk museum that traces the early farm life of the area. From Voss it's an easy drive along lovely Oppheimsvann Lake to Stalheim, where you can see Stalheimskleiv gorge and waterfalls. From here, travel down to the village of **Gudvangen** and return to your ship.

Geirangerfjord is one of Norway's most celebrated fjords; and what a sight it is to cruise by, passing the cascading Seven Sisters Falls. Nestled at the head of this waterway is the charming hamlet of the same name, **Geiranger,** one of the most popular resorts in the country. From here you may drive five thousand feet up to Mount Dalsnibba for a panoramic view of glaciers, waterfalls, lakes, and more mountains. You may even see your ship below like a tiny toy at anchor. If you begin your overland trip from **Hellesylt,** you will enjoy the same beautiful panorama of snowcapped peaks, glaciers, and the Geirangerfjord.

Molde's sheltered location and gentle climate warmed by the Gulf Stream make it the center of the country's rose industry, which gives it the nickname of City of Roses. Many of the buildings in Molde are recent because bombs and fire destroyed two-thirds of the town in 1940. Molde Church is the largest postwar church to be built in Norway. Its modern style is a great attraction in this tourist center, and over the baptismal font is a charred reminder of the bombed ruins. On the outskirts of town is the Romsdal Museum, an open-air complex of over two dozen wooden houses dating from the Viking period to the fifteenth century. During the cruise season, local children in regional costumes perform Norwegian folk dances and provide a colorful scene for photographers. Following the performance, take time out for the fabulous view of the eighty-seven peaks of the "Romsdal Alps" and the island-studded fjord below. Both can be seen from the deck of the Vardestua Restaurant some 1300 feet high.

From Molde you can travel overland to **Andalsnes.** Take a ferry across Romsdalsfjord to Vestnes, and then go by bus along Storfjord and Norddalfjord to the town of Valldal, noted for its mountain scenery and its abundant strawberries. From here the drive will take you along one of Norway's serpentine roads among the King, Queen, and Bishop mountains and by the 500-foot Stigfoss Waterfall, then down through the valley to the small village of Andalsnes on the banks of the Rauma River. (Or if you've had enough of fjords and high drives at this point, and it's the first week in August, check in Molde for the International Jazz Festival, fast becoming Europe's best.)

Trondheim is Norway's third largest city (after Oslo and Bergen) and one of its most interesting. It lies on the south bay of the Trondheimfjord, some 425 miles north of Bergen, and was founded by the Viking king Olav Tryggvasson in the tenth century. Trondheim was both the medieval capital of the country until the thirteenth century and the most important religious center in all of Scandinavia. Nidaros Cathedral, dating from the eleventh century, drew many a medieval pilgrim who came to worship at the shrine of the canonized King Olav. Ten Norwegian kings are buried here, and this was also the coronation site of King Haakon VII in 1906. Other attractions in Trondheim are the folk museum complex, with old timbered houses and a gold-colored stave church, and the Museum of Musical History at Rinvge Manor. This mansion, birthplace of a Norwegian sea hero, is often considered the highlight of the Trondheim tour, for it contains a collection of approximately two thousand musical instruments from all over the world. During the summer season daily tours in English are offered in the morning. Your guide will play a selection of the instruments, demonstrating their position in musical history.

If you're looking for the Midnight Sun, you'll find it in **Narvik**, a town situated 250 miles north of the Arctic Circle on the Ofotfjord. This industrial town that dates from 1903 has continuous sunshine from late May to mid-July, although August is known for having its share of mysterious lighting. Tours from Narvik may include a train trip to Riksgrensen in Lapland or to Gratangen for the thrilling panorama of fjords and mountains. **Tromso** is another town about 250 miles north of the Arctic Circle. Tromso, a boomtown, is very expensive now because of the North Sea oil projects. Skip it if you like, unless you're interested in visiting the world's northernmost university, which dates from 1972.

Hammerfest, the most northerly major town in the world, was founded in 1787 and then totally destroyed during World War II. Now very much rebuilt, it is a lively, ice-free port where fish and furs are loaded onto ships. Since it is also a shopping center for Lapps, you may see reindeer in town, so keep your cameras in focus. Here, too, the sun does not set from mid-May to the end of July; to offset this feat, it doesn't rise from late November to late January. The world's northernmost village and gateway to the North Cape is **Honningsvag,** on the southern side of Mageroy Island. Also situated on this island is **Skarsvag,** considered the most northerly point in Europe. Skarsvag offers a wonderful view of the Arctic Ocean from its 1000-foot elevation.

NORTHERN CAPITALS

Hamburg is one of those cities that belongs to the "Venice of the . . ." society. In this instance it is called the Venice of the North because of its many canals and its traditional coexistence with the sea. With nearly two million inhabitants, Hamburg is Germany's largest port, welcoming ships and sailors from every flag imaginable. It is the perfect starting point for the itinerary known as the Northern Capitals. A harbor cruise is a sensible way to begin a tour of this city, followed by a drive through the St. Pauli district to City Hall, the twelfth-century St. Petri church and the Altmannbrucke commercial center. Continue around the shores of Aussenalster, a lovely sheet of water in the center of the city, to millionaires' row and then to Poseldorf for some shopping and browsing.

The capital of tiny Denmark, **Copenhagen,** is as friendly and lively a city as one can find in the Baltic area. Here beautiful palaces and parks, great museums and shops share top billing with the world's greatest amusement park, Tivoli. Copenhagen, a charming port touched by the magical spirit of Hans Christian Andersen, is home to the Little Mermaid who sits in the harbor, a patient subject for your photographs. But where should you go first? There is so much to see—the dazzling display of the Danish crown jewels at Rosenborg Castle; Amalienborg Palace, where Queen Margrethe II lives; Gefion Fountain, named in honor of the Danish goddess who, in a single night, ploughed the island of Sealand out of Sweden, and the many fine art museums. But the best views come from the countryside of North Sealand and tours of the castles—Frederiksborg, built by King Christian IV in 1620 and now the National Historic Museum; Fredensborg Palace built in 1723 and still a summer residence of the royal family; and Kronborg in Elsinore. Renowned as the dramatic setting for Shakespeare's *Hamlet,* Kronborg was built by Frederick II between 1574 and 1585. Or, if you prefer more rural atmosphere, visit the open-air museum of Frilandsmuseet covering some forty acres. Here the Danish farmlife of yesteryear flourishes, with windmills, country houses, and period pieces and utensils. A drive back to Copenhagen will take you through even more countryside to Frederiksdal, one of the most beautiful areas in all Denmark. After dark, Tivoli, offers diversions for all ages—a pantomime theater, a concert hall, ballet, clowns, acrobats, and aerialists—in a fantasy world of merry-go-rounds, swans and boats on the tiny lake, games of chance, a ferris wheel, and plenty of places to dine. If this isn't enough, visit a brewery. It's free and you can drink all you want at either the Carlsberg or Tuborg breweries, where guided tours are available two or three times each weekday.

Oslo, at the mouth of the island-studded 60-mile-long Oslofjord, is Norway's capital and largest city. It is, however, neither its most interesting nor cosmopolitan city (those honors go to Bergen). Oslo, founded by a Viking king in the eleventh century, was made capital of the country around 1300 by King Haakon V. In square miles, Oslo is one of the largest cities in the world but has a population of less than half a million, who live amid great natural beauty. In fact, many of the city's great attractions are out-of-doors, including the 75-acre Frogner Park where the city financed 175 sculptures by Norway's A. Gustav Vigeland—a monumental project that took some thirty years to finish. The 35-acre grounds of the Norwegian Folk Museum on Bygdoy Peninsula exhibit other fine examples of local craft. The museum comprises 170 old buildings transported from all over the country, representing all facets of Norwegian life; it even includes the reassembled study of playwright Henrik Ibsen just as it was left at his death in 1906.

Also on the Bygdoy Peninsula are three of the famous Viking longboats, eighth- and ninth-century relics excavated at Gokstad and Oseberg, and the balsa-wood raft, *Kon Tiki*, that in 1947 Norwegian scientist Thor Heyerdahl and five colleagues sailed from Peru to Polynesia. The raft is housed in its own museum along with exhibits pertaining to Heyerdahl's projects, including his visit to Easter Island. You can also drive out to see Holmenkollen ski jump, one of the best known in the world and the highlight of the annual winter ski festival. A ski museum at the base of the jump houses many interesting exhibits. Your drive should also take you past City Hall (noted for both its modernity and ugliness) and Akershus Castle, built in 1300 and used as a fortress and royal residence for several centuries. Last but not least, save a little time for the Edvard Munch Museum, with its vast collection of works by Scandinavia's leading painter who is most known for his melancholy and morbid depictions.

Stockholm, capital of Sweden, is a city built on fourteen islands. The water in every direction provides a good excuse to tour this beautiful archipelago by launch. After traveling the canals and waterways, under bridges of every shape and size and past all the important and historic buildings you may wish to visit some of the more imposing structures—such as the eighteenth-century baroque-style Royal Palace or the thirteenth-century Riddarholm Church, the second oldest in Stockholm. The royal flagship *Wasa* is a Scandinavian vessel of renown that also has its own museum. The *Wasa* was raised from Stockholm harbor just twenty years ago, after she lay at the bottom for three centuries from the ignominious sinking on her maiden voyage in 1628. This capital also has a 75-acre open-air museum, known as Skansen, where 150 eighteenth- and nineteenth-century dwellings have been reassembled. The museum offers continual exhibits of the country's crafts through many historical stages. For more modern artworks, visit the sculpture garden-by-the-sea of Carl Milles, Sweden's foremost sculptor and friend of Rodin (who is also represented here). The garden, on the residential island of Lidingö, provides a lovely setting as giant ships pass by on their way out to the Baltic.

On another island, in Lake Mälaren, sits the eighteenth-century palace and theater known as Drottningholm. The palace is still visited by the royal family, and the theater still uses the original stage machinery and scenery. The delightful performances here complement the entire compound, one of the most charming attractions in all of Scandinavia. Before you return to your cruise vessel, make a walking tour of Gamla Sta'n or Old Town, which has wonderful antique shops, narrow cobblestone streets, and a historic marketplace.

Although the island of **Gotland** is not a capital, it is a popular call on Baltic cruises, for the walled city of **Visby** is considered one of the medieval jewels of Europe. The short-lived seat of the Hanseatic merchants from the late twelfth to early thirteenth century, the commercial Queen of the Baltic was sacked in 1316 by the Danes, and the island drifted into obscurity—not emerging as a tourist center until recent times, when its medieval ruins became known as the best in northern Europe. A tour will take you to the old Hanseatic harbor, past the town's oldest building (Kruttornet), and by two of the more famous towers in the old walls—Maiden's Tower, where a peasant girl was buried alive for helping a Danish nobleman, and Powder Tower, the most ancient fortification in Visby. Then you will drive by Gallow Hill, a medieval hanging station used until the mid-nineteenth century, and explore the ruins of the thirteenth-century monastery of St. Nicholas where operas are staged for the Visby summer festival. Finally, a fine historical museum and the Botanical Gardens give Visby its title, the City of Ruins and Roses.

Helsinki, the white city of the North, is one of Europe's most underrated capitals. Although founded in 1550 by King Gustavus Vasa of Sweden, most of the city belongs to the twentieth century and is a tribute to modern Finnish design. Helsinki, built on a peninsula, is skirted by islands that dot the harbor. The marketplace at the water's edge, the most active and colorful square in town (especially in the early morning), is a good place to begin your tour. From here, you can take a ferry to Suomenlinna Fortress, known as the Gibraltar of the North, which has guarded the entrance to the harbor for two centuries. Another island to visit, Seurasaari, has its own open-air museum, which offers a view of Old Finland with seventeenth- and eighteenth-century structures, including an original sauna. In the summer, folk dancing delights many museum visitors.

Pride of the Finns, though is **Tapiola**, a self-contained city-within-a-city, a look at the world of tomorrow. Perfectly planned, this striking area six miles west of the capital has parks, fountains, well-designed homes and apartment buildings, playgrounds, shopping centers, schools, and churches. If you're hungry, you can eat at a self-service restaurant that sits atop a large office building. Another area worth visiting is **Hvitträsk,** a center for Finnish art and handcraft. Built in 1902 by three of Finland's noted architects—Saarinen, Lindgren, and Gesellius—for their residences and studios, the site features buildings made of natural stone and logs, which blend into the surrounding forest, lake, and majestic cliffs. Saarinen's house is open to the public, and the grounds outside contain many sculptures by all three artists. For a look at other artisans, pay a visit to the Finnish Design Center, which has a permanent exhibition and shop, and the Arabia ceramic house, which exports both utility pieces and artworks. A first-rate restaurant, sauna, beach, and natural park enhance the experience.

Many cruise vessels also call at the western seaport of **Turku,** just 102 miles from Helsinki. Turku is Finland's oldest city and considered the cradle of Finnish civilization, because it was an ecclesiastical center in the thirteenth century and the capital until the early nineteenth century. Among the sights here are Turku Cathedral, dating from the thirteenth century and one of the most important medieval monuments in the country; the equally old castle at the mouth of the Aura River, now the Turku Museum; and the open-air handcraft museum, perfectly preserved from the eighteenth century, in the only part of the city that survived the great fire of 1827. The houses of this compound— original, not reassembled, dwellings—are now the homes of craftsmen.

Leningrad, the second largest city in the Soviet Union, was the capital of the Russian empire until 1918. It was founded in 1703 by Peter the Great, who named St. Petersburg after himself. In 1914 it became Petrograd. Ten years later, the name changed again to honor Lenin after his death. By any name, this city is also called the Venice of the North for its many canals that connect some one hundred islands. The city boasts over one thousand architectural and historical monuments and houses great cultural riches in more than fifty museums and two thousand libraries. Leningrad was the city of the Czars, great art collectors who also admired fine buildings and churches. The finest of all the buildings, the baroque Winter Palace now known as the Hermitage Museum, has more than one thousand rooms and reception halls, almost two thousand windows, and over one hundred staircases. Many of the rooms have been decorated in semiprecious stones—malachite, jasper, and agate. A ton of malachite was used for just the columns in what is known as Malachite Hall. Amid all this splendor are more than eight thousand paintings, a collection of artistic treasures almost unparalleled anywhere in the world. If you pay attention to nothing else in Leningrad, a visit to the Hermitage will make your trip worthwhile. Here are two dozen Rembrandts, a whole room of Rubens, numerous works representing five centuries of French painters, and masterpieces from the ancient world. Even the Impressionists are well represented (if you can make it to the top floor), with early works by Gauguin and Van Gogh that few people have ever seen. Truly one of the world's greatest museums.

Driving through Leningrad will acquaint you with the Admiralty built by Peter the Great, St. Isaac's Cathedral and Square, the Blue Bridge (which was once a serf market), St. Nicholas' Cathedral, and the Kirov State Theater. But a more popular excursion takes you fourteen miles south to the town of Push-kin (named in honor of the poet), where Catherine the Great built a palace and fine parks. Go four miles more and arrive at Pavlovsk, the site of another eighteenth-century palace and English-style park. Visits are allowed into the park only, which has interesting sculptures, artificial ponds, and wet jokes (if you happen to step under the wrong arbor, you will be drenched).

PORTUGAL

Portugal's capital on the Tagus River, **Lisbon,** is a low-key city that may seem drab in comparison to other European capitals, but visitors soon appreci-ate its special character. Legend says that Ulysses founded the town, but the credit to the Phoenicians in 1200 B.C. is more believable. Historically, Lisbon has gained many honors, for the great discoverers Vasco da Gama (the Indies) and Pedro Alvares Cabral (Brazil) set out from here in the late fifteenth century when Portugal reigned as a major maritime power.

Medieval Lisbon, the city's most fascinating section, begins with St. George's Castle overlooking the sea, then winds down into the Santa Cruz quarter of narrow streets and old houses. Between the Tagus and the castle is the Alfama, or former Moorish section, with stair-streets, tiny squares, and blind alleys lined with sixteenth- to eighteenth-century houses. Walking is the best way—indeed, the only way—to get around. From the castle, you can walk all the way down to the Praca do Comercio (Commerce Square) on the water. Here, where the Stock Exchange has replaced the former Royal Palace, the Portuguese king would walk down to greet every returning ship to collect incoming gold and riches.

Manueline Lisbon is up the Tagus in a suburb called Belem. A sixteenth-century monastery lies along the harbor here, its cloister a masterpiece of rich sculptured stone. On the riverside is a Monument to the Discoveries, erected in 1960 to honor the 500th anniversary of Prince Henry the Navigator. Nearby are the museums of popular art, ancient art, and the Coach Museum. The latter is installed in the former riding school of Belem Palace and holds some of the most ornate royal coaches from the sixteenth to nineteenth centuries. Most of them appear well-used, while others served merely as small gifts of apprecia-tion between monarchs. All look extremely uncomfortable! Another museum worthy of a visit, the Gulbenkian, shows the extensive collection of an Arme-nian who willed his entire cache of artworks to his adopted country, Portugal, at his death in 1955.

Europe's longest suspension bridge spans the Tagus River. Originally called the Salazar Bridge after Portugal's hardy dictator, its name was changed after the 1974 revolution to the April 25th Bridge. Across the bridge are some inter-esting towns, especially those on the Atlantic coast—the quaint fishing village of Sesimbra; Setúbal, with its sardine boats and twelfth-century castle; and Arrabida, where the scenery from mountain to sea is spectacular. Estoril, that fashionable gambling resort where deposed monarchs live out their twilight days in splendor, is only about fifteen miles south of Lisbon, and a few minutes more is charming Cascais, where former royalty also resides. But the most beautiful destination for a day trip from the capital is Sintra, nestled high in the Sierra de Sintra range; Lord Byron once called it a "glorious Eden."

At the end of the day in Lisbon, you must do what the Portuguese do—have a glass of red wine and listen to a little fado, haunting songs of fate sung to the accompaniment of romantic guitars. Early tradition held that only women sang these sad songs, but recently males have also sung them.

The 35-mile long island of **Madeira,** 560 miles southwest of Lisbon and on the same latitude as Casablanca, is often called the Pearl of the Atlantic because of its mild climate year-round, its lush subtropical vegetation, and its vast panoramas of volcanic landscapes. The Portuguese refer to Madeira proudly as the "floating garden" because the floral splendor includes bougainvillea, jacaranda trees, hibiscus, frangipani, poinsettia, Bird of Paradise, and all varieties of orchids. Madeira arose from the sea floor as the result of a volcanic eruption in the Tertiary Period. Thus, its rocky shoreline abuts right into high cliffs, and the only beaches are on the small, nearby island of Porto Santo. Inland, Madeira's mountains are so steep that farmers must not only dig out narrow terraces on which to plant, but also build *palheiros*—small thatched sheds—in which to keep their cows (lest the cows miss their step and fall over the cliff).

Funchal, capital and chief port of Madeira, was named for the sweet smell of fennel. When Portuguese explorer Joao Gonclaves Zarco "discovered" the island in 1419, called it Madeira (wooded isle), and claimed it in the name of Prince Henry the Navigator, he also named Funchal. The English relate a more romantic tale: they say the island was first found by the English adventurer Robert Machim, who was shipwrecked here (with his mistress) in 1346. Perhaps because of this story, but more likely because of the comfortably mild climate, the English love Madeira.

Cruise ships dock in Funchal, which lies at the end of a beautiful bay. Most of the city's 98,000-plus inhabitants live in charming white houses perched on terraces in the surrounding hills. At night the twinkling city lights give off a fantasy-land feeling. And if you're an early riser, just a few steps from the cruise ship pier you can find the small flower market where local women in traditional costumes are as colorful as their merchandise. If you wish to "have some Madeira, m'dear," this is the right place. The Madeira Wine Association on Avenida Arriaga has a tasting lodge (as do all the local firms) where you can sample as much as you like, from the sweetest Malmsey (Duke of Clarence is the most popular brand) to the driest Sercial. Whatever you wish to purchase will probably be packed in a locally made wicker basket. Wicker and exquisite embroidery are two of the island's best known cottage industries; both products are worth the entire visit.

Your sightseeing excursions should include a visit to Quinta das Cruzes, a villa (built by Zarco) that is now a museum surrounded by a beautiful orchid garden; Camara de Lobos, the fishing village Sir Winston Churchill painted on his visits to the island; further along the coast, Cabo Girao, the world's second highest sea cliff (at 1900 feet), with a proper railing so you can look without falling off. And if you like a thrill now and then, take a tobogan ride down to Funchal from Monte, four miles away. Two straw-hatted professionals who wear rubber-tire shoes will guide your toboggan, a wicker basket on wooden runners, as you slip and slide down the smooth pebble path. Each toboggan holds two people, so you can cling together during the fast turns.

The area around Funchal has many good restaurants and smart hotels. My favorite is the famous, old Reid's Hotel (again, where Churchill loved to stay) where the terrace view of the harbor is lovely. Reid's also has a wonderful garden, and if you're confused about the name of a particular plant or flower, the manager might just get out his book and look it up for you. Closer to town is the ultra-modern Casino Park Hotel, designed by the renowned Brazilian architect Oscar Niemeyer, in a complex that includes the Casino of Madeira (so if you like roulette, blackjack, French bank, and slot machines, drop in between 4 p.m. and 3 a.m.). If you hunger for real country food, take a taxi up into the hills where the restaurant A Seta serves hot, crusty bread, *espetada* (beef on a spit); pitchers of local wine; and Madeira honey cake for a bargain price.

SPAIN

As your cruise ship sails into the harbor of **Barcelona,** your senses will tell you that full enjoyment lies ahead. For Spain's second largest city and principal port has character, beauty, and charm. The people who live here call themselves Catalans and speak their own language, which they insist is not a combination of French and Castilian Spanish. But they, and the city in which they live, are certainly influenced by the proximity to neighboring France as well as to the varied cultures that have come through this port since the third century B.C.

Barcelona has wide boulevards lined with sidewalk cafes and elegant shops; flowers everywhere and palm trees (which tell you about the climate); a gothic quarter with narrow streets and thirteenth- to fifteenth-century buildings (visit the Palacio Real where Columbus paid a visit following his return from the New World); Montjuich Park and Tibidabo Mountain; the Ramblas section; and the historic port section with a statue of Columbus, a replica of the *Santa Maria*, and an interesting Maritime Museum. While touring the city, every visitor must stop to pay respects to two favorite sons: Pablo Picasso and Antonio Gaudi, the latter a surrealist architect who died in 1926 (run over by a tram). Gaudi left behind some crazy concoctions, the most famous of which is the church of the Sagrada Familia (Holy Family), begun in 1884 and still unfinished because he left no plans (and so far, no one has been able to interpret his motives). Other examples of "gaudy" works are Guell Lodge and Park and some luxury flats on the Paseo de Gracia. By contrast, the Picasso Museum will seem like an old friend. Located in the fourteenth-century Aguilar Palace at 15 Calle Montcada (the street is lined with medieval Catalan architecture, so be sure to walk the entire length), the museum contains some 2500 works donated by Picasso. The artist lived here as a young man, in Bohemian style down near the port. Some of his wonderful early sketches of Barcelona show us what the city was like around the turn of the century.

Malaga is the undisputed capital of the Costa del Sol, Spain's sun coast and a year-round tourist spot. It is also the most important town on the Mediterranean side of Andalusia. The Moors, who occupied this part of Spain for eight centuries, gave it the name Andalusia, and the Arab influences are still very much felt in Malagan houses, folklore, and colorful native costumes. Some say the best flamenco, the soul of Andalusia, can be seen here—a good complement to gazpacho, the region's gastronomic specialty. Malaga, prosperous and lively, is protected by mountains in the north and the sea to the south. Not far from the harbor and the lovely, park-lined Paseo de Cintura del Puerto are two fortresses that made Malaga one of the major strongholds of Andalusia. The higher one, Gibralfaro, commands a spectacular view from its fourteenth-century ramparts. The lower, Alcazaba, was built over a Roman amphitheater and has lovely Moorish gardens, art, and atmosphere. Walk back to the seafront via the sixteenth-century cathedral and the fascinating shops along Larios Street. Stop at a local cafe for a glass of wine, some crusty bread, and a bowl of iced gazpacho.

Only one small town in Sicily gets as much sunshine as Malaga, I've heard, so when you're ready for the beach, take a tour to Torremolinos where the white, sandy beach is five miles long. It's no longer a quaint little village supported by the sugar cane industry. Now it's row upon row of modern, high-rise hotels and apartment houses. When you've had enough of this impersonal air, you can always return to the Old World atmosphere of Malaga, the Arab-Spanish-gypsy town that gave birth to Pablo Picasso at 15 Plaza de la Merced.

The port of **Vigo,** on Spain's Atlantic coast just north of the Portuguese border, has been an important natural harbor since Roman times. Primarily, it is the point of entry for **Santiago de Compostela,** Spain's holiest of cities. Since the Middle Ages, pilgrims from all over the world have made their way to Santiago where, it is believed, the remains of the Apostle St. James the Greater were buried. The relics were discovered early in the ninth century, and by the eleventh century a pilgrimage to St. James' shrine in Santiago de Compostela ranked equally with a visit to Jerusalem or Rome. The Apostle became Patron Saint of Spain during the Reconquest. For the half to two million pilgrims a year, a Pilgrim Guide existed, written in the late twelfth century by Cluny monks. It described the best routes to take and what sights to enjoy along the way (this may have been the first guidebook ever written).

Santiago de Compostela has changed little since medieval times. One can still wander the winding, stone streets that lead to the plaza and cathedral, just as devoted Christians have done for centuries. The present cathedral, believed to be on the very site where the Apostle's tomb was found, dates from the eleventh through thirteenth centuries. Its huge edifice is always welcoming the faithful and curious who come to pay their respects to the thirteenth-century statue of St. James and to his relics. If you happen to visit the cathedral on a holy day, as I did a few years ago, you may be able to observe the ceremony of the incense, when a huge, smoking pot is thrown from side to side in front of the altar. I was lucky; in the crowd that day was Spain's handsome King Carlos who had come to pay his respects, and he personally greeted everyone within sight, including a friend and me! In 1982 Santiago de Compostela celebrated a Holy Year Jubilee, a year-long fête that occurs only when July 25, the Day of St. James the Apostle, falls on a Sunday. The jubilee officially begins on December 31 of the previous year, and the Holy Doors on the east face of the cathedral are opened at this time. Like the Holy Doors at St. Peter's Basilica, these doors are allowed to be opened only during a jubilee year.

A tour to Santiago is not complete without a visit to the Hotel de Los Reyes Catolicos on the cathedral square. This remarkable *parador* (government-run inn) was founded by Ferdinand of Aragon and Isabella of Castile in the late fifteenth century as a pilgrim inn and hospital. Most of the original carved columns and grillwork are still intact; enjoy them as you walk through the four beautiful patios, large dining room, and lovely, antique-filled guestrooms. On the same Plaza de Espana (the cathedral square) are the twelfth-century Bishop's Palace, the eighteenth-century Raxoy Palace (now the Town Hall), and the seventeenth-century San Jeronimo College. Take your camera. All are worth several thousand words!

BALEARIC ISLANDS: One of Spain's forty-nine provinces is the Balearic archipelago, which consists of Mallorca, Minorca, Ibiza, and the small Formentera. Capital of the group and most popular tourist center is **Palma de Mallorca,** a port city spread around the back of a beautiful, wide bay. Palma has a mild climate year-round, lovely old mansions of the fifteenth and sixteenth centuries, and an interesting harbor. It claims to receive more visitors (by air and sea) than any other place in Spain. The island has been a part of Spain for most of its discovered life (with the exception of three hundred years during Moorish occupation) and boasts its own school of painting (from the fourteenth to fifteenth centuries) and at least one well-known native son, Junipero Sera (1713–1784). Born in Petra (a town near the center of the island), Sera became a Franciscan, went to the New World to work with Indians in Mexico and California, and founded several missions and the cities of San Diego, Monterey, and San Francisco. Not bad work for a local boy.

Along the waterfront you can see the cathedral, which took from the thirteenth century to the year 1601 to complete; the Bishops' Palace; Almudaina, former residence of the Moorish kings; and Lonja, a fifteenth-century commercial exchange. But save some energy for a stroll through the Old Quarter with its many beautiful old mansions, public buildings, and Moorish Baths left behind from the days of Palma's caliphate. A long climb westward (about two miles) brings you to the site of the fourteenth-century Bellver Castle, summer residence of Mallorcan kings and later a prison. If you still have the energy to climb the winding steps of the tower, you will enjoy a panoramic view of Palma Bay. And if you are in the mood for shopping, you will find good quality leatherwork here. For a view of the countryside take a tour to Vall-demosa, an old Mallorcan village and Carthusian monastery that harbored two famous visitors during the winter of 1838—composer Frederick Chopin and French author George Sand.

The second largest of the Balearic Islands is the cavernous **Minorca** where the remains of a Bronze Age people have been found in the form of talayots. These great stones, used to cover funeral chambers, perhaps also formed the bases of primitive houses. The thirty-mile island is dotted with them. Other interesting finds include Stone Age monuments called navetas, or upturned boats, that may have been tombs. Check the Archaeological Museum at Conquista Square in Mahon, the capital, for more complete information on and examples of the findings. Minorca is quite a different island from Mallorca, and suffers from its second-best rating. Tourism is less developed here, and the atmosphere is more peaceful and subdued. A certain eighteenth-century British influence flourishes, attributable to a British occupation of the island. Admiral (Lord) Nelson is said to have visited briefly and even put the finishing touches on a book here during the fall of 1799. And the fishing is reputed to be superb around Minorca. The locals even claim to have invented mayonnaise to serve with their catch of the day.

Tourism is growing on **Ibiza,** the third largest of the Balearic Islands, often called the White Island because of its many whitewashed, limestone buildings with terraced roofs designed to catch rainwater. This mountainous island, with a population of only 35,000 on its twenty-five miles, has been important to Mediterranean trade routes since the tenth century B.C. when the Phoenicians stopped here en route from Spain to Africa. They left behind a splendid grave-yard, a necropolis, overlooking the main harbor, with some two thousand tombs. La Ciudad—the city—is the primary port town, with about twenty thousand inhabitants, busy streets lined with shops, and open-air cafes along the waterfront. In the fishermen's quarter the cubic, whitewashed houses are built one atop the other, leaving space for nothing in between. The pine forests, which fringe the island, explain why the Greeks called this place Pitiousa, or Pine Island. But there are other trees: almonds, olives, figs, and palms. Just three and one-half nautical miles south of Ibiza lies the Wheat Island, the eight-mile long Formentera. Fourth in size of the Balearics, Formentera has little to attract tourists, but your cruise vessel will probably sail by closely enough so you can see the small harbor of Cala Sabina.

CANARY ISLANDS: Another island-province of Spain, the Canaries lie just 72 miles northwest of Africa and 650 miles south of Europe. The islands comprise Furteventura, Grand Canary, Lanzarote, and Tenerife. Cruises often call at the popular ports of Las Palmas and Santa Cruz de Tenerife. Las Palmas, capital and main seaport of Grand Canary, is a scallop-shaped island with steep cliffs on the north and south coasts. Founded in a plam grove in 1478, Las Palmas was visited by Christopher Columbus at the commencement of each of his discovery voyages to the New World. Where he actually stayed in 1502 became the palace of the island's first governors and is now a museum of fine arts with a collection of fifteenth-century maps, charts, and navigational equipment used at the time of these voyages.

Like the whole chain, volcanic **Grand Canary** offers some spectacular views from the mountainous areas of black sand beaches over lush fruit trees and tropical flowers. Wonderful excursions begin at Las Palmas, the most interesting of which is to Cruz de Tejeda where, at 4750 feet, you can see a petrified forest. Actually, it's the village of Tejada that stands in a huge volcanic basin. If you climb even higher, to 6496 feet, you can see the island's meterological station as well as a panoramic view of the countryside, the coastline, and the sea.

Tenerife, largest of the Canary Islands, possesses the highest summit on Spanish territory, the snowcapped volcanic peak named Mount Teide, on the Las Canadas plateau. For one of the most breathtaking views in the world, visit the cone. You can do so from Santa Cruz, the island's capital and main port. The drive from Santa Cruz passes through La Laguna, the oldest town on Tenerife (founded in 1496) and its first capital. Travel on to the floral paradise of Orotava where the ascent begins. The road up to Teide is twenty-four miles long, past the Aguamansa woods, by the Dornajito and Monteverde springs, and then to the Altavista Resthouse where the funicular will whisk you up to the cone. From here, it's a 45-minute climb to the edge, where at 11,664 feet, you'll get one of the thrills of your lifetime. If you prefer to stay in town, Santa Cruz, a free port since 1852, has some charming old houses with wooden balconies that are typical of the island.

8. / GOING ASHORE

On a small tender loaded with sleepy passengers last summer, I overheard a woman with a Texas accent say, "I wouldn't dream of getting up at 6 a.m. in Dallas, so why am I doing it in Dikili?" Well, she spoke for everyone in the boat; what were we all doing anyway? It was the first morning of a week's cruise to Turkey and the Greek islands, and because the *Stella Solaris* had anchored out we were en route in the small boat to explore the ruins of the ancient city of Pergamum. Later, lunching on deck as the ship sailed for Istanbul, we savored every moment of the early-hour excursion.

Some people never go ashore. They just love ships, sailing, and the whole concept of a cruise; they feel no need ever to set foot in port. However, most of us eagerly await each port of call and, in fact, we often choose our cruise holidays as much by the itinerary offered as by the passenger vessel. According to Rod McLeod, a Royal Caribbean Cruise Line executive (former chairman of Cruise Lines International Association), port selection ranks as top priority after ship design. Rod says that his line selects ports only after a careful analysis of several factors. They consider integration of on-board and onshore activities, convenience and comfort for passengers, availability of sightseeing attractions and shopping opportunities, and rigid navigation safety standards. It is safe to assume that what happens ashore affects your entire cruise experience. The physical facilities for every potential port of call must meet stringent standards and offer adequate vessel accommodations. Most ship lines prefer ports with dockside berthing, since it is more convenient for passengers to walk ashore. Most lines also seek ports which have sufficient emergency facilities (doctors, dentists, hospitals, ambulances), just in case. Many ports offer everything, while others may excel in history and archaeology or be just the place for sunbathing.

I pay particular attention to destination, hours spent in each port, arrival time and day of the week (are the shops open, is it a holiday, is there a strike of some sort?). These questions are very important, because I try to plan as much exploration time as possible, while also calculating how much time to allow for shopping and indulging in local specialties. Thus, it can be most disappointing if the program changes without your knowledge. I overheard another woman on the same Greek islands/Turkey cruise complain that she had been promised a longer stay in Istanbul. Unfortunately, she booked the cruise on the basis of an old itinerary, and the morning call in Dikili was substituted for a late evening departure from Istanbul.

INFORMATION ON PORTS OF CALL: Long before each port of call looms over the horizon, a member of the cruise staff will give an on-board briefing detailing the latest information on arrival and departure times (they tend to vary according to sailing conditions and any unforeseen circumstances), the vessel's moorning plans, dress suggestions considering local custom and weather, currency rates, shore excursions (if you have not already bought the full package), and free time. If you plan to do any exploring alone or in a private group, you will also wish to know taxi and other transportation rates, where to eat and shop, and how long it takes to get from place to place. The briefings may even include a short film or slide show to acquaint you with the location of famous sights. However, most of these port talks provide only adequate information, and you may want to supplement them. A map is always helpful, whether you join the organized tour or not. Most ships sell maps in the purser's office (but the supply is limited so get there early). The best maps have famous sites sketched on, so that even if the taxi driver cannot read English, he can at least recognize the monument (this was a godsend in China). On Royal Cruise Line each passenger receives a map of the port that indicates the primary points of interest as well as the ship's location and return directions.

Guidebooks furnish both background material and practical information concerning your ports of call. Historical novels are a good source for atmosphere, and since port cities were often the first settled or colonized, plenty has been written about most of them. Friends and colleagues may offer tips, and perhaps your travel agency has its own cache of materials. If you are booked on a serious cruise (Swans Hellenic, Raymond & Whitcomb, Society Expeditions, or Lindblad), you may receive a reading list to prepare yourself for the sights and sounds ahead. And if you're really lucky, you may discover some picture books and such in the ship's library. (When Raymond & Whitcomb charters a vessel other than the *Argonaut*, it stocks a whole section of the library with reading matter related to the itinerary.) In addition, I try to have some local currency ready so I can purchase a book or two in port. Although many are not bound very well and tend to fall apart with use, the local books, usually written by native scholars, are a good primary source.

BUYING SHORE EXCURSIONS: You may prefer to purchase every shore excursion available and leave the driving and the thinking to someone else. Buying the complete package of port tours when you book is the very best way to purchase these tours, because the price quoted should include all the extras, and you're done with it. Procuring shore excursions piecemeal can be bad psychologically; you begin to think too much about price and lose your enthusiasm. Of course, if you have booked a cruise operated by Swans Hellenic, Raymond & Whitcomb, Society Expeditions, Lindblad, Galapagos Cruises or on many of the lovely barges in Europe, the shore tours are all-inclusive (and how excellent they are).

The average shore excursion, developed between the ship line and a local tour operator in each port of call, is generally well organized and well managed. You don't have to worry about safety or buses running out of fuel, because the ship line plans carefully. What the company cannot control is the turnover in tour guides, some of whom are in it only for the money. Beware of guides who put green dots on your collar or flowers in your buttonhole for identification. Guides may use these symbols to tip off shops that you are a "wealthy" tourist. (It's an old trick and still used worldwide.) If you feel your guide has not fulfilled her/his duties gracefully or has attempted to obtain extra charges from the bus group, complain at once to the purser's office. You deserve a rewarding and hassle-free experience in return for the price paid.

Shore excursions are expensive for many reasons. Often, the ship line must deal with countries where the cost of fuel and vehicles is almost prohibitive. Add this to the greed that tourism breeds, and you have inflated prices. I understand that tour guides in the Caracas area want $500 a day, which explains why a short morning tour of Caracas from La Guaira costs over $35 per person. Then, remember that you buy the tour from the ship line, which buys from the tour organizer, which buys from someone else. Each party marks the price up a little bit. Actually, ship lines claim that they only add a little to the price to cover the expenses (and commission to the travel agent). However, as a friend at a ship line told me, "If we didn't make any money from shore excursions, we wouldn't sell them." In an attempt to cut prices as much as possible, some lines eliminate tour organizers and organize and sell their own tours.

Some ports of call practically require packaged shore excursions to fill out your cruise experience. For example, why sail to Alexandria and miss the thirteen-hour excursion to Cairo? (That is, if you have not been there before and are not the shipbound type.) The Cairo tour does mean six hours round trip through the hot and dusty desert and is hideously expensive (nearing $100), but it offers a splendid view of Africa's largest and most exciting city as well as lunch across from the Pyramids. The same applies to the Holy Land tours from Haifa or Ashdod and for the archaeological sites of Pergamum, Ephesus, and

Delos. The only tour in this area that I found unsatisfactory was in Heraklion, Crete, because the guides were brusque, and neither the museum nor the palace was designed to handle large crowds (such as occur when two ships land in port at the same time). I learned more and had more fun by letting the crowds pass ahead, while I followed a local guidebook (*Crete, A Complete Traveler's Guide* by J. M. Christoforakis).

Many other areas in the cruise world demand—price be damned—the shore excursions. These include the USSR and China (where it's obligatory for the most part), North Africa, the Red Sea (especially to Petra), some South American and North Cape calls, and Alaska. One of the most popular but very expensive excursions on Alaskan cruises is a seaplane tour which, if it includes lunch at the charming Taku Lodge, can run over $90 per person. A 45-minute helicopter tour of Sitka Sound, St. Lazari Island National Bird Reserve, Mt. Edgecumbe, and a quick landing nearby to see goats, seals, whales, and bears costs almost as much. But, all who take this short ride say it is the highlight of the entire Inside Passage sailing.

ON-YOUR-OWN SHORE EXCURSIONS: If you are counting pennies, you can save by touring many ports on your own, especially if they have few tourist sites and are more renowned for their beauty and fine beaches than their costlier attractions; try the Mexican Riviera or many of the Caribbean Islands (especially Puerto Rico and St. Thomas) for this. Toss aside frantic sightseeing tours of these ports and indulge in a leisurely catamaran cruise in the harbor or a stroll through the narrow back streets to reward yourself. I have also been told that, although the Hawaiian island tours are excellent, many passengers arrange to drive off on their own in a rental car. Plan ahead if you do this, because the number of cars is limited. In some port cities, knowledge of the area and a friend to help share taxi expenses make for a thrifty and enjoyable exploration, especially in the northern capitals of Europe, Athens, and Hong Kong. Some excursions—sailing the Orinoco River or transiting the Panama Canal, for example—are exciting enough in themselves, and you never need to go ashore. However, I would not miss the temple tour in Bangkok, the Japanese garden tour in Kyoto, or any tour of that "Morning of the World" island, Bali. Nor would I forgo the horse/donkey ride up to La Citadelle La Ferriere at Cap Haitien, or any trips to the temples and monuments along the Nile (no matter what the temperature or the hour).

Many of the local cruise and beach tours around the Caribbean sound splendid, and some ship lines even arrange their own. Norwegian Caribbean has offered a very successful beach party on Grand Cayman and now adds turtleburgers to the luncheon spread. Its other vessels have dropped anchor off one of the uninhabited Berry Islands, and the *Norway* uses Little San Salvador to treat its passengers to sun, sail, waterski, and snorkel between rounds of beer and soda, hamburger and hotdogs. Snorkeling is a popular pastime at many calls in the Caribbean and should be included in your shore excursion budget, for it's pretty hard to beat the beauty and excitement of this underwater world.

Activities like these also present a wonderful way to meet other people on the ship with shared interests. You may even make lasting friendships. Often, passengers will become friendly during an organized tour in one port and decide to share expenses and explore together during the next call.

If you do decide to explore alone, pay particular attention to checking off and on the ship and allowing plenty of time for coming back aboard. (Many cruise staff personnel insist they will not wait for returning passengers.) If the port is small and lacks the proper facilities, your vessel may have to anchor out. This means "tendering in," which cuts your time in port considerably; remember it is your responsibility to know the times of the last tender. Frequently, the boats leave the ship every fifteen minutes or so for the first hour and then begin returns every hour on the half hour. Ship lines often leave a crew member on the pier to check your boarding tag numbers, especially if you opt for the last launch back, to prevent anyone's being left behind. But you never know. The port calls and shore periods have been carefully planned by the ship line for passengers' fullest enjoyment. To make it work, you have to be on time.

CHANGES IN ITINERARY: If weather or some other unforeseen circumstance prevents your cruise ship from completing the full itinerary in the time allotted, you can do nothing but accept the situation gracefully. Hurricanes in the Caribbean and monsoons in the South China Sea are "acts of God," so we can't hold the ship line responsible. If this happens to you, be grateful for the competency of the captain and thank him when it's all over. On the other hand, if the boilers break down and the entire cruise is ruined, you will definitely receive some recompense—which may be a one hundred percent refund, a discount on a future cruise, or both. No ship line wishes to have anything but happy passengers, and its employees will try everything to please you.

9. / SHOPPING

Shopping wins without contest as the number one diversion on cruises, after eating and drinking. And why not? You have the opportunity to complete your entire Christmas list, add the odd trinket or two to your collection, as well as replace that tired tie, broken bowl, or even last year's bikini. And all at tax-free prices! From boutiques aboard cruise vessels, I have bought some lovely Nina Ricci silk ties for my husband, countless bottles of perfume for just about everyone, scarves and hankies, and various pieces of gold. Only the tip of what was on display, these items have filled my suitcases—Russian fur hats and jackets, liquor and cigarettes, handmade sweaters from Norway, antiques, leather wear, and designer clothes.

SHIP-BOARD SHOPPING: Whether exploring my new "home away from home" before getting underway or inspecting a line-up of ships in port, I always head straightaway for the boutiques and gift shops on board. For here, as I peer through the bars at the many items on display, I learn a great deal about this cruise vessel and its passengers. Most of the shops, franchised and run by people outside the ship line, obviously stock to satisfy the clientele. Higher prices and better quality merchandise appear on the more elegant ships, while cruises that cater to a more middle-class set indulge in quantity and sale items in their shops.

Stores on board the *Norway,* along the Champs Elysee and Fifth Avenue promenades on International Deck, are all spacious, well lit, and designed to entertain as well as to entice, since the *Norway* spends so much time at sea in the guise of the largest floating resort in the world. These most impressive duty-free shops offer everything from dental floss to Cartier-designed jewelry, which is exactly the range one might be seeking! For example, chic beachwear is available in Dimensions, It's A Small World features toys to computer games, and the Golden Touch has—you guessed it! Scandinavia offers whatever you can't live without from Norway, Sweden, Denmark (and Switzerland), and East of Eden sells just what you can find in any Chinatown. Upstairs at the Downstairs has unusual gift items, like fine china, crystal, and porcelains for yourself or friends, plus a selection of fine watches. Below (or downstairs) is Le Drugstore for sundries, cigarettes, magazines, film, liquor, and souvenirs. In case all this shopping makes you thirsty or hungry, the ice cream parlor is conveniently located to dish up Svens favorite flavors.

The *Island Princess* and *Pacific Princess* have elegant boutiques and gift shops, while the *Sun Princess'* ships cater to a more casual crowd. Nonetheless, the items stocked range from Scottish cashmere sweaters to Aynsley china, embroidered sweaters, and silk items from the People's Republic of China. The usual shelves of perfume, jewelry, watches, and other trinkets of great value are there, too. During the summer season in Alaska these boutiques and gift shops sell local merchandise for passengers' convenience. The items stocked for these cruises might include soapstone or ivory curios, Russian-style dolls, and jewelry in jade or hematite (Alaskan black diamond), at prices that are on a par with shops in the forty-ninth state.

Shopping aboard the *Queen Elizabeth 2* can take a full day, and the displays appeal to both the fish'n' chips crowd as well as to the beef Wellington set. You can find all the shops on the gallery above the transatlantic-class Double Down Room (aft of the deluxe staterooms and theater balcony). If you want to spend money, you'll love the diamond-encrusted watches. If you've forgotten your dress shirt and you don't mind ruffles faced with blue or black, you can pick one up here. One shop devotes its shelves to nothing but perfume, and you'd better buy early because lines begin to form as the vessel sails closer to port. Knit dresses sell like hot cakes when the transatlantic weather does not cooperate (and the air-conditioning in your cabin won't turn off). Holland America's flagship, the *Rotterdam*, also has a huge shopping area; the cases display Waterford crystal sets, Royal Worcester egg coddlers, Royal Copenhagen ashtrays, Cardin handbags and scarves, watches, and jewelry. To move the merchandise more quickly from the storeroom to your suitcase the shops have occasional sales, so wait until that Waterford decanter is fifteen percent off and you'll feel even more proud of your purchase.

The shops aboard Home Lines' *Oceanic*, diverse and rather scattered among the decks, encourage browsing—if you can locate them all. Two large gift shops on Riviera Deck stock designer clothes and accessories, gold items from Greece, and a huge collection of perfumes. You can also buy Hummel figurines, Florentine-style boxes, and Royal Copenhagen products. Down on Atlantic Deck is yet another gift shop (with more souvenir items) and a drugstore.

Home Line's spanking new *Atlantic* boasts a most tempting array of gift items, sundries, souvenirs, perfumes, and jewels in the shops along Belvedere Deck, between the Bermuda and Atlantic lounges. The Norwegian-flag vessels carry lovely hand-knit sweaters with silver buttons; and all that glitters on Greek ships is truly gold, whether dipped or 24-Karat. Most ship-board shops now accept the whole family of credit cards and stay open from morning to evening except in port, when the customs authorities make them close.

SHOPPING AT PORTS OF CALL: Enticements lie around the corner of every street and lane in your current port of call! Tax-free temptations are just too irresistible, no matter how hard I try. On several visits to **Bermuda** I have managed to collect an entire set of Herend hand-painted china from Hungary at forty percent below New York prices. Other good and frequent purchases from Trimingham's and Smith's and Cooper's include shetland pullovers in beautiful colors, Liberty of London prints, and Bermuda bags with cedar handles. After I check Blucks' once again to convince myself a new piece of Herend has not snuck into the shop, I never fail to feed another addiction. I pay a call on the island's artist laureate, Alfred Birdsey, to add a few more watercolors to my collection. No one has brought the spirit of Bermuda to paper so well as Birdsey. (I have called him an eccentric elsewhere and I shall continue to do so, because he loves it!) If your cruise vessel is **Bahamas**-bound or if you just pop over for the weekend out of Miami, you will want to save a few pennies to spend at the Straw Market in Rawson Square for bags and hats and such. This is about the only fun shopping left in the Bahamian capital, as Bay Street is no longer very interesting unless you have a hankering for American-fast-food-chain chicken or hamburger.

In the **Caribbean** most cruise vessels aim their bows straight for St. Thomas, USVI, and do not even bother to pass go, for the charming town of Charlotte Amalie might just well be the bargain center of the entire Western Hemisphere. Most travelers consider it such, and even U.S. customs waxes so enthusiastic that returning citizens are allowed double duty-free purchases from here ($600 per person). As a bonus you may even bring back a gallon of liquor acquired here (versus the quart from elsewhere). Liquor is such a popular item for purchase in St. Thomas that the larger (and more aggressive) stores will come aboard, take your orders, and deliver the five-pack in bond before you have the chance to say "boo." Of course, if you prefer to walk the streets and alleyways of Charlotte Amalie, you will find many other ways to break the bank. For example, Hummel figurines, Irish Beleek, Limoges, perfumes, cameras and lenses, tape machines and other grown-up toys, watches galore, and jewels will knock your eyes out. The town even has a Hans Stern outlet as well as Little Switzerland, Gucci, St. Michael (the Marks and Spencer people), a store just for tablecloths, and T-Shirt World. If you buy something that is made or bottled here, a 100-year-old work of art, or a contemporary painting, you may bring them home duty-free. Now you understand why cruise passengers go bananas when the captains say "St. Thomas."

Throughout the Caribbean you can buy some lovely handcrafts as well as tax-free European imports. Haiti is known for its primitive paintings, voodoo drums, and Iron Market. San Juan has *Santos* (small religious wooden figures that are handcarved and very traditional), a Bacardi Rum factory, and a Hathaway shirt outlet in the center of the shopping district. I don't recommend Barrachina, which has promised free piña coladas (a thimbleful) and two-dollar rides to the airport. When I went, the place was dirty and overpriced (and extremely rude when I refused to buy). You can find delft jugs and orange liqueur in Curaçao, lovely filigree jewelry and Dunhill pipes in Trinidad, perfumes and French crystal in Martinique, and straw items wherever your cruise calls.

Silver jewelry in **Mexico** is no longer a bargain but it's still beautiful, and the resort clothes in Acapulco are a dream. Embroidered peasant blouses, fresh and dainty, bring compliments long after your visit. **Alaska** offers ivory curios, totem pole souvenirs, colorful wooden doll sets from Russia, and jewelry made from jade and hematite (Alaskan black diamond).

If your cruise includes ports in **South America,** you will have even more fun shopping. Favorite items in the popular port of Cartagena include tooled leather goods (a traditional Colombian art form), macrame purses, and jewelry of gold and emeralds. Hans Stern, who lives in Rio de Janeiro, is a jeweler known throughout the world for his good and sometimes gaudy designs featuring gold and Brazilian semiprecious stones. His stores will literally follow you around South America, and he has also opened in New York, Paris, Lisbon, Madeira, Frankfurt, Tel Aviv, and Jerusalem. The stores are reputable, as far as I can gather, and the tag prices prevail (no bargaining). In Caracas you can buy jewelry made from cacique coins, the familiar Hand of Fatima, *chinchorros* (hammocks), handbags, and sandals. Rio combines Acapulco and Monte Carlo, with its high-style and very expensive shops touting gold and stones, the latest fashions from the Continent, and the briefest of bikinis.

If your vessel calls at Montevideo, you may want to pick up a few amethysts (they are considered the best in the world here), a suede or antelope jacket, and nutria or seal coats. Or perhaps a nice gaucho hat with boots to match. Chilean specialties include colorful, hand-woven ponchos, vicuna rugs, and artisan copper work. Chilean contemporary art is extremely interesting, and the rock shops feature locally mined lapis lazuli, jade, amethyst, agate, and onyx. Although Lima overflows with silver and gold, you should also look for the many Indian items available, such as baskets, gourds, textiles, and rugs of alpaca and llama fur. When you get to Ecuador, you have landed where the very finest Panama hats are made. Ecuador has some lovely early Indian artifacts, and some fine contemporary painters gain their inspiration from the pottery. The country has presented an artistic medal of honor to Olga Fisch, who turns out one-of-a-kind carpets and wall-hangings with early Indian motifs. They are worth every penny.

If your ship sails to the heart of the **Pacific islands,** pick up a muumuu or two in Honolulu, some sarongs in Tahiti, finely woven placemats in Samoa, and a few baskets in Suva. Although koala bears are not for sale in Sydney, Maori carvings are the thing to buy in New Zealand (along with anything wooly, of course).

If you're bound for the **Far East,** head straight for Hong Kong; it has every-thing anyone has ever wanted, and for the best price! While not the idyllic shoppers' paradise it once was, Hong Kong is still the number one shoppers' call on world cruises. Singapore tries to match Hong Kong as a free port but has never succeeded (there is less choice in products and the prices are slightly higher, probably because the shelves are cleaner). It's simple to spend money in Hong Kong, as it's rather difficult to find anything else to do. Your ship docks right at Ocean Terminal, itself a huge shopping complex and only a short walk from the Nathan Road area where buying and selling is practically a religion. Here you can still have a silk dress made in forty-eight hours (but don't expect it to fit like standard-size clothes), find a setting for your new stones, buy photographic and stereo equipment, and even pick up a Betamax at prices lower than anywhere else in the world (if you pay cash). If you insist upon using a credit card, the shop may charge you an additional seven percent to cover the carrying charges. However, it is pretty hard to beat Hong Kong's prices if you shop carefully and follow the advice of the free *Stop and Shop Bargain Guide* (issued by the Hong Kong Tourist Association) which outlines licensed dealers for every type of equipment and product sold and gives sug-gested retail prices (which I have always found to be quite accurate). It is especially important to follow this guide for photographic equipment pur-chases. I am still staggered that my husband recently got more trade-in allow-ance for a lens than I originally paid in Hong Kong eight years ago. Such is Hong Kong.

If you must skip the People's Republic of China, you can make do with one of the many terrific Chinese department stores, completely owned and operated by the PRC and often offering better prices than in Guangzhou (Canton) or Beijing (Peking). These department stores market lovely silks and embroideries, carpets, jade, Ming dynasty-style vases, and gold (the gold is only 9-karat, I believe). The best department store, China Arts and Crafts, has a Kowloon branch catty-corner to the Star Ferry Building (the one with the clocks), on the left hand side as you walk from Ocean Terminal to Nathan Road. Hong Kong has also become quite a diamond center, but check first with the Hong Kong Tourist Association for their list of reputable dealers. And never pay attention to people on the street who offer you gold watches and such. They think they can always spot a victim, so prove them wrong!

If your Far East cruise does include China, spend some time shopping in this fascinating country. The Chinese now accept travelers' cheques as well as some credit cards in the government-run Friendship Stores. You may browse in other stores, of course, such as the famous Number One Department Store in Shanghai, which has a money exchange on the top floor and is quite ac-customed to foreign guests. If you enter the smaller shops, be certain to have plenty of Renminbi with you. The most popular items are Mao jackets and hats that now come in extra large sizes to fit the Western figure. Silk pajamas and lounge suits abound, but often the prices are better in Hong Kong where there is more competition. If you get into a government-controlled antique shop, you will be staggered by the prices; take care in what you buy. Nothing really old is allowed out of China these days, so you may be the owner of an authentic reproduction (despite the dynasty chart the sweet little girl explains to you in great detail). Good buys in China are jade (if you have lots of money with you), embroidered silks and linens, souvenirs like sandalwood fans or hand-painted silk fans, and handkerchiefs. The silk fans are my favorite item, however, for they make wonderful spur-of-the-moment gifts and only cost about the equivalent of thirty cents. If you're lucky enough to visit a silk fan factory, buy them there and save a penny.

Shopping in Japan, a subtle and sensitive art form, includes the play of nimble fingers over an abacus to finish every deal. Although prices remain out of sight, the Japanese make some of the most beautiful things in the world. This is the land of pearls, woodblock prints, happy coats and kimonos, exquisite lacquer ware, and imaginative folk crafts. *Mingei* (folk art), found primarily in paper, wood, and pottery, make the local shops seem like art galleries, they are so bursting with charming designs. The tape recorders and computer products are better bought in Hong Kong, where fierce competition keeps the prices low. For the real experience of shopping Japanese-style, stick to the arts and crafts of Japan.

Elsewhere on your Far Eastern cruise, find brilliant silks in Thailand, as well as shops full of rings set with semiprecious stones. Singapore is a clean version of Hong Kong, and Penang has little but Malaysian batiks. Indonesia offers beautiful, rich brown and blue batiks (and the antique irons used to make them are wonderful bookends). Buy dolls of old coins in Sumatra, wayang puppets in Bandung (wonderful souvenirs), and art (paintings, carvings, sculpture) in Bali. In the Philippines you will find the wonderful pina fiber (made from pineapples) that the *barong tagalog* shirt and ladies' pantsuits and dresses use (but no matter how interesting they look, beware; they can be very hot!) Taiwan is a shopper's paradise for brass, baskets, and tailoring at low prices. Semiprecious stones sparkle in Sri Lanka, which has sapphires, chameleonlike alexandrites, cat's eyes, rubies, and aquamarines. And if your vessel calls at Bombay, seek out some lovely saris and exquisite Moghul miniatures that are mostly fakes (but never mind if you don't pay too much).

Cruising **Europe**'s waters brings you into contact with many familiar items, but before long you realize that many of your favorite things are actually cheaper at home. Most European countries have Value Added Tax (VAT) which raises the price of luxury items by as much as 33.33 percent. Unfortunately, this tax is unavoidable if you buy less than $100 at a time and carry the item back on board. The Scandinavian countries have the highest goods taxes in Europe (Iceland—23.5 percent, Sweden—17.7 percent, Denmark—22 percent, Norway—20 percent) but other countries are not far behind. Spain and Portugal are still wonderful countries in which to shop, and Lisbon is a popular shopping port call, but if you have the luck of stopping by Madeira, you are very fortunate. Here amid a floating garden, are wonderful wicker products, exquisite hand-fingered embroideries, and plenty of the local brew.

Specialties along the shores of the **Mediterranean** include whatever you can find in the famous souks of Morocoo, wonderful white filigree birdcages from

Tunisia, scarabs from Egypt as well as busts of Nefertiti and jellabas and caftans. Actually, the most popular Egyptian souvenir is the cartouche, an insignia bearing a pharaoh's name in hieroglyphics; you can buy it as a necklace, in gold or silver. If you would rather have a Muslim charm, the Hand of Fatima is here, too. Since most cruise vessels that call in Egypt now also continue on to Israel, prepare yourself for the woven and hand-stitched crafts available, as well as the olive wood items, the copper and brass work, pottery and basket ware.

On a Greek island and Turkey cruise, you will be tempted by rugs, rugs, and more rugs. All are fascinating and if you buy one, carry it home. The covered bazaar in Istanbul is a wonderful place to get lost and you will be approached time and time again by people pushing rugs. (I even had an offer of a flying carpet.) Turkey also has wonderful brass and copper items, spices, leather coats and jackets, and meerschaum pipes. Everything in Greece is a temptation, and I have a very hard time resisting, especially among the various island ports. Crete offers impressive red rugs (they're best as wall hangings), and Mykonos displays the most splendid looking, handmade sweaters in the world, and Rhodes (glorious Rhodes) has just about everything. I buy all my gold jewelry in Rhodes, among the shops just off the Palace of the Knights, and I always dream about the pieces left behind! Souvenir items in Greece include fine reproductions of pottery found in the ancient tombs—hand-painted and very reasonably priced.

U.S. CUSTOMS: "Sailing Through Customs" is Norwegian Caribbean Cruise Lines' catchphrase for declaring all your new purchases. According to the U.S. Customs laws, each returning resident may bring back up to $300 worth of acquired merchandise (including gifts), duty free, every thirty days. The only exception is from the U.S. Virgin Islands, American Samoa, or Guam, where the allowance is $600 (if you return directly and at least half of your bundle was purchased here). Original works of art and antiques (at least one hundred years old) are exempt from duty, as are any items made on these U.S. territories (perfume, clothing, jewelry, and handbags). If you travel as a family, the duty-free allowance lets you pool your purchases, which means that a family of four has a combined allowance of $1200. If your acquisitions exceed this (and the customs officials are very lenient), a flat rate of ten percent is assessed on the first $600 over the limit. After that the rate of duty reverts to the old laws and varies widely. If all your purchases were made in U.S. territories, the flat rate is only five percent for the first $600 worth of goods over the allowance.

If you plan to return with tobacco and liquor, first check your state laws, for federal and state regulations differ widely. For example, California residents should be aware that importing more than one bottle of wine is illegal. Basically, your duty-free limit is one carton (two hundred) of cigarettes per person or one hundred cigars. Each U.S. resident (age twenty-one and over) is also allowed one quart of liquor duty free. Cruise passengers returning from the U.S. Virgin Islands may import one gallon (five fifths), provided at least four fifths were bought in St. Thomas. It is also forbidden to bring any live plant, piece of fruit or vegetable, plant cutting or seeds, or unprocessed plant product into this country. Other items banned include Haitian goat skins, certain ivory items, alligator products, and any articles made from the skins of endangered species. Trademarked products may be imported now for personal use only; the limit is one item.

If you plan to send gifts from abroad, restrict yourself to one per address and no more than $25 worth, duty free ($40 if sent from St. Thomas) to stay within the limit. When you send presents through the mail, be careful which countries you choose; know the regulations and be certain to insure the packages properly. Write in large letters on the outside of the wrapping, "Gift enclosed, value under $25" ($40 if from St. Thomas).

The Generalized System of Preferences, instituted in 1976 to help developing countries improve their financial or economic condition through export trade, provides for duty-free importation of certain products from certain nations. Many of these are tourist items. The list, which is renewed each year, includes 107 nations, 32 dependent territories, and approxiamtely 2700 items—Turkish rugs, loose semiprecious stones, rattan (other than furniture), shell products (except from the Philippines), toys (except from Hong Kong and Taiwan), and wigs (except from South Korea) to name a few. If your cruise encompasses a great many calls in developing nations and territories, you may wish to check which potential purchases might be duty free. Under the Trade Act, however, certain items—like most footwear, textiles, watches, some electronic products, and some glass and steel products—are specifically excluded from any GSP benefits. The U.S. actually prohibits importation of many articles, such as many types of ivory, skins from endangered species, plants and animals, and foodstuffs that could carry contamination. If you feel a buying spree approaching, contact your nearest U.S. Customs office for updated information. Or write to: Department of the Treasury, U.S. Customs Service, Washington, D.C. 20229 for "GSP & the Traveler" and "Customs Hints—Know Before You Go." If you contemplate purchases of ivory, skins, fur, etc., contact the U.S. Fish and Wildlife Service, Department of the Interior.

For most cruise vessels returning to U.S. ports, Customs officials will come aboard (along with Immigration) to check each passenger's Customs forms. Declare all dutiable goods at this time, and pay any charges when you collect your baggage later on the dock (the baggage is generally stacked according to the first letter of your surname). Bear in mind that a U.S. customs official has the right to check your baggage at any time, and you can be severely fined for underestimating the total value of goods acquired abroad. Most inspectors seem more mellow these days because of the increase in duty-free allowances (as well as previous complaints of their rudeness). However, they can be very strict (and comb your suitcases) if you are returning from countries with heavy traffic in drugs or diamonds.

10. / INLAND WATERWAYS

ABERCROMBIE & KENT INTERNATIONAL, INC.

1000 Oak Brook Road
Oak Brook, Illinois 60521
tel: (312) 887–7766

Abercrombie & Kent is certainly not Abercrombie & Fitch (that wonderful wooden-floored sportsman's paradise on Madison Avenue of a more genteel era) but I suspect that it would like to be recognized as the A & F of travel. The tours are selective, for small groups who like personalized service. Hence, A & K has chartered the twenty-passenger *Abu Simbel* for one- and two-week Nile cruises that are combined with some land arrangements. The 1978-built barge has just ten cabins, a dining room that seats all passengers, a main lounge, and library/game room section. The vessel is small and therefore lacks some of the open-deck/swimming pool amenities of other ships that offer Nile sailings, but A & K insists that their attention to personal service is more important.

The brochure is both impressive and enticing, as Geoffrey and his wife, Jorie Butler Kent, are featured in before-the-Pyramids-photographs. Although the Nile cruises are relatively recent endeavors, Geoffrey Kent is a second-generation travel expert from Kenya. He is quite accustomed to managing safari-like groups—a similarity in ambiance to the *Abu Simbel* Nile sailings. Pre-cruise information includes a reading list, a personalized itinerary, a notebook full of travel tips, and an especially edited history of Egypt. Kent's reputation is very sound, indeed, but I wonder how much time he spends with his tour company considering he is also an accomplished and renowned polo player who travels the world following the "season."

CONTINENTAL WATERWAYS

11 Beacon Street
Boston, Massachusetts 02108
tel: (617) 227–3220

Anyone who sees the emblem of Continental Waterways will understand the joys of barge cruising as my friend Barbara Hess introduced it to me. Picture a little fat chef in toque and mini-trident chasing a snail and you understand everything. What Continental began in the mid-1960s has become "the rage" of experienced travel folk. Good food and a tour through the heart of Europe's waterways combine to make one of the most enjoyable experiences possible.

For this season, Continental is offering seven different barges in France and England, carrying six to twenty-four passengers each. The smaller boat is available on a full-charter-only basis (take along your friends), and two are brand-new conversions. Continental opened an office on this side of the Atlantic a few years ago, and the American cousins seem to be discovering quickly the art of barging. Information and reservations are also handled through any Air France office.

It does not take long to be utterly captivated by barge cruising, where nothing is more relaxing to the mind or refreshing for the spirit than to drift slowly along a waterway, watching life unfold on both banks. You become an integral part of the passing scene before you even realize it. A completely different atmosphere from ocean voyages, here you travel through the heart of the countryside, observing the everyday and mundane, which often turns out to be utterly charming and exquisite. The barges vary in size and style, but all are rather small—English narrow boats measure only seven feet wide, while the waterways of France can handle boats of sixteen feet at beam. If you happen to be tall or big, however, you just may not fit. Life on board a barge is rather cozy; you are thrown together in close quarters with people with whom you hope you will be compatible. During the day the boats move slowly along the water while you are out touring or bicycling along the towpath. Calm evenings with an early tie-up invite a stroll before dinner and a visit to the local village later. Family-style meals on board are very tasty. This is home cooking at its best and the gourmet touch is evident! Table wines are available at luncheon and dinner, and you can buy other types if you wish. Each barge has a cozy sitting and dining room with bar where you can sign for drinks and pay later (in local currency, please). The atmosphere, casual but very polite, necessitates your consideration because of the cramped quarters. Leave the silks and satins behind; a simple pair of slacks and long skirt will do. And remember, don't take up too much room!

To know the *Palinurus* is to love her! She is not the most luxurious nor glamorous barge on the French waterways, but the one with great personality and history. Emily Kimbrough wrote a book about her and her crazy owner-captain, the English francophile named Richard Parsons. Richard and his colleague, Guy Bardet, are credited with developing most of this fine art of barging, and the *Palinurus* is their first (and still favorite) boat. The barge has eleven cabins on two decks, with no facilities (but no one seems to care as there are plenty of water closets and three showers). The vessel has been situated in The Midi for some time, and has a popular following. Her route runs from Castets to Sète along the Canal Lateral a la Garonne and the famous Canal du Midi. The most popular part of the route is the six-day cruise between Toulouse and Carcassonne, some of the most picturesque of medieval France.

The slightly larger *Mark Twain* (eight passengers) is Continental's most elegant and gracious barge. Built in Holland at the end of the last century, the *Mark Twain* has a gracious, old-world atmosphere with a brass-and-teak-fitted lounge and four pleasant twin cabins with private facilities. The small capacity allows Captain Charlie Pope, and his wife Beth, to care very much; and this is considered a "gourmet barge." Included in the six-day cruise price is dinner at one of eastern France's top restaurants: L'Auberge de l'Ill at Illhaeusern, Chateau d'As at Baume, La Gentilhommiere at Nancy, or Chateau de Rigny at Gray. The *Mark Twain*'s route lies in a triangle with Nancy, Strasbourg, and Dijon at its corner, but it takes some six or seven weeks to snail around the entire circuit. Both the barge and the itinerary are highly rated.

A recent addition is the 22-passenger *Lafayette*, also cruising in France's Alsace region between Nancy, Strasbourg, and Montbeliard. Passengers are picked up at hotels in Strasbourg on Wednesday afternoon, and returned on Tuesday morning replete with the local foie gras and white, fragrant wines. The *Lafayette* has six twin, four double, and two single cabins (all with private facilities).

La Litote ("the understatement") will always be my favorite Continental barge. Twenty passengers offers a good mix and the barge's route through Burgundy is perfectly beautiful. *La Litote* has a spacious lounge and dining area, sun deck midships and a small area forward for photographing the passing scenery. There are four cabins on the upper deck (two twins, two doubles), with large picture windows that cost a bit more but would be well worth it. All cabins seem spacious with big beds—six-and-a-half feet long. Cabins J and K even have beds seven feet long! All have private facilities, with showers that you can even turn around in—what bliss.

For this season, *La Litote* will be cruising between Auxerre, Montbard, and Dijon in eastern Burgundy, while the 24-passenger *L'Escargot* ("the snail") takes a western Burgundy route between Nevers, Briare, Nemours, and Auxerre. *L'Escargot* was refitted a few years ago and upgraded to twelve twin/double cabins with private facilities. Buddy Bombard was so pleased that he occasionally uses this barge for his air/land/waterway programs.

Continental represents one six-passenger barge available for full-charter only—the *Berendina*, which cruises between Nevers, Digoin, and Dijon, in southern Burgundy.

New on the River Thames—often called the Queen's Highway—is the twenty-four passenger *Princess*, named in honor of Britain's favorite Royal— the Princess of Wales. This luxurious barge replaces the former *Clemence* and *Cadence*, which were familiar figures around this *Wind in the Willows* area. The *Princess* cruises between Tower Bridge in London and Henley-on-Thames, the site of the famous boating races. The six-day journey passes Putney, Mortlake, Richmond, Kingston-on-Thames, Runnymede, Staines, Windsor and Eton, Bray, Maiden Head, and Marlow. The Monday-to-Sunday program returns passengers by bus to London. Meals on board are regional English and, if the *Clemence* is any prior judgment, are surprisingly good. But that chef was a Canadian-born Cordon Bleu graduate!

Accommodations aboard the *Princess* are quite spacious and all berths are six-and-a-half feet long. The two twin cabins on the upper deck, undoubtedly, will always be booked first. The sun deck, lounge, and dining area are all very comfortable, and the *Princess* is a nice addition to Britain's most historic waterway.

ESPLANADE TOURS

38 Newbury Street
Boston, Massachusetts 02116
tel: (617) 266–7465

My friend Jackie Keith represents what is probably the most "posh" hotel barge in Europe, *Etoile de Champagne*. (Picture two Daimler limousines awaiting passengers along the river bank.) Owned and operated by the charming and handsome Australian Peter Evans, *Etoile de Champagne* is a familiar sight just below Place de la Concorde on the river Seine. Evans, who has been in the barging business since 1968, offers two different routes from Paris. My favorite is the Champagne Cruise, which takes passengers up the Marne Valley to Epernay (or vice versa), where that extraordinary monk named Dom Perignon "discovered" how to keep bubbles in wine. Visits to the eighteen miles of Moet et Chandon cellars highlight this cruise.

Evans' other itinerary from Paris features the Chablis country, and the *Etoile* cruises between the French capital and Joigny on the Yonne River. Here, passengers climb into the waiting Daimlers for a tour of the vineyards and the small town of Chablis—with some tastings definitely in order. Evans has also devised a third program, between Ste. Florentine and Montbard in the Burgundy area for the months of July and August. Built in 1979, *Etoile de Cham-*

pagne is one of the largest barges afloat (2,400 square feet of passenger area) but carries only twelve guests. Fully heated or air-cooled, the vessel has large cabins where you can enjoy Continental breakfast in bed. Other meals are gourmet and the complimentary wines are all *appellation controlle*. And the two Daimlers can't help but make one feel *trés riche*, indeed!

On the Canal du Midi, Jackie represents the twelve-passenger *Athos*, a new hotel-barge that cruises between Toulouse and Beziers. Over 100 feet long, the *Athos* is the largest size possible to still negotiate the 300-year-old locks along this historic canal. The design of the barge was planned with American clients in mind, and the *Athos* contains many "creature comforts" to make this journey as cozy as possible. Cruise lengths are seven and ten days, and the barge is also available for full-charter (about $1,000 per day).

Esplanade has also developed a series of programs in conjunction with Salen Lindblad Cruising, aboard the *Lindblad Polaris*. Three cruises in the spring sail from Suez to Syracuse, from Syracuse to Lisbon, and from Lisbon to Copenhagen. Three fall cruises depart Lisbon for Civitavecchia (Rome), from Civitavecchia to Piraeus, and from Piraeus through the Greek Islands and Asia Minor. All are two weeks in length and feature full sightseeing programs and guest lecturers. And I can predict that each of the lucky seventy-nine passengers on these cruises will enjoy the port calls all the more!

EUROPEAN HOTEL BARGES AMSTERDAM

% Aventours Travel, Ltd.
801 Second Avenue
New York, N.Y. 10017
tel: (212) 867–8770
(or any KLM office)

European Hotel Barges in Amsterdam is owned and operated by a jolly Dutchman named Maarten C. Groen, who has persevered to find success with two different types of vessels in his native land. Groen's 130-foot *Rembrandt* carries eighteen passengers in two suites (Rembrandt and Van Gogh), six twin and two single cabins below deck. Above is a spacious lounge with bar, and separate dining area with round tables, pink cloths, and candelabra! In good weather, passengers spend most of their time on the sun deck forward. Invitations to the wheelhouse and kitchen are also extended often. Food aboard the *Rembrandt* is very Dutch, which means that there is too much of it! Breakfasts are cooked to order from about 8:30 a.m. onward; lunches vary in strength, and dinners tend to be on the heavy side. (I suggested to the chef that Americans did not want to eat so much, but he would have none of my advice). The chef, however, is such a personality that passengers soon forgive him for the extra calories. And, he is very generous about sharing the recipes of some favored hors d'oeuvres—although he claims not to remember the exact proportions.

The *Rembrandt* offers two different itineraries; the standard Heart of Holland Cruises from Amsterdam with excursions to The Hague, lunch at the famous North Sea resort of Scheveningen, the Frans Hals Museum in Haarlem, a walking tour of Alkmaar (although the picturesque Cheese Market is another day), a cruise in the Zuider Zee and along the River Vecht, and a week aboard that featured Keukenhof tulip nurseries and the once-every-decade Floriade in Amsterdam. Both were lovely experiences.

A new Friesland itinerary is also available; it includes Lemmer, Stavoren, Sneek, Leeuwarden, Dokkum, Zoutkamp, and Groningen. Our friend Ellinor Malin-Berger refers to it as the "land of contented cows" which appeals to me, for I find most of Holland's waterways too commercial for my taste. More poetic landscapes are always preferable!

Maarten Groen's other vessel is the clipper ship, *Vios*. Since 1979, the 99-foot *Vios* has taken eighteen young passengers a week on exciting sailings through the Zuider Zee and into the lakes of Friesland and around northern Holland's Wadden Sea. The young people do their own household chores and help with the sailings. There is a spacious recreation/dining area and everyone loves the hearty Dutch meals! The *Vios* is available on group charter only, from approximately $4,000 per week (including all meals and taxes).

FLOATING THROUGH EUROPE

271 Madison Avenue
New York, N.Y. 10016
tel: (212) 685–5600

Self-styled boatniks, Jarrett and Stanley Kroll own and operate Floating Through Europe, a hotel-barge company begun in the mid-1970s that has cruised its way throughout France, Holland, Belgium and England. The Krolls began researching the inland waterways of Europe, wrote a book about their experiences, and are totally dedicated to this mode of vacation travel. As Stanley now spends most of his waking hours in the marketplace of high finance, Jarrett runs the company with the capable Jennifer Ogilvie at her elbow. There are now seven barges in four countries. The company also represents a number of self-drive river and canal boats that can accommodate from two to eight persons on lengths of up to sixty feet. (Queries should be directed to the New York office.) And, if you care to read before you go—a number of beautiful books are available by mail, including the Kroll's *Cruising the Inland Waterways* of Europe and John Liley's *France, the quiet way*.

Floating Through Europe caters to people who know better and like it. Not everyone is suited to the spirit and intimacy of barge travel—but those who are, certainly enjoy cheerful cabins (albeit tiny) and memorable meals. They are also pleased with well-planned excursions in the barge's own mini-bus, that miraculously appears at every mooring. The FTE fleet of seven all offer comfortable accommodations, good private facilities, charming public areas, and pleasant crew. FTE does not stint, especially when satisfying passengers' palates! Young Cordon Bleu graduates do the planning, shopping, and cooking; and the meals are mainly nouvelle cuisine (no matter which country one happens to be cruising through)! Fresh produce is purchased almost daily from the local markets, and you can count on plenty of wonderful and interesting cheeses, pates, breads, and salads, not to mention the local bottled grape that is carefully chosen to complement the menus.

Flagship of the FTE fleet is still the 126-foot *Janine*, a most luxurious barge launched in Burgundy in 1979 that carries 24 passengers in high style, plus a crew of eight. The vessel is noted for her superb food. In fact, the *Janine* became the first nonperson to be honored by a French Wine Society, when she was made a member of the Confrerie St. Vincent et Disciples de la Chanteflute de Murcurey. In addition, the *Janine*'s 28-year old American-born chef de cuisine was named a Commandant of the Commanderie des Cordons Bleus de France (whose only other American honorèe has been Julia Child). The *Janine* is also noted for the excellent tours available through the Cote d'Or area, under the direction of Jean Michel Lafond (professor of gastronomy at Dijon University and popular raconteur).

Among the many exciting cellars and vineyards visited by *Janine* passengers are Clos Vougeot, Nuits-St. George, Gevrey-Chambartin, and Beaune. The six-day cruises between Lyon and Dijon also feature a five-course Burgundian lunch at La Rotissiere du Chambertin and wine tastings. In addition to the Burgundy Wine Cruises, the barge also offers a series of mini-Wine Cruises of three days only in late spring and early fall. But, *pièce de résistance* is the Trois Glorieuses Cruise in November which highlights the famous wine auction at Hospice de Beaune.

The 112-foot *Linquenda*, a former Dutch Klipper barge, was converted to luxury standards in 1980. The vessel sails in northern Burgundy on four different programs. Three-day Chateaux Cruises that ply the waters between Tanley and Montbard are available on Fridays and Mondays in early April and the fall. Burgundy Chateaux Cruises, that run between Pouillenay and Tanlay, visit the Chateau de Tanlay, Chateau Ancy-le-Franc, the forge of Buffon, the ancient town of Montbard, the abbey at Fontenay, Alise-Ste.-Reine, and the fortified hill town of Semur-en-Auxois. The Burgundy Historic Towns itinerary cruises between Tanley and Sens, beginning on the Canal de Bourgogne or the River Yonne. There are also Yonne Valley Cruises scheduled for the *Linquenda*, between Sens and Clamecy.

The eight-passenger *Bonjour*, one of the most delightful hotel-barges afloat, cruises in the Midi between Carcassonne and Toulouse and between Marseillan and Carcassonne. This is among France's most historic waterways, and the most enchanting way to enjoy the region is by barge. The Canal du Midi is Europe's oldest—designed by Pierre Paul Riquet and opened in 1681.

What Floating Through Europe calls the Languedoc Coast Cruise is equally as impressive as the Medieval Midi itinerary, both of which visit an assortment of historic sites, old fortresses, and other highlights. The *Bonjour* also offers three-day cruises in the spring and fall, highlighting Beziers and Oppidum d'Enserune. There is plenty of open deck space aboard the *Bonjour* to enjoy the scenery, but watch out for mosquitoes in this area (take along plenty of repellent). For such a small barge, it is also wise to choose your fellow travelers, since one "rotten apple" can certainly spoil the fun.

The charming twelve-passenger *Lys*, a former grain-carrying Sheffield Keel from England's Humber River, was moved from the canals of Holland to historic Flanders and now cruises between Antwerp and Ghent and Bruges. This is a beautiful area, especially for art lovers, since all three of these ancient towns are filled with inspiring monuments. (Two of my favorites are the Memling Museum in St. John's Hospital in Bruges and Rubens' Antwerp residence.) Unfortunately, many of the Belgian waterways are not that poetic. The river Lys, however, is lovely, and the towns along the way are full of character. On a recent trial run, the Historic Flanders itinerary was most enjoyable, with exemplary crew and superb food. When not creating ambitious dishes, the young chef Philippe could be found making heavenly smelling French-rolled cookies for tea and dessert. The *Lys* is also scheduled for some three-day Flanders Cruises between Ghent and Bruges in addition to some three-day Tulip and Spring Flower Cruises back in Holland from Amsterdam to Haarlem, Zaanse Schans, Zuider Zee seaports, and Alkmaar.

The new girl in town, though, is the 24-passenger *Juliana*, which began cruising the Dutch canals in June of 1982. Cabins on this barge are among the most cheerful I've ever inspected, and the bathrooms are very well designed, indeed. Nothing seems to have been spared in on-board amenities, from sheets to stainless steel flatware. All is in good taste, and I hope *Juliana* passengers appreciate the tender care shown here. The barge was built in three sections so each area of four cabins is its own entity (with its own stairwell). This feature might be especially appealing to groups of eight planning to travel together. Fleet Commodore Edwin Parks managed the construction of the *Juliana* and is now her Captain. He has a fine crew of seven eager young people. The *Juliana* makes a few Dutch Tulip Cruises before she begins her Golden Age of Holland itinerary, which departs from Amsterdam's River Amstel for various Netherland spots. Dutch Country Cruises also depart from Amsterdam, as does an annual Dutch Masters Art Cruise with guided tours of the Rijksmuseum, Vincent Van Gogh Museum, Stelijkmuseum, and Historic Museum in Amsterdam as well as others along the route.

In the heart of Shakespeare Country on the River Avon, a pair of traditional English "wideboats" painted with Roses & Castles insignia are known as the *Beverly* and *Jean*. They have been cruising this river together since 1978, one with the motor and the other following behind. The *Beverly* is the service boat, with small salon/dining area, front deck, galley, and crews' quarters. The *Jean* accommodates twelve passengers, and the only problem seems to be that sometimes the private facilities are not alongside when you need them most! The crew, however, is a young, dedicated group of five. The food is delicious, the wines only so-so (this is not France); but the ambiance is fun. The barges cruise along side by side; everyone runs topside to help with the self-service locks; and this is a lovely, peaceful waterway. The weekly cruises between Stratford-upon-Avon and Tewkesbury feature, among other things, at least one play, half-timbered Tudor houses, a Norman-origin Abbey, the Vale of Evesham, and a tour through the Royal Worcester Porcelain Factory. Three-day cruises between Stratford-upon-Avon/Evesham/Tewkesbury are also available.

The least elegant of the Floating Through Europe barges is the twelve-passenger *Actief*, another former Dutch Klipper converted a few years ago. The *Actief* plys the famous Queen's Highway (also known as the Thames) between Windsor and Oxford, calling at such familiar place names as Cliveden, Hurley, Sonning, Pangbourne and Shillingford. Three-day cruises are also available between Windsor and Henley-on-Thames or Oxford and Henley-on-Thames. Robert Burns once said that Father Thames was liquid history. It is the Royal River and most enjoyable on a sunny English day (but take along your rain gear, just in case).

HILTON INTERNATIONAL

P.O. Box 257
Cairo, Egypt
(or any Hilton International hotel)

The Nile Hilton in Cairo operates two of the most popular boats that cruise the Nile River—the 270-foot, 124-passenger twin vessels, the *Isis* and *Osiris*, which sail between Luxor and Aswan on four night/five day excursions year-round. These vessels are alike, simple but very comfortable and considered as floating hotels of Hilton International standards. A number of top-quality tour operators who specialize in Egypt, such as Lindblad and Maupintour, use the twins.

The *Isis* and *Osiris* have four passenger decks and are fully air-conditioned. The cabins, small and simple, can sleep from one to three persons in all outside accommodations with private facilities. On the top, or Bridge Deck, are a small swimming pool, open sitting area with awning, and enclosed lounge. The first deck has a pleasant dining room with bar, a lounge, and small boutique. The front office and beauty salon are located on the main deck, along with passenger cabins, and the lower deck is all accommodations. Although Egypt bills itself as a year-round destination, the best time for cruising along the Nile falls between September and the end of May, when the days are sunny and warm and the nights cool. From December through February the weather is also pleasant, although the evenings can be chilly. June through August should be avoided if you cannot take heat and bone-dry air (the vessels are well air-conditioned, but the monuments are not). At all times of the year, though, the sightseeing excursions occur only during early morning and late afternoon hours, because the Egyptians fully agree that "only mad dogs and Englishmen" are crazy enough to sit in the midday sun.

The ships alternate sailing every five days from Luxor to Aswan and vice versa. The Luxor Aswan itinerary includes the great temples of Luxor, Karnak, and Abydos. You will visit the Temple of Hatour, Thebes' Necropolis, Valley of the Kings, and Tomb of Tutankhamon. The Temple of Queen Hatshepsut at Deir al Bahri, the romantic Valley of the Nobles, the Valley of the Queens, the Temple of Medinet Habu, and the famed Colossi of Memnon will awe you. Then, an early morning departure for Esna takes you to the Temple of Esna and on to the Temple of Horus (237 B.C.), the most complete example of the remaining Egyptian temples. During your last day you will see the Ptolemic Temple of Kom Ombo, with its beautiful murals, fascinating reliefs, and fine view of the river. A morning sailing to Aswan includes a visit to the Botanical Island and Mausoleum of Agha Khan by *feluccas* (small native sailing craft).

HORIZON CRUISES

215 North 75th Street
Belleville, Illinois 62223
tel: (618) 397–7524
(or any Air France office)

Horizon Cruises operates five luxury hotel-barges on the canals of France for charter or individual passage from mid-April through October. The cruises combine charming and delightfully decorated boats, gourmet meals, and chateau-bottled wines—plus interesting side excursions by bicycle or mini-bus. The company is owned by Midwest attorney Rex Carr, who took his family on a barge trip through France five years or so ago. His vacation was almost aborted when the French authorities seized the barge for nonpayment of debts. So, the story goes, Carr saved the barge and his vacation by putting up the necessary funds. Now in business with five barges, the company also offers the twelve-person *Chateau de Cezy* as an optional week in France following your elegant cruise.

Most luxurious of these hotel-barges is the sixteen-passenger *Nenuphar*, a 126-foot by 17-foot vessel originally built in Belgium, converted from her mercantile ancestry in the late 1970s. The *Nenuphar*, which means water lily, is completely furnished in French antiques. It has two suites (Antoinette and Louis XV) and seven cabins below deck, all with private facilities. The top deck has the dining room, a saloon/lounge, and a sun deck. A crew of seven includes Captain Don Porter (one of the barge's owners) and his wife, Gail, a cordon bleu chef. The *Nenuphar* cruises between Nemours and Briare, between Briare and Nevers, covering the Canal du L'oing, the Canal de Briare, and the Canal Lateral a la L'oire. The one-week cruises include transportation between Paris and the mooring.

The twelve-passenger *Horizon,* originally built in 1908 at one of the great shipyards on the River Clyde in Scotland, was completely refitted in the mid-1970s and carries a dining/saloon/bar area, three double cabins, two twins, and two singles—all on one deck. The cabins lack private facilities but do have hot and cold running water. Topside of the 126-foot long barge is a large sun deck for watching the Burgundy countryside go by. A crew of six includes Captain Krishna Lester and his wife Sarah, another cordon bleu chef. The *Horizon* cruises on a Sunday to Saturday schedule between Pouilly en Auxois and Montbard, Montbard and St. Florentin, or Pouilly en Auxois and Dijon. Transportation between Paris and the mooring is provided.

The classic, six-passenger and three-crew *De Hoop* was originally built in 1906 to sail the Zuider Zee. Converted in 1971 to a luxury barge at the same shipyard that created her, the boat belonged to a Dutchman who wished to cruise the waterways of Europe in style. The 65-foot long by 13-foot wide boat has two double cabins, one twin, and communal water closet and showers. Midships on the single deck is a dining room, with a saloon aft and two sun decks topsides. Englishman Roger Collins captains the barge while his wife Yvette, a native of Burgundy and premier chef, oversees the food preparation. The *De Hoop* (The Hope) cruises between Villeneuve-sur-Yonne and Clamecy and between Clamecy and Chatillon-en-Bazois, covering the Yonne River and the Nivernais Canal. Transportation from Paris to the mooring is provided for these Saturday to Friday cruises.

The two newer additions to the Horizon barge family are the ten-passenger *Liberte,* a two-masted Dutch sailing *tjalk* converted in 1981, and the six-passenger *Sara Jane.* The *Liberte* has just four twin/double cabins plus the Versailles Suite, a saloon, dining room, and sun deck. The vessel is stationed on the Charente River, between St. Savinien and Angouleme. The *Sara Jane,* available for full-charter only, cruises between Castelnaudary (near Toulouse) and Marseillan (near Sete) on the Midi Canal. Formerly a fully rigged Dutch *tjalk,* the *Sara Jane* has only three cabins, and two bathrooms with showers for guests.

Horizon also operates a fleet of eight self-drive boats on the canal systems of France; each sleeps up to eight people and costs under one thousand dollars per week, but this is a "bare boat" charter rate. You must provide the fuel and food and be somewhat knowledgable about navigation and the French lock system.

K.D. GERMAN RHINE LINE

Rhine Cruise Agency
170 Hamilton Avenue
White Plains, N.Y. 10601
tel: (914) 948–3600

KD German Rhine Line has spent over 150 years operating passenger services on the river that flows through the very heart of Europe. The Rhine has often determined the course of European history. It flows from the romantic Alps of Switzerland and France to the rugged North Sea—820 miles of important trade routes, historic towns and cities, and cultural monuments that give a fine taste of the civilizations that developed here for several centuries. The river touches upon the banks of four European countries—Switzerland, France, Germany, and Holland—and the variety of scenery you pass through and impressions you receive will seem endless. It's exhilarating to cruise along this stalwart waterway trying to absorb almost two thousand years of art and history.

This is the "rich and romantic" Rhine, where the famed Lorelei reclined some 433 feet above, combing her locks and singing a siren song that lured fishermen to the rocky shores. Here Caesar's legions bridged the floodwaters and General Eisenhower battled the army of Hitler. Industrial areas spew saffron smoke into the air, a stark contrast to the castles dating from the twelfth century when you could almost see the dragons who inhabited the cliffs. Wooded hills, vineyards, and the spire of a distant church all tease the senses.

KD German Rhine Line operates some twenty-eight different passenger vessels, including eight comfortable cruise liners: the *Deutschland*, *Britannia*, *France*, *Nederland*, *Austria*, *Italia*, *Helvetia*, and *Europa*. The ships average about 330 feet long and 40 feet wide, and sail about 10 miles per hour upstream, 16 miles per hour downstream. Each vessel carries about 200 passengers in clean and simple all-outside cabins, which have one sofa-bed, one folding bed, a large window, and private facilities. The public areas feature a spacious observation lounge with double-length windows for uninterrupted views of the river and a cozy bar, reading room, dining room, and shopping arcade.

All the ships have large sun decks and, except for the *Italia* and *Austria*, all have a heated outdoor swimming pool. The cuisine on board favors German specialties, with plentiful Rhine and Moselle wines at moderate prices. On four of the vessels—the *Europa*, *Austria*, *Helvetia*, and *Italia*—simple dining offers buffet breakfasts and three-course luncheons and dinners. This, instead of served breakfasts and five-course meals the rest of the day, results in lower prices (by about thirty percent) as compared to ships with deluxe service.

These eight vessels sail from the source of the Rhine to its mouth between April and the end of October, with some special cruises offered in November and December. It takes one week to "do" the river, but most of the sailings range from two to five days in either direction. Major cities along the way include Basel, Strasbourg, Worms, Mainz, Koblenz, Bonn, Cologne, and Nijmegen. The ships anchor each evening along the riverbank, so passengers can take a stroll after dinner or go into the nearest village for a beer, and get underway again in the wee hours of the morning.

Special cruises include a five-country, six-day sailing from Basel to Antwerp, Rhine/Moselle cruises of six days from Rotterdam or from Basel, a wine seminar from Basel to Rotterdam of seven days on the Rhine and Moselle rivers, and both Christmas and New Year's cruises from Cologne (five days). Since the 1982 season KD offers the Bed and Breakfast Cruise, an attractively priced concept that lets you discover the Rhine River. The idea keeps costs down, and only a few hearty travelers would want three full German meals. The only problem I find with this company is that some of the ships are far better than the others (at least for Americans), and it is often difficult to know exactly which vessel you will embark until you do so.

SHERATON NILE CRUISES

% The Sheraton Corporation
60 State Street
Boston, Massachusetts 02109
Tel: (617) 367–3600
or
Sheraton Hotels
P.O. Box 125
Orman, Giza
Egypt

Sheraton Hotels in Egypt operates four identical hotel-barges year-round on the Nile River between Luxor and Aswan. These 89-cabin vessels built in Scandinavia, named the *Tut, Aton, Anni,* and *Htop,* have a total of about twenty-five sailings each month of either four or seven nights. The 235-foot barges carry 178 passengers in two-berth cabins (some have an additional berth for a third person). All accommodations have private facilities, air conditioning, and lots of wardrobe space. In addition, each barge has a large restaurant and lounge/bar that reverts to a disco in the evening. Live entertainment, a swimming pool, and a sun deck that is popular at cocktail time provide pleasant distractions. Two meal seatings offer lunch at noon or 1:15 p.m. and dinner at 7 p.m. or 8:15 p.m. All meals, plus afternoon tea, shore excursions, and entertainment are included in the cruise fare.

The four-night cruises visit the temples at Luxor and Karnak, the Valley of the Kings, Esna, Edfu, Kom Ombo, and Aswan. The seven-night itinerary features Luxor and Karnak, Thebes, Nag 'Hammadi, Abydos, Dendera, Esna, Edfu, Kom Ombo, and Aswan/Elephantine/Kitchener/Aga Khan Mausoleum as well as the High Dam/Old Dam, granite quarries, and Philae Temple. The order of sites reverses when the barges sail from Aswan to Luxor. These are spacious vessels—perfect for travelers who enjoy having a little legroom.

11. / THE CRUISE LINES

AMERICAN CANADIAN LINE

461 Water Street
Warren, Rhode Island 02885
tel: (401) 245–1350 or
    (800) 556–7450 for outside R.I.

American Canadian Line has been operating mini-cruises along the New England coastline and the inland waterways of Canada for well over a decade, and its small vessels have sailed many more than a million miles. Last year the line launched the *New Shoreham II*, a 150-foot, 72-passenger cruiser with three decks and a draft of only six feet—allowing her to dock just about anywhere.

The *New Shoreham II* sails out of Warren, Rhode Island, during the summer season on New England coastal and island cruises, which include a series of three-night weekend cruises to Block Island, Martha's Vineyard, Cape Cod, and Newport. The longer sailings call at Mystic, Connecticut; Cape Cod; Long Island; and Nantucket. From June to August twelve-day cruises are available between Warren and the Saguenay River (with connecting buses for the return trip). On these voyages the vessel cruises the Hudson River, the Erie Canal, Lake Ontario, and the St. Lawrence and Saguenay rivers. Fall foliage cruises take place in October, and in November the *New Shoreham II* sails from Warren to Palm Beach, Florida, en route to her winter home.

During the winter months the *New Shoreham II* is based in Nassau for twelve-day cruises to the Bahama Out Islands. Two itineraries are offered. One cruises around Eleuthera and Exuma Cays and the other sails in and out of Grand Bahama and Great Abaco islands. Swimming, snorkeling, bonefishing, sailing (the ship carries small boats), and collecting shells are the order of the day. Life is very casual on board. The cabins are rather small, so luggage should be kept to a minimum. Days are spent playing in the water or walking on the beach, and in the evening you are left to your own entertainment devices. The dining room seats all passengers at one time, and meal service is family style, with menus geared to American taste buds. There is no need to dress up; a nice sports shirt for men and a long cotton skirt for women are appropriate. The brochure advises to BYOB (bring your own bottle), although sodas are supplied. No money on board is necessary other than any gratuities you wish to present at the end of your wonderful cruise.

AMERICAN CRUISE LINES

1 Marine Park
Haddam, Connecticut 06438   *tomorrow.*
tel: (203) 345–8551

This very small, very American cruise line, located at Steamboat Landing in Haddam, Connecticut, operates three vessels built especially for coastal sailing. These delightful little ships provide another dimension in leisure cruising, for they are able to call at out-of-the-way islands and quaint, tiny harbors in perfect comfort. The summer cruises hug the coast, bays, and sounds of New England (you are seldom out of sight of land), while the southern routes follow the beautiful Atlantic Intracoastal Waterway all the way to Florida. This waterway is an inland passage of interconnecting rivers, canals, landcuts, locks, and sounds that form a protected route. The southern cruises depart from Baltimore, Maryland; Savannah, Georgia; or Fort Meyers, Florida. The New England Islands sailings depart from home port in Haddam or Rockland, Maine.

American Cruise Lines is owned and operated by a most energetic and enterprising fellow in his early forties named Charles A. Robertson. A former airline pilot who hung around shipyards while growing up in New Jersey, Robertson's simple success story is an inspiration to all Americans who want to do their own thing. When he retired from commercial flying, Robertson chose affluent, upper-strata Connecticut as the base for his new leisure-oriented company and began by offering day-cruises out of Haddam.

He designed and built the 49-passenger *American Eagle* in 1975, and the following year launched the 78-passenger *Independence*. He also acquired the shipyard in which she was built, and saved considerable time and money in construction. He eventually moved the ship-building facilities to Salisbury, Maryland, and completed the *America* in April, 1982. Because of his no-nonsense, get-the-job-done philosophy, Robertson's shipyard has had recent queries from officials who operate the Staten Island ferry as well as others running hotel boats along the Nile.

The passengers Robertson attracts on these three vessels are people who just love to cruise, and many have recently disembarked the *QE2* or *Rotterdam*. Aboard American Cruise Lines, these passengers are able to enjoy the American shoreline in a most relaxed manner. There is no commercial bar in the lounge, although the Captain hosts about three cocktail parties per cruise. Otherwise, it's bring your own bottle (BYOB), and don't worry about the sodas and ice (they're always set up). In the past, many passengers have come all the way from California to enjoy the sights along the Eastern seaboard. The Smithsonian and National Trust for Historic Preservation are also good customers, and their members love the cruises along the intracoastal waterway for history and wildlife.

Although Haddam will continue to be home port for the company, Robertson is planning more and more sailings from Baltimore. He has found the cruise to Savannah so popular that he plans to offer more sailings there. Also in the future is another ship, built at his own yard, designed to carry over one hundred passengers in riverboat style (with private verandas on many staterooms). It is certainly rewarding to spend time aboard these vessels as well as to watch this small company grow as it offers so many lovely cruises along our very own shores.

All the staterooms of the 49-passenger *American Eagle* are on the outside and above the main deck; all also contain a large opening window, twin beds (except one double and one single), and private facilities. The atmosphere on board, congenial and homey, flourishes in the Nantucket Lounge, with comfortable, parlorlike furniture, an electric player piano, card table, self-service bar (with complimentary set-ups), and small library. The dining room seats all passengers for family-style meals, and menus are posted daily on the bulletin board. Dinner hours, strictly nonglamorous, begin at 6 p.m., while breakfast is served from 7:30 to 9 a.m. and lunch at 12:30 p.m. Breakfasts are hearty, lunches are light (soup, sandwiches, salads), and dinners feature American specialties like Cornish game hen or freshly caught seafood. When not touring the various ports of call, you are left to your own devices for entertainment. Chances are you will enjoy the company of your fellow passengers for conversation, bridge, or watching the coastline. During October the vessel offers Hudson River Foliage Cruises from Haddam.

A newer member of this American-flag fleet is the 78-passenger *Independence*, built in Maine 1976, a year later than her sister ship. Similar in appearance and construction to the *American Eagle*, the *Independence* has thirty-seven doubles, four singles, and two triple cabins, all with opening window and private facilities. The Nantucket Lounge and dining room function in the same manner as the *Eagle*, and both vessels have two spacious sun decks. As cruising speed is about eleven knots per hour, life is relaxed and casual on board both ships.

The newest member of the growing fleet is the M/V *America*, launched in Baltimore's Inner Harbor in April 1983. This 83-passenger vessel, the country's largest coastal cruise ship thus far, is just slightly larger than her sister ship

Independence. Each of the 47 cabins have two regular beds, large picture windows that open, the standard glass-enclosed Nantucket Lounge with player piano and color TV, and two sun decks—and a crew of 17 fresh, young faces. The dining area has round tables set for six and some of the staterooms can be made into suites if there is a demand. Standard on all three American Cruise Line vessels are the complimentary bar setups in the lounge, freshly-baked cookies for morning coffee and afternoon tea, and cheese snacks during cocktail hour.

AMERICAN HAWAII CRUISES   *seamen union*

One Embarcadero Center   *808 521·0384*
San Francisco, California 94111   *604 FORT ST*
tel: (415) 392–9400   *Honolu Ha, 96813*

The C. Y. Tung family, Hong Kong-based ship owners (remember the *Queen Elizabeth* and the ill-fated Seawise University?) are behind this new company, formed to operate inter-Hawaiian island cruises aboard the *Oceanic Independence*. This 30,090-ton vessel is the former *Independence* of American Export Lines, built in 1951 at the Bethlehem Quincy Shipyard in Massachusetts. The *Independence*, well known in her heyday, offered long cruise itineraries and boasted fine first-class interiors which were designed under the direction of the popular Henry Dreyfuss. In her twilight years, however, the *Independence* suffered along with her colleagues from lack of interest in cruises. A very sad picture of her in my favorite passenger ship history book (*Sail, Steam and Splendour* by Bryon S. Miller) shows her sailing out of port with psychedelic stripes and a huge sunburst lady painted on her exterior. According to the caption, it was an attempt to capture a younger crowd for cruising and pay-as-you-eat meals, but the experiment failed and the vessel was retired. C. Y. Tung's Atlantic Far East Line picked her up and rechristened her the *Oceanic Independence* in 1974.

When American Hawaii Cruises was formed with plans to operate the *Oceanic Independence* in American waters again, cruising passengers from port to port, a special bill had to be approved by Congress and signed into law by the President. Accomplished in November 1979, the bill allows an American-built (and subsidized) vessel that had been decommissioned (that is, sold to a foreign concern) to return to American waters and carry the U.S. flag.

With this approval, a spruced-up and sparkling *Oceanic Independence* began interisland Hawaiian cruises in June 1980, painted sparkling white like the former Matson liners that dominated these waters in the good old days. Although the vessel island-hops, the passengers must stay aboard for the full seven days, because Federal shipping regulations restrict the ship line from carrying anyone from point to point. So don't jump ship at your favorite Aloha port, if you please.

The week-long cruises depart Honolulu's Aloha Tower at midnight every Saturday, and you spend the first day at sea sailing slowly around Molokai,

Maui, and Lanai. The vessel calls at Hilo, on the Big Island of Hawaii, from 8 a.m. Monday to midnight. Take your time on Tuesday exploring the other side of the island from the lovely Kona coastline; passengers must tender in here, as there are no docking facilities. On Wednesday the *Oceanic Independence* calls at Kuhului, Maui. Thursday and Friday are devoted to Kauai and the port of Nawiliwili. The vessel returns to Honolulu on Saturday at 7 a.m. and excellent air-sea programs from throughout the mainland are available to take you home. Shore excursions have been planned well at each of these ports of call, but many passengers prefer to have a rental car waiting (book ahead) and drive around themselves for the day.

The 30,000-ton *Constitution,* sister ship of the *Oceanic Independence* and also built at Bethlehem Quincy Shipyards in Massachusetts in 1951 for American Export Line, was also returned to U.S.-flag status by executive order in the early months of 1982. At inauguration the late Princess Grace of Monaco smashed a bottle of champagne against the ship's bow in Kaohsiung, Taiwan, where the vessel was being refurbished for inter-Hawaiian-island cruises. The *Constitution* was always a favorite of the Princess. As Academy-award-winning movie star Grace Kelly, she sailed aboard the *Constitution* to her fairy-tale wedding and principality on the Côte d'Azur. She later boarded the vessel with her Monarch-of-Monaco husband, Prince Rainier, and then took an additional voyage alone.

The 800-passenger *Constitution* began service from Honolulu in June 1982 on the same course as the *Oceanic Independence* but in reverse order. The vessel boasts four bars and two each of lounges, swimming pools, and dining rooms.

American Hawaii Cruises has also reinstituted a series of trans-Pacific sailings from either Honolulu or West Coast ports (Los Angeles, San Francisco, and Seattle) aboard the *Oceanic Independence* in response to a demand for the romantic, old days of the Matson Line. After all, many a romance began on these crossings between California and our fiftieth state . . . at least so the movies say . . . so why not revive a wonderful tradition?

ASTOR UNITED CRUISES

P.O. Box 13140
Port Everglades Station
Fort Lauderdale, Florida 33316
tel: (305) 523–3200
    (800) 432–3611 (in Florida)
    (800) 327–8152 (elsewhere in U.S.)

This German-financed cruise line is still in the trial stage for North American credentials. The cruise company operates one vessel—the 18,000-ton *Astor,* which can carry approximately 683 passengers. The company recently built this first-rate $55 million vessel and then announced that it was after the "five-star" market. This market, however, has grown accustomed to ships far more spacious than the *Astor,* and to cabin and bathroom facilities that are better, and to ships with a higher passenger-to-crew ratio (at the very least, two to one). The fact that none of the standard-cabin bathrooms feature tubs is sloughed off by a company spokesman who presumes that people between the ages of fifty and 100 years don't take baths. Nonsense! (We understand that their "no-bath" savings also included no curtains for the showers.)

The *Astor* appears to be a welcome addition to the North American cruise market; but for true success, the company should not attempt overwhelming aspirations. If the mix of eighty percent Americans during Caribbean season and some fifty percent during the summer in Europe is accurate, then the English spoken on board must be perfected by many of the service crew.

The *Astor* seems to have a most impressive itinerary. The vessel sails in the Caribbean, along the central eastern seaboard of South America (from Belem to Buenos Aires) and into Manaus on the Amazon, across the Atlantic, and into the Baltic Sea, the North Cape, and the Arctic/Iceland area. In addition, it plans to make an Egypt/Israel cruise.

BAHAMA CRUISE LINE

61 Broadway
New York, N.Y. 10006
tel: (212) 480–0177

The little-known Bahama Cruise Line underwent a rebirth recently and is finding a well-deserved place in the cruise industry. Formerly part of the Transway freight company, Bahama Cruise Line is now a wholly owned subsidiary of a British shipping firm called Common Brothers Ltd. One might say that Common Brothers Ltd. has been in travel since 1890, when the firm was established to transport British troops to Hindustan!

Common Brothers also owns Bahama Cruise Line's only vessel at present, the *Veracruz I,* which sails from Tampa during the winter season and between New and Montreal all summer. Both itineraries are imaginative and most successful (and the copycats are following quickly). The seven-hundred passenger *Veracruz I* has been flying the Panamanian flag for Bahama Cruise Line since 1973, although the vessel has been around much longer. She was built in 1957 as war reparations by the German Government, and known then as the *Theodor Hertzl* of Zim Lines. Following a period of trans-Atlantic service, the vessel was sold for cruises and renamed the *Freeport. Veracruz I* suits the 10,595-ton vessel very well, indeed.

Bahama Cruise Line has not only developed new ports of embarkation and some exciting itineraries in the past few years, but has also added a choice of lengthy shore excursions for their passengers. From mid-October to June, the vessel sails from Tampa to the Yucatan every Saturday. Passengers who wish to explore more of the Land of the Maya may opt for a seven-day sail, visiting Merida, Uxmal, Chichen Itza, the Lagoon at Xel-Ha, Tulum, and Cancun before taking the cruise back to Tampa. For water sports enthusiasts, the line offers a number of snorkeling and scuba diving adventures for both the novice and experienced. In addition to the Mexican ports, the vessel calls at Key West for a brief introduction to one of America's quaintest towns.

It is just this interest in North America that will prove to make the new Bahama Cruise Line image a success. The summer program between Montreal and New York is one of the best itineraries available for it combines the history, beauty, and big-city life of the Northeast. Passengers traveling to Montreal may take the train back to New York along a very scenic route, fly, or receive a discount on the return cruise. This is certainly a wonderful way to enjoy a beautiful part of the world!

Bahama has spent a few million dollars upgrading the engine room and plans to refurbish some of the public areas. There is not much one can do about the size of the cabins (small), but they are kept very well and the service personnel from some sixteen countries are very pleasant and helpful.

BERGEN LINE

505 Fifth Avenue
New York, N.Y. 10017
tel: (212) 986–2711

This Norwegian-based company operates ferry services between Bergen/Oslo/ England/Holland/Germany, and acts as U.S. general agent for a number of other Scandinavian shipping interests all in cooperation with SAS. Among these are the Silja Line cruises between Sweden and Finland (Stockholm/ Turku/Mariehamn/Helsinki) that no longer visit the USSR, and the Jahre Line passenger/car ferry operated between Oslo and Kiel.

Bergen's best offer is the Norwegian coastal service, operated by a conglomerate of four local steamship companies. Simple but congenial cargo/mail/ passenger vessels make the 2500-mile scenic voyage through the Norwegian fjords and to the North Cape in eleven days round trip from Bergen, calling at as many as thirty-three ports along the way. They operate year-round, and rates vary according to season. With spare but clean, almost first-class accommodations, and three meals daily, these ships do not compare to the luxury cruise vessels that find their way to the North Cape every summer, but neither do the prices. If you're interested in enjoying the fjordlands as the natives do, waving as the townsfolk come out to greet the vessel (often a source of communication), and spending one-quarter of what other vessels cost, you will enjoy this experience! And you'll probably make many interesting friends. If you prefer, a twelve-day voyage from Bergen to Spitsbergen and return is available from mid-June to the end of August. The highlight is sailing above the Arctic Circle and receiving a certificate from Father Neptune! Passengers sixty-seven years of age and over will be entitled to a discount during all periods except the summer season—May 22 to August 12. (Proof of age is required.)

CARNIVAL CRUISE LINES

820 Biscayne Blvd.
Miami, Florida 33132
tel: (305) 377–4751

Carnival Cruise Lines, slick and sales-oriented, is operated by a young set of officers who have no strong link to the old world of shipping. A hard-hitting, competitive, and forceful company, it peddles its products nonstop to singles, honeymooners, families, old and young, and just about everyone who will listen. While I do not always agree with what these people have to say, I admire the exuberance and enthusiasm that has brought them over the past years to their present fleet. The company operates four large vessels that have boasted an average occupancy rate of well over one hundred percent for years; they may even set some kind of record for these fun-filled ships.

Carnival launched the first of this new-born fleet with the flagship *Mardi Gras* in 1973. This 27,250-ton vessel, carrying an easy 906 passengers, was the former *Empress of Canada*. A year later Carnival developed the "Fun Ship" theme, which soon became associated with sparkling white exteriors and a red, white, and blue smokestack that is recognized in every Caribbean port. In 1976 the ship line launched the *Carnivale*, the former *Empress of Britain*, sister ship of the *Mardi Gras*. Both vessels were converted from North Atlantic sailings to full-time Caribbean cruising, but both still have the old-time, less-than-elegant look of their past. However, these ships do well, catering to the night owl set, who love to eat, drink and be merry on into the wee hours. The *Carnivale* set occupancy records since her launching, carrying well over the 950-passenger complement forecast.

Then, the 38,175-ton *Festivale* joined the fleet in 1978. The former SA *Vaal* of Trans-Vaal Castle Line carries just over 1400 passengers and has done very well since her relaunching as a Caribbean cruise ship.

Carnival recently introduced its much-touted ship of the eighties to cruise clientele in the Caribbean. Called the *Tropicale*, the $100 million, Danish-built vessel has a capacity for 1,200-plus passengers and is considered by the ship line to be *the* fun ship of their now four-fun-ship-fleet. The vessel has been well-designed, with plenty of deck space for the swinging crowd, an enormous casino, and just enough spit-and-polish to be vaguely impressive. Cabins are comfortable and, with the exception of twelve veranda-suites on Verandah Deck, all are the same size with large windows, closed-circuit color television, and twin beds that can be joined for a king-size treat. Emphasis is on having a good time and dropping lots of money in the casino or at any of the several bars. A note of caution from my own experience: watch the bartender when you order a drink, especially if you wish to have some liquor in it. A ship line spokesperson once admitted that more money was made on the bars than in the casinos, and I found it obvious why.

Carnival has already announced a decision to build three jumbo-size cruise vessels over the next six years or so. Each vessel is expected to cost about $150 million, be around 45,000 tons, and carry up to 1,800 passengers (if every available berth were sold). The first of the series is scheduled to be delivered by mid-1984, which seems rather optimistic as of this writing. Carnival, however, is just the company to perform such a miracle—if anyone can!

The *Tropicale* sails from Los Angeles to Puerto Vallarta, Mazatlan, and Cabo San Lucas. Other destinations include Alaskan/Canadian waters for Westours.

CHANDRIS, INC.

666 Fifth Avenue
New York, N.Y. 10019
tel: (212) 586–8370

The founder of Chandris, Inc., John D. Chandris, bought his first vessel in 1915 and entered the passenger shipping business in 1922 with the 300-ton *Chimara*. Today Chandris is run by the younger son of the founder (Dimitrios) and by the grandchildren. The first Chandris was born in Chios, an island off the coast of Turkey that is renowned for supplying shipping tycoons to modern Greece. This particular native son not only started the successful ship line, but also began a shipyard and built hotels all around the Aegean—which means that you can spend a week on a vessel (mainly the *Romanza*) and a week in one of the Chandris hotels on Corfu, Chios, Crete, or in Athens. All of these hotels are attractive and convenient except for the new Athens property, which is rather out of the way for ardent sightseers but just right for those who prefer horse racing and beach life.

The Chandris fleet, extensive but extremely confusing, keeps you guessing from month to month exactly which vessels will be employed, which will be chartered to other concerns, or which will be returned to mothballs. I think many of these cruise ships should be permanently retired, as they are rather old and worn. According to the latest roundup filed with Cruise Lines International Association, an organization of cruise line operators, Chandris still counts the *Amerikanis* (the former *Kenya Castle*), the *Ariane* (formerly the *Ariadne* and *Bon Vivant*), the *Britanis* (former *Monterey*), *Ellinis* (former *Lurline*), *Italis* (formerly the *America* and *Australis*), *Regina Prima* (former *President Hoover*), *Romanza* (former *Aurelia*), and *Victoria* (former *Dunottar Castle*). Built as early as 1932 and 1939, some vessels are considerably older than many of the passengers on board.

The 25,000-ton *Britanis* is on charter to a firm that calls itself Fantasy Cruises and sails from New York on "party cruises," from overnight to five days. From late December through April, the 15,000-ton *Victoria* alternates itineraries on a Monday to Monday schedule calling one week at Curaçao, La Guaira, Grenada, Martinique, and St. Thomas on Itinerary A. Simply substitute Aruba for Curaçao for Itinerary B. The *Amerikanis*, under a charter agreement to Costa Line year-round from Miami on three- and four-day cruises to Nassau and Freeport in the Bahama Islands.

Chandris's Europacruises feature sailings around the entire Mediterranean and Aegean, the Canary Islands, and the North Cape on three different vessels. The 7500-ton *Romanza* departs from Venice every Saturday from mid-May to mid-October to the Greek islands, calling at Dubrovnik, Corfu, Heraklion, Kuşadasi, Patmos, and Piraeus. You may also embark the *Romanza* at Piraeus for Thursday to Thursday sailings. Meanwhile, the *Victoria* begins the summer season by sailing from Amsterdam on fourteen-day cruises to the northern capitals, North Cape and Spitsbergen, and North Cape/Norwegian fjords. She then repositions herself in Genoa for the month of October for two fourteen-day cruises in the eastern Mediterranean. In December departs Genoa for the westbound transatlantic voyage to San Juan, and passengers are invited aboard for the crossing that calls at eastern Mediterranean and Caribbean ports along the way.

COMMODORE CRUISE LINE

1015 North America Way
Miami, Florida 33132
tel: (305) 358–2622

This Florida-based cruise line, with offices right on Dodge Island in the heart of the active Port of Miami, operates two vessels with West German registry and officers. This "Happy Ship," the *Boheme*, is comfortable and geared to a young, active crowd not particularly interested in the luxury-class ships. Commodore offers good value and fills a need for cruises in this category.

The 11,000-ton *Boheme*, built in Finland in 1968 and refurbished in 1977, carries five hundred passengers every Saturday from Miami to Puerto Plata, St. Thomas, San Juan, and Cap Haitien. Named by its Swedish owner after his favorite opera, *La Boheme* by Puccini, the vessel's interior design reflects Paris in the romantic era of the early 1800s. You can find works of art by painters Ann Bergson, Zoia, and Angelo Romano throughout the public rooms, which are named after characters in *La Boheme* as well as for famous areas in which artists gathered in the Paris of this period. Marcello Lounge and Cafe des Artistes are on Promenade Deck; the Rodolfo Lounge, Puccini, and Paris dining rooms and Salle Musetta on Main Deck. Main Deck also houses Le Club Mimi and Place Montmartre, which opens onto the shopping area.

The food on the vessel has a good—but not gourmet—reputation, and the ship line makes a point of saying that it does *not* concession any of its food and beverage services, as so many ships in the Caribbean do. Lively entertainment on board befits the type of passengers, and the line specializes in Oktoberfest cruises, with lots of good German beer, pretzels, and all the trimmings during the month of October. Other theme cruises are available, and families are encouraged to bring their entire entourage during the summer months. Reasonable prices and the four-port itinerary attract many passengers.

COSTA CRUISES

733 Third Avenue
New York, N.Y. 10017
tel: (212) 632–7520
    (800) 223–8908
    (800) 522–2288 for New York State

Costa Cruises considers itself the largest cruise fleet in the world, with eleven ships in constant motion. Costa is also one of the oldest privately owned maritime firms in Italy, established in 1924 with the purchase of the freighter *Ravenna*, although the Genoa-based family has been in the olive oil business since 1860. Over a century ago, Giacomo Costa and his brother began importing the oil from Sardinia, refining it, and exporting it throughout Europe. To do so, they needed vessels and a soon-booming cargo business led to passengers and cruises. The company claims it pioneered Caribbean cruises from San Juan in 1968, and today home-ports at least three vessels in Puerto Rico. Frankly, I have always felt that Costa is synonymous with "confusion," not only because of the vast numbers of relatives who pass through the company but also because one never knows where the fleet actually is. In my experience, Costa will announce a year-round program (say, from San Juan), then abruptly charters that vessel to another company for the summer . . . and so on. This constant state of waves must drive travel agents bonkers!

According to the latest statistics, the Costa fleet consists of: the 748-passenger *Carla C* (everyone's absolute favorite!) which sails mostly year-round from San Juan to the lower Caribbean; the 426-passenger *World Renaissance* (on long-term charter from Epirotiki Lines) which also sails from San Juan, although some successful eastern seabord (Jacksonville, Philadelphia, Baltimore, and Charleston) cruises to Bermuda from May through July will most likely be offered; the 465-passenger sister ships *Daphne* and *Danae* (on long-term charter from the defunct Carras Cruises) which sail mainly from San Juan during the winter months, sometimes in the Mediterranean through summer, and anywhere else you could imagine; the venerable but beloved 617-passenger *Amerikanis* (on long-term charter from Chandris, Inc.) which offers three- and four-day cruises from Miami to the Bahamas. The *Amerikanis* was originally scheduled to cruise out of Port Everglades, but was repositioned last year to replace the *Flavia*, which the company sold to another line.

The Costa fleet also contains a number of vessels that only sail in European and South American waters. Possibly through the export of olive oil to South America, the company discovered a goldmine in the passenger business and began carrying immigrants in 1948 with the *Anna C*. She was succeeded by a number of other ships, all named after Costa grandchildren. Today, any one of the *Enrico C.*, *Federico C.*, *Eugenio C.*, *Andrea C.*, *Italia*, or *Columbus* can be seen South of the border, primarily offering cruises between Rio, Buenos Aires, and the tip of the continent. Shopping spree cruises to Miami from South America were also popular a while ago, but Costa keeps a low profile on much of this business.

During the summer, the better vessels in the fleet are employed in the Mediterranean, where Costa innovated air-sea programs as early as 1959 from Genoa and in 1967 from Venice. These well-priced programs from the U.S. are popular, especially for travelers who love Italians and want to see Europe in a most relaxed manner (but don't mind if every corner of the ship is not spic and span). Costa's cruises have a great deal of charm and certainly provide an element of romance that is lacking on many other ships—it must be that Italian crew and kitchen!

At this writing, the *Amerikanis* will sail all year from Miami to the Bahamas on three- and four-day cruises (until replaced by a newer vessel). From San Juan, the *Carla C.*, *Daphne* and *World Renaissance* will sail every week on splendid itineraries to the lower Caribbean. The *World Renaissance* will also sail from East Coast ports to Bermuda from late spring to summer, and the *Daphne* will again be in the Alaska/Canada cruise market during the season. In the Mediterranean from May through October, the *Italia* will probably offer seven-day Sunday sailings from Venice to the Greek Islands, the *Enrico C.* will sail on Saturdays from Genoa to the western Mediterranean, the *Federico C.* will offer ten-day cruises from Genoa to the Canary Islands and North Africa, and the *Danae* will sail on alternate Saturdays from Venice to the Greek Islands/Egypt and Israel. Flagship of the fleet is the *Eugenio C.*, which sails from Genoa on eleven- and thirteen-day cruises to the Black Sea, eastern Mediterranean and Africa/Canary Islands. My best advice is—see your travel agent to be sure . . . but don't miss the boat!

CUNARD LINE

555 Fifth Avenue
New York, N.Y. 10017
tel: (212) 880-7500

Cunard Line, which started life as the British and North American Royal Mail Steam-Packet Company just over 140 years ago, was the first to offer regular transatlantic passenger service and has remained the last. The visionary behind such an undertaking was a merchant from Halifax, Nova Scotia, named Samuel Cunard, who took an idea to London in 1839: scheduled mail service on the North Atlantic was possible. A few passengers could come along too, he added. Cunard cajoled a mail contract out of the British Admiralty, and a year later he launched the *Britannia* which left Liverpool on July 4, 1840. The voyage to Boston took fourteen days and eight hours, and the *Britannia* received a tumultuous welcome. The Boston citizenry were so proud of this new service that they presented Cunard with an enormous sterling silver loving cup as a memento. Miraculously, the cup has survived 140 years of stormy seas and wars, and is on view just as you enter the Columbia Dining Room of the QE2.

The *Britannia* was a wooden paddle-steamer of 1150 tons with a 207-foot hull. She carried noteworthy passengers including novelist Charles Dickens, who sailed to Boston in 1842 and was shocked to discover his stateroom was nothing more than a closet, even though he had booked deluxe accommodations. He called it "utterly impractical, thoroughly hopeless, and a profoundly preposterous box." However, he and his two roommates finaly agreed that the cabin could be quite spacious, especially if they all turned around in unison!

In 1847 Cunard added the port of New York to the transatlantic itinerary, and the Admiralty agreed to increase his mail subsidy. By the end of the decade the fleet had doubled and the North Atlantic was becoming "crowded," Cunard cried. But in 1856 he launched the biggest ship ever—the *Persia*—twice the length of the *Britannia*, with paddles that were no less than forty feet in diameter, a capacity for three times the passengers than before, and a record speed of fourteen knots. Although Cunard Line never formally recognized the famous "Blue Riband," the award to the fastest ship on the Atlantic service presented from the 1880s to the end of the 1960s, the launching of the *Persia* began a racetrack atmosphere.

Hence, the history of passenger service on the North Atlantic closely parallels the development of Cunard Line (and you might say, its denouement). At the end of the nineteenth century Cunard was building ships in pairs, following specifications laid down by Lloyds and decorating them in the manner of the day—Victorian—with velvet drapes, stained-glass cupolas, and wooden paneling. The twentieth century brought the turbine engine and such sister ships as the *Carmania* and *Caronia*, *Mauretania* and *Lusitania*.

But the most famous of all Cunard's vessels are, undoubtedly, the *Queen Mary* and *Queen Elizabeth*. These two ships were planned with dollar signs in the eyes of company officials, so that every week of the year (with the exception of brief overhaul periods) one Queen would depart Southampton, the other New York, at a speed of about twenty eight and one-half knots. The *Queen Mary* was launched in 1937 and, by the next year, was the fastest ship in Atlantic service. The *Queen Elizabeth* did not fare so auspiciously at first, but began life stealing across the North Atlantic under the cover of wartime gray. The vessel did not carry any paying passengers until after the war. During the war the two *Queens* had together transported over a million troops back and forth across the seas. Of this service Winston Churchill commented, "The world owes them a debt that it will not be able to measure."

In the postwar years when Europe was again reachable, life was heady for Cunard Line. The two *Queens* were the most prestigious ships on the transatlantic run, not for their cuisine especially but for their traditional British-style service and for afternoon tea and violins among the palms—and for all the elegant people (not to mention the misplaced royalty) who sailed aboard them! But within two decades, the dream faded. In September 1967 the *Queen Mary* tooted to her younger sister, the *Queen Elizabeth*, for the last time as they passed midway across the Atlantic. Less than one year later, the *Elizabeth* was retired and on her way to an ignominious end—to be ravaged by fire in Hong Kong harbor.

Cunard was not without a *Queen* for long. In the spring of 1979 Queen Elizabeth II used the same pair of gold scissors to cut the launching cord of the

QE2 that her mother and grandmother had used while christening the two ships named after them. It was a lovely beginning for the splendid new 67,107-ton vessel filled with the latest in transport technology. Her 1700 passengers have thirteen decks and fourteen public rooms through which to roam, as well as four swimming pools, two gymnasia, several saunas, and a complete hospital. One can get lost but not bored on the QE2. And the old lady hangs in there, offering the only regular passenger service from New York to Southampton between April and December, interspersed with more lucrative short cruises. From January to April she circumnavigates the world—sometimes in as little as eighty days, just because she's the only ship that can do so.

The Queen's schedule was disrupted in 1982; the British government requisitioned her for war service in the Falkland Island crisis. The interior of the vessel was stripped down to carry troops, and helicopter pads were welded to the top decks. Over seven hundred members of her crew volunteered for service and received combat pay as well as a citation from Her Majesty's government. Fortunately, the vessel received no damage, just a heroine's welcome upon her return to Southampton in July. She was completely refurbished, more outdoor dance space was designed, and the ship was fitted with a floating Golden Door health spa for all passengers' use. The QE2 returned to service on August 14, 1982, a wiser and more respected lady of the sea.

The Queen usually offers a world cruise, but in 1983 she departs New York for a Circle Pacific and Orient Odyssey tour. The exciting 1983 voyage features six maiden arrivals for the vessel and a call in China (Qingdao). Passengers who do not wish to spend the full 89 days aboard may take shorter segments, with excellent air-fare allowances as an added enticement.

Cunard also operates two warm-weather, short-cruising vessels, the Cunard Countess and the Cunard Princess. In the ship line's tradition, the two vessels were designed identically and built simultaneously. In August 1976 the Countess was launched in San Juan by Mrs. Neil Armstrong (wife of the first man to walk on the moon) who was chosen to symbolize the vessel's interior astrotheme. The Princess was launched in New York harbor by the late Princess Grace of Monaco in March 1977. Both 17,500-ton ships carry up to eight hundred passengers, primarily to ports in the lower Caribbean. The Countess sails from San Juan every Saturday year-round for La Guaira, Grenada, Barbados, Martinique, and St. Thomas. The Princess winters in San Juan, sailing every Saturday (October to May) for St. Kitts, St. Maarten, Guadeloupe, Iles de Saintes, St. Lucia, St. Thomas, Virgin Gorda, and Tortola. This Seven-Plus itinerary offers nine different port/island calls. From the end of May to mid-September, she cruises from Vancouver to Alaska's Inside Passage. In between these two assignments, she offers repositioning cruises through the Panama Canal—westbound in May, eastbound in September.

Because Cunard Hotels is a sister company, passengers aboard the three cruise vessels—the QE2, the Princess, and the Countess—have an excellent opportunity to stay in any of several fine properties in England and the Caribbean. For Princess and Countess passengers, a special Sail 'n Stay two-week package is available that combines a seven-day cruise with another seven days at either Hotel La Toc in St. Lucia or the Paradise Beach Hotel in Barbados (free nine months of the year). About four years ago Cunard Hotels took over London's famed Ritz and spent some $15 million bringing the historic place back to its grand style of 1906. Across Picadilly is the Bristol, another Cunard hotel. Both are convenient for QE2 transatlantic passengers. On a much less elegant scale is the Cunard International Hotel between Heathrow and London, but golfers will enjoy the Cambridgeshire Hotel & Golf Club in Cambridge, England.

Two years ago Sir Samuel Cunard was posthumously inducted into the Travel Hall of Fame as a recognition of his lasting contributions to and vision in the travel industry. Cunard's plan not only to inaugurate transatlantic service between England and America, but also to insure a regular schedule certainly deserves kudos. As with many who had imagination and perseverance, Sir Samuel Cunard altered and advanced the course of (maritime) history.

DELTA LINE CRUISES

2700 Stewart Street Tower   One World Trade Center
One Market Plaza   Suite 3647
San Francisco, California 94106   New York, N.Y. 10048
tel: (415) 777-8300   tel: (212) 432-4700

Delta Lines, basically a cargo company (based on New Orleans), now operates the famous 100-passenger cargo liners that sailed under the Prudential name for almost a decade. This cargo/passenger service that concentrates on South American ports is an outgrowth of the famed Grace Line and the tall-sparred clipper ships of the 1860s. Since the 1960s a few name changes reflected changing ownership—from Grace to Prudential to Delta—but the service to South America has not been interrupted.

The company runs four 100-passenger, 20,000-ton liners (*Santa Maria, Mariana, Mercedes,* and *Magdalena*) that were launched in 1963–64 and run on a continual schedule from Vancouver down the West Coast, through the Panama Canal, and around South America in a clockwise direction. The schedule is such that one of the four Santa liners leaves Vancouver every two weeks. Because these are basically cargo ships, their time in any port of call is rather flexible, and in fact, the itinerary may change somewhat during the sailing. Rarely a problem to the passengers these ships draw, the definitely older, retired set seem to have both the time and money to spend on this type of cruise vacation. The itinerary from Vancouver and through the Strait of Magellan features calls at Tacoma, San Francisco, Los Angeles, Manzanillo, Balboa (the Panama Canal), Cartagena, Puerto Cabello, La Gauira (for Caracas), Salvador, Rio de Janeiro, Santos (for São Paulo), Parangua, Buenos Aires, Valparaiso, Callao (for Lima), Guayaquil, and back to the West Coast ports. The complete Grand Circle cruise takes approximately fifty-four days, and the highlight of the trip is always the passage through the Strait of Magellan, which is often called "the greatest natural wonder on earth." It is home to thousands of marine animals and birds (who play with the ships that occasionally pass through) as well as such landmarks as Cape of a Thousand Virgins, Useless Bay, and Desolation Island. The breathtaking scenery (which competes with Alaska's Inside Passage and Norway's fjordland for its icy grandeur) is at its best during the Southern Hemisphere's winter months of June, July, and August.

A number of land and cruise options are available around South America, and passengers can disembark in one port and meet the vessel a week or so later. Also popular are the air-sea programs on which travelers fly one way and cruise back. Magellan Club members (repeat passengers) also receive special bonuses in reduced fares and complimentary shore excursions.

Delta Lines also operates a group of twelve-passenger cargo vessels from New York to the Caribbean and the west coast of South America, calling at ports in the Dominican Republic, Columbia, Panama, Ecuador, Peru, and Chile—the *Delta Bolivia*, *Delta Columbia*, *Delta Ecuador*, *Delta Panama*, *Delta Peru*, *Delta Venezuela*, *Delta Caribe*, *Delta Chile*, and *Delta Canada*. If you are interested in cruises of three- to six-weeks aboard such vessels and can afford to be flexible in your itinerary (it all depends upon the cargo), contact the New York office of Delta Lines. These cargo carriers can be tremendous fun and truly relaxing, provided your fellow passengers are congenial (and love to play bridge). But bear in mind that twelve passengers is the legal limit without the required certified doctor on board—so sail in good health!

DELTA QUEEN STEAMBOAT COMPANY

511 Main Street
Cincinnati, Ohio 45202
tel: (513) 621-1445

The Delta Queen steamboats are as much fun to think and write about as they are to sail upon. As the only two paddle-wheel overnight boats left in America, they are charged with the glorious mission of keeping alive a more than 150-year tradition as they cruise over 35,000 miles each along the Mississippi and Ohio rivers, at the speed of some eight miles per hour. Between these two paddle-wheelers, a dozen states are visited each year as well as hundreds of large and small river towns.

The *Delta Queen*, last of the old-time steamboats, was constructed in 1926 with no expense spared in the teakwood handrails, stained-glass windows set with copper instead of lead, brass fittings and posts, and paneling of either oak or mahogany. These irreplaceable features cost $850,000 at the time. During World War II the U.S. Navy commissioned the *Delta Queen* to ferry wounded and healthy troops across San Francisco Bay. In 1946 she was sold to the president of Greene Line Steamers (the former name of the Delta Queen

Steamboat Company) who had the paddle-wheeler towed home to New Orleans. (It was a long journey down the Pacific Coast, through the Panama Canal, and across the Gulf of Mexico, even if in a crate!) From there, the *Delta Queen* traveled to Pittsburgh for a thorough remodeling and refitting. She began her new life in the Mississippi River in June 1948.

For the next two decades this steamboat cruised slowly up and down the main arteries of the Midwest, offering her passengers the treat of experiencing American river life. Then the controversy began—a new Safety at Sea law required all vessels carrying over fifty passengers overnight to be constructed entirely of steel. Facing threats that the venerable old lady might be forced to retire, her loyal subjects rallied and not only obtained six subsequent exemptions from the law, but also enjoined the Department of the Interior to list the *Delta Queen* in the National Register of Historic Places. The current exemption expires in 1988.

The *Delta Queen* follows an itinerary of two- to twelve-night cruises that stop along the Mississippi and Ohio rivers from early February through December. The final sailings of the season are pre-Christmas fetes with old-fashioned holiday atmosphere. A recent annual summer event for the sister *Queens* is the Great Steamboat Race during the eleven-night Mississippi Explorer itinerary from New Orleans to St. Louis (in June). Steamboat racing was a colorful pastime on American rivers during the last century, and the Delta Queen Steamboat Company was able to revive the tradition a few years ago. The *Mississippi Queen* won the coveted Golden Antlers in 1979 and '80, but her venerable sister took the honors the next year. The 1982 race was another colorful occasion, as both ships were making eleven-day cruises from New Orleans to Cincinnati, via Natchez, Memphis, Louisville, and Madison. It's wonderful fun with races between the steamboats and contests between the complement of passengers. Streamers, shouting, clapping, New Orleans jazz, and nonstop libations add to the excitement.

While some aficionados prefer spring and others wouldn't miss the fall foliage, any time of the year on the river is special, for life is relaxing and the livin' is easy aboard these boats. I suggest comfortable sportswear for both men and women, and good walking shoes are helpful for visiting plantations, small towns, and such along the way. Jackets and ties, although not required for dinner, are in good taste for the formal evenings on board. There are two seatings for each meal, and shore tours are arranged at most stops. The cruise director will advise you of all activities in the daily *Steamboat Times*, so nothing will pass you by. Service on board both *Queens* is special. The average age of the crew is about thirty years old, and all are totally dedicated to their work on the river. During the summer you may find occasional students who have joined the staff hoping to get a flavor of life on the Mississippi, but all are perfectly professional and should be treated with the same courtesies (that means tips) as the crew aboard a large cruise ship.

The enthusiastic entertainment on board both steamboats is strictly river-oriented (that's what you came for), sweeping you up with singalongs, Dixieland jazz bands, barbershop quartets, and concerts of river songs. How long has it been since you've heard "Bill Bailey," "My Old Kentucky Home," "Camptown Races," and everyone's favorite tune "Ole Man River"? As the entertainment fires up spontaneously at times, you may find yourself the recipient of a tableside serenade at dinner, which by the way, is strictly American fare. Expect the menu to offer such items as southern fried catfish from Arkansas (an old Mark Twain favorite, they say), creole dishes, peanut butter soup, and cornbread in all disguises. And whether you've ordered them or not, you'll probably find grits with your scrambled eggs at breakfast. Wines tend to be domestic, and the bloody marys are famous for being hot and spicy.

Life on board the *Mississippi Queen* is slightly more formal because of her size, her greater luxury, and her well air-conditioned public rooms (which means more dressing up). Personally I prefer the *Mississippi Queen*, especially during the summer months because she has a small pool, a much appreciated amenity when the river gets too hot. This newest stern-wheeler, launched in 1976 (at a final cost of $27 million) and Old World in concept is a thoroughly splendid and modern machine. In appearance, the two boats are similar, although the *Mississippi Queen* is much larger by approximately one hundred feet and almost three thousand tons. But both have the same layer cake look and both seem to cruise along the rivers leading with their tongue, or "stage" that sticks straight ahead. The *Mississippi Queen*, however, has benefited from the most advanced technology, for her huge thirty-five by twenty-five foot paddle wheel is turned by a four-cylinder "horizontal tandem compound condensing steam engine." Her automatic boilers (which use oil like everything else) and her steam turbine generators can provide enough electricity to power a small city. Inside, her mouldings, mirrors, polished steel, and brass all evoke the past in nineteenth-century detail, but nothing is made of wood. Even her calliope, considered to be the world's largest and lustiest, is computerized so that both professionals and passengers can play onto a digital tape, push a button, and hear it all come back. And if you happen to be sitting on the top deck near the swimming pool, you really hear it!

The Mark Twain Association has been formed recently for repeat passengers, who receive special gifts, enjoy a champagne reception with the Captain, and hear new itineraries before the general public. Delta Queen also has an official historian and anecdotist, named Don Deming, who offers tidbits of river lore and legend in his writing and lectures around the country. The Steamboat Calliope, published four times a year for passengers and agents, has a regular column by Deming as well as many other articles of interest.

EASTERN STEAMSHIP LINES/WESTERN STEAMSHIP LINES

1220 Biscayne Blvd.
P.O. Box 010882
Miami, Florida 33101
tel: (305) 373-7501

140 Sixth Street
San Pedro, CA 90731
tel: (305) 373-7501

Eastern Steamship Lines, the oldest cruise company sailing from the port of Miami, dates from the year 1953 when the name plus two vessels (*Evangeline* and *Yarmouth*) were purchased from Boston owners. From Miami's original terminal on Biscayne Boulevard, the two vessels sailed for Havana and Nassau on one- and two-week cruises. Very few of the cabins had private facilities but no one much cared, for these were strictly party cruises. In the decade of the 60s, the ship line operated the *Bahama Star* and *Ariadne* in the Caribbean. In the early 70s, the company bought the former *President Roosevelt* and renamed her the *Emerald Seas*. She remains Eastern's sole vessel and is popular on the three- and four-day Bahamas run.

Eastern boasts a number of employees who began their career in the 50s and remain loyal to the company. Whatever Eastern seems to do, it does right. The vessel is spacious but not glamorous; yet many in the industry swear by her. Eight-hundred-odd passengers enjoy cabins with large windows, closed circuit television, swimming pool, casino with a full house of games, gift and duty-free shopping. For the short hop, this is the vessel to Nassau and Freeport.

The company started a western subsidiary in 1980, with the purchase of the former *Calypso* of Ulysses Lines. Renamed the *Azure Seas*, the vessel sails from San Pedro on three- and four-day cruises to Mexico (Ensenada). Again, the theme is partying and gambling, and it seems to work. Eastern/Western seems to have developed a good formula for both coasts.

EPIROTIKI LINES

551 Fifth Avenue
Suite 1900
New York, N.Y. 10017
tel: (212) 599-1750

This family-owned Greek shipping company is thriving under the fourth generation leadership of brothers George and Andreas Potamianos, great-grand-sons of the adventurous youth from the island of Cephalonia who first hauled cargo and a few passengers up and down the Danube River in the 1850s. The company was named after Epirus, the hometown in northwestern Greece where Tassos Potamianos, grandson of the originator and a pioneer of cruising in the Aegean and Mediterranean, first launched his ships. It was Tassos who created the company symbol, a stylized gold Byzantine cross on a sky-blue background, which has now become a familiar sight in cruise ports around the world.

World headquarters of the ship line is the Epirotiki Building, a modern, steel and tinted-glass structure right on the harbor in Piraeus. From this building, which has already become a city landmark, the brothers command the largest Greek-flag cruise fleet in the world, a total of ten passenger vessels that sail most of the year, either on company-operated cruise programs or on charter. A good eighty percent of the ship line's business comes from the chartering of their vessels to tour operators in the U.S., the U.K., and Germany.

Epirotiki is considered the pioneer in Greek cruising. In 1930 and 1939 the company organized and operated the first cruises in the Aegean, for American archaeological groups. In 1946 Epirotiki operated the first passenger ship linking the Ionian Islands, and the next year introduced the largest vessel available for Greek coastal service. In 1954 the Greek National Tourist Organization joined with Epirotiki to undertake a new concept in European holidays—regularly scheduled cruises around the Aegean. This experiment was such a success that it spurred the growth of cruises throughout the world. The first passenger-plus-car ferry service between Brindisi (Italy) and Patras (Greece), launched in 1959 by Epirotiki, opened up another new type of European vacation car touring. In 1960 Epirotiki extended this service to link Europe with Asia (Turkey).

From 1965 to 1973 Epirotiki launched seven ships that were either newly built or recently refurbished specifically for the cruise market. The first to usher in this new era of cruising was the 200-passenger *Argonaut*, a vessel originally built in 1929 as a private yacht. The *Argonaut*, still considered the flagship of the fleet, sails under the auspices of Raymond and Whitcomb of New York City, a tour operator that specializes in high-caliber programs for members of museums, college alumni associations, and special interest groups. The *Argonaut* is positioned in the Red Sea during the winter season, in the Mediterranean and Aegean in spring and autumn, in the British Isles and waterways of France during the summer months, and in dry dock at the end of the year.

In 1966 the newly built *Jason* made its debut. The refurbished *Orpheus* and *Apollo* both arrived in 1970. The 9000-ton *Jupiter*, which debuted in 1971 in both the Aegean and Caribbean, became the largest of the ships thus far. Epirotiki launched the 4,000-ton *Neptune* in 1972, and the next year cruise passengers saw the 16,000-ton *Atlas* (first built in 1951 as the *Ryndam*) in both the Aegean and Caribbean. In 1977 Epirotiki introduced the 2500-ton *Hermes* for seasonal one-day cruises to the Saronic Gulf islands, and some 300,000 tourists now take this ship annually. Two more vessels joined the fleet in 1978: the 12,000-ton *Oceanus*, which began life in 1952 as the *Jean Laborde* of French Line (currently on charter to Lauro Line) and the 12,000-ton *World Renaissance*, which was built in 1966 as the flagship of Paquet French Line (then named the *Renaissance*). Within the very week that Epirotiki purchased the latter vessel, she was leased on a long-term basis to Costa Line. "It was like getting a ship for free," said a company spokesman, "because the charter fee pays the mortgage."

Epirotki runs a good, solid fleet that is not luxurious by any standards, but the ships are well-maintained and the service is reported to be excellent. With so many cruise vessels to care for, Epirotiki manages its own workshop for repairs. The company also has had a long and fruitful relationship with American interior designer Maurice Bailey, who moved to Greece in 1962 to design the interior of the Athens Hilton and who now has more than one hundred hotel interiors to his credit. A few years after he arrived in Greece, Bailey took on the interiors of the *Argonaut*, followed closely by the *Jason*, *Orpheus*, *Apollo*, *Jupiter*, *Neptune*, and *Atlas*. Bailey and his artists, namely Arminio Lozzi and Russell Holmes, have integrated the mythological tales and escapades of the legendary figures after whom each ship is named, into the cabin murals, beautiful tapestries and sculptures in the public rooms, mosaics in the swimming pool, and even into the carpet designs. Delightful and appealing schemes appear throughout each ship. The *Neptune* has trident carpets and a large Poseidon tapestry in the Lounge of the Tritons as well as handmade brass lamps depicting Poseidon's Castle. The main lounge bar of the *Jason* displays a huge tapestry of Jason yoking the wild bulls in the sacred field of Ares. Walking up from the *Jason's* reception hall, you see a sculpture of *Argo*, the ship that carried Jason and his Argonauts on their search for the Golden Fleece. And each cabin in the *Jason* has my favorite mural—a scene of the mysterious island of Santorini (Thíra).

EXPLORATION CRUISE LINES

1500 Metropolitan Park Building
Olive Way at Boren Avenue
Seattle, Washington 98101
tel: (206) 625-9600

The relatively young Exploration Cruise Lines of Seattle is offering the same philosophy on the West Coast that makes American Canadian Line and American Cruise Lines so successful on the East Coast—that is, small vessels with a casual atmosphere that can navigate the rivers and byways often ignored by innovators in the industry. The company's fleet of three 100-ton cruisers are yachtlike in appearance and ambiance. All are built in the U.S and carry an eager, all-American crew along with a qualified naturalist/lecturer. The vessels can cruise in ice, close to glaciers; and they have a draft of only eight feet, allowing bow landings in many areas. In addition, inflatable boats are carried for launch service at difficult shore stops. The imaginative itineraries of all three vessels are a wonderful way to enjoy nature's beauty unhindered.

The company inaugurated the *Pacific Northwest Explorer* in the spring of 1981 for cruises on the Columbia and Snake rivers. During that summer the 80-passenger *Explorer* sailed in Puget Sound and along the Canadian coastal waterways. In late autumn the vessel moved down to San Francisco for Stockton and Sacramento river cruises, and was then chartered to Special Expeditions (Sven-Olaf Lindblad) for the popular Baja California circumnavigations.

The 88-passenger *Majestic Explorer* began operating in March 1982 on the Sacramento and San Joaquin rivers through California's delta country, then cruised from May through August between Ketchikan and Skagway. The ship was originally to be named *Majestic Alaska Explorer*, but the Alaska was dropped to expand potential use in California and other parts of the world. Indeed, during the winter of 1982/83, the *Majestic Explorer* will begin a most interesting series of French Polynesia cruises from Papeete (Tahiti) to Huahine, Bora Bora, Raiatea, and Moorea. The sailings depart Papeete every four and five days (some omit the call at Huahine). During the summer the vessel will return to the Ketchikan-Skagway circuit.

Newest on line of this young fleet is the 96-passenger *Great Rivers Explorer*, a ship similar to the *Majestic Explorer*, and used for cruises along the Columbia, Willamette, and Snake rivers. This three-state, 900-mile round-trip adventure begins at Portland, Oregon, and ranges inland as far as Lewiston, Idaho. During the winter the *Great Rivers Explorer* will pioneer weekly cruises in Panama between Balboa and Colon. The vessel will make five-day sailings through the Panama Canal with calls at the Pearl Islands, Darien Jungle and San Blas Islands (or four-day sailings omitting the Pearl Islands). The cruise is one-way, with rail to either Colon or Panama City. Sounds different, to say the least, but the Panama Canal, one of man's greatest achievements, is exciting to transit. The vessel will return to Portland for the three-river adventure in mid-May.

GALAPAGOS CRUISES

c/o Adventure Associates
5925 Maple Street
Suite 116
Dallas, Texas 75235
tel: (214) 357-6187

Galapagos Cruises, a division of Metropolitan Touring of Quito, Ecuador, was the pioneer in offering pleasure cruises to the Galapagos Islands. Ecuadorean Eduardo Proano, president of Metropolitan Touring, is deeply concerned with both promoting and preserving these enchanted islands. He brings in most (if not all) of the allotted twelve thousand tourists annually. Proano opened the area to tourism in 1968.

Flagship of Galapagos Cruises is the 1500-ton *Santa Cruz*, a ninety-passenger, all first-class vessel built in Spain in 1979 especially for these cruises. The *Santa Cruz* offers a three-, four-, or seven-day program among the islands, but the best is a seven-day itinerary (a combination of the three- and four-day), with flights to and from the ship. In addition, the company operates the 38-passenger yacht *Delfin* on three- and four-night cruises and the sixteen-passenger *Isabela* on one-week programs. It also charters schooners, ketches, and sloops, equipped and crewed for four to ten passengers, and develops itineraries to suit your needs. During the various Galapagos programs that highlight the most popular islands, guides trained by the Darwin Research Station come aboard each vessel.

Galapagos Cruises also operates a three-deck, 56-passenger flotel *Orellana* on Ecuador's Napo River for two- to four-night jungle cruises. The two- to four-berth cabins all have private facilities, and the flotel has a large sun deck, salon, and dining room. Shore excursions into the rain forests in motorized dugout canoes travel to such places as the Jivino River, Monkey Island, Primavera, Limoncocha, and Lake Taracoa—not for the timid, but worth it for the colorful scenery and thousand new sounds.

HAPAG LLOYD AG

Gustav Deetjen Alee 2/6
Postfach 10/79-47
2800 Bremen, West Germany
tel: (0421) 35-50-11

The much-respected Hapag Lloyd shipping line is the result of a 1970 merger between the famous Hamburg-America line (Hapag) and North German Lloyd (NDL). Lloyd dates from 1857 and began service between Germany and North America in 1858 with the steamer *Bremen*; Hapag was founded a decade earlier. The two companies were constant rivals in both service and speed as they carried passengers between the Old World and the New. By 1881, NDL's steamer *Elbe* had reduced crossing time between Southampton and New York to only eight days, 12 hours, and 50 minutes. A Hapag ship, the *Fürst Bismarck*, set a record of six days, 11 hours and 44 minutes on the same route in 1889. NDL retaliated with a fleet of four-funnel class vessels capable of making the North Atlantic crossing in less than six days. The battle for the Blue Riband had begun!

Even before the century turned, the two companies were expanding dramatically worldwide. In 1913 the ten-millionth passenger was recorded aboard a Lloyd vessel, while Hapag was reportedly the largest shipping line in the world. These golden days, however, ended with the advent of World War I. When it was over, only a few vessels remained to both companies. But by 1930, NDL boasted two Blue Riband winners—the *Bremen* and the *Europa*. Again, such glorious times were fleeting, and World War II brought total destruction to both fleets.

Today, Hapag Lloyd's strength lies in freighters and container ships that carry their cargo all over the world. The company also operates one cruise vessel, the *Europa*, and has just replaced the old stand-by (formerly the *Kungsholm I*) with a spanking new 34,000-ton ship. The new *Europa*, built in the Hapag-Lloyd yard in Bremerhaven, was launched last year and began her inaugural cruise season in Europe in June 1982. The vessel boasts twelve decks, "an overall design ahead of its time," noiseless and spacious cabins, and a passenger capacity of between 600 and 1,000 plus crew space for about 300. The vessel is scheduled to follow the sun all over the world beginning in North America in the spring and fall of 1983. Passengers are advised that the official language aboard the *Europa* is German. Nonetheless, she sounds like a splendid addition to the cruise world.

HELLENIC MEDITERRANEAN LINES

200 Park Avenue
New York, N.Y. 10017
tel: (212) 697-4220

Hellenic Mediterranean Lines was formed in 1929 to represent the overseas services of Hellenic Coast Lines, which operated some thirty-three passenger vessels at the time. However, the Greek government requisitioned the entire fleet during World War II, and all but two vessels were sunk by enemy action. Just over two decades ago Hellenic Mediterranean Lines built the *Egnatia* for passenger/car ferry service between Italy and Greece. This successful service now represents four vessels that operate between Patras, Hegoumenitsa, Corfu, and Brindisi: the *Egnatia, Castalia, Appia,* and *Espresso*. The *Neptunia* travels between Ancona, Piraeus, and Haifa; and the *Appollonia* serves Venice, Piraeus, Rhodes, Limassol, and Haifa.

Hellenic Mediterranean Lines launched the 4800-ton *Aquarius* in 1972 for seven-day cruises from Piraeus in the spring and summer. The 280-passenger vessel, a charming but small ship, sails on Fridays for Thira, Heraklion, Rhodes, Kuşadasi, Istanbul, and Mykonos. The *Aquarius* offers a good alternative for passengers who prefer a more intimate vessel on their Greek island/Turkey cruises.

HOLLAND AMERICA CRUISES

Two Penn Plaza
New York, N.Y. 10121
tel: (212) 760-3800

The beginning of Holland America Line fits into modern history. The future of Rotterdam as a port looked rather bleak in the early 1870s because ship owners seemed to prefer rival Amsterdam. Therefore, to try to develop some necessary trade between Holland and America, two young Dutchmen commissioned the SS *Rotterdam*, an iron vessel of 1700 tons that could carry eight passengers in first-class accommodations and 380 in steerage, as well as 1500 tons of cargo. Her maiden voyage took place in October, 1872, and her subsequent voyages were so successful that the two young partners joined with a third to form the Netherlands-American Steam Navigation Company in April, 1873. It became known simply as Holland America Line in 1896.

From the very beginning, Holland America's flagship has been named the *Rotterdam*, one in a fleet that features such names as *Nieuw Amsterdam, Potsdam, Ryndam, Noordam, Maasdam,* and *Statendam*. In addition to weekly service between Rotterdam and New York, the company began cruises to Copenhagan as early as June 1895 aboard the *Rotterdam* (the second). Another cruise offered during the first decade of the twentieth century, aboard the *Statendam*, included a visit to the Holy Land. A few years later the company ordered a new 32,000-ton *Statendam*, which was destined to become a giant among passenger vessels, but alas, never carried a paying passenger. The ship launched just as World War I broke out, was fitted to transport troops, only to be sunk at sea—a U-boat victim.

Another new *Statendam*, ordered in the mid-1920s, sailed on her maiden voyage in April 1929, arriving in New York on the three hundredth anniversary of the landing of the Dutch ships that carried the founders of the settlement once known as New Amsterdam. The decade of the 1930s was a slump time for shipping, due to the world economic situation. By May 1940 Germany had invaded Holland and Dutch shipping ground to a standstill. At this time, however, Holland America transferred its headquarters to Curaçao in the Dutch West Indies, where it remains.

In the postwar period Holland America launched the 15,000-ton *Ryndam* (most recently the *Atlas* of Epirotiki Line) and the *Maasdam* (now the *Stefan Batory* of Polish Ocean Line). The former *Statendam* (fourth of her name), launched in 1957, was recently sold to Paquet French Cruises and now sails as the *Rhapsody*. In 1958 Queen Juliana launched the fifth *Rotterdam*; her maiden voyage took place a year later. Both vessels easily converted to one-class cruising shps to accommodate the demand of the past few decades.

Holland America's present fleet also includes the sister ships *Veendam* and *Volendam*, originally built in 1958 as the *Argentina* and *Brazil*, having had brief flings as the *Monarch Star* and *Monarch Sun* of Miami.

The 23,000-ton sister ships sail from New York to Bermuda between April/May and October, and into the Caribbean all winter. Holland America has now positioned the 715-passenger *Volendam* in Port Everglades on a fourteen-day pattern that is also offered in seven-day segments between Florida and Barbados. The 713-passenger *Veendam* will be based in Tampa from November until May, offering seven-day cruises to Mexico, Montego Bay, and Grand Cayman.

The 38,000-ton *Rotterdam*, flagship of Holland America's fleet, begins 1983 with the Silver Cruise—a very special global voyage celebrating the twenty-fifth anniversary of this prestigious event for the line. Passengers aboard the 82-day, 28,700-mile voyage will call at twenty-one ports on four continents and have the time of their lives. Silver keepsakes, a souvenir book (written as the cruise progresses), dancing to a specially created song, new gustatory creations, and selected vintage wines bottled exclusively for the cruise are all planned for the Silver Jubilee celebration. And one full-cruise passenger will win a Rolls Royce Silver Spirit as the ultimate memento. In addition, the line has scheduled gala Bon Voyage parties for all passengers in New York, Port Everglades, and Los Angeles. What a way to travel!

The *Rotterdam* returns from this superlative event on the first of April in New York harbor. Following a two-week cruise from New York to the Caribbean, the vessel repositions in Vancouver for seven-day sailings to Alaska from June through mid-September. Joining the *Rotterdam* on the Inside Passage is Holland America's $150 million new vessel, the *Nieuw Amsterdam*. The 32,000-ton cruise ship was built in St. Nazaire, France, for 1,200 passengers and a crew of 536.

The *Nieuw Amsterdam* is the first step in Holland America's fleet modernization program, and scheduled for inaugural service in May. Following the summer season in Alaska/Canada, the vessel will be based on the West Coast. A second new vessel, the *Noordam*, will be identical to the *Nieuw Amsterdam* and is expected to be commissioned in the spring of 1984. The names of both vessels have been bestowed previously upon ships in Holland America's fleet, and are both familiar and respected names in the history of North Atlantic crossings.

The ship line's fleet is all registered in the Netherlands Antilles, has Dutch officers and an Indonesian crew. In fact, Holland America, which is proud of its staff, operates its own training school in Jakarta. The line implemented a No Tipping Required policy a few years ago and insists that it's the *spirit* of the policy that works so well, that the crew works for your smile and not your cash. However, "exceptional service" is not expected to go unrewarded, so tipping aboard these ships is not a bad word; it's just not a continual word. The line also introduced what it calls the Impulse Cruise, a money-saver to Bermuda, whereby passengers apply early and deposit $200 but are only confirmed on a space-available-basis one week before sailing date. This is an excellent way to fill up a ship and, if all goes well, encourage repeat clientele.

Holland America's new management team believes in what it terms "theming," offering passengers something immediately identifiable. For example, the theme of the *Nieuw Amsterdam* will be that of a seventeenth-century ship sailing between Holland and America; the interior of the vessel will be adorned will beautiful artifacts of the period. The sistership, *Noordam*, will feature an eighteenth-century atmosphere, with an interior decorated accordingly. The company has also uncomplicated its cruise schedules, so that all ships will depart Saturdays at 7 p.m. on either seven- or 14-day sailings from New York, Port Everglades, or Tampa. After wintering in Miami for many years, Holland America has moved to the less-congested Florida ports and plans to open up even more new vistas as the decade unfolds. Would that the company returns to cruising in the Indonesian archipelago, which it pioneered so successfully in the 70s!

HOME LINES

One World Trade Center
Suite 3969
New York, N.Y. 10048
tel: (212) 775-9041

Home Lines is an American-based company, owned by a foundation chartered in Canada that has charitable interests in Greece. Home Lines began operation with the first postwar passenger service between Italy and South America in 1947. Two years later the ship line established regular passenger service between the Mediterranean and New York, with such well-remembered vessels as the *Italia* and the *Atlantic*. In 1955 the company added the former *Mariposa* to the fleet as the *Homeric* to provide deluxe Caribbean cruises during the winter season. As cruises became more important to the ship line, the *Italia* became the flagship for one-week sailings between New York and the Bahamas.

In the early 1960s Home Lines built the *Oceanic* in Italy and changed the design midstream from a transatlantic passenger ship to the first vessel ever commissioned especially for cruises. The *Oceanic*, launched in 1965, and has had nothing but the best of reputations during her years of service from New York to Bermuda, the Bahamas, and the Caribbean. In 1974 the *Homeric* was retired, and the line brought the *Doric* (the former *Hanseatic* of German-Atlantic Line and *Shalom* of Zim Line) into the Florida cruise market. The *Doric* was a sturdy, well-run vessel that enjoyed many successful years of cruising from New York to Bermuda from spring to fall, and from Port Everglades to the Caribbean during the winter season. Home Lines sold the vessel in February 1982 to Royal Cruise Line, and she has been renamed the *Royal Odyssey*. (An executive of Royal Cruise Line mentioned that, true to Home Lines' reputation, the vessel was as immaculately maintained on the day of delivery as on the day of first sighting). You can always be assured of both safety and excellent service aboard any Home Lines vessel.

In addition to the 39,241-ton *Oceanic*, which carries a total of 1034 passengers on ten decks, Home Lines recently inaugurated the 30,000-ton *Atlantic* for the Bermuda run from New York and for Caribbean cruises from Port Everglades. This $100 million vessel was built in La Seyne-sur-Mer (near Toulon), France, and like the *Oceanic*, carries just over one thousand passengers on ten decks. She is a beauty if you consider that this is a cruise ship of the 1980s and not of two decades ago. Public areas are spacious and comfortable—never crowded—and special attention has been paid to good cabin size. Approximately seventy-five percent of the 543 cabins are situated outside, and there are 180 deluxe staterooms as well as six large suites. At first glance, the decor tends to appear a bit old-fashioned, but I think it is decidedly more appealing than many of the super-modern vessels coming on line. At least, passageways are wide enough for two adults abreast and the dining room is most attractively appointed. My only criticism of the ship's design is the portholes, which surely could have been more imaginatively conceived (i.e., larger in both cabins and dining room).

Frankly, it is difficult to fault any aspect of Home Lines' cruises (my husband's favorite), and I hope that passengers appreciate the apparent quality aboard both the *Atlantic* and *Oceanic*. Both vessels are registered in Panama (obviously, for tax reasons) but carry all-Italian officers and crew. The ships are so efficiently managed and so spotless, that one suspects both an iron hand and loving care are responsible. "Ask and ye shall receive" seems to be the motto. The dining rooms are a joy both in service and food. Cabin attention is overwhelming. Soap is refreshed almost every time you use it, and there are plenty of towels in the well-appointed bathrooms. Breakfast in bed arrives promptly, and the steward is aware that there are still such things as china and linen. Grease spots on cloths disappear even before noticed, and night things are always laid out on the bed (one favorite Home Lines' trick is to give everyone an eighteen-inch waist)!

During the New York season—between April and Novmber—the Home Lines pier is awash with well-wishers. As many as 4000 visitors come aboard both vessels weekly, which is good for business but costs the line plenty in refurbishing the passageway carpets. Nonetheless, it is always a thrill to see so many enthusiastic cruise passengers and their friends at the Bon Voyage. Unfortunately, the *Oceanic* has forsaken her home port of New York during the winter and now sails from Port Everglades. The *Atlantic* joins her for the Caribbean season, but also has two interesting trans-Panama Canal cruises scheduled. It is good to watch both vessels being utilized to the fullest.

K-LINES HELLENIC CRUISES

Olympic Tower
645 Fifth Avenue
New York, N.Y. 10022
tel: (212) 751-2435

In 1910 one vessel owned by Philippos Kavounides started K-Lines Hellenic Cruises. By the outbreak of World War I he had a fleet of five passenger ships but lost three to enemy torpedoes. However, the old Greek bounced back with a fleet of four just in time to be destroyed, again, by the enemy during World War II. Through all this, Kavounides today claims the longest running passenger ship service to Greece and the longest continuous passenger ship service since the war. A great force within the industry, the company, now owned and operated by the grandsons of the founder, displays a familiar "K" on the smokestack of cruise ships in the Aegean and eastern Mediterranean.

K-Lines Hellenic Cruises operates the 2500-ton *Kentavros* (which joined the family in 1964), the 6200-ton flagship *Orion* (1969), the 5500-ton *Galaxy* (1971), the 5500-ton *Atlantis* (1975), and the 12,500-ton *Constellation* (1980). Of the five vessels, the *Orion, Galaxy, Kentavros,* and *Atlantis* are sailing during this season in the Aegean. The *Kentavros* had been positioned in Salonica (Thessaloníki) for cruises to Macedonia and the northern Greek islands, but after two years of not "catching on" (even with a Greek government subsidy), the vessel has been repositioned. It is a pity, because the itinerary, innovative and interesting, included rarely visited islands well off the beaten tourist path—Kavala and Thasos; Lesbos, with its petrified forest; Skopelos and Skiathos, perfect for snorkeling; and Lemnos, where Zeus supposedly hurled Hephaestus to earth.

After refurbishing and some indecision for the past few years, Epirotiki has finally launched the 415-passenger *Constellation* and named her flagship of the fleet. This 12,500-ton vessel began life as the Brazilian cruise ship *Anna Nery*, but has been reborn as a very fine vessel with spacious all-outside staterooms with two lower beds, interesting public areas, split-level disco, and several bars. During her inaugural season during the summer of 1982, the *Constellation* sailed every other week from Genoa to Barcelona, Palermo, Heraklion, Port Said, Ashdod, Kusadasi, Piraeus, and Capri. A most interesting and relaxing itinerary.

Beginning Dec. 24, 1982, the *Constellation* will be operated under the aegis of March Shipping Passenger Services on one-week cruises to the Caribbean from St. Petersburg (Florida) as well as trans-Panama Canal sailings and a summer cooling-off in Alaska/Canada from a base in Vancouver. We look forward to seeing this vessel, as she sounds most charming and ALL Greek!

LINDBLAD TRAVEL, INC.

8 Wright Street
Westport, Connecticut 06880
tel: (203) 226-8531

Explorer, conservationist, and travel pioneer Lars-Eric Lindblad and his company have been devising tours since the 1950s that draw special groups of people. Adventurous travelers pay top dollar for the privilege to join a Lindblad tour. And what a privilege it is. Each itinerary opens new and exciting vistas on this earth we inhabit, from the "roof of the world" (Tibet) to a sub-Antarctic cruising expedition. As Lindblad lives out the fantasies of his Swedish childhood, he plans each itinerary to be more exotic than the last. Expense also increases. Forty intrepid passengers who wanted to visit relatively untouched area demanded that Lindblad and company arrange a new sub-Atlantic cruise; this required Lindblad to arrange for his ship's refueling by sending gas, oil, and a complete pumping station down to Kerguelen (a French possession in the sub-Antarctic).

It is certainly a challenge to match Lindblad's ingenuity. One of his latest cruise coups is the thirty-six passenger *Kun Lun*, a 277-foot riverboat on China's Yangtze Kiang. The *Kun Lun*, built in 1962, originally entertained ministers of state, visiting heads of state, and other foreign dignitaries. Passenger vessels of similar design and tonnage, which belong to the East is Red fleet, hold from seven hundred to nine hundred Chinese passengers on their travels from port to port along the third longest river in the world (after the Amazon and the Nile). *Kun Lin* passengers, however, are accommodated in eighteen twin-bed cabins with private facilities. Open seating is standard, with Western breakfasts and Chinese lunch and dinners. One main lounge and three smaller lounges grace the three-deck vessel and offer pleasant surroundings for a chat with a Chinese speaking sinologist, a Lindblad hostess, or Luxingshe (China International Travel Service) guide or interpreter who will be on board.

Two new members of the Lindblad family are the 10,000-ton *Yao Hua* for China coastal and Yangtse River cruises, and the 79-passenger *Lindblad Polaris* for Scandinavia sailings in the summer and Red Sea cruises during the winter. Both were launched in 1982 and are now members of the Salen Lindblad Cruising fleet, aong with the *Lindblad Explorer*. All three are prominent in Lindblad's famous Intrepids Club that offers a number of special features for previous participants in at least one Lindblad tour. For an annual fee of approximately $25, members are entitled to the beautiful *Intrepid Magazine*, a special pin, reduction on all Lindblad Travel offerings, exclusive tours for members, an Annual Meeting somewhere wonderful and a photographic competition with prizes. Not to mention that Intrepids make and renew many warm friendships on all their Lindblad adventures.

The *Lindblad Explorer* cruises around Australasia, the Philippine and Indonesian archipelagos, and the Coral Sea (Australia's Great Barrier Reef and New

Zealand's fjordland) as well as Antarctica, the sub-Antarctic islands, and the Ross Sea. Operated by the Swedish American Line, this vessel welcomes field guides, lecturers, ornithologists, and other extraordinary people dedicated to the spirit of adventure and exploration. The vessel also carries a fleet of Zodiacs, specially designed rubber inflatable boats that enable passengers to penetrate otherwise inaccessible rivers, streams, swamps, and marshes (and gives them a feeling of being part of the scenery). The *Lindblad Explorer*, a very popular little vessel, is always filled with interesting passengers.

The *Explorer* used to offer cruises among the Galapagos Islands, but since the Ecuadorian government banned all foreign vessels, Lindblad now charters the new *Santa Cruz* for its programs several times a year. This splendid small vessel hires excellent guides to give tours of the islands.

Lindblad also programs boats to cruise up and down the Nile River, considered some of the best tours available. A Thousand Miles Up The Nile cruise uses the twin vessels operated by Hilton Hotel, the *Isis* and *Osiris*. Actually, you only spend five nights aboard these 141-passenger vessels—between Luxor and Aswan—and the thousand miles refers to the view from the high cliffs that house the temple of Abu Simbel. You can actually see the thousand-mile point on the Nile (if you begin counting at the delta). Lindblad also reveals the Nile by private yacht—two twenty-passenger riverboats called the *Aswan* and the *Abu Simbel*. Each vessel has ten cabins with private facilities, a twenty-four seat dining room, and a spacious bar/living room. The fourteen-day cruise between Cairo and Aswan calls at El Wasta, El Minya, Beni Hasan, Asyūt, El Balyana, Dendera, Esna, Edfu, and Kom Ombo. The fully air-conditioned boats sail year-round (except July and August), and an egyptologist accompanies each cruise.

One of Lindblad's divisions is Special Expeditions, supervised by son Sven-Olaf Lindblad, featuring the MV *Pacific Northwest Explorer*, a brand new cruiser—1980 vintage—of ninety-nine tons and just seventy-four passengers. Lindblad built this vessel to sail in Alaskan waters during the summer months; during the winter he charters it for some fascinating sailings around the Sea of Cortez, a body of water, also called the Gulf of California, that is about six hundred miles long and not more than ninety miles wide, just west of the Baja Peninsula. It harbors an extremely rich assortment of marine life as well as the world's second largest animals, the fin whales, which are the sleekest of their kind and which can reach eighty feet in length. From the end of January to the end of March fifteen-day programs set out to observe the whales, seals, and all types of sea birds. Prices are high for these sailings, but each is accompanied by a well-known naturalist, and each is another unique and unforgettable Lindblad experience.

Lindblad Travel is also general U.S. sales agent for the 10,000-ton, Portuguese-owned cruise vessel *Funchal* for a series of fifteen-day itineraries around the North Cape, Iceland and the Faroes, and western Europe. The vessel, built in Denmark in 1961, is owned by the Portuguese government and was recently refurbished in the Netherlands. She carries 395 passengers and a crew of 185 on fifteen-day programs that cost fifty to sixty percent less than other ship lines in the area, and she usually has an interesting mixture of Americans and Europeans on board. The facilities although not "world class," meet the approval of many hard-to-please Lindblad loyalists.

MARCH SHIPPING PASSENGER SERVICES

1001 Franklin Avenue
Garden City, New York 11530
tel: (516) 747-8880
    (212) 347-4310 in Manhattan
    (800) 221-3254 from other areas

March Shipping Passenger Services is a fine old company, head-quartered in Montreal, that acts as North American representative for most of the Russian, as well as some Chinese and Yugoslav ship lines. In addition, March is the general agent for the recently rebuilt *Constellation*, flagship and pride of K-Hellenic Lines, and also operates independent cruises on the Volga, Danube, and St. Lawrence rivers.

The 415-passenger *Constellation* has been in the refurbishing stage for a few years, but K-Lines could not quite decide where to position this fine vessel. Finally launched in the summer of '82 for fourteen-day cruises from Genoa, the *Constellation* begins a new life in the Caribbean sailing from St. Petersburg, Florida, under Regency Cruise Lines (jointly owned by K-Lines and March). Then she sails through the Panama Canal to San Francisco and Vancouver, for a series of seven-day cruises to Alaska. The ship looks lovely, with oversized outside staterooms, spacious lounges, a split-level discotheque, enclosed sports deck, and even a sunken bar!

Because of great success with ten-day cruises of the *Alexandr Pushkin* on the mighty Volga River, March will continue with this series. The 21-day air/land/ sea tours in conjunction with Finnair and Intourist feature sightseeing in Moscow and Rostov-on-Don prior to the cruise.

March has also offered seven-day St. Lawrence cruises from June to September aboard another newcomer, the 240-passenger *Regina Maris*. This Singapore-registered vessel is owned by a West German company and was recently refurbished and brought to North American waters. The same program leaving from Montreal will be repeated but possibly aboard a larger vessel.

For many years March Shipping has been synonymous with the cruises offered in North America by the Black Sea Shipping Company of Odessa. This ship line is but one of the many passenger-related divisions of Morposflot, the USSR state-run maritime agency that commands one of the biggest fleets in the world. Familiar names in the Black Sea family are the *Maxim Gorki* (a most popular ship in the 1970s), the *Odessa*, and the *Kazakhstan*. The two latter vessels, built in England in 1975 and Finland in 1976 respectively, enjoyed some loyal following on cruises from New Orleans to the Caribbean during the winter months, from Vancouver to Alaska/Canada during the summer season. At one point, the *Odessa* could boast that it was the only cruise vessel from a U.S. port to call at Havana. Politics however, have intervened and the *Odessa* was no longer welcome in North American waters—as a national protest again Russian military maneuvers in Poland.

Another important money-maker in Morposflot is the Baltic Shipping Company that runs ferry services between Leningrad and other Northern European capitals. The company also commands two large liners, the 19,860-ton *Alexandr Pushkin* and the *Mikhail Lermontov*, both of which accommodate about 600 passengers. The *Lermontov*, recently refurbished and upgraded, now sails from Tilbury (Great Britain) on twelve- to thirty-night cruises. The *Pushkin* is employed on the Volga during the summer, where March Shipping has set aside 100 deluxe cabins for North American passengers.

Also sailing out of Tilbury are the 350-passenger *Kazakhstan*, the 240-passenger *Mikhail Kalinin*, and the 600-passenger *Kareliya*. A new program in the Far East will be successfully repeated this season, which involves the 200-passenger *Turkmenia* from Singapore and offers ten- to eighteen-day cruises. Ports of call include Manila, Hong Kong, Kobe, the Inland Sea, Takamatsu, Phuket, Penang, Bangkok, Kuching, Kota Kinabalu, Rangoon, Madras, and Colombo—but of course, not all on the same sailing!

March also offers river cruises along the Volga and Don, the Dnieper (which is supposed to rank third among Europe's great waterways) and along the not-so-blue Danube. The Danube course travels through eight countries from either Passau or Vienna, as well as on to Izmail on the Black Sea coast of the Soviet Ukraine and Yalta in the Crimea.

I was never very fond of either the *Odessa* or the *Kazakhstan* and am not sorry to see them leave our shores. I must admit, however, that many of the above sailings sound very interesting—especially the river cruises available. In the Far East, I feel that I would rather be more comfortable aboard a vessel catering to Western tastes (because the climate in most of ports visited demands it). I do admire Morposflot, however, for allowing the *Turkmenia* in Singapore and offering a most exciting itinerary that is too often overlooked.

NORWEGIAN AMERICAN CRUISES

29 Broadway
New York, N.Y. 10006
tel: (212) 422-3900

Norwegian American Cruises made the wise decision to take the *Sagafjord* off the market in 1980 and refurbish her. Some $12 million later, the company proudly inaugurated the splendid new vessel complete with fifteen Sundeck suites. Thirteen of these staterooms are terraced and are among the most tastefully designed accommodations afloat. The *Sagafjord* is an ever-popular vessel, and it is never surprising to find that more than half the passenger complement are not only repeaters but active members of the ship line's Fjord Club. This organization offers tender and loving care to its members, and frequent cocktails, luncheons, and dinners are held throughout the country as well as on board. Gifts are often bestowed upon frequent cruise passengers, and you can accumulate quite a collection of Scandinavian glassware!

With the 1983 season NAC has introduced what it calls a new approach to marketing, "Cruising Plus". In essence, this term means that passengers receive all-inclusive pricing for their NAC holiday immediately. Every NAC cruise will be rated to include the time aboard ship, the round-trip airfare between home gateway and vessel plus transfers, sightseeing, and deluxe hotel accommodations where applicable. Although the prices appear rather high initially, they do include the entire package and are substantially less than if passengers booked their own air and land portions. In addition, NAC plans to provide all the air tickets as well as ship documentation, so travel agents can sit back and relax and pay more attention to clients. With the Cruising Plus concept is the encouragement for experienced passengers to "custom tailor" their own cruise holidays and choose any segment of the long sailings that appeal to them. The company now has computerized reservation systems, and can easily match the demands of individual air and land arrangements. One exciting voyage, from Southampton to Port Everglades aboard the *Vistafjord*, even features a British Airways Concorde flight from New York or Washington, D.C. How swish!

To launch the new year, the *Sagafjord* departs Port Everglades on its annual three-month Great World Cruise. An exciting diversion this year is the four-night stay in Hong Kong, where passengers will disembark for a glamorous sojourn at the Hong Kong Regent Hotel, while the vessel enters a local drydock for maintenance. The Regent Hotel overlooks the most beautiful harbor in the Far East (perhaps the world), and the company president will fly out for a gala dinner-dance during this time. Following her return to South Florida, the *Sagafjord* will make three two-week Caribbean cruises before departing through the Panama Canal to the West Coast and Alaska/Canada.

Following six sailings northward from San Francisco, the *Sagafjord* is scheduled for a two-month Hawaii/Orient/China cruise from Los Angeles in August. A Shanghai call is featured on this 58-day cruise. The *Sagafjord* returns to the West Coast in October and departs again on a 56-day voyage to the South Pacific and South America, which includes a call in the Galapagos Islands. The final cruise of the year is a three-week Christmas/New Year's sailing from Los Angeles to Mexico and through the Panama Canal to the Caribbean and Port Everglades.

The elegant *Vistafjord* celebrates a tenth anniversary on May 15, and the ship line has assuredly planned some glamorous events to mark the occasion. The *Vistafjord* begins 1983 a little early, with a three month sailing from Genoa around the African continent in mid-November. In February, the vessel departs Southampton for a three-week westbound transatlantic crossing and cruise that ends in Florida. The eastbound crossing departs in March from Port Everglades and ends in Genoa, where the vessel homeports for several spring-time eastern Mediterranean cruises. By early June, the *Vistafjord* is repositioned in Hamburg for North Cape and Scandinavia/Baltic sailings. At the end of August Wine Lover's Cruise along the coastline from Southampton to Genoa sets the stage for another eastern Mediterranean voyage and then a long East Africa and India departure at the end of October. A week before Christmas, the *Vistafjord* sails again on a 56-day Middle East/India/Far East cruise that ends in Hong Kong. Passengers who wish to do so may re-embark in Hong Kong in February for the 56-day voyage back to Genoa!

The *Vistafjord* was the site of several filmings last year, including the European version of *Love Boat*. The vessel has always been especially popular with Europeans, and a six-part TV series of *Traumschiff* ("Dreamboat") has not hurt cruise sales. More recently, a Jon Voight feature-length film named *Table for Five* was filmed aboard, and one of the NAC executives made his acting debut as the purser!

NORWEGIAN CARIBBEAN LINES

One Biscayne Tower
Miami, Florida 33131
tel: (305) 358-6670

It seems a long way from hauling coal around Scandinavia at the turn of the century to buying one of the most famous ships afloat and converting her into a fun-filled resort called the *Norway*, but that is just the history of the family Kloster. The *Norway* is the latest coup of the grandson of the original Kloster ship owner, who bought his first steamer of 830 tons in 1906. Knut Utstein Kloster, whose Oslo-based company (Klosters Rederi A/S) owns Norwegian Caribbean Lines, has a reputation for doing the unexpected and doing it with panache. His first venture into the cruise business occurred in 1966 with the introduction of the *Sunward* on three- and four-day cruises to the Bahamas from Miami. Since that time Caribbean cruises and this company have grown so rapidly that NCL can now carry approximately 250,000 passengers each year on five different vessels. (Not to mention that its estimated gross revenue for 1981 is approximately $200 million.)

The original *Sunward* (now retired) was soon followed by the 16,000-ton *Starward* in 1968, which pioneered weekly cruises to Jamaica. In 1970 the company introduced the 16,250-ton *Skyward* on weekly cruises that featured a call at Cap Haitien, home of the renowned Citadel Laferriere. Two years later NCL launched the 16,607-*Southward* on fourteen-day cruises, but then changed her itinerary to a seven-day program in 1975. Then, NCL bought the ailing Cunard *Adventurer*, completely refitted her, and changed her personality to fit three- and four-day Bahama cruises. She took to the seas again in 1976 as the *Sunward II* on sailings that featured Nassau as well as an Out Island, just for the fun of it! The ship line made a rather bold move when it decided to just plop people down on a beautiful beach for a day, disregarding vacationers' gambling and shopping instincts. It has been a noteworthy success. As one contented passenger said recently, "It was the most relaxing five hours I have ever spent. When I saw those sparkling sands, I knew what it was like to be a beach bum!"

Sometime during this history, Kloster bought real estate in Jamaica, so passengers aboard the *Starward* could enjoy a cruise-and-stay holiday at Jamaica Hill near Port Antonio. Unfortunately, the 44-villa resort on an old estate with acres of lawn, tennis courts, and a swimming pool overlooking miles of beautiful beaches, has not been a success and is no longer part of the NCL package. But the biggest coup of all was the purchase of the SS *France* and her conversion into a $100 million floating resort, the *Norway*. No one said it would work, but once again Kloster succeeded (despite some severe problems). A handsome vessel, with the most beautiful public rooms on the sea and a wonderful spirit from top to bottom, it charms even those who knew her as the *France* to say that her reincarnation was well planned and well done. The 1035-foot *Norway* is truly her own cruise destination and has proved to be one of the most relaxing one-week holidays available.

Just for the *Norway*'s passengers, Kloster bought an island in the Bahamas. Located nine miles east southeast of Eleuthera Point, this $3.5 million worth of sand dunes and palm trees, called Little San Salvador, has already become NCL's own Fantasy Island for beach parties, picnics, snorkeling and sunfishing, or just loafing.

Someone once called Norwegian Caribbean Lines the "Chevrolet" of the cruise industry, which I agree with when I consider the company's three seven-day vessels, the *Skyward*, *Southward*, and *Starward*. Good, solid ships, they don't pretend to be elegant but offer interesting ports of call, fine onboard service, and average food instead. Passengers can depend upon these vessels and are rarely disappointed. If you are in the mood for just three or four days in the Bahamas, the *Sunward II* has a fine reputation for onboard service, food, and just plain fun. For a more glamorous time of doing very little but entertaining yourself, NCL's fourth seven-day ship, the *Norway*, would be my number one choice. The entertainment potential aboard this beautiful vessel is almost unlimited. The ports of call are minimal—St. Thomas to satisfy one's shopping instincts; Nassau and Little San Salvador to enjoy one of the sparkling sandy beaches of the Bahamas. Although passengers must use the ship's own 400-person launches to get ashore, I understand the crew handles the situation with maximum efficiency and courtesy and a minimum of discomfort. You might then consider the *Norway* the Lincoln Continental of the fleet.

Always an innovator in the cruise industry, NCL emphasizes good clean fun that is very popular with its passengers. One of the most memorable programs available is the Dive In, for which a staff of some fifteen certified diving instructors offers lessons, equipment, and guidance on undersea tours around the Caribbean. Since its debut in 1978 aboard the *Sunward II*, the Dive In program has led some half a million NCL passengers in colorful explorations below the water. All five NCL vessels now offer the program, and you do not even have to swim to participate and enjoy! (A safety vest protects nonswimmers from danger.) Most of the Dive In programs occur on the ship line's Bahamian Out Island, but other ports of call are now also included. In fact, the *Southward's* one-week cruises to Cozumel, Grand Cayman, Ocho Rios, and the Out Island now features Dive In at every call!

Knut Kloster and his cruise company have had their moments the past few years, with abrupt changes in management and the problems of the *Norway*, but that is all behind and the coming season looks like a winner. The *Norway* has sailed away full ever since her return from dry-docking in Bremerhaven. She departs every Saturday for St. Thomas, Nassau, and the Out Island. Every Friday the *Sunward II* sails for Nassau and the Out Island, and every Monday the vessel sails for Nassau, the Out Island, and Freeport. The *Southward* sails each Saturday, while the *Starward* and *Skyward* depart on Sundays. The one-week itinerary is Nassau, San Juan, St. Thomas, and the Out Island. A Mexican Fiesta program aboard the *Skyward* complements the ports of call—Playa del Carmen (for Cancun and Tulum), Cozumel, and an Out Island.

P & O CRUISES

c/o Princess Cruises
2029 Century Park East
Los Angeles, California 90067
tel: (213) 553-1770

The Peninsular and Oriental Steam Navigation Company, England's largest and most prestigious passenger and cargo line, began in the early 1800s and grew steadily in the nineteenth and twentieth centuries through a series of astute acquisitions (and some romantic seafaring history). The company flag, a combination of the blue and white national colors of Portugal, quartered with the red and yellow colors of Spain, symbolizes the highest of honors which both countries bestowed upon the ship line in the 1830s, commemorating valuable services rendered to Queen Maria of Portugal and Queen Isabella of Spain. Another interesting episode in the annals of P & O history dates to the opening of service between Egypt and India, which added a new word to the English language: *Posh* appeared stamped on certain steamship tickets to indicate that the passenger had bought the best (and coolest) cabin—which happened to be "Port Out (to India), Starboard Home." Since this cabin was in the most expensive category, the new word began to connote wealth and elitism.

According to company correspondence, P & O Line had such a fine reputation in the Victorian nineteenth century that even its shipwrecks were considered the best of any passenger fleet! In a letter dated 1863, from a Mrs. Dulcimer to her friend, Laura, the writer advises, "If you are ever shipwreckd, do contrive to get the catastrophe conducted by the Penninsular and Oriental Company. I believe other companies drown you sometimes and drowning is a very prosaic arrangement fit only for seafaring people and second class passengers. I have just been shipwrecked under the auspices of P & O and I assure you that it is the pleasantest thing imaginable. It has its little hardships to be sure, but so has a picnic, and the wreck was one of the most agreeable picnics you can imagine." What a recommendation!

Today the P & O passenger division operates two large cruise ships under its own flag (*Canberra, Sea Princess*) as well as the *Uganda* of BI Discovery Cruises (a P & O subsidiary); it also owns Princess Cruises of Los Angeles, *Island Princess, Pacific Princess, Sun Princess*). In all, the ship line runs a total cruise capacity of 146,474 gross tons and carries a potential of 5450 passengers when all six ships sail. That's quite an impressive set of figures, and P & O now has closer marketing cooperation between Los Angeles and London. In addition, the ship line has disclosed plans for a new *Princess* vessel of 40,000 tons and a capacity of 1200 passengers, to be delivered in late 1984. Although sailing for Princess Cruises from the West Coast, the vessel replaces the *Oriana* now out of service.

Unfortunately for P & O, 1982 proved to be rather a disruptive year as the British government requisitioned both the *Canberra* and the *Uganda* for service in the Falkland Island crisis. Although exposed to repeated air attacks while in San Carlos Sound, the *Canberra* was fortunate not to suffer any structural damage. She returned to Southampton in mid-July and was completely refitted with the aid of the government. Temporary helicopter landing pads were taken off her decks, and the entire interior of the vessel received new furnishings, carpeting, and paint. A peak-condition *Canberra* was returned to P & O for the resumption of her cruise schedule in September. Meanwhile, the *Uganda* served as a hospital ship, with a red cross gracing the familiar black and white funnel, and the vessel was scheduled to resume cruises by late fall.

The 45,000-ton *Canberra*, the third largest passenger liner in the world, is the pride of P & O's fleet. With an officer and crew complement of 800, and a capacity of 1700 passengers, the *Canberra* was the largest British post-war passenger vessel at the time of her launch in 1961. She was named in honor of the capital of Australia and has served faithfully on the Southampton-to-Sydney run as well as around the world. Upon her return to service, the *Canberra* sailed from Southampton on three 14-day cruises to the Mediterranean before departing on an eleven-week voyage to Australia. For 1983, the vessel will make thirteen cruises to the Canaries and the Mediterranean, beginning April 15 from Southampton. The sailings of twelve to twenty-one nights each run through October.

P & O's most luxurious cruise liner is the *Sea Princess*, the former *Kungsholm* of Flagship Cruises. This beautiful 28,000-ton vessel, originally built for Swedish America Line on the famous River Clyde in Scotland, now carries 840 passengers plus a crew of approximately 400. During the first three months of 1983, the *Sea Princess* is carrying the P & O flag around the world. On her exciting global voyage, the vessel will call at five continents and visit twenty-one ports in 90 days. Passengers not wishing to take the full voyage may break the journey in Sydney or Singapore and fly back (or vice versa).

Returning to Southampton on April 7, the *Sea Princess* offers a series of two- to three-week cruises to the Mediterranean, Red Sea, Scandinavia, the Canaries, and the Caribbean through January 8, 1984 (when another world cruise is presumably in order).

P & O never dissolved the name of the British India Steam Navigation Company, with which it merged in 1913. Under the aegis of BI Discovery Cruises, P & O offers educational cruises aboard the 17,000-ton *Uganda* (a former troop ship in the India and Burma area). The vessel carries three hundred cabin passengers on the upper decks as well as six hundred students in the former troop quarters. The two groups do not mingle on the eleven- to fourteen-night cruises on itineraries that range from the Baltic to the Holy Land. The more than seventy ports of call are often away from the well-trodden tourist path, and the primary shore excursion in each port is included in the cruise fare. The *Uganda* also features special interest sailings, such as fine arts lectures on board, theater-at-sea, and musical cruises.

A few years ago P & O started the Posh Club for repeat passengers, offering a number of Posh Club Cruises each year that entice passengers with special discounts as well as complimentary, escorted shore excursions. The *Canberra* and *Sea Princess* sail on these Posh cruises, but the quarterly newsletter sent to members is beginning to discuss the merits of the three *Princess* ships based on the West Coast. P & O views Australia and the South Seas as new growth areas in cruising and predicts that the old, established cruise clientele in the Caribbean will venture to the faraway South Seas, only to be replaced by a whole new set of Caribbean lovers. There's certainly room for everyone!

PAQUET FRENCH CRUISES

1370 Avenue of the Americas
New York, N.Y. 10019
tel: (212) 757–9050

This French cruise company traces its beginnings back to 1860 when Nicola Paquet and some friends started service between Marseilles and Morocco with a chartered 350-ton steam and sailing ship named the *Languedoc*. Apparently, Paquet and his *amis* found many contented passengers to shuttle back and forth between these two ports, because within three years they formed Compagnie de Navigation Paquet and extended service to the Canary Islands and Senegal. Soon, routes to the eastern Mediterranean, to Turkey, and into the Black Sea were added. Although Paquet now belongs to a Paris-based transportation conglomerate (which also has controlling interest in UTA French Airlines), the cruise company still works out of Marseille and still runs a regular ferry service to North Africa. *Quelle Fidélité!*

A few decades ago, Paquet boasted a dozen or so passenger vessels, but times have changed. Even the *tres charmante,* 450-passenger *Renaissance,* launched in 1966 as the flagship, has been sold and now belongs to Epirotiki Lines (on long-term charter to Costa). This vessel, now known as the *World Renaissance,* was well known for her Mayan cruises during the winter season in the Caribbean and for the Music Festivals at Sea. In 1970 Paquet introduced the 550-passenger *Mermoz* to cruise in the Caribbean. From mid-December through March she sails from San Juan on ten- and eleven-day cruises, and during the summer months she resides in the Mediterranean.

Paquet is now marketing the European schedule of the *Mermoz* as well as the 700-passenger *Azur* that the company acquired in 1976. Formerly a car-ferry named *Eagle,* the *Azur* is what I consider a comfortable but most unbeautiful vessel for the fun-set. A recent $20 million renovation may have improved her facilities somewhat; while she cruises around the Mediterranean at least, some seventy bicycles as well as several windsurf boards, small sailboats, and launches for water skiing are available to passengers through two full-time sports directors.

Paquet's most valuable contributions to the cruise world are the twice-yearly Music Festivals at Sea, now aboard the *Mermoz.* While the vessel is nothing to shout about, and the gourmet food reported to be a borderline case, all is forgiven during the two weeks of wonderful concerts at sea and in various ports of call. Although many of the great names are too busy and too expensive these days to participate, artists like Maurice André and James Galway are no slouches in the music world. Dancers, a chamber orchestra, and a few soloists usually complete the bill. The cruises are expensive (but well worth the price for serious music lovers) and usually occur at the end of the summer around Europe, early January in the Caribbean.

In conjunction with Ulysses Cruises, Paquet operates the 12,500-ton *Dolphin* (formerly the *Ithaca*) on three- and four-day cruises from Miami to the Bahama Islands. The 565-passenger vessel is registered in Panama, has a Greek-influenced crew, but a little French flair. Paquet serves unlimited bottles of its Sommelier red and white at dinner. A fourth vessel entered the Paquet family last year with the purchase of Holland America's *Statendam.* Now called the *Rhapsody,* with a French captain and an American in Paris Lounge, the vessel makes one-week cruises from Miami all winter, and from Vancouver during the Alaska/Canada season.

PEARL CRUISES OF SCANDINAVIA

Pier 27
San Francisco, California 94111
tel: (415) 391–7941   391, 7808
  (800) 792–0944 (in California)
  (800) 227–5666 (Continental U.S.)

Formed in the fall of 1981, Pearl Cruises of Scandinavia is a joint venture of two long established and respected Scandinavian cruise and shipping companies: I.M. Skaugen of Norway (one of the owners and maritime operator of Royal Caribbean Cruise Lines) and J. Lauritzen of Copenhagen (parent company of a multi-faceted group comprising shipyards, industry, and shipping companies including Scandinavian World Cruises of Miami). The new line was formed to "meet the needs of a growing travel market to China and Asia" and will be the only major cruise company offering sailings around Asia throughout the year.

Utilizing a recently refurbished vessel called *Pearl of Scandinavia*, with a passenger capacity of just under 500, the ship line will offer 29 sailings a year. The 14-day cruises focus on ports in the People's Republic of China for eight months of the year, then move south to the Indonesian Islands and Malaysia for the remaining four months. With six different itineraries available, passengers can combine the cruises and sail for 28 or 42 days at a stretch!

Ports of call for the new cruise line include Amoy, Shanghai, Qingdao, Dalian, Whampoa (Huang-pu), Xingang (for Beijing) in China; Kobe and the Inland Sea of Japan; Pusan, South Korea; Hong Kong; Singapore; Manila and Cebu in the Philippine Islands; Muara in Brunei; Kota Kinabalu, Kuching, and Penang in Malaysia; Belawan, Sibolga, Nias, Jakarta, Surabaya, and Bali (Padang Bay) in the Indonesian Archipelago.

The 17,400-ton *Pearl of Scandinavia*, formerly known as the *Finnstar*, began her new life on June 5, 1982, sailing from Hong Kong to China and Japan. With the recent $15 million renovation and a Scandinavian decor, the vessel sounds most comfortable and as deluxe as possible in this area of the cruising world. There are fourteen new suites on Sky Deck for those with the money to rent such space. An interesting array of guest lecturers have been scheduled to advise passengers on Asian history and culture, Chinese cooking, where and how to shop for silks and semi-precious jewels, and politics (both ours and theirs). The itineraries appear to be very well-planned, with just enough days at sea (three) to relax from the rigors of sightseeing. There is, of course, no deviation in the China excursion program and the entire complement of passengers travels as a group. All other shore tours are optional and sold separately. The Indonesian Archipelago cruises, although not quite so imaginative as the late and lamented *Prinsendam* used to perform, certainly satisfy that desire for an unusual yet luxurious travel experience.

Chief executive officer of the company is John Traina, a veteran of twenty-five years in the shipping and cruise industry, whose name is familiar to all who have enjoyed the Prudential/Grace/Delta cruises around South America on the Santa liners. Captain of the *Pearl of Scandinavia*, Erik Bjurstedt, has spent more than three decades at sea and was most recently with Royal Caribbean Cruise Lines in Miami. The officers are a mix of Scandinavian and American, working with European hotel management and Filipino stewards. By all standards, the company appears sound and is a welcome addition to the wonderful world of cruising.

POLISH OCEAN LINES

c/o McLean Kennedy, Inc.
410 St. Nicholas Street
Montreal, Quebec H2Y 2P5
tel: (514) 849–6111

Polish Ocean (Gdynia America Line) is a very old and established shipping company whose only entry into the cruise market is the 15,000-ton *Stefan Batory*, the former Dutch liner *Maasdam* of Holland America Line. The *Stefan Batory*, flagship of Polish Ocean, was bought by the government in 1968 and refitted with modern furniture and air conditioning. The vessel accommodates 779 passengers in comfortable but hardly elegant cabins (in my opinion). More than half the cabins are inside and some fifteen percent lack private facilities. For a wonderful adventure, however, this is one of the best ships around and chances are that you will feel that your time and money were very well spent.

The *Stefan Batory* sails between Gdynia, Poland, and Montreal, Canada, from April through November, with the exception of some St. Lawrence/ Saguenay River cruises of seven days each during the month of July. The Saguenay sailings from Montreal call at St. Pierre, Miquelon, Charlottetown (Prince Edward Island), and Quebec City. The transatlantic sailings depart Montreal and call at London and Rotterdam before arriving in Gdynia. On certain sailings the ship line has developed a schedule so that you can visit your favorite places in Europe and then catch the vessel on her westbound voyage. Sailing on the *Stefan Batory* both ways, though, entitles you to a big discount. During the winter months the *Stefan Batory* sails from London on some very economical cruises to the Canary Islands and the West Indies, and in the spring to the Mediterranean and Black seas. For true economy, if you can do without much fuss and bother, consider this vessel. The crew doesn't even expect tips. Some friends and colleagues rave about the *Stefan Batory* but add that children may miss the companions and activities that other ships offer.

PRINCESS CRUISES

2029 Century Park East
Los Angeles, California 90067
tel: (213) 553–1770

Yes, Princess Cruises is the "Love Boat" ship line; and the company enjoys it immensely! If you're lucky, you may even catch the filming of this popular television comedy series while you sail on the *Island Princess* or *Pacific Princess* . The film crew of about 150 comes aboard for location shots. (I ran into "Doc," the doctor and "Julie," the social director last summer in San Juan on board the *Island Princess*; it was great fun). With an audience of approximately thirty million people each week, the series unwittingly promotes Princess and cruises in general. When asked, many passengers on board respond that the television series encouraged them to take a cruise. Why not? Princess operates three top-rate vessels, and the British officers actually do wear those short, sexy uniforms.

Princess Cruises, formed in 1965 by Seattle industrialist Stanley McDonald, started cruises from the west coast of California to the west coast of Mexico and through the Panama Canal into the Caribbean. He also pioneered sailings to the now-popular Inside Passage and Glacier Bay National Monument in Alaska. McDonald sold his Los Angeles-based company in 1968, but bought it back in 1970 only to resell it again in 1974 to P & O Line. Although all three vessels belonging to Princess Cruises have British registry and crew, their home port is San Pedro, outside of Los Angeles.

The ship line operates the beautiful sister ships, *Island Princess* and *Pacific Princess*, both built in West Germany in the early 1970s to carry six hundred passengers in all first-class accommodations. These 20,000-ton vessels offer plenty of open deck space and large, gracious public rooms. Both have British officers and crew in addition to Italian stewards who tend the dining room. The third vessel in the Princess fleet, the Italian-built 17,000-ton *Sun Princess* (the former *Spirit of London*), carries seven hundred passengers in smaller, less elegant accommodations. But this last vessel fosters a reputation as the fun ship of the fleet, sailing on seven- to eighteen-day itineraries to the Mexican Riviera, Alaska, and the Caribbean. All three vessels summer in Alaska, where they offer over 35 sailings!

In 1983 Princess Cruises began two new itineraries for the *Pacific Princess*, as well as continued her successful and familiar pattern that she shares with the other two vessels. The *Pacific Princess* departs from Los Angeles on a 70-day roundtrip cruise to the South Pacific and the Orient, which is also available in four shorter segments of 24 to 46 days each. Tours and fly-free programs are available. During the rest of the year the *Pacific Princess* sails on six- to fourteen-day cruises to the Mexican Riviera, and twelve-day cruises from San Francisco to Alaska and the Inside Passage.

The *Island Princess* is occupied on two-week trans-Panama Canal cruises between Los Angeles and San Juan, except from June to mid-September when she sails from Vancouver on an eight-day itinerary to Alaska/Canada. The *Sun Princess* also sails from Vancouver during the summer season, but on a one-week circuit. From October through March, she is based out of San Juan for one-week lower Caribbean cruises. Longer repositioning cruises between San Juan/West Coast/Vancouver via the Panama Canal are also available.

Princess has expanded its Seabird Air program from 35 to 67 gateway cities for 1983. Other good news is that all transcanal as well as the two long *Pacific Princess* cruises are fly-free for all passengers. One-week Caribbean cruises are fly-free for Atlanta passengers, while those coming from Los Angeles add $100 per person for air fare. The ship line is also allowing third persons to travel free, if occupying a cabin with two full-fare passengers, and a five percent discount for payment in full six months or more before sailing.

Not to be outdone by other lines announcing new tonnage, Princess has ordered a "super love boat" from the Wartsila shipyards in Helsinki. To be delivered in late 1984, the 40,000-ton vessel will cost approximately $150 million and be designed to carry 1200 passengers. Norwegian architect Njal R. Eide has been commissioned for the ship's interiors, along with the American design firm of Hirsch/Bedner & Associates. Structural design will be directed by the naval architectural firm Knute E. Hanson Company. Princess plans to keep certain "innovative features" and configuration confidential for some time. The British-registered new vessel will be home-ported in Los Angeles, but a name and areas of cruising have not yet been selected. Worldwide operation is not out of the picture at this writing.

By my standards, Princess Cruises definitely rates as one of the top American-based ship lines, and you can always count on splendid itineraries, modern ships, and excellent service.

RAYMOND AND WHITCOMB CO.

400 Madison Avenue
New York, N.Y. 10017
tel: (212) 759–3960

If you belong to a museum, private club, or college alumni association, chances are you have received Raymond and Whitcomb brochures from time to time, detailing specially designed cruises aboard the *Argonaut*. Designing cruises for members and friends of a variety of organizations around the U.S. is the specialty of this company that claims to be the oldest travel firm in the country, dating from 1879 when two young Bostonians (Walter Raymond and Irvine Whitcomb) first offered weekend excursions by train. These trips actually began as a service to people who swore they would never travel in a group, but who soon became converts when they discovered how enjoyable group travel could be when handled well. And for over a century Raymond and Whitcomb has built a reputation for handling group travel very well, indeed.

The small, yachtlike *Argonaut*, an Epirotiki Lines vessel that Raymond and Whitcomb has chartered for more than a dozen years, handles each cruise. The *Argonaut*, not a luxury ship, retains a comfort and congeniality that match the superb service. Basically, the ship cruises the Aegean in the spring and fall for the Greek islands and Turkey. She offers the Island World of Britain and the Waterways of France cruises during the summer, the Mediterranean and Iberian "idylls" fill the repositioning sails, and she winters in the

Red Sea/Suez area. The vessel spends November and December in dry dock.

If Raymond and Whitcomb offers the Waterways of France itinerary for your college alumni association, for example, the company will invite a full-time lecturer from your college to join the cruise (which features the Loire and Gironde rivers, Brittany and the Channel coast); but lectures are not mandatory to your enjoyment (you can always "deck-chair it" with a bloody mary). If a museum or other nonprofit public institution sponsors the cruise, your fare will automatically include a tax-deductible donation to the sponsoring institution. In addition to the *Argonaut*, chartered vessels occasionally sail for custom-made cruises, such as the Smithsonian-sponsored expedition aboard the *Neptune* a few summers ago that drew such well-known Americans as Lady Bird Johnson and the Lawrence Rockefellers. Recent agendas offered the Northeast Passage (from New York to New England and Canada), sponsored by the Metropolitan Museum of Art and the National Trust for Historic Preservation, in September and the North Cape (Norway's fjordland) in August, aboard Royal Viking Line vessels. The beginning of the decade coincided with a new Amazon River expedition aboard the *World Discoverer*, arranged in cooperation with Society Expeditions Cruises, Inc. of Seattle—an alliance that is expected to continue.

ROYAL CARIBBEAN CRUISE LINE

903 South America Way
Miami, Florida 33132
tel: (305) 379–2601

In the highly competitive world of cruise companies based in Miami for sailings around the Caribbean, Royal Caribbean Cruise Line consistently earns top honors in quality of its ships, itineraries, and on-board amenities. The fifteen-year old ship line is a partnership of three respected Norwegian companies, long experienced in offering solid products worldwide: I.M. Skaugen is involved with supertankers; Anders Wilhelmsen operates the Barber Line freighters among other shipping interests; Gotaas Larsen has tankers and freighters, and is involved with Eastern and Western Cruise Lines of Miami and Los Angeles. While Royal Caribbean's headquarters and fleet is registered in Oslo, its North American management team is in Miami and very aware of passenger preferences and fluctuations. In the past decade there has been very little changeover in the line's decisionmakers—an example of the company's solidity and performance.

RCCL (as the company is affectionately called) now boasts a fine fleet of four vessels, all built in the famed Wartsila shipyard near Helsinki, Finland, for warm-water cruising. All four sail exclusively in the Caribbean (although a few cruises will be offered to Bermuda in 1983). The *Song of Norway* began service in November 1970 and for a decade made a consistent seven-day pattern, often filled with first-time RCCL passengers. Sister ships *Nordic Prince* and the *Sun Viking* arrived in 1971 and 1972 respectively, to be placed on two-week itineraries that departed Miami on alternate Saturdays. As originally designed and constructed, all three vessels were approximately 18,600 tons and carried some seven hundred passengers. Each ship is immediately recognizable in any Caribbean port by the distinctive, circular Viking Crown Lounge, which sits about ten stories above the sea and is cantilevered from the smokestack. (The only unfortunate aspect of this spectacular bar/lounge is its sole accessibility by an outside and often windy stairway).

The very popular *Song of Norway* returned to her place of birth, Wartsila shipyard in Helsinki, to be enlarged in 1978. The *Song* became the first of several cruise ships to be "stretched," a sophisticated method of adding tonnage and capacity to its midsection. The *Song* (and later the *Nordic Prince*) both had 85-foot-long insertions, increasing the ships to 23,000 tons and capacity for just over one thousand passengers. Public rooms were increased in size and space for about eighty crew members added. The already impressive vessels became more so.

Royal Caribbean's newest member of the fleet, the *Song of America*, arrived on schedule in Miami on December 5, 1982, for her maiden season. The vessel was four years in the planning/construction, and her design is based on the Finnjet approach that places most of the cabins in the forward section to eliminate unnecessary noise problems. The ship's main lounge has a multi-level seating arrangement to improve passengers' visibility of entertainment, and the Madame Butterfly dining room has a U-shape configuration with two terraced galleries for dramatic ocean viewing while eating. But the cantilevered Viking Crown Lounge, hallmark of the ship line, provides the most dramatic departure of all. It completely encircles the funnel some twelve decks above the waterline and provides a 360 degree panorama for its 140-person capacity.

The public rooms on all four Royal Caribbean vessels are themed after hit Broadway musicals. The *Song of Norway* has The King and I, My Fair Lady, and South Pacific lounges; the *Nordic Prince* boasts Camelot, Carousel, and Showboat; HMS Pinafore, The Merry Widow, and Annie Get Your Gun can be found on the *Sun Viking*; and the *Song of America* inaugurates Can Can, Oklahoma, and Guys and Dolls. Deck space is superb on all four vessels and the outdoor pools are among the best afloat. In addition to the distinctive Viking Crown Lounge, the late-night spots have simultaneous slide presentations put together by the ship line's own photographer who roams the world in search of good shots. Dining-room service is excellent and once again, each night of the week is themed with different table settings and menus. Waiters seem to be hired as much for their ability to take "orders" as for their agility in singing and entertaining guests.

Royal Caribbean never did much for a writer's copy during its first decade of operation, for the company found a successful formula for seven-and fourteen-day cruises and stuck by it year after year. The ship line, however, seems to have leapt into the volatile 1980s with a new vessel and some innovative itinerary changes. The softening of the world economy has also prompted the line to offer free airfare from over seventy gateways, and now includes such annoying trivia as port taxes in a one-time, easy to understand cruise price. Since the addition of port taxes to passengers' fares is a consumer "rip-off," I applaud RCCL for publishing an all-inclusive rate that is among the very best value in the Carribean.

Royal Caribbean's attention to quality is evident in its highly rated food and service, entertainment that rotates weekly among the fleet, and cabin cleanliness. Passengers report that breakfast arrives promptly every morning when requested, ice and fruit are replenished daily, covers are turned down with soft lights turned on, and a chocolate is on every pillow before bedtime. Recently, a few thousand members of a Northeast-based cruise society (who seem to spend almost all of their time in the Caribbean by the ships surveyed) voted all three RCCL vessels (*Sun Viking, Song of Norway,* and *Nordic Prince*) as the top in their category. The only way RCCL can top this is to entice these cruise buffs aboard the *Song of America* in 1983!

This year, RCCL vessels are covering the Caribbean as no fleet has ever done before.

ROYAL CRUISE LINE

One Maritime Plaza
San Francisco, California 94111
tel: (415) 956–7200

Royal Cruise line was formed in 1972 in Greece "for the explicit purpose of constructing a fleet of new, super-deluxe cruise ships to operate cruises in the Mediterranean, Scandinavian, and Western Hemisphere waters for passengers from the United States." Founder and president of the company is Pericles S. Panagopoulos, a well-know Greek shipper who runs Royal Cruise Line from his headquarters in Piraeus, Greece. The North American office in San Francisco is responsible for marketing the *Golden Odyssey* and the *Royal Odyssey.*

Flagship of Royal Cruise Line's fleet is the 10,500-ton *Golden Odyssey,* built in 1974 in Elsinore, Denmark, under the direction of Tage Wandborg, one of the world's leading naval architects. The vessel holds 460 passengers comfortably. From the very beginning Royal Cruise Line concentrated on two basic concepts: offering air-sea packages and drawing passengers from the West Coast. The *Golden/Royal Odyssey* cruise, pushed on the West Coast and sold as an all-inclusive air-sea package, flies passengers from Los Angeles and San Francisco to meet the ships either in the Caribbean during the winter months or the Mediterranean during the summer season. (Passengers who wish to buy their own air transportation can buy "cruise only" portions of the program, if they wish.)

The *Golden Odyssey* earns a deservedly high reputation in my opinion and seems to suit the American/California market perfectly. Although I have never sailed aboard this vessel, I have been continually impressed by the concern for both the ship and her passengers shown by her shore personnel. An unusual attention to detail is especially impressive. (Perhaps this is only possible when a company operates just one ship, but I don't think so.) It pays off, though, because overwhelming evidence points to happy and satisfied passengers who come back for more cruises. On one particular sailing last year, almost half the passengers were repeaters and members of the exclusive Odyssey Club. For repeat passengers the ship line always arranges something special—a cocktail party or a special dinner on shore. (Many ship lines offer this courtesy, but Royal Cruise seems to pay special attention to it.)

The *Golden Odyssey* also has a fine reputation for service. Menus geared to California tastes offer an abundance of beef and fresh fruit, although more Continental-style cuisine is now offered at the table. The dining room presents a number of special nights: Greek Night, Pirate Night, Pastel Night, Carnival, and the special Welcome Aboard dinner and Captain's Gala evening. In addition to wine lists and full bar, take advantage of the special drink of the day (Calypso Cocktail, Golden Adventure, Ancient Mariner) which still only costs about a dollar. What a bargain.

Royal Cruise Line's long search for another vessel was finally over in late 1980, with the intent to purchase the 800-passenger *Doric* from Home Lines. Royal Cruise acquired the vessel last winter, spent several million dollars renovating and refurbishing, changed her registry to Greek and relaunched her as the *Royal Odyssey* during the recent Mediterranean season. A new Greek-style decor was created by interior designer Michael Katzourakis, using the colors of sand, sky, sea, and sun (apparently to alternately soothe and dazzle the passengers). Katzourakis designed all the fabrics and most of the furnishings especially to suit the vessel. Bathrooms throughout were among the facilities modernized, and all cabins now feature all-American amenities.

Among changes in the public areas are the multileveled Odyssey Lounge, the Ambrosia Dining Room with ocean-view windows, a larger on-deck swimming pool, and a casino. There are now 22 superior deluxe suites, 33 junior suites, plus 279 outside and 71 inside staterooms. Each deck is "color coded," which the ship line finds convenient for both passengers and baggage handlers in finding their way about.

The *Royal Odyssey* will keep her sister ship, *Golden Odyssey*, in good company this year while following the sun around the Caribbean before repositioning in the Mediterranean. From December to March both vessels offer twelve-day air-sea cruises between San Juan and Acapulco. The *Royal Odyssey* also sails between Miami and Acapulco this winter, while the *Golden Odyssey* makes four round trips from San Juan. In late March, both vessels begin the Mediterranean season from Lisbon to Athens (Piraeus) and then share a series of Mediterranean programs. During the height of summer, the *Golden Odyssey* returns to the Black Sea, while the *Royal Odyssey* sails from London (Tilbury) to the land of the Norsemen. Two-night London theatre packages are available pre- or post- all cruises.

All 1983 winter cruises aboard both vessels will feature a number of retired military officers as hosts, adding an extra dimension of "sociability" on the dance floor as well as at the card table and cocktail parties. Wine seminars will also be offered this season, with representatives of California wineries conducting complimentary tastings. Evening entertainment will continue to delight, with both present and past celebrities on board to perform.

The shore excursion programs provide another example of Royal Cruise Line's attention to detail. (Shore excursions can be purchased before departure and this is often recommended.) Prior to docking at each port of call, the cruise staff distributes a detailed map of the area as well as the Pocket Port of Call. The latter, printed on different colored stiff papers, explains how to pronounce the names of foreign ports and details a few pertinent facts and bits of history, the excursions of the day, shopping opportunities, and what to do on your own. No shipboard lecture can possibly be as informative as what you can read for yourself and carry around with you! You will be grateful for the well-organized and handy hints contained on each sheet, especially when you want to get away from your group.

Although I suspect Royal Cruise Line likes to think it attracts more and more younger passengers on its cruises (indeed, all ship lines have this in mind), the majority of its vacationers are from the middle-aged to retired set, drawn by marketing and aimed at the so-called Leisure World communities so popular in California. Again, the high cost of per diem travel aboard this ship (about $200 per day minimum, per person on the European sailings) influences the age group on board. And like all ship lines, Royal Cruise Line offers its favorite passenger stories—the travel agent who has sailed so often the crew refer to her as "Mama" or the middleaged bachelor who found his wife on board, married her, and returned with her for their honeymoon.

ROYAL VIKING LINE

One Embarcadero Center   ATTN:
San Francisco, California 94111
tel: (415) 398–8000

Royal Viking Line, one of North America's top-class cruise companies, operates three identical sister ships whose white hull and crimson sea eagle emblems on the smokestack are familiar sights in ports of call throughout the world. The ship line was formed in Oslo around 1970 by three separate Norwegian firms (A.F. Klaveness, Bergen Line, and Nordenfjeldske) who each commissioned the construction of one vessel. Today the 22,000-ton, 500-passenger *Royal Viking Star* (1972), *Royal Viking Sky* (mid-1973), and *Royal Viking Sea* (December 1973) are owned and operated by the latter two companies, since Klaveness bowed out in the mid-1970s.

The Royal Viking ships keep Norway alive in spirit and style and carry on the great Viking tradition of exploring the world. The three vessels are renowned for their fine service, cuisine, and itineraries, which create alternating patterns around the globe. To keep track of all these comings and goings, RVL publishes an annual Cruise Atlas that features fine photographs, inventive maps of the popular cruising areas, and brief tempters on ports of call. The brochure also describes an overwhelming number of sailings available each year in addition to an endless variety of cruise options. For example, a 45-day cruise round trip from Florida to the Mediterranean and Black seas is forty-two days round trip from New York, twenty days from Florida to Piraeus (port for Athens), and seventeen days from New York. Or if you prefer to embark in Greece, you may enjoy a 24-day cruise to New York. Five different options within one cruise!

Basically, the itineraries RVL schedules for its three vessels each year feature a series of very long cruises (South Seas, Circle Pacific, Around South America, Around the World) as well as a variety of short and longer sailings to Alaska/Canada, the Caribbean, Mexico, Tahiti/Hawaii, New England/Canada, North Cape, Northern Capitals, and Mediterranean/Adriatic/Black Sea. New for 1983 is a series of four 14-day cruises between Hong Kong and Kobe, with port calls at Shanghai, Dalian and Hsingang in China as well as Nagasaki and Kagoshima in Japan. These cruises take place from April 25 through a June 6 sailing, and shore excursions include overnight visits to Tientsin and Beijing. Land programs in Japan and Hong Kong are also available. Passengers may purchase cruise only, beginning at $2,826 per person for double occupancy, or pay for a complete package with air transportation, stopovers in Hawaii, and land programs in Japan and Hong Kong.

Royal Viking inaugurated a Gateway to Gangway program last year for its Panama Canal/Caribbean/Mexico itineraries, featuring guaranteed air fare, greeting upon arrival at airport (if ~ame day as sailing), baggage handling and transfers. The program is extended this year for all RVL cruises, from over 40 North American gateway cities. Passengers who wish to arrive early and make their own land arrangements at ports of departure, will still have guaranteed air fare but will lose eligibility for baggage handling and transfers between airport and ship.

In an attempt to prevent being priced right out of the marketplace, RVL has revised its rate structure and added two more categories at the lower end of the span, allowing passengers more choice. The two new categories are noted as G and GG and cover the new, mid-section outside doubles on Mediterranean Deck only. Even lower priced are the F and FF category outside doubles in the forward section of Mediterranean deck, and J refers to all inside cabins for which rates have been considerably lowered this year. Other good news is that single travelers no longer need pay 100% more for occupying a double cabin. The maximum charge has been lowered to 1.6 of the double occupancy fares. Additionally, many cruises have been shortened (Alaska/Canada from 14 to 12 days) to make them more appealing and better-priced.

In the summer of 1980, Royal Viking Line revealed plans to "stretch" its existing fleet of three ships by adding a 93-foot mid-section to each vessel. These additions were scheduled to be performed in Bremerhaven, West Germany over a period of three years or so, increasing the size of each vessel to 28,000 tons, the length to 674 feet, and the passenger complement to about 725. The total cost of the three-ship expansion project was expected to be around $100 million, the approximate price of a brand-new 600-passenger vessel in today's market (provided the construction was well-subsidized by a foreign government).

The *Star,* first to be launched was first to be stretched, and returned to service in the Caribbean around Christmastime 1981. Although her passenger capacity is now around 725, the one-seating dining room was retained by enlarging the existing space and then breaking it up into smaller areas that don't intimidate the diners so much. Penthouse suites, with private verandas, additional deluxe cabins, a new Venus Lounge adjacent to the Stella Polaris Room, a second outdoor pool, the Sky Deck and Lido bar were all part of the renovations. From many reports, the high standard of RVL service, cleanliness and food has been well maintained throughout and passengers are responding well to the larger vessel. To add even more excitement, RVL has re-assessed its menu plans and introduced more 'nouvelle cuisine' to the daily fare (and at least the women passengers appreciate the lighter dishes).

Second on the stretch-schedule was the *Sky,* which was returned to service on December 5 in the Caribbean sporting her new mid-section. At this writing, the *Sea* is expected to depart Port Everglades for Bremerhaven on February 28 for cosmetic surgery and sail June 10 from Southampton.

Royal Viking Line celebrated a proud tenth anniversary in 1982 and presented its passengers with gold and silver certificates toward future cruises. Its Skal Club for repeat passengers was one of the first organized and remains one of the most active. Repeaters receive sets of aquavit glasses (about the size of a thimble), decanters and glass bowls for their loyalty. Some 70% of the 1982 world cruise was repeat passengers, and some afficiandos boast as many as 20, 25, 30 and 35 cruises in the past decade aboard all three vessels. One woman, we understand, went through the Panama Canal three times and around the world last year, and only disembarked to see her husband and children!

SALEN LINDBLAD CRUISING

133 East 55th Street
New York, N.Y. 10022
tel: (212) 751–2300

This company was formed in July 1982 to operate and market *Lindblad Explorer,* the *Lindblad Polaris* and the *Yao Hua.* Both the *Polaris* and *Explorer* now sail under Swedish flag and offer unusual cruises worldwide. The *Yao Hua* is a Chinese-owned vessel that cruises between Hong Kong and Nanjing with longer air-land-sea programs from the U.S.

The Salen Group operates approximately two hundred cargo vessels and has a number of subsidiary marine services around the world. Headquarters of the new company is in New York and Salen has sent over Swedish president and overseer Lars Wikander.

The *Lindblad Explorer,* which had her maiden voyage in December 1969, is well known to that intrepid group of cruise passengers who enjoy exploring areas out of the way and spending time in the Antarctic as well as the South Pacific and North Cape. Fiji, Bora Bora, Easter Island, the Sea of Cortez, the Aleutians and Bering Sea and Asmat are like home to this vessel. She has a very loyal following and one can be assured of a fascinating itinerary as well as stimulating fellow passengers.

Along the China coastline, the *Explorer* has been replaced by the *Yao Hua* for cruises between Hong Kong and Nanjing, with air tours to Beijing and back. The ship is less comfy than the *Explorer* but one of best and most reliable around. Because of her small size (10,000 tons), the vessel can call at ports that many other cruise ships can not. It is an exciting program for people who want to taste a bit of China with excellent guides and well-planned shore excursions.

Newest of the group is the 79-passenger *Lindblad Polaris*, inaugurated in May 1982 for cruising in the Baltic and Scandinavia during the summer months, around Europe in the spring and fall, and through the Red Sea during the winter season. The *Polaris* visits both the cities of renown as well as small islands full of marine and plant life. Zodiacs are carried on top, much like the *Explorer*, so passengers can tender into the lesser available coves. The ship combines a sense of adventure with solid European comfort and food and one can be assured of meeting stimulating colleagues aboard.

Salen Lindblad Cruising is a welcomed addition and hopefully will produce a solid, compact brochure soon that details all its programs in simple and realistic terms. Intrepid Club members will continue to be invited on special sailings and meet many old friends.

SCANDINAVIAN WORLD CRUISES

1290 South America Way
Miami, Florida 33132
tel: (305) 377–9000

Scandinavian World Cruises, a cruise line formed about 1980 in Miami, grew from the distinguished century-old United Steamship Company of Denmark, known worldwide as DFDS. The DFDS group is one of the largest shipping concerns in Europe, with sixteen modern container ships and twelve passenger vessels that serve ports in the North Sea, the Atlantic, the Baltic, and the Mediterranean. The passenger vessels do not actually operate cruises, as I define the word, but it does primarily transport people from one place to another.

The company launched its Sea Escape program in February 1982 with two vessels sailing from two different Florida ports. The 1000-passenger *Scandinavian Sea* departs daily from Port Canaveral in the morning and returns about eleven hours later. The 1000-passenger *Scandinavian Sun* sails daily from Miami in the early morning and returns about midnight. Both connect in Freeport for a few hours. The cruises appeal to the young set, and many parents bring along the children for an exciting day at sea. On-board activities on both vessels are aimed at the active types, with an emphasis on water sports, exercise, snorkeling, and dancing. There are cabaret-type shows to fill the dark hours on the return cruise. Day cabins are available on both vessels for a per-room charge ranging from $15 to $50. Suites are $100 on the *Sun* only. There is a no-reservation, guaranteed departure system during weekdays.

At this writing, the port of New York was still waiting for the 35,000-ton flagship, *Scandinavia*, to arrive for service. Scheduled for a late 1982 inaugural, the $100 million vessel just built in France, will carry 1000 passengers comfortably but have a full capacity for 1600 people and 400 cars. She will sail every fifth day from New York to Freeport, arriving on Grand Bahama island on the morning of the third. Passengers may drive their own cars off (after paying a hefty inspection fee to the Bahamian government) or transfer them to the *Scandinavian Sun* or *Sea* for the short sail to Florida. A number of land programs are available in all ports. Alternatively, passengers may stay aboard the *Scandinavia* and sail her back to New York. A recent promotional offer features the return cruise free of charge.

The Scandinavian-designed cabins sound most comfortable and offer 24-hour room service as well as feature films on TV screens. The Windows of the World restaurant serves buffet-style for breakfast and lunch, but breaks up into more intimate specialty restaurants for dinner. There is a 40-foot swimming pool with retractable roof, a shopping alley worthy of St. Thomas, several bars and lounges and a complete fitness center with hot tub! It all sounds very entertaining.

Last year, the company announced the acquisition of yet another vessel for the Bahamas cruise market. To be renamed the *Scandinavian Star*, the former *Tor Britannia* was built in 1975 and carries a complement of 1300 passengers. Considered a lavish cruise ship and scheduled to be placed on the three- and four-day run from Miami to the Bahamas, the *Star* sounded like an instant success. The parent company of DFDS decided, however, to postpone her entry in North American waters and use the vessel in European service between Denmark and Holland via the North Sea. Pity, as the short cruises to the Bahamas certainly need some more modern and attractive vessels.

SITMAR CRUISES

10100 Santa Monica Boulevard
Los Angeles, California 90067
tel: (213) 553–1666

The Beverly Hills-based Sitmar Cruises is just one small arm of the V-Group, a large shipping operation headquartered in Monte Carlo, which explains why a large "V" graces the smokestack of every vessel. The company formed about 1970 when it bought two old Cunard liners, the former *Carinthia* and *Sylvania*, and rebuilt them for luxury cruising. The ships were then registered in Liberia, manned with seaworthy Italians, and renamed the *Fairsea* and *Fairwind*, respectively. Another vessel operated by Sitmar, based in Sydney, is considerably more casual than the other two. This is the *Fairstar* which, when boarded in Hong Kong recently, was full of happy Australians sitting around a publike lounge drinking beer. The floor was covered with sawdust and the dartboards were an obvious source of entertainment. The company also used to operate the *Fairsky* from Australia, but apparently that vessel was scratched and a new namesake is on the way for late 1983. The new *Fairsky* will be 38,000 tons and carry a passenger complement of 1200. The vessel is being constructed near Toulon in France (where both the *Sagafjord* and *Atlantic* were built) and is expected to cost around $150 million. The proposed itinerary will be from California.

Sitmar vessels have a reputation for good organization and service, and particular attention to detail. Passengers' comments are computerized and graded, so the company always knows what goes on and what the popular entertainment and ports of call are. The ship line is well-known for its theme cruises, especially those that bespeak of nostalgia. It's all a matter of taste, and obviously Sitmar's clientele love the likes of Mel Torme and Sid Caesar. However, younger passengers and entire families are now being courted—especially during the summer months when about a dozen staff members are on board each vessel to entertain the youth from 9 A.M. to midnight. If you do take your youngsters aboard, the ship line recommends an early dinner sitting (which may be the only time the whole family is together).

Sitmar's air-sea programs have been renowned for being one-step ahead of any other company. Now all cruises are fly-free and as long as passengers are aware that Something is never given away for Nothing (it's included in the cruise rate), then everyone is happy. Fly-free is a very creative gimmick that is being copied by many other ship lines.

The *Fairwind* is homeported in Port Everglades for a series of cruises to the Caribbean. Within the familiar framework for this season are some unusual sailings to the western Caribbean, with partial-transits of the Panama Canal. The vessel sails on one- to two-week cruises year-round. The *Fairsea* is based in San Pedro, the port for Los Angeles, for Mexico cruises (Cabo San Lucas, Mazatlan, Zihuatanejo and Puerto Vallarta) for the winter season. Two Panama Canal transits of fourteen days each are on the schedule. During the summer season, the vessel sails from San Francisco on two-week cruises to Canada and Alaska's Inside Passage. The vessel makes a series of fourteen-day trans-Panama Canal sailings between Los Angeles and San Juan in the spring, fall, and winter months and cruises to Mexico on alternate dates. These alternate sailings, primarily to the Mexican Riviera, range from seven days (three ports) to eleven days (five ports) duration.

SOCIETY EXPEDITIONS CRUISES

723 Broadway East
Seattle, Washington 98102
tel: (206) 324–9400

Society Expeditions Cruises was formed in September 1979 to handle the cruises aboard the *World Discoverer* for members of the Society for the Preservation of Archaeological Monuments (incorporated in Washington state). Sole stockholder and director of this corporation is a fellow who signs himself T.C. Swartz (and for two years I have been curious what the initials mean—Theodore Charles). The cruises offered aboard the *World Discoverer* are very much like those that have made the *Lindblad Explorer* world famous. Each cruise is called a "project" and visits exotic centers around the world where naturalists and photographers and ornithologists love to roam. You can count on cruising expeditions to the Amazon and Antarctic, Melanesia, Indonesian archipelago, the Indian Ocean area, the Red Sea, Iceland and Greenland, and North Africa—not to mention the Amazon, Easter Island, and New Guinea.

The 3,150-ton *World Discoverer* was built in Bremerhaven in 1974, and is still owned by a West German firm. The vessel was built especially for the adventurous traveler who enjoys sailing to the remote places of the world (and converse about it later). In fact, the *Discoverer* was once charted by Lindblad Travel but his clients thought it "too big." She is now on charter to Society Expeditions until January 1984. She carries 140 passengers, with a crew of 70. She also carries ten motorized Zodiacs (German-designed rubber rafts used as launches that accommodate fifteen to twenty persons).

To inaugurate this season, Society Expeditions is offering a 121-day seven-continent cruise beginning January 18 in Antarctica, then traveling through New Guinea and the Great Barrier Reef, Singapore and the Seychelles, and Arabia/Red Sea. Of course, this cruise is broken into many different segments of two to three weeks each, for passengers who don't wish to spend up to $55,000 at one stretch! Other sailings during the year feature Morocco and West Africa, the Norwegian fjords and Spitsbergen, Iceland and Greenland, and the Amazon River.

Passengers can be assured that each cruise is carefully planned and a goodly number of naturalists, ethnologists, historians, and fellow explorers are on board. As with most cruises of this type, only the healthy need apply, since some of the shore excursions can be rigorous. Simply climbing in and out of the Zodiacs takes some agility—especially in the rain! The vessel is very comfortable and sells itself. There are plenty of diversions on board, even a swimming pool and gymnasium/sauna. And nothing but adventure lies over the horizon!

SPECIAL EXPEDITIONS

133 East 55th Street
New York, N.Y. 10022
tel: (212) 888–7980

Special Expeditions was formed a few years ago by Sven-Olaf Lindblad to use travel to focus on a greater depth of exposure in a few select areas of the world. The company caters to small groups with an interest in obtaining an intimate view of marine and shore life, especially at times of migrations. One of the most popular programs that Special Expeditions offers is the Baja California Circumnavigated aboard the *Pacific Northwest Explorer*. The program features six two-week circumnavigations of Baja California from January through March, between San Diego and San Felipe. Passengers visit such wondrous areas as Isla San Martin, Bahia de Ballenas (Bay of Whales), Magdalena Bay, Cabo San Lucas, Espiritu Santo, etc. Naturalists, lecturers, photographers, artists and writers accompany the voyages, and a log is kept of the wildlife spotted. During the first season, some 122 different birds, 108 fish, 68 plants, and 14 marine mammals (including six species of whales) were recorded.

During the month of September, Special Expeditions charters the *Majestic Explorer* for ten-day cruises along the Alaskan coastline to watch migrating birds and follow whales. The cruises sail from Ketchikan to Sitka (and vice versa). Needless to say, it's an interesting time to be in the Northwest, watching nature prepare herself for winter.

Special Expeditions is a division of Lindblad Travel.

SUN LINE CRUISES

One Rockefeller Plaza
New York, N.Y. 10020
tel: (212) 397–6400

Although Sun Line is an affiliate of the Marriott Corporation (which has an overall majority interest), the family firmly behind this cruise company is Mr. Ch. A. Keusseoglou, his wife Isabella, and his two sons. Ch. A. (as he calls himself) remains president of the company he formed at the end of the 1950s. A former executive with Home Lines, Keusseoglou launched the *Stella Maris I* as Sun Line's first vessel for Aegean cruises from the port of Piraeus. In 1963 the *Stella Maris II* replaced her namesake, and the *Stella Oceanis* became a Sun Line ship in 1967. Flagship and pride of the fleet, the *Stella Solaris*, had her maiden voyage in 1973. Isabella Keusseoglou supervised the interior design of all three Sun Line vessels and still takes an active part in the day-to-day "housekeeping" from the family home in Monaco and a suite in the Plaza.

The 18,000-ton *Stella Solaris* is certainly one of the premier vessels in the Aegean, and she cruises from Piraeus every week between April and October. An alternating pattern calls among the Greek Islands and Turkey one week, returns to port and sails again for Egypt, Israel, Turkey and the Greek Islands. During the winter season, the Solaris is based in Galveston and has made a big hit with the Texans! Her schedule begins with a long Christmas and New York cruise that double-transits the Panama Canal. From January until March the *Solaris* makes a series of ten-day cruises (between Galveston and Curaçao) that feature a Panama Canal transit. Passengers fly to either Texas or the Caribbean for embarkation. In March the vessel departs Port Everglades on Primavera III, a 22-day transatlantic cruise to Piraeus; rates include economy airfare from Athens back to New York.

The 6,000-ton *Stella Oceanis* is the least charming of the three vessels. From April to October, she sails every Monday and every Friday from Piraeus to the Greek Islands. The Turkish port of Kusadasi (for Ephesus) is offered on the longer cruise. During the winter season, the *Oceanis* sails from San Juan on 13-, 14- and 15-day cruises called Leeward to the Orinoco. This most inventive itinerary takes passengers up the Orinoco River to Ciudad Guayana, where an optional excursion takes passengers to the jungle resort of Canaima and by plane over Angel Falls. This is definitely one of the most interesting cruises available in the Caribbean.

The 4,000-ton *Stella Maris II* is baby of the fleet and everyone's favorite. Carrying over 180 passengers and a crew of 100, the vessel sails from Piraeus on three- and four-day Greek Island/Turkey cruises beside the *Oceanis* during the spring and fall months. During the summer she offers one of the best itineraries in the Mediterranean, on weekly sailings between Nice and Venice. This popular cruise is sold out early, so hurry!

During the 1982/83 winter the *Maris* is on charter for Red Sea cruises. This itinerary has not quite taken off, but perhaps this year will be the exception.

SWANS HELLENIC CRUISES

c/o Exprinter (General Sales Agents)
500 Fifth Avenue
New York, N.Y. 10110
tel: (212) 719–1200

The prestigious London travel firm of W. F. and R. K. Swan has been operating Mediterranean cruises since 1954 on a regular schedule and Nile cruises since 1960, in addition to the quality tours arranged to more than forty different countries since the 1930s. In 1980 R. K. Swan (the indefatigable son of the founder and a most distinguished gentleman in his early 60s) inaugurated Around Britain cruises. For the first time in twenty-five years he repeated an itinerary. This was an earth-shattering event, for Swan prides himself on never duplicating cruise itineraries.

Swans Hellenic Cruises, as they are called, are more than just cruises. The ship is mere transportation, but coupled with mini-courses in the archaeology, history, and culture of the area visited the cruises attract travelers who wish to learn as much as possible from their experiences. Lecturers on board each cruise, drawn from the corridors of Cambridge, Oxford, and other notable colleges (even from Princeton and Yale) entertain and enlighten passengers on what they are about to see and do. Although this may sound a little too cerebral, it's really not because R. K. Swan remembers that his clients are "on holiday" after all. You can just as well sit in a deck chair with a beer, or you can listen to the lectures in the privacy of your cabin. But the high-caliber, optional lectures are well worth the effort to attend. The Archbishop of Canterbury, a well-known classicist, used to lecture and his wife, I understand, was very miffed when her husband accepted his present job, because it meant no more "free" cruises with R. K. Swan!

R. K., as he is known to his colleagues, believes in delivering as much value for the money as possible to his passengers. Included in the cruise fare are all port taxes, shore excursions, site fees, gratuities, and literature. And the literature is superb! Each cruise has its own special handbook with maps, a quick reference of selected dates and historical events, a short description of each place visited, and a glossary of technical terms. If you don't wish to carry the whole book, take a tear sheet, available for each separate excursion, with you. Most tours, planned as only half-day events, leave plenty of time for study and relaxation. Often an artist will be along to take care of a group of sketchers, because R. K. insists that you cannot do both—sketch and listen to the guide!

Swans Hellenic Cruises all use the 51,250-ton *Jason* of Epirotiki Lines, a Greek-flag vessel of adequate comfort (it is not a luxurious ship by any means and doesn't pretend to be) that carries just over two hundred passengers. This cruise season features sailings in the eastern Caribbean from April through June, Around Britain cruises in July, Western Europe in August, and the eastern Mediterranean area again in September. All sailings are fourteen days, and Swan provisionally charters DC-10 aircraft in London for the convenience of passengers meeting the ship.

On the Nile River, where R. K. pioneered by offering long cruises to the many temple sites and cities, the company launched a new vessel in September 1980. The 68-passenger *Nile Star*, a two-deck fully air-conditioned riverboat, offers fourteen-day cruises from Cairo to Aswan (and vice versa) throughout the year (except July and August when the river is just too hot). According to R. K., late January to late March are the most popular months on the Nile and was the traditional period when the Edwardian English "went out" to winter in Egypt (anything to escape the climate at home). It all reminds me so much of "Death on the Nile," only instead of David Niven on board, there's a qualified egyptologist. Of course.

I have never taken a Swans Hellenic Cruise (you might say that I'm saving the best for last), but I highly recommend all of them, for in this age of masses and tour buses led by obnoxious guides, I am touched by the concern that R. K. feels for his clients and for the attention to detail that he pays each itinerary. I also think that I would meet an interesting group of passengers, for forty percent are repeaters and a low twenty to thirty-five percent are Americans.

12. / THE SHIPS AND THEIR RATINGS

The ship ratings given below are based entirely on my own opinion and are drawn from my own experiences as a cruise passenger and reporter and from conditions as they existed at the time I inspected the ships. Hollow stars indicate my tentative rating for a brand-new ship that I have evaluated from deck plans and other factors prior to her launching.

My ratings are not a grade for luxury. Rather, I have tried to consider the type of cruise experience each line tries to provide and to evaluate how well the line achieves its goal. Thus, while the *World Discoverer* is not a top luxury ship, I have given her a high rating because I believe that the passenger looking for adventure will find her cruises unique and thrilling.

★★★★AMERICA/INDEPENDENCE

American Cruise Lines; American registry and crew; America built in Maryland in 1981; Independence built in Maine in 1976; 1,000 tons each; 174 and 172 feet long, respectively; 37 feet at beam; 83 and 78 passengers, respectively; crew of about 18; cruising speed of 13 knots; 3 passenger decks.

These sister ships are almost identical twins, and both were designed and built especially for the coastal cruises they offer along the Eastern seaboard from Ft. Myers in Florida to homeport in Haddam, Connecticut. With an American registry and spirit, these two charming vessels offer seasonal sailings around New England from spring to fall, from Baltimore to Savannah and down to Florida during the winter months. Especially popular is the fourteen-day East Coast Inland Passage cruise from Baltimore to St. Michael's, Oxford, and Annapolis before the middle of Chesapeake Bay.

There are Harbor Hopping cruises, according to President and Chairman Charlie Robertson, where passengers are met along the way by members of local historical societies for personalized tours of their ports and towns. A nicer way to tour is seldom possible! Most excursions are inclusive in the cruise rate; those that are not are subsidized by American Cruise Lines.

Life aboard both vessels is pleasant and casual. The Nantucket Lounge is the scene of most on-board activities, from mid-morning coffee and freshly baked cookies to the congeniality of cocktail hour and snacks. As neither vessel has a commercial bar aboard, passengers are encouraged to BYOB (bring your own bottle), and the staff provides ice, mixers, and plentiful hors d'oeuvres. The Captain hosts about three formal cocktail hours per week, with ample supplies of beverages. Meals in the dining room are also casual, family-style around tables set for six. The all-American menu features home-baked bread and pastries and local produce. Seafood aficionados can rejoice that fresh lobster and shrimp are served at least weekly, and special menus will be provided for those that need them (with advance notice).

Cabins aboard both vessels are functional, but quite roomy for what are really two large yachts. All cabins are equal (although a few suites are destined for the *America*), with large sea-view windows, two lower beds, adequate wardrobe space, and private facilities (with showers). There is little need for "dressing up" on board, but the vessels moor each night in port so passengers can wander about for a change of pace.

From early October through June, the *America* and *Independence* sail from Baltimore, Savannah, or Ft. Myers (Florida) along the Southeastern seaboard. The seven- and fourteen-day cruises cover the famous Inland Passage, the Carolina coasts and Golden Isles, and Okeechobee and the southern waterways. by June both vessels are on their way home to Haddam, Connecticut, for one-week sailings around New England and neighboring islands. In early autumn, Hudson River cruises are in order to view the foliage while vessels are en route back to Baltimore. Maryland is becoming a more and more important base for American Cruise Lines as well as an increasing source for passengers. The company opened an office in Baltimore's World Trade Center last year and moved its shipbuilding facilities to the Chesapeake Bay area earlier.

★★★★AMERICAN EAGLE

American Cruise Lines; American registry and crew; built in Maine in 1975 especially for coastal cruises; 600 tons; 150 feet long; 30 feet at beam; 49 passengers; crew of 16; cruising speed of 13 knots; 3 passenger decks.

The original of the Harbor Hopping fleet, the *American Eagle*, was commissioned in 1975, followed a year later by the larger *Independence*. More like a private yacht than a cruise vessel, the *Eagle* has a casual atmosphere and a great following. In 1982, one-week sailings from Rockland, Maine, were inaugurated aboard the *Eagle* and proved to be very popular. From mid-June through mid-September the cruises called in the port of Castine, then sailed through Penobscot Bay to Vinalhaven—the largest of the neighboring islands. The *Eagle* then carried passengers past Metinic and the Monhegan Islands into popular Boothbay Harbor, then up the Kennebec River to Bath. Before returning to Rockland, the vessel called at Wiscasset which claims to be Maine's prettiest village. What a wonderful way to visit Maine's rugged and historic coastal towns! A repeat is promised.

The *American Eagle* has but twenty-four twin cabins and one single, all with large windows and private facilities. Main ship-board activities take place in the Nantucket Lounge with adjoining sun deck and player piano. The dining room serves all passengers at one seating, with American home-cooking and family-style service. Life aboard this vessel is as casual and congenial as can be. There is no commercial bar, so passengers are encouraged to BYOB (bring your own bottle). The ship line provides plenty of hors d'oeuvres, ice, and soft drinks. Most shore excursions are included in the Harbor Hopping rate; others may have a minimal extra charge. Evening entertainment is on your own (books/cards/TV).

★★★AMERIKANIS

Chandris Inc.; Greek registry and Greek/Italian officers; international crew; on long-term charter to Costa Line; originally built in 1952 and formerly named Kenya Castle; rebuilt in 1971; 19,377 tons; 576 feet long; 74 feet at beam; 617 passengers; crew of 250; cruising speed of 18 knots; 8 passenger decks.

I have a very nice feeling for the *Amerikanis*. She may be a bit on the older side, but she's no slouch in the cruise trade. I enjoyed a very pleasant week aboard this vessel just before the transfer to three- and four-day Bahamas cruises. There are certainly more glamorous and elegant vessels afloat, but few are more seaworthy and with whom a passenger feels more "in tune." The cabins and public areas are so spacious that you never feel intimidated by your fellow passengers. In fact, it's difficult to realize that there may well be over 600 other people aboard! Well, breakfast in bed and lunch outdoors at the Aquamarine Bar does give a sense of freedom. In the evening, opt for dinner at the late sitting in either the Silvercarte dining room or the Silverleaf. Between the two, just over 300 passengers can be accommodated, and this lends an air to intimacy. I've found the food is average to good.

Cabins are definitely old-world but very comfortable. There is plenty of space for turning around (even doing a few push-ups), and the wardrobe/dresser facilities are plentiful. Bathrooms are vintage (often with bidets) but the flow of clean towels more than compensates for any minor inconvenience. I would, however, recommend requesting a cabin in the forward section of the vessel, as the engines are noisy and cause nightly vibrations that can make you nervous.

The Athens Deck is the main public area, with the Neptune Lounge, the Library/Writing/Card rooms, the Casino Gallery, the Rendezvous Bar and the Mayfair Ballroom. One deck up, the Galaxy Club swings until the very wee hours. Entertainment (from all reports) is okay, but I really couldn't comment upon it with any element of truth. While aboard, I read the *Winds of War* straight through twice (which left little time for any nightlife).

The *Amerikanis* is a member of the Chandris family and has Greek registry and some Greek/Italian officers. The crew, however, is international and most pleasant. In fact, one reader (and letter writer) has informed me that she had such a good time ". . . was always dodging crew members." For some single women, that makes for a good cruise! This same young lady from Houston, Texas, reported that she got so sunburned during the call in Nassau that she did not disembark the vessel in Freeport, but rather spent $5 with the ship's doctor for some medicine. Her closing is that she had a wonderful time on the four-day Bahamas cruise, with better accommodations than friends on the *Dolphin*, and . . . "I don't see any better (or cheaper) way to take a vacation!" Another contented passenger that wants to spend a full week at sea this year . . . providing there are plenty of singles on board.

★ANDREA C.

Costa Line; Italian registry and crew; originally built in 1942 and formerly named the Ocean Virtue; refurbished and rebuilt in 1976; 8,600 tons; 467 feet long; 57 feet at beam; 400 passengers; crew of 180; cruising speed of 15 knots; 5 passenger decks.

The *Andrea C.* is Costa Line's smallest vessel and, to some, its most appealing. Her diminutive size reveals a charming intimacy. The *Andrea C.* has 115 outside cabins and 71 inside, all with private facilities. Be forewarned; the configuration of the ship makes for what I consider small cabins. The public areas are also compact. Two lounges serve the passengers—the Varazze on Lounge Deck with the adjoining Portofino Bar (all Italian ships seem to have a Portofino something or other) and the Remini on Promenade Deck, which also doubles as a late-night disco. The Viareggio Dining Room on Promenade Deck has two seatings for both meals, and ample, open deck space surrounds the ship's two swimming pools.

The *Andrea C.* sails out of Genoa every Saturday from the end of May to mid-October, to Barcelona, Palma de Mallorca, Tunis, Palermo, and Naples/Capri (at least some summers). During the winter season the *Andrea C.* sails from South American ports.

★★★★AQUARIUS

Hellenic Mediterranean Lines; Greek registry and crew; built in 1972; 4,600 tons; 340 feet long; 45 feet at beam; 280 passengers; crew of 125; cruising speed of 18 knots; 6 passenger decks.

The *Aquarius* is a charming vessel with an intimate atmosphere and friendly Hellenic crew. She has 120 outside cabins and 20 inside; all with private facilities. The rooms, with attractive polished wood furnishings, are very modern-looking and cheerful. All cabins are located on Lyra, Norma, and Vela decks and have the usual amenities as well as both shower and bathtubs in addition to televisions in the deluxe staterooms. Service is very personal and attentive. The public rooms are all located on the Promenade Deck, including the Belvedere and Constellation lounges with bars. The library is also situated in the Belvedere Lounge, and blackjack tables open nightly for those who wish to try their hand. The Constellation Lounge, larger of the two, is the scene of after-dinner entertainment, dancing, and on-board festivities like the Captain's Welcome cocktail party. Some of the best entertainment available is the program of Rhodian folk dances performed by members of the crew.

The swimming pool and sun area are also situated on Promenade Deck, and a cold buffet lunch is served by the pool from noon to 2 P.M. daily. Afternoon tea can be found on this deck too, as well as the ship's third bar and a few slot machines. The dining room on Vela deck seats just 250 people in a cozy, attractive atmosphere. The ambiance and service here is certainly a cut above most other Aegean cruises—with Rosenthal china, fine crystal, Cristofle flatware, and fresh flowers at every table. The food is equal to the surroundings, as the *Aquarius* boasts European chefs and freshly purchased produce at every port. On the seven-day itinerary, you can expect the traditional Greek Taverna night as well as other themes. For the wee hours, a disco on Dorado deck that is open until 2 A.M. features a steel-tiled dance floor, a bar, and a real-live disc jockey!

Every Friday between the end of March and November, the *Aquarius* sails weekly from Piraeus to Thíra, Heraklion (Crete), Rhodes, Patmos, Kuşadasi, Istanbul, and Mykonos. Touring the Greek Islands on a small ship is advantageous because you can dock right in port and do not have to anchor out, as some of the larger vessels must do.

★★★ARGONAUT

Epirotiki Lines; Greek flag and crew; originally built in 1929 and rebuilt in 1965; 4,500 tons; 330 feet long; 47 feet at beam; 150 passengers; crew of 102; cruising speed of 14 knots; 4 passenger decks.

The *Argonaut* is on a long-term charter agreement to Raymond and Whitcomb, the travel firm that specializes in cruise programs for museums, private clubs, and college alumni associations. Billed as the "exceptional" *Argonaut* and originally built as the world's largest private yacht (for an American in 1929), the ship was rebuilt and refurbished in 1965 and launched as the flagship of Epirotiki Lines. This small vessel can carry two hundred passengers, but Raymond and Whitcomb keep the capacity to 150 to insure greater comfort.

Although it lacks a certain luxury, the *Argonaut* is a pleasant and charming vessel with a congenial personality and a crew that prides itself on offering excellent service. A graciousness and warm informality that is lost on larger vessels exists on the smaller *Argonaut*. The only large public room is the Golden Fleece Lounge, but smaller coffee and garden lounges often hold art lectures. The dining room is simple and large enough to accommodate all passengers at the same time, permitting free seating. The Greek/Continental cuisine is definitely modified to suit American taste—another plus. The vessel also has two cozy bar areas, a small pool, boutique, and beauty shop, but my favorite feature is the central winding stairway.

☆☆☆☆**ASTOR**

Astor United Cruises; West German registry and European crew; built in Hamburg in 1981; 18,800 tons; 538 feet long; 74 feet at beam; 600 plus passengers; crew of 220; cruising speed of 20 knots; 6 passenger decks.

The brand new *Astor*, named after the illustrative Anglo-American family, made her cruising debut in the Caribbean during the [1982/83] season. The $55 million vessel, owned by a Hamburg-based ship line called Hadag, has been positioned in Port Everglades for a series of Caribbean and South American sailings. The already much-touted *Astor* is reported to be a well-appointed cruise vessel, with impressive decor throughout the public areas. The cabins however, appear to be a little too small, and the passenger/crew ratio a little too low, in my opinion, for the super-deluxe type of ship the company is promoting.

Service and food aboard the *Astor* has been reported as excellent, although there seems to be a communication problem with some of the European waiters that do not speak fluent English. (As the company expects up to eighty percent Americans on board, I would expect this problem to be solved). And although the *Astor* had been in service for less than six months, advertisements were already boasting an award from the International Chaine des Rotisseurs for "unparalleled gourmet standards." I wonder about such honors bestowed so quickly upon a new product . . . especially since most culinary prizes take years to win.

The public areas feature an English-style pub on Bridge Deck (well aft of where the Captain does his job), which dispenses plenty of German draft beer. Below, on Boat Deck, is the outdoor pool and sun area as well as the Lido Bar where luncheon buffets are served and calypso comes on for dancing in the evening. There are two seatings in the Waldorf Astoria dining room, which also has two private rooms astride (called Waldorf and Astoria). Mid-ships on Promenade Deck is an apparent replica of Harry's New York Bar (one assumes it is after the original in Venice and not the various clones), while the Redoute Lounge, where a European-style cabaret entertains after dinner, is in the forward section. A card room and library as well as a gallery for watching the passing scene complete the Promenade Deck.

Below on C-Deck is a complete fitness center, with heated pool, exercise room, sauna/massage, and a solarium. Located next door is the ship's hospital, which is equipped with dialysis machinery for passengers who need constant treatment. The company is also planning to install a casino, with slot machines and blackjack tables. It will be small, according to a company spokesman, because of the space limitations on board the vessel.

The *Astor* begins her 1983 program from Port Everglades with a 13-day Caribbean cruise, ending in San Juan. A 16-day cruise ends in Manaus, Brazil, and then the vessel flirts around South America until she returns to Barbados on March 12, just prior to a 19-day transatlantic sailing to Genoa. The vessel makes three 14-day cruises in the Mediterranean and Black Sea from Genoa, before repositioning in Germany for northern European sailings. The *Astor* returns to Port Everglades on November 3, for 10-, 11- and 12-day cruises to the Caribbean through January 9, 1984.

★★★★★ATLANTIC

Home Lines; Panamanian registry and all Italian crew; built in 1982 in La Seyne-sur-Mer, France; 30,000 tons; 672 feet long; 90 feet at beam; 1,067 passengers; crew of 600; cruising speed of 21 knots; 10 passenger decks.

It is always a pleasure to be aboard a Home Lines' vessel and the new *Atlantic* is no exception. Only inaugurated on April 17, 1982, and still a little fresh around the edges, the *Atlantic* began her career on the run from New York to Bermuda. This vessel was designed for passengers' comfort. Public rooms are spacious and well appointed. Cabins and bathrooms are larger than average, and even the passageways can hold two persons abreast. At first glance, the *Atlantic* looks a bit old-fashioned for this modern age, but that impression soon passes into a feeling of being "very much at home" aboard. The portholes could have been bigger and better placed, and the cabin lights look like something from the Folies Bergére, but these are moot points in an otherwise spectacular cruise ship.

The *Atlantic* is large and finding one's way about this vessel is no small feat. Although Continental Deck holds the Purser's Office and departments, the main public areas are atop on Belvedere and Lido decks. Two large lounges—Bermuda and Atlantic—accommodate the passengers comfortably, whether for the Captain's Welcome Aboard cocktail or after-dinner entertainment. Night life aboard the *Atlantic* is considerable, and the Casino and Disco are both very swinging. Up on Lido Deck, the line for the Midnight Buffet in the Observation Lounge is surprisingly long (it must have been the early seating).

Food aboard the *Atlantic* is typical Home Lines' fare, which means wonderful! The attractive dining room on Restaurant Deck has two seatings but you would never suspect it. Stewards are so attentive at the late seating that you would never dream this was a repeat performance. And despite the difficulty of keeping "good help" these days, it is a delight to look around the *Atlantic* dining room and see so many familiar faces from both the *Oceanic* and *Doric*.

(Somebody must be doing something right). If any of these nice people ever opened a restaurant in New York, I would be the first customer. Pasta lovers will love the *Atlantic*—and the Italian wines are not bad, either!

The room stewards also deserve special praise. Both friends and we found exemplary service, and breakfast in bed is a must. Cabins are spotless and the bathrooms are better than home, with soap and towels refreshed frequently. There is 24-hour room service (but pizza is served in both the Disco and Bermuda Lounge at 1:30 A.M.). No matter what time you arise or retire aboard the *Atlantic*, there are both activities and snacks.

During her first season the *Atlantic* cruised weekly from New York to Bermuda. Coming into the archipelago is a beautiful sight and during a recent run, I was able to fulfill a life-long ambition—tooting to the *Oceanic* (which was already at anchor in the harbor). For the winter months the *Atlantic* will sail from Port Everglades on a series of Caribbean cruises. The vessel will also make an exciting trans-Panama Canal cruise in February between Port Everglades and Los Angeles, with the return in March. Bravo for a splendid new ship!

★★ATLANTIS

K-Lines Hellenic Cruises; Greek registry and crew; originally built in 1965 and formerly named the Adonis; refurbished in 1976–78; 5,500 tons; 350 feet long; 53 feet at beam; 296 passengers; crew of 125; cruising speed of 15 knots; 6 passenger decks.

The *Atlantis* is the sister ship of Sun Lines' *Stella Oceanis*. Small and cozy, the *Atlantis* carries only 296 passengers in 108 outside cabins and 41 inside, all with private facilities. The accommodations, small and very pleasant, all have television (although in the Greek Islands you will have little time between shore excursions to do anything but rest). The public rooms are inviting—the main lounge, discotheque, and two bars on Paris Deck, as well as the dining room, garden cafe, and card room. A smaller lounge and bar are situated on Santorini Deck, and the swimming pool and sunning area is up on Nireus Deck. Named after the legendary lost continent, the *Atlantis* was refurbished a few years ago and still looks cheerful.

The *Atlantis* sails on her three- and four-day cruise itinerary from Piraeus between April 10 and October 26. The Monday departures call at Mykonos, Heraklion, Thíra, Rhodes, Kuşadasi, and Patmos. The Friday sailings visit Delos, Mykonos, Rhodes, Heraklion and Thíra. These cruises are an excellent way to see some of the Greek islands in a short period of time.

★ATLAS

Epirotiki Lines; Greek registry and crew; originally built in 1951 as the Ryndam; refurbished in 1973 and relaunched as the Atlas; 16,000 tons; 510 feet long; 70 feet at beam; 568 passengers; crew of 297; cruising speed of 15 knots; 8 passenger decks.

As one of the larger vessels in the Epirotiki fleet, the *Atlas* is often on charter to other companies offering cruises in both the Aegean and the Caribbean. Occasionally, the *Atlas* does sail with the fleet, as occurred in 1982 on weekly cruises to Egypt/Israel. An older vessel, the *Atlas* has been redecorated recently, but is still not a member of the luxury set.

The *Atlas* has 180 outside cabins, 104 inside, with decor by fleet designer Maurice Bailey. The Esperides Lounge is the main activity area, although small rooms are available for reading, writing, cards, and relaxing. The Pleiades dining room has two seatings for all meals. The ship has one indoor and two outdoor swimming pools, with sauna/massage areas. There is also a large theater.

You never know exactly when or where the *Atlas* will be seen in cruising waters. In past summers, she sailed from Piraeus weekly to Rhodes, Ashdod, Port Said, Patmos, and Kusadasi. If the demand is great, Epirotiki will no doubt repeat this schedule.

★★★AZUR

Paquet French Cruises; French registry and crew; originally built in 1971 and named the Eagle; rebuilt and renamed Azur in 1976; 13,600 tons; 465 feet long; 72 feet at beam; 700 passengers; crew of 300; cruising speed of 16 knots; 7 passenger decks.

The *Azur* is Paquet's answer to Club Med at sea. To compensate for the decidedly unluxurious quality of this former car-ferry, Paquet decided to concentrate on appealing to the younger sets who are involved in water sports and the like. Down below, where the cars were stored, are two sports areas for volleyball, squash, Ping-Pong, and judo. Also on board are about seventy bicycles for passengers' use during shore tours. For those who prefer to do their own thing in the water, the vessel carries equipment for windsurfing, water skiing, and sailing. Two full-time sports directors are ready to instruct and encourage.

Although a member of the Paquet family since 1976, the *Azur* was only brought to the attention of American travelers last year when a $20 million renovation was completed. Apparently, Paquet also changed the language of communication on board to English in an attempt to attract more American passengers. The renovations included additional cabins, a second swimming pool on Sun Deck, the Rialto cinema, and the Tahiti nightclub. The public rooms were also upgraded, especially the Grand Salon and the dining areas. The small and intimate Eden Roc Grill is for deluxe cabin passengers, while the Riviera Restaurant accommodates the others in pleasant surroundings framed by large, sea-view windows. Food on board has been European in the past, but the menu has been modified to more American tastes. Large breakfasts with eggs and bacon as well as American coffee are available. Mid-morning bouillon and luncheon buffets are served on deck in good weather, and a midnight deli table features meat, cheese, and pastries. French wines are complimentary at both lunch and dinner, and the youthful crew provides sprightly service. The *Azur* should attract an interesting and energetic group of passengers (I enjoyed a most charming cruise to Elba and Capri a few years ago). Prices for the air-sea excursions from the U.S. are quite reasonable, but you must remember that the majority of cabins on this vessel are now inside (187). There are 132 outside cabins and 24 deluxe staterooms.

The *Azur's* homeport is Toulon, on the edge of the beautiful Cote d'Azur, and from here the vessel makes a circuit of the Mediterranean and the Aegean from July to December. She calls at ports in Italy, Greece, Turkey, Israel, and Egypt.

★AZURE SEAS

Western Steamship Lines; Panamanian registry and international crew; originally built in 1955 and formerly named the Southern Cross, then Calypso; 20,000 tons; 603 feet long; 78 feet at beam; 734 passengers; crew of 300; cruising speed of 21 knots; 9 passenger decks.

Western Steamship Lines, a subsidiary of Eastern Steamship Lines of Miami, began operating three- and four-night cruises from Pier 93 in San Pedro (the port for Los Angeles) to Ensenada in Baja, California, in mid-November 1980. The cruises, billed as "Let's Go" and "party" sailings, offer a fully equipped casino and top nightclub entertainment on board. The cruises schedule one full day at sea on the three-night sailings and two full days at sea on the four-night sailings.

The *Azure Seas* departs San Pedro every Friday at 8 P.M., arrives in Ensenada on Saturday at 10 A.M. and departs on Sunday at 1 A.M. The vessel then spends its day at sea before returning to port on Monday at 8 A.M. The four-night midweek cruise departs San Pedro on Monday at 5 P.M., spends all day Tuesday at sea and arrives in Ensenada on Wednesday at 10 A.M. The vessel departs the Baja city at 1 A.M. on Thursday, spends its second entire day at sea, and then returns to San pedro on Friday at 8 A.M.

The *Azure Seas* has 217 outside and 150 inside cabins, all with private facilities. Public areas feature an enormous casino (with slot machines) on Boat Deck; the Rendezvous Lounge, the Mayfair, and Cafe Miramar on Promenade Deck; and the Caravelle Restaurant on Caravelle Deck. In addition to these areas the ship has a disco (on Disco Deck), the double-tiered Rialto Theater, library, card room, swimming pool, and huge sun deck. Two seatings apply for all meals, and passengers embarking on Fridays are invited to an extensive buffet beginning at 5 P.M.

★BOHEME

Commodore Cruise Line; West German registry and officers, international crew; originally built in 1968 in Wartsila, Finland; refurbished in 1977; 11,000 tons; 450 feet long; 65 feet at beam; 500 passengers; crew of 220; cruising speed of 20 knots; 7 passenger decks.

The *Boheme* is one of the last old-style vessels to be built in the Wartsila shipyard in Finland, where the super-modern and glamorous Royal Caribbean ships were later built. The *Boheme* does not pretend to be glamorous, or even modern, but she is billed as a "happy ship," and Commodore calls her "cozy" as well. The *Boheme* has 149 outside and 79 inside cabins that are comfortable and sturdy, with private facilities (hand showers), lovely use of old woods, and plenty of wardrobe space. Eight cabins have double beds and eleven have full bathtubs. While the vessel lacks a certain beauty, she displays many photographs and memorabilia of Puccini's opera, *La Boheme*, her namesake. Even the public rooms carry on the theme. On Promenade Deck the Cafe des Artistes overlooks the swimming pool, and the Marcello Lounge is a nightclub-cum-disco. On Main Deck you will find the Rodolfo Lounge and Le Club Mimi (now a full casino with blackjack, roulette, and other games), the Salle Musetta Reading Room, and two dining rooms (Puccini and Paris). There are two seatings at all meals, as the dining rooms only hold 100 and 150 people respectively. Commodore manages its own food service; it is not catered like many other ships in the Caribbean.

The majority of passengers on this happy, cozy ship come from the southern states and the Midwest and find good value in the four-port itinerary. The *Boheme* is the first vessel to leave Miami every Saturday and the last one to return the following week, according to a Commodore spokesman. The four ports of call are Puerto Plata, St. Thomas, San Juan (for one night and the better part of the next day), and Cap Haitien. Rates are very favorable for this "adult summer camp" atmosphere (about $130 per day minimum). The ship line must be doing something right because the average stay for the crew is ten years, and at last report the *Boheme* sailed at 114 percent capacity. Perhaps it's those electronic games (Space Invaders, Blue Shark, Lunar Lander, and Sea Wolf) that were installed for children—but who knows who plays them the most?

★BRITANIS

Chandris Inc.; Greek registry and crew; 25,245 tons; originally built in 1932 and formerly named the Monterey; *refurbished in 1970; 642 feet long; 79 feet at beam; 1,474 passengers; crew of 420; cruising speed of 21 knots; 8 passenger decks.*

The *Britanis* is a large vessel with a reputation for offering economical seven-day cruises of the Caribbean on a year-round basis. The vessel carries a large passenger complement on eight decks, in 199 outside cabins and 356 inside cabins, not all with private facilities. Many of these cabins have one or two additional berths, and four cabins (774, 775, 816, and 819 in Category) can accommodate six berths each. The *Britanis*, built for carrying passengers from one point to another in the cheapest and most convenient way possible, definitely lacks your usual cruise ship configuration.

Public rooms include two large lounges and one smaller lounge on Promenade Deck, a huge casino, a card room, and a writing room. The swimming pool and Veranda Bar are situated on Upper Deck, and a children's playroom and gymnasium are located on Main Deck. The dining rooms, on B Deck, announce two seatings for all meals, and the theater down on D Deck entertains both children and adults. Sports facilities can be found up on Sun Deck.

The *Britanis* is on charter to Fantasy Cruises, a division of Gogo Tours, for party-type cruises from New York that range from overnight to four and five days to Bermuda or Halifax.

If you are looking for a taste of the cruise life on board one of the most economical vessels possible, you should consider the *Britanis*. But don't expect more than you pay for. A good solid ship with a smiling Greek crew, it does not pretend to be in the top-class category. A teenaged reader, however, recently complained of debris-filled decks, green cabin water, and "lousey" meal service.

★★ to ★★★★CANBERRA

P & O Line; British registry and crew; 45,000 tons; 819 feet long; 107 feet at beam; 1,735 passengers; crew of 802; cruising speed of 26 knots; 10 passenger decks.

Flagship of the P & O fleet, the *Canberra* is the last remaining passenger liner to carry on that old-world tradition. With the *Oriana* now out of northern service, the *Canberra* is the third largest vessel afloat (after the *QE2* and *Norway*) and the most respected of them all. Launched in 1961 when shipboard travel was still the traditional way to cross oceans, her ambiance remains that of a great liner. She has ten passenger decks and a wealth of open space. Just four times around her Promenade Deck is equal to one mile. There are three swimming pools, fifteen public rooms, nine bars, two restaurants, four shops, a children's playroom, launderettes, and several other amenities. Many cabins are inside and do not have private facilities.

According to P & O Line, the galleys on board cater to an average of 7,500 meals each week, with approximately 4,840 eggs cracked and 6,500 rolls baked daily. The *Canberra News* publishes 1,500 copies daily, and the ship photographers shoot some 4,000 pictures per two-week cruise. The vessel was named after the capital of Australia, an Aboriginal word meaning "place by the water" or "meeting place." And passengers on board the *Canberra* can meet at any one of some forty different activities, not including special events like instruction in bridge or dancing offered by selected guest celebrities on special cruises.

Passengers in the more luxurious staterooms (1 to 102) dine in the Pacific Restaurant (where slightly more menu choices are available), while all others (cabins 201 to 333) dine in the Atlantic Restaurant. There are two seatings for all meals. The vessel draws people of all interests worldwide, and children are well entertained during the day with their own activities. In addition to the many large lounges, some more intimate areas are the very-English Cricketers Tavern and the Crystal Room (often used for private parties).

The *Canberra* begins the year Down Under and sails from Sydney to South-ampton in March, calling at Los Angeles along the way. From mid-April through October, she sails from Southampton on a series of thirteen different cruises of one to three weeks each into the Mediterranean, the Red Sea, the Canary Islands, and the Norwegian fjords. Special Standby Fares are available on a limited basis, with savings of up to fifty-three percent. The ship line also offers group discounts and special rates for four adults sharing the same cabin. Sounds cozy but interesting!

★★★CARLA C.

Costa Line; Italian registry and crew; originally built in 1952 and formerly named the Flandre; refurbished in 1976; 20,477 tons; 600 feet long; 80 feet at beam; 748 passengers; crew of 370; cruising speed of 22 knots; 8 passenger decks.

Of the many cruise vessels Costa operates from San Juan, the *Carla C.* is the only one owned by the company. The *Carla C.* sails year-round every Satur-day for Curaçao, La Guaira, Grenada, Martinique, and St. Thomas (except for annual dry-dock period from the end of July to October). This is a typical Costa vessel—comfortable but not glamorous, with good Italian food and wines and a most helpful and pleasant crew. Costa has added some very attrac-tive stewardesses in recent years who have proved to be every bit as intriguing as their male counterparts. Definitely the ship line's most popular vessel!

The *Carla C.* has 191 outside cabins and 183 inside, all with private facili-ties. The cabins are fairly spacious, as befits an older vessel, but to me they are not especially elegant and certainly do not evoke any special feeling. You will probably want to spend your free time in the public areas, which include the Grand Salon, Observation Lounge, theater, and Lido Deck area with swim-ming pool. The dining room has two meal seatings. The food aboard the *Carla C.* is good, emphasizing Italian specialties and a good selection of Italian wines at very reasonable prices. The steak, spaghetti, and pizza are tempting, but also try the veal scallopini, homemade cannelloni, and anchovy patties. Service both in the dining room and on the deck is excellent. And many passengers find it difficult not to fall for at least one of the handsome Italian stewards and stewardesses!

☆☆☆CONSTELLATION

K-Lines Regency Cruises; Greek registry and crew; originally built in 1962 and named the Anna Nery; refurbished and rebuilt in 1981 and rechristened Con-stellation; 12,500 tons; 492 feet long; 66 feet at beam; 392 passengers; crew of 190; cruising speed of 18 knots; 8 passenger decks.

This is the current flagship and pride of K-Lines Hellenic Cruises, but in 1983 she is sailing in North American waters under the aegis of Regency Cruises—a fifty-fifty ownership shared by K-Lines and March Shipping Passenger Service (the North American agent). The *Constellation* has been in the refitting stage for more than a few years and is a welcome addition to the world of cruises. The sparkling white vessel is very comfortable, and all cabin space has been designed for outside locations, with two lower beds and bathtubs in the majority of private facilities. Exclusive three-room apartments and suites are supposedly unparalleled (but I have to be very careful with superlatives)!

On-board amenities include a two-level Sagittarius disco/bar on the upper decks, Lion and Gemini lounges, Capricorn Casino, Constellation foyer, two duty-free shops, a theater, gym and sauna, and the Ambrosia dining room that seats 330 passengers. Cabins are reported to be more spacious than usual. Following her maiden voyage during the summer of 1982, the *Constellation* sails from St. Petersburg, Florida, to the Caribbean and then summers in Alaska. The programs sound very interesting and the rates are excellent.

The Caribbean program begins on Christmas Eve and extends through April, sailing every Saturday in season to Grand Cayman, Montego Bay, and Cozumel. In January, the *Constellation* departs Florida for an 18-day northbound trans-Panama Canal cruise, ending in Los Angeles. The vessel turns around on January 25 and returns to St. Petersburg on the eleventh of February. She departs again in May for the summer season from Vancouver to Alaska/Canada Inside Passage.

☆☆☆CONSTITUTION

American Hawaii Cruises; American registry (returned) and mostly Hawaiian crew; originally built in the U.S. in 1951 and named the Constitution; owned by the C. Y. Tung conglomerate but placed under American custody for cruising in Hawaiian waters; 30,090 tons; 682 feet long; 89 feet at beam; 800 passengers; crew of 340; cruising speed of 17 knots; 9 passenger decks.

Sister ship of the *Oceanic Independence* and rechristened last spring by the late Princess Grace in Kaohsiung, Taiwan (who sailed the vessel to her famous wedding in Monaco), the *Constitution* once again flies the American flag. She departs from home port of Honolulu every Saturday (giving the Sunday departure to the *Independence*), for Nawiliwili, Kona, Hilo, and Kahului. With the inaugural of the *Constitution* last June, American Hawaii Cruises now has a capacity of 1,550 passengers for intra-Hawaiian Islands sailings.

The *Constitution* boasts some 23,000 square feet of deck space, 18 suites, 58 deluxe inside cabins, 47 deluxe outside cabins, and so on down the line. There are four bars (Tradewinds Terrace, Starlight Lounge, Beachcomber Bar, and Lahaina Landing). The two restaurants are called Bird of Paradise and Hibiscus. The two lounges are named Constitution and Friendship Bridge Lounge. There are also two swimming pools, a nightclub/conference room called the Tropicana (don't tell the I.R.S.), barber/beauty salon, shopping arcade, children's playroom, hospital, and photo gallery.

Like the *Oceanic Independence*, the *Constitution*, I suspect, needs considerable time to find her way in terms of proper service and meals.

★★★CUNARD COUNTESS

Cunard Line; British registry and officers, international crew; built in Italy and launched in 1976; 17,500 tons; 537 feet long; 76 feet at beam; 800 passengers; crew of 350; cruising speed of 20.5 knots; 6 passenger decks.

One of two sister ships especially designed for short, warm-weather cruises and high passenger capacity, the *Countess* was christened in San Juan in August, 1976, by Janet Armstrong, wife of former U.S. astronaut Neil Armstrong, who was the first man to walk upon the moon. Although all Cunard vessels have been christened by prominent women, most of the ships extended the honor to British subjects and members of the royal family. The decision to invite Mrs. Armstrong was prompted by America's 1976 bicentennial celebration and was in keeping with the contemporary concept of the vessel and the astro-theme interior. Not to mention the fact that Cunard predicted (accurately) that the majority of *Countess* passengers would be Americans. Huge photos taken from space decorate the Splashdown Bar on Sun Deck (adjacent to the swimming pool) as well as other sections. (At least two of these photos were taken by Neil Armstrong.) The ship also has the Gemini Dining Room; Nova Suite, a theater/conference center; Galaxy Lounge and Club Aquarius; and Starlight Lounge, which is adjacent to the casino.

Like the *Princess*, the *Countess* has 259 outside and 121 inside cabins, all with private facilities and all very small. The beds fold over to make sofas by day, but this doesn't help the lack of space very much. I found the cabins very "plastic" and "pre-fab," so be rather careful about slamming dresser drawers and such, or you may jolt your next-door neighbor right out of bed (this happened to me)! In my view, even the so-called deluxe rooms on this vessel tend to be small. But there is plenty of public space, both in the lounges and on deck. In addition to using the swimming pool/Splashdown Bar area on Sun Deck, you can shape up at the putting green/driving range and on the paddle tennis court. The cruise staff is very competent, and the captains, who rotate from the QE2 to the smaller vessels, are at the top of their profession.

The calls for the two seatings in the dining room are harbingers of food that I consider only "fair." Expect to have one Medieval night. The English breakfasts include kippered herrings, Nova Scotia salmon, steamed finnan haddie, and even French onion soup—a quick pick up for the morning after. Or you can breakfast al fresco at the charming cafe on Five Deck, which also serves hamburgers at lunchtime. The wine list has a limited but varied selection of American and European vintages, and after-dinner liquered coffees are featured in the lounges after dinner.

The *Countess* sails every Saturday year-round from San Juan for La Guaira, Grenada, Barbados, Martinique, and St. Thomas. Within this one-week framework, passengers may choose a few options. For example, if you have the time for a two-week "Sail 'n Stay" holiday, you may disembark at either the Cunard-owned Paradise Beach Hotel in Barbados or the Hotel LaToc in St.

Lucia for seven days, then reboard the vessel and continue your cruise. Or you may prefer to take the *Countess* round trip from La Guaira. With four different ports for embarkation/disembarkation, the *Countess* serves as both a cruise vessel and passenger transport in the lower Caribbean. One thing is certain—you will not be seeing the same faces throughout a seven-day cruise.

★★★ + CUNARD PRINCESS

Cunard Line; Bahamian registry and international crew; built in Italy and launched in March 1977; 17,500 tons; 537 feet long; 77 feet at beam; 800 passengers; crew of 370; cruising speed of 20.5 knots; 6 passenger decks.

The Cunard *Princess* has the distinction of being the only passenger vessel ever christened in New York harbor. The late Princess Grace of Monaco did the honors in 1977, and a lovely portrait of the former actress hangs in the main stairwell of the vessel. The *Princess* is identical to the *Countess*, with private facilities in all 259 outside and 121 inside cabins. Be careful about engaging in loud conversations or slamming drawers in your cabin, as everything can be heard next door (See Cunard *Countess*)! Your sleeping quarters become sitting rooms by day, with beds that make up into sofas, but as on the *Countess* you won't want to spend much time here since the spaces are rather small.

Public rooms aboard the *Princess* include the Meridian Dining Room, Steamer Row (a casual lounge along the starboard side aft), and the Clipper Suite (theater/conference center). Eight Bells and Showboat Lounge are situated on Boat Deck, and Sun Deck features the Lido Bar (adjacent to the swimming pool) and the Topsail Lounge (with casino). I saw the late Princess Grace having the time of her life, playing the slot machines at the Topsail Lounge. Like the *Countess*, the *Princess* also has a putting green/driving range and a paddle tennis court.

The Meridian Dining Room has two seatings for all meals, but you can opt for breakfast served al fresco in the cafe on Five Deck. And you can stay on for hamburgers at noon if you're still hungry. The food is average, in my opinion, but the service is pleasant and the cruise staff very professional. The *Princess* is considered to have a slight edge over the *Countess*, because she is registered "off shore" in the Bahamas (which means that Cunard does not have to contend with the British unions quite so closely and can hire an international blend of service personnel). The *Princess* also seems to have more fun in the world of cruises, and for 1983 has a new itinerary called Seven Plus.

The new itinerary from San Juan features nine different island or port visits on the seven-day sailing, some to less frequented Caribbean destinations. A stopover at Iles des Saintes will allow a sunrise hike, for willing passengers, before a longer call on Guadeloupe that same day. The Virgin Gorda visit features a pre-breakfast swim before the vessel calls at Tortola, the largest of the British Virgin Island chain. On St. Lucia, the *Princess* will anchor off the Cunard-owned resort of La Toc and the day will be spent in an exchange.

Hotel La Toc guests will spend the day aboard the *Princess*, and cruise passengers will be treated to a beach party/barbecue with snorkeling, sailing, tennis, and the lot! As on the *Countess*, Sail 'n Stay options of a week at either La Toc or Paradise Beach in Barbados are available in conjunction with the seven-day sailing.

During the summer season, the *Princess* cruises the Inside Passage/Alaska under the aegis of Westours.

★★★DANAE/DAPHNE

Carras Cruises; Greek registry and crew; Danae on long-term charter to Costa Line; originally built in 1956; rebuilt and relaunched in 1976; 15,560 tons; 432 feet long; 74 feet at beam; 465 passengers; crew of 250; cruising speed of 21 knots; 5 passenger decks.

These two cruise vessels were former Cunard sister ships, refitted and made into luxury liners by Greek ship owner John Carras, who began his Delian cruise operation in 1975. Carras designed these two ships for very special people who wanted high-quality itineraries, lecturers, good food and accommodations, and printed brochures that were works of art. Unfortunately, his concept was not marketed properly and the two vessels are now on charter to other companies; they are used in a manner that (to me) does not approach the spirit in which they were redesigned.

The *Danae* is one of my favorite ships afloat. I have the fondest memories from cruising aboard her from Bangkok to Hong Kong (including a four-day storm on the South China Sea), and then sailing up the Pearl River in the dark of night to Whampoa (Huang-pu). It was February 1977, and the *Danae* made cruise history as the first Western passenger vessel to dock in a mainland Chinese port since 1948. It was an exciting voyage for her passengers and crew, and although there were some minor mishaps, the *Danae* sailed through the choppy waters as smoothly as possible. I think of her on this cruise with memories of impeccable service, delicious food (you could order anything you wanted, even if not on the menu), and top-class entertainment. I especially remember a hot, foamy bath that I slipped into upon my return from dusty Canton—simply glorious!

Accommodations aboard the *Danae* are splendid, no matter what category. There are 161 outside cabins with two lower beds, plus 21 deluxe suites. In addition, on Thalia Deck, six super suites have a balcony, king-sized beds, separate sitting rooms, and enormous bathrooms. Nineteen inside, double cabins have full bathrooms and tubs. The same attention has been paid to all accommodations, and the Greek decor features original artwork and hand-woven curtains and bedspreads. The public rooms are also attractive. The Muses Lounge, spacious and elegant, features a small bar area in the rear that opens onto the deck in good weather. The very pleasant dining room accommodates all passengers at one seating—one of the criteria for a truly first-class vessel. There is also a small dining veranda for private cocktail parties and dinners. A card room and library are situated between the lounge and dining area.

Other facilities include a comfortable theater with bar, a small children's playroom, an attractive bar/disco on the top deck, swimming pool and Lido area (plus children's wading pool), and well-equipped gym and sauna. Everything was planned with great care, and the vessel is a good size for getting around easily.

The *Daphne*, launched one year earlier than the *Danae*, was considered the flagship of the Carras fleet. This vessel has the same interior/exterior configuration. Both are on long-term charter to Costa.

The *Daphne* sails from San Juan early January to May, calling at Curaçao, La Guaira, Grenada, Guadeloupe, and St. Thomas. Costa plans to repeat her most successful Alaska/Canada season this summer by offering seven-day cruises from Vancouver to Ketchikan, Sitka, Juneau, and Glacier Bay. The vessel will also make two complete San Juan/Vancouver sailings through the Panama Canal. The *Danae* spends the summer in the Mediterranean, departing Venice every other Saturday from May to October for ports of call in the Greek Islands, Egypt, and Israel. During the winter season this vessel is a welcome sight cruising from San Juan to the Lower Caribbean each week.

★★★★DELTA QUEEN

Delta Queen Steamboat Company; American crew and registry; 1,650 tons; 285 feet long; 58 feet at beam; 188 passengers; crew of 77; 12 miles per hour maximum speed; 4 passenger decks; listed in the National Register of Historic Places.

The *Delta Queen* has ninety outside, double staterooms with facilities, plus four inside cabins without facilities (I115, I116, I121, I122). The superior staterooms which former president Carter and his wife occupied during their summer of 1979 cruise are on Sun Deck (A339 and A340). Amy bunked next door in G338, and we are told she had an impromptu slumber party with her new friends on board. That same year the *Delta Queen* extensively refurbished both her public rooms and cabins. Real, "sit-down-in" upholstered furniture and velvet curtains were put into the Forward Cabin Lounge. The Texas Lounge and Orleans Restaurant were also redone. The vessel was not exactly returned to her former glory, but more to what passengers feel she must have looked like in the 20s, according to the interior designer. Her finishings throughout are reminiscent of those floating river palaces of long ago: stained-glass windows, paneling and beams in the public areas, and a polished Siamese ironbark floor in the Orleans Room. Passenger accommodations have also been refurbished and the air-conditioning system upgraded.

With so much history and with a cozy passenger capacity, the *Delta Queen* is an intimate paddle-wheeler. Not many minutes will pass by after you board before old friends are reacquainted and new ones made. Master of the vessel is

Captain Jim Blum, a St. Louis resident. Also on board is the only female river pilot licensed in the United States, Lexie Palmore. She embarked on *DQ* (as intimates call the vessel) as a passenger from her hometown in Tyler, Texas, fell in love with river life, returned as a maid, and worked herself up to her present position. That's what it's all about!

Since the *Delta Queen* began steamboating life on the rivers of America in 1927, this carefully preserved and beloved antique entered into the National Register of Historic Places in 1970, has cruised more than 30,000 miles annually, and has visited more than fourteen states from her home port in New Orleans. While watching the banks drift by is still the favored pastime, passengers can also enjoy spontaneous sing-alongs, kite flying over the paddlewheel, calliope-playing contests, locking through on the Upper Mississippi and Ohio rivers, first-run films in the lounge, lectures by staff members and visiting guests on river history and commerce, and boat tours.

The *Delta Queen*'s schedule features eighteen different itineraries beginning with four- and five-day roundtrip cruises from New Orleans, then with a twelve-day cruise up the Mississippi River to reposition the vessel into Cincinnati, followed by two-, four-, and five-day trips which depart Cincinnati through May (with at least one between St. Louis and return). In June a four-day cruise is scheduled roundtrip from St. Louis, and then the vessel returns downriver to New Orleans. The Great Steamboat Race leaves New Orleans in tandem with the *Mississippi Queen* at the end of June, and both vessels finish in St. Louis on July 4. The remainder of the summer features *Delta Queen* cruises from St. Louis, Cincinnati, Pittsburgh (on the Ohio River), and even a sailing from St. Paul. She returns to New Orleans and home port in October for more four-, five- and seven-day cruises of the lower Mississippi through the year.

★★DOLPHIN

Paquet Ulysses Cruises; Panamanian registry and international crew; originally built in 1956 and formerly named the Ithaca; 12,500 tons; 501 feet long; 65 feet at beam; 565 passengers; crew of 280; cruising speed of 15 knots; 7 passenger decks.

During a recent inspection tour of the *Dolphin* in Miami, I was rather surprised at the shabby quality of what I considered a charming vessel. (Put her alongside the *Sunward II* and there is almost no comparison). Some of the outside accommodations do have a "butcher block" feeling, with wooden furnishings and double beds, but the rest of the cabins (206 outside; 78 inside) are very average. The public areas are pleasant, but nothing fancy. There is a very nice Lido pool area with wooden decking, where buffet luncheons and barbecues are held. The Rendez-Vous Lounge is the scene of afternoon and early-evening entertainment, and the Cafe Miramar for continuous snacks and refreshments. Insomniacs will also want to locate the disco down on Dixie Deck. There is a Monte Carlo casino, duty-free shopping, and the Club Royale midships on Promenade Deck. The Barbizon Restaurant can be found on Barbizon Deck, and here Paquet has added a French flair in the menus and complimentary table wines at dinner. In addition to three meals daily (with two sittings), the late-night buffet is also served in the Barbizon Restaurant.

The *Dolphin* sails every Friday afternoon for Nassau. She sails every Monday afternoon for Freeport and Nassau. The schedule offers plenty of time in port for passengers. There are also a number of Cruise & Stay programs to Miami, Miami Beach, and Walt Disney World available from the ship line.

★EMERALD SEAS

Eastern Steamship Lines; Panamanian registry and international crew; originally built in 1944 as the President Roosevelt; 24,458 tons; 622 feet long; 75 feet at beam; 920 passengers; crew of 400; cruising speed of 18 knots; 7 passenger decks.

The *Emerald Seas*, a familiar and respected sight, plys the waters between Miami and the Bahamas twice a week. This vessel operates on a three- and four-night schedule out of Miami, which gives passengers plenty of time to enjoy the beaches, nightlife, and gambling of the Bahamas. Strictly an entertainment cruise for people who like both casinos and top-class nightclub acts, the *Emerald Seas* departs every Friday afternoon, sails for Nassau when she docks from Saturday morning to Sunday afternoon, and returns to Miami Monday morning. She departs again on Monday afternoon for Nassau to spend Tuesday through Wednesday evening there. Then she cruises to Freeport for Thursday, spends the day in port, and returns to Miami on Friday morning.

The *Emerald Seas* has 245 outside cabins and 145 inside, all with private facilities. The cabins, spacious and well kept, all have closed-circuit television for viewing on-board entertainment. The public rooms are also large and very lively. They include the Mayfair Ballroom, Aquarius Club, and Rainbow Lounge on Rainbow Deck. The vessel also has its own casino, a bank of slot machines, the Picadilly Game Room, discotheque, and good swimming pool with adjacent French cafe. The dining room on Ruby Deck has two seatings for all meals.

★ENRICO C.

Costa Line; Italian registry and crew; originally built in 1950 and formerly named Provence; 16,000 tons; 579 feet long; 73 feet at beam; 700 passengers; crew of 300; cruising speed of 20 knots; 7 passenger decks.

The *Enrico C.* is one of the eleven vessels operated by Costa Line and by my standards certainly not one of the best (but then again, not one of the worst either). The vessel has a total of 147 outside cabins and 116 inside cabins. All have private facilities and some have been enlarged and refurbished (especially the forward cabins on A, B, and C decks). The public areas include two dining rooms and two lounge/bars on Upper Deck, a small lounge and a tavern on Promenade Deck, and the large Alassio Lounge on Lounge Deck. The *Enrico C.* also has three swimming pools, children's playroom, library, and theater.

From June to mid-October the *Enrico C.* sails from Genoa every Saturday to Barcelona, Palma de Mallorca, Bizerte, Palermo, and Naples. During the winter this vessel cruises among ports along the eastern coast of South America.

★★★EUGENIO C.

Costa Cruises; Italian registry and crew; originally built in Italy in 1966; refurbished last in 1976; 30,000 tons; 713 feet long; 96 feet at beam; 1,100 passengers; crew of 475; cruising capacity of 27 knots; 9 passenger decks.

Flagship and pride of the Costa fleet, the *Eugenio C.* is the largest vessel the Costa group has ever built. This is also one of the most luxurious ships available on the Mediterranean to South America run. The vessel has a total of 638 outside cabins, and 184 inside (although some 157 do not have private facilities). The *Eugenio C.* is a most comfortable vessel nonetheless, and always the one employed by Costa on its around-the-world cruise each year. Ordinarily the *Eugenio C.* is not marketed to the North American clientele, but Costa has offered some eastern Mediterranean/Black Sea/African and Canary Island cruises aboard this vessel recently.

The *Eugenio C.* boasts seven bars, three dining rooms (Flauto, Etrusca, and Genova), four lounges, a nightclub and a theater. The vessel also has three outside swimming pools, a gymnasium/sauna, children's playroom, and several other amenities. Some cabins have both telephones and television, but this is not standard equipment. The vessel cruises around the world from January to April, does several South American runs during the spring, and sometimes spends the summer in Europe (one can never be quite sure with Costa). In 1982 the *Eugenio C.* sailed from Genoa on several eleven-day cruises to the eastern Mediterranean, Israel, and Egypt, the Black Sea, and even to Africa and the Canary Islands.

☆☆☆☆EUROPA

Hapag Lloyd; German registry and crew; built in Bremerhaven and commissioned in 1982; 35,000 tons; 650 feet long; 95 feet at beam; 600 plus passengers; crew of 280; cruising speed of 28.9 knots; 12 passenger decks.

Hapag Lloyd's new flagship *Europa* appears to be an impressively designed and spacious vessel. With twelve passenger decks and some 12,000 square feet of outdoor space, there is plenty of room for the six-hundred-plus passengers. Cabins are larger than average (especially for new ships) and are reported to be noiseless, as all are situated in the forward and central section of the vessel. There are some beautiful suites on Sun Deck forward, named after famous composers (Haydn, Wagner, Mozart, Beethoven, Handel, and Schubert). The

Europa has two outdoor swimming pools, several bars and nightspots, a large health center, theater, casino, spacious restaurant, and Europa Salon (the main lounge). German-speaking readers will certainly enjoy this exciting vessel for worldwide cruises.

For her first full season of sailings, the *Europa* will begin 1983 with a seven-teen-day Genoa to Dakar cruise. She will then sail around the world between February 10 (from Genoa) and June 4 (return to Genoa), offering a choice of segments. Following a short cruise to the Greek Islands and the Bosporus in June, the *Europa* is repositioned in Bremerhaven for northern European sail-ings the rest of the summer. From mid-September to late October she is sched-uled for a forty-day cruise to Canada, the eastern seaboard (Boston, New York, Baltimore, etc.) and the Caribbean. (This cruise is also offered in segments). Following some cruises along the eastern coast of South America, the *Europa* crosses to West Africa, circumnavigates that continent, passes through the Red Sea and Suez Canal, returns to Genoa on January 8, 1984. An ambitious and exciting program for a brand new vessel!

There is no doubt that the *Europa* will enjoy great success. A couple on her inaugural cruise have written that the ship is very beautiful and kept in "apple pie condition;" the food and service were excellent, and the sailings handled efficiently. The only complaint was a rather "amateurish" type of evening en-tertainment. Sounds like a good book would be in order here.

★★★★★FAIRSEA/FAIRWIND

Sitmar Cruises; Liberian registry, Italian officers and crew; originally built in 1956 at the famous John Brown & Co. shipyard on the River Clyde in Scotland and formerly named the Carinthia, then Sylvania; rebuilt and relaunched in 1971 and 1972 as the Fairsea and Fairwind, respectively; 25,000 tons; 608 feet long; 80 feet at beam; 830/900 passengers; crew of 500; cruising speed of 20 knots; 11 passenger decks.

These sister ships operated by Sitmar in North American waters, the *Fairsea* and *Fairwind*, are both spacious and comfortable and can accommodate as many as nine hundred passengers with great ease. In refitting these former Cunard liners, Sitmar did a fine job of creating larger than average accom-modations and public areas that flow well. The vessels are exactly alike in interior configuration, although the decor is rather different, as are the names of the public spaces. Some refurbishing is scheduled for all the seating furnish-ings, and I hope brighter colors are used. Attention to detail, the lifeboat drill, and housekeeping on both vessels gets high marks. The all-Italian crew is atten-tive and cheerful, a clear indication that the ships are well managed and re-ceive good care. Cuisine is also better than average, with Italian specialties like pasta and pizza outshining the rest. These cruises attract a solid, rather staid clientele that often brings the entire family along. In fact, Sitmar's summer Caribbean cruises feature a special program for teens and juniors that keeps the young ones occupied daily from 9 a.m. to midnight—by no fewer than a dozen staff members. It's a wonderful way for *everyone* to relax and vacation at sea.

Both the *Fairsea* and *Fairwind* have 234 outside cabins and 237 inside, all with private facilities. The ship offers two swimming pools for adults and a splash pool for children as well as children's playroom and nursery (opposite the card room on Europa Deck). The nightclub (named Dolphin on the *Fairsea* and Mistral on the *Fairwind*) is located on Ocean Deck, just forward of the deluxe cabins and suites. The main public areas, on Promenade Deck, include three lounges, shops, a small casino, writing room, library, and some bars. Both vessels have two dining rooms (two seatings each) and a meeting room on Riviera Deck. Other features are a self-service laundromat, beauty salon, bathtubs on reservation, and two-tiered theater between Continental and D-Deck.

The *Fairsea* sails out of San Pedro, the port for Los Angeles, on three separate schedules. In the winter, spring, and fall she makes a series of fourteen-day trans-Panama Canal cruises between the West Coast and San Juan. Alternatively, the vessel sails from the West Coast to the Mexican Riviera on cruises that range from seven days and three ports to eleven days and five ports. The calls include Cabo San Lucas, Mazatlán, Acapulco, Zihuatanejo, and Puerto Vallarta. From early June to the end of August the *Fairsea* sails out of San Francisco on fourteen-day round trips to Alaska's Inside Passage, calling at Vancouver, Nanaimo, Ketchikan, Juneau, Glacier Bay (cruising only), Sitka, and Victoria.

The *Fairwind*, based in Port Everglades for seven- to fourteen-day cruises to Caribbean ports and an occasional Panama Canal transit between Florida and Acapulco, Mexico, calls in the Caribbean at San Juan, St. Thomas, St. John, Aruba, Cartagena, Panama Canal (Gatun Lake), and San Blas Islands. New for 1983 are stops at Montego Bay and Grand Cayman, as well as at Barbados and St. Croix. Sitmar says its *Fairwind* is the only cruise vessel to call at all three of the Virgin Islands this year. All cruises on both ships include a Fly Free plan for both adults and children.

Watch for the 38,000-ton, 1,200-passenger *Fairsky* somewhere from California later this year. She sounds like a beautiful vessel.

★★★FESTIVALE

Carnival Cruise Line; Panamanian registry, Italian officers, and international crew; originally built in 1961 and formerly named the S.A. Vaal; refurbished in 1978 and launched as the Festivale; 38,175 tons; 760 feet long; 90 feet at beam; 1,400 passengers; crew of 570; cruising speed of 24.5 knots; 9 passenger decks.

I must admit at once I have not sailed on this vessel and that my tour of the *Festivale* took place at the worst possible time. The vessel was due to sail for dry dock within the hour, so I could only walk through the ship as quickly, but thoroughly, as possible. I began at the top and worked my way down, which seemed the appropriate thing to do. The pool area and Lido bar/grill/snack place is very pleasant on Sun Deck, with an observation area on the above deck. Below, on Verandah Deck, there is a smaller swimming pool as well as the sauna/massage/gymnasium and the deluxe cabins and suites. These accommodations are the best on the ship, and all are spacious and pleasant. Some have separate sitting areas and ten include a small veranda. Most of these cabins also have full bathrooms. On Promenade Deck are the main public areas. Midships is the Gaslight Club Casino with the Carnivale Lounge, Le Cabaret nightclub, and Fanta Z disco. In the foreward section of the deck are the Copacabana Lounge, the Gaslight Saloon, and the Trade-Winds Club. The Trade Winds Club and the Library were the only lounges I liked very much. The decor of the other areas struck me as rather garish, in colors of shocking pinks and purples, and certainly not soothing to my spirit. But this is billed as a "Fun Ship" and these lounges were designed for the night-owl set who love to prowl the ship in the wee hours.

The remainder of the 272 outside and 309 inside cabins are located below on Empress, Upper, Main, and Riviera decks. These cabins are definitely more spacious than the average Caribbean-size found on other vessels, but I thought them less elegant. Despite the multi-million-dollar conversion that this vessel underwent, the *Festivale* still gave me the feeling of a trans-oceanic transport and did not have the light and airy atmosphere that is associated, with good reason, with seven-day cruises to the Caribbean. In the Continental Restaurant on Main Deck, an orange and brown decor reminded a friend I was with of MacDonald's. Despite its lack of windows, it is cheerful and looks very efficient. The restaurant accommodates 700 persons at one seating, and Carnival has assumed its own food service and expects to offer passengers better than average fare as well as around-the-clock food service in the cabins. Daily ice-carvings and a "can-do" attitude will be part of the new service.

The *Festivale* is ready to welcome just about anyone who wants to have constant fun and activity. If you are single, newly married, old-married, or a young family member, you will not lack entertainment aboard this cruise ship. Great emphasis is put on all kinds of musical entertainment, and the casino is open more than twelve hours each day. Or if you prefer to entertain yourself with a good book, the library is one of the original rooms on board and, hands down, my favorite. The *Festivale* sails every Saturday for Nassau, San Juan, and St. Thomas, three full days at sea for all that fun.

★★★★FUNCHAL

Owned by Portuguese government; on charter to Fritidskryss of Sweden; Portuguese flag and crew; built in Denmark in 1961; 10,000 tons; 450 feet long; 395 passengers; crew of 185; 5 passenger decks.

When the *Funchal* slid off the ways at the shipyard in Elsinore some twenty years ago, she was the largest vessel ever built in Denmark. Now the 395-passenger vessel is considered "yacht-like" but her Scandinavian decor is still intact. Owned and operated by the Portuguese government, the *Funchal* is on long-term charter to a Swedish tour operator named Fritidskryss. Lindblad Travel is the general U.S. sales agent and receives an allotment of cabins for each sailing.

The vessel has comfort and charm. All cabins sold by Lindblad are air-conditioned, and most have private facilities. Room service is available and the multilingual staff speak English, Swedish, and German. The public areas are spacious, with three bars, a no-smoking lounge, library and card room, and outdoor swimming pool. Two dining rooms seat all passengers for each meal and the food is a mixture of Scandinavian and international. Expect Swedish buffet breakfasts and the sumptuous smorgasbord for lunch almost daily!

During the spring/summer season the *Funchal* offers fifteen-day air/sea programs via SAS (at reasonable rates) to the North Cape, the British Isles and Coast of France, and the shores of western Europe. All sailings are roundtrip from Gothenburg and the North Cape cruises are considered excellent value. Shore excursions in each port of call are optional. Further information is available from Lindblad Travel, 8 Wright Street, Westport, CT 06880. Telephone: (203) 226-8531.

★★GALAXY

K-Lines Hellenic Cruises; Greek registry and crew; originally built in 1957 and formerly named the Scottish Coast; refurbished in 1971; 5,500 tons; 342 feet long; 52 feet at beam; 286 passengers; crew of 125; cruising speed of 16 knots; 6 passenger decks.

The third of the K-Lines fleet, the *Galaxy* is a good value for a three- or four-day cruise of the Greek islands. The vessel carries just 286 passengers in 112 outside cabins and 31 inside, all with private facilities and television. The accommodations are simple and pleasant, and many are designed to include a third person on a sofa-bed in an upper berth. Public areas are minimal but adequate, with the Get Together Lounge on Athinai Deck; the Upper Lounge, swimming pool, and solarium on Piraeus Deck; a conference room and discotheque on Upper Deck; and the dining room on Creta Deck.

The *Galaxy* sails on Fridays and Tuesdays from Piraeus, between April 3 and October 27, on three- and four-day itineraries of the Greek islands. The longer, Friday sailing calls at Mykonos, Kuşadasi, Patmos, Rhodes, Heraklion, and Thíra. The Tuesday departure visits Delos, Mykonos, Rhodes, Heraklion, and Thíra. Both itineraries offer a fine taste of the Greek islands.

★★★★GOLDEN ODYSSEY

Royal Cruise Line; Greek crew and registry; built in Elsinore, Denmark, in 1974 especially for the American cruise market; 10,500 tons; 427 feet long; 63 feet at beam; 460 passengers; crew of 200; 22.5 knots maximum speed; 7 passenger decks.

The *Golden Odyssey* has 237 staterooms, of which 181 are outside doubles, 48 are inside, and eight are deluxe suites. Some cabins accommodate three and four persons and some connect. The cabins are all decorated in bright, Mediterranean colors with reproductions of Greek embroideries from the Benaki Museum in Athens on the walls. Each has two lower beds in a parallel or "L" arrangement that are made up to look like sofas by day. All cabins have wall-to-wall carpeting, individual air-conditioning control, three-channel music, rosewood furniture, vanities, three closets, and tiled bathrooms with showers. Full bathtubs are found in the deluxe suites on Riviera Deck; and in rooms 703, 704, and 710; and in rooms 536–553, 436–453, and 327–343 (not including inside rooms). Continental breakfast and snacks on a 24-hour basis are served in the cabins. By modern cruise ship standards, the cabins are adequate in size, and I would certainly not expect to find them any larger on a vessel of this size.

The Lotus Restaurant on Odyssey Deck seats about 250 passengers at a time in tables of two to eight persons. Breakfast is open seating, while luncheon is served from noon (main) and 1:30 p.m. (late). Dinner hours are 6:45 p.m. (main) and 8:30 p.m. (late). Next to the Lotus dining room is a small, private room for cocktail parties. Among the five bars on board, one is on the swimming pool deck where an outdoor buffet is served at lunchtime. The main public area, the Ulysses Lounge, accommodates the full passenger list for afternoon lectures, classes, evening cabaret (an English theatrical group performs scenes from popular musicals), folkloric shows, and Greek night performances as well as dancing. For night owls, the Calypso Lounge on Riviera Deck becomes the late-night disco. And for those who have not had enough to eat, the Midnight Buffet begins at 11:30 p.m. in the Lotus Restaurant (again!). The *Golden Odyssey* also has a library/writing room, card room, gym with saunas, beauty salon, and hospital. Deck chairs and games are complimentary.

The *Golden Odyssey* continues her success program of offering air-sea cruises between San Juan and Acapulco in January; then a series of five round-trip departures from San Juan, beginning with a tennis cruise; and continuing sailings through March. Late March brings the vessel from Lisbon to Piraeus to reposition for a series of eastern Mediterranean and Greek Isles cruises in April (value season), May, July, and August. The *Golden Odyssey* also returns to Lisbon via Mediterranean ports in May, September, and October. A Lisbon to Piraeus cruise takes place in June and September. Rounding out the *Golden Odyssey*'s European season are two Piraeus-to-Venice Seas of Ulysses and Black Sea departures in June and July, and two Venice-to-Piraeus sailings in June and August. Passengers fly to meet the vessel in one port, disembark, and fly home at the other.

☆☆☆☆**GREAT RIVERS EXPLORER**

Exploration Cruise Lines; American registry and crew; built on Whidbey Island, Washington, and commissioned in 1982; 100 tons; 152 feet long; 31 feet at beam; 92 passengers; crew of 19; cruising speed of 12 knots; 4 passenger decks.

The *Great Rivers Explorer* is the third member of the Exploration Cruise Lines fleet. The 92-passenger vessel was inaugurated May 1982 for cruises along the Columbia, Snake, and Willamette rivers until mid-October. The Saturday departures from Portland cover three states and 900-roundtrip-miles of adventure, traveling as far inland as Lewiston, Idaho. Much of the journey follows the route marked by Lewis and Clark in 1804.

During the seven days of cruising, the vessel transits eight locks and eight dams, watches salmon swim up their own ladder, and takes a number of offbeat shore excursions. Among these shore trips are a castle on the Columbia River, meetings with both the Umatilla and Nez Perce Indians, and a jet boat into Hell's Canyon on the Snake River (which claims to be the deepest gorge in North America). One former passenger has termed this cruise a "thoroughly delightful learning experience" about one's own country. Several museums along the route and even a "tasting" at a local winery are included in the tour.

The *Great Rivers Explorer* moves to Panama for the winter season to pioneer weekly cruises between Balboa and Colon that feature a transit of the famed Panama Canal, considered to be one of man's greatest masterpieces. Through April the *Explorer* will sail from Balboa to the Pearl Islands, Darien Jungle, transit the Panama Canal, call at the San Blas Islands, and end in Colon (or vice versa). Passengers take the railway either to or from the ship. Another ambitious adventure for this company!

The *Great Rivers Explorer* is sister ship to the *Majestic Explorer*, but has two additional outside cabins. Life aboard is the same—casual and congenial—and main activities take place in the glass-enclosed Vista View Lounge or the Explorer dining room. As on the other vessels, the meals are all-American and served family-style around small tables. An extensive wine list offers selections for purchase, and the ship's bar is next to the player piano in the main lounge. With a draft of just eight feet and the bow-to-shore stairway, the vessel can call at out-of-the-way coves and harbors.

★★★★ILLIRIA

Chartered by Travel Dynamics, Inc.; Greek registry and crew; built in Italy in 1962; refurbished in 1981; 4,000 tons; 333 feet long; 48 feet at beam; 130 passengers; crew of 65; cruising speed of 16 knots; 3 passenger decks.

The *Illiria* must be one of the best-kept secrets in the Aegean! Known as the "diamandi de Aegon" (diamond of the Aegean), this vessel underwent a complete refurbishing two years ago just so she could handle specialized cruise programs. Among her special features are an elegant decor by designer Michael Katzourakis of Athens, with food managed by the famous Ligabue Catering of Venice. And the engine rooms are supposed to be as immaculate as the galleys!

Although the 4,000-ton vessel could accommodate about 198 passengers in comfort, Travel Dynamics limits the capacity to between 120 and 130 on each of its special cruises. Each sailing is custom-designed for special interest groups and appeals to college alumni associations, museums, and cultural organizations. Among the contented voyagers aboard the *Illiria* last year were members of the National Trust for Historic Preservation, the Friends of the Philadelphia Museum of Art, the Los Angeles County Art Museum, and Stanford College alumni. The ship makes two-week cruises in the Aegean, the Adriatic, the Tyrrhenian and the Mediterranean as well as along the Atlantic coastline of Europe. Each sailing brings together travelers with the same interests and curiosity plus well-known scholars to enhance the cruise experience (although attendance at any lecture is hardly mandatory). Still, it's fun to hobnob and feel that you are receiving value for money well spent.

The *Illiria* is probably the very best small vessel on this type of circuit. Certainly, I'd say she outranks the vessels chartered by Raymond and Whitcomb and R. K. Swan. Her red, white, and blue exterior has a gracious appearance. All but eight cabins are outside, with private facilities and telephone. Public areas include the main lounge on Lido Deck (with impressive sea views), a large bar, and a wind-protected swimming pool. Joggers may run around the Promenade areas at appointed hours. The dining room on Main Deck seats all passengers at one time—a most important requisite to being a first-class vessel. This is a highly recommended cruise experience, and groups interested in chartering her should contact Travel Dynamics, Inc., 1290 Avenue of the Americas, NYC 10014; (212) 247-6363.

★★★★★ISLAND PRINCESS/PACIFIC PRINCESS

Princess Cruises; British registry and crew (with Italian dining room personnel); sister ships built in West Germany and launched in 1970 (Pacific Princess) and 1972 (Island Princess); 20,000 tons; 550 feet long; 80 feet at beam; 630 passengers; crew of 352; cruising speed of 20 knots; 7 passenger decks.

The *Island* and *Pacific Princess* rank high in the most attractive cruise ship category; with the distinctive Princess Cruises logo atop their smokestacks, these are the most luxurious vessels in the P & O family. Although identical in design and ambience, they differ somewhat in decor. However, once you find your way around one of these *Princesses*, you'll feel right at home aboard the twin. You'll also be very pleased with your choice of vessels!

With a total of thirteen different public rooms you feel the spaciousness aboard these vessels—from the gracious Purser's Lobby, with its dramatic staircase and gallery, to the romantic Starlight Lounge in the forward section of Sun Deck. This lovely hideaway has wraparound windows that allow wonderful views of the sea and sky. On Riviera Deck the Carib/Pacific lounge, bar, and club; the Princess Theater; and the Carousel lounge and bar offer a variety of entertainment. And if you're a night owl, the Skal Bar turns into a disco at midnight. For games and more serious pursuits, you can seek out the Bridge and International lounges or the library/writing room one deck below. Both vessels have the Coral Dining Room (located on Coral Deck) with two sittings for luncheon and dinner, and two swimming pools. The Crystal Pool on Sun Deck is the most glamorous, with its Sun Dome for inclement weather (of course, it is rarely needed).

Accommodations aboard both these Princess vessels are splendid. The deluxe suites are spacious and delightful. The sitting areas are perfect for private gatherings, and you can find large beds in cabins 346, 348, 349, and 350. The deluxe outside twin cabins are as large as mini-suites, and the standard twin gains space by day with one bed that folds into the wall while the other becomes a sofa. The crew aboard both vessels is friendly, attractive, and helpful; and the British officers are stunning in their short white uniforms and knee socks! In the dining room the Italian chef and stewards dish up a cuisine that has both a fine reputation and sex appeal. Needless to say, the food is another outstanding feature on these two vessels, so plan to enjoy yourself and forget about calories.

During the summer season the *Pacific Princess* sails to Alaska's Inside Passage on twelve-night cruises from San Francisco. The *Island Princess* offers the same itinerary for eight nights from Vancouver, with calls at Ketchikan, Juneau, Skagway, Glacier Bay (cruising), and Sitka. The two vessels are familiar sights and totally committed to Alaskan waters from June until mid-September. During the rest of the year the *Island Princess* makes two-week cruises between Los Angeles and San Juan via the Panama Canal. Special theme cruises offered include Classical Music, Big Band, Bridge/Backgammon, and Film Festivals.

The *Pacific Princess* begins this year with a series of one-week Mexican Riviera cruises between Los Angeles and Acapulco. The ship acts as hotel in Acapulco for two nights each way. In March the *Pacific Princess* departs Los Angeles on a seventy-day cruise to the South Pacific and Orient that features an inaugural visit to the People's Republic of China. The itinerary is impressive, with four separate segments available: 46 days Los Angeles to Hong Kong; 26 days Los Angeles to Sydney; 44 days Sydney to Los Angeles; and 24 days Hong Kong to Los Angeles. Princess is also offering free air fare for both full cruise and all segments, plus complimentary hotels in Hong Kong or Sydney to the segment passengers and complimentary sightseeing to the full-cruise passengers. A special overland tour of China is also being arranged, on an optional basis.

Following her summer in a cooler climate, the *Pacific Princess* returns to Los Angeles for a fall series of Mexican Riviera cruises. In December the vessel departs again on another long and exciting itinerary—to Tahiti and Hawaii. The 26-day sailing spends a full week at sea, before calling at Nuku Hiva (Marquesas Island), Moorea (Society Islands), Pepeete (Tahiti), Bora Bora, Christmas Island, Honolulu, Lahaina, Kailua, Nawiliwili, and the Hamakua Coast. Christmas Day is spent crossing the Equator, and the vessel returns to Los Angeles in January of the next year. A third person traveling in the same cabin with two full-fare passengers is free (but does not qualify for the free air).

★★★JASON

Epirotiki Lines; Greek crew and registry; built in Italy in 1965; refurbished and launched as Jason in April 1967; 5,250 tons; 346 feet long; 53 feet at beam; 275 passengers; crew of 112; cruising speed of 15 knots; 6 passenger decks.

The *Jason* is my favorite of the Epirotiki fleet, not only for her pleasant gold and orange decor, but also for her ambience which I suspect is due, in large part, to the charming Captain Claudatos, and his American-born wife, who he met during an Alaskan cruise. The vessel has 134 cabins situated among four decks, and all but 30 have outside views. All have private facilities with stall showers. The only full baths found on the ship are in suites A1 through A6 on Apollo deck. The cabins, small but very pleasant, have fold-over sofa arrangements for day. Large murals reminiscent of the island of Thíra and curtain designs that feature shields of ancient Greek heroes make the rooms even more pleasant.

The *Jason* is justifiably proud of the many fine artworks on board, which add to her appeal as a cruise vessel. Up on Jupiter Deck an unusual fountain supplies fresh seawater to the Argo Pool, while the mosaic tabletops in the adjoining Argonaut Bar reflect the designs of ancient warrior shields. Below, in the Orpheus Nightclub (a disco after 10 p.m.), a life-size bronze and copper figure of Orpheus plays his lyre. On Dionysos Deck (also called Main Deck), the Jason Bar stands out with its tapestry of Jason yoking the wild bulls in the sacred field of Ares, and the corridor to the Golden Fleece Lounge boasts a monumental brass sculpture, Sunburst, which is said to be the largest bronze work cast in Greece since the classical age. It's impossible to sail aboard this vessel and not become interested in Greek mythology.

Some lovely tapestries inside and around the Eros Dining Room deck the cheerful restaurant that seats the entire complement of passengers at one time. The gold and orange room has large, bright windows to constantly remind you of the excitement of the sea. The food and service are reported to be good, especially the Greek dishes and fine selection of local wines. Epirotiki has concocted a special drink for each ship, and this one is known as Jason Night; it consists of one ounce of gin, two ounces fresh lemon juice, syrup, and a splash of apricot brandy. It sounds as though it would burn beautifully!

The *Jason* has replaced the *Orpheus* as the R. K. Swan vessel. (See under Swan for the schedule.) You can be sure that the library is well stocked with reading matter and there is one seating in the dining room. All gratuities to the crew are included in the cruise price, per R. K. Swan policy.

★★JUPITER

Epirotiki Lines; Greek flag and crew; originally built in 1961 and named the Moledet; rebuilt and refurbished in 1971 as the Jupiter; 9,000 tons; 415 feet long; 65 feet at beam; 450 passengers; crew of 212; cruising speed of 16 knots; 7 passenger decks.

The *Jupiter* is one of the larger vessels belonging to the Epirotiki fleet, and it has many modern amenities such as the fine theater/conference center and the Hygcia sauna/hcalth studio, both located on Poseidon Deck. The vessel has 187 cabins, of which 143 are outside and 88 interconnect to form two-room suites, each with private facilities. All cabins convert to a sitting room by day, with a fold-over sofa arrangement. The *Jupiter* has a total of seven public rooms, including an art gallery and two cocktail lounges. A number of fine tapestries relate the tales of Jupiter (Zeus to the Greeks), king of the heavens, and his paramours. The dining room is called Leda and the Swan, and the Gannymede Club for young people is next door. You can find Kronos sun bar on Jupiter Deck and the Evropi lounge/bar next to the swimming pool area. The main lounge, Lounge of the Titans, honors old Atlas, who bore the heavens on his shoulders. The vessel also has a Zeus Bar, Adonis beauty salon, and Semiramis Agora (boutique) as well as the Praxiteles art gallery. In my opinion this ship is certainly the most complete and spacious of the Epirotiki line in the Aegean, and from all reports, a most enjoyable cruise vessel on three-, four-, or seven-day sailings.

★★★★★KUN LUN

East is Red; Chinese registry and crew; riverboat launched in December 1962; relaunched by Lindblad in 1979 for American tourists; 2,300 tons; 277 feet long; 36 passengers; crew of 80; 3 passenger decks.

This beautiful riverboat was built in China especially for entertaining ministers, visiting heads of state, and other foreign dignitaries. Named *Kun Lun* after the Kunlun mountain range that extends from the Pakistan/China border to the Sichuan basin, the boat was designed to accommodate only thirty-six passengers in large cabins with private facilities (they range from 230 square feet to 650 square feet), although other vessels of this size carry from 700 to 900 passengers up and down the river. Said to be a miniature version of the transatlantic liners of the 1930s, the entirely air-conditioned *Kun Lun* has eighteen cabins, a main lounge with bar, and library plus three smaller lounge areas, a shop, beauty salon, bank, laundry service, and resident doctor. The dining room seats all passengers and serves Western breakfasts, and Chinese lunches and dinners (Western food can be ordered twenty-four hours in advance).

The *Kun Lun* sails up and down the Yangtze River, China's longest waterway and the third largest in the world (after the Amazon and the Nile). The four-thousand-mile Yangtze (which the Chinese call Chang Jiang or Long River) flows through ten provinces of China and has over seven hundred tributaries. Its fertile basin, inhabited by more than 300 million people, covers some 60 million cultivated acres which produce at least seventy percent of China's aquatic rice and one-third of its cotton crop. The river cuts west to east through the heart of China and has been the traditional division between the north and south for centuries.

The Yangtze River expedition is a complete 25-day tour from San Francisco (to Hong Kong, Guangzhou, Shanghai, and Suzhou), with twelve days spent aboard the *Kun Lun*, cruising between Nanjing (Nanking) and Chongqing (Chunking). Calls are made at Jiujiang (Kiukiang) to visit the mountain retreat of Lu San, Wuhan, Shashi (Shashih), Wan Xian (Wanshien), and Shibao Block. In addition, you will spend an entire day on board traversing the Three Gorges of the Yangtze, considered to be some of the most spectacular river scenery in the world. And every night a Chinese banquet—what more could a person desire? Departure dates for these exciting cruise expeditions take place from the end of March to the end of November (it's cold and chilly during the rest of the year). The participating air carrier is Pan Am.

★★★★★LINDBLAD EXPLORER

Salen Lindblad Cruising; Swedish registry; European and American crew; built in Finland in 1969; 2,500 tons; 250 feet long; cruising speed of 15 knots; 6,000 mile cruising range; 92 passengers; crew of 60; 5 passenger decks.

The *Lindblad Explorer*, dedicated to the spirit of adventure, made her maiden voyage on December 14, 1969, through the tropical Atlantic to the southern polar ice pack. She is a familiar sight in the most interesting and exotic areas the world has to offer. Specific itineraries are planned with scientific institutions, explorers, and naturalists; a voyage never takes place without several experts on board. Each cruise also includes lectures, discussions, and films designed to prepare passengers for the areas they are visiting. A simple laboratory has even been installed for scientific work.

The *Lindblad Explorer* has fifty outside cabins with private facilities, and all but a few have twin beds. The cabins are practically identical in size; the price difference varies with location on the ship. A crew of sixty (including a doctor) takes care of the ninety-two passengers. Public areas include the Penguin Room (so called because of the mural painted by wildlife artist Keith Shackleton) for briefings, films, and lectures and the Explorer Lounge for games, drinks, and relaxation. A small library, a shop, beauty/barber salon, laundry facilities, swimming pool, and dining room that seats the full passenger complement at all meals fills out the public space. The vessel also carries a fleet of Zodiacs, specially designed rubber inflatable boats powered by outboard motor. These serve as landing craft for the ship and allow passengers to explore otherwise inaccessible areas. They also give passengers a new perspective and a more personal feeling for these areas. (The Zodiac is supposed to be as comfortable as a deck chair but, admittedly, slightly wetter at times!)

The *Explorer* no longer cruises along the Chinese coastline, due to the 1982 launching of the *Yao Hua*. Hence, the vessel offers a more diverse program during the spring. In early March 1983, the *Explorer* is scheduled for a Melanesia cruise to the "Golden Isles of Papua, New Guinea" between Sydney and Port Moresby. Another two-week cruise sails between Manila and Singapore, calling at ports in the Philippines, Borneo, and Malaysia. From Singapore, the *Explorer* sails to Malacca, Burma and the Bay of Bengal, ending in Colombo. The Islands of the Indian Ocean, namely the Seychelles and Maldives, are ports of call on a cruise from Colombo to Mombasa in late April. A mid-May sailing from Hodeidah passes through the Red Sea and Suez Canal to Cyprus, Crctc, and Corfu.

During the summer season, the *Lindblad Explorer* journeys to the Arctic and Greenland from Copenhagen and Reykjavik. In the fall, the vessel will make her famous Amazon River cruises both upstream and downstream.

★★★★★LINDBLAD POLARIS

Salen Lindblad Cruising; Swedish registry and crew; originally built in Aalborg, Denmark, in 1960 and employed as an overnight ferry within Scandinavia; rebuilt in 1982 and relaunched as Lindblad Polaris; 2,124 tons; 218 feet long; 42 feet at beam; 79 passengers; crew of about 40; cruising speed of 16 knots; 4 passenger decks.

I shall always think of the *Lindblad Polaris* as a sanctuary against the wild weather one might encounter in the Baltic Sea in early spring. When the *Polaris* was launched on May 1, 1982, about sixty members of the Intrepid Club joined Lars and his wife Cary, other members of the Lindblad family, and some friends for an inaugural cruise from Stockholm to Copenhagen. It was a typical Lindblad adventure—with the proper balance in visiting the familiar as well as the far flung. Only the weather didn't cooperate, which is why I have such fond memories of the *Polaris* as a refuge from the wind and the rain (and one day, the snow)!

An unpretentious vessel that has been nicely refurbished, the *Polaris* carries just seventy-nine passengers and handles like a yacht (according to the Captain). Cabins are small but well-fitted; passengers requiring more space should definitely book the #300 line on Wasa Deck or #122 and #125 on A Deck. Bathrooms are functional, although the showers were made for midgets (watch out or everything in sight will be drenched). The pleasant Scandinavian decor throughout, with light woods and sleek comfortable furniture, is enhanced by some original works of Sweden's foremost artist—Roland Svensson. It was also Svensson who arranged the impressive volumes available for browsing in the vessel's small Strindberg Library, and even added much of his own personal collection.

The Wasa Restaurant, with its panoramic view and tables set for six, accommodates all passengers at open sitting. Breakfast is buffet-style, and everything from local fruit-flavored yogurts to coldcuts and cheese is available. The charming waitresses serve coffee and take orders for eggs and bacon. Lunch is strictly a Swedish smorgasbord, and anyone who enjoys herring in at least a dozen sauces will be in heaven here! (Wash it down with a Tuborg beer or two, and take the rest of the day off.) Three-course, European-style dinners are more formal, and a compact but worthy wine list is available. On Thursday evenings (at least, on the Baltic cruises), the traditional Swedish meal of pea soup, thin pancakes of jam, and warm Arrak punch is served—an interesting touch that I thought once was certainly enough. Some meals on the Baltic itinerary are served ashore, and the most noteworthy were a luncheon across from the former homes/studios of Finnish architects Saarinen/Lindgren/Gesellius, as well as a dinner at Tallinn's number-one-tourist-hotel where the food was as much a surprise as our spruced-up guides!

Life aboard the *Polaris* is casual/chic and stimulating, to say the least. Lindblad's cruises sell themselves because they always attract well-educated and well-traveled people. Most of the passengers on the inaugural cruise had met one another in the past, and some were veterans of over a dozen Lindblad adventures worldwide. There is no after-dinner entertainment, other than an occasional lecture. You might see some slides and hear of personal experiences on Tristan de Cunha or enjoy a humorous lecture on how the Scandinavian languages were formed. Bird watchers can discuss their daily findings, and the cruise director will advise on the use of the Zodiacs, the German-built rubber rafts carried atop the vessel and employed in getting ashore at remote harbors.

The *Polaris* represents a homecoming for Lars-Eric Lindblad, who has spent over three decades sending travelers on adventures to all other parts of the world. Now he is bringing his friends and clients to Scandinavia, to share with them the excitement of his native land. From May to mid-September, the *Lindblad Polaris* will sail around the Baltic, visiting not only the great northern European capitals but also a number of less-known islands famous for their flora and fauna. A favorite call is at Stora Karlso where guillemots (narrow-billed birds that resemble penguins) can be sighted when the weather is good. With luck, there will be cloud formations over another island, Bla Jungfrun, so passengers can enjoy the unusual silhouettes that often appear.

The vessel also makes several calls at major Russian ports, such as Riga (capital of Latvia), Leningrad, and Tallinn (capital of Estonia). Here, as elsewhere, all shore excursions are inclusive of the cruise rate and the time spent ashore is "visa free." There is no deviation from the program in the Russian ports, but passengers feel that because of Lindblad's fine reputation some extra special courtesy is very evident.

During the winter months, the *Polaris* will be situated in the Red Sea/Sinai Peninsula area, offering a series of the most exciting and well-planned programs ever! Several other companies have failed at cruises in this part of the world, because proper guides and historian/archaeologist lecturers must be on board at all times. Anyone with an interest in Egypt and the Middle East should definitely sign on! The spring and summer program will feature some early April cruises in the Aegean, a three-week sailing from Syracuse to Copenhagen, followed by several one-week cruises in the Baltic between Copenhagen, Helsinki, and Stockholm.

☆☆☆☆MAJESTIC EXPLORER

Exploration Cruise Lines; American registry and crew; built on Whidbey Island, Washington, and commissioned in 1982; 100 tons; 152 feet long; 31 feet at beam; 88 passengers; crew of 19; cruising speed of 12 knots; 4 passenger decks.

The second member of the Exploration Cruise Lines fleet is the slightly larger *Majestic Explorer*, which arrived in February 1982. The vessel began operation on the Sacramento and San Joaquin rivers through California's "delta country" in March, then repositioned in Alaska for the May through August season. She will repeat the same schedule in 1983, cruising weekly between Ketchikan and Skagway every Sunday. Ports of call are Misty Fjords, Wrangell, Sitka, Tracy Arm and Juneau, Skagway, Haines, Glacier Bay cruising, Petersburg and Le Conte Glacier before returning to Ketchikan. A variety of optional extensions are available.

During the winter season, the *Majestic Explorer* will inaugurate a series of unusual cruises around the French Polynesian islands, departing from Papeete.

This *Explorer* is just 100 tons and carries 88 passengers with a crew of 19 all-Americans. The ship can call in often-bypassed coves and harbors because of an eight-foot draft and ingenious bow-to-shore stairway. Cabins are comfortable but very functional, and life on board is casual/congenial. Both the panoramic Vista View Lounge and the Explorer dining room accommodate all passengers. The lounge has a player piano and the ship's bar. Meals in the dining room are hearty, family-style and a selection of wines is available for purchase. It is a charming vessel with an impressive set of itineraries year-round.

★★★MARDI GRAS/CARNIVALE

Carnival Cruise Lines; Panamanian registry, Italian officers, and international crew; Mardi Gras was originally built in 1961 and formerly named the Empress of Canada; the Carnivale was originally built in 1956 and formerly named the Empress of Britain; refurbished in 1973 and 1976, respectively; 27,250 tons; 760 feet long; 87 feet at beam; 1,100 passengers; crew of 510; cruising speed of 21 knots; nine passenger decks.

The *Mardi Gras* was the first launched of what Carnival Cruise Lines hopes to be a fleet of seven or eight by the end of this decade. The *Carnivale* is her sister ship and, although ten feet shorter in length, actually carries a few more passengers. Both vessels have been refurbished but still seem to retain what I call a cold weather atmosphere with their enclosed promenades and public areas that do not flow into one another. The use of wood and brass throughout these vessels is impressive and a definite sign of their vintage, but I think these ships lack a real Caribbean character. It was very difficult for me to believe that these ships were warm-water cruisers except around the pool or on the Sports Deck.

The spacious cabins aboard both vessels are roomier than what I call Caribbean-size. Again, the warm woods and old-time feeling abound throughout the accommodations (except for a few recently added cabins); it must have been quite an experience to cross the Atlantic in these surroundings. Because these were former transatlantic vessels, inside cabins outnumber outside cabins. While both ships have 264 inside cabins, the *Mardi Gras* has 193 outside cabins, and the *Carnivale* has 217. All have private facilities and 24-hour room service. Since both ships emphasize *fun*, the public areas feature full casinos (operated by the ship line) that are active from mid-morning into the wee hours of the next day, a number of different nightclubs and discos (that become active in the evening), three bands (steel, orchestral, and romantic), and several bars. There are also children's playrooms and counselors (during holiday times), indoor pools and saunas, outdoor pools and sports areas on the upper decks. Because these are older vessels, the dining rooms are below deck and do not offer sea views, but you can always have breakfast in your room or a luncheon buffet served near the pool.

Carnival is attempting quite seriously to upgrade its food and service image, in order to encourage passengers to return another time. The ship line does very well in bringing first-time cruisers into Miami, but the repeat ratio is low by comparison to other lines. It seems that the young/fun set returns to other vessels for that second- and third-time out. Nonetheless, the emphasis on both these ships is for all passengers to have a good time, to eat and be merry, enjoy the sun and the sea and the shore excursions, and the late-night entertainment. There are sumptuous midnight buffets to encourage the night owls, and the casino closes when the last group goes. Both vessels have been recently refurbished, to lend more of an 80s air.

The *Carnivale* sails from Miami every Sunday for Samana, San Juan, and St. Thomas. The *Mardi Gras* also sails on Sundays for Cozumel, Grand Cayman, and Ocho Rios. Both vessels feature three full days at sea during the one-week cruises.

★★★MERMOZ

Paquet Ulysses Cruises; French registry and crew; originally built in 1957 and formerly named the Jean Mermoz; launched in 1970 as the Mermoz; 13,800 tons; 530 feet long; 66 feet at beam; 550 passengers; crew of 230; cruising speed of 17 knots; 5 passenger decks.

The *Mermoz* celebrated her tenth anniversary in 1979 with champagne and roses and special gourmet salutes during her Caribbean cruise season. This, alas, is very short for North Americans, for the *Mermoz* only sails in the Western Hemisphere between mid-December and the end of March each year. During this time she is based in San Juan for ten-, eleven-, and twelve-day cruises to fun ports in the Caribbean and archaeological sites in Mexico. During the summer months the *Mermoz* cruises from the south of France into the Mediterranean, the Baltic, and North Cape, and even the Red Sea. A *pièce de résistance* that, if you have the interest and the money, is well worth everything—the bi-annual Music Festival at Sea (previously offered aboard the *Renaissance*). Usually scheduled in late summer and early winter, the music festival features some of the most exciting artists of the world today (they may not necessarily be the top by my standards but they are the most entertaining), including the entire Rostropovich family (Mstislav, daughters Olga and Elena, and wife Galina Vishnevskaya), trumpeter Maurice Andre, known balletomanes, and favorite lecturers such as Karl Haas (who appears daily on New York and Detroit radio programs, among other things). Although I rate the cruises as very expensive for these musical festivals (and you should really be more a music lover than a cruise buff), they are worth every penny. Paquet insists upon offering them twice a year, despite the high costs (and probable losses) to the line. How can you fault a cruise company that still endures this?

Although I think she looks rather like a bucket from the outside, the *Mermoz* is known for her French menus (a nice change from most Caribbean cruise cuisine) and complimentary table wines at both luncheon and dinner. The vessel has 230 outside and 60 inside cabins, all with private facilities. Most of the cabins are average, Caribbean-size. The deluxe staterooms and suites are located on Grand Salon Deck, which also holds the Grand Salon, card room, shops, and beauty facilities. Above on Grill Deck are the reading room, grill room (where luncheon buffets are served with salads, hot dishes, and complimentary table wines), and swimming pool. Another outdoor pool is located on Lido Deck and Sun Deck features many beauty and exercise preparations and performances. The main dining room is down on Restaurant Deck, the disco on Caverne Deck, and cinema down on Movie Deck (one cannot get much lower). Although passenger comments to me range from excellent to poor in the housekeeping department, if you wish to practice your French and cruise the Caribbean or Mediterranean at the same time, this is the ship. And if you don't expect it to be Scandinavian-scrubbed, you'll love it. And I hear the captain is veeery sexy!

★★★★MISSISSIPPI QUEEN

Delta Queen Steamboat Company; American crew and registry; built by Jeffboat in Jefferson, Indiana; launched July 1976; 4,500 tons; 382 feet long; 68 feet at beam; 377 passengers; crew of 142; 14 miles per hour maximum speed; 7 passenger decks.

When the *Mississippi Queen* was commissioned on July 25, 1976, in Cincinnati, Ohio, it was the culmination of a ten-year project that cost $27 million and involved the craftsmen of both England and America. This *Queen* was the largest and most spectacular riverboat ever built, and special arrangements were made for her to be constructed in Jeffersonville, Indiana, where nearly 5,000 steamboats had been born during the nineteenth century.

The *MQ* is over one hundred feet longer, ten feet wider at beam, and almost 3,000 tons larger than her venerable sister, the *Delta Queen*. She also carries twice the passenger and crew capacity. Her exterior was devised by James Gardner of London, who also participated in the design of Cunard Line's flagship, the *Queen Elizabeth 2*. The interior of the vessel has been conceived very carefully to offer every nuance of the ambiance of nineteenth-century river life, without breaking the Safety at Sea Law that states all materials must be as inflammable as possible. Although none of the fine old polished woods of the *DQ* are possible here, the mouldings, mirrors, highly polished steel and brass everywhere and the plush carpeting throughout the public areas certainly recall the opulence of the great steamboat era.

The *MQ* has 131 outside cabins, of which 80 have private verandas just like the good old days. The cabins are well-designed, some with pullman-type berths, and 79 are on the inside. As on the *Delta Queen* this year, children under 16 years of age may cruise free of charge when sharing accommodations with two paying adults. The public rooms are spacious and comfortable. The Grand Saloon holds the entire passenger complement for afternoon tea dances and evening entertainment, and opens out onto an observation area.

At the other end of the Observation Deck is the Dining Saloon, with windows so large the river is always at your elbow. There are two sittings for all meals, the only awkward aspect of the entire program. The Dining Saloon opens onto the Upper Paddlewheel Lounge, overlooking a double-tiered space sheathed in glass just forward of that ever-churning red paddlewheel. The lounge is where the day's fun usually begins and ends: Dixieland, barbershop quartet, and jazz are all live continually as the libations flow on. You will always meet new friends in this lounge—and find old ones!

Promenade Deck aft is the location of the famous Calliope (claimed to be the largest in the world) and the Calliope Bar. Passengers try their talent on the "steam pianna" throughout the cruise, and it's even computerized so sour notes can be heard again. Midship on Promenade Deck is a small jacuzzi pool, open year-round and heated to suit the temperatures of the day, as well as a small gym, massage areas, and sauna. A library is the most recent addition to Observation Deck, and history lovers will enjoy the many books covering "steamboating" and the Old South. The library provides quiet and relaxation; next to it on the port side is an expanded Steamboatique, with over 400 selections of gifts and souvenirs from porcelain dolls to riverboat gambler sets. The *MQ* also has a nice theater, situated next to the beauty parlor on Lower Deck, where first-run films are offered. I saw "Showboat" there, during the inaugural cruise, and have not forgotten it!

The *MQ* has a loyal following and attracts a more active and energetic crowd than those devoted to her elder sister. Captain Gabriel Chengary from Pittsburgh, PA, is only in his mid-30s and the rest of the crew is younger. Life aboard ship revolves a great deal around the Paddlewheel Lounge, and there is plenty of local entertainment in the Grand Saloon or up in the Calliope Bar. Kite flying, exercise sessions, riverboat bingo, calliope contests, lectures, shore gazing, pilot house turns, locking through the Upper Mississippi, and eating well are all part of on-board life. Passengers also love the Big Band Cruises with the Glen Miller Orchestra during the month of February. As on the *Delta Queen*, the *MQ* offers Mardi Gras Cruises, Spring Pilgrimage Cruises, the Great Steamboat Race, Fall Foliage Cruises, Old Fashioned Holiday Cruises, plus golf and tennis options on seven-day cruises calling all day in Natchez or Vicksburg.

★★NEPTUNE

Epirotiki Lines; Greek crew and registry; built in 1955 in Denmark; refurbished and relaunched as Neptune in April 1972; 4,000 tons; 300 feet long; 45 feet at beam; 180 passengers; crew of 97; cruising speed of 14 knots; 6 passenger decks.

The *Neptune* is the smallest of the Epirotiki fleet, even smaller than the "private yacht" *Argonaut*. The vessel has only ninety-six cabins (of which twenty-four are inside), all with private facilities and a fold-over sofa arrangement for daytime use. You will find full baths in only three Special Staterooms (HS, HS1, HS2) located on Hera Deck, just inside the observation area. The cabin decor features murals depicting the underwater Palace of Poseidon (Neptune), with curtains on which "happy waves" seem to play in blues and greens or gold and brown tones. As on all Epirotiki vessels, interior designer Maurice Bailey and artists Arminio Lozzo and Russel Holmes have integrated the mythological tales of the ship's namesake throughout.

The vessel has *Poseidon* painted in Greek on the stern, but *Neptune* in Roman characters on the bow (for the American passengers, no doubt). However one calls this fellow, he was Lord of the Sea; and this ship's tapestries, mosaics, brass sculptures, and other artworks indicate this. The Lounge of the Tritons, the main public area, has three large tapestries of Neptune with his trident. Next door in the Poseidon Bar, a large, swirled mosaic made me think of the *Poseidon Adventure* (which I doubt was the intention). In the passageways handmade brass lamps represent the house of Poseidon, and more tapestries hang in the Dining Room of the Sirens, a cheerful restaurant in purples and pinks that seats the full complement of passengers. The large viewing windows also add to the pleasant effect.

Another nice spot is up on Hera Deck in the solarium, located between the swimming pool and the Mermaid Bar. Here you can catch a bit of the sun, enjoy the excitement of the sea, and appreciate the highlight of this floating art gallery—the magnificent mosaic by the swimming pool. And while you're up here, try a Neptune Wave, the ship's specialty that consists of one ounce tequila, two ounces fresh orange juice, and one-quarter ounce Grenadine. I know that it's served with a smile!

★★★NEW SHOREHAM II

American Canadian Line; American registry and crew; built in Warren, Rhode Island, and commissioned in 1979; 100 tons; 150 feet long; 32 feet at beam; 72 passengers; crew of 15; cruising speed of 12 knots; 3 passenger decks.

The tiny coastal cruiser *New Shoreham II* was designed and built by Luther Blount at his very own shipyard in Warren, Rhode Island. Mr. Blount also owns and operates American Canadian Line, and he designed this vessel with a shallow draft so she could cruise right up on the shore. In fact, the front section of the bow opens to disembark passengers. The *New Shoreham II* has just 36 cabins, some of which will accommodate third persons, but the quarters could be rather close. Most cabins have large sea-view windows and private facilities. Those in the thrifty category are inside, with facilities across the hall. The vessel has one lounge and a dining room on Atlantic Deck. There is no commercial bar, so passengers are encouraged to bring along their own bottle for the cruise.

Life aboard the *New Shoreham II* and the itineraries are for the agile and young at heart. During the summer season, the vessel sails from Warren, Rhode Island, on Saguenay River Cruises; in the fall, foliage cruises up the Erie Canal are in order, with return bus to Rhode Island. The vessel sails down to Florida in late autumn, to spend the winter in the Bahama Islands offering cruises from Abaco, and between Exuma and Eleuthera. These are popular with passengers who enjoy crystal Bahamian waters and snorkeling.

☆☆☆☆NIEUW AMSTERDAM

Holland America Cruises; Netherlands Antilles registry; Dutch officers and Indonesian crew; built at St. Nazaire in France and scheduled for commissioning on March 31; 32,000 tons; 689 feet long; 89 feet at beam; 1,200 passengers; crew of 536; cruising speed of 21 knots; 11 passenger decks.

This exciting new vessel, ordered by Holland America a few years ago, is designed by Dutch architect F. de Vlaming with a modern and most abrupt-looking squared-off stern. The vessel will feature the very latest in technological equipment as well as satellite navigation and communication equipment. For the approximately $150 million price-tag, passengers will find spacious lounges, two swimming pools (plus an additional wading pool for children), a 700-person dining room with large ocean-view windows, a casino, theater, Lido Restaurant for buffet breakfasts and luncheons, nightclub and disco, large gymnasium with sauna, and an observatory lounge on the Top Deck that becomes an intimate piano bar by night.

On the seven decks from Navigation Bridge to "C," there will be 430 outside cabins and 170 on the inside, all the usual private facilities and individually controlled air conditioning/heating. All 600 cabins will also feature closed-circuit color television, music/news selections, and push-button telephones with message indicators. Twenty of the outside cabins are considered "deluxe," with king-size beds and sofa areas for conversation.

The vessel is being constructed to be carefully insulated from sound throughout, and the range/maneuverability of the new ship will allow unrestricted deployment possibilities worldwide. For the first year of service, the new luxury liner will be homeported in San Francisco for cruises from Vancouver during the summer season, and to Mexico and the Caribbean in the winter months. The *Nieuw Amsterdam* will be joined at the end of January 1984 by a sister ship, built to the very same specifications in the same place, called the *Noordam*.

This is the third vessel named *Nieuw Amsterdam* in the 111-year-old company of Holland America. The first vessel called *Nieuw Amsterdam* sailed on her maiden voyage from The Netherlands to the United States on April 7, 1906, with 417 First Class passengers, 391 Tourist Class and 2,300 Third Class passengers on the transatlantic run. Although she was not fast (16 knots maximum) and she was the last of the fleet to carry sails for emergency use, the vessel was a favorite of the company and clients for her comfort, cuisine, and service. The second *Nieuw Amsterdam* was launched in 1936 and refitted in the late 1950s, innovating a new trend for ocean liners that featured a large complement of passengers with run-of-the-ship and a small number of First Class passengers stuck in their own tight quarters above.

Although the newest *Nieuw Amsterdam* will soon be one of the most modern vessels afloat, her ambiance will be that of a seventeenth-century ship sailing between Holland and America, adorned with beautiful artifacts of the period. The *Noordam* will feature an eighteenth-century atmosphere within the most modern framework possible.

★★★★NORDIC PRINCE

Royal Caribbean Cruise Line; Norwegian registry and officers, international crew; built in Wartsila shipyard in Helsinki and originally launched in 1971; refitted and lengthened in 1980; 23,000 tons; 635 feet long; 80 feet at beam; 1,038 passengers; crew of 400; cruising speed of 16 knots; 8 passenger decks.

Second of the famed RCCL fleet to be stretched, the *Nordic Prince* gained 85 feet and 4,500 tons, allowing space for 310 more passengers and 80 additional crew. As a result of this process, the ship now has 339 outside and 180 inside cabins, all with private facilities. The size of the cabins has not changed—there are just many more of them. However, the dimensions of the public areas are much larger, especially the Camelot dining room, the Showboat Lounge (and theater), and the Carousel Lounge. In addition, the Midsummer's Night Lounge on Promenade Deck and the pool area with a new pool cafe for luncheon buffets have both increased considerably in size. Food and service aboard the *Nordic Prince* is on par with the other RCCL vessels, and the entertainment is exactly the same. Royal Caribbean uses the same nightclub attractions on all three ships and flies them from port to port, so you see each act only once. In short, this vessel is another fine RCCL product—the only differences are the names of the public areas and the ports of call which are generally in Caribbean and southeastern coastal waters.

★★★★+NORWAY

Norwegian Caribbean Lines; Norwegian registry and officers, international crew; originally built in France in 1961 and launched as the flagship of French Line; relaunched in 1980 as the Norway; 69,500 tons; 1,035 feet long; 110 feet at beam; 2,000 passengers; crew of 800; cruising capacity of 18 knots; 10 passenger decks.

Knut Kloster, whose company owns Norwegian Caribbean Lines, says he bought the former *SS France* because she smiled down at him from her forlorn dock in Le Havre (where the vessel had been tied since being ignominiously pulled from service in 1974), and he wanted to see her smiling for the next twenty or so years. So as a good part of the world looked upon the project with great skepticism, Kloster plunked down eighteen million dollars for the vessel, once considered the best French restaurant in the world, and transformed her three cold-weather classes into a one-class floating Caribbean resort. Several million dollars later, no one who sees this beautiful blue and white vessel docked in Miami can help but be overwhelmed, for she looks ten blocks long, and she certainly is smiling!

Danish naval architect Tage Wandborg, who has more than thirty modern cruise ships and more than a hundred conversions to his credit, supervised the reincarnation and left behind his distinctive and stylish trademark. For the decoration of the public areas, Kloster hired interior designer Angelo Donghia of New York, who has some famous clients and is a familiar figure in the new hotel and nightclub circuit. Donghia and his staff of eighty came up with the decor of 74 suites, 871 other staterooms and cabins, and 14 public rooms, among others. Some of Donghia's achievements are the disco, "A Club Called Dazzles," with portholes into a lighted swimming pool and a glass dance floor that reflects the discotheque lighting; the cabaret, "Checkers," with red and black decor and a rug that looks like a checkerboard; the "Windjammer Bar," small and nautical; and the "Monte Carlo Room," with a carpet of kings and queens. By far, everyone's favorite room aboard is the "Club Internationale" in which Donghia has definitely evoked the glamorous and elegant days of trans-atlantic crossings. This room, by day or night, is subdued and very romantic in an Art Deco manner. The 1800 pieces of art worth nearly one million dollars were commissioned and placed under the supervision of a husband and wife team from Oslo who dealt primarily with Scandinavian artists. The *Norway's* largest public room is the North Cape Lounge, located aft on Pool Deck, which can accommodate a mere 650 passengers.

The *Norway* has two most attractive dining rooms, both decorated in soft browns and beiges, and there are two seatings for all meals. Passengers in the aft section of the vessel dine in the double-deck Leeward, while those in the forward section use the Windward dining room. Many other places to eat include the Great Outdoor Restaurant and the Cafe de Paris, or Svens, where you can buy gooey ice cream concoctions. And fourteen bars, manned by a staff of eighty, let you relax without being seen in the same place too often!

Aside from eating and watering, activities abound on board this floating resort—two outdoor pools and an indoor pool/gymnasium/sauna complex, a full casino, cinema (with feature films), exercise classes, lectures, fashion shows, two "streets" lined with elegant shops (Champs Elysses and Fifth Avenue), bridge and backgammon tournaments, and a very pleasant library. You don't even have to leave your cabin for much of this, because a full closed-circuit television service begins each morning at nine. In the evening, the 541-seat

Saga Theater presents super-duper productions of "Sea Legs" and "My Fair Lady" in addition to any number of guest entertainers who play throughout the lounges and nightclubs.

The *Norway* offers twenty-three different categories of cabins as befits a ship of her great size. These range from Grand Deluxe Suites on Viking Deck (with two bedrooms, sitting room, and private dining room) that are available on request only and cost about ten thousand dollars for the week to an Inside Stateroom (upper and lower berths) that is about seven hundred dollars per person for the week's cruise. Even the inside cabins are spacious with the high ceilings of yesteryears. Many cabins still have the old wall fans from transatlantic days, and all the former first-class cabins have large bathtubs and bidets, along with roomy wardrobe space. The ship line added several new cabins in the conversion, including some mini-suites on Pool Deck that are small but special and very pleasant. These Pool Deck Suites have unusual, super-large windows that were once part of an enclosed promenade area. Since the suites are several stories up, you never need to close the drapes—ah, moonlight!

Following a much-publicized drydocking in the Hapag Lloyd Shipyard in Bremerhaven for about three months, the *Norway* returned to Caribbean service in July. A total of $15 million had been spent, mainly in the engine room where three new diesel generators were installed and three main boilers were totally retubed. In addition, a new television monitoring system for the entire engine room area and a new boiler control panel were installed. The vessel also received two new propellers to reduce fuel consumption by seven percent, new satellite communication equipment, and thirty tons of paint. Five hundred new television sets were installed in cabins; all 931 cabins received some refurbishment, with more than 250 being completely redone. Twenty-five of the cabins, including some of the very large suites, remain as they were originally built because some irreplaceable materials in them (bronze and gold leaf) are still in excellent condition.

On her second cruise upon return to service, the *Norway* never looked better. The vessel was filled to capacity, Rita Moreno was the headliner and gave exciting performances, and the crew could not have been more capable. NCL has accomplished the ultimate—the *Norway* is the greatest floating resort in the Caribbean. There are so many activities that one couple complained the ship line forgot to program any time for sleep! Another passenger spent his entire time jogging, dancing to exercise, and enjoying swimnastics; and I'm quite sure he left the cruise a far healthier person than he embarked (despite occasional indulgences in the dining room). A couple I met from Miami were already planning their twenty-fifth anniversary cruise next year (with the entire family).

The vessel is certainly its own best advertisement—from the attractive Captain Aage Hoddevik (who enjoys dramatic entrances in the dining room) to the charming and helpful room steward (born of Chinese parents on Jamaica). Everything seems to work well, and the days at sea become quite overwhelming with activity. A TV Times brings news, features, interviews, films, and exercises into the cabin from 7 a.m. on. There are three swimming pool, some 65,000 square feet of open deck space, and the usual lectures available on bridge, astrology, memory, etc. The various shops on board are tempting, indeed, and a new men's boutique has recently opened. Children seem to have their own corner and counselors, even a new video game room.

I hope the food aboard the *Norway* improves somewhat as the season progresses, although there are always plenty of alternatives. You can avoid the dining room at breakfast and lunch by eating *al fresco* in The Great Outdoor Restaurant on plastic trays. There is always room service (finger sandwiches available from 7 a.m. to 11 p.m.), or you can gorge at the soda fountain (one scoop 60¢, two scoops 80¢) for a bargain. The wine list is rather unsophisticated, and the drinks are tasty but full of sugar calories, not alcohol. This does not however seem to cramp anyone's style—especially in the Windjammer Bar around midnight!

The only serious complaint I heard aboard the *Norway* concerned the amount of walking necessary from one section to the other. As the vessel is over one thousand feet long, it is not a good choice for the less than agile (wheelchair victims fare very well, however). The size of the *Norway* also prevents her coming alongside in port, and passengers must use 88-foot tenders that hold about 400 persons. The *Norway* carries two of these 55-ton open boats in the forward section of Pool Deck, and they are lowered by cranes when needed. The system works quite efficiently because the crew and staff have been well trained.

Every Saturday, the *Norway* sails from Miami about 6 p.m. for St. Thomas, Nassau, and that Bahamian Out Island. NCL's popular Dive In program is available to *Norway* passengers as well.

★★★★★OCEANIC

Home Lines; Panamanian registry and Italian crew; built in Trieste and launched in 1965; 39,241 tons; 774 feet long; 97 feet at beam; 1,034 passengers on short cruises, 875 on long cruises; crew of 600; cruising speed of 23 knots; 10 passenger decks.

The *Oceanic* is the flagship of Home Lines and the pride of the company for excellent reason. This is an elegant, sleek, and most splendid vessel that carries her great load of passengers and crew very well. Because she was designed and built at a time when space was not yet considered a too-costly luxury, both her public rooms and staterooms are spacious and most luxurious. She has a total of 524 cabins and 22 public rooms plus a large double-swimming pool complex covered by a retractable dome—the first of its kind. In addition, the vessel is beautifully maintained and comes replete with interesting artwork that was especially created for her. In the staircase niches are fifty-two anodized aluminum and ceramic panels (with historical notes) that were created by European artists and should not be passed by without notice. Other works of art on the vessel are also of museum quality. My favorite work of art adorns the wall of the little-used Escoffier Grill and is little appreciated. Look for it!

The *Oceanic* has a record number of public rooms, of which the largest is the attractive Aegean Lounge, a gathering place for horseracing and bingo in the afternoon, after-dinner entertainment later. The lounge was completely refurbished a few years ago, and although I can do without the icicle-clad columns, the velvet chairs in red, orange, or magenta are stunning. More forward on Riviera Deck (the main public area) are the Mayfair Bar and Italian Hall, where the captain always holds his Welcome Aboard cocktail party. Aft are the even larger Skal Bar and European Observation Lounge as well as a card room, casino, writing room, and some excellent gift shops (the *Oceanic* has some of the very best on-board shops).

Belvedere, a deck of deluxe cabins with double-sized windows, separates the two main public areas. Up on Lido Deck are the twin swimming pool with magrodome. (The retractable, transparent glass roof closes automatically in bad weather.) The Montmartre Club (after-hours disco) and the Fun-O-Rama room and soda fountain for the very young set are also on Lido Deck. Forward are the Eden Roc and Escoffier Grill, used primarily for private parties and for extravaganza luncheon buffets. The Oceanic Restaurant, down on Restaurant Deck, has two seatings (early and late) with tables that handle from two to eight people. The food is excellent, and a long list of Italian wines are reasonably priced. The stewards are so attentive that if you come aboard a second time your waiter will likely still remember your face, if not your name.

While even the inside cabins are comfortable (and spacious) the vessel has some superior accommodations that many other lines have copied—the penthouse suites up on Sun Deck, with their own private terraces, one and one-half baths, and bar/refrigerator. (I hinted that double beds were more appropriate for these accommodations, but was told by the ship line that this was uneconomical. I say, forget the economics and bring in the romance—where it belongs!)

I'd rate entertainment aboard the *Oceanic* as fair to good. First-run movies appear in the two-level cinema/theater and participatory games fill the daytime hours. The evening performances at sea were not very stimulating for me, and I was relieved to have along a thousand-page novel. That was the cruise on which my husband and I threw a bottle overboard. The poem it contained was returned to us just six months later by a member of the US Navy who had found it washed ashore on the island of Eleuthera. My faith in waves was certainly restored!

★★★OCEANIC INDEPENDENCE

American Hawaii Cruises; American registry and crew; originally built in the U.S. in 1951 and originally named the Independence; 30,090 tons; 682 feet long; 89 feet at beam; 750 passengers; crew of 300; cruising speed of 17 knots; 9 passenger decks.

The former *Independence*, the flagship of American Export Lines, was a three-class vessel which carried approximately a thousand passengers across the Atlantic and on long cruises throughout the world. She has been converted into a one-class vessel accommodating approximately 750 passengers, with an all-American (30% Hawaiian) crew of just 300. From all reports, this refitting has been very successful, for passengers admire the many public areas, the 23,000 square feet of deck space, and the larger-than-usual cabins. One passenger who enjoyed the ship immensely told me the Aloha spirit was everywhere: "If you expect a deluxe cruise, you will be disappointed. But if you relax and fall into the swing of Hawaiian lifestyle, you'll love it!" He especially noted that the vessel was clean and spacious, food rated better than average, and service was good (but shaky in the dining room). The usual five meals a day are supplemented with outdoor breakfast and luncheon buffets.

The *Oceanic Independence* has 20 suites, 27 deluxe cabins, 107 outside cabins with two lower beds, 8 outside with double beds, and 6 outside with upper/lower berths. There are 141 inside cabins with 2 lower beds, 17 inside with double beds, 60 inside doubles with upper/lower berths, and 11 inside singles with lower berths. All cabins have private facilities and are definitely larger than average for cruise space. On-board facilities include two outdoor swimming pools, a full Sports Deck, Barefoot Bar overlooking the Sun Deck pool, and Latitude 20° with a glass wall over the Upper Deck pool. The Palms dining room, down on Aloha Deck, does not have sea views but is divided into smoking and non-smoking sections. What was once another dining room on Main Deck is now a conference center, booked in advance on many cruises for groups who wish to combine business with pleasure. Midships on Promenade Deck is the Independence Lounge, while the huge Pacific Showplace (for evening entertainment) and the Commodore's Terrace are aft. The Hunt breakfast is served on deck, and morning bouillon and afternoon tea are available in the Parisian-style Sidewalk Cafe on Upper Deck, which also houses shops and the children's playroom. A cinema is down on Coral Deck.

Life aboard the *Oceanic Independence*, described as casual and "very Hawaiian-style," means that women do not have to pack anything more formal than a muumuu and men may show up in aloha shirts or sports jackets (no tie is necessary) for dinner. If you want to learn the hula, take part in a daily dance lesson. Two seatings for all meals precede nightly entertainment in the Pacific Showplace. First-run movies are offered nightly in the theater.

Once each week the *Oceanic Independence* departs Aloha Tower and sails slowly around the islands of Molokai, Lanai, and Maui all day Sunday. The vessel spends all day Monday in Hilo and then sails around the other side of the Big Island of Hawaii to dock off the coast of Kona (passengers must tender in from here). All Wednesday is spent at Kahului on Maui, and Thursday and Friday are devoted to Nawiliwili on Kauai. Return to Honolulu Saturday morning. A full range of shore excursions is available at every island, including Hilo volcanic tours, Maui to Hana drives, and a three-hour Kauai luau. However, as mentioned before, many passengers prefer to order rental cars in advance and have them waiting at the dock. If you are in an adventurous mood, I suggest you do this, but plan ahead.

At this writing, American Cruise Lines of Haddam, Connecticut has brought suit in United States District Court against American Hawaii Cruises over the intended name change of the *Oceanic Independence* to the *Independence*. American Cruise Lines has had a vessel named *Independence* since 1976 and claims it has spent some $4 million advertising the product and the cruises. According to the suit filed, "the renaming of the *Oceanic Independence* to the *Independence* affects the business reputation of American Cruise Lines and diminishes the distinctive character and quality of both American Cruise Lines and its vessel, the *Independence*."

★★★OCEANUS

Epirotiki Lines; Greek registry and crew; formerly known as Ancona; rebuilt in 1978 and relaunched as Oceanus; 14,000 tons; 488 feet long; 65 feet at beam; 500 passengers; crew of 200; cruising speed of 16 knots; 6 passenger decks.

The *Oceanus* is Epirotiki's latest acquisition, and she was completely refurbished for her rebirth by the line's favorite architect/interior designer, Maurice Bailey. The new design includes artworks that reflect the name of the vessel. Bailey has made what I consider a pleasant but not deluxe ship, with 188 outside and 68 inside cabins, all with private facilities and fold-over beds for use as daytime sofas. The public areas, which I consider limited, include only one large lounge, the Modern Odyssey Lounge, on Apollo Deck. A smaller gathering place, situated one deck above, on Jupiter, is called the Old Athens Club, and lies adjacent to a bar and the Selene Discotheque as well as to a shopping gallery. Outside on deck is a small swimming pool. The Byzantine Dining Room, located on Dionysus Deck, has two seatings for all the Greek/European meals.

During the summer months (May through September) through 1983, the *Oceanus* is on charter to Lauro Lines for fourteen-day cruises from Genoa to Naples, Alexandria, Port Said, Haifa, Kuşadasi, Istanbul, Piraeus, and Capri. During the winter season the vessel is on charter to other European interests for Caribbean cruises.

★★★ORION

K-Lines Hellenic Cruises; Greek registry and crew; originally built in 1952 and formerly named the Achilleus; refurbished in 1969 and 1978; 6,200 tons; 414 feet long; 55 feet at beam; 243 passengers; crew of 125; cruising speed of 16.5 knots; 6 passenger decks.

The *Orion* is the flagship of the K-Lines fleet—that is, until the *Constellation* was launched. This ship has a good reputation for comfort, with one of the friendliest crew in the Greek islands. A discerning friend who sailed aboard the *Orion* recently, on the Greece/Israel/Egypt cruise, returned raving about the itinerary, the fine service, and the warm feeling throughout the ship. After the long, hot days of touring (especially in Port Said and Ashdod), coming back aboard the *Orion* "was like being with the family again," she said. This is the best compliment a ship can receive, especially one that does not pretend to be world class. For if the crew does not make you feel welcome, you may as well get off at the first port of call . . . and stay off.

Two of the *Orion's* best features are her small size and her relatively spacious cabins. She carries only 243 passengers in 128 all-outside cabins with private facilities. All feature a bathtub and television. Many can also accommodate a third person on a sofa-bed or in an upper berth. All the public rooms are on Lido Deck (except the Athenian Disco on Diana Deck), which has the large Athenian Lounge, Garden Lounge, smoking room, Pan Bar, card room, and Olympia Dining Room. Lido Deck also features the swimming pool and deck games area. Food service is Greek but caters to American taste.

The *Orion* sails every Tuesday from Piraeus, between April 14 and October 27, for Port Said, Ashdod, Rhodes, Kuşadasi, and Patmos—an excellent itinerary. I highly recommend this vessel.

★★★ORPHEUS

Epirotiki Lines; Greek flag and crew; originally built in 1952 as the Munster; rebuilt in Greece in 1969 and renamed the Orpheus; 5,000 tons; 353 feet long; 51 feet at beam; 300 passengers; crew of 139; cruising speed of 15 knots; 6 passenger decks.

Until recently on long-term charter to R. K. Swan (who prefers the *Jason* for this year's programs) the *Orpheus* has returned to the Epirotiki family. A new schedule features eleven two-week cruises for the *Orpheus*, from Venice, Genoa, and Amsterdam. The first two sailings from Venice call at Dubrovnik and Corfu, transit the Corinth Canal, then sail amongst the lesser-visited Greek Islands before skirting the Peloponessus and returning to the Adriatic. A cruise from Venice to Genoa calls at North African ports, and is followed by a two-week Genoa-to-Amsterdam repositioning. With Amsterdam as a base, the *Orpheus* will make three cruises to the Norwegian fjords and one to the Northern Capitals of the Baltic. Then the vessel reverses the program, and three final sailings are offered between Amsterdam and Piraeus.

The *Orpheus* holds over three hundred passengers, if the inside cabins are used. Accommodations are not plush, but very comfortable and cheerfully decorated. Public rooms include the Argonaut Lounge, the Lounge of the Muses, and the Jason Taverna where buffet luncheons are served. The Dionysus dining room serves some tasty Greek-style dishes and wines. There is also a small library on board.

★★★★PACIFIC NORTHWEST EXPLORER

Exploration Cruise Lines; American registry and crew; built in Warren, Rhode Island, and launched in 1981; 97 tons; 144 feet long; 28 feet at beam; 80 passengers; crew of 16; cruising speed of 12 knots; 4 passenger decks.

The young and innovative Exploration Cruise Lines took delivery of its first vessel, the *Pacific Northwest Explorer*, in January 1981 to introduce unusual cruises through Northwest and Canadian waterways. Because the vessel is only 144 feet long and has a draft of 7½ feet, shorelines often bypassed can be visited comfortably by passengers. Bow landings are often possible, and disembarkation is via a forward-thrust ladder. (Only the agile need apply, here). As if this were not enough adventure, the vessel carries rubber rafts for use as service launches.

The yachtlike vessel has forty cabins, all with private facilities. The Vista View Lounge and Explorer dining room seat all passengers, and life aboard is casual and congenial. Hearty American meals are served family-style and a selection of wines is available for purchase. The ship's bar is located next to the player piano in the glass-enclosed main lounge. But, most passengers find little time on board during the four- and five-day cruises departing Seattle from June through September.

★★★PEARL OF SCANDINAVIA

Pearl Cruises of Scandinavia; Bahamian registry; Scandinavian and American officers; European hotel management; Filipino crew; originally built in 1967 in Finland and named Finnstar; rebuilt in 1982 and rechristened the Pearl of Scandinavia; 17,400 tons; 502 feet long; 66 feet at beam; 473 passengers; crew of 200; cruising speed of 20 knots; 9 passenger decks.

The *Pearl of Scandinavia* inaugurated a new and exciting program in the Far East on June 5, 1982, and from all reports is doing very well, indeed. Prior to her new life, the vessel underwent a $15 million renovation and conversion in Aalborg, Denmark. Fourteen new luxury suites were added to the top deck, just behind the bridge. All other cabins were upgraded, colorfully decorated and furnished in Scandinavian style. This is a top-class vessel and all cabins feature refrigerator, multichannel music, individually controlled air-conditioning and heating, and telephone; and many have both tub and shower in the bathroom. There are seven different floor plans available for both inside/outside cabins, singles and doubles. The majority of cabins are on Main Deck and A-Deck, with a few forward and aft on B-Deck. In addition to the top suites, other luxury cabins can be found forward of the officer's quarters on Captain's Deck and in the forward section of Promenade Deck. Only one cabin, #156, has a separate bedroom. There is round-the-clock service in all accommodation categories.

The vessel is compact and the public areas are more than adequate for the passenger complement. A Veranda Lounge, outdoor bar, and sun deck are located on the Promenade Deck. Below, on Salon Deck are the Galaxy Lounge, dining room, card room, ballroom with bar, and outdoor swimming pool. There is also a small shopping area (Main Deck), hairdresser (C-Deck), and indoor pool with sauna, plus a small cinema on D-Deck. Just enough space for comfort, not too much to get yourself lost. There are two passenger elevators and the vessel is equipped with gyro fin stabilizers, should the need arise during monsoon time in the South China Sea area.

Four months of the year (mid-January through March, mid-November and December), the *Pearl of Scandinavia* sails from Singapore on fourteen-day cruises to Malaysia and Indonesia. Because of her convenient draft (less than six meters), the vessel can call in such places as Nias in Indonesia so passengers can visit the Stone Age warrior culture of the Nias Batak people. The vessel also offers a series of cruises between Singapore and Hong Kong, and the China Explorers Cruises from spring through fall months. All rates include roundtrip economy air transportation via Pan Am from the West Coast (or the equivalent fare in credit and you make your own arrangements). The China Explorers Cruise also includes all land arrangements in the People's Republic of China. All other shore excursions are optional and sold on an individual basis.

★★★★ + to ★★★★★ + QUEEN ELIZABETH 2

Cunard Line; British registry and crew; built on the River Clyde and launched in May 1969; named after Her Majesty Queen Elizabeth II; 67,107 tons; 963 feet long; 105 feet at beam; 1,815 passengers; crew of 1,000; cruising speed of 28.5 knots; 13 passenger decks.

The *Queen* is back. Long live the *Queen!* Cunard's famed flagship, *Queen Elizabeth 2*, had a short but dramatic role in the so-called Falkland Islands crisis and returned to service in August of 1982 with a $10 million facelift, an amenable crew, and unprecedented sentiment from both sides of the Atlantic. According to Ralph Bahna, Cunard's chief executive officer, a replacement for this last of the great liners would cost approximately $400 million; therefore, a commitment to "keep pace without compromise" and launch the vessel into the 1980s has been made.

The "new" QE2 has a pearly gray and white exterior, with the familiar orange-and-black funnel. Interior refurbishment includes new decor in the Queen's Grill/Lounge area, and the transformation of the former Q4 hideaway into Club Lido. This space has been opened onto the Quarter Deck with smoky-glass windows and a plastic bubble for dining and dancing within view of the stars. A new half-million-dollar kitchen has been installed, and elegant Golden Door Spa has gone to sea! Located on Six Deck, the spa is under the direction of perfectionist Deborah Szekely, founder of the California-based original. A well-trained staff guides passengers daily (no charge) through exercise routines in the pool or cheerful mirrored-space, suggests one of three Jacuzzis for relaxation, and oversees a special salad bar at Club Lido buffets. (There are also low-calorie luncheon and dinner suggestions on every menu). Although the QE2 is not the first to follow the physical-fitness-at-sea trend, here is where the style is!

With a crew of almost one thousand, it is no mean feat to carry out the daily chores of operating this superliner. There are a total of 946 cabins (which can accommodate over 1,900 passengers in a pinch) and some number near to fourteen public rooms, four swimming pools, four restaurants, and a dozen different watering holes. In addition to the new spa at sea, there are a Player's Club (casino), a fully operating hospital with cute nurses known as "sisters," a two-tiered theater in use several times daily, children's playroom, kennel, car park, and plenty of open deck space. (Fit and trim have always been golden words aboard this vessel, and the youthful sixty-ish Eric Mason has been leading passengers through his jogging and yoga courses for years.)

There are three separate and distinct classes of accommodations and service aboard the *Queen*, dependent entirely upon the number of zeros you can bear to write. Mere mortals dine in Tables of the World and play in the Double Up/ Down Room (where all the action is, anyway). Tables of the World seats 800 persons, but has been divided into different "theme" areas to ameliorate that Madison Square Garden atmosphere. The food here is considered very good and there are two seatings for all meals.

First Class passengers dine in the slightly-less-vast Colombia Restaurant on Quarter Deck, graced by an enormous silver loving cup presented by the city of Boston to Samuel Cunard in 1840. (The cup was only relocated in a second-hand shop several years ago and certainly deserves better respect than being stuffed with a hideous artificial floral arrangement). Nonetheless, the menu here is on a par with other five-star vessels and Cunard boasts a 20,000-bottle wine cellar. To the whim of your maitre d', ordering "off the menu" may be encouraged—and can become a habit.

Super Class (my term) passengers (from D grade through Penthouse Suites overlooking the bridge) play where they like, but meal service is exclusive to the grill rooms. Here, the maitres d' treat guests like minor royalty (indeed, there may be some seated nearby), suggest exotic dishes to suit one's fancy, and serve an abundance of caviar nightly. (Cunard claims it is one of the world's largest buyers of caviar, consuming over five percent of the total annual production)! While the food and service in both grills is equal to any top-rated European-style restaurant, many prefer the more intimate (80 person) Princess Grill. Decorated in bordello-red plush velvet and reached by its own elevator (if you can ever find it), the Princess offers romance, full sea-view windows and a dignified double-height space.

The recently refurbished Queen's Grill (about 180 persons) has a greater mix of fellow Super Class passengers; and the tender care of one's silver-plated stomach more than offsets the inelegant space and the view into your very own lifeboat. (If you happen to find David, Norman, Georges, and Carlos in your corner, however, chances are you would never consider dining elsewhere). The Queen's Grill is perfect for single travelers, couples, and families, especially those who wish to partake in an adjoining conversation from time to time. It also has a super attractive lounge for quietude and cocktails, far away from the crowd.

Cunard has spent considerable effort in revising its food service and the results are commendable. According to Chief Chef John Bainbridge, menus vary according to the passenger mix and itinerary. A Japanese chef arrives on board during the long Pacific cruise; game and other hearty dishes are stored for our English cousins; Americans prefer less rich sauces and smaller portions; and there is even a store of some 50 lbs. of dog biscuits for canine friends on the transatlantic crossings!

Mention should be made of another new convenience for passengers, the QE2 Passport, which enables you to sign—right up to disembarkation—for beverages, laundry, massage, telephone, etc. by establishing credit with any of several cards. A copy of the itemized account will be sent to your home, and the total charge appears on your credit card bill. Photographs, shops, flowers, hair, and medical (a seasick shot is $10) are payable separately.

Cunard touts the QE2 as the "greatest ship in the world" (and even Norman Vincent Peale says so in his Sunday sermon); certainly, there is no other vessel afloat that offers so much in itinerary and excitement. She even has the highest price tag on two super suites: the Queen Mary and Queen Elizabeth each sell for $275,000 during the three-month Pacific and Orient cruise. But a Super Class crossing is the memorable experience, and the QE2 is scheduled for 24 transatlantic sailings in 1983 as well as some three-day "party cruises" and a few longer calls in European ports. Transatlantic passengers reap great benefits by flying one-way via British Airways. Cunard also offers irresistible rates at its famous Ritz Hotel in Picadilly as well as the Bristol on Berkeley Street and the International.

★★★REGINA MARIS

Deilmann Reederei; Singaporean registry and international crew; originally built in 1966 for about 300 passengers; rebuilt in 1980 in Germany as a first-class vessel; 5,800 tons; 387 feet long; 54 feet at beam; 190 passengers; crew of 160; cruising speed of 17.5 knots; 5 passenger decks.

This small vessel, owned by a German firm, was recently redesigned for an exclusive passenger complement—less than 200 people catered by a crew of about 160. The vessel was destined for North American waters, but was trouble-plagued for most of the past summer. The new cruise company that leased the vessel was sued over a name-similarity and was forced to regroup. The *Regina Maris* sailed in the St. Lawrence under the aegis of a general agent, but the Canadian government seized the gambling equipment with the claim that her casino operation was illegal!

The *Regina Maris* boasts larger than average cabins (11' by 13' excluding bathrooms and closet space), and approximately 80 percent are on the outside. The passenger/crew ratio is supposed to guarantee around-the-clock room service. The owner, Peter Deilmann, is proud of the fact that the vessel was originally constructed for 450 passengers, rebuilt later for about 250, then refurbished last year for about 190. Officers are German, with a German and Filipino service staff.

There are six spacious suites on Boat Deck, along with the Monte Carlo piano bar aft and the main lounge area in the forward section. The Casino Royale lounge is located just below on Riviera Deck, with the dining room which accommodates all passengers at one seating. The ship also has a fresh water (sic) swimming pool, healthclub and sauna, casino, and an array of shops.

There is talk that the *Regina Maris* may be cruising in South American waters in 1983. But, you never know for sure.

☆☆☆RHAPSODY

Paquet French Cruises; Bahamian registry and international crew; built in Holland in 1957 and sailed as Statendam until 1982; refurbished and renamed Rhapsody by Paquet; 24,500 tons; 642 feet long; 79 feet at beam; 800 plus passengers; crew of about 400; cruising speed of 19 knots; 9 passenger decks.

This is the former *Statendam*, a much-respected vessel that sailed for Holland America for a quarter-century. Anyone who has ever been aboard the former *Statendam* has very pleasant memories (as I have), especially if it took place in the good old days of transatlantic trade. Because Holland America has two new vessels arriving on line in the next two years, the company sold the *Statendam* to Paquet who immediately renamed her the *Rhapsody* (with no explanation). How much has been spent on the refurbishing is a mystery, but Paquet has renamed some of the decks and most of the public rooms. The former Aquarius dining room is now called the Cordon Bleu restaurant (and whether it lives up to this illustrious name is anyone's guess), the Stuyvesant Lounge has been renamed Rhapsody and the Hudson Lounge/Disco is a combination of the Can Can Bar and American in Paris Lounge. Most other areas have remained the same. Paquet has added Captain Jean M. Guillou, but the ship's Bahamian registry allows a mixed crew (mainly from the Caribbean). The menu will be mainly French-inspired and wine parties will be featured often. (A No Tipping Policy is obviously no longer in effect.)

The *Rhapsody* began her new life, French-style, with seven-day cruises from Miami on November 21, 1982. The itinerary features calls at Playa del Carmen, Cozumel, Grand Cayman and Ocho Rios. Then, from May through September, the *Rhapsody* sails from Vancouver. Fourteen-day Westbound/ Eastbound Panama Canal cruises are offered twice a year, in May and October. Paquet French Cruises has offered mostly free air fare in the past and may be continuing this into the next season.

★★★ROMANZA

Chandris, Inc.; Panamanian registry, Greek and Indian crew; built in 1939 and formerly named the Aurelia; refurbished in 1971; 7,538 tons; 488 feet long; 60 feet at beam; 600 passengers; crew of 250; cruising speed of 15.5 knots.

Of all the vessels Chandris operates, I think the *Romanza* is the most charming and has the atmosphere of a real cruise ship. Her diminutive size and small number of passengers make her popular and fun, especially with younger Europeans. The ship has 137 outside and 160 inside cabins, all with private facilities (shower and toilet). Most of the accommodations are designed for two berths; only fifteen inside cabins are sold as four-berth, and thirty-five others on Capri Deck can accommodate a third or fourth person. The public areas feature four bars, a large lounge, card room, casino, discotheque, theater, children's playroom, swimming pool, and dining room (for two seatings at all meals). The atmosphere and crew throughout the vessel are all Greek, with the exception of Indian stewards in the cabins.

From May 16 through the October 10 sailing the *Romanza* departs every Saturday from Venice for Dubrovnik, Corfu, Heraklion, Kuşadasi, Patmos, and Piraeus. The cruises are also sold as seven-day itineraries from Piraeus with embarkation/disembarkation on Thursdays from May 21 through the October 8.

★★★★ROTTERDAM

Holland America Cruises; Netherland Antilles registry, Dutch officers, and Indonesian crew; originally built in the Netherlands in 1959 and christened by former Queen Juliana; 38,000 tons; 748 feet long; 94 feet at beam; 1,050 passengers (short cruises), 850 passengers (long cruises); crew of 560; cruising speed of 21 knots; 10 passenger decks.

They don't build ships like the *Rotterdam* anymore. Her sleek black and white hull exudes confidence and comfort and a seaworthiness that is hard to find these days. She has an Old World charm that grew on me, even though I thought she got left behind in the beauty and glamour department. However, this vessel has some very fine features and a very loyal following, especially on long cruises. My friends Karen and Hugo spent their honeymoon aboard her, on a three-month Around the World voyage. Karen is especially sentimental about this ship and still becomes misty-eyed when she discusses the food, the friendly Indonesian crew, the first-rate entertainment, and the fine shore briefings. Woe to another cruise that does not approach the standard Karen has set for the *Rotterdam*'s global voyage!

Although no great beauty on the inside the *Rotterdam* has some wonderful public areas, and you can get rather lost from forward to aft. You enter the vessel via Main Deck, near the front office and beauty parlor. Two flights up is Promenade Deck, which extends from the vast swimming pool area to the 450-seat theater in the forward section. In between are the pleasant Lido Terrace, a large Lido Restaurant for breakfast and buffet luncheons, a card/game room, the Lynbaan shopping center, the Ocean Bar, and the Queens Lounge with a bust of Juliana surveying all those who enter. One deck up are two nightclubs, the Ambassador Room and the Ritz Carlton, the latter of which has an elegant winding staircase up to a terrace and open deck area. But one cannot bypass the smoking room, the Tropic Bar, more shops, and a pleasant theater balcony that seats 160 passengers. The dining rooms down on B-Deck are called Odyssey and La Fontaine. In the tradition of vessels designed for the transatlantic run, these dining rooms do not have a sea view, but they are very well planned and comfortable. The vessel also has indoor swimming pool/sauna/massage areas, casino, and self-service laundry and ironing facilities.

The *Rotterdam* has 304 outside cabins and 246 inside, all with private facilities. While not glamorous by my standards, the accommodations are sturdy, functional, and spacious—nothing tacky nor prefab about them. The crew is eager to please, friendly, and forever smiling, offering gracious service. Holland America runs its own training school in Djakarta for crew aboard three of its vessels, and does a fine job. Although all Holland America ships have a no-tipping policy on board, many passengers on long cruises do tip their room and dining room stewards to show appreciation for extra-special service. And no one turns away such gratuities. But if any member of the crew were to solicit them, he or she could be fired and sent home.

Entertainment aboard the *Rotterdam* is one of her finest features. Whether on long or short cruises, the vessel always has top show and nightclub acts. Experts also come on board from time to time to teach passengers the latest in bridge, backgammon, and even diet tricks (such as the Slimways cruises). On the Around the World voyage a number of interesting personalities sail for a time to lecture on this and that (as they do on all the vessels making this global voyage) to help break up the days at sea. Prominent people on past world cruises included Moshe Dayan of Israel, Ivor Richard of Great Britain, Fei Yiming of the Chinese People's Congress, and a former CIA director. Not bad for rubbing elbows on the high seas. During the official visit of Queen Beatrix and Prince Claus, to honor the two centuries of American/Dutch relations, the *Rotterdam* was the site of a state dinner. Honored guests joined the Queen and her consort on board for an elegant, many-course meal as well as a sail around Manhattan and fireworks over Battery Park. The April 1982 party was a great success, and one Holland America official called it the "most expensive Circle Line cruise in history"!

The *Rotterdam* heralds the New Year with an 82-day Silver Jubilee World Cruise, a global voyage designed to surpass any other on record! Silver mementoes, a special book written as the cruise progresses, a song composed especially for the occasion as well as a new dance, gourmet innovations and complimentary vintage wines between Honolulu and Hong Kong, a Silver Cruise Ball and the drawing of a Rolls Royce Silver Spirit are all part of the celebration of Holland America's twenty-fifth world cruise. The 28,700-mile voyage will visit seventeen countries, calling at twenty-one different ports.

Following a two-week Easter cruise, the *Rotterdam* sails for the West Coast and the summer season in Alaska/Canada beside the *Nieuw Amsterdam*. Both vessels will sail from Vancouver under the aegis of Westours, a sister company to Holland America Cruises under the tourism group of Holland America Line U.S.A. The *Rotterdam* will sail on one-week cruises from Vancouver, beginning in June.

☆☆☆☆ROYAL ODYSSEY

Royal Cruise Line; Greek crew and registry; originally built in 1964 and former names were Hanseatic, Shalom, and most recently Doric; refitted and refurbished in 1982 and relaunched as Royal Odyssey; 25,500 tons; 627 feet long; 81 feet at beam; 806 passengers; crew of 350; cruising speed of 21 knots; 9 passenger decks.

Just completing her first season for Royal Cruise Line, the *Royal Odyssey* should prove to be as popular as her sister ship, the *Golden Odyssey*. The Royal Cruise concept is attention to detail, good organization in itineraries and air-sea programs, and excellent care of passengers. The vessel was completely refitted early in 1982 with interior designs by Greek artist Michael Katzourakis, who created colorful schemes throughout. Fabrics Katzourakis designed were woven in Belgium by the house of Van Havere. English Crossley carpets were laid, and Brown Jordan rattan with custom upholstery now graces the glass-enclosed Calypso Lounge making it cheerful by day and intimate as a nightclub.

The multitiered Odyssey Lounge, where theatrical entertainment occurs in the evening, has an Italian parquet dance floor designed by David Legno, as well as a reportedly spectacular lighting system. Both indoor and outdoor pools have been refurbished and tiled with French Briare ceramics. The Ambrosia Dining Room has been opened up, with windows to the sea, and Greek-designed tapestries and mirrored abstracts grace landings and corridors. All staterooms are accented with silkscreen panels, and even the Ice Cream Parlor has been brightened.

The *Royal Odyssey* now boasts a total of 405 cabins: 22 superior deluxe suites; 33 junior suites; 279 outside cabins; and 71 inside cabins. Bathrooms have been modernized and many have tubs as well as showers. All cabins have individual air-conditioning, American electrical outlets, twin beds, full vanities with long mirror, music, and telephone for 24-hour room service. In addition to the four lounges, the vessel is equipped with five bars, card room casino, library and writing room, theater, gymnasium, sauna, and hairdresser. She is well organized and spacious enough for the full complement of passengers. There are two sittings in the dining room: luncheon at 12 noon (main) and 1:30 (late); dinner at 6:45 (main) and 8:45 (late). Luncheon buffets are also served poolside, and a midnight buffet begins around 11:30 p.m. for those that feel deprived.

The *Royal Odyssey* winters in the Caribbean from December to March along with the *Golden Odyssey*. Both vessels offer a number of air-sea cruises in the Mediterranean from late spring to early fall. While the *Golden Odyssey* sails around the Black Sea, the *Royal Odyssey* plans to repeat popular cruises inaugurated last year from London (Tilbury) to the Land of the Norsemen.

★★★★★ + ROYAL VIKING SEA/ROYAL VIKING SKY

Royal Viking Line; Norwegian registry and European crew; 28,000 tons; both built in Helsinki and both launched in 1973; both rebuilt in Bremerhaven (the Sky in 1982 and the Sea in 1983), with a 93-foot midsection added and returned to service the same year; 725 passengers each; crew of 400 plus; 674 feet long; 83 feet at beam; cruising speed of 21 knots; 7 passenger decks.

By June 10, 1983, when the *Sea* returns to service from Southampton, all three Royal Viking Line vessels will have been "stretched" from their former 500-passenger size to just over 700, with an additional 6,000 tons of space and 93 feet in length. Although these enlargements have altered the shape and ambiance of the vessels, the philosophy behind a Royal Viking Line cruise experience has not been changed. The *Sea* and *Sky* are very similar in appearance and atmosphere, and it is often difficult to tell at first glance which ship is which. And, as both vessels alternate in their cruising itineraries throughout the world, it doesn't really matter which one you choose.

With the renovations, nine new penthouse suites have been added as well as a new outdoor pool and Lido bar on Sky Deck. The elegant Discovery/Windjammer rooms with their plush seating and dramatic views of the ocean or port remain the same in the forward section of each vessel. All suites have separate sitting areas, partitioned bed and vanity rooms, two bathrooms, refrigerator, and closed-circuit television. The Scandinavia Deck dining rooms, with their oversized windows on the sea, have been enlarged to still offer one-seating meals (which I consider the true sign of a first-class vessel). Other new features include a small chapel, a private room off the dining room for cocktail parties, and enlarged reception and shopping areas. It is a credit to Royal Viking Line that "bigger has actually become better" in both spaciousness and service.

There is plenty of closet space in all cabin categories, and you truly need not only an extensive wardrobe on these vessels but also the correct apparel. As a friend who deals daily with the rich and beautiful at her glamorous spa in California once said, "One must dress right on Royal Viking Line." Many of the bathrooms (with full tubs) are a touch too small with awkwardly placed doors, but it's all a matter of opinion. Service is excellent and full breakfasts in bed include eggs, cheese, and meats, along with the usual accoutrements of fruit and coffee. A sense of humor, however, is not often found aboard here, and I feel that the stewardesses should introduce themselves to passengers and make a few pleasantries. (I left a tip on one cruise for someone I had never met, although I appreciated a job well done.)

There are plenty of activities offered daily aboard all three vessels, although bingo always seems to be the most popular. Occasional speakers, self-acclaimed experts in their fields, offer enrichment lectures on many cruises. Expect to find authors touting their own works, although few of them push the product. If you buy the shore excursions, well-written briefs on each port will be presented. Otherwise, ask the librarian (if you can find same) for some good background material, or bring along your own as I always do.

In 1983, the *Royal Viking Sea* makes three trans-Panama Canal cruises between San Francisco and Port Everglades, then sails to Bremerhaven on February 28 for her "stretching." She returns to service on June 10 from Southampton to Copenhagen, visiting the Northern Capitals of Europe and Russia. On June 24 and July 8, she sails from Copenhagen to the North Cape and back, and then does another Russia/Europe cruise on July 22. (This schedule has been planned for passengers who wish to take back-to-back cruises with different itineraries). On August 5, the vessel offers a North Cape/Iceland/Canada/New England cruise of 21 days, ending in New York. On August 26 and September 9, the *Sea* sails from New York on fourteen-day New England/Canada cruises, then departs New York on September 23 (from Port Everglades on September 26) for a trans-Panama Canal/Caribbean/Mexico cruise, ending in her home port of San Francisco. On October 13, the *Sea* offers a 47-day Around South America sailing that ends in Port Everglades. On November 29, she departs Florida for an 18-day trans-Panama Canal cruise to the West Coast. A Christmas/New Year 1984 cruise departs the West Coast on December 17/18 for Tahiti, the South Sea Islands, and Hawaii.

The *Royal Viking Sky* (newly stretched) sails from Port Everglades on January 13 for a complete 88-day Around the World Cruise. She returns to Florida on April 11 and departs that day for Piraeus. From April 25 through the May 23 sailing, the *Sky* offers fourteen-day cruises in the Adriatic. On June 6, she departs Greece through the Mediterranean to reposition in Copenhagen. From July 1 through the August 12 sailing, the *Sky* offers North Cape and Russia/Europe on the same alternate itineraries available aboard the *Sea*. The August 12 Russia/Europe cruise ends in Southampton, and the August 26 cruise from Southampton through the Mediterranean ends in Piraeus. From September 8 through the October 30 sailing, the *Sky* cruises to the Black Sea and Greek Isles, or to the Holy Land and Mediterranean. A 24-day cruise from Piraeus to Florida visits ports along the Mediterranean and North Africa. From Port Everglades, the *Sky* completes her 1983 season with a seven-day Caribbean cruise on December 6 and a 28-day Christmas and New Year cruise.

★★★★★ + ROYAL VIKING STAR

Royal Viking Line; Norwegian registry and European crew; 28,000 tons; built in Helsinki especially for RVL and launched in 1972; renovated in Bremerhaven in 1981 with 93-foot mid-section added; 725 passengers; crew of 400 plus; 674 feet long; 83 feet at beam; cruising speed of 21 knots; 7 passenger decks.

As first-launched of the three-vessel Royal Viking fleet, the *Star* has always been the innovator (although no vessel is considered the flagship). She is just enough different in concept to stand slightly apart from her sister ships, the *Sea* and *Sky*. As the first-stretched of the fleet, the *Star* has become a real beauty of the sea. Nine penthouse suites, a new swimming pool, and 202-passenger Venus Lounge were added to Sky Deck, which before could only boast the very popular Stella Polaris Room (with its wonderful leather lounge chairs and bar with dramatic ocean views).

The nine penthouse suites have a separate bedroom and vanity room, private wood-deck verandas and spacious sitting areas. There is plenty of closet space (one needs a considerable and very chic wardrobe for these cruises), and each suite has refrigerator, television, and two bathrooms. Four of the suites also have convertible sofa-beds for a third person. The passage from the twin beds into the sitting area, however, was designed for midgets. Considering the fact that these suites sell for approximately $600 per person, per day, and that passengers who can afford such rates are often less agile (and occasionally less slim) than the rest of us, I wonder about the design. Perhaps this will be modified in the *Sea* and *Sky* renovations.

The *Royal Viking Star* departs San Francisco for a 45-day tour of the South Sea Islands, New Zealand, and Australia. Upon her return, she sails for the South Pacific, ending in Kobe. Then she begins a new program of fourteen-day China/Orient cruises between Kobe and Hong Kong. The *Star* next departs Kobe for an eighteen-day trans-Pacific cruise to San Francisco and begins a series of six twelve-day cruises to Alaska/Canada. In the fall the vessel returns from annual drydocking with a four-day party cruise to Ensenada, then makes four complete transits of the Panama Canal to Florida and return. The season's final sailing from Port Everglades calls also in New Orleans to embark passengers, and returns to San Francisco long after the New Year bells have rung.

The Venus Lounge is the least impressive of the public rooms aboard the *Star*, but it is utilized primarily for card and bingo games and late-night entertainment. Ten additional deluxe cabins, which feature a sitting area, refrigerator, and television, have been added to Promenade Deck. The Lido Bar now serves drinks, hamburgers, and sandwiches outside to sunbathers who cannot trouble themselves to walk down a few decks to the more elaborate luncheon buffet by the larger pool.

Otherwise, business is as usual aboard the *Star*. The dining room seats all passengers at one time, but is well designed with its own sections so that you need never feel caught in a cavernous space. The midnight buffet (cold meats and cheese) is laid out in the Stella Polaris Room, but few people admit hunger pains after the lovely and well-served dinners that now feature more *nouvelle cuisine*. Entertainment is offered nightly in the Bergen Lounge, but the room empties out quickly (about 10:30 p.m.), as most passengers prefer their beauty rest to carousing. The Galaxy (night) Club is the scene of officers relaxing plus a very few of the younger set aboard staying after hours.

The *Star* also boasts a fine theater for first-run films on Mediterranean Deck, a small chapel on Pacific Deck, beauty/barber shops, a hospital, launderette, enlarged reception area and shops, saunas and a recommended masseuse. The Scandinavian decor is very pleasant and cared for lovingly, and the cabins (even suites) are average size. With the re-evaluation of the lower-priced categories, cruises aboard the *Star* are no longer so far out of line in the marketplace.

★★★★★ + SAGAFJORD

Norwegian American Cruises; Norwegian registry and Northern European crew; launched in 1965; 25,000 tons; 629 feet long; 82 feet at beam; 505 passengers; crew of 350; cruising speed of 20 knots; 10 passenger decks.

The *Sagafjord* is a great lady of the sea—some say without equal. While her physical beauty is certainly surpassed by the Royal Viking fleet, there is a special quality of contentment aboard this cruise ship. In addition to top-grade food and service, there is an obviously well-treated crew that shows concern and warmth for all passengers. Room stewardesses, especially, are a smiling lot and many are married to other crew members. Cabins are kept spotless, and the company cares enough to send along a bottle of the bubbly for that Bon Voyage sip (usually German sparkling wine, although long-time passengers get the real thing).

Following a $12 million refurbishing a few years ago, under the direction of Norwegian designer Njal R. Eide, the *Sagafjord* has a more modern look bestowed upon its cabins, and several Sun Deck terraced staterooms were added. The rooms are small but truly elegant; twelve doubles and a single all have private verandas and a separate sitting area. Two panoramic suites, Saga (101) and Vista (102), have separate sitting rooms and a better view than that from the bridge. All other cabins aboard the *Sagafjord* are spacious, and ninety percent have full bathtubs (plus showers). There are a total of 240 outside cabins and 32 inside cabins.

Promenade Deck is the location of the main public rooms, but most of the action takes place around the swimming pool and Lido Bar on a sunny day. Even on a not so sunny day, you can always get a "Stabilizer" (half port wine/half brandy) to settle the stomach. Morning bouillon, luncheon buffets, afternoon tea, and a midnight snack are all served in the Veranda Cafe looking out on the pool area. Lectures, evening entertainment, and the Captain's Welcome Aboard are held in the Ballroom midships. Often, the Fjord Club Cocktail Party for repeat passengers is held here as well, because the guest numbers are so great. The North Cape Bar and Garden Lounge are also favorite places to pass the time, and the waiters will always remember your preference. Club Polaris opens nightly at 11 p.m. and presents a show just before midnight.

The dining room on Main Deck has a dramatic double staircase entrance (very tempting to slide down the bannister)! The area is spacious enough so passengers can exchange tables from time to time. It was, however, designed when everyone dined "down under" and hence has no glorious sea views like the *Vistafjord*. Food is Continental, Nouvelle, Scandinavian—whatever you wish—and the wine list is quite worthy. Other ship-board amenities include a small casino, library, fitness center with sauna and indoor pool, and small launderette (unfortunately tucked down on C-Deck). A most comfortable theater on Veranda Deck shows first-run feature films and plays host to visiting lecturers.

The *Sagafjord* begins every new year with the Great World Cruise. The vessel departs Port Everglades for the Panama Canal, Galapagos Islands, South Pacific islands, New Zealand and Australia, and the Philippines. The ship arrives in Hong Kong and all continuing passengers disembark for a four-night stay at the superb Regent Hotel. During this time, a gala dinner dance will be hosted by the company president. (And the *Sagafjord* enters a local drydock for an annual check-up.) The vessel sails again for Port Everglades with stops including Singapore, Bombay, Suez, Casablanca, Funchal, and Bermuda. The cruise is available in three shorter segments, with special air rates.

The vessel makes some Caribbean, Mexico, and Bermuda cruises in April and May before sailing northward to New England and Canada, then southward again through the Panama Canal to San Francisco. From mid-June through August, the *Sagafjord* sails from San Francisco on cruises to Alaska and Canada. Several more trans-Panama Canal cruises and a New England/Canada sailing complete the year, prior to the annual Christmas and New Year itinerary in the Caribbean.

★★★★SANTA CRUZ

Galapagos Cruises of Quito, Ecuador; Ecuadorean crew and registry; designed and built in Spain exclusively for Galapagos cruises; launched December 1979; 1,500 tons; 230 feet long; cruising speed of 15 knots; 4 passenger decks; American Bureau of Shipping highest international safety classification.

The *Santa Cruz* is a first-class ship accommodating ninety passengers in forty-five cabins, far superior to anything before found in the Galapagos Islands. All twin and triple cabins are outside, and five single, inside cabins are on Main and Upper deck. All cabins have private facilities and are well designed with comfortable beds and a feeling of spaciousness. The vessel has a large sundeck, a pleasant one-seating dining room, and an attractive lounge area with bar. The bar hours are flexible to passengers' wishes, and bartender Pepe makes terrific Pisco Sours—the local cocktail. Mixed drinks are rather expensive since most supplies are imported by air, and wine can run to ten dollars per bottle. Beer and cigarettes cost about a dollar each. The food on board is good, but not gourmet to my taste. Breakfasts are wonderful (omelets, pancakes, fruit, and fresh juices), but my coffee was powdered Nescafe. The dinners of fresh fish and fresh lobster tails are superb.

Life on board the *Santa Cruz* is decidedly casual, as each passenger is restricted to twenty pounds of luggage. Men are required to wear nothing more formal than a short-sleeved pullover, while women may want a more dressy outfit for the evening. After all, the charming Carlos, captain of the *Santa Cruz*, may invite you to dine at his table!

★★★★SANTA MARIA
SANTA MARIANA
SANTA MERCEDES
SANTA MAGDALENA

Delta Lines; American crew and registry; 20,000 tons each; 546 feet long; 79 feet wide; 100 passengers; crew of 90; cruising speed of 20 knots; 5 passenger decks; classified as cargoliners.

These four identical "Santa liners" carry both cargo and passengers with tender loving care on complete sailings around South America. The Grand Circle Cruise from Vancouver takes approximately fifty-four days, but you are encouraged to take any segment of it that suits your interest. Air-sea programs that range from a few days to as many as forty-one are available. One of the most popular portions of this itinerary is the cruise from Buenos Aires through the Strait of Magellan to Valparaiso. This voyage lasts exactly seven days, so if you wish to plan a two-week holiday, you will have plenty of time to explore both Buenos Aires and Chile before your flight home. You are not restricted to any published program, and Delta Lines will work with you and your travel agent to customize a land and cruise program that appeals to you.

The accommodations aboard these liners are absolutely spectacular, and you'll never be homesick because they will remind you of personally decorated bedrooms. There are forty-three outside staterooms with either large twin beds or a large double bed. Some staterooms are as spacious (or more so) as other ships' suites. And if you're mad about suites, four stunning combinations are available on Sun Deck, but if you have to ask the price (very expensive), you don't want them! Each vessel also has ten inside cabins that feature one sofa bed and one upper wall-bed, but these are often suggested for single travelers, especially on the long cruises. The public rooms aboard are spacious and attractive, albeit only three (plus a pleasant swimming pool area), but there is plenty of deck space for lounging both in the open and under cover.

The Vista Dining Room on Promenade Deck has tables for four and six, as well as cozy banquette seating for two, and terrific views from its "wall of glass" windows. Food and service are both very American, and the stewards are known for their warmth and graciousness. Buffet luncheons and South American-style barbecues are served on deck in good weather, and the wine list leans heavily on California and South American vintages. Cocktails are served in the Club Andes and on Promenade Deck, which has a small dance floor and adjoins a covered terrace. Overlooking the stern of the ship, the smaller Bolivar Lounge is set for bridge and piano music and opens onto the Sports Deck.

For such limited facilities, these Santa Liners pack in a great deal for passengers. They offer movies under the stars, local entertainers in the Club Andes at each port, gift shop, beauty/barber shop, laundry, baggage room, and medical department. But rates are high, *very* high in my opinion, and range from eight thousand to sixteen thousand dollars per person for the full 54-day cruise from Vancouver that covers a total of eighteen thousand miles (smaller segments are prorated). The most popular time of the year to cruise for those who live in the Northern Hemisphere is during the winter months when it's sunny and warm below the Equator. However, the rugged 640-mile channel called the Strait of Magellan is supposed to be at its best during the cool months of June, July, and August when the glacial scenery is even more breathtaking than usual. These are also the "bonus months" for Delta Lines when passengers are treated to complimentary shore excursions in many ports.

With high per diem rates and a lengthy cruise itinerary, the Santa liners carry an average passenger who often is older, retired, and pretty well-heeled, as well as a many-times-over world traveler eager for new and exciting vistas. If you fit into these categories, book before the popular winter months are sold out. To have a taste of South America in the most leisurely and comfortable manner available (not to mention the peace and quiet on board), a Santa liner is a good bet. In fact, I can't think of anything better for the right passenger!

☆☆☆SCANDINAVIA

Scandinavian World Cruises; Bahamian registry and international crew; built in France and launched in 1982; 35,000 tons; 604 feet long; 87 feet at beam; 1,000 passengers; 400 cars; crew of 400; cruising speed of 21 knots; 8 passenger decks.

The $100 million *Scandinavia*, ordered for construction a few years ago when the world economy looked more optimistic, is scheduled to become the flagship of this cruise line whose concept is mass-market, short haul sailing. The *Scandinavia* has the capacity to carry up to 1,600 passengers and four hundred automobiles from New York to Freeport, Grand Bahama, on a five-day round-trip program. There will be no charge for the vehicles (at least, initially). Promotional offers during the first six months of operation will also feature the return trip free of charge, either by air or aboard the *Scandinavia*.

This most modern vessel is designed with picture-windowed outside cabins, full-size twin beds that can be converted to doubles, in-cabin TV for feature films, 24-hour room service, and Scandinavian decor. All cabins are 16 feet by 8 feet and many conect for the convenience of families with small children. Public areas include the Vita Course for joggers, a health center and water sports complex, Broadway main lounge, Blue Riband night club, Las Vegas casino, John Paul Jones' Pub, Windows on the World, Galaxy discotheque, and Bookworm library/card room.

On a space-available basis, passengers may travel with their cars and use them in Freeport or transfer to the *Scandinavian Sun* or *Sea* for passage to Miami. Seemingly limitless programs are available on a hassle-free method of getting you and your transportation to Florida, while leaving the positioning driving to someone else. DFDS, the parent company of Scandinavian World Cruises, is very successful in Europe with this concept. I wonder how North

Americans will accept it, especially when the driving on Grand Bahama is British-style (left side), but the company reports quite overwhelming bookings early on.

★★★SCANDINAVIAN SEA

Scandinavian World Cruises; Bahamian registry and international crew; originally built in 1967 as the Blenheim; 15,000 tons; 500 feet long; 66 feet at beam; 1,000 passengers; 200 cars; crew of 400; cruising speed of 20 knots; 5 passenger decks.

The *Scandinavian Sea* began one-day Cruises to Nowhere from Port Canaveral, Florida, in February 1982. The ship accommodates 400 passengers in day cabins, and up to 600 deck passengers. The company recently lowered the rate for the 11 a.m. to 10 p.m. sailing from $70 to just $29 per person, with a $15 supplement for meals. Day cabins are $15/$25 and children under the age of 12 may accompany parents for a $10 meal charge.

Public areas aboard the vessel are a casino, Sea Escape Disco on Sun Deck, a pool with Lido Bar and changing facilities. The vessel also carries up to 200 cars and is scheduled to connect with the *Scandinavia* sailings for passengers who wish to sail to central Florida with their vehicles.

The on-board Sea Escape activities are not quite so glamorous as those available on the *Scandinavian Sun*, but there is plenty of music and merrymaking. Special Cape Canaveral launch cruises will be offered as the NASA shuttle program becomes more and more of a reality. Thus far, the TV camera people have found the *Scandinavian Sea* a great site for their own "shoot."

★★★SCANDINAVIAN SUN

Scandinavian World Cruises; Bahamian registry and West Indian crew; originally built in 1968 as the Svea Star; also named Freeport II and Caribe; 11,000 tons; 441 feet long; 70 feet at beam; 1,000 passengers; 200 cars; crew of 200; cruising speed of 20 knots; 6 passenger decks.

This vessel, the former *Caribe* of Commodore Cruise Lines, has recently been converted for $10.5 million into a mass-market day-cruiser from Miami to Freeport, Grand Bahama. The vessel now carries up to 1,000 deck passengers for sixteen hours of fun and sun on the sea. The round-trip cruise sails daily from Miami at 8 a.m. for a four-hour layover in Freeport after lunch. The Sun returns to her home port about midnight. During the cruise, which costs about $100 per person, three full meals are served buffet-style, entertainment is non-stop, and the Sea Escape Casino is a popular site. Those who prefer deck activities may swim and sun. Lockers for changing clothes are available free of charge on a first-come, first-served basis, and there are also shower stalls in the changing areas.

The *Scandinavian Sun* has 95 cabins for day use on Andros and Bimini decks for a surcharge of $50 per cabin, as well as six suites on either side of the

Sea Escape Casino for $100. All has been pleasantly refurbished. The two attractive dining rooms, Lucaya East and West on Bahamas Deck, are the scene of all food service, and you can expect long lines when the hunger pains (or just plain curiosity) begin. There is plenty of entertainment to while away the nighttime hours (at least until that midnight arrival). There are two shows in the Goombay Club, a 1950s dance band in the Castaways Lounge, plus calypso music. There is also the Breakaway Disco and a theater for first-run films.

In addition to the one-day Sea Escapes aboard the *Scandinavian Sun*, the cruise line has a number of two-night hotel packages on Grand Bahama, as well as sports and honeymoon packages and extended stays in South Florida. Through a recent agreement with Budget Rent-a-car, passengers to Florida may take the *Sun* sailings for about fifty percent discount from the published rate.

★★★★★SEA CLOUD

Owned by Windjammer Segeltouristik GMBH of Hamburg; registered in Cayman Islands with German/international crew; custom-built in Kiel, Germany, in 1931 and originally christened Hussar; name changed to Sea Cloud in 1936; renovated and refurbished for luxury charter market in Germany in 1979; 2,300 tons; 316 feet long; 49 feet at beam; 70 passengers; crew of 67; cruising speed of 17 knots; 3 passenger decks.

Possibly the most romantic ship afloat . . . certainly, the only square-rigged, four-masted barque with twenty-nine sails covering some 34,000 square feet that anyone with the time and money can cruise aboard. This is believed to be the largest private yacht ever built (named *Hussar*) and it was a million-dollar wedding present from E.F. Hutton to Marjorie Merriweather Post in 1931. Someone was obviously listening to the young bride's dream of glory, for the bathroom fixtures were of fourteen-karat gold (so they would never need to be polished) and knickknacks included Sevrès vases glued to the table tops. "Her" suite had a canopy bed, working fireplace, and a Louis XVI spirit. "His" (across the corridor) featured Georgian sensibility, with classical embellishments in the polished wood paneling and marble fireplace. In the old days, there was a crew of seventy-two on board, and the yacht played frequent host to royalty—some of whom were still enthroned.

When Mrs. Post divorced E.F. Hutton and married a Washington lawyer named Joseph E. Davies, she kept the yacht and rechristened her *Sea Cloud*. While Davies was U.S. Ambassador to Russia from 1936 to 1938, the capitalist *Sea Cloud* had the proletariat distinction of being moored in the Neva River at Leningrad. During this time, it is reported, the couple served two tons of American frozen foods to a startled diplomatic corps. The *Sea Cloud* was moved to Ostend, Belgium, when Davies accepted an ambassadorship to that country in 1938. Alas, after a few cruises in the North Sea, the Second World War intercepted such pleasurable politics and the yacht was chartered to the

U.S. government for $1 a year. The Navy sailed her in the North Atlantic and claimed that several U-boats spotted by those aboard were later sunk.

In the mid-1950s, Mrs. Post divorced the former Ambassador and sold the *Sea Cloud* to Rafael Trujillo (dictator of Santo Domingo) for about half a million dollars. Life for this beauty of the sea was downhill from then until 1978, when Captain Hartmut Paschburg discovered the vessel in derelict condition in Panama's Colon Bay. Envisioning a rebirth of the *Sea Cloud*, Paschburg formed a consortium with eight other Germans and they bought the vessel. They spent approximately $7 million in refurbishing and by 1979, she was considered as "good as new" and listed 100-A1 by North German Lloyds. The original splendor and elegance have been maintained throughout the vessel, and seventy passengers now sleep in twenty-eight new staterooms as well as the thirteen original suites. The officers are mainly German but the sixty-odd crew comes from all over the world and considers it a privilege to run up the mast and get paid just over $200 a month for the adventure.

Travel Dynamics, Inc. of New York City (1290 Avenue of the Americas, NY 10014; 212-247-6363) charters the *Sea Cloud* for about nine months per year. This company specializes in well-respected and refined cruises for college alumni associations, museums, and cultural organizations. For example, past schedules have included alumni from Dartmouth, Yale, Stanford, William and Mary, as well as members of the National Trust for Historic Preservation and the Los Angeles County Museum. Special lecturers were part of the program for cruises among the Lesser Antilles in the Caribbean, the Greek Islands/ Sicily on a Rome-to-Athens air-sea package, or along the Tyrrhenian and Adriatic seas. The vessel spends from December to April in the Caribbean, and from May to October in the Mediterranean area. The other few months are available for other charters. Interested parties should contact the owner's representative in New York (Joseph H. Conlin, 516 Fifth Avenue, NY 10036; 212-575-1234).

From all reports, life aboard the *Sea Cloud* is glamorous, thrilling, and a delightful experience. To sit on deck under full sail, to see the lighted rigging at night from the shore, to enjoy formal dinners with German white wines and French reds, to come into harbors that other cruise vessels cannot enter—all these are part of the *Sea Cloud*. Both breakfast and luncheons are buffet-style, we are told, and the food tends toward German/Continental. Rates are high as you might imagine (about $17,000 for the owner's suite for fourteen days, about $10,000 for two lower berths in one of the new cabins). I was also informed that there is considerable "tendering" into shore, so this is not a ship for the less than agile.

★★★★★SEA PRINCESS

P & O Line/Princess Cruises; British flag and officers; Goanese and Pakistani crew; built by John Brown on the River Clyde in 1966 and launched as Kungsholm of Swedish America Line; refitted and relaunched in 1979 as Sea

Princess; 28,000 tons; 600 feet long; 87 feet at beam; 750 passengers; crew of 400; cruising speed of 20 knots; 6 passenger decks.

The *Sea Princess* is one of the most gracious ships afloat, and many who knew her as the *Kungsholm* were disappointed to see her sold and leave North American waters. However, it is pleasing to know that P & O Line has given this former sister ship of the *Gripsholm* (the late *Navarino*) a splendid rebirth with a fine crew and some exciting itineraries. Sailing from Sydney year-round, the *Sea Princess* replaced the beloved *Arcadia* (which gave twenty-five years of service to P & O) on cruises to the Far East and the exotic islands of the South Seas. What a way to go!

The ambience on board the *Sea Princess* is gracious and just enough Old World to be enjoyable. No doubt the addition of British officers in their sexy short uniforms will liven the atmosphere (which was rather stiff under the Flagship team). Although P & O tightened up the vessel somewhat, with the addition of eighty cabins, the public rooms are still intact and as inviting as ever. My favorite place is the Lookout Bar in the forward section of Promenade Deck, where the lovely bay windows allow good daytime viewing and then add romance when it becomes a nightclub. The large lounge aft now has a carousel theme and a circular dance floor. Buffet luncheons are served around the nearby pool. During this time the Carousel Lounge becomes a Lido bar for the pool; at night, it is transformed into the ship's disco. Another Lido bar and pool are located in the center of Promenade Deck.

Enjoy the many public rooms on Verandah Deck. You can feel pampered and decadent in the plush, magenta-colored Tiffany's Bar or retreat to the quiet of the library and card rooms that flank the 300-seat Princess Theater. The elegant dining room, renamed the Tasman Restaurant, displays porcelain. To work off those extra calories a keep-fit paradise is located on D-Deck, with indoor swimming pool, gymnasium, sauna, and massage rooms.

During a recent inaugural call in New York some friends and I inspected the former *Kungsholm*. We were all overwhelmed by the sparkling quality and the immaculate care the vessel boasts. Throughout the old-world, solid-ship quality of the *Sea Princess* is an evident concern for maintenance. In fact, Captain King informed us, there is a full-time French polisher on board whose sole responsibility is the beautiful teak paneling throughout the ship. And if Captain King (who plays his role most proficiently) is typical of the *Sea Princess'* masters, P & O is fortunate. One of the English ladies on this three-week cruise to Bermuda and the East Coast slipped a note into the Suggestion Box that read, "The Captain is the nicest man on this ship"!

In May 1982, P & O repositioned its most luxurious liner to Southampton where the vessel sailed on two- and three-week warm-weather cruises. In 1983, the *Sea Princess* replaces the nine-year veteran *Canberra* on P & O's annual global circumnavigation. Offering more intimate and deluxe service, the vessel departs Southampton in January for ninety days to such ports as Madeira, Bermuda, the Dutch Antilles, through the Panama Canal to Mexico and the

West Coast, across the Pacific to Hawaii, Samoa, Fiji, and Australia. The vessel then sails to Indonesia, Malaysia, Singapore, and Sri Lanka before heading home via the Cape with scheduled calls at Mauritius, Durban, Dakar, and Portugal. The three-month cruise is available in shorter segments between Southampton/Sydney/Singapore, with Fly Free one way.

Returning to Southampton in April, the *Sea Princess* begins her 1983 season with shorter cruises to the Mediterranean, Red Sea, Egypt and the Holy Land, Scandinavia, Madeira, the Canary Islands, and the Caribbean. The final sailing of 1983 is a 23-day cruise to Bermuda, the Carribean, and Madeira departing in December. The *Sea Princess* returns to Southampton in January of the new year—just in time for another world cruise!

★★★SKYWARD

Norwegian Caribbean Lines; Norwegian registry and officers, international crew; originally built and launched in 1970; 16,250 tons; 525 feet long; 75 feet at beam; 790 passengers; crew of 306; cruising speed of 16 knots; 8 passenger decks.

Similar to the *Starward* in design, the *Skyward* also has a wonderful bubble-top Tropicana Bar overlooking the Sun Deck dance floor (where much of the daytime action takes place). The two-tiered theater is between Biscayne and Caribbean decks, and the main public areas are on Rainbow Deck, which includes the Starlight Dining Room aft and the Paradise Lounge forward. In between is the Pot O' Gold room, where you can relax with a drink and try your luck at the same time. The swimming pool and Lido bar are one deck up on the Boat Deck.

The *Skyward* has 221 outside and 141 inside cabins, all with private facilities. As on all three NCL seven-day vessels, the inside cabins have double beds and an upper folding berth, but don't plan on more than two people if you can help it. During a recent visit the *Skyward* looked to me in need of refurbishing, but the Lido bar served the best piña coladas in Miami.

The *Skyward*'s Mexican Fiesta theme begins the moment passengers step aboard the vessel; it has become a great success for the line. The *Skyward* sails every Sunday from Miami for Playa del Carmen, Cancun, Cozumel, and a Bahamian Out Island. On board are Mexican actors and strolling musicians as well as plenty of food and drink typical of that land South of the Border. To enhance the experience, a multi-media presentation and souvenir guidebook acquaint passengers with the mystery of the Mayas. A small Maya Museum, a large pyramid-temple gracing the ship's top deck, and a simulated archaeological dig are all part of the program.

Shore excursions include tours of the Mayan ruins at Chichen Itza, Tulum, and Coba. The call at Cancun offers plenty of sun and snorkeling on the beautiful beaches, and a party in Cozumel features Mexican refreshments and plenty of the local folk in full regalia. Passengers return to Caribbean basics at the NCL-hosted Out Island beach party where rum punch, hot dogs, and a calypso band are in order.

☆☆☆☆SONG OF AMERICA

Royal Caribbean Cruise Line; Norwegian registry and international crew; built in Wartsila Yard in Helsinki and launched in 1982; 32,000 tons; 705 feet long; 94 feet at beam; 1,400 passengers; crew of 500; cruising speed of 16 knots; 7 passenger decks.

With the inaugural service of the *Song of America* on December 5, 1982, Royal Caribbean Cruise Line became a four-fleet company at last. The new vessel was three years in the planning and over a year in the construction, at a final cost of approximately $140 million. Interior design of the vessel has been executed by two of Scandinavia's best: Mogens Hammer of Denmark and Finn Nilsson of Norway. The ship has a total of 707 cabins plus 21 deluxe staterooms and one super suite, all with pleasing Scandinavian decor and complementary Caribbean colors. The walls are off-white and natural tones. All cabins have 110-volt current for American-made hair dryers, curlers, and electric shavers, in addition to modular bathrooms with showers.

The *Song of America* boasts the well-recognized RCCL trademark, the cantilevered Viking Crown Lounge. However, this one encircles the funnel stack some twelve decks above sea level and offers a complete 360 degree panorama. On a clear day, you can see some twenty miles (so they say). The lounge also holds about 140 passengers comfortably, almost three times more than those above the rest of a fleet, and an elevator whisks you into the center with nary a hair out of place! The vessel also has a proper theater for first-run films on Cabaret Deck. Other public areas include the Can Can and Oklahoma lounges on Cabaret Deck, and the main dining room on Main Deck. This large facility is divided into the Madame Butterfly restaurant, the Ambassador Room, and the Oriental Terrace, all of which will change settings and specialties at each dinner service. The late-night spot can be found in the Guys and Dolls Lounge on Promenade Deck. Sun-seekers will love the two huge pools, with bar and outdoor Verandah Cafe on Sun Deck, and fitness buffs should not miss the gymnasium and saunas on Bridge Deck. The Mast Bar and Sun Walk are located up on Compass Deck.

The *Song of America* sails every Sunday from Miami to Nassau, San Juan, and St. Thomas. RCCL has excellent air-sea programs, and it is never a surprise to find the huge California contingent already on board and enjoying a light lunch soon after their Miami arrivals.

★★★★SONG OF NORWAY

Royal Caribbean Line; Norwegian registry and officers, international crew; built in Wartsila shipyard, Helsinki, and originally launched in 1970; refitted and lengthened by 85 feet in 1978; 23,005 tons; 635 feet long; 80 feet at beam; 1,040 passengers; crew of 400; cruising speed of 16 knots; 8 passenger decks.

The *Song of Norway* was the first-born of the RCCL fleet and she remains one of the most popular, simply because the numbers on the seven-day cruises are greater than each of the sister ships on a two-week pattern. In fact, the ship line often said that first-time cruise passengers tried their waterwings on the *Song*, then graduated to the *Nordic Prince* and *Sun Viking*. Following eight years of success, the vessel was returned to Wartsila shipyard in Helsinki for a "stretching," which added 85 feet to her midsection and increased her passenger complement by thirty percent. Public rooms were also increased in size, and the vessel has one of the most beautiful sun-and-pool areas afloat.

Like all RCCL vessels, the *Song's* public rooms have been named after hit Broadway musicals. There is The *King and I* dining room, the *My Fair Lady* forward lounge, the *South Pacific* aft lounge. The famous cantilevered Viking Crown Lounge on the funnel stack still accommodates only 67 passengers comfortably, and the panorama is impressive. The Lounge of the Midnight Sun nightclub was enlarged and has simultaneous slide shows happening on several wall areas, so it's best to stay sober and enjoy! Entertainment quality is very high, as on all RCCL ships, and passengers never see the same nighttime attraction twice. The dining service is themed each night, with costumes for the waiters and different table settings as well as menu offerings.

The *Song of Norway* has a total of 535 cabins, most of them rather small but compact. Third and fourth persons in them make it very cozy, indeed. The stretching of the vessel, however, allowed for several new outside deluxe and larger cabins (13 even have bathtubs). On-board amenities are excellent, and the ship has a reputation for being beautifully managed and maintained. There is plenty to occupy the days at sea, and plenty of space in which to be active. The *Song of Norway's* only competitor on the seven-day circuit is the new *Song of America*. Every Saturday the vessel sails for the western Caribbean to Grand Cayman, Montego Bay, and Cozumel. The ship offers free air from 71 gateways and all rates are inclusive of port taxes and transfers. California passengers board Pan Am's famous "red eye" service to Miami, but are whisked onto the ship early for a light lunch and rest. By sailing time, they are refreshed and ready to enjoy themselves.

★★★SOUTHWARD

Norwegian Caribbean Lines; Norwegian registry and officers, international crew; originally built and launched in 1972; 16,607 tons; 536 feet long; 75 feet at beam; 738 passengers; crew of 302; cruising speed of 16 knots; 9 passenger decks.

When the *Southward* was placed into service in 1972, she was the first cruise vessel to sail on a fourteen-day itinerary from Miami. She did so until 1975 when the growing appeal of shorter cruises dictated the change. However, this vessel has retained something of her longer cruise atmosphere, and is considered by many to be the most regal of the three Norwegian Caribbean seven-day vessels. The *Southward* has 259 outside and 111 inside cabins, all with private facilities and all of the same Caribbean-size. Ten very pleasant, deluxe outside staterooms with separate sitting area and full baths are on Boat Deck, just forward of the El Dorado Dining Room. The main public areas are located on Mayflower Deck: the lovely Clipper Lounge, the health center, casino, library and card room, art gallery, and cocktail lounges. The swimming pool and Lido bar comprise Beach Deck, and the Crow's Nest nightclub can be found up on Tropicana Deck. A game room and shops are down on Atlantic Deck, and the two-tiered theater is between Biscayne and Caribbean decks. It's a simple ship on which to get around, and it has a cozy ambience despite its more than 700-passenger capacity. Food, service, and housekeeping amenities are as on all NCL vessels. Coffee, tea, and juice are available in the cabin around-the-clock. Finger sandwiches are available from 7 a.m. to 11 p.m. Continental breakfast service only.

The *Southward* sails every Saturday for Cozumel, Grand Cayman, Ocho Rios, and a Bahama Out Island port, with beach parties planned at Grand Cayman and the Out Island. Shore excursions in Cozumel feature the Mayan ruins of Tulum, and in Ocho Rios you can climb the breathtaking Dunn's River Falls before you head for the beach and a calypso/limbo/fire dancers performance.

★★★STARWARD

Norwegian Caribbean Lines; Norwegian registry and officers, international crew; built and launched in 1968; refurbished in 1976; 16,000 tons; 525 feet long; 75 feet at beam; 740 passengers; crew of 325; cruising speed of 16 knots; 7 passenger decks.

First launched of NCL's present five-vessel fleet, the *Starward* has enjoyed a fine reputation as a high-density seven-day cruise ship. She is a nice, middle-class vessel with Caribbean-size cabins. My cabin had a double bed that took up the entire allotment of space; it was not possible to get into the curtained closet or even sit at the vanity without climbing over the bed. There are a few suites with double beds and small sitting area and full bathroom on Atlantic and Caribbean decks. On Galaxy Deck the public areas include the Neptune Dining Room (two seatings at all meals), the Venus Lounge, and the Orion Club (with adjacent card room and conference room). A large swimming pool area and Lido bar are located on Boat Deck, and another swimming pool with dance floor and topside Garden Lounge are situated on Sun and Compass decks. The Garden is a splendid hideaway during the day and pleasant for private cocktail parties in the evening.

The *Starward* sails every Sunday for Nassau, San Juan, St. Thomas, and a Bahamian Out Island. On a seasonal basis, Puerto Plata is substituted for the Nassau call (whatever that means). As on all NCL ships, there is great emphasis on sports activities both aboard and in port, an ambitious Las-Vegas-style revue, and a special Viking Night with Norwegian dishes on the menu and complimentary Akavit. The stewards all appear in Viking headpieces, and if you're lucky, you may find a paper facsimile at your table. Also featured aboard is a Country and Western Night, a poolside party complete with hoedown, clogging, and barbecue. (Attendance is optional, I am sure).

★★STEFAN BATORY

Polish Ocean Lines; Polish registry and crew; originally built in 1954 and formerly named the Maasdam; rebuilt in 1971 and relaunched as the Stefan Batory; 15,024 tons; 503 feet long; 69 feet at beam; 700 passengers; crew of 340; cruising speed of 16.5 knots; 7 passenger decks.

My friend Frank Braynard, ship buff/historian/artist and the person who knows more about cruise vessels than anyone, says the *Stefan Batory* is the nicest ship on the Atlantic. Just back from a voyage between Montreal and Tilbury (port for London), Frank reported the vessel was spotless throughout and the service superb. If anything, the dining room stewards were almost too obliging and the food too good! Not Polish-oriented, as one might suspect, but very continental, the cuisine aboard the *Stefan Batory* has been commended even by the French. In addition, the table settings and menus were splendid. Frank even brought home his menus as keepsakes because he admired the artwork so much.

The public rooms aboard the *Stefan Batory* are very comfortable, but the staterooms are spare and small and few of them have private facilities. Of the 322 total cabins, only 35 have private facilities. However, there are plenty of sparkling clean rest rooms for both men and women throughout the vessel. The First Class section on Boat Deck has fifteen staterooms with private facilities; these passengers also have their own dining room and lounge. Entertainment includes an hour each day of classical records and some very fine Polish dance exhibitions, complete with colorful costumes. "The place really jumps!" said Frank.

See Montreal for schedule. As the vessel is always full, book well in advance to enjoy this very fine Polish cruise ship.

★★★★STELLA MARIS II

Sun Line; Greek registry and crew; originally built in 1960; rebuilt in 1966; 4,000 tons; 300 feet long; 45 feet at beam; 180 passengers; crew of 100; cruising speed of 16 knots; 4 passenger decks.

The *Stella Maris II* is a little gem, one of the most charming vessels around. She really is "yachtlike" with an intimate feeling throughout and a very special ambience. The ship has eighty outside cabins and thirteen inside, all with private facilities and all with a decor of cool colors. The sixteen deluxe cabins are done in beige with either blue or red velvet chairs and accents. The public areas are also decorated in cool velvets: the Salon Athinai and Belvedere lounges on Sun Deck and a small swimming pool aft, and the small and friendly Poseidon Restaurant on Aegean Deck with bright-blue chairs and green tablecloths. Life aboard the *Stella Maris II* has a style all of its own. If you have an ambulatory handicap, be forewarned; this vessel has no elevator.

During the summer season the *Stella Maris II* cruises between Venice and Nice. The one-week itineraries are exceptionally well planned to offer the best possible shore experiences in this central part of the Mediterranean. The Saturday departures from Venice to Nice call at Dubrovnik, Corfu, Malta, Tunis, Costa Smeralda, Elba, and Portofino. On alternate Saturdays the *Maris* sails from Nice to Venice, calling at Portofino, Costa Smeralda, Tunis, Malta, Katakolon, Corfu, and Dubrovnik. Air France is offering good air-sea programs between the U.S. and France for these cruises. In the spring and fall, the *Stella Maris* follows the same Friday and Monday departures from Piraeus to the Greek Islands/Turkey as the *Stella Oceanis*.

During the winter the *Stella Maris II* is on charter to such exciting places as the Red Sea.

★★★STELLA OCEANIS

Sun Line; Greek registry and crew; originally built in 1965 and formerly named the Aphrodite; rebuilt in 1967 and relaunched; 6,000 tons; 350 feet long; 53 feet at beam; 300 passengers; crew of 140; cruising speed of 17 knots; 6 passenger decks.

The *Stella Oceanis*, with three hundred passengers and six thousand tons, is the middle member of the Sun Line fleet. This is a very pleasant vessel, but it lacks the class of the *Solaris* or the unique charm of the *Maris II*. The *Oceanis* has a total of 159 cabins, of which 113 are on the outside. All have private facilities. There are twenty deluxe accommodations—many of them are connecting—and six deluxe suites. The public rooms are few but more than adequate for the size of the vessel. With the exception of the Plaka Taverna, a terrific room on Lido Deck that becomes the late-night disco and is available for movies or private parties, the public space is centered on Oceanis Deck. Here the Salon Minos with gold carpets and velvet chairs seats the entire ship complement amid the murals of Minos the Bull. The main lounge has a pleasant bar and a small club in the aft for private gatherings. A boutique and casino lead the way to the Aphrodite Restaurant, also designed with gold and blue accents, with pleasant ocean-view windows. There are two meal seatings.

During the summer season, from early April through October, the *Stella Oceanis* is at home in Piraeus for cruises to the Greek islands and Turkey. The four-day sailings departing Monday evenings call at Hydra, Thíra (weather permitting), Heraklion, Rhodes, Kuşadasi, and Mykonos. The Friday morning sailings of three days visit Delos, Mykonos, Rhodes, Heraklion, and Thíra (weather permitting). From mid-December to mid-March the *Stella Oceanis* is based in San Juan for unusual and interesting two-week cruises that are true to

Sun Line form, and which include, for example, a stop in Ciudad Guayana; a town 180 or so miles up the Orinoco River in Venezuela. The vessel remains here for about thirty-three hours; passengers may opt for an air excursion to the jungle resort of Canaima and over Angel Falls, the tallest waterfall in the world. Between the Orinoco River adventure and these "off the beaten track" islands, this itinerary is one of the best you can find and a terrific investment in adventure. What a conversation piece!

★★★★STELLA SOLARIS

Sun Line; Greek registry and crew; formerly named the Camboge; rebuilt in 1973 and launched as the Stella Solaris; 18,000 tons; 550 feet long; 72 feet at beam; 650 passengers; crew of 310; cruising speed of 20 knots; 8 passenger decks.

The *Stella Solaris* is the flagship of Sun Line fleet and a beautifully maintained vessel. She has an excellent and charming captain and a fine cruise staff under the direction of a dynamic Greek-American woman from Chicago named Irene. True to Sun Line form, the itineraries are unusual and very satisfying to her passengers, who are a good mix of Texans, other Americans, and Europeans. This is one of the best Greek ships found cruising the Aegean during the summer season.

The *Stella Solaris* has a total of 329 cabins with private facilities, of which 250 cabins are on the outside (218 have full bathtubs). Of the 66 deluxe staterooms, 28 suites on Boat Deck can accommodate a third person on the sofa bed. All the cabins are nicely furnished. I would avoid cabins called "outside communicating rooms," which I think are badly designed with partitions that are too thin to afford adequate privacy. The public spaces are very pleasant. The main lounge is the center of activity for briefings and entertainment, although the Piano Bar is more popular with those who like cocktails at sunset or sailing away. Other public areas are the Monte Carlo Room and bar/grill (mainly for drinks) on Solaris Deck, a card room on Boat Deck (aft of the deluxe cabins), and the Lido bar and swimming pool on Lido Deck (where a fine buffet luncheon is served). The vessel also has a small gymnasium/massage/sauna and a children's room on Golden Deck, a lovely theater on Sapphire Deck, and a disco way down on Main Deck (if you can ever find it).

The dining room, located in the forward section of Solaris Deck, is beautifully decorated, if a bit crowded with tables. Two seatings for all meals are given when the ship is full. When the ship is half full, everyone is crammed in for one seating (which I discovered eliminated tables for two and the chance to change your table if the companions were not well suited). I also found that service in the dining room varied from section to section (and depended on whether I happened to be sitting with a member of the staff). The food could have been a lot better for such a top-class vessel, I thought, and hopefully has improved since my visit. Local dishes and wines were excellent, but dinner, I found, was a grave disappointment. Breakfast is open seating, unless you insist that you be placed at your own table (and firmness is the password every time).

From April to October, the *Stella Solaris* sails the Mediterranean from Piraeus on the now-popular double itinerary which includes a return to Piraeus before setting out for Port Said, Ashdod, Haifa, Rhodes, Kuşadasi and Samos. Passengers can take back-to-back cruises and never duplicate a port of call. In fact, fifteen-day air/sea programs from the U.S. are now available.

In late November, the *Solaris* makes a three week or more transatlantic crossing, calling at ports along the Mediterranean as well as in West Africa. Then she repositions in Galveston, Texas, just before Christmas. She begins the winter season with a seventeen-day Christmas and New Year cruise that includes a double transit of the Panama Canal. From the beginning of January through the beginning of March, the vessel sails between Galveston and Curaçao on a ten-day itinerary. Passengers may embark in either port and return by air from the other. Following that cruise, the *Stella Solaris* departs Port Everglades on a 22-day "Primavera III" that begins in the Caribbean, crosses the Atlantic, and makes a few European stops before ending in Piraeus. Cruise rates include the return flight from Athens to New York.

★★★SUN PRINCESS

Princess Cruises; British registry and crew (with Italian dining room personnel); built in Italy and launched in 1972; 17,370 tons; 535 feet long; 75 feet at beam; 700 passengers; crew of 300; cruising speed of 20 knots; 7 passenger decks.

The *Sun Princess*, an attractive and inviting cruise vessel, has an inherent lively and fun-loving atmosphere for her seven-day cruises out of San Juan in the winter and Vancouver during the summer months. This is a high-density vessel designed strictly for this shorter, sun-filled cruise pattern and cannot be considered in the same gracious and stylish league as the *Island* or *Pacific Princess*. The *Sun Princess* has 241 outside and 118 inside cabins, all with private facilities but all seemed to me on the very small side and obviously made for passengers who wish to spend their time on deck. Four rather nice suites are well worth the extra prices (PR 6, 7, 21, and 24).

The public rooms feature the large International Lounge (where terrific entertainment is offered every evening), the pleasant and romantic Starlight Lounge up on Observation Deck, and the swinging Union Jack Bar. Near the swimming pool on Lido Deck is the Union Jack, a great place for grilled, juicy hamburgers, which you can enjoy in your bathing suit—an added treat! Life aboard the *Sun Princess* is definitely more casual, and the passengers are quite a bit younger (and more often single) than on the line's other two vessels. In fact, this is a good choice for singles—as evidenced by the many happy faces I saw disembarking in San Juan recently.

The *Sun Princess* spends the summer season in Vancouver departing on seven-night cruises to Alaska's Inside Passage and calling at Juneau, Skagway, Glacier Bay (cruising), Ketchikan, and Misty Fjord (cruising). From mid-December through May she sails every Saturday from San Juan. This season she offers an alternate itinerary on these popular weekly Caribbean cruises, so you could stay aboard for fourteen nights and have a wonderful voyage. The *Sun Princess* also features an eleven-day Christmas cruise and a ten-day New Year's sailing, both of which depart from San Juan.

★★★★SUN VIKING

Royal Caribbean Cruise Line; Norwegian registry and officers, international crew; built in Wartsila shipyard, Helsinki and launched in 1972; 18,559 tons; 550 feet long; 80 feet at beam; 728 passengers; crew of 320; cruising speed of 16 knots; 8 passenger decks.

The *Sun Viking* is the last of the Royal Caribbean vessels of her original size and configuration. Last to be launched in the cruise market, the *Sun Viking* may be stretched like her sister ships in 1983, so she now looks small compared to her companions, especially if you are standing in the main entrance hall and looking fore and aft along Karl Johans Gate (where Information, cruise director's office, and gift shops are located). Like her sisters, the *Sun Viking*'s public areas are named after Broadway hit musicals. Located on Restaurant Deck are the HMS Pinafore Dining Room, the Merry Widow Lounge, and the Annie Get Your Gun Lounge (with its Sitting Bull Bar over to the side). But my favorite place on this and other Royal Caribbean ships is the circular, cantilevered Viking Crown Lounge ten stories above the sea and reachable only by outside staircase. This lounge is intimate, for it holds just sixty persons, whether for a predinner cocktail or quiet, romantic evening drink. The second most attractive lounge on the vessel is the nightclub/disco, Lounge of the Northern Lights, which features on-the-wall entertainment, a travelogue picture story with slides taken by RCCL's own photographer, who travels the globe in search of this material.

The *Sun Viking* has 266 outside and 114 inside cabins, all with private facilities. They are not the most spacious afloat, but are beautifully serviced. It has the same food service and entertainment features as the *Song of Norway*, plus a sauna/massage center adjacent to the topside midships swimming pool.

Last year, the *Sun Viking* was named Ship of the Year by a society of cruise passengers who spend most of their time in the Caribbean (judging from the ships mentioned in the survey). Nonetheless, it's a great honor for the vessel and I'm quite certain that she deserves the accolade. Through March, the *Viking* will make ten- and eleven-day cruises from Miami to familiar ports in the Eastern Caribbean. Beginning in April, she will assume the *Nordic Prince*'s two-week itinerary also in the Caribbean. The sailings are also available as "SunVenture I" (Miami to Barbados and return by air) or "SunVenture II" (fly to Barbados and sail back to Miami) for a reasonable air supplement.

★★★+SUNWARD II

Norwegian Caribbean Lines; Norwegian registry and officers, international crew; originally built in 1971 and formerly named the Cunard Adventurer;

rebuilt and relaunched in 1977 as the Sunward II; 15,000 tons; 485 feet long; 70.5 feet at beam; 718 passengers; crew of 279; cruising speed of 19 knots; 7 passenger decks.

The *Sunward II* is yet another Norwegian Caribbean Lines success story, and she ranks far, far above the other ships in the short-cruise category. This vessel was the former ailing Cunard *Adventurer* that some travelers said was on her last legs and no longer seaworthy (even though not even five years old). But NCL bought the vessel and transformed her into a fun-filled and sunny ship for three- and four-day cruises to the Bahamas. NCL scheduled the usual ports of Nassau and Freeport, but added an Out Island just for sunning, snorkeling, and swimming. It has worked so well that many passengers choose this cruise just for the beautiful "Bahamarana" beach party in the Berry Islands. The ship has about fifty Sunfish, rental equipment for snorkeling, and five instructors on board for the beach call. Cabanas have been built past the sand dunes, and the ship's band plays on while you play and party (food and drink are brought ashore). The Dive-In program is Number One here.

The *Sunward II* has 238 outside and 121 inside cabins, all with private facilities. The accommodations are standard but well designed, and there are plenty of suites and larger-than-average outside staterooms. This vessel was refurbished with a few days of good fun in mind, and that is the feeling projected throughout the public areas: the split-level Sunburst Dining Room, the Bahamarana Lounge on Boat Deck where the onboard Las Vegas-style revues are staged, the Crow's Nest Nightclub, and the Lido Cafe/Disco. In addition, there is a slot machine casino with bar, a theater, and a large swimming pool area with sauna and massage rooms.

Every Friday the *Sunward II* departs Miami for Nassau and one of the Bahamas' most beautiful atolls in the Berry Islands. The vessel returns to Miami on Monday morning. Every Monday afternoon the *Sunward II* sails for Nassau, the Berry Islands, and Freeport. The vessel returns to Miami on Friday morning.

★★★TROPICALE

Carnival Cruise Lines; Liberian registry; Italian officers and international crew; built in Aalborg, Denmark, especially for Carnival Cruise Lines; commissioned in January 1982; 36,674 tons; 656 feet long; 86.3 feet at beam; 1,200 passengers; crew of 500; cruising speed of 22 knots; 10 passenger decks.

The $100-million *Tropicale* made her debut in January 1982, and Carnival Cruise Lines called their new vessel the eighth largest cruise ship afloat. Certainly, she was the first of several new ships scheduled to make waves during the decade of the 80s. The 1,200-passenger *Tropicale* has a distinctive outward appearance, with a winglike funnel that was originally planned for aesthetics-sake but has proved to be effective in moving the smoke outward. Other innovative features include a below-water bulbous bow for fuel efficiency (makes the vessel appear to be on water skis), and computerized engine room and bridge. A satellite reception dish brings TV signals into the cabins but does not seem too successful more than several miles from shore. The vessel is energy-efficient and even recycles about eighty tons of nonpotable water each day for maintenance functions. A squared-off stern was apparently designed for economy in building the accommodations section.

The 511 passenger cabins were installed fabricated; even the lavatories were constructed as entire units. Cabin size is unusually spacious for a modern-day vessel, and the majority have large sea-view windows as well as twin beds that can be converted to king-size configuration. Wardrobe and storage spaces are both plentiful (beds are built high enough for suitcases to slide easily under them), and all cabins are card-coded which means you can never forget your number. Closed-circuit televisions overhead bring feature films several times daily, and 24-hour room service is also available. As this vessel is not expected to cater to exotic fancies, request nothing more than an automat-type cheese sandwich and an apple. Even properly ordered breakfasts arrive on paper plates, with plastic utensils. If you can't manage plastic in the cabin, go upstairs to the Boiler Room and eat your scrambled eggs hot and out on deck.

The Boiler Room, aft on Lido Deck, is also the scene of hot dogs and hamburgers at lunchtime and afternoon tea with cakes. There is plenty of deck space on the *Tropicale*, although even three (albeit small) swimming pools are inadequate for the size of the passenger complement. Popular on tropical evenings is the Patio Bar, which remains open until an unorthodox 6 a.m., where a calypso band plays for dancing and fountains take over in the main pool. The Grand Midnight Buffet is also served here. Otherwise, passengers flock to the Tropicana Lounge where extravaganzas are offered nightly after dinner, or to the Islands in the Sun lounge on deck above which appears to be a bit more cozy (but is actually, huge)! The late-night set frequents the Extra-Z Disco or the casino, both of which close only when the last group goes.

The 658-capacity Palm Restaurant, surprisingly, is located down on Riviera deck (the current trend is to enjoy sea views). Meal presentation is fine and the dinner menus quite a departure from the usual Carnival fare. Special theme nights break the monotony. All beef dishes are excellent and obvious care is used in the selection of top-grade meat. I found neither the wine carte nor the service spectacular.

The *Tropicale* boasts twelve suites up on Verandah Deck, with their own sea-view balconies, bars, and bathtubs plus separate conversation areas. The suites are pleasant, although the sitting areas seem less bright and cheerful than the average cabin. Beginning in mid-September 1982, the vessel calls Los Angeles home port and sails every Sunday for Puerto Vallarta, Mazatlan and Cabo San Lucas. During the summer, the *Tropicale* will sail from Vancouver for Westours. The Saturday departures will call at Ketchikan, Juneau, Glacier Bay, and Sitka. The *Tropicale* is a typical ship for the fun set. No serious thoughts should be brought aboard on this one!

★★★UGANDA

BI Discovery Cruises; British crew and registry; 17,000 tons; 540 feet long; 71 feet at beam; 300 cabin passengers; 600 students in former troop quarters; crew of 350; cruising speed of 18 knots; 4 passenger decks.

The *Uganda*, a former troop/cargo vessel, is now used for educational cruises under the aegis of BI Discovery Cruises, a division of P & O Line. The vessel carries three hundred cabin passengers on the upper four decks, and some six hundred students below in the former troop quarters. Because of plenty of deck area for the cabin passengers and unpretentious and friendly life on board, each cruise has a high percentage of repeat passengers. Cabins are simple but clean and comfortable. Public rooms include a smoking room, music room with dance space, two side verandas, and two bars. There is also a small swimming pool and aft veranda. A large theater/assembly hall is used for lectures, and the dining saloon on C Deck has two seatings. Continental breakfast is served in the cabins.

Despite a reputation as a sturdy, no-nonsense vessel, the *Uganda* has a loyal following and is popular with people who enjoy a different type of cruise experience. The clublike atmosphere on board brings together many old friends, for at least half the passenger complement on each sailing is repeat clientele. Many are teachers. During this season, the *Uganda* will follow her traditional course, visiting well over seventy ports (many off the tourist route) on a year-long program of twenty-four cruises. Passengers fly from London's Gatwick Airport to Malta, Naples, Athens, Venice, or Split to embark the vessel and fly home from another port two weeks later. Those wishing to spend a month in the Mediterranean may take back-to-back cruises with no duplication in port calls.

One of the year's highlights is a pre-Christmas cruise to the Holy Land, that also calls at Port Said, Messina, Alanya, and Nauplia. The *Uganda* also returns to post-earthquake Kotor, as well as to familiar destinations like Alexandria, Istanbul, Haifa, Rhodes, and Dubrovnik. A cruise to the Black Sea calls at Varna and Constanta. Departures from Edinburgh will sail to Portugal and the Northern Capitals. Cruise aficionados who have sailed aboard the *Uganda* swear by the stimulating and quite unique experience enjoyed.

★★VEENDAM/VOLENDAM

Holland America Cruises; Netherlands Antilles registry; Dutch officers and Indonesian crew; built in 1957 for Moore-McCormack Lines and originally named Argentina and Brazil; also known briefly as the Monarch Star/Monarch Sun; 23,500 tons; 617 feet long; 88 feet at beam; 715 passengers; crew of 340; cruising speed of 21 knots; 7 passenger decks.

The *Veendam* and the *Volendam* are full-fledged members of the Holland America family. These sister-ship vessels are practically identical, although the

Volendam has a cruise capacity of two more passengers than her sister. Both have 285 outside cabins and suites, with 73 inside. The accommodations are more spacious than you would find on most newer vessels, and certainly the partitions between the cabins are somewhat more noise resistant. The decor in the cabins is Indonesian batik, in your choice of "flavors;" and the housekeeping gets high marks. Service is rendered with not just a smile but a toothy grin, and the company's No Tipping Required policy is working well. Contented and well-cared-for passengers do tip and with pleasure, not because it is an obligation.

The *Veendam* and *Volendam* are very comfortable vessels, not glamorous, but you must sail them to love them—as they say. With the exception of a small observatory lounge on Sun Deck, the main public area is located on Promenade Deck where the main lounge is midships. Forward are the nightclub, casino, card room, and library, while the Lido Lounge is aft, where you serve yourself breakfasts and luncheons (if you want) within full view of the swimming pool and sun deck. Holland America is proud of the Lido Lounge idea and feels its success lies in the No Tipping Required policy. Promenade Deck also has some good duty-free shops as well as the Photo Center. The Purser's Office, Shore Excursion Office, and restaurant are located two decks down, on Main. The theater is one deck below.

From early April through October, the *Veendam* sails from New York every Saturday for Hamilton, Bermuda, while sister ship *Volendam* departs on Sundays for both St. George's harbor and Hamilton. Both are popular, fun-filled vessels on this Bermuda run and it's not unusual to see bridal parties scurrying aboard early for the nuptial ceremony (bring your own preacher) and reception. Holland America has also instituted the successful Impulse Cruise for these sailings, whereby passengers can book ahead at lower rates with a $200 deposit and receive confirmation a week before departure (on a space-available-basis).

During the winter season, the *Veendam* sails from Tampa every Saturday for Playa del Carmen, Cozumel, Montego Bay, and Grand Cayman. The *Volendam* is based in Port Everglades on two-week sailings to the Caribbean that are also offered as seven-day air/sea between Florida and Barbados. The "Seafarer" departs Port Everglades every Saturday for St. John, St. Maarten, Martinique, and Barbados. The "Wayfarer" sails every Saturday from Barbados for Antigua, San Juan, St. Thomas and Port Everglades. The two-week cruises visit all ports with no duplication.

★★★VERACRUZ

Bahama Cruise Line; Panamanian registry and international crew; built in Hamburg in 1957 and reconstructed in 1975; 10,600 tons; 488 feet long; 64 feet at beam; 700 passengers; crew of 300; cruising speed of 18 knots; 8 passenger decks.

It's time the secret of the *Veracruz* was out! What some people once considered somewhat of a "tub" has become a delightful vessel on which to cruise. The size of the cabins has not changed (small) and the decor often leaves something to be desired, but the sixteen-or-so nationality crew is pleasant and helpful. They are also a smiling lot, which means that someone is treating them right. Since Bahama Cruise Line was reborn recently with a new owner, things have changed and both the vessel and the itineraries are to be commended. Since the beginning of the 1980s, the company has pioneered two very interesting programs—to the Land of the Maya during the winter and to the so-called Northeast Passage all summer.

The winter program departs from Tampa, a port that is becoming more and more popular for cruise ships due to the over crowding of southern Florida. The Saturday afternoon sailings spend Monday in Playa del Carmen (for Cancun) and Tuesday at Cozumel. Thursday is spent at Key West, Florida. Passengers aboard the seven-day cruises may also opt for a Cruise-and-Stay program into the Yucatan, and re-embark the *Veracruz* the following Tuesday. The land route include Uxmal, Merida, Chichen Itza, Tulum, and Xel-ha Lagoon.

The ship line has also developed a popular Aquasports Adventures program that features both snorkeling and scuba diving. Participants will explore the reefs at each port of call, supplemented with on-board lectures, slide shows, and films. For certified divers, there is a Cruise 'N Dive program that offers seven dives and use of equipment. There is also a Learn to Dive for novices as well as a Snorkeling Safari that includes instruction plus a take-home set of equipment for just $75. The addition of Key West is another example of Bahama Cruise Line's interest in North America. Bravo!

During the summer months, the *Veracruz* sails between New York and Montreal on one-week cruises through the Northeast Passage. Again, the ports of call are of great interest to all North Americans, for they combine our continent's natural beauty with cultural capitals. New Bedford and Fall River, Massachusetts, offer passengers a glimpse of the old whaling days and the Gold Coast in Newport, Rhode Island boasts old mansions from the days when money was no object for some of the successful. Sydney and Halifax in Nova Scotia are full of historical significance and French-English confrontations in the New World. Bonaventure Island and the Saguenay River cruising both show nature at her best (on a sunny day), and the Canadian cultural capitals of Quebec and Montreal are like being in Europe (with none of the effort or expense).

The seven-hundred passenger *Veracruz* is a survivor. Built in 1957 by the German government as war reparations, the ship has been through a few lives already but was rebuilt in La Spezia shipyard in Italy in 1975. She flies the Panamanian flag of convenience, has a handsome young West German captain named Jens Thorn, and a crew that includes nationals from Korea, the Philippines, France, Jamaica, England, America, and Canada. As I mentioned earlier, the service is very pleasant indeed, somewhat better in the dining room than in the cabins. Accommodations are small but good value for the money. Entertainment is mediocre, but the food is certainly on a par with many other mid-category ships. The vessel itself is small but very compact, and the Denny Brown stabilizers are rarely utilized. A casino and lounge are very popular during the proper hours; the New Orleans coffee shop is great for Continental breakfasts and late-night snacks. It also serves complimentary hot dogs and hamburgers during the noon hour. Some refurbishing includes making the Lido bar area into a dancing-under-the-stars, upgrading the Casino Lounge, and creating a proper recreation room atop for the young.

Life aboard the *Veracruz* is considered very casual. Jackets and ties are only necessary twice during the cruise (at the Captain's Hail and Farewell parties). There are two seatings in the dining room and table assignments are made on embarkation only. Smoking and non-smoking is available. There is a small theater, offering good feature films, and a small reading/writing room on Galleon Deck. The swimming pool is small but does the job, and there seems to be plenty of complimentary deck chairs to accommodate everyone.

★★VICTORIA

Chandris, Inc.; Panamanian registry, Greek and Indian crew; originally built in 1939 and formerly named Dunottar Castle; refurbished in 1971; 14,917 tons; 572 feet long; 72 feet at beam; 562 passengers; crew of 300; cruising speed of 16 knots; 7 passenger decks.

Although definitely a vintage vessel, the *Victoria* is considered one of Chandris' best, for she was nicely refurbished in the early 1970s. Since becoming a member of the Chandris fleet a few years ago, the *Victoria* has increased her capacity from 480 passengers to the present 562, with the addition of 42 inside and 32 outside cabins. The ship now totals 218 outside and 67 inside accommodations, all with private facilities. Public areas include two lounges, a double-deck theater with wide screen, a casino, library/card room, the Bamboo Club, and Roman Restaurant (where two seatings take place for all meals). She also has two swimming pools back to back on Lido Deck and a gymnasium/sauna up on Pearl Deck. I think it's too bad much of the outdoor deck space had to be reduced to add the extra cabins on Pearl Deck. I also find the cabin space adequate but not overly generous. The attendants come from India, while the officers, crew, and atmosphere are all Greek.

The *Victoria* sails from San Juan every Monday, from just before Christmas through April, on two different itineraries, both cruising the Caribbean. During the summer season the *Victoria* sails from Amsterdam on a series of fourteen-day cruises to the Northern Capitals and the North Cape. The *Victoria* then departs Amsterdam for a fourteen-day repositioning cruise to the Mediterranean followed by an itinerary that includes Piraeus, Alexandria, Haifa, Limassol, Kuşadasi, Corfu, Dubrovnik, and Venice. She then sails from Venice for Katakolon, Piraeus, Kuşadasi, Alexandria, Haifa, Crete, and Dubrovnik.

In early December the *Victoria* departs Genoa for the winter, via a fifteen-day transatlantic voyage to San Juan calling en route at Madeira, Barbados, Guadeloupe, Antigua, and St. Thomas. Arriving in San Juan just before

Christmas, the vessel begins her Caribbean season of seven-day sailings every Monday through April.

★★★★★ + VISTAFJORD

Norwegian American Cruises; Norwegian registry and northern European crew; launched in 1973; 25,000 tons; 628 feet long; 82 feet at beam; 635 passengers; crew of 350; cruising speed of 20 knots; 8 passenger decks.

The *Vistafjord* is one of my favorite cruise vessels for her onboard ambience and the beauty of her interior. She even cuts a striking figure on the outside, with a beige hull and striped smokestack. I rate her at the top of the first-class line of cruise ships, and this is reflected everywhere—from cabin service to itineraries. To begin with, Norwegian American Cruises presents you with a complimentary bottle of champagne as you check into your stateroom, a thoughtful gesture and a most gracious way to begin any cruise holiday. The accommodations are lovely and well kept (you never have the feeling that some little bit of decor needs replacing), and all rooms are serviced by ingratiating stewardesses, many of whom are girlfriends or wives to the male half of the crew. The vessel has a total of 294 outside and 46 inside cabins, all with the most modern private facilities (including precision-dialed temperatures for those with bathtubs), and twenty-four-hour room service.

A striking characteristic of the vessel is the interior staircase, perfect for grand entrances and make-believe (children love it too). In the beautiful Vista Dining Room you can have both a delicious meal and a wonderful view, and I especially like having the entire passenger complement accommodated (with room to spare) at one seating. The food is truly Continental, with many Scandinavian specialties (like herring fixed in an endless number of ways). Other public rooms include a Grand Ballroom in the grand old tradition (with a capacity for seven hundred), a more casual Garden Lounge, Norse Lounge, and North Cape Bar (where everyone congregates). The Club Viking on Promenade Deck is the spacious nightclub-cum-disco. The *Vistafjord* also has two swimming pools (one indoors with massage, saunas, and gym adjacent), a dance studio (for classes), a fine Sports Deck, casino, library, and writing room.

The *Vistafjord* was completely refurbished in late 1981 and the $6 million seems to have been well spent. Passengers who can afford suites will be entranced by the Vista and Star penthouses as well as the deluxe accommodations up on Sun Deck. The vessel's four other suites, named after the Norwegian monarchs Magnus, Harald, Olav, and Haakon, are located on Promenade Deck. As this elegant vessel will be celebrating a tenth anniversary of service on May 15, 1983, passengers can expect some special events aboard their spring and summer cruises.

The *Vistafjord* is a favorite with Europeans and is scheduled to spend most of her time sailing from Genoa and Hamburg this year. Some even call her the Dreamboat *(Traumschiff)* after a German TV series that was filmed abroad.

Look for the ship also in a new Jon Voight feature film named *Table for Five*. As 1983 arrives, the *Vistafjord* will be on the first segment of a complete circumnavigation of the African continent. Her schedule calls for a December 18 departure from Genoa for the Suez Canal and Red Sea, the Indian Ocean and Cape Town, before sailing up the western Coast of Africa to Southampton. Following some transatlantic crossings, that include calls in the Caribbean and Cape Canaveral, the vessel returns to Genoa for the spring season in the Mediterranean and Black Sea. A repositioning in June, via the Iberian Peninsula, finds the *Vistafjord* in Hamburg for two-week cruises to the North Cape, the Baltic, and Northern Capitals. Pre-Christmas cruises will be offered again from Genoa to the Mediterranean ports.

★★★★ + WORLD DISCOVERER

Society Expeditions; Singapore registry, West German officers, and Indonesian crew; built in 1974 in Germany; 3,200 tons; 285 feet long; 140 passengers; crew of 70; cruising speed of 14.7 knots; 6 passenger decks.

The *World Discoverer* was designed especially for cruising to confined and remote areas of the world. A shallow draft allows the vessel to sail safely into places that are inaccessible to other ships. She is also exceptionally easy to maneuver and has an especially strengthened and ice-hardened hull to feel right at home among the icebergs! Her navigational equipment is the most sophisticated possible, and she carries both super-launches and inflatable rubber boats for exploring narrow tributaries and otherwise nonnavigable waters.

The interior of the *World Discoverer* is comfortable and practicable but hardly meant to be luxurious. The standard two-berth cabins have showers and two lower beds (one foldaway into the wall). All seventy-five cabins are outside, and a few can accommodate a third person. Two suites are available on A Deck (99 and 114). The dining room is also situated on A Deck; it accommodates the full passenger complement at one seating for all meals (no breakfast in bed, please). There are four Swiss chefs on board who deliver an excellent menu with local specialties. Public rooms include the Seven Seas Lounge, High Tide Bar, and library on Boat Deck, and a lecture room/cinema combination on Observation Deck. The vessel also has a small swimming pool and a gymnasium/solarium/sauna area. There are two Sun decks, but one is rather full of the rubber landing craft, so there is not much space left for passengers. Entertainment means a pianist in the lounge, first-run movies late at night, dance music, or occasional "crew shows."

The theme aboard the *World Discoverer* is conservation and preservation of wildlife and cultures around the world. Itineraries are planned for travelers who have a keen sense of curiosity and adventure and the flexibility of mind needed for spontaneous exploration. Naturalists on board the vessel net fish and other sea life for display in the *Discoverer*'s aquaria. Microscopes, plant presses, and other scientific equipment are also available for passengers' use. Along with the 70 crew members, there are approximately seven lecturers on board (as well as three members of the Society Expeditions staff). Briefings on the itinerary and program are held daily in the lecture room with an enclosed deck/observation area or in the lounge before dinner. At the beginning of every cruise, there will be instruction regarding the use of the motorized Zodiacs for landing on dockless shores.

In January, November, and December 1983, the *World Discoverer* will sail around Antarctica, then move in February to Milford Sound, the Great Barrier Reef, and New Guinea. In March, the vessel sails among the Indonesian archipelago visiting the remote islands and villages (when it is convenient to the Indonesian government), and arrives in Singapore by April for a sailing to the Seychelles and vicinity. Springtime finds the *Discoverer* in the Red Sea, cruising from Djibouti up through the Suez Canal. During July, the vessel can be found in the Arctic, sailing among the Norwegian fjords to Spitsbergen, then Iceland and Greenland. In mid-September the *Discoverer* cruises the Amazon River, and so it goes.

★★★WORLD RENAISSANCE

Epirotiki Lines; on long-term charter agreement to Costa Line; Greek registry and crew; originally built in 1966 and named Renaissance; 12,000 tons; 492 feet long; 69 feet at beam; 426 passengers; crew of 200; cruising speed of 18.5 knots; 8 passenger decks.

This charming vessel was the flagship and pride of Paquet French Cruises but was sold in an economy measure to Epirotiki Lines. Epirotiki changed her registry and crew to Greek, renamed her *World Renaissance*, and chartered her out on a long-term basis to Costa. The *World Renaissance* is a small, very cozy ship and a familiar sight in the Caribbean where she now sails every Saturday in season from San Juan.

She has 173 outside and 40 inside cabins, all with private facilities. Although I'd say that in general the cabins are on the small side and the rates on the high side, rooms 601 and 602 on Sun Deck are excellent value ($1,170 per person, double occupancy). The vessel has an agreeable Grand Salon that accommodates the entire passenger complement, a pleasant dining room with one seating for meals, and a charming Cafe de Paris for drinks and snacks by the pool. Other facilities include a second pool up on Sun Deck, a small theater/cinema, and a nightclub/disco on Taverne Deck.

Of course, it is anyone's guess, but the word is that the *World Renaissance* will repeat a series of most successful Eastern Seaboard departures to Bermuda from May through July. These seven-day cruises depart from Jacksonville (Florida), Philadelphia, Baltimore, and Charleston and call at St. George's, the island's first capital and a most enchanting port. At the end of July, look for a cruise from Charleston to La Guaira (Venezuela) via Cape Canaveral, Nassau, and Curaçao. This cruise features an overnight at the Caracas Hilton and a return flight to American gateways.

Some readers have complained about the cleanliness aboard this vessel, but the price you pay does not mean a scrubwoman cleans every hour. As rates on this (and all other Costa vessels) are very reasonable, I can only suspect that some passengers expect more than they deserve (and their travel agents should set them right.) I have always found the *World Renaissance* a most appealing ship and I can easily forgive her sometime drawbacks (and I am not easy to please). I sincerely feel that on this type of vessel, you should book middle-of-the-line (if possible) for maximum comfort and satisfaction. I can understand being upset at cabins located "below the water line" or above the engines. We have all been there—but the activities aboard and the ports of call should more than compensate for (perhaps) an unfortunate draw of cabins.

★★★★★YAO HUA (BRILLIANCE)

Salen Lindblad Cruising; Chinese registry and crew; built in France in 1967; 10,000 tons; 385 feet long; 66 feet at beam; 176 passengers; crew of 220; cruising speed of 15.5 knots; 4 passenger decks.

The *Yao Hua* ("brilliance") is one of three vessels now being marketed by Salen Lindblad Cruising. The Salen Group (which owns the *Lindblad Polaris*) spent $1 million on this vessel and, in a joint venture with China Ocean Shipping Company, inaugurated China coastal cruises aimed at the American market. The *Yao Hua* has a capacity for 176 passengers in 88 cabins; most are twins with private baths, but there are several deluxe accommodations, including two suites. All accommodations are now located on the outside of Promenade, A, B, and C decks. Public rooms include the Club Lounge (on Promenade Deck adjacent to the swimming pool), a small writing room and casino, the Dragon Boat Lounge, the conference room, some shops, and a dining room that holds all passengers on an open-seating basis.

The food aboard the *Yao Hua* is reported to be excellent and just the perfect combination of Western and Chinese. Breakfasts are buffet-style, with plenty of breads and fruit and eggs, as well as yoghurt for those who wish to live to be 100. The more adventuresome may also wish to try the rice gruel and stir-fried Chinese noodles with scallions and bits of pork. Ship-board lunches on days at sea feature the traditional Swedish smorgasbord, with herring in several different sauces, cold dishes plus some familiar-looking leftovers, fruit, and cheese. In addition, the Captains hosts two very Swedish dinners which are considered the Welcome Aboard and Farewell evenings. Otherwise, the *Yao Hua* is considered one of the best floating Chinese restaurants in the neighborhood.

Two-week programs from the U.S., in conjunction with Pan Am, give passengers plenty of time for sightseeing/shopping in both Hong Kong and Peking plus the six-day cruise. Ports of call in the People's Republic are Xiamen (Amoy), Shanghai, and Nanjing, as well as a full day sailing the Yangtse River. Passengers fly between Beijing and Nanjing, but cruise to and from Hong Kong. There is talk that the *Yao Hua* may be found in the South Pacific during the winter season.

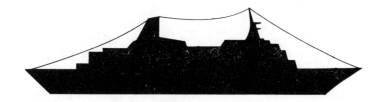

13. / WORLDWIDE SHIP SCHEDULES

Itineraries and prices in the following pages (and elsewhere in the book) are based on the latest information available, and occasional changes are to be expected. Since cruise rates skyrocketed so much in the past few years, however, many ship lines have already announced that there will be no change in rates from 1982 to 1983. Others have lowered the base rate per person for the minimum accommodations and raised the prices for the deluxe suites, allowing a greater than ever range. I hope this will encourage a healthier mix of younger and older passengers aboard some of the more luxurious vessels. Please check with your travel agent and the ship line to confirm sailing dates and itineraries, and check whether the cruise rate includes any air fare. Free air fare has become the byword for many 1983 sailings!

AEGEAN/MEDITERRANEAN

FROM CIVITAVECCHIA

LINDBLAD POLARIS—Oct. 7 to Palermo, Taormina, Otranto, Dubrovnik, Split, Urbino, Venice, Rab and Zadar, Corfu, Katakolon, Milos, and Piraeus (14 days). $3,850 to $5,990 per person, double.

FROM DUBROVNIK

JASON—April 13 to Corinth Canal, Piraeus, Mt. Athos, Cape Helles, Istanbul, Troy, Pergamum, Antalya, Rhodes, Delos, Mykonos, Heraklion, and Venice (14 days); air-sea from London.

JASON—Sept. 21 to Piraeus, Santorini, Heraklion, Alexandria, Rhodes, Bodrum, Ephesus, Delos, Mykonos, Tinos, Corinth Canal, and Venice (14 days); air-sea from London.

FROM GENOA

ASTOR—March 31 and Oct. 1 to Piraeus, Alexandria, Haifa, Limassol, Rhodes, Syracuse (14 days). $2,370 to $5,357 per person, double; (Easter Cruise) $2,426 to $5,498.

ASTOR—April 14 to Messina, Catania, Heraklion, Rhodes, Kos, Izmir, Delos, Mykonos, Piraeus, Katakolon, Naples, and Civitavecchia (14 days). $2,341 to $5,293 per person, double.

ASTOR—April 28 to Piraeus, Mudanya, Varna, Yalta, Odessa, Istanbul, Katakolon (14 days). Same rates as April 14 cruise.

ASTOR—May 12 to Malaga, Cadiz, Casablanca, St. Cruz, Funchal, Lisbon, Vigo, Corunna, St. Malo, and Cuxhaven (16 days). $2,680 to $6,091 per person, double.

ASTOR—Oct. 15 to Palma de Mallorca, Malaga, Funchal, St. Cruz, Barbados, Martinique, St. Kitts, St. Thomas, San Juan, and Port Everglades (21 days). $3,245 to $7,426 per person, double.

VISTAFJORD—Dec. 17 (1982) to Port Said, Suez, Safaga, Port Sudan, Aden, Mahe, Nossi-be, Mutsamudu, Zanzibar, Mombasa, Tamatave, Port Louis, Maputo, Durban, Port Elizabeth, Cape Town, Walvis Bay, Jamestown, Lagos, Lome, Tema/Accra, Abidjan, Freetown, Dakar, Tenerife, Funchal, Lisbon, and Southampton (60 days). $10,290 to $36,750 per person, double, plus port taxes.

VISTAFJORD—March 26, April 9 and 23, Sept. 24, and Oct. 9 to Stromboli, Straits of Messina, Heraklion, Patmos, Kos, Antalya, Alanya, Haifa, Alexandria, Santorini, Piraeus (14 days). $3,430 to $9,850 per person, double (Cruising Plus).

VISTAFJORD—May 8 and Sept. 11 to Stromboli, Straits of Messina, Piraeus, Canakkale, Mudanya, Bosporus Sea, Varna, Yalta, Constanta, Istanbul, Dardanelles, Mykonos, Heraklion, Valletta (14 days). $3,430 to $9,850 per person, double (Cruising Plus).

VISTAFJORD—May 22 to Malaga, Gibraltar, Tangier, Casablanca, Agadir,

Lisbon, Vigo, Guernsey, Southampton, and Hamburg (13 days). $3,340 to $9,290 per person, double (Cruising Plus).

VISTAFJORD—Oct. 23 to Port Said, Suez, Safaga, Aden, Mogadiscio, Mombasa, Zanzibar, Mutsamudu, Madagascar, Mauritius, Seychelles, Male, Colombo, Bombay, Oman, Djibouti, Safaga, Suez, Suez Canal, Port Said, Haifa (49 days). $9,200 to $31,660 per person, double (Cruising Plus). Also available in segments.

VISTAFJORD—Dec. 17 to Izmir, Haifa, Port Said, Suez, Suez Canal, Safaga, Aden, Bombay, Male, Colombo, Kuala Lumpur, Singapore, Kota Kinabalu, Zamboanga, Makassar, Surabaya, Bali, Jakarta, Singapore, Pattaya, Labuan, Cebu, Keelung and Hong Kong (56 days). $12,290 to $39,150 per person, double (Cruising Plus). Also available in segments.

FROM MALTA

UGANDA—Jan. 16 to Alexandria, Alanya, Piraeus, Gythion, Syracuse, and Naples (13 days). £612 to £1,288 per person, double, air-sea from Gatwick.

UGANDA—March 9 to Piraeus, Istanbul, Haifa, Bodrum, Kotor, and Split (13 days). £680 to £1,431 per person, double, air-sea from Gatwick.

UGANDA—April 17 to Santorini, Haifa, Istanbul, Nauplia, Messina, and Naples (13 days). £697 to £1,467 per person, double, air-sea from Gatwick.

UGANDA—Dec. 7 to Messina, Port Said, Ashdod, Alanya, Nauplia, and Naples (13 days). £629 to £1,324 per person, double, air-sea from Gatwick.

FROM NAPLES

JASON—May 11 to Taormina, Rhodes, Patmos, Ephesus, Pergamum, Istanbul, Samothrace, Mykonos, Delos, Tinos, Piraeus, Corinth Canal, Corfu, and Venice (14 days); air-sea from London.

SEA PRINCESS—Oct. 19 to Rhodes, Port Said, Safaga, Elat, Suez, Port Said, Limassol, Haifa, and Piraeus (15 days). £1,335 to £2,415 per person, double, air-sea from Gatwick.

SEA PRINCESS—Nov. 16 to Port Said, Safaga, Aqaba, Elat, Suez, Port Said, Haifa, Rhodes, and Piraeus (15 days). £1,185 to £2,130 per person, double, air-sea from Gatwick.

UGANDA—Jan. 29 to Itea, Alexandria, Haifa, Patmos, Izmir, and Piraeus (13 days). £680 to £1,431 per person, double, air-sea from Gatwick.

UGANDA—April 30 to Bizerta, Loutraki, Alexandria, Antalya, Mykonos, Delos, and Piraeus (13 days). £714 to £1,503 per person, double, air-sea from Gatwick.

UGANDA—Dec. 20 to Haifa, Mersin, Rhodes, Piraeus, Monemvasia, and Split (13 days). £740 to £1,557 per person, double, air-sea from Gatwick.

FROM NICE

STELLA MARIS—Alternate Saturdays in June, July, and August to Portofino, Costa Smeralda, Tunis, Malta, Katakolon, Corfu, Dubrovnik, and Venice (7 days). $1,050 to $1,800 per person, double, plus $30 port taxes.

FROM PIRAEUS

AQUARIUS—every Friday from March 25 through Nov. 4 to Santorini, Heraklion, Rhodes, Kuşadasi, Istanbul, Mykonos (7 days). $795 to $1,275 per person, double, off season (March 25; April 1, 8, 15; Oct. 21, 28; Nov. 4); $995 to $1,500 low season (April 22, 29; June, July, and August; Oct. 14); $1,100 to $1,700 (May, September, and October 7); plus $55 port taxes.

ATLAS—every Monday from April 11 through October to Rhodes, Alexandria, Port Said, Ashdod, Patmos, and Kuşadasi (7 days). $1,140 to $2,080 per person, double, plus $55 port taxes.

GOLDEN ODYSSEY—April 4 and 16; April 28, May 10, July 11, Aug. 16 and 28 to Kuşadasi, Istanbul, Mykonos, Rhodes, Alexandria, Haifa (14 days air-sea from U.S.). $2,978 to $4,298 per person, double; $2,858 to $4,198 on April 4 and 16 (value season).

GOLDEN ODYSSEY—May 22, Sept. 9, Oct. 5 to Mykonos, Naples, Livorno, Nice/Villefranche, Palma, Malaga, Gibraltar, and Lisbon (15 days air-sea from U.S.). $3,168 to $4,498 per person, double.

GOLDEN ODYSSEY—June 17, July 23 to Odessa, Yalta, Istanbul, Izmir, Mykonos, Corfu, Bay of Kotor, Dubrovnik, and Venice (14 days air-sea from U.S.). $2,978 to $4,298 per person, double.

JUPITER—Every Friday from April 15 to Nov. 11 to Mykonos, Rhodes, Patmos, and Kuşadasi (3 days). $480 to $680 per person, double, plus $25 port taxes.

JUPITER—Every Monday from April 11 to Nov. 7 to Mykonos, Heraklion, Santorini, Kos, Rhodes, Patmos, and Kuşadasi (4 days). $640 to $915 per person, double, plus $27 port taxes.

JUPITER—March 28 and Apr. 4 to Rhodes, Alexandria, Port Said, Ashdod, Patmos, and Kuşadasi (7 days). $1,140 to $2,080 per person, double, plus $55 port taxes.

LINDBLAD POLARIS—Oct. 21 to Volos, Skiros/Skiathos, Thessaloniki, Samothrace, Istanbul, Dikili, Chios/Samos, Mykonos, Santorini, Kasos/Karpathos, Lindos, and Rhodes (14 days). $3,850 to $5,990 per person, double.

NEPTUNE—March 25 and Apr. 8 to Mykonos, Rhodes, Patmos, and Kuşadasi (3 days). $480 to $680 per person, double, plus $25 port taxes.

NEPTUNE—March 21 and Apr. 4 to Mykonos, Santorini, Kos, Rhodes, Patmos, and Kuşadasi (4 days). $640 to $915 per person, double, plus $27 port taxes.

NEPTUNE—Apr. 15 through May 13 to Heraklion, Santorini, Rhodes, Patmos, Kuşadasi, Istanbul, and Mykonos (Delos optional) (7 days). $1,140 to $2,080 per person, double, plus $55 port taxes.

NEPTUNE—May 27; June 17; July 8, 29; Aug. 19; Sept. 9 to Canakkale (for Troy), Varna, Constanta, Odessa, Yalta, Istanbul, Kuşadasi, Patmos, Santorini, and Mykonos (10 days). $1,330 to $2,200 per person, double, plus $80 port taxes.

NEPTUNE—June 6, 27; July 18; Aug. 8 and 29 to Canakkale (for Troy), Varna, Constanta, Yalta, Sochi, Sukhumi, Istanbul, Kuşadasi, Santorini, and Mykonos (11 days). $1,460 to $2,420 per person, double, plus $100 port taxes.

ROYAL ODYSSEY—Sept. 20; Oct. 2 and 14. Same rates and itinerary as May 10 *Golden Odyssey*.

ROYAL ODYSSEY—April 9. Same itinerary as May 22 *Golden Odyssey*, with value season rates from $3,068 to $4,198 per person, double.

ROYAL ODYSSEY—May 5 to Heraklion, Capri, Livorno, Villefranche/Nice, Palma, Malaga, Lisbon, and Tilbury (17 days air-sea from U.S.). $3,328 to $4,668 per person, double.

ROYAL VIKING SKY—April 25, May 9 and 23 to Catania, Livorno, Villefranche, Kotor, Dubrovnik, Venice (14 days). $2,156 to $7,882 per person, double, plus port taxes.

ROYAL VIKING SKY—June 6 to Gibraltar, Lisbon, Southampton, Amsterdam, and Copenhagen (11 days). $1,694 to $6,193 per person, double, plus port taxes.

ROYAL VIKING SKY—Sept. 8 and 21, Oct. 4 to Varna, Odessa, Yalta, Istanbul, Kuşadasi, Patmos, Mykonos, Rhodes, Heraklion (13 days). $2,249 to $8,112 per person, double, plus port taxes.

ROYAL VIKING SKY—Oct. 17 and 30 to Istanbul, Kuşadasi, Rhodes, Alexandria, Port Said, Haifa, Heraklion (13 days). $2,093 to $7,683 per person, double, plus port taxes.

ROYAL VIKING SKY—Nov. 12 to Catania, Malaga, Gibraltar, Lisbon, Casablanca, Las Palmas, Dakar, St. Thomas, and Port Everglades (24 days). $3,480 to $13,512 per person, double, plus port taxes.

SEA PRINCESS—May 2 to Haifa, Limassol, Mersin, Istanbul, Corfu, and

Venice (13 days). £975 to £1,755 per person, double, air-sea from Gatwick.

SEA PRINCESS—May 28 to Istanbul, Skiathos, Izmir, Kos, Palma, Praia da Rocha, and Southampton (14 days). £1,036 to £1,834 per person, double, air-sea from Gatwick.

SEA PRINCESS—Sept. 23 to Alexandria, Alanya, Izmir, Corfu, Dubrovnik, and Venice (13 days). £1,157 to £2,093 per person, double, air-sea from Gatwick.

SEA PRINCESS—Nov. 3 to Alexandria, Haifa, Istanbul, Volos, Messina, and Naples (13 days). £1,118 to £1,989 per person, double, air-sea from Gatwick.

SEA PRINCESS—Dec. 1 to Aghios Nikolaos (Crete), Alexandria, Haifa, Limassol, Alicante, Gibraltar, and Southampton (14 days). £910 to £1,638 per person, double, air-sea from Gatwick.

STELLA OCEANIS/STELLA MARIS—Every Friday from May 6 through October to Kos, Rhodes, Heraklion, Santorini (3 days). $435 to $875 per person, double, plus $15 port taxes.

STELLA OCEANIS/STELLA MARIS—Every Monday from May 2 through October to Hydra, Santorini, Heraklion, Rhodes, Kuşadasi, and Mykonos (4 days). $585 to $1,170 per person, double, plus $25 port taxes.

STELLA SOLARIS—Alternate Mondays from May 2 through October to Port Said, Ashdod, Haifa, Rhodes, Kuşadasi, and Samos (7 days). $995 to $2,050 per person, double, plus $50 port taxes.

STELLA SOLARIS—Alternate Mondays from May 9 through October to Dikili, Istanbul, Izmir, Rhodes, Heraklion, Santorini, Delos/Mykonos (7 days). $995 to $2,050 per person, double, plus $50 port taxes.

STELLA SOLARIS—Alternate Sundays from May through October (15 days air-sea from U.S. combining the two above itineraries). $2,890 to $5,000 per person, double, plus $100 port taxes.

UGANDA—Feb. 11 to Istanbul, Rhodes, Limassol, Haifa, Nauplia, and Venice (13 days). £680 to £1,431 per person, double, air-sea from Gatwick.

UGANDA—May 13 to Varna, Constanta, Trabzon, Istanbul, Volos, and Split (13 days). £714 to £1,503 per person, double, air-sea from Gatwick.

UGANDA—June 6 to Izmir, Volos, Palermo, Cagliari, Port Mahon, Lisbon, and Southampton (14 days). £714 to £1,503 per person, double, air-sea from Gatwick.

UGANDA—Oct. 2 to Kavalla, Istanbul, Haifa, Limassol, Kotor, and Venice (14 days). £751 to £1,580 per person, double, air-sea from Gatwick.

UGANDA—Oct. 29 to Volos, Alexandria, Dikili, Rhodes, Corfu, and Split (13 days). £680 to £1,431 per person, double, air-sea from Gatwick.

FROM SPLIT

UGANDA—March 22 to Skiathos, Izmir, Alexandria, Rhodes, Heraklion, and Venice (13 days). £680 to £1,431 per person, double, air-sea from Gatwick.

UGANDA—May 26 to Itea, Haifa, Alanya, Santorini, and Piraeus (11 days). £619 to £1,302 per person, double, air-sea from Gatwick.

UGANDA—Nov. 11 to Navarino, Istanbul, Piraeus, Mykonos, Delos, Dubrovnik, and Venice (13 days). £646 to £1,359 per person, double, air-sea from Gatwick.

FROM VENICE

GOLDEN ODYSSEY—June 29, Aug. 4 to Dubrovnik, Bay of Kotor, Corfu, Mykonos, Izmir, Istanbul, Odessa, Yalta, and Piraeus (14 days air-sea from U.S.). $2,978 to $4,298 per person, double.

JASON—March 30 to Olympia, Heraklion, Alexandria, Rhodes, Bodrum, Ephesus, Delos, Mykonos, Syros, Piraeus, Corinth Canal, Mycenae, Corfu, and Dubrovnik (14 days); air-sea from London.

JASON—April 27 to Olympia, Corinth Canal, Piraeus, Delos, Mykonos, Mt. Athos, Thasos, Pergamum, Sardis, Izmir, Ephesus, Mylasa, Bodrum, Heraklion, Malta, Tunis, and Naples (14 days); air-sea from London.

JASON—May 25 to Olympia, Heraklion, Rhodes, Bodrum, Mylasa, Ephesus, Cape Helles, Troy, Istanbul, Princes' Islands, Samothrace, Mt. Athos, Mykonos, Delos, Tinos, Piraeus, Corinth Canal, Kotor Fjord, Dubrovnik, Split, and Venice (14 days); air-sea from London.

JASON—June 8 to Korcula, Dubrovnik, Corfu, Delphi, Corinth Canal, Santorini, Patmos, Ephesus, Cape Helles, Troy, Istanbul, Princes' Islands, Samothrace, Thasos, Mykonos, Delos, Tinos, Piraeus, and Venice (14 days); air-sea from London.

JASON—Aug. 10 to Corinth Canal, Piraeus, Delos, Mykonos, Mt. Athos, Thasos, Samothrace, Cape Helles, Troy, Istanbul, Princes' Islands, Izmir, Sardis, Rhodes, Santorini, Corfu, Korcula, and Venice (14 days); air-sea from London.

JASON—Aug. 24 to Korcula, Dubrovnik, Corfu, Santorini, Patmos, Ephesus, Cape Helles, Troy, Istanbul, Princes' Islands, Mt. Athos, Delos, Mykonos, Tinos, Piraeus, Corinth Canal, and Venice (14 days); air-sea from London.

JASON—Sept. 7 to Corfu, Heraklion, Santorini, Rhodes, Patmos, Ephesus, Cape Helles, Troy, Istanbul, Princes' Islands, Samothrace, Salonica, Mykonos, Delos, Piraeus, Corinth Canal, and Dubrovnik (14 days); air-sea from London.

SEA PRINCESS—May 15 to Itea, Naples, Alexandria, Izmir, Volos, and Piraeus (13 days). £975 to £1,755 per person, double, air-sea from Gatwick.

SEA PRINCESS—Oct. 6 to Itea, Haifa, Piraeus, Kos, Messina, and Naples (13 days). £1,118 to £1,989 per person, double, air-sea from Gatwick.

STELLA MARIS—Alternate Saturdays in June, July, and August to Dubrovnik, Corfu, Malta, Tunis, Costa Smeralda, Elba, Portofino, and Nice (7 days). $1,050 to $1,800 per person, double, plus $30 port taxes.

UGANDA—Feb. 24 to Dubrovnik, Kos, Alexandria, Haifa, Heraklion, and Malta (13 days). £697 to £1,467 per person, double, air-sea from Gatwick.

UGANDA—April 4 to Heraklion, Bodrum, Istanbul, Patmos, Itea, and Malta (13 days). IAPS Educational Cruises charter. Rates on request.

UGANDA—Oct. 16 to Dubrovnik, Katakolon, Heraklion, Alexandria, Izmir, and Piraeus (13 days). £697 to £1,467 per person, double, air-sea from Gatwick.

UGANDA—Nov. 24 to Itea, Rhodes, Alexandria, Haifa, Aghios Nikolaos, and Malta (13 days). £697 to £1,467 per person, double, air-sea from Gatwick.

CARIBBEAN

FROM BARBADOS

ASTOR—March 12 to Martinique, St. Kitts, St. Maarten, San Juan, Bermuda, Ponta Delgada, Funchal, Malaga, and Genoa (19 days). $2,755 to $6,470 per person, double.

NORDIC PRINCE—Alternate Saturdays to Martinique, St. Maarten, San Juan, St. Thomas, and Miami (7 days). *SunVenture* 2. $1,210 to $1,435 per person, double, all air fare and port charges.

VISTAFJORD—March 2 to St. Lucia, Martinique, St. Croix, Port-au-Prince, Nassau, Cape Canaveral, and Port Everglades. $2,590 to $7,630 per person, double (Cruising Plus).

VOLENDAM—Jan. 29, Feb. 12 and 26, March 12 and 26, April 9 to Antigua, San Juan, St. Thomas, and Port Everglades (7 days). $815 to $1,790 per person, double, including air fare where applicable.

FROM CURACAO

STELLA SOLARIS—Jan. 17, Feb. 6 and 26 to Aruba, Cartagena, Panama Canal transit (partial), Balboa, San Blas Islands, Montego Bay, Grand Cayman, Playa del Carmen/Cozumel, and Galveston (10 days). $2,100 to $3,895 per person, double, plus $55 port taxes.

FROM NASSAU

NEW SHOREHAM II—Jan. 21, Feb. 4 and 18, March 4 and 18, April 1 and 15, May 1 to Spanish Wells, the Bluff and Current on Eleuthera, Hatchet Bay, Governor's Harbour, Cape Eleuthera, Exuma Sound, Sampson Cay, Staniel Cay, Halls Pond Cay and Highborne Cay (12 days). $750 to $1,250 per person, double.

NEW SHOREHAM II—April 26 to Berry Islands, Harbour Island, Gorda Cay, Cave Cay, Crown Haven, Green Turtle Cay, Treasure Cay, Man-O-War Cay, Marsh Harbour, Guana Cay, and Freeport (12 days). Same rates as *New Shoreham II* above.

FROM SAN JUAN

ASTOR—Jan. 16 to St. Maarten, St. Barthelemy, Dominica, Martinique, St. Lucia, Grenada, Trinidad, French Guiana, Belem, Amazon Delta, Almerin, Rio Tapajos, Santarem, Boca do Valeria, and Manaus (16 days). $2,480 to $5,816 per person, double.

ASTOR—Nov. 16 and Dec. 7 to St. Thomas, Martinique, Grenada, La Guaira, Aruba, Port-au-Prince, Nassau, and Port Everglades (10 days). $1,992 to $4,484 per person, double; (Thanksgiving Cruise) $1,914 to $4,301.

CARLA C.—Every Saturday from Jan. 8 to Curaçao, La Guaira, Grenada, Martinique, and St. Thomas (7 days). $895 to $1,995 per person, double, plus $25 port taxes. Some free and/or discounted air fare.

CUNARD COUNTESS—Every Saturday to La Guaira, Grenada, Barbados, Martinique, and St. Thomas (7 days). $1,069 to $1,965 per person, double, air-sea from 40 cities.

CUNARD PRINCESS—Every Saturday to St. Maarten, Iles des Saintes/Guadeloupe, St. Lucia, St. Kitts, St. Thomas, Virgin Gorda/Tortola (7 days). Same rates as *Cunard Countess* above.

DAPHNE—Every Saturday from Jan. 8 through March 18 to Curaçao, La Guaira, Grenada, Guadeloupe, and St. Thomas (7 days). $995 to $1,875 per person, double, plus $29 port taxes. Some free and/or discounted air fare.

FAIRSEA—Jan. 29, March 19, Oct. 22 to St. Thomas, Aruba, Cartagena, San Blas Islands, Panama Canal transit, Acapulco, Cabo San Lucas, and Los Angeles (14 days). $2,485 to $4,830 per person, double, plus port taxes (value season); $2,625 to $4,970 (peak season). Free air fare.

FAIRSEA—May 21. Same itinerary as *Fairsea* above, ends San Francisco. Value Season rates.

GOLDEN ODYSSEY—Jan. 7 to La Guaira, Aruba, Cartagena, San Blas Islands, Panama Canal transit, Balboa/Panama City, and Acapulco (12 days air-sea from U.S.). $2,248 to $3,398 per person, double.

GOLDEN ODYSSEY—Jan. 29; Feb. 7, 16, and 25; March 6 to St. Barthelemy, St. Maarten, St. Lucia, Barbados, La Guaira, Curaçao, St. Thomas (10 days air-sea from U.S.). $1,898 to $2,898 per person, double.

ISLAND PRINCESS—Jan. 29, Feb. 26, March 26, April 23, May 21, Oct. 8, Nov. 5, Dec. 10 to St. Thomas, La Guaira, Curaçao, Panama Canal transit, Panama City, Acapulco, Cabo San Lucas and Los Angeles (14 days). $3,206 to $6,202 per person, double, plus port taxes (Jan. 15 through April 9; Oct. 22 through Dec. 10); $2,982 to $5,796 per person, double (April 23 through May 21; Sept. 24 through Oct. 8).

MERMOZ—Jan. 3 to Colombia, Curaçao, Barbados, St. Lucia, Guadeloupe, and St. Croix (11 days). *Music Festival at Sea.* $2,730 to $6,015 per person, double, plus $19 port taxes. Free air fare from most cities.

MERMOZ—Jan. 25, Feb. 15 and March 8 to St. Barthelemy, Guadeloupe, Curaçao, La Guaira, Martinique, Antigua, and St. Croix (10 days). $1,445 to $2,455 per person, double, plus $19 port taxes. Free air fare from most cities.

MERMOZ—Jan. 14, Feb. 4 and 25, March 18 to St. Thomas, Guadeloupe, Curaçao, La Guaira, Tobago, Barbados, Martinique, and St. John (11 days). $1,570 to $2,685 per person, double, plus $19 port taxes. Free air fare from most cities.

STELLA OCEANIS—Jan. 7 and 14, Feb. 4 and 18 to St. Maarten, Iles des Saintes, Dominica, St. Lucia, Barbados, Tobago, Ciudad Guayana, Palm Island, St. Vincent, Bequia, Antigua, Montserrat, St. Kitts, and St. Thomas (14 days). $2,370 to $4,620 per person, double, plus $40 port taxes. (Subtract $200 for Jan. 7 cruise).

STELLA OCEANIS—March 4 to St. Maarten, Iles des Saintes, Dominica, St. Lucia, Barbados, Tobago, Ciudad Guayana, Union/Palm Islands, St. Vincent, Bequia, Antigua, Montserrat, St. Kitts, and St. Thomas (13 days). $2,170 to $4,420 per person, double, plus $40 port taxes.

SUN PRINCESS—Alternate Saturdays from Jan. 8 through April 30; Oct. 29 through Dec. 10 to Curaçao, La Guaira, Palm Island, Martinique, and St. Thomas (7 days). $1,477 to $2,779 per person, double, plus port taxes (Jan. 29 through March 25; Oct. 22 through Dec. 10); $1,407 to $2,646 (Jan. 8 through Jan. 22; April 2 through May 7).

SUN PRINCESS—Alternate Saturdays from Jan. 15 through May 7; Oct. 22 through Dec. 3 to Barbados, Palm Island, Martinique, St. Maarten, and St. Thomas (7 days). Same rates as *Sun Princess* above.

SUN PRINCESS—Dec. 17 to Curaçao, La Guaira, Barbados, Palm Island, Martinique, St. Maarten, and St. Thomas (11 days). $2,420 to $4,576 per person, double, plus port taxes.

SUN PRINCESS—Dec. 28 to Curaçao, La Guaira, Barbados, Palm Island,

Martinique, St. Maarten, and St. Thomas (10 days). $2,200 to $4,160 per person, double, plus port taxes.

SUN PRINCESS—May 14 to St. Thomas, La Guaira, Curaçao, Panama Canal transit, Panama City, Acapulco, Cabo San Lucas, and Los Angeles (14 days). $2,716 to $5,572 per person, double, plus port taxes.

VICTORIA—Jan. 3, 17, 31; Feb. 14, 28; March 14, 28; April 11, 25; May 9 to St. Thomas, Guadeloupe, La Guaira, Curaçao (7 days air-sea from New York). $999 to $1,475 per person, double, plus $27.50 port taxes.

VICTORIA—Jan. 10, 24; Feb. 7, 21; March 7, 21; April 4, 18; May 2 to St. Thomas, Martinique, La Guaira, and Aruba (7 days). Same rates as *Victoria* above.

WORLD RENAISSANCE—Jan. 2 to St. Maarten, Antigua, St. Lucia, Martinique and St. Thomas (6 days). $765 to $1,500 per person, double plus $29 port taxes. Some free and/or discounted air fare.

WORLD RENAISSANCE—Every Saturday from Jan. 8 to mid-May to St. Maarten, Martinique, Barbados, St. Lucia, Antigua, and St. Thomas (7 days). $875 to $1,750 per person, double, plus $29 port taxes. Some free and/or discounted air fare.

CENTRAL AND SOUTH AMERICA

FROM BALBOA

GREAT RIVERS EXPLORER—Jan. 3, 12, 22, 31; Feb. 9, 19, 28; March 9, 19, 28; April 6 to Pearl Islands, Darien jungle, Panama Canal transit, San Blas Islands, and Colon (6 days). $798 to $1,198 per person, double (5 days omitting Pearl Islands, $649 to $949).

FROM BUENOS AIRES

LINDBLAD EXPLORER—Jan. 20 to King George Island, Deception Island, Paradise Bay, Port Lockroy, Le Maire Channel, Peter Island, Cape Royds, McMurdo Base, Scott Base, Cape Hallett, Cape Adaore, Balleny Islands, Macquaire Island, Campbell Island, Auckland Islands, Snares Island, Stewart Island, and Auckland (20 days). $8,700 to $10,000 per person, double, inclusive.

FROM COLON

GREAT RIVERS EXPLORER—Jan. 8, 17, 26; Feb. 5, 14, 23; March 5, 14, 23; April 2, 11 to San Blas Islands, Panama Canal transit, Pearl Islands, Darien jungle, and Balboa (6 days). $798 to $1,198 per person, double (5 days omitting Pearl Islands, $649 to $949).

FROM GUAYAQUIL/QUITO

SANTA CRUZ—Jan. 27, March 2, April 7, May 12, June 16, July 21, Aug. 25, Sept. 29, Nov. 3 and Dec. 8 to Hood Island, James Bay, Espumilla Beach, Academy Bay, Plaza Island, Bartolome Island, Tower Island, Isabela Island, Narborough Island, Baltra Island (7 days). $990 to $1,400 per person, double, plus return air fare.

SANTA CRUZ—Jan. 6 and 13; Feb. 3, 10, and 17; March 10, 17, and 24; April 14, 21, and 28; May 19 and 26; June 2, 23, and 30; July 7 and 28; Aug. 4 and 11; Sept. 1, 8, and 15; Oct. 6, 13, and 20; Nov. 10, 17, and 24; Dec. 15, 22, and 29 from Baltra to North Seymour, Hood Island, Floreana, Santa Cruz, Plaza, James Bay, Espumilla Beach, and Baltra (4 days). $610 to $850 per person, double, plus air fare.

SANTA CRUZ—Jan. 3, 10, and 17; Feb. 7, 14, and 21; March 14, 21, and 28; April 18 and 25; May 2, 23, and 30; June 6 and 27; July 4 and 11; Aug. 1, 8, and 15; Sept. 5, 12, and 19; Oct. 10, 17, and 24; Nov. 14, 21, and 28; Dec. 19 and 26 from Baltra to North Seymour, Bartolome, Tower, Isabela, Narborough, and Baltra (3 days). $470 to $660 per person, double, plus air fare.

SANTA CRUZ—Jan. 20, Feb. 24, March 31, May 5, June 9, July 14, Aug. 18, Sept. 22, Oct. 27, and Dec. 1 to Baltra, Bartolome, Isabela, Narborough, Tower, North Seymour, Hood, Gardner Bay, Santa Cruz, Plaza, and Guayaquil (7 days). $990 to $1,400 per person, plus one-way air fare.

FROM MONTEVIDEO

ASTOR—Feb. 19 to Buenos Aires, Santos, Rio de Janeiro, Salvador de Bahia, Recife, Fortaleza, Belem, and Barbados (21 days). $3,086 to $7,244 per person, double.

FROM PUNTA ARENAS

WORLD DISCOVERER—Jan. 6 to Strait of Magellan/Beagle Channel, Cape Horn, Drake Passage, Antarctic Peninsula, Drake Passage, Beagle Channel/Tierra del Fuego (16 days). $3,990 to $7,500 per person, double, plus air fare.

WORLD DISCOVERER—Jan. 18 to Antarctica, Great Barrier Reef, New Guinea, Indonesian archipelago, Singapore and the Seychelles, Arabia and the Red Sea, plus land stay in Paris (121 days). *Journey to Seven Continents.* $24,000 to $55,000 per person, double, plus air fare. Also available in segments.

WORLD DISCOVERER—Dec. 13 to Strait of Magellan, Falkland Islands, South Georgia Islands, South Orkney Islands, Antarctic Peninsula, Drake Passage, Beagle Channel (25 days). $6,090 to $11,250 per person, double, plus air fare.

FROM RÍO DE JANEIRO

WORLD DISCOVERER—Nov. 24 to Montevideo, Falkland Islands, Drake Passage, Antarctic Peninsula, Drake Passage, Beagle Channel, and Punta Arenas (24 days). $4,490 to $10,720 per person, double, plus air fare.

FAR EAST

FROM HONG KONG

PEARL OF SCANDINAVIA—Jan. 1, April 5, Nov. 5 (1983); Jan. 7 and Oct. 27 (1984) to Whampoa, Manila, Cebu, Kota Kinabalu, Brunei, Kuching, and Singapore (14 days). *South China Sea Cruise.* $2,870 to $8,050 per person, double, including air fare.

PEARL OF SCANDINAVIA—May 21, June 18, July 16, Aug. 13, Sept. 10, Oct. 8 (1983); April 14, May 12, June 9, July 7, Aug. 4, Sept. 1 and 29 (1984) to Xiamen, Shanghai, Qingdao, Dalian, Hsingang (for Beijing), Pusan, Sea of Japan cruising, and Kobe (14 days). *China Explorers Cruise.* $3,370 to $8,550 per person, double, including air fare and China shore excursions.

ROYAL VIKING STAR—May 9, June 6 to Shanghai, Dalian, Hsingang (for Beijing), Nagasaki, Kagoshima, Inland Sea cruising, and Kobe (14 days). $3,629 to $9,649 per person, double, including air fare to and from California and all China shore excursions.

YAO HUA—March 13, 27; April 10, 24; May 8, 22; June 5, 19; July 3, 17, 31; Aug. 14, 28; Sept. 11, 25; Oct. 9, 23; Nov. 6 (northbound) and March 20; April 3, 17; May 1, 15, 29; June 12, 26; July 10, 24; Aug. 7, 21; Sept. 4, 18; Oct. 1, 16, 30; Nov. 13 (southbound) to Xiamen, Shanghai, Yangtze River, Nanjing, and air to Beijing (14 days). $1,975 to $5,050 per person, double, inclusive.

FROM KOBE

PEARL OF SCANDINAVIA—June 4; July 2, 30; Aug. 27; Sept. 24; Oct. 22 (1983) and April 28; May 26; June 23; Aug. 18; Sept. 15, Oct. 13 (1984) to Inland Sea cruising, Pusan, Hsingang (for Beijing), Dalian, Qingdao, Shanghai, Xiamen, and Hong Kong (14 days). *China Explorers Cruise.* $3,370 to $8,550 per person, double, including air fare and China shore excursions.

ROYAL VIKING STAR—April 25, May 23 to Inland Sea cruising, Kagoshima, Nagasaki, Hsingang (for Beijing), Dalian, Shanghai, and Hong Kong (14 days). $3,629 to $9,649, including air fare to and from California, transfers, and all China shore excursions.

ROYAL VIKING STAR—June 20 to Yokohama, Honolulu, Lahaina, Los Angeles, and San Francisco (17 days). $2,118 to $8,733 plus port taxes.

FROM MANILA

LINDBLAD EXPLORER—March 28 to Coron Island, Cuyo Island, Cagayan Island, Zamboanga, Sandakan, Kota Kinabalu, Brunei, Kuching, Kuala Trengganu, Redang Island, Perhentian Islands, Tioman Island, and Singapore (21 days). $5,300 to $7,100 per person, double, plus air fare.

FROM SINGAPORE

LINDBLAD EXPLORER—April 12 to Malacca, Penang, Phuket, Rangoon, Madras, Trincomalee, and Colombo (20 days). $5,220 to $7,380 per person, double, plus air fare.

PEARL OF SCANDINAVIA—Jan. 15 and 29, Feb. 12 and 26, March 12 and 26, Nov. 19, Dec. 3 to Penang, Belawan, Sibolga, Nias, Jakarta, Bali, Surabaya (14 days). $3,110 to $8,500 per person, double inclusive.

PEARL OF SCANDINAVIA—April 9, May 7, Dec. 24 to Kuching, Brunei, Kota Kinabalu, Cebu, Manila, Whampoa, and Hong Kong (14 days). $2,870 to $8,050 per person, double inclusive.

WORLD DISCOVERER—April 1 to Malacca, Penang, Phuket, Andaman Sea, Rangoon, Bay of Bengal, Colombo, Cochin, Maldive Islands, and Seychelles (28 days). $6,780 to $12,300 per person, double, plus air fare.

INDIAN OCEAN/RED SEA

FROM COLOMBO

LINDBLAD EXPLORER—April 29 to Male, Haddummoti Atoll, Bird Island, Aride and Praslin, La Digue, Mahe, Alphonse, Farquhar, Cosmoledo, Aldabra, Lamu, and Mombasa (24 days). $5,800 to $7,900 per person, double, plus air fare.

FROM DJIBOUTI

WORLD DISCOVERER—April 30 to Aden, Hodeida, Red Sea cruising, Port Sudan, Jidda, Safaga, Aqaba, Mount Sinai peninsula, Suez Canal, and Suez (18 days). $4,700 to $7,990 per person, double, plus air fare.

FROM HODEIDAH

LINDBLAD EXPLORER—May 22 to Port Sudan, Mukawwar Island, Safaga, Aqaba, Sharm el Sheikh, Ras Muhammad, Suez Canal transit, Alexandria, Limassol, Rhodes, Heraklion, Calamata, and Corfu (25 days). $6,400 to $8,200 per person, double, plus air fare.

FROM SAFAGA

LINDBLAD POLARIS—Jan. 2, 16, 30; Feb. 13, 27; March 13, 27 to Aqaba, Geziret el Fara'un, Nuweiba, El Tur, and Suez (8 days). $1,560 to $2,820 per person, double, plus $42 domestic air fare.

FROM SUEZ

LINDBLAD POLARIS—Jan. 9, 23; Feb. 6, 20; March 6, 20 to El Tur, Ras Muhammad, Sharm el Sheikh, Nuweiba, Geziret el Fara'un, Aqaba, and Safaga (8 days). $1,560 to $2,820 per person, double, plus $42 domestic air fare.

NORTH AMERICA

FROM ACAPULCO

FAIRWIND—Feb. 19 to Panama Canal transit, San Blas Islands, Cartagena, Aruba, Curaçao, St. Thomas, and Port Everglades (14 days). $2,625 to $4,970 per person, double, plus port taxes. Free air fare.

GOLDEN ODYSSEY—Jan. 19 through Panama Canal to Cristobal/Panama City, San Blas Islands, Cartagena, Aruba, La Guaira, and San Juan (12 days air-sea from U.S.). $2,248 to $3,398 per person, double.

ROYAL ODYSSEY—Jan. 3 and 25; Feb. 16 through Panama Canal, Cristobal/Panama City, San Blas Islands, Cartagena, Ocho Rios, and Miami (12 days air-sea from U.S.). $2,198 to $3,358 per person, double.

ROYAL ODYSSEY—March 10. Same itinerary and rates as Jan. 19 *Golden Odyssey*.

PACIFIC PRINCESS—Alternate Saturdays from Jan. 8 through March 19 and from Sept. 17 through Nov. 26, to Ixtapa/Zihuatanejo, Puerto Vallarta, Mazatlan, Cabo San Lucas, and Los Angeles (7 days). $1,498 to $2,842 per person, double, plus port taxes (Jan. 8 through 22); $1,575 to $2,996 (Jan. 29 through March 19; Sept. 10 through Nov. 26).

FROM ANCHORAGE

CUNARD PRINCESS—Alternate Saturdays from June 11 through Sept. 17 to Prince William Sound, Skagway, Juneau, Tracy Arm, Misty Fjords, Behn Channel, and Vancouver (7 days). $1,090 to $2,195 per person, double, plus port taxes.

FROM BALTIMORE

AMERICA—April 23 and Oct. 29 to St. Michael's, Annapolis, Oxford, Crisfield, Yorktown, Norfolk, Great Bridge, Coinjock, Belhaven, Morehead

City, Wrightsville Beach, Bucksport, Charleston, Beaufort, and Savannah (14 days). *East Coast Inland Passage Cruise.* $1,456 to $1,596 per person, double.

AMERICA—May 21, 28; June 4, 11, 18 to St. Michael's, Oxford, Cambridge, Crisfield, Yorktown, and Annapolis (7 days). *Chesapeake Bay Cruise.* $728 to $798 per person, double.

AMERICA—June 25 to Chesapeake Bay, South Street Seaport (New York City), Port Jefferson, and Haddam (7 days). *Chesapeake Bay to New England Cruise.* $728 to $798 per person, double.

INDEPENDENCE—April 3 to St. Michael's, Annapolis, Oxford, Crisfield, Yorktown, Norfolk, Great Bridge, Coinjock, Belhaven, Morehead City, Wrightsville Beach, Bucksport, Charleston, Beaufort, and Savannah (14 days). *East Coast Inland Passage Cruise.* $1,456 to $1,596 per person, double.

INDEPENDENCE—May 29; June 5, 12, and 19 to St. Michael's, Oxford, Cambridge, Crisfield, Yorktown, and Annapolis (7 days). *Chesapeake Bay Cruise.* $728 to $798 per person, double.

INDEPENDENCE—June 26 to Chesapeake Bay, South Street Seaport (New York City), Port Jefferson, and Haddam (7 days). *Chesapeake Bay to New England Cruise.* $728 to $798 per person, double.

FROM FT. MYERS (FLORIDA)

AMERICA—Jan. 18, Feb. 8, March 1, Nov. 29, and Dec. 27 to Lake Okeechobee, Vero Beach, Fort Pierce, Kennedy Space Center, St. Augustine, Jacksonville Beach, Fernandina Beach, Sea Island, St. Simons, and Savannah (10 days). *Okeechobee and Southern Waterways Cruise.* $1,040 to $1,140 per person, double.

INDEPENDENCE—Feb. 9 and March 2 on same itinerary as *America* above (if there is a demand) (10 days). *Okeechobee and Southern Waterways Cruise.* $1,040 to $1,140 per person, double.

FROM GALVESTON

STELLA SOLARIS—Jan. 7, 27 and Feb. 16 to Playa del Carmen/Cozumel, Grand Cayman, Montego Bay, Panama Canal transit, Balboa, San Blas Islands, Cartagena, Aruba, and Curaçao (10 days). $2,100 to $3,895 per person, double, plus $55 port taxes.

FROM HADDAM (CONNECTICUT)

AMERICA—June 25; July 2, 9, 16, 23, 30; Aug. 6, 13, 20, 27; Sept. 3, 10, 17, 24 to Block Island, Nantucket and Martha's Vineyard, Newport (7 days). *New England Islands Cruise.* $728 to $798 per person, double.

AMERICA—Oct. 1, 8, 15 to Greenport, South Street Seaport (New York

City), Port Jefferson, and West Point (7 days). *Hudson River Foliage Cruise.* $728 to $798 per person, double.

AMERICA—Oct. 22 to Port Jefferson, South Street Seaport (New York City), West Point, and Baltimore (7 days). *Hudson River to Chesapeake Bay Cruise.* $728 to $798 per person, double.

AMERICAN EAGLE—June 1 and Aug. 3 to Block Island, Gloucester, Boston, New Bedford, Portsmouth/Strawberry Banke, and Rockland (Maine) (10 days). *Maine Coast Cruise.* $1,040 to $1,140 per person, double.

AMERICAN EAGLE—Oct. 1, 8, and 15 to Greenport, South Street Seaport (New York City), Port Jefferson, and West Point (7 days). *Hudson River Foliage Cruise.* $728 to $798 per person, double.

INDEPENDENCE—July 3, 10, 17, 24, 31; Aug. 7, 14, 21, 28; Sept. 4, 11, 18 to Block Island, Nantucket and Martha's Vineyard, and Newport (7 days). *New England Islands Cruise.* $728 to $798 per person, double.

FROM HALIFAX

LINDBLAD EXPLORER—Aug. 21 to Labrador, Killinek Island, Padloping Island, Cambridge Fjord, Pond Inlet, Arctic Bay cruising, Prince Leopold Island, Devon Island, Clyde River, Pangnirtung, Brevoort Island, Lake Harbour, Cape Dorset, Akpatok Island, Labrador, Nova Scotia, and Bar Harbor (30 days). $8,400 to $10,500 per person, double, plus air fare.

FROM KETCHIKAN

MAJESTIC EXPLORER—Sundays from May through September to Misty Fjords, Wrangell, Sitka, Tracy Arm/Juneau, Skagway/Haines, Glacier Bay cruising, Petersburg (7 days). $1,197 to $1,799 per person, double.

FROM LOS ANGELES

ATLANTIC—March 2 to Cabo San Lucas, Puerto Vallarta, Manzanillo, Acapulco, Balboa, Panama Canal transit, Cristobal, Aruba, La Guaira, St. Thomas, and Port Everglades. $2,940 to $5,795 per person, double, plus port taxes.

AZURE SEAS—Every Friday to Ensenada (3 days). $385 to $570 per person, double, plus $11 port taxes.

AZURE SEAS—Every Monday to Ensenada (4 days). $440 to $610 per person, double, plus $11 port taxes.

CONSTELLATION—Jan. 25 to Puerto Vallarta, Acapulco, Balboa, Panama Canal transit, Cristobal, Cartagena, Montego Bay, Cozumel (18 days). $2,295 to $4,295 per person, double, plus port taxes.

DAPHNE—Saturdays from April 23 to May 21; Sept. 24 to Nov. 5 to Mazatlan and Puerto Vallarta (7 days). $795 to $1,695 per person, double, plus port taxes.

DAPHNE—Nov. 5 to Mazatlan, Acapulco, Punta Arenas, Panama Canal transit, Cartagena, Montego Bay, Cozumel/Playa del Carmen, and Miami (17 days). $1,895 to $4,120 per person, double, plus port taxes.

FAIRSEA—Jan. 15, March 5, May 7 to Acapulco, Panama Canal transit, San Blas Islands, Cartagena, Aruba, St. Thomas, and San Juan (14 days). $2,485 to $4,830 per person, double, plus port taxes (value season); $2,625 to $4,970 (peak season). Free air fare.

FAIRSEA—Jan. 8, April 2 and 30, Nov. 5, Dec. 3 and 10 to Cabo San Lucas, Mazatlan, Puerto Vallarta (7 days). $925 to $995 per person, double, plus port taxes (value season); $995 to $2,135 (peak season). Free air fare.

FAIRSEA—Feb. 12, April 9, Nov. 12, Dec. 17 to Cabo San Lucas, Mazatlan, Acapulco, Zihuatanejo, Puerto Vallarta (11 days). $1,435 to $3,230 per person, double, plus port taxes (value season); $1,545 to $3,340 (peak season). Free air fare.

FAIRSEA—Feb. 23, April 30, Nov. 23, Dec. 28 to Cabo San Lucas, Mazatlan, Acapulco, Zihuatanejo, Puerto Vallarta (10 days). $1,365 to $2,985 per person, double, plus port taxes (value season); $1,465 to $3,085 (peak season). Free air fare.

ISLAND PRINCESS—Jan. 15, Feb. 12, March 12, April 9, May 7, Sept. 24, Oct. 22, Nov. 26, and Dec. 24 to Acapulco, Panama Canal transit, Cartagena, Aruba, Martinique, St. Thomas, and San Juan (14 days). $3,206 to $6,202 per person, double, plus port taxes (Jan. 15 through April 9; Oct. 22 through Dec. 10); $2,982 to $5,796 (April 23 through May 21; Sept. 24 through Oct. 8).

ISLAND PRINCESS—June 4 to San Francisco, Vancouver, Ketchikan, Juneau, Skagway, Glacier Bay cruising, Sitka, and Vancouver (11 days). $2,057 to $4,301 per person, double, plus port taxes (10 days from San Francisco, $1,870 to $3,910).

PACIFIC PRINCESS—March 26 to Lahaina, Honolulu, Christmas Island, Bora Bora, Papeete, Moorea, Pago Pago, Niuafoo, Suva, Auckland, Sydney, Great Barrier Reef, Port Moresby, Bali, Singapore, Manila, Hong Kong, Shanghai, Japan Inland Sea cruising, Kobe, Yokohama, Honolulu, and Los Angeles (70 nights). $13,720 to $25,900 per person, double, plus port taxes; $10,166 to $19,550 (46 nights to Hong Kong); $6,266 to $11,570 (26 nights to Sydney); $9,724 to $18,700 (44 nights Sydney to Los Angeles); $5,784 to $10,680 (24 nights Hong Kong to Los Angeles).

PACIFIC PRINCESS—Jan. 2 to Cabo San Lucas, Mazatlan, Puerto Vallarta, Manzanillo, and Acapulco (6 days). $1,284 to $2,436 per person, double, plus port taxes.

PACIFIC PRINCESS—Alternate Saturdays from Jan. 15 through March 12; Sept. 24 through Nov. 19. Same itinerary as *Pacific Princess* above (7 days). $1,575 to $2,996 per person, double, plus port taxes ($1,498 to $2,842 on Jan. 15).

PACIFIC PRINCESS—Dec. 12 to Nuku Hiva, Moorea, Papeete, Bora Bora, Christmas Island, Honolulu, Lahaina, Kailua, Nawiliwili, Hamakua coast (26 days). $5,928 to $11,752 per person, double, plus port taxes.

RHAPSODY—Oct. 1 to Acapulco, Balboa, Panama Canal transit, Cristobal, San Blas Islands, Cartagena, Ocho Rios, and Miami (14 days). $2,075 to $4,185 per person, double, plus $19 port taxes.

SAGAFJORD—Aug. 29 to Honolulu, Yokohama, Kobe, Pusan, Shanghai, Hong Kong, Pattaya, Singapore, Kota Kinabalu, Manila, Guam, Honolulu, Hilo (58 days). $10,130 to $36,020 per person, double (Cruising Plus). Also available in segments.

SAGAFJORD—Oct. 26 to Honolulu, Apia, Suva, Noumea, Sydney, Auckland, Rarotonga, Papeete, Moorea, Pitcairn Island, Easter Island, Callao, Guayaquil, Galapagos Islands, Acapulco, Cabo San Lucas (56 days). $9,500 to $34,070 per person, double (Cruising Plus). Also available in segments.

SAGAFJORD—Dec. 21 to Puerto Vallarta, Acapulco, Balboa, Panama Canal transit, Cristobal, Cartagena, La Guaira, Bridgetown, St. Thomas, and Port Everglades (19 days). $4,200 to $14,210 per person, double (Cruising Plus).

SANTA MARIA, MAGDALENA, MERCEDES, AND MARIANA—Every other week to Puerto Vallarta, Buenaventura, Balboa, Panama Canal transit, Cartagena, Porto Cabello, La Guaira, Salvador, Rio de Janeiro, Santos, Buenos Aires, Strait of Magellan, Valparaiso, Callao, Guayaquil (52 days). $8,775 to $16,900 per person, double.

SUN PRINCESS—Oct. 8 to Acapulco, Panama Canal transit, Cartagena, Aruba, Martinique, St. Thomas, and San Juan (14 days). $2,716 to $5,572 per person, double, plus port taxes.

TROPICALE—Every Sunday to Puerto Vallarta, Mazatlan, Cabo San Lucas (7 days). $900 to $1,695 per person, double, plus $18 port taxes.

FROM MIAMI

AMERIKANIS—Every Friday to Nassau (3 days). $270 to $535 per person, double (off season); $285 to $555 (on season) plus $16 port taxes.

AMERIKANIS—Every Monday to Freeport and Nassau (4 days). $355 to $650 per person, double (off season); $375 to $685 (on season); plus $17 port taxes.

BOHEME—Every Saturday from March 19 to Puerto Plata, St. Thomas, San Juan, and Cap Haitien (7 days). $750 to $1,400 per person, double, plus $17 port taxes.

CARNIVALE—Every Sunday to Samana, San Juan, St. Thomas (7 days). $850 to $1,655 per person, double (value season); $900 to $1,705 (peak season); plus $20 port taxes. Includes free air fare.

DAPHNE—April 8 to Port Antonio, Cartagena, Panama Canal transit, Cristobal/Balboa, Acapulco, Manzanillo, and Los Angeles (15 days). $1,695 to $3,635 per person, double.

DOLPHIN—Every Friday to Nassau (3 days). $240 to $490 per person, double (off season); $255 to $505 (peak season); plus $15 port taxes.

DOLPHIN—Every Monday to Freeport and Nassau (4 days). $315 to $595 per person, double (off season); $335 to $620 (peak season); plus $16 port taxes.

EMERALD SEAS—Every Friday to Nassau (3 days). $265 to $565 per person, double (off season); $280 to $580 (peak season); plus $15 port taxes.

EMERALD SEAS—Every Monday to Freeport and Nassau (4 days). $345 to $685 per person, double (off season); $370 to $725 (peak season); plus $16 port taxes.

FESTIVAL—Saturdays to Nassau, San Juan, and St. Thomas (7 days). $850 to $1,655 per person, double (value season); $900 to $1,705 (peak season); plus $20 port taxes. Free air.

MARDI GRAS—Sundays to Cozumel, Grand Cayman, and Ocho Rios (7 days). Same rates as *Festival* above.

NORDIC PRINCE—Alternate Saturdays through March 26 to Ocho Rios, Aruba, Curaçao, Barbados, Martinique, St. Maarten, San Juan, and St. Thomas (14 days). $1,965 to $4,990 per person, double, all-inclusive. Free air fare from 90 gateways. Also available as *SunVenture I* (Miami to Barbados and return by air) or *SunVenture II* (air to Barbados and sail to Miami); $1,060 to $1,435 per person, double, plus $50 to $175 for air.

NORDIC PRINCE—June 11 and Aug. 6 to Bermuda and Nassau (8 days). $1,240 to $1,870 per person, double, all-inclusive. Free air fare from 71 gateways.

NORDIC PRINCE—April 16, May 14, July 9, Sept. 3, Oct. 15, Nov. 12, Dec. 10 to Bermuda and Nassau (8 days). Same rates as *Nordic Prince* above.

NORDIC PRINCE—April 24 and Aug. 14 to Key West, New Orleans, Playa del Carmen, Grand Cayman, and Ocho Rios (10 days). $1,540 to $3,495 per person, double, all-inclusive. Free air fare from 90 gateways.

NORDIC PRINCE—April 6, May 4, June 1, July 27, Aug. 24, Oct. 5, Nov. 2 and 23, Dec. 28 to St. Croix, Martinique, Barbados, Antigua, and St. Thomas (10 days). Same rates as *Nordic Prince* above.

NORDIC PRINCE—May 22, July 17, June 29 to Port Canaveral, Savannah,

Bermuda, and Nassau (10 days). $1,540 to $3,795 per person, double, all-inclusive. Free air fare from 90 gateways.

NORDIC PRINCE—June 19, Sept. 25, Oct. 23, Nov. 20, and Dec. 18 to St. Thomas, Antigua, Barbados, Martinique, and St. Croix (10 days). Same rates as *Nordic Prince* above.

NORDIC PRINCE—March 26 to St. Thomas, La Guaira, Curaçao, Ocho Rios, and Port-au-Prince (11 days). $1,705 to $3,795 per person, double, all-inclusive. Free air fare from 90 gateways.

NORWAY—Every Saturday to St. Thomas, Nassau, and Bahamas Out Island (7 days). $960 to $4,620 per person, double, plus $18 port taxes. Free air fare.

RHAPSODY—Jan. 2 to Ocho Rios, Playa del Carmen, and Cozumel (6 days). $665 to $1,180 per person, double, plus $18 port taxes. Mainly free air fare.

RHAPSODY—Every Saturday from Jan. 8 through May 7 to Playa del Carmen, Cozumel, Grand Cayman, and Ocho Rios (7 days). $935 to $1,655 per person, double ($835 to $1,475 on Jan. 8) plus $18 port taxes. Mainly free air fare.

RHAPSODY—Nov. 5 and Dec. 17. Same itinerary as *Rhapsody* above, with rates from $905 to $1,605 per person, double, plus $18 port taxes.

RHAPSODY—May 14 to Ocho Rios, Cartagena, San Blas Islands, Cristobal, Panama Canal transit, Balboa, Acapulco, and Los Angeles (14 days). $2,075 to $4,185 per person, double, plus $19 port taxes.

ROYAL ODYSSEY—Jan. 14 *Tennis Cruise*; Feb. 5 and 27 to Ocho Rios, Cartagena, San Blas Islands, Panama Canal transit, Balboa/Panama City, and Acapulco (12 days air-sea from U.S.). $2,198 to $3,358 per person, double.

SCANDINAVIAN SUN—Daily to Freeport. $89 per person, plus $10 port taxes. Day cabins optional, $50 or $100.

SKYWARD—Every Sunday to Playa del Carmen, Cancun/Cozumel, Bahamas Out Island.

SONG OF AMERICA—Sundays to Nassau, San Juan, and St. Thomas (7 days). $995 to $1,965 per person, double, all-inclusive. Free air fare from 71 gateways.

SONG OF NORWAY—Saturdays to Grand Cayman, Montego Bay, and Cozumel (7 days). $995 to $1,835 per person, double, all-inclusive. Free air fare from 71 gateways.

SOUTHWARD—Every Saturday to Cozumel, Grand Cayman, Ocho Rios, Bahamas Out Island (7 days). $1,000 to $1,865 per person, double, plus $24 port taxes. Free air fare.

STARWARD—Every Sunday to Nassau, San Juan, St. Thomas, and Bahamas Out Island (7 days). $1,000 to $1,610 per person, double, plus $24 port taxes. Free air fare.

SUN VIKING—Jan. 2, 23; Feb. 13; March 6 to St. Thomas, Antigua, Barbados, Martinique, and St. Croix (10 days). $1,415 to $2,400 per person, double, all-inclusive. Free air fare from 90 gateways.

SUN VIKING—March 23 to St. Croix, Martinique, Barbados, Antigua, and St. Thomas (10 days). $1,540 to $2,330 per person, double, all-inclusive. Free air fare from 90 gateways.

SUN VIKING—Jan. 12; Feb. 2, 23, March 23 to St. Thomas, La Guaira, Curaçao, Ocho Rios, Port-au-Prince (11 days). $1,560 to $2,610 per person, double, all-inclusive. Free air fare from 90 gateways.

SUN VIKING—Alternate Saturdays from April 2, to Ocho Rios, Curaçao, Aruba, Barbados, Martinique, St. Maarten, San Juan, and St. Thomas (14 days). $2,160 to $3,265 per person, double, all-inclusive. Free air fare from 90 gateways. Also available as SunVenture I or II between Miami and Barbados; $1,160 to $1,385, plus $50 to $175 for air.

SUNWARD II—Fridays to Nassau and Bahamas Out Island (3 days). $270 to $550 per person, double (low season); $300 to $605 (high season); plus $18 port taxes.

SUNWARD II—Mondays to Nassau, Bahamas Out Island and Freeport (4 days). $370 to $750 per person, double (low season); $410 to $785 (high season); plus $20 port taxes.

FROM MONTREAL

VERACRUZ—Alternate Fridays from June 17 through Sept. 16 to Quebec, Saguenay Fjord cruising, Halifax, Fall River, and New York (7 days). $795 to $1,065 per person, double, plus $10 port taxes. Suites extra.

FROM NEW YORK

ATLANTIC—Saturdays from April 16 through Oct. 15 to Bermuda (7 days). $855 to $1,725 per person, double, plus $28 port taxes (economy season); $880 to $1,805 (intermediate season); $925 to $1,855 (high season).

OCEANIC—Saturdays from April 2 through Nov. 12 to Bermuda and Nassau (7 days). $825 to $1,600 per person, double, plus $32.20 port taxes (economy season); $855 to $1,650 (intermediate season); $880 to $1,700 (high season).

QUEEN ELIZABETH 2—Jan. 4 to St. Thomas, St. Kitts/Nevis, Martinique, Barbados, Grenada, La Guaira, and Curaçao (12 days). $1,820 to $6,085 per person, double.

QUEEN ELIZABETH 2—Jan. 17 to Port Everglades, Curaçao, Cartagena, Cristobal, Panama Canal transit, Balboa, Acapulco, Los Angeles, San Francisco, Papeete, Moorea, Rarotonga, Auckland, Wellington, Sydney, Brisbane, Great Barrier Reef/Whitsunday Islands, Port Moresby, Bali, Singapore, Pattaya, Hong Kong, Qingdao, Kobe, Yokohama, Honolulu, Kona, Los Angeles, Acapulco, Balboa, Panama Canal transit, Cristobal, La Guaira, St. Thomas, Port Everglades (89 days). *Circle Pacific and Orient Odyssey.* $15,440 to $78,500 per person, double, plus port taxes, for 89 days NYC/NYC; $14,195 to $71,750 for 75 days LA/NYC or NYC/LA; $12,950 to $65,000 for 61 days LA/LA; including air fare. Shorter segments also available.

QUEEN ELIZABETH 2—April 16, June 4, 21; July 4, 27; Aug. 14, 28; Sept. 9, 20; Oct. 23; and Nov. 21 to Southampton. Transatlantic crossing (5 days). $1,185 to $5,350 per person, double (thrift season); $1,360 to $5,865 (intermediate season); $1,435 to $6,185 (high season).

QUEEN ELIZABETH 2—June 1, Aug. 25, Oct. 13 to Nowhere (3 days). $585 to $970 per person, double.

QUEEN ELIZABETH 2—Aug. 7 to Bar Harbor, Halifax (7 days). $1,195 to $3,600 per person, double, plus port taxes.

QUEEN ELIZABETH 2—Oct. 16 to Nassau and Bermuda (7 days). $1,195 to $3,600 per person, double, plus port taxes.

QUEEN ELIZABETH 2—Nov. 11 to Caribbean (10 days). $1,695 to $5,140 per person, double, plus port taxes.

QUEEN ELIZABETH 2—Dec. 21 to Caribbean (14 days). $2,795 to $9,895 per person, double, plus port taxes.

ROTTERDAM—January 8 to Port Everglades, Cartagena, Cristobal, Balboa, Acapulco, Los Angeles, Honolulu, Hong Kong, Shanghai, Hong Kong, Singapore, Colombo, Bombay, Safaga, Suez, Port Said, Haifa, Piraeus, Naples, Cannes, Tangier, Gibraltar, Lisbon, Madeira, Port Everglades (82 days). *Silver Cruise.* $15,585 to $35,275 per person, double; from Port Everglades (78 days), $15,285 to $34,975 per person, double; Los Angeles/New York (69 days), $13,280 to $30,195 per person, double.

ROTTERDAM—April 2 to Port Everglades, Curaçao, La Guaira, Barbados, Martinique, St. Maarten, St. Thomas, and Port Everglades (14 days). $2,020 to $3,520 per person, double, including air fare where applicable.

ROYAL VIKING SEA—Aug. 26, Sept. 9 to Nantucket, Halifax, Charlottetown, Montreal, Quebec, Bar Harbor, Boston, Newport (14 days). $2,366 to $9,660 per person, double, plus port taxes.

ROYAL VIKING SEA—Sept. 23 to Port Everglades, St. Thomas, Santo Domingo, Cartagena, Panama Canal transit, Acapulco, Zihuatanejo, Puerto

Vallarta, Los Angeles, and San Francisco (20 days). $2,911 to $12,116 per person, double, plus port taxes.

SAGAFJORD—May 20 and Sept. 15 to St. John, Halifax, Quebec, Montreal, Gaspé, Charlottetown, Bar Harbor, Gloucester (14 days). $3,680 to $14,420 per person, double, plus port taxes (May 20); $3,800 to $15,100 (Sept. 15).

SCANDINAVIA—Every five days from January 5 through December 31 to Freeport (5 days). $469 to $1,010 per person, double, round trip through May 31; $760 to $1,150 (season); $660 to $1,080 (off season); plus $16 port taxes. Automobiles carried free of charge for round-trip passengers.

VEENDAM—Saturdays from April 2 through Oct. 22 to Bermuda (7 days). $760 to $1,395 per person, double, plus $28 port taxes.

VERACRUZ—Alternate Fridays from June 10 through Sept. 23 to New Bedford, Cape Cod Canal cruising, Sydney, Bonaventure Island, Saguenay Fjord cruising, Quebec, and Montreal (7 days). $795 to $4,065 per person, double, plus $40 port taxes. Suites extra.

VOLENDAM—Sundays from April 24 through Oct. 23 to Bermuda (7 days). $760 to $1,395 per person, double, plus $28 port taxes.

FROM PORT CANAVERAL

SCANDINAVIAN SEA—Daily to Freeport. $29 per person, plus port taxes. Meals and day cabin additional.

FROM PORT EVERGLADES

ASTOR—Jan. 3 to Puerto Morelos, Grand Cayman, Ocho Rios, Aruba, La Guaira, Tobago, Barbados, Guadeloupe, St. Thomas, and San Juan (13 days). $2,048 to $4,807 per person, double.

ASTOR—Nov. 5 and 26 to Puerto Morelos, San Andres Islands, Cristobal, San Blas Islands, Cartagena, Curaçao, and San Juan (11 days). $2,086 to $4,705 per person, double.

ASTOR—Dec. 17 to Puerto Morelos, Grand Cayman, Ocho Rios, Port-au-Prince, San Juan, and Nassau (11 days). $2,246 to $5,069 per person, double.

ASTOR—Dec. 28 to St. Thomas, St. Kitts, Martinique, St. Lucia, Barbados, Tobago, La Guaira, Aruba, and San Juan (12 days). $2,431 to $5,509 per person, double.

ATLANTIC—Jan. 2 to St. Thomas, St. Maarten, Antigua, and San Juan (9 days). $1,395 to $2,830 per person, double, plus port taxes.

ATLANTIC—Jan. 11 to Santo Domingo, St. Thomas, Antigua, Barbados, Montserrat, and St. Maarten (11 days). $1,695 to $3,995 per person, double, plus port taxes.

ATLANTIC—Jan. 22 to Curaçao, La Guaira, Grenada, Martinique, and St. Thomas (10 days). $1,640 to $3,290 per person, double, plus port taxes.

ATLANTIC—Feb. 1 to St. Thomas, Martinique, Barbados, Grenada, La Guaira, and Aruba (11 days). $1,800 to $3,560 per person, double, plus port taxes.

ATLANTIC—Feb. 12 to Montego Bay, Cartagena, San Blas Islands, Cristobal, Panama Canal transit, Balboa, Acapulco, Zihuatanejo, Puerto Vallarta, Mazatlan, Cabo San Lucas, and Los Angeles (17 days). $2,940 to $5,795 per person, double, plus port taxes.

ATLANTIC—March 19 to San Juan, St. Thomas, and St. Maarten (7 days). $1,115 to $2,235 per person, double, plus port taxes.

ATLANTIC—March 26 to Bermuda (7 days). $1,115 to $2,235 per person, double, plus port taxes.

ATLANTIC—April 2 to St. Thomas, Martinique, Barbados, Grenada, La Guaira, Aruba, Port Everglades, and New York (14 days). $1,990 to $4,055 per person, double, plus port taxes.

FAIRWIND—Jan. 8, March 26, April 2, May 14 and 21, June 18, Aug. 27, Sept. 24, Dec. 3 and 10 to Nassau, St. Thomas, and San Juan (7 days). $995 to $2,175 per person, double, plus port taxes (value season); $1,065 to $2,245 (peak season). Free air fare.

FAIRWIND—Jan. 26, March 16, April 20, June 8, July 6 and 27, Aug. 17, Sept. 14, Oct. 12, Nov. 2 and 23, Dec. 28 to St. Thomas, Antigua, Barbados, Martinique, St. Croix (10 days). $1,430 to $3,060 per person, double, plus port taxes (value season); $1,530 to $3,160 (peak season). Free air fare.

FAIRWIND—April 9 and 30, June 25, July 16, Aug. 6, Sept. 3, Oct. 1, Dec. 17 to Curaçao, Caracas, Martinique, St. Thomas, St. John's and Nassau (11 days). $1,485 to $3,305 per person, double, plus port taxes (value season); $1,595 to $3,415 (peak season). Free air fare.

FAIRWIND—Jan. 15, March 5, and May 28 to Nassau, Cartagena, San Blas Islands, Panama Canal, Jamaica, and Grand Cayman (11 days). $1,485 to $3,305 per person, double, plus port taxes (value season); $1,595 to $3,415 (peak season). Free air fare.

FAIRWIND—Oct. 22 and Nov. 12 to Nassau, Cartagena, San Blas Islands, Panama Canal, San Andres, Cancun (11 days). $1,485 to $3,305 per person, double, plus port taxes. Free air fare.

FAIRWIND—Feb. 5 to St. Thomas, Curaçao, Aruba, Cartagena, San Blas Islands, Panama Canal transit, and Acapulco (14 days). $2,485 to $4,830 per person, double, plus port taxes (value season); $2,625 to $4,970 (peak season). Free air fare.

OCEANIC—Jan. 2 to San Juan, St. Thomas, and St. Maarten (6 days). $795 to $1,970 per person, double, plus port taxes.

OCEANIC—Every Saturday from Jan. 8 through March 12 to San Juan, St. Thomas, and St. Maarten (7 days). $990 to $2,425 per person, double, plus port taxes ($930 to $2,300 on Jan. 8 and 15).

OCEANIC—March 19 to Freeport and Nassau (4 days). $530 to $1,190 per person, double, plus port taxes.

ROTTERDAM—April 16, 23, 30 and May 7 to St. Thomas, St. Maarten, and Nassau (7 days). $815 to $1,650 per person, double, including air fare where applicable.

ROYAL VIKING SEA—Jan. 24 and Nov. 29 to St. Thomas, Santo Domingo, Cartagena, Panama Canal transit, Acapulco, Zihuatanejo, Puerto Vallarta, Los Angeles, and San Francisco (17 days). $3,203 to $10,920 per person, double, plus port taxes (Jan. 24); $2,485 to $10,343 (Nov. 29).

ROYAL VIKING SKY—Jan. 13 to Cartagena, Panama Canal transit, Acapulco, Puerto Vallarta, Los Angeles, Honolulu, Majuro Atoll, Guam, Hong Kong, Pattaya, Singapore, Penang, Colombo, Victoria, Durban, Cape Town, Tristan de Cunha cruising, Rio de Janeiro, Salvador, Martinique, and St. Thomas (88 days). $14,168 to $52,008 per person, double, plus port taxes.

ROYAL VIKING SKY—April 11 to Malaga and Piraeus (14 days). $1,694 to $6,986 per person, double, plus port taxes.

ROYAL VIKING SKY—Dec. 6 to St. Thomas, St. Maarten (7 days). $952 to $3,941 per person, double, plus port taxes.

ROYAL VIKING SKY—Dec. 13 to St. Maarten, Antigua, Martinique, Barbados, St. Vincent, La Guaira, Curaçao, St. Thomas, San Juan, Cartagena, San Blas Islands, Grand Cayman, Playa del Carmen/Cozumel, New Orleans (28 days). $5,628 to $20,300 per person, double, plus port taxes.

ROYAL VIKING STAR—Oct. 15. Same itinerary and rates as Jan. 24 *Royal Viking Sea*.

ROYAL VIKING STAR—Dec. 14 to New Orleans, Playa del Carmen/Cozumel, Grand Cayman, Ocho Rios, Curaçao, Cartagena, Panama Canal transit, Acapulco, Mazatlan, Puerto Vallarta, Los Angeles, and San Francisco (24 days). $5,488 to $17,763 per person, double, plus port taxes.

SAGAFJORD—Jan. 7 to Cristobal, Panama Canal transit, Balboa, Galapagos Islands, Nukuhiva, Moorea, Papeete, Rarotonga, Auckland, Sydney, Brisbane, Port Moresby, Torres Straits, Zamboanga, Hong Kong, Pattaya, Singapore, Colombo, Bombay, Port Sudan, Safaga, Suez, Port Said, Genoa, Strait of Gibraltar, Casablanca, Funchal, Hamilton, and Port Everglades (91 days). *World Cruise.* $16,890 to $60,290 per person, double, plus port taxes. Also sold in segments.

SAGAFJORD—April 9 and 23, May 7 to Playa del Carmen, Cozumel, Grand Cayman, Aruba, La Guaira, Guadeloupe, St. Thomas and San Juan (14 days). $2,260 to $7,990 per person, double (Cruising Plus).

SAGAFJORD—May 21 to Grand Cayman, Montego Bay, Cartagena, Cristobal, Panama Canal transit, Balboa, Acapulco, Mazatlan, Cabo San Lucas, Los Angeles, and San Francisco (16 days). $2,870 to $10,210 per person, double (Cruising Plus).

STELLA SOLARIS—March 8 to Puerto Plata, St. Thomas, St. Barthelemy, St. Maarten, Antigua, Las Palmas, Casablanca, Gibraltar, Monte Carlo, Livorno, Capri, Messina, Katakolon, and Piraeus (22 days). $3,250 to $5,500 per person, double, plus port taxes.

VISTAFJORD—March 11 to Cap Haitien, San Juan, St. Thomas, Funchal, Casablanca, Malaga, and Genoa (16 days). $3,460 to $10,080 per person, double (Cruising Plus).

VOLENDAM—Jan. 22, February 5 and 19, March 5 and 19, April 2, to St. John's, St. Maarten, Martinique, Barbados, Antigua, San Juan and St. Thomas (14 days). $1,630 to $3,280 per person, double, including airfare where applicable. Also sold in 7-day segments between Port Everglades/Barbados, for $815 to $1,790 per person, double including airfare where applicable.

FROM PORTLAND

GREAT RIVERS EXPLORER—Saturdays from mid-May through mid-October to Oregon City, Astoria, Hood River, Clover Island, Lewiston, Sacajawea Park (7 days). $1,197 to $1,799 per person, double (subject to change).

FROM ROCKLAND, MAINE

AMERICAN EAGLE—June 11, 18, 25, July 2, 9 and 16, Aug. 13, 20 and 27, Sept. 3 and 10 to Wicsasset, Bath, Castine, Vinalhaven, Bar Harbor and Boothbay Harbor (7 day). *Maine Coast Cruise.* $728 to $798 per person, double.

AMERICAN EAGLE—July 23 and Sept. 17 to Portsmouth/Strawberry Banke, New Bedford, Boston, Gloucester, Block Island, and Haddam, Conn. (10 days). *Maine Coast Cruise.* $1,040 to $1,140 per person, double.

FROM SAN DIEGO

PACIFIC NORTHWEST EXPLORER—Jan. 8 and 22, Feb. 5 and 19, March 5 and 19 to Isla San Martin, Islas San Benitos, Bahia de Ballenas, Magdalena Bay, Boca de Soledad, Cabo San Lucas, Espiritu Santo and Partida South, La Paz, Isla Santa Catalina, Isla San Pedro Martir, Bahia de Los Angeles, Canal de Ballenas, Isla Angel de la Guarda, and San Felipe (or vice versa) (15 days). $2,650 to $3,680 per person, double (land/cruise).

FROM SAN FRANCISCO

FAIRSEA—June 4, July 16 and 30, Aug. 13 and 27 to Vancouver, Alert Bay, Prince Rupert, Ketchikan, Juneau, Glacier Bay cruising, Sitka, Victoria, Astoria (14 days). $2,195 to $4,545 per person, double, plus port taxes (Value Season); $2,335 to $4,685 (Peak Season). Free air fare.

FAIRSEA—June 18, July 2 to Victoria, Prince Rupert, Juneau, Malaspina Glacier, Seward, Valdez, Columbia Glacier, Vancouver (14 days). $2,335 to $4,685 per person, double, plus port taxes. Free air fare.

FAIRSEA—Sept. 10 to Cabo San Lucas, Acapulco, Panama Canal transit, San Blas Islands, Cartagena, Aruba, and San Juan (14 days). $2,485 to $4,830 per person, double, plus port taxes. Free air fare.

NIEUW AMSTERDAM—Alternate Saturdays from Oct. 1 through 1983 to Mexico (14 days).

PACIFIC PRINCESS—June 6, 18, 30; July 12 and 24; Aug. 5, 17, and 29 to Vancouver, Prince Rupert, Juneau, Skagway, Glacier Bay cruising, Sitka and Victoria (12 days). $2,676 to $5,256 per person, double, plus port taxes.

PACIFIC PRINCESS—Sept. 1 to Cabo San Lucas, Mazatlan, Puerto Vallarta, Manzanillo, and Acapulco (7 days). $1,575 to $2,996 per person, double, plus port taxes.

ROYAL VIKING SEA—Jan. 7 and Feb. 11 to San Diego, Mazatlan, Puerto Vallarta, Panama Canal transit, Cartagena, Curaçao, Ocho Rios, and Port Everglades (16 days). $3,020 to $10,296 per person, double, plus port taxes. (Substitute Los Angeles for San Diego on Feb. 11.)

ROYAL VIKING SEA—Oct. 14 to Acapulco, Callao, Valparaiso, Puerto Montt, Strait of Magellan, Punta Arenas, Rio de Janeiro, Salvador, Bridgetown, and Port Everglades (46 days). $6,603 to $27,482 per person, double, plus port taxes. (Cruise leaves Oct. 13 from Los Angeles.)

ROYAL VIKING SEA—Dec. 17 to Los Angeles, Nukuhiva, Moorea, Papeete, Bora Bora, Honolulu, Lahaina, San Francisco, and Los Angeles (26 days). $5,824 to $18,850 per person, double, plus port taxes.

ROYAL VIKING STAR—Jan. 13 to Los Angeles, Moorea, Papeete, Nuku' Alofa, Auckland, Hobart, Sydney, Suva, Niuafo'ou cruising, Apia, Honolulu, San Francisco, and Los Angeles (45 days). $7,245 to $26,595 per person, double, plus port taxes.

ROYAL VIKING STAR—Feb. 27 to Los Angeles, Papeete, Moorea, Nuku' Alofa, Auckland, Sydney, Great Barrier Reef cruising, Cairns, Bali, Singapore, Hong Kong, Shanghai, Dalian, Hsingang, Nagasaki, Kagoshima, Inland Sea cruising, and Kobe (56 days). $9,097 to $33,392 per person, double, plus port taxes.

ROYAL VIKING STAR—July 8 and 20, Aug. 1, 13, and 25, Sept. 6 to Victoria, Juneau, Skagway, Glacier Bay cruising, Sitka, Prince Rupert, Vancouver (12 days). $2,052 to $7,884 per person, double plus port taxes.

ROYAL VIKING STAR—Sept. 24 to Ensenada (4 days). $544 to $2,252 per person, double plus port taxes.

ROYAL VIKING STAR—Sept. 28, Nov. 27 to Los Angeles, Mazatlan, Puerto Vallarta, transit Panama Canal, Cartagena, Curaçao, Ocho Rios, and Port Everglades (16 days). $2,343 to $9,752 per person, double plus port taxes.

SAGAFJORD—June 19; July 3, 17, 31; Aug. 14 to Vancouver, Prince Rupert, Juneau, Skagway, La Perouse Glacier, Columbia Glacier, Valdez, Sitka, Victoria (14 days). $2,890 to $10,260 per person, double (Cruising Plus).

SANTA MARIA, MAGDALENA, MERCEDES, MARIANA—Every other week to Los Angeles, Puerto Vallarta, Buenaventura, Balboa, Panama Canal transit, Cartagena, Porta Cabello, La Guaira, Salvador, Rio de Janeiro, Santos, Buenos Aires, Strait of Magellan, Valparaiso, Callao, Guayaquil, Los Angeles (53 days). $9,155 to $17,630 per person, double.

FROM ST. PETERSBURG

CONSTELLATION—Every Saturday from Feb. 12 through April 30 to Grand Cayman, Montego Bay, Cozumel (7 days). $895 to $1,695 per person, double plus port taxes.

CONSTELLATION—Jan. 7 to Cozumel, Montego Bay, Cartagena, Cristobal, Panama Canal transit, Balboa, Acapulco, Puerto Vallarta, and Los Angeles (18 days). $2,295 to $4,295 per person, double plus port taxes.

CONSTELLATION—May 7. Same itinerary as above, with San Francisco, and Vancouver (22 days). $2,795 to $5,250 per person, double plus port taxes.

FROM SAVANNAH

AMERICA—Jan. 8, 29 and Feb. 19 to St. Simons, Sea Island, Fernandina Beach, Jacksonville Beach, St. Augustine, Kennedy Space Center, Fort Pierce, Vero Beach, Lake Okeechobee, and Ft. Myers (Fla.) (10 days). *Okeechobee and Southern Waterways Cruise.* $1,040 to $1,140 per person, double.

AMERICA—March 12, 19 and 26, April 2, 9 and 16 to Hilton Head, Beaufort and Charleston, South Carolina plus St. Simons, Georgia (7 days). *Carolinas and Golden Isles Cruise.* $728 to $798 per person, double.

AMERICA—April 23 to Beaufort, Charleston, Bucksport, Wrightsville Beach, Morehead City, Belhaven, Coinjock, Great Bridge, Norfolk, Yorktown, Crisfield, Oxford, Annapolis, St. Michael's, and Baltimore (14 days). *East Coast Inland Passage Cruise.* $1,456 to $1,596 per person, double.

INDEPENDENCE—Feb. 20 (10 days). *Okeechobee and Southern Waterways Cruise.* $1,040 to $1,140 per person, double.

INDEPENDENCE—April 17 and 24, May 1 and 8 to Hilton Head, Beaufort and Charleston, South Carolina plus St. Simons, Georgia (7 days). *Carolina and Golden Isles Cruises.* $728 to $798 per person, double.

INDEPENDENCE—May 15 to Beaufort, Charleston, Bucksport, Wrightsville Beach, Morehead City, Belhaven, Coinjock, Great Bridge, Norfolk, Yorktown, Crisfield, Oxford, Annapolis, St. Michael's, and Baltimore (14 days). *East Coast Inland Passage Cruise.* $1,456 to $1,596 per person, double.

FROM SEATTLE

PACIFIC NORTHWEST EXPLORER—Alternate Saturdays from June 4 through September 10 to La Conner, Vancouver, Howe Sound, Victoria, American San Juan Islands (4 days). $636 to $956 per person, double (subject to change).

PACIFIC NORTHWEST EXPLORER—Alternate Mondays and Wednesdays from June 1 through September to Puget Sound, Agate Pass, Vancouver, Princess Louisa Inlet, Pender Harbour, Victoria, American San Juan Islands, Friday Harbour, Whidbey Island (5 days). $797 to $1,197 per person, double (subject to change).

FROM TAMPA

VEENDAM—Every Saturday from January 1 through April 30 to Playa del Carmen, Cozumel, Jamaica, Grand Cayman (7 days). $815 to $1,790 per person, double including airfare where applicable.

VERACRUZ—Jan. 2 to Cozumel and Key West (6 days). $555 to $845 per person, double plus $20 port taxes.

VERACRUZ—Every Saturday from Jan. 8 through June to Cancun, Cozumel and Key West (7 days). $645 to $1,040 per person, double plus $20 port taxes.

FROM VANCOUVER

CONSTELLATION—Every Sunday from May 29 through Sept. 18 to Wrangell, Skagway, Juneau, Tracy Arm/Endicott Arm, Ketchikan (7 days). $945 to $1,775 per person, double plus port taxes.

CUNARD PRINCESS—Alternate Saturdays/from June 4 through Sept. 10 to Behn Channel, Misty Fjords, Tracy Arm, Juneau, Skagway, Prince William Sound, and Anchorage (7 days). $1,090 to $2,195 per person, double, plus port taxes.

DAPHNE—Every Friday from May 27 to Sept. 16 to Wrangell, Endicott Arm, Juneau, Skagway and Ketchikan (7 days). $795 to $1,850 per person, double plus port taxes (Value Season); $860 to $1,850 (Peak Season).

ISLAND PRINCESS—June 9, 17, 25; July 3, 11, 19, 27; Aug. 4, 12, 20, 28; Sept. 5 and 13 to Ketchikan, Juneau, Skagway, Glacier Bay cruising, Sitka (8 days). $1,744 to $3,648 per person, double plus port taxes. (Sept. 13 cruise also 11 days to Los Angeles, $2,057 to $4,301).

NIEUW AMSTERDAM—Every Sunday from June 26 through September 18 to Ketchikan, Juneau, Sitka, Glacier Bay National Monument (cruising only) (7 days). $1,305 to $2,475 per person, double plus port taxes.

RHAPSODY—Every Tuesday from May 31 through Sept. 27 to Ketchikan, Juneau, Glacier Bay cruising, and Sitka (7 days). $1,075 to $1,995 per person, double (May 31 and June 7); $1,120 to $2,075 (June 14 and 21, Sept. 6 to 20); $1,175 to $2,180 (remainder) plus $19 port taxes.

RHAPSODY—Sept. 27 to San Francisco, and Los Angeles (4 days). $485 to $895 per person, double plus $19 port taxes.

ROTTERDAM—Every Saturday from June 4 through Sept. 3 to Ketchikan, Juneau, Sitka, Glacier Bay National Monument (cruising only) (7 days). $1,125 to $2,475 per person, double plus port taxes.

SANTA MARIA/MAGDALENA/MERCEDES/MARIANA—Jan. 14, 28, Feb. 11, 25, and every two weeks or so through 1983—to Tacoma, San Francisco, Los Angeles, Puerto Vallarta, Buenaventura, Balboa, Panama Canal transit, Cartagena, Porto Cabello, La Guaira, Salvador, Rio de Janeiro, Santos, Buenos Aires, Strait of Magellan, Valparaiso, Callao, Guayaquil, Los Angeles, San Francisco, Vancouver, Tacoma, etc. (54 days). $9,630 to $18,545 per person, double.

SUN PRINCESS—Saturdays from June 4 through Sept. 17 to Juneau, Skagway, Glacier Bay cruising, Ketchikan, Misty Fjord (7 days). $1,379 to $2,912 per person, double (June 4 through 18, Sept. 3 through 17); $1,456 to $3,066 from June 25 through Aug. 27.

TROPICALE—Every Thursday from June 9 through September 1 to Ketchikan, Juneau, Glacier Bay and Sitka (7 days). $860 to $1,595 per person, double plus $20 port taxes.

FROM WARREN (RHODE ISLAND)

NEW SHOREHAM II—May 29, June 10 and 26, July 8 and 24, Aug. 5 and 21, Sept. 2 to Long Island Sound, Hudson River to Waterford, Erie Canal to Little Falls, Oswego, Prescott, Ontario, Montreal, Quebec City, Saguenay-Tadoussac, Quebec City and Montreal (12 days). $825 to $1,390 per person, double. (Cruises are one-way, with bus connections to Rhode Island).

NEW SHOREHAM II—June 23, July 21 and Aug. 18 (Weekend Island Hop) to Block Island, Martha's Vineyard and Newport (2½ days). $210 to $285 per person, double.

NEW SHOREHAM II—Sept. 18 to Waterford, Little Falls, Oswego, Alexandria Bay, Sylvan Beach, Fort Johnson, West Point, New York City, Mystic, Newport (12 days). $750 to $1,290 per person, double.

NEW SHOREHAM II—Oct. 2 (Fall Foliage) to Waterford, Little Falls, Oswego, Sylvan Beach, Lake Oneida, Schenectady, West Point, Port Jefferson, Greenport, Mystic, Block Island, and Newport (12 days). Same rates as above.

NEW SHOREHAM II—Nov. 6 to New York City, Annapolis, Norfolk, Belhaven, Wrightsville Beach, Georgetown, Charleston, Thunderbolt, St. Simons Island, St. Augustine, Titusville, Jensen Beach and West Palm Beach (14 days). $875 to $1,650 per person, double.

PACIFIC OCEAN/SOUTH SEAS

FROM CAIRNS (AUSTRALIA)

WORLD DISCOVERER—Feb. 28 to Lizard Island, Great Barrier Reef, Coral Sea, Milne Bay area, Woodlark Island, Rabaul, Garove Island, Madang, Sepik River, Murik Lakes, Umboi, Trobriand Islands, and Port Moresby (17 days). $3,840 to $7,200 per person, double, plus air fare.

FROM HONOLULU

CONSTITUTION—Every Sunday to Nawiliwili, Kona, Hilo, Kahului (7 days). $895 to $2,295 per person, double, plus $19 port taxes. (Add $100 per passenger for Christmas/New Year cruises.)

OCEANIC INDEPENDENCE—Every Saturday to Hilo, Kona, Kahului, Nawiliwili (7 days). $895 to $2,295 per person, double, plus $19 port taxes. (Add $100 per passenger for Christmas/New Year cruises.)

FROM PAPEETE

MAJESTIC EXPLORER—Jan. 4, 18, 23; Feb. 1, 6, 15, 20; March 1, 6, 15, 20, 29; April 3, 12, 17 to Huahine, Bora Bora, Raiatea, Moorea (6 days). $899 to $1,349 per person, double.

MAJESTIC EXPLORER—Jan. 14, 28; Feb. 11, 25; March 11, 25; April 8 to Raiatea, Bora Bora, Moorea (5 days). $749 to $1,098 per person, double.

FROM PORT BLUFF (NEW ZEALAND)

WORLD DISCOVERER—Feb. 15 to Milford Sound, Tasman Sea, Lord

Howe Island, Queen Elizabeth and Middleton Reefs, Coral Sea, Heron Island, Swain Reefs, Whitsunday Passage, Flinders Reef and Cairns (18 days). $3,540 to $6,760 per person, double, plus air fare.

FROM PORT MORESBY (PAPUA NEW GUINEA)

WORLD DISCOVERER—March 13 to Daru, New Guinea south coast, Asmat, Aru/Gorong, Banda, Lucipara/Gunungapi, Larantuka, Savu, Komodo, Bali, Semarang, Jakarta, Krakatoa, and Singapore (23 days). $5,440 to $10,000 per person, double, plus air fare.

FROM SYDNEY

LINDBLAD EXPLORER—March 7 to Dunk Island, Cairns, Samarai, Engineer Group, Calvados Chain, Jomard and Punawan Islands, Deboyne Lagoon, Renard and Misima Islands, Woodlark and Ginefu Islands, Madau Island, Gawa and Iwa Islands, Tuam Island, Madang, and Port Moresby (19 days). $5,600 to $7,600 per person, double, plus air fare.

WESTERN EUROPE

FROM BERGEN

WORLD DISCOVERER—July 10 to Olden, Rost, Bear Island, Spitsbergen, and Tromso (15 days). $4,500 to $7,980 per person, double, plus air fare.

FROM COPENHAGEN

LINDBLAD POLARIS—May 28, June 25, July 23, Aug. 20 to Ronne/Christianso, Riga, Tallinn, Leningrad, Helsinki, Korpo, Graso/Vaddo Canal/Stockholm, Bjorko/Mariefred/Sodertalje Canal, Visby and Kalmar (15 days). $3,525 to $7,425 per person, double, plus air fare.

LINDBLAD POLARIS—June 11, July 9, Aug. 6 and Sept. 3 to Arhus/Alborg, Gotland/Trollhatte, Lake Vanern, Lysefjord, Sognefjord, Geiranger, Trondheim, Andalsnes, Nordfjord, Bergen, Stromstad, and Oslo (15 days). $3,525 to $7,425 per person, double, plus air fare.

ROYAL VIKING STAR—June 24, July 8 to Geiranger, Trondheim, Honningsvag, Tromso, Molde, Flaam, Gudvangen, Bergen, Stavanger, Oslo (14 days). $2,688 to $9,660 per person, double, plus port taxes.

ROYAL VIKING SEA—July 22 to Amsterdam, Hamburg, Gdynia, Leningrad, Helsinki, and Stockholm (14 days). $2,688 to $9,660 per person, double, plus port taxes.

ROYAL VIKING SEA—Aug. 5 to Lerwick, Bergen, Geiranger, Honningsvag, Tromso, Reykjavik, St. John's, St. Pierre, Bar Harbor, Boston, Newport, and

New York (21 days). $3,549 to $14,490 per person, double, plus port taxes.

ROYAL VIKING SKY—June 17, July 15 and 29. Same itinerary and rates as June 24 *Royal Viking Sea*.

ROYAL VIKING SKY—July 1. Same itinerary and rates as July 22 *Royal Viking Sea*.

ROYAL VIKING SKY—Aug. 12 to Leningrad, Helsinki, Stockholm, Gdynia, Hamburg, Amsterdam, and Southampton (14 days). $2,688 to $9,660 per person, double, plus port taxes.

FROM CUXHAVEN

ASTOR—May 28 to Oslo, Copenhagen, Swinoujscie, Visby, Stockholm, Turku, Helsinki, Leningrad, Gdynia, Bornholm Island, and Kiel (14 days). $2,592 to $5,880 per person, double.

ASTOR—June 25 and July 13 to Invergordon, Torshavn, Reykjavik, Akureyri, Spitsbergen, Skarsvag, Hammerfest, Hellesylt, Geiranger, and Bergen (18 days and 17 days). $3,312 to $7,554 (18 days), $3,138 to $7,157 (17 days), per person, double.

ASTOR—July 30 to Vik, Sognefjord, Gudvangen, Naerofjord, Andalsnes, Romsdalsfjord, Trondheim, Hammerfest, Skarsvag, Tromso, Narvik, Hellesylt, Geiranger, Olden, Bergen, and Kiel (14 days). $2,648 to $6,006 per person, double.

FROM GOTHENBURG

FUNCHAL—June 10, 21; July 13, 24; Aug. 4 to Skagerak/Norwegian coast, Storfjord/Geiranger, Lofoten/Arctic Circle, Honningsvag, Tromso, Norwegian Sea/Lofoten Islands, Molde, Olden, Bergen, Lysefjord (12 days). $1,290 to $2,600 per person, double, plus air fare.

FUNCHAL—July 2 to North Sea, Orkney Islands, Oban, Dublin, Cork, St. Mary's (Scilly Islands), Cherbourg (12 days). $1,290 to $2,600 per person, double, plus air fare.

FUNCHAL—May 29 to North Sea, Amsterdam, San Sebastian, Bordeaux, St. Nazaire, Zeebrugge (12 days). $1,290 to $2,600 per person, double, plus air fare.

LINDBLAD EXPLORER—July 1 to Stavanger, Geirangerfjord and Hellesylt, Rostoy, Fugloya, Honningsvag, Bear Island, Hopen, Tjuvfjorden, Svenskoya and Sorgfjord, Hinlopen and Moffen Island, Amsterdamoya, Maddalenafjord and Ny Alesund, Longyearbyen, Sveagruva, Jan Mayen, Westmanoya and Surtsey Island, and Reykjavik (25 days). $6,800 to $9,600 per person, double, plus air fare.

FROM HAMBURG

ASTOR—Sept. 17 to Tilbury, St. Malo, Corunna, Vigo, Lisbon, Tangier, Malaga, Palma de Mallorca, and Genoa (14 days). $2,341 to $5,293 per person, double, plus port taxes.

VISTAFJORD—June 4, July 30, Aug. 13 to Gdynia, Leningrad, Helsinki, Stockholm, Copenhagen, Oslo, London (14 days). $3,870 to $11,100 per person, double (Cruising Plus); $4,080 to $11,860 (July and August).

VISTAFJORD—June 18, July 2 and 16 to Molde, Andalsnes, Trondheim, Narvik, Tjeldsund, Harstad, Magdalena Bay, Ice Barrier, Ny Alesund, Lilliehood Fjord, Longyear City, Barentsburg, Bear Island, North Cape, Hammerfest, Tromso, Geiranger, Hjorundfjord, Oye, Bergen (14 days). $3,920 to $11,290 per person, double (Cruising Plus); $4,080 to $11,860 (July).

VISTAFJORD—Aug. 27 to Southampton, Pauillac, Oporto, Lisbon, Casablanca, Cadiz, Gibraltar, Ceuta, Mahon and Genoa (15 days). $3,890 to $10,760 per person, double (Cruising Plus).

FROM KIEL

ASTOR—June 11 to Vik, Gudvangen, Andalsnes, Trondheim, Hammerfest, Skarsvag, Tromso, Narvik, Hellesylt, Geiranger, Olden, Bergen, and Cuxhaven (14 days). $2,648 to $6,006 per person, double.

ASTOR—Aug. 13 to Bornholm, Gdnyia, Leningrad, Helsinki, Stockholm, Visby, Warnemunde, Copenhagen, Oslo, and Hamburg (14 days). $2,592 to $5,880 per person, double.

FROM LEITH (for Edinburgh)

UGANDA—June 24 to La Pallice, Gibraltar, Malaga, Tangier, Praia da Rocha (14 days). £714 to £1,503 per person, double.

UGANDA—July 8 to Travemunde, Stockholm, Helsinki, Bornholm, Copenhagen (13 days). £663 to £1,395 per person, double.

FROM LISBON

GOLDEN ODYSSEY—March 23 and Oct. 18 to Cadiz, Palma, Nice/Villefranche, Livorno, Naples, Messina, and Piraeus (14 days air-sea from U.S.). $2,858 to $4,198 per person, double.

GOLDEN ODYSSEY—June 4 and Sept. 22 to Gibraltar, Malaga, Palma, Nice/Villefranche, Livorno, Naples, Mykonos, and Piraeus (15 days air-sea from U.S.). $3,168 to $4,498 per person, double.

ROYAL ODYSSEY—March 28. Same itinerary and rates as March 23 *Golden Odyssey.*

ROYAL ODYSSEY—April 22. Same itinerary as June 4 *Golden Odyssey,* with value season rates from $3,068 to $4,198 per person, double.

LINDBLAD POLARIS—April 30 to Oporto, Corunna, La Pallice, Belle-Ile-en-Mer, Rouen, Bruges, Amsterdam, Kiel Canal transit, Aero, and Copenhagen (14 days). $3,850 to $5,990 per person, double.

LINDBLAD POLARIS—Sept. 23 to Portimao, Cadiz, Casablanca, Tangier, Motril, Alicante, Barcelona, Sete, Marseille, Calvi, Livorno, Maddalena, and Civitavecchia (14 days). $3,850 to $5,990 per person, double.

FROM REYKJAVIK

LINDBLAD EXPLORER—July 25 to Angmagssalik, Prince Christian Sound, Narssarssuaq, Broughton Island, Sam Ford Fjord, Pond Inlet, Coburg Island, Grisefjord, Bylot Island, Padloping Island and Cape Searle, Pangnirtung, Brevoort Island, Lake Harbour, Cape Dorset, Walrus and Coates Islands, Digges Island, Akpatok, Red Bay, and Halifax (30 days). $8,400 to $10,500 per person, double, plus air fare.

FROM SYRACUSE

LINDBLAD POLARIS—April 17 to Palermo, Porto Empedocle, Malta, Sousse, Tunis, Cagliari, Mahon, Motril, Tangier, Cadiz, Portimao, and Lisbon (14 days). $3,850 to $5,990 per person, double.

FROM SOUTHAMPTON

CANBERRA—April 15 to Malaga, Messina, Volos, Istanbul, Haifa, Piraeus, Gibraltar (21 days). £1,218 to £2,688 per person, double, plus port taxes.

CANBERRA—May 6 to Gibraltar, Barcelona, Cannes, Elba, Naples, Palma (14 days). £812 to £1,708 per person, double, plus port taxes.

CANBERRA—May 20 to Lisbon, Praia de Rocha, Tenerife, Las Palmas, Madeira, Vigo (13 days). £767 to £1,625 per person, double, plus port taxes.

CANBERRA—June 2 to Gibraltar, Dubrovnik, Corfu, Messina, Palma (14 days). £854 to £1,792 per person, double, plus port taxes.

CANBERRA—June 16 to Hardangerfjord, North Cape, Narvik, Andalsnes, Bergen, Olso (13 days). £806 to £1,768 per person, double, plus port taxes.

CANBERRA—July 1 to Malaga, Haifa, Izmir, Piraeus, Gibraltar (16 days). £1,024 to £2,160 per person, double, plus port taxes.

CANBERRA—July 17 to Vigo, Madeira, Tenerife, Ibiza, Praia de Rocha (13 days). £858 to £1,794 per person, double, plus port taxes.

CANBERRA—July 30 to Gibraltar, Palermo, Loutraki, Corfu, Palma (14 days). £966 to £2,030 per person, double, plus port taxes.

CANBERRA—Aug. 13 to Rosas, Cannes, Genoa, Elba, Palma (13 days). £910 to £1,937 per person, double, plus port taxes.

CANBERRA—Aug. 26 to Malaga, Piraeus, Rhodes, Port Said, Gibraltar (16 days). £1,072 to £2,272 per person, double, plus port taxes.

CANBERRA—Sept. 11 to Palma, Naples, Marseille, Alghero, Malaga (14 days). £924 to £1,932 per person, double, plus port taxes.

CANBERRA—Sept. 25 to Vigo, Tenerife, Las Palmas, Madeira, Lisbon (12 days). £804 to £1,704 per person, double, plus port taxes.

CANBERRA—Oct. 7 to Malaga, Messina, Port Said, Haifa, Gibraltar (16 days). £1,024 to £2,160 per person, double, plus port taxes.

QUEEN ELIZABETH 2—April 29, May 27, June 16 and 27, July 22, Aug. 2 and 20, Sept. 3 and 15, Oct. 8, Nov. 5 and Dec. 16 to New York (transatlantic 5 days). $1,185 to $5,350 per person, double (thrift season); $1,360 to $5,865 (intermediate season); $1,435 to $6,185 (high season).

QUEEN ELIZABETH 2—April 22 and Oct. 29 to Canary Islands (7 days). $1,195 to $3,600 per person, double, plus port taxes.

QUEEN ELIZABETH 2—May 15 and Sept. 26 to Mediterranean (12 days). $2,055 to $6,165 per person, double, plus port taxes (May 15); $1,950 to $5,855 (Sept. 26).

QUEEN ELIZABETH 2—June 10 to Iberia (6 days). $1,025 to $3,085 per person, double, plus port taxes.

QUEEN ELIZABETH 2—July 10 to North Cape (12 days). Same rates as May 15 QE2.

QUEEN ELIZABETH 2—Dec. 13 to Nowhere (3 days). $585 to $970 per person, double.

ROYAL VIKING SEA—June 10 to Bergen, Arendal, Oslo, Leningrad, Helsinki, Stockholm, and Copenhagen (14 days). $2,688 to $9,660 per person, double, plus port taxes.

ROYAL VIKING SKY—Aug. 26 to Guernsey, Bordeaux, Vigo, Lisbon, Gibraltar, Valletta, and Piraeus (13 days). $2,249 to $8,112 per person, double, plus port taxes.

SEA PRINCESS—Jan. 6 to Madeira, Bermuda, Port Everglades, Curaçao, Panama Canal transit, Acapulco, San Francisco, Honolulu, Pago Pago, Suva, Sydney, Bali, Jakarta, Singapore, Penang, Colombo, Mauritius, Durban, Cape Town, Dakar, Lisbon (90 days). *World Cruise*. £6,985 to £12,950 per person, double, plus port taxes. Also sold in segments: U.K. to Sydney (45 days), £3,574 to £6,556; Sydney to U.K. (44 days), same rates; U.K. to Singapore (58 days), £4,391 to £8,088; Singapore to U.K. (36 days), £2,855 to £5,127.

SEA PRINCESS—April 18 to Gibraltar, Palma, Alexandria, Kos, Izmir, Santorini, and Piraeus (14 days). £1,008 to £1,792 per person, double, air-sea.

SEA PRINCESS—June 11 to Malaga, Ciudadela, Barcelona, Tangier, Vigo (13 days). £1,027 to £1,846 per person, double, plus port taxes.

SEA PRINCESS—June 24 to Madeira, Martinique, Barbados, Grenadines, Dominica, Vigo (22 days). £1,694 to £3,058 per person, double, plus port taxes.

SEA PRINCESS—July 16 to Amsterdam, Copenhagen, Oslo, Geirangerfjord, Andalsnes, Bergen (13 days). £1,118 to £1,989 per person, double, plus port taxes.

SEA PRINCESS—July 29 to Praia da Rocha, Alicante, Leghorn, Cannes, Cadiz (14 days). £1,218 to £2,198 per person, double, plus port taxes.

SEA PRINCESS—Aug. 12 to Ponta Delgada, Horta, Madeira, Tenerife, Lisbon (13 days). £1,157 to £2,093 per person, double, plus port taxes.

SEA PRINCESS—Aug. 27 to Gibraltar, Marseille, San Remo, Alghero, Palma (13 days). £1,118 to £1,989 per person, double, plus port taxes.

SEA PRINCESS—Sept. 9 to Lisbon, Gibraltar, Ibiza, Messina, Gythion, Haifa, and Piraeus (14 days). £1,134 to £2,044 per person, double, air-sea to Gatwick.

SEA PRINCESS—Dec. 16 to Bermuda, San Juan, Antigua, Martinique, Barbados, Madeira (23 days). £1,886 to £3,358 per person, double, plus port taxes.

UGANDA—Aug. 2 to Lisbon, Tangier, Cadiz, Madeira, Ponta Delgada (14 days). £751 to £1,580 per person, double, plus port taxes.

UGANDA—Aug. 16 to Kristiansand, Copenhagen, Helsinki, Leningrad, Travemunde, and Tilbury (13 days). £663 to £1,395 per person, double, plus port taxes.

UGANDA—Sept. 18 to Lisbon, Ciudadela, Civitavecchia, Gythion, Rhodes, Santorini, and Piraeus (14 days). £714 to £1,503 per person, double, plus port taxes.

VISTAFJORD—Feb. 20 to Tenerife, Barbados, St. Lucia, Martinique, St. Croix, Port-au-Prince, Nassau, Cape Canaveral, and Port Everglades (19 days). $4,435 to $14,605 per person, double (Cruising Plus).

FROM TILBURY

ROYAL ODYSSEY—May 20; June 1, 13, 24; July 7, 19, 31; Aug. 12, 24; to Kiel Canal transit, Leningrad, Helsinki, Stockholm, Copenhagen, Bergen, Hardangerfjord (14 days air-sea from U.S. to London). $2,778 to $4,118 per person, double.

ROYAL ODYSSEY—Sept. 5 to Lisbon, Malaga, Palma, Villefranche/Nice, Livorno, Capri, Heraklion, and Piraeus (17 days air-sea from U.S.). $3,323 to $4,668 per person, double.

FROM TROMSO

WORLD DISCOVERER—July 22 to Bear Island, Spitsbergen, Scoresby Sound, Angmagssalik, Breidafjord, Heimaey, Faroe Islands, Orkney Islands, and Leith (23 days). $6,600 to $11,500 per person, double, plus air fare.

INLAND WATERWAYS

ALSACE CANALS

LAFAYETTE—Wednesdays from April 6 through Nov. 2 between Nancy, Strasbourg and Montbeliard (6 days each). $1,280 per person, double. Inaugural Season.

MARK TWAIN—Wednesdays from April 6 through Nov. 2 from Epinal to Port-sur-Saone to Dole to Montbeliard to Strasbourg to Nancy (6 days each). $1,440 per person, double. Gourmet Cruises.

THE AMAZON RIVER

FROM ANTIGUA

LINDBLAD EXPLORER—Oct. 3 to Amazon River upstream to Iquitos (25 days). $5,600 to $7,400 per person, double, plus air fare.

FROM IQUITOS

LINDBLAD EXPLORER—Oct. 22 to Amazon River downstream to Belem (25 days). $6,200 to $8,200 per person, double, plus air fare.

FROM MANAUS

ASTOR—Feb. 1 to Boca do Valeria, Rio Tapajos, Belem, Fortaleza, Salvador de Bahia, Rio de Janeiro, and Montevideo (18 days). $2,861 to $6,722 per person, double.

THE RIVER AVON

BEVERLY AND JEAN—April 10 through Oct. 23 between Stratford-upon-Avon and Tewkesbury, visiting Welford, Bidford, Evesham, Pershore, and Twining (or vice versa) (6 days). $850 per person, double, in April and October; $995 May through September.

BEVERLY AND JEAN—April 10 through Oct. 23 between Stratford-upon-Avon and Tewkesbury (3 days). $425 per person, double, in April and October; $550 May through September.

BEVERLY AND JEAN—March 31 (4 days). $550 per person, double. *Easter Cruise.*

BURGUNDY CANALS

ETOILE DE CHAMPAGNE—Saturdays from July 3 through Aug. 21 between Ste. Florentine and Montbard. $1,500 per person, double.

HORIZON—Sundays from April 17 through October between Pouilly en Auxois and Montbard, Montbard and St. Florentin, Pouilly en Auxois and Dijon (6 days each). $995 per person, double.

JANINE—Fridays and Mondays from Feb. 28 to April 22, Oct. 28 to Nov. 11 and 25, and Tuesday, Nov. 22, between Dijon and Tournus, visiting Canal de Bourgogne and Verndun, or Chalon and St. Jean de Losne (3 days). $495 per person, double. *Wine Cruises.*

JANINE—Alternate Wednesdays from April 27 through Oct. 12 from Dijon to Lyon, visiting Gissey, St. Jean de Losne, Chalon, Tournus, Trevoux (6 days). $1,495 per person, double ($1,270 on April 27). *Burgundy Wine Cruises.*

JANINE—Alternate Wednesdays from May 4 through Oct. 19 from Lyon to Dijon, visiting Trevoux, Tournus, Chalon, Canal de Bourgogne, St. Victor (6 days). $1,495 per person, double.

JANINE—Nov. 16 from Lyon to Dijon. $1,870 per person, double. *Special Trois Glorieuses Cruise.*

LA LITOTE—Wednesdays from April 6 through Nov. 2 between Auxerre, Montbard, and Dijon (6 days each). $1,280 to $1,380 per person, double.

L'ESCARGOT—Wednesdays from April 6 through Nov. 2 between Nemours and Auxerre (6 days). $1,280 per person, double.

LINQUENDA—Fridays and Mondays from April 1 to 11; Oct. 21 to Nov. 25 between Tanlay and Montbard (3 days). $430 per person, double. *Chateaux Cruises.*

LINQUENDA—Saturdays from April 16 through May 14; June 18 and 25; Aug. 6 through 27; and Oct. 1 through 15 between Pouillenay and Tanlay, visiting Les Laumes, Montbard, Cry, Ancy-le-Franc (6 days). $1,395 per person, double. *Burgundy Chateaux Cruises.*

LINQUENDA—Saturdays, May 21, June 11, July 2 and 30, Sept. 3 and 24 between Tanlay and Sens, visiting Tonnerre, Flogny, St. Florentin, Brienon, River-Yonne to Joigny, Villeneuve-sur-Yonne (6 days). $1,395 per person, double. *Burgundy Historic Towns Cruises.*

CANAL DU MIDI

ATHOS—April through October between Toulouse and Beziers (7 to 10 days). Approximately $200 per person, double, per night; or for full-charter only.

BONJOUR—Fridays and Mondays, April 1 to 11; Oct. 28 and 31, Nov. 4 to 21 visiting Beziers, Fonserrannes, Libron Sluice, Percee de Malpas and Oppidum d'Enserune (3 days). $430 per person, double.

BONJOUR—Saturdays, April 16, 23, and 30; May 7 and 14; June; July 15, 23, and 30; Aug. 6 and 27; Sept. 3 and 24; and October between Marseillan and Carcassone, visiting Agde, Beziers, Colombiers, Argeliers, Homps, and Trebes (6 days). $995 per person, double (April departures); $1,325 thereafter.

BONJOUR—Saturdays, May 21 and 28; July 2 and 9; Aug. 13 and 20; Sept. 10 and 17 between Toulouse and Carcassone, visiting Villedubert, Carcassonne, Bram, Castelnaudary, Gardouch, Port Sud (6 days). $1,325 per person, double.

PALINURUS—Wednesdays from April 6 through Nov. 8 between Bordeaux and Sete, visiting Castets, Meilhan, Buzet, Agen, Moissac, Montauban, Toulouse, Castelnaudary, Carcassonne, Narbonne, Beziers (6 days). $1,140 per person, double.

SARA JANE—Sundays from mid-April through October between Marseillan/Argeliers and Argeliers/Castelnaudary, visiting Agde, Beziers, Colombiers, Carcassonne, and Bram. Available for full-charter only. Rates upon request.

VIRGINIA ANNE—Wednesdays from April 6 through November 8 between Agde, Narbonne, and Carcassonne. Available for full-charter only. Rates upon request.

CANAL DU NIVERNAIS

DE HOOP—Saturdays from mid-April through October between Villeneuve-sur-Yonne and Clamecy, visiting Gurgy, Auxerre, Mailly-le-Chateau, Chatel Censoir (6 days). Full-charter only. Rates upon request.

DE HOOP—Saturdays from late-April to mid-October between Clamecy and Chatillon-en-Bazois, visiting Tannay, Chitry-les-Mines, Sardy-les-Epiry, Baye (6 days). Full-charter only. Rates upon request.

LINQUENDA—Saturdays, May 28, June 4, July 9 and 16, Sept. 10 and 17 between Sens and Clamecy, visiting Chatel-Censoir, Cravant, Vaux, Joigny (6 days). $1,395 per person, double.

SECUNDA—Sundays from mid-April through October between Nemours, Joigny, Clamecy, Chatillon, Ancy-le-Franc, and Briare (6 days between each stop). $1,205 per person, double.

CHARENTE RIVER

LIBERTE—Saturdays from mid-April through October between St. Savinien and Angouleme, visiting Saintes, Cognac, Jarnac, St. Simeux (6 days). $1,300 per person, double.

DUTCH CANALS

JULIANA—Saturdays from April 2 through May 7 from Amsterdam to Keukenhof Gardens, Haarlem, Zaanse Schans, Alkmaar, Zuider Zee (6 days). $1,040 per person, double (April 2 and 9); $1,295 thereafter. *Tulip and Spring Flower Cruises.*

JULIANA—Saturdays on May 14, 21; June 4, 11, 25; July 2, 16, 23; Aug. 6, 13, 27; Sept. 3, 17, 24; Oct. 8 from Amsterdam to Kaag, Delftshaven, Gouda, the River Vecht, Ouderkerk (6 days). $1,295 per person, double ($1,040 on Oct. 8). *Golden Age of Holland Cruises.*

JULIANA—Saturdays on May 28, June 18, July 19 and 30, Aug. 20, Sept. 10, Oct. 1 from Amsterdam to Kaag, Zaanse Schans, De Haukes, Medemblik, Hoorn, Ouderkerk (6 days). $1,295 per person, double ($1,040 on Oct. 1). *Dutch Country Cruises.*

JULIANA—Oct. 15 from Amsterdam to Oudewetering, Gouda, Maarsen, Zaanse Schans, Haarlem, and Ouderkerk (6 days). *Dutch Masters Art Cruise.* $1,295 per person, double.

LYS—Fridays and Mondays in April from Amsterdam to Keukenhof Gardens, Haarlem, Zaanse Schans, Alkmaar, Zuider Zee (3 days). $445 per person, double (April 1 through 18); $520 (April 22 through 29). *Tulip and Spring Flower Cruises.*

REMBRANDT—Sundays on April 3, 10; May 15, 22, 29; June 5, 26; July 3 through 31; Aug. 21, 28; Sept. 4 through 25; and Oct. 2 through 23 from Amsterdam to Kaag, Haarlem, Alkmaar, Purmerend, Muiden (6 days). $990 per person, double ($1,060 from May 15 through Oct. 23). *Heart of Holland Cruises.*

REMBRANDT—Sundays on April 17 and 24, May 1 and 8 from Amsterdam to Keukenhof Gardens, Kaag, Haarlem, Alkmaar, Purmerend, Muiden (6 days). $1,200 per person, double. *Tulip Cruises.*

REMBRANDT—Sundays on June 12 and 19, Aug. 7 and 14 between Lemmer and Groningen, visiting Stavoren, Sneek, Leeuwarden, Dokkum, and Zoutkamp (6 days). $1,060 per person, double (June 12 and 19); $990 (Aug. 7 and 14). *Friesland Cruises.*

LOIRE VALLEY

L'ESCARGOT—Wednesdays from April 6 through Nov. 2 between Nemours and Briare, visiting Montargis, Montbouy, Rogny (6 days). $1,280 per person, double.

NENUPHAR—Mondays from mid-April through October between Nemours and Briare, Nevers and Briare, visiting Marseilles, Les Aubigny, La Charite, Sancerre, Maimbray or Rogny, Montbouy, Montargis, and Nargis (6 days each). $1,275 per person, double.

THE RIVER LYS

LYS—Saturdays from May 7 through Sept. 24 between Antwerp and Bruges, visiting Oostende-Ghent Canal, Ghent, Ooidonck Castle, Ringvaart, Antwerp Harbor, Kempen Canal (6 days). $1,195 per person, double. *Historic Flanders Cruises.*

LYS—Mondays and Fridays, Sept. 30 through Oct. 28 between Ghent and Bruges (3 days). $520 per person, double (Sept. 30 through Oct. 7); $445 thereafter. *Flanders Cruises.*

THE MARNE

ETOILE DE CHAMPAGNE—Saturdays from May 1 through June 5 and Sept. 18 through Oct. 23 between Paris and Epernay, visiting Thorigny-sur-Marne, Meaux, Jouarre, Chateau Thierry, Mont St. Pere (6 days). $1,500 per person, double. *Champagne Cruises.*

THE MISSISSIPPI RIVER

FROM MEMPHIS

MISSISSIPPI QUEEN—May 6 and 20, June 3, July 22 to Greenville, Vicksburg, Natchez, St. Francisville and Houmas House, and New Orleans.

MISSISSIPPI QUEEN—June 17 to Vicksburg, Natchez, St. Francisville, Houmas House, and New Orleans (6 nights). $570 to $1,860 per person, double.

MISSISSIPPI QUEEN—Aug. 26 to Kentucky Lake, Evansville, Louisville, Madison, and Cincinnati (7 nights). $665 to $2,170 per person, double.

FROM NEW ORLEANS

DELTA QUEEN—Feb. 9, 14, 23, and 28 *(Mardi Gras Cruises)*; Dec. 2 and

7 *(Old Fashioned Holiday Cruises)*; to Houmas House, Baton Rouge, Natchez, and St. Francisville (5 nights). $475 to $1,425 per person, double.

DELTA QUEEN—March 4, 9, 18, 23 and April 1 *(Pilgrimage Cruises)*; April 6, 15; Oct. 28; and Nov. 2, 7, 12 to Houmas House, Baton Rouge, Natchez, and St. Francisville (5 nights). $475 to $1,525 per person, double.

DELTA QUEEN—Feb. 14 and 28 *(Mardi Gras Cruises)*; March 14 and 28 *(Pilgrimage Cruises)*; April 11 and 20; Nov. 17 and 28 to Natchez and St. Francisville (4 nights). $380 to $1,220 ($1,140 on Feb. 14 and 28) per person, double.

DELTA QUEEN—April 24 to Natchez, Memphis, Evansville, Louisville, Madison, and Cincinnati (12 nights). *19th Annual Kentucky Derby Steamboat Race.* $1,140 to $3,660 per person, double.

DELTA QUEEN—June 23 to Houmas House, St. Francisville, Natchez, Vicksburg, Memphis, Cairo, and St. Louis (11 nights). *Great Steamboat Race Cruise.* $1,045 to $3,355 per person, double.

DELTA QUEEN—Oct. 21; Nov. 21; Dec. 12, 19, 26 *(Old Fashioned Holiday Cruise)* to St. Francisville, Vicksburg, Natchez, and Baton Rouge (7 nights). $665 to $2,135 ($1,995 on Dec. 12) per person, double.

MISSISSIPPI QUEEN—Jan. 24 *(Mardi Gras Cruise)*; July 11 to Natchez and St. Francisville (4 nights). $380 to $1,240 ($1,120 on Jan. 24) per person, double.

MISSISSIPPI QUEEN—Jan. 28 and Feb. 4, 11 *(Mardi Gras Cruises)*; Feb. 18, 25 *(Mardi Gras and Glen Miller Orchestra Cruises)*; March 4, 11, 18, 25 and April 1 *(Pilgrimage Cruises)*; April 8, 15, 22 and July 29 and Aug. 5, 12 and Oct. 28 and Nov. 11; Nov. 18, 25 and Dec. 2, 9, 16, 23, 30 *(Old Fashioned Holiday Cruises)* to St. Francisville, Vicksburg, Natchez, and Baton Rouge (7 nights). $665 to $1,960 (Jan. 28 through March 11; Dec. 2 through 16); $2,170 (March 18 through Nov. 25; Dec. 23 and 30).

MISSISSIPPI QUEEN—April 29; May 13, 27; June 10; July 15; Aug. 19 to Houmas House, St. Francisville, Natchez, Vicksburg, and Memphis (7 nights). $665 to $2,170 per person, double.

MISSISSIPPI QUEEN—June 23 to Houmas House, St. Francisville, Natchez, Vicksburg, Memphis, Cairo, and St. Louis *(Great Steamboat Race Cruise)* (11 nights). $1,045 to $3,410 per person, double.

FROM ST. LOUIS

DELTA QUEEN—July 8, Aug. 12 and 26 to Hannibal, Dubuque/Galena, Prairie Du Chien, Wabasha, and St. Paul (7 nights). $665 to $2,135 per person, double.

DELTA QUEEN—June 9, July 4 to Burlington/Nauvoo and Hannibal (4 nights). $380 to $1,220 per person, double.

DELTA QUEEN—May 15, July 22, Sept. 9 and 28 to Cairo, Louisville, and Cincinnati (5 nights). $475 to $1,525 per person, double.

DELTA QUEEN—June 13 to Cairo, Memphis, Vicksburg, Natchez, St. Francisville, Houmas House, and New Orleans (10 nights). $950 to $3,050 per person, double.

MISSISSIPPI QUEEN—July 4, Oct. 21 to Cairo, Memphis, Vicksburg, St. Francisville, and New Orleans (7 nights). $665 to $2,170 per person, double.

MISSISSIPPI QUEEN—Sept. 9 and 23, Oct. 10 *(Fall Foliage Cruises)* to Hannibal, Dubuque/Galena, Prairie Du Chien, Wabasha, and St. Paul (7 nights). $665 to $2,170 per person, double.

FROM ST. PAUL

DELTA QUEEN—July 15, Aug. 19, Sept. 2 to LaCrosse, Prairie Du Chien, Dubuque/Galena, Burlington/Nauvoo, Hannibal, and St. Louis (7 nights). $665 to $2,135 per person, double.

MISSISSIPPI QUEEN—Sept. 16 and 30, Oct. 14 *(Fall Foliage Cruises)* to LaCrosse, Prairie Du Chien, Dubuque/Galena, Burlington/Nauvoo, Hannibal, and St. Louis (7 nights). $665 to $2,170 per person, double.

THE MOSELLE RIVER

EUROPA—Every four days from July 1 through Aug. 26 upstream between Koblenz and Trier, calling at Beilstein, Alf, Traben-Trarbach, and Bernkastle (3 days). $155 to $180 per person, double.

EUROPA—Every four days from July 3 through Aug. 28 downstream between Trier and Koblenz, calling at Trittenheim, Zeltingen, Zell, Alf, Beilstein, and Cochem (3 days). Same rates as *Europa* above.

THE NILE RIVER

ABU SIMBEL—Jan. 6, 13; Feb. 17, 24; March 31; April 7; Oct. 13, 20; Nov. 25; Dec. 1 between Aswan and Luxor, visiting Nag Hamadi, Dendera, Luxor, Esna, Edfu, Kom Ombo (7 days). $2,517 to $2,617 per person, double, for 15-day land and cruise program, inclusive.

ABU SIMBEL—Jan. 20; Feb. 3; March 3, 17; April 14, 28; May 26; Sept. 29; Oct. 27; Nov. 10; Dec. 8, 22 between Cairo and Luxor, visiting Giza, Mazghouna, Ayat, Beni Suef, Beni Hassan, Tell El Amarna, Assyut, Ballyana, Nag Hamadi, Luxor, Esna, Edfu, Kom Ombo (14 days). $3,262 to $3,462 per person, double, for 19-day land and cruise program, inclusive.

ANNI/ATON/TUT—Every fifth day throughout 1983 from either Luxor or Aswan, calling at Kom Ombo, Edfu, and Esna (5 days). $480 per person, double, until May 15; $330 after May 16; inclusive of all shore excursions.

HTOP—Tuesdays alternating from either Luxor or Aswan throughout 1983, calling at Esna, Edfu, and Kom Ombo (7 days). $744 per person, double until May 15; $462 after May 15; inclusive of all shore excursions.

ISIS/OSIRIS—Every fifth day throughout 1983 from either Luxor or Aswan, calling at Kom Ombo, Edfu, and Esna (5 days). $480 per person, double, through May, inclusive of all shore excursions.

NILE STAR—Jan. 11; Feb. 8; March 8; April 5; May 3, 31; Aug. 30; Sept. 27; Oct. 25; Nov. 22; Dec. 20; Jan. 17 (1984); Feb. 14; March 13; April 10; May 8; June 5 from Cairo to Aswan, visiting Gizeh, Hawamdieh, Sakkara, Memphis, El Wasta, Beni Suef, Meidum, Minieh, Beni Hassan, El Ashmunein, Tuna El Gebel, Tell El Amarna, Abydos, Dendera/Karnak/Luxor, Thebes and the Valley of the Kings, Valley of the Queens and Luxor, Esna, Edfu, Kom Ombo/Aswan (optional tours to Abu Simbel and Philae). Air-sea from London (17 days). $2,654 to $3,600 per person, double.

NILE STAR—Jan. 23; Feb. 20; March 20; April 17; May 15; June 12; Sept. 11; Oct. 9; Nov. 6; Dec. 4; Jan. 1 (1984), 29; Feb. 26; March 25; April 22; May 29; June 17 from Aswan to Cairo, visiting same sites as above in reverse order. Air-sea from London (17 days). $2,654 to $3,600 per person, double.

OHIO RIVER

FROM CINCINNATI

DELTA QUEEN—May 10, June 4, Aug. 7, Sept. 23 to Louisville, Evansville, Cairo, and St. Louis (5 nights). $475 to $1,525 per person, double.

DELTA QUEEN—May 31 to Gallipolis and Ripley (4 nights). $380 to $1,220 per person, double.

DELTA QUEEN—May 29 and July 27 to Louisville (2 nights). $190 to $610 per person, double.

DELTA QUEEN—May 6 to Louisville, Madison *(Kentucky Derby Cruise)* (4 nights). $455 to $1,465 per person, double.

DELTA QUEEN—May 20 and July 29; Sept. 14 and Oct. 3 *(Fall Foliage Cruises)* to Huntington, Marietta, and Wheeling, and Pittsburgh (5 nights). $475 to $1,525 per person, double.

MISSISSIPPI QUEEN—Sept. 2 Louisville (2 nights). $190 to $620 per person, double.

MISSISSIPPI QUEEN—Sept. 4 to Louisville, Evansville, Cairo, and St. Louis (5 nights). $475 to $1,550 per person, double.

FROM PITTSBURGH

DELTA QUEEN—Oct. 10 *(Fall Foliage Cruise)* to Wheeling, Marietta, Huntington, Cincinnati, Louisville, Memphis, Vicksburg, St. Francisville, and New Orleans (11 nights). $1,045 to $3,355 per person, double.

DELTA QUEEN—May 25, Aug. 3, Sept. 19 to Wheeling, Marietta, and Cincinnati (4 nights). $380 to $1,220 per person, double.

DELTA QUEEN—Oct. 8 *(Fall Foliage Cruise)* to Wheeling (2 nights). $190 to $610 per person, double.

THE RHINE RIVER

AUSTRIA/ITALIA—March 31, April 5; every Tuesday and Saturday from April 12 until Oct. 11 upstream between Nijmegen and Basle, calling at Cologne, Braubach, Speyer, and Strasbourg (4 days). $400 to $435 per person, double. *Europa Class Four-Country Cruises.*

AUSTRIA/ITALIA—April 9; every Saturday and Wednesday from April 16 until Oct. 15 downstream between Basle and Nijmegen, calling at Mannheim and Cologne. $360 to $395 per person, double. *Europa Class Four-Country Cruises.*

BRITANNIA/FRANCE/DEUTSCHLAND—Every three days from April 21 through Oct. 13 downstream between Basle and Rotterdam, calling at Strasbourg, Rudesheim, Dusseldorf, and Cologne (4 days). $610 to $675 per person, double. *First Class Four-Country Cruises.*

BRITANNIA/FRANCE/DEUTSCHLAND—Every three days from April 16 through Oct. 8 upstream between Rotterdam and Basle, calling at Dusseldorf, Koblenz, Speyer, Strasbourg, Cologne, and Konigswinter (5 days). $645 to $705 per person, double. *First Class Four-Country Cruises.*

BRITANNIA—Sept. 13 from Rotterdam to Dusseldorf, Cologne, Linz, Cochem, Mainz, Speyer, Strasbourg, and Basle (7 days). $770 to $840 per person, double. *Floating Wine Seminar.*

FRANCE—Sept. 8 from Rotterdam to Dusseldorf, Cologne, Linz, Cochem, Mainz, Speyer, Strasbourg, and Basle (7 days). $770 to $840 per person, double. *Floating Wine Seminar.*

HELVETIA—Every 10 days from May 1 through Oct. 18 downstream between Basle and Amsterdam, calling at Strasbourg, Rudesheim, Cologne, and Nijimegen (5 days). $344 to $412 per person, double. *Bed and Breakfast Four-Country Cruises.*

HELVETIA—Every 10 days from May 6 through Oct. 13 upstream between Amsterdam and Basle, calling at Dusseldorf, Koblenz, Speyer, and Strasbourg (5 days). $344 to $412 per person, double. *Bed and Breakfast Four-Country Cruises.*

NEDERLAND—Every Monday from May 2 until Sept. 26 upstream between Rotterdam and Strasbourg, calling at Dusseldorf, Boppard, Speyer, and Cologne (4 days). $370 to $435 per person, double. *Three-Country Cruises.*

NEDERLAND—Every Friday from May 6 until Sept. 23 downstream between Strasbourg and Rotterdam, calling at Rudesheim, Dusseldorf, and Cologne (3 days). $330 to $395 per person, double. *Three-Country Cruises.*

THE THAMES

ACTIEF—April 10 through Oct. 23 between Windsor and Oxford, visiting Shillingford, Pangbourne, Mapleduram, Sonning, Henley-on-Thames, Hurley, Cookham Lock, Cliveden Reach, Windsor (or vice versa) (6 days). $895 per person, double, in April and October; $1,050 from May through September.

ACTIEF—April 10 through Oct. 23 between Windsor and Oxford (3 days). $450 per person, double in April and October; $595 May through September.

ACTIEF—March 31 (4 days). *Easter Cruise.* $595 per person, double.

THAMES PRINCESS—April 4 through Nov. 6 between Tower Bridge and Henley-on-Thames, visiting Putney, Kew Kingston, Windsor, Marlow, Henley-on-Thames (or vice versa) (6 days). $1,280 to $1,380 per person, double.

THE YANGTZE RIVER

FROM HONG KONG

KUN LUN—April 17, May 15, June 12, Sept. 11, Oct. 9 (downstream); March 31, April 28, May 26, June 23, Aug. 25, Sept. 22, Oct. 20 (upstream) to Guangzhou, Shibao Block, Wanxian Gorges, Yichang, Shashi/Jingzhou, Yueyang, Wuhan, Jiujiang/Mt. Lushan, Nanjing, Yangzhou, Zhenjiang, Shanghai (26 days air/land/sea). $5,900 to $7,600 per person, double, inclusive.

KUN LUN—July 7, 14, and 21 to Guangzhou/Chongqing, Shibao Block/Wanxian, White King City/Fengje, Three Gorges/Yichang, Shashi/Jingzhou, Chenglingji/Yueyang, Wuhan, Shanghai (19 days air/land/sea). $4,000 to $5,250 per person, double, inclusive.

THE YONNE RIVER

ETOILE DE CHAMPAGNE—Saturdays from March 20 through April 24, June 12 through June 26, August 28 through Sept. 11, and Oct. 30 and Nov. 6 between Paris and Joigny, visiting Melun, Fontainebleau, Moret-sur-Loing, Pont-sur-Yonne, Villeneuve-sur-Yonne (6 days). $1,500 per person, double. *Chablis Cruises*.

INDEX

General

Air-sea packages, 19–20, 22, 37
Alcoholic beverages, 16, 23, 39, 46–48, 195

Cabins, selection of, 33–35
Children, 17, 24, 25, 29, 43, 49
Clothing, 27–28, 40, 49
Costs, 17, 19–20, 24–25, 36
Credit cards, 38
Cruise Lines International Association (CLIA), 8–9, 24, 188
Customs & duties, 39, 199–200

Deck plans, 29, 30–31, 32
Documents, 38

Electrical current, 38–39
Embarking, 39–40
Entertainment, *see* Ship-board facilities

Families, *see* Children
Freshwater cruising, 17, 19, 21–22

Gambling, 23, 51

Handicapped travelers, 24
History of cruising, 15–17

Itinerary, 18–19
Itinerary changes, 192

Luggage, 37, 39

Meals, 29, 42–46
Medical services & problems, 37–38, 40–41

Port taxes, 8, 25

Retired travelers, 23

Shake-down cruises, 33
Ship-board facilities, 29, 48–52
Ship personalities, 20–21
Ship personnel, 39, 48–50
Ship safety & sanitation, 29–30, 40
Shopping, 193–200
Singles cruises, 23
Special interest cruises, 22–23

Tickets, 36–37
Tipping, 25–26
Travel agents, 9, 20, 23, 38, 39

VAT (Value Added Tax), 198

Ships and Ship Lines

Abercrombie & Kent International, Inc.,
    201–202
Abu Simbel, 201–202, 243, 401, 402
Actief, 209, 404
America/Independence, 21, 215–217, 271, 372,
    373, 386
American Canadian Line, 21, 214–215, 309
American Cruise Lines, 21, 215–217
American Eagle, 21, 215, 216, 272–273, 373,
    384
American Hawaii Cruises, 21, 217–218, 283,
    315
Amerikanis, 222, 224, 225, 273–274, 376
Andrea C., 224, 274
Anni, 213, 402
Apollo, 233
Aquarius, 237, 274–275, 360
Argonaut, 23, 189, 233, 256–257, 275–276
Astor United Cruises, 218–219
Astor, 219, 276, 358, 364, 365, 368, 369, 381,
    390, 391, 396
Atlantic, 239–241, 277–278, 374, 379, 381
Atlantis, 241, 278
Atlas, 233, 238, 278–279, 360
Aton, 213, 402
Austria/Italia, 212, 403
Azur, 252, 279–280
Azure Seas, 232, 280, 374

Bahama Cruise Line, 219–220, 350
Bergen Line, 220
Beverly, 208, 396
BI Discovery Cruises, 22, 250, 349
Boheme, 223, 280–281, 376
Bonjour, 207–208, 397
Brilliance of China, see *Yao Hua.*
Britanis, 222, 281–282
Britannia/France/Deutschland, 212, 403

Canberra, 45, 249–251, 282–283, 392, 393
Carla C., 225, 283, 365
Carnival Cruise Lines, 20, 23, 35, 46,
    221–222, 293, 305, 347
Carnivale, 221, 376
Carras Cruises, 287
Chandris, Inc., 20, 222–223, 273, 281, 323,
    352

Chateau de Cezy, 210
Commodore Cruise Line, 20, 223, 280
Constitution, 218, 283–284, 388
Constellation, 241, 244, 284, 374, 385, 387
Continental Waterways, 21, 202–204
Costa Line, 20, 224–225. 274, 283, 290, 291
Cunard *Countess*, 20, 23, 29, 43, 44,
    227–228, 285–286, 365
Cunard Line, 8, 19, 20, 21, 23, 24, 33, 47,
    225–228, 285, 286, 320
Cunard *Princess*, 20, 23, 29, 43, 44, 227–228,
    286–287, 365, 374, 376, 387

Danae/Daphne, 224, 225, 287–288, 365, 374,
    376, 387
De Hoop, 211, 397, 398
Delta Lines, 21, 23, 228–229, 288, 332
Delta Queen, 21, 23, 93, 229–231, 288–289,
    400, 401, 402, 403
Delta Queen Steamboat Company, 93,
    229–231, 307
Dolphin, 23, 46, 252, 289–290, 376

Eastern Steamship Lines, 231–232, 290
Emerald Seas, 23, 232, 290, 376
Enrico C., 224, 225, 290–291
Epirotiki Lines, 20, 232–234, 275, 278, 300,
    309, 317, 318, 355
Esplanade Tours, 204–205
Etoile de Champagne, 204–205, 396, 399, 405
Eugenio C., 224, 225, 291
Europa, 236, 291–292, 401
European Hotel Barges Amsterdam, 205–206
Exploration Cruise Lines, 234–235, 298, 304,
    318

Fairsea/Fairwind, 265–266, 292–293, 360,
    362, 365, 371, 381, 382, 392
Fairsky, 265–266
Festivale, 221, 293–294, 376
Floating Through Europe, 21, 206–209
Funchal, 243, 294–295, 390, 391

Galapagos Cruises, 190, 235
Galaxy, 241, 295
Golden Odyssey, 20, 259–261, 295–296, 360,
    362, 365, 371, 392
Great Rivers Explorer, 22, 235, 298–299, 367,
    383

Hapag Lloyd Ag, 236, 291
Hellenic Mediterranean Lines, 20, 236–237,
    274
Hilton International, 209–210
Holland America Cruises, 21, 24, 25, 33, 39,
    52, 237–239, 310, 324, 349

Home Lines, 20, 24, 44, 239–241, 277, 314
Horizon, 211, 396
Horizon Cruises, 21, 210–211
Htop, 213, 402

Illiria, 23, 299
Independence, 372, 373, 386
Isis, 209, 243, 402
Island Princess/Pacific Princess, 20, 194, 250, 255–256, 296–298, 366, 372, 375, 384, 387

Janine, 207, 396
Jason, 22, 23, 300, 358, 359, 362
Jean, 208, 396
Juliana, 208, 398
Jupiter, 233, 300–301, 360

Kazakhstan, 21, 244, 245
K.D. German Rhine Line, 211–213
K-Lines Hellenic Cruises, 20, 45, 241, 278, 284, 295, 317
Kun Lun, 242, 301–302, 404

Lafayette, 203, 395
La Litote, 203–204, 396
L'escargot, 203–204, 396, 399
Liberte, 211, 398
Lindblad Explorer, 22, 242, 243, 263–264, 266, 302, 367, 370, 371, 373, 389, 391, 392, 395
Lindblad Polaris, 19, 22, 205, 242, 263–264, 302–304, 357, 360, 371, 389, 392
Lindblad Travel, Inc., 8, 9, 20, 22, 24, 123, 189, 190, 209, 242–244, 268, 295, 301
Linquenda, 207, 397, 398
Lys, 208, 398, 399

Majestic Explorer, 22, 234, 235, 268, 304–305, 374, 389
Mardi Gras, 221, 305–306, 377
Mark Twain, 203, 395
Mermoz, 20, 46, 252, 306–307, 366
Mississippi Queen, 21, 23, 93, 229–231, 307–308, 399, 400, 401, 403

Nederland, 212, 404
Nenuphar, 210, 399
Neptune, 233, 234, 257, 309, 360, 361
New Shoreham II, 21, 214–215, 309–310, 365, 388
Nieuw Amsterdam/Noordam, 237, 238, 239, 310–311, 384, 387
Nile Star, 22, 270, 402
Nordic Prince, 257–259, 311, 364, 377
Norway, 18, 23, 29, 34, 41, 43, 45, 52, 72, 191, 193–194, 247–248, 311–314, 377
Norwegian American Cruises, 8, 9, 20, 27, 29, 43, 44, 46, 49, 245–247, 330, 353
Norwegian Caribbean Cruises, 20, 21, 23, 25, 36, 40, 72, 191, 247–249, 311, 338, 340, 341, 346

Oceanic, 239, 240, 314–315, 379, 382
Oceanic Independence, 46, 49, 217–218, 315–317, 389
Oceanus, 233, 317
Odessa, 21, 245
Orion, 241, 317–318
Orpheus, 233, 318
Osiris, 209, 243, 402

Pacific Northwest Explorer, 22, 234, 243, 267–268, 318–319, 384, 386
Palinurus, 203, 397
P & O Cruises, 20, 22, 249–251, 282, 336
Paquet Cruises, 251–252, 279, 289, 306, 323
Pearl Cruises of Scandinavia, 253–254, 319
Pearl of Scandinavia, 253–254, 319–320, 369, 370
Polish Ocean Lines, 22, 44, 254, 342
Princess Cruises, 20, 47, 250–251, 254–256, 296, 336, 345

Queen Elizabeth, 9, 16, 20, 27, 34, 44, 46, 49, 51, 104, 194, 226–228, 320–322, 379, 380, 393

Raymond & Whitcomb Co., 23, 189, 190, 256–257, 275
Regina Maris, 322–323
Rembrandt, 205–206, 398, 399
Rhapsody, 238, 252, 323, 375, 377, 378, 387
Romanza, 222, 223, 323–324
Rotterdam, 27, 193, 237, 238, 324–325, 380, 382, 387
Royal Caribbean Cruise Line, 21, 43, 45–46, 188, 257–259, 311, 339, 346
Royal Cruise Line, 20, 24, 37, 189, 259–261, 295, 326
Royal Odyssey, 240, 259–261, 326, 361, 371, 372, 378, 392, 395
Royal Viking Line, 8, 9, 20, 27, 43, 44, 47, 261–263
Royal Viking Sea/Royal Viking Sky, 9, 21, 261–263, 327–328, 361, 380, 382, 383, 384, 385, 390, 394
Royal Viking Star, 9, 261–263, 328–330, 369, 370, 383, 385, 390

Sagafjord, 9, 245–246, 330–331, 375, 380, 383, 385
Salen Lindblad Cruising, 263–264, 302

Santa Cruz, 235, 243, 331, 368
Santa Liners (*Magdalena, Maria, Mariana, Mercedes*), 228–229, 332–333, 376, 385, 387
Sara Jane, 211, 397
Scandinavia, 264–265, 333–334, 380
Scandinavian Sea, 264–265, 333, 334, 380
Scandinavian Sun, 264–265, 333, 334–335, 378
Scandinavian World Cruises, 264–265, 333, 334
Sea Cloud, 23, 335–336
Sea Princess, 249–251, 336–338, 359, 361, 362, 394
Sheraton Nile Cruises, 213
Sitmar Cruises, 20, 24, 25, 44, 265–266, 292
Skyward, 29, 247–248, 338–339, 378
Society Expeditions Cruises, 22, 189, 190, 257, 266–267, 354
Song of America, 258–259, 339, 378
Song of Norway, 34, 35, 257–259, 339–340, 378
Southward, 29, 247–248, 340–341, 378
Special Expeditions, 267–268
Starward, 29, 247–248, 341–342, 378
Stefan Batory, 16, 22, 238, 254, 342
Stella Maris II, 20, 24, 268–269, 342–343, 360, 362, 364
Stella Oceanis, 28, 268–269, 343–344, 362, 366
Stella Solaris, 28, 44, 47, 51, 134, 151, 188, 268, 344–345, 362, 364, 373, 383
Sun Line Cruises, 28, 268–269, 343, 344
Sun Princess, 20, 23, 33, 44, 194, 250, 345–346, 366, 376, 388
Sun Viking, 257–259, 346, 378
Sunward II, 23, 29, 247–248, 346–347, 378, 379
Swans Hellenic Cruises, 20, 22, 51, 123, 189, 190, 269–270

Thames Princess, 204, 404
Travel Dynamics, 23, 299
Tropicale, 221–222, 347–348, 376, 388
Tut, 213, 402

Uganda, 22, 249–251, 349, 359, 362, 364, 391, 392, 394

Veendam/Volendam, 238, 349–350, 364, 380, 383, 386
Veracruz, 219–220, 350–352, 379, 380, 387
Victoria, 222, 352–353, 367
Virginia Anne, 397
Vistafjord, 9, 245–247, 353–354, 358, 364, 383, 391, 395

Western Steamship Lines, 231–232, 280
World Discoverer, 22, 257, 266–267, 354–355, 368, 369, 370, 371, 388, 389, 395
World Renaissance, 225, 233, 252, 355–356, 367

Yao Hua, 22, 242, 263–264, 356, 370

Ports of Call

Acapulco, Mexico, 91, 371–372
Aegean, 357–364
Ajaccio, France, 126
Alaska and the Inside Passage, 17, 19, 20, 88–89
Alexandria, Egypt, 121
Alsace Canals, 395
Amazon R., 17, 19, 395–396
Anchorage, 372
Andalsnes, Norway, 176
Antigua, Brit. Leeward Is., 76–77, 395
Apia, Western Samoa, 160
Aqaba, Jordan, 148
Argentina, 162–163
Aruba, Neth. Antilles, 84
Ashdod, Israel, 137
Athens, Greece, 19, 126, 127–128, 360–362
Auckland, New Zealand, 158–159
Australia, 38, 157–158
Avon, River, 396

Bahama Is., 18, 71–72
Balboa, Canal Zone, 103, 367
Balearic Is., Spain, 185–186
Bali, 103–104
Baltimore, 372
Bangkok, Thailand, 119–121
Bantry Bay, Ireland, 174
Barbados, 29, 76, 364
Barcelona, Spain, 183–184
Bar Harbor, ME, 98
Baton Rouge, LA, 94
Bay of Islands, New Zealand, 159
Beijing (Peking), China, 107–109
Bergen, Norway, 175, 389
Bermuda, 18, 23, 29, 72–74
Black Sea, 74–76
Boka Kotorska (Gulf of Kotor), Yugoslavia, 154–155
Bonaire, Neth. Antilles, 84
Bora Bora, Society Is., 161
Boston, MA, 98
Brazil, 163–164
Bridgetown, Barbados, 76
British Isles, 17, 19, 22, 23, 171–174

British Leeward Is., 76–77
British Virgin Is., 77–78
British Windward Is., 78–79
Buenos Aires, Argentina, 19, 162–163, 367
Bulgaria, 74
Burgundy Canals, 396–397

Cabo San Lucas, Mexico, 90
Cagliari, Italy, 143
Cairns, Australia, 158, 388
Cairo, Egypt, 121–122
Cairo, IL, 95
Callao, Peru, see Lima
Canal du Midi, 397
Canal du Nivernais, 397–398
Canary Is., 186–187
Cancun, Mexico, 92
Cannes, Frances, 125
Cap Haitien, Haiti, 82
Caracas, Venezuela, 170–171
Caribbean, 17, 18, 19, 20, 21, 23, 25–26, 28, 37, 38, 40, 46, 76–87, 364–367
Cartagena, Colombia, 165
Casablanca, Morocco, 145–146
Cayman Is., 79
Central America, 102–103, 367
Channel Is., 172
Charente River, 398
Charlotte Amalie, USVI, 87
Charlottetown, Prince Edward I., 99
Chichén-Itzá, Mexico, 19, 92
Chile, 164–165
China, 20, 22, 104–109
Cincinnati, OH, 101
Civitavecchia, 357
Colombia, 165
Colombo, Sri Lanka, 118–119, 370
Colon, 367
Constanta, Romania, 74–75
Conway, Wales, 173
Copenhagen, Denmark, 177–178, 389–390
Corfu, Greece, 129
Corsica, France, 126
Cozumel, Mexico, 92
Crete, Greece, 136
Curaçao, Neth. Antilles, 83–84, 364
Cuxhaven, 390
Cuzco, Peru, 169

Delos, Greece, 129–130
Delphi, Greece, 128
Denpasar, Bali, 103
Dikili, Turkey, 150
Djibouti, 371
Dominican Republic, 28, 79
Dover, England, 172
Dubrovnik, Yugoslavia, 154, 358
Dubuque, IA, 96

Dutch Canals, 398–399
Dutch Windward Is., 80

Easter I., 165
Ecuador, 166–167
Edinburgh, Scotland, 172–173, 391–392
Egypt, 17, 19, 121–123
Eidfjord, Norway, 175
Eire, see Ireland
Elba, Italy, 143
English Harbour, British Leeward Is., 76–77
Ensenada, Mexico, 90
Ephesus, Turkey, 151
Evansville, IN, 101

Far East, 17, 22, 38, 103–121, 369–370
Fiji, 159–160
Flam, Norway, 175
Florence, Italy, 139
Fort-de-France, Martinique, 80
Fort Myers, FL, 372–373
France, 23, 123–126
Freeport, Bahama Is., 28, 72
French Polynesia, 160–161
French Riviera, 123–126
French West Indies, 80–81
Funchal, Portugal, 182–183

Gaillard Cut (Panama Canal), 102–103
Galapagos Is., 17, 19, 22, 38, 167–168 ·
Gallipolis, OH, 102
Galveston, TX, 373
Galway Bay, Ireland, 174
Gaspé Peninsula, Canada, 99
Geiranger, Norway, 175
Genoa, Italy, 138, 358–359
Gibraltar, 126
Glacier Bay National Monument, AK, 89
Gothenburg, Sweden, 390–391
Gotland, Sweden, 179
Grand Canary, Canary Is., 187
Great Barrier Reef, Australia, 157–158
Great Wall, China, 108
Greece, 17, 18, 19, 28, 126–136
Grenada, Brit. Windward Is., 78–79
Guadeloupe, 81
Guangzhou (Canton), China, 104–105
Guayaquil, Ecuador, 166, 368
Gudvangen, Norway, 175

Haddam, CT, 373
Haifa, Israel, 137
Haiti, 28, 81–82
Halifax, Canada, 98–99, 373
Hamburg, Germany, 19, 177, 391
Hammerfest, Norway, 177

Hannibal, MO, 96
Hawaii (state), 17, 19, 21, 155–156
Hawaii (island), HI, 155–156
Hebrides, Scotland, 173
Hellesylt, Norway, 175
Helsinki, Finland, 19, 179
Heraklion (Iraklion), Greece, 136
Hilo, HI, 155–156
Hodeidah, 371
Holyhead, Wales, 173
Hong Kong, 110–111, 369
Honningsvag, Norway, 177
Honolulu, HI, 19, 155, 388–389
Houmas House (Mississippi R.), 93–94
Hull, England, see York

Ibiza, Spain, 186
Iles Des Saintes, French West Indies, 81
Indian Ocean, 370–371
Inland Waterways, 201–213, 395–405
Iquitos, Peru, 395
Ireland, 171, 173–174
Israel, 17, 19, 137–138
Istanbul, Turkey, 151–154
Italy, 138–144
Itea, Greece, 128

Jamaica, 82–83
Japan, 38, 111–115
Juneau, AK, 89

Kahului, HI, 156
Kailua-Kona, HI, 156
Kauai, HI, 156
Kavalla, Greece, 132
Kiel, 391
Ketchikan, AK, 88–89, 374
Kobe, Japan, 113, 369
Kos, Greece, 133
Kralendijk, Neth. Antilles, 84
Kusadasi, Turkey, 151
Kyoto, Japan, 113–114

La Goulette, Tunisia, 149
La Guaira, Venezuela, see Caracas
Leith, Scotland, see Edinburgh
Lemnos, Greece, 133
Leningrad, USSR, 180–181
Lesbos, Greece, 132–133
Lihue, HI, 156
Lima, Peru, 169–170
Limon Bay (Panama Canal), 102
Lisbon, Portugal, 181–182, 392
Livorno (Leghorn), Italy, 139
Loire Valley, 399
Los Angeles, CA, 374–379

Louisville, KY, 101
Lys, River, 399

Machu Picchu, Peru, 170
Madeira, Portugal, 182
Madison, IN, 101
Malaga, Spain, 184
Malaysia, 115
Malta, 144–145, 359
Manaus, Brazil, 396
Manila, Philippines, 115–116, 370
Manzanillo, Mexico, 91
Marne, 399
Marrakesh, Morocco, 146
Marseille, France, 125–126
Martha's Vineyard, MA, 97
Martinique, 80
Mas, Bali, 103–104
Maui, HI, 156
Mazatlán, Mexico, 90
Mediterranean, 20, 22, 28, 121–155
Memphis, Egypt, 122–123
Memphis, TN, 95
Menton, France, 124–125
Mexico, 19, 23, 90–92
Miami, Florida, 18, 39
Ming Tombs, China, 108
Minneapolis, MN, 97
Minorca, Spain, 186
Mississippi R., 17, 19, 21, 92–97, 399–400
Molde, Norway, 175–176
Montego Bay, Jamaica, 83
Montevideo, 368
Montreal, Canada, 18, 22, 379
Moorea, French Polynesia, 161
Morocco, 145–146
Moselle, 401
Mt. Agung, Bali, 104
Mykonos, Greece, 130

Nantucket, MA, 97–98
Naples, Italy, 139–140, 359
Nara, Japan, 113
Narvik, Norway, 176
Nassau, Bahama Is., 23, 29, 71–72, 364–365
Natchez, MS, 94–95
Nauvoo, IL, 96
Nawiliwili, HI, 156
Netherlands Antilles, 83–84
Nevis, Brit. Leeward Is., 76–77
New Guinea, 22
New Harmony, IN, 101
New Orleans, LA, 19, 21, 93, 400
Newport, RI, 98
New York, NY, 18, 19, 39, 379–380
New Zealand, 158–159
Nice, France, 123–124, 360
Nile River, 17, 19, 20, 22, 123, 401–402

North America, 88–102, 371–388
North Cape, 19, 174–177
Northeast Passage, 19, 21, 24, 97–102
Northern Capitals, 17, 19, 177–181

Oahu, HI, 155
Oak Alley Plantation (Mississippi R.), 93
Ocho Rios, Jamaica, 83
Odessa, USSR, 75–76
Ohio River, 402–403
Olympia, Greece, 128–129
Oranjestad, Aruba, 84
Orkney Is., Scotland, 173
Oslo, Norway, 178

Pachacamac, Peru, 170
Pacific, the, 155–159, 388–389
Pago Pago, American Samoa, 160
Palma de Mallorca, Spain, 185–186
Panama Canal, 19, 25, 102–103
Papeari, Tahiti, 161
Papeete, Tahiti, 161, 389
Patmos, Greece, 134
Penang, Malaysia, 115
Pergamum, Greece, 150–151
Peru, 169–170
Petra, Jordan, 148
Philippines, 115–116
Piraeus, Greece, see Athens
Playa del Carmen, Mexico, 92
Point-à-Pitre, Guadeloupe, 81
Port Antonio, Jamaica, 82–83
Port-au-Prince, Haiti, 82
Port Bluff, New Zealand, 389
Port Canaveral, 380
Port Everglades, Florida, 381–383
Portland, OR, 383
Port Moresby, New Guinea, 389
Portofino, Italy, 138–139
Port of Spain, Trinidad, 86
Port Said, Egypt, 147
Portugal, 181–183
Prairie Du Chien, WI, 96
Prince Edward I., Canada, 99
Puerto Montt, Chile, 164
Puerto Plata, Dominican Republic, 79
Puerto Rico, 84–86
Puerto Vallarta, Mexico, 90–91
Punta Arenas, Chile, 368

Quebec City, Canada, 99–100
Quito, Ecuador, 19, 166–167, 368

Rabat, Morocco, 146
Raiatea, Leeward I., 161
Red Sea, 19, 22, 23, 147–148, 370–371

Reykjavik, Iceland, 392
Rhine, 403–404
Rhodes, Greece, 135–136
Rio de Janeiro, Brazil, 163–164
Ripley, OH, 101
Rockland, ME, 384
Romania, 74–75
Rome, Italy, 140–141

Safaga, Egypt, 147–148
Saguenay R., Canada, 99
St. Barthelemy, French West Indies, 81
St. Croix, USVI, 86
St. Francisville, LA, 94
St. George, Bermuda, 73–74
St. John's, USVI, 87
St. Kitts, Brit. Leeward Is., 77
St. Louis, MO, 95–96, 401
St. Lucia, Brit. Windward Is., 78
St. Paul, MN, 97, 401
St. Petersburg, FL, 385–386
St. Pierre, Martinique, 80
St. Thomas, USVI, 29, 87
St. Tropez, France, 125
St. Vincent, Brit. Windward Is., 78
Samoas, the, 160
Samos, Greece, 134
San Diego, CA, 384
San Francisco, CA, 19, 88, 384–385
San Juan, 19, 84–86, 365–367
Santiago, Chile, 165
Santiago de Compostela, Spain, 184–185
Santo Domingo, Dominican Republic, 79
Santorini, see Thíra
Santos, Brazil, see São Paulo
São Paulo, Brazil, 164
Sardinia, Italy, 143–144
Savannah, GA, 386
Seattle, WA, 386
Seychelles, 19, 22
Shanghai, China, 105–107
Sicily, Italy, 144
Singapore, 19, 20, 116–117
Sint Maarten, Dutch Windward Is., 80
Sitka, AK, 89
Skarsvag, Norway, 177
Skiathos, Greece, 132
Skopelos, Greece, 132
South America, 17, 19, 20, 21, 38, 367–369
Southampton, England, 171–172, 392–395
South Pacific, 159–161, 388–389
Spain, 183–187
Split, 362–363
Sri Lanka, 118–119
Stavanger, Norway, 174
Stockholm, Sweden, 178–179
Strait of Magellan, 19, 170
Stromboli, Italy, 143
Suez, Egypt, 147, 371

Suez Canal, 147–148
Sydney, Australia, 19, 157, 389
Syracuse, Italy, 392

Tahiti, 160–161
Tampa, FL, 386–387
Tapiola, Finland, 179–180
Taxco, Mexico, 91–92
Tenerife, Canary Is., 187
Thailand, 119–121
Thames, 404
Thasos, Greece, 133
Thessaloniki (Salonika), Greece, 131–132
Thíra (Santorini), Greece, 130–131
Tianjin (Tientsin), China, 107
Tobago, 86
Tokyo, Japan, 112–113
Tonga, 160
Tortola, Brit. Virgin Is., 77–78
Toulon, France, 125
Trinidad, 86
Tromso, Norway, 176, 395
Trondheim, Norway, 176
Tulum, Mexico, 19, 92
Tunis, Tunisia, 149
Tunisia, 149–150
Turkey, 17, 18, 19, 28, 150–154
Turku, Finland, 180

Ubud, Bali, 103
USSR, 38, 75–76
U.S. Virgin Is., 86–87

Valletta, Malta, 144–145
Valparaíso, Chile, 19, 164–165
Vancouver, Canada, 18, 19, 88, 387–388
Varna, Bulgaria, 74
Venezuela, 170–171
Venice, Italy, 142–143, 363–364
Vicksburg, MS, 95
Victoria, Canada, 88
Vigo, Spain, 184–185
Visby, Sweden, 179
Voss, Norway, 175

Wabasha, MN, 97
Waimea, HI, 156
Warren, RI, 388
Waterford, Ireland, 174
Wellington, New Zealand, 158
Western Europe, 171–187, 389–395
Willemstad, Curaçao, 83–84

Yalta, USSR, 75
Yangtze R., 22, 404–405
Yokohama, Japan, 111–112
Yonne, 405
York, England, 172
Yucatan Peninsula, Mexico, 92
Yugoslavia, 154–155

Zihuatanejo, Mexico, 91